Surveillance Law

Surveillance Law

Michael Cousens
Barrister, Chambers of Richard Ferguson QC, 2–4 Tudor Street

LexisNexis™ UK

Members of the LexisNexis Group worldwide

United Kingdom	LexisNexis UK, a Division of Reed Elsevier (UK) Ltd, Halsbury House, 35 Chancery Lane, LONDON, WC2A 1EL, and 4 Hill Street, EDINBURGH EH2 3JZ
Argentina	LexisNexis Argentina, BUENOS AIRES
Australia	LexisNexis Butterworths, CHATSWOOD, New South Wales
Austria	LexisNexis Verlag ARD Orac GmbH & Co KG, VIENNA
Canada	LexisNexis Butterworths, MARKHAM, Ontario
Chile	LexisNexis Chile Ltda, SANTIAGO DE CHILE
Czech Republic	Nakladatelství Orac sro, PRAGUE
France	Editions du Juris-Classeur SA, PARIS
Germany	LexisNexis Deutschland GmbH, FRANKFURT, MUNSTER
Hong Kong	LexisNexis Butterworths, HONG KONG
Hungary	HVG-Orac, BUDAPEST
India	LexisNexis Butterworths, NEW DELHI
Ireland	LexisNexis, DUBLIN
Italy	Giuffrè Editore, MILAN
Malaysia	Malayan Law Journal Sdn Bhd, KUALA LUMPUR
New Zealand	LexisNexis Butterworths, WELLINGTON
Poland	Wydawnictwo Prawnicze LexisNexis, WARSAW
Singapore	LexisNexis Butterworths, SINGAPORE
South Africa	LexisNexis Butterworths, DURBAN
Switzerland	Stämpfli Verlag AG, BERNE
USA	LexisNexis, DAYTON, Ohio

© Reed Elsevier (UK) Ltd 2004

A CIP Catalogue record for this book is available from the British Library.

ISBN 0 406 97115 3

Typeset by Columns Design Ltd, Reading, Berkshire
Printed and bound in Great Britain by Hobbs the Printers Ltd, Totton, Hampshire

Visit LexisNexis UK at www.lexisnexis.co.uk

Preface

The reason for writing this book was primarily to gather together material relating to the Regulation of Investigatory Powers Act 2000 (RIPA 2000) to enable criminal practitioners such as myself to get to grips with what is a central aspect of modern pro-active policing. Even as I write, there is no other publication including the Act available to help the beleaguered barrister. It was originally intended that as well as the relevant Act and its accompanying Codes there would be a short handbook-style commentary designed to highlight the more important aspects of the Act. It rapidly became clear that not only was the subject significantly wider, but that the potential effect of the powers was much greater than I had anticipated. The point is made elsewhere that over 950 public authorities have the right to use one or other of the surveillance powers contained within. Many of those authorities will never before have had to consider, let alone get to grips with, the use of such powers and the consequences that could lie in store for unauthorised snooping.

The book has tried to remain true to its intention of containing all the relevant materials together with a commentary. In so far as it is possible, the commentary has been designed with both lawyers and non-lawyers in mind. In an attempt to clarify the authorisation procedures, some parts have been highlighted and others omitted. Any form of selection involves a degree of distortion for which I take full responsibility. In view of the undistinguished history of the courts in construing the 'impenetrable' Interception of Communications Act 1985 and the difficulty experienced by the Court of Appeal in interpreting the 'particularly puzzling' RIPA 2000, it may seem foolhardy even to venture into such territory. I take full responsibility for doing so and acknowledge the certainty that I will have made mistakes. I hope I will be forgiven.

I should like to acknowledge the 1998 Justice Report 'Under Surveillance' and also Professor David Ormerod whose articles in the Criminal Law Review in February 2003 and January 2004, and in the Journal of Criminal Law 2004 have helped throw light on an area that has received inadequate scrutiny in the past.

This area of law is one that is likely to develop significantly in the future.

As I write, the House of Lords has declared in favour of Miss Naomi Campbell in her case against the Mirror newspaper. The result effectively destroys the comment made by Lord Nolan in *R v Khan*, an important decision on surveillance, to the effect that there was in English law nothing unlawful about a breach of privacy. That the legal landscape has been changed by that case and by the Human Rights Act 1998, s 6 is clear. What is not so clear is the effect that the change will have in the months and years to come.

Michael Cousens
June 2004

Contents

Table of statutes

References to *Statutes* are to Halsbury's Statutes of England (Fourth Edition) where the annotated text of the Act may be found. References in the right-hand column are to paragraph number. Paragraph references printed in **bold** type indicate where the Act is set out in part or in full.

S

Table of Statutory Instruments

References in the right-hand column are to paragraph number. Paragraph references printed in **bold** type indicate where the Statutory Instrument is set out in part or in full.

Table of Cases

S

T

V

W

Chapter 1

Surveillance

Introduction

1.1 The 1984 decision of the European Court of Human Rights (ECt HR) in *Malone v United Kingdom*[1] produced a concurring judgment by Judge Pettiti in which he stated that:

> 'the mission of the Council of Europe and its organs is to prevent the establishment of systems and methods that would allow "Big Brother" to become master of the citizen's private life.'

He had earlier in the judgment pointed out that:

> 'the danger threatening democratic societies in the years 1980–1990 stems from the temptation facing public authorities to "see into" the life of the citizen. In order to answer the needs of planning and of social and tax policy the State is obliged to amplify the scale of its interferences. In its administrative systems, the State is being led to proliferate and then to computerise its personal data-files. Already in several of the member states of the Council of Europe each citizen is entered on 200 to 400 data-files. At a further stage, public authorities seek, for the purpose of their statistics and decision-making processes, to build up a profile of each citizen. Enquiries become more numerous; telephone tapping constitutes one of the more favoured means of this permanent investigation.'

The UK government responded to the adverse decision by enacting the Interception of Communications Act 1985 (IOCA 1985).

1   (1984) 7 EHRR 14.

1.2 In its leading article of 6 March 1985, on the day of the second reading (of IOCA 1985), *The Times* newspaper referred to weaknesses in the chain of accountability:

> 'The Bill to be debated today provides an opportunity for remedying those weaknesses. But as it stands it goes very little way towards doing so. It is one of

this government's "dumb insolence" measures ... in which the minimum action possible is grudgingly taken to comply with the letter of rulings under international agreements. In this case the ruling is by the European Court and the action in response is effectively to make legal the practice that the court complained had no legal sanction. [It contains] unnecessarily wide measures to protect confidentiality or reference in any court or tribunal to the possibility that official sources could engage in illegal tapping ... and it fails to provide for the control of bugging devices not connected to public communications networks though the issues are exactly the same ... The system is nominally controlled by warrants issued by one of five secretaries of state, but the warrants can be drawn loosely and run for long periods ... The Royal Commission on Criminal Procedure recommended warrants issued by a judge ... The Commissioner will be able only to consider whether procedure has been followed and whether unauthorised disclosures have been made. He will have nothing to say if any procedures are defective or if abuses are carried out with punctilious observance of procedure.'

1.3   IOCA 1985 remained in force for 15 years. The unnecessarily wide measures to prevent reference to the possibility that official sources could indulge in illegal wiretapping have resulted in five trips to the House of Lords (see **Chapter 6**). During that period, the government of the day suffered numerous further adverse decisions in Europe, including those of *Hewitt and Harman v United Kingdom*,[1] *Khan v United Kingdom*[2] and *Halford v United Kingdom*,[3] each of which was instrumental in the somewhat piecemeal development of further legislation.

This included the Security Service Act 1989, the Intelligence Services Act 1994 (ISA 1994) (see **Chapter 4**), the Police Act 1997 (see **Chapter 5**) and the Regulation of Investigatory Powers Act 2000 (RIPA 2000), which repealed IOCA 1985 (see **Chapters 6–9**). The Security Service Act 1989 has also been effectively repealed by ISA 1994. The regimes for surveillance established by that Act and Part III Police Act 1997 survive. Together with the regimes established by RIPA 2000 there are now a total of 9 overlapping regimes.[4]

1   (1989) 14 EHRR 657.
2   (2001) 31 EHRR 45.
3   (1997) 24 EHRR 523.
4   Justice Human Rights Audit 2000.

1.4   As their name implies, the first three acts were concerned with the activities of specific services. One of the unsatisfactory features of IOCA 1985 was that it did not specify who (or what) was entitled to apply for an interception warrant. The position has now been clarified by RIPA 2000, s 6(1) (see **para 6.52**), which makes it clear that all three services are entitled to apply for an interception warrant. The purpose of Security Service Act 1989 and ISA 1994 was not only to give for the first time statutory recognition to the respective services, namely MI5, MI6 and GCHQ, but also to entitle them to apply for a property warrant to enter on and interfere with property. Part III of the Police Act 1997 somewhat belatedly gave the police, Customs and Excise (HMCE), the National Criminal Intelligence Service (NCIS) and the

National Crime Squad (NCS) similar powers. None of the three acts gave to the respective service any other more generalised powers of surveillance such as have now been included in RIPA 2000, Pt II.

1.5   RIPA 2000, Pt II and relevant sections of Pt IV came into force on 25 September 2000. Chapter I of Pt I and most of the remaining sections of Pt IV came into force on 2 October 2000, the same day as did the Human Rights Act 1998 (HRA 1998). Apart from replacing IOCA 1985, the main purpose of RIPA 2000 was said somewhat inaccurately to be 'to protect human rights' (see Foreword by the Home Secretary to the Consultation Paper 'Interception of Communications in the United Kingdom', Cmnd 4368). In fact the main purpose of RIPA 2000 is not to protect human rights but to provide protection for a large number of public authorities from the consequences of actions that would otherwise be unlawful under HRA 1998.

The structure of RIPA 2000

1.6   As indicated above, RIPA 2000, Pt I, Ch I replaces IOCA 1985. Part I, Ch II is entitled 'Acquisition and Disclosure of Communications Data' and did not come into force until 5 January 2004. The public authorities entitled to use these powers are set out in RIPA 2000, s 25(1). The original plans to widen the number of authorities so entitled met with such opposition when published in the summer of 2002 that the government was forced to withdraw them. The compromise position is now set out in SI 2003/3172, but still represents a significant extension in the number of authorities entitled to use at least some of the powers contained in Ch II. For reasons that are unclear, Ch II did not deal with the question of retention of such data which is now the subject of the Anti-terrorism, Crime and Security Act 2001, Pt 11, which came into force on 14 December 2001. RIPA 2000, Pt II is entitled 'Surveillance and Covert Human Intelligence Sources' (CHIS). It is the powers in this Part to which the large number of authorities set out in SI 2003/3171 have access (**para 8.12**).

RIPA 2000, Pt III is entitled 'Investigation of Electronic Data Protected by Encryption etc' but is not yet in force. As at the date of writing in April 2004, the government have given no indication as to when the commencement date might be. A summary of its main effects is, however, set out in **Chapter 9**. Part IV is entitled 'Scrutiny etc of Investigatory Powers and of the Functions of the Intelligence Services' and is the subject of **Chapter 10**. It includes s 71, which provides for the issue and revision of Codes of Practice, as to which see **para 1.8** below. Part V is entitled 'Miscellaneous and Supplemental'. An unusual and somewhat confusing feature of RIPA 2000 is that it contains no less than five interpretation sections, namely ss 2, 20, 25, 48 and 81.

The importance of statutory instruments

1.7   As can be seen from the above, statutory instruments play a very important part in the practical application of RIPA 2000. Section 78 refers to 13 instruments subject to the affirmative resolution procedure. Other important instruments to which reference will be made during the course of the text include the Telecommunications (Lawful Business Practice) (Interception of Communications) Regulations 2000 (SI 2000/2699) (**Chapter 6**) and the Investigatory Powers Tribunal Rules 2000 (SI 2000/2665) (**Chapter 10**).

The importance of Codes of Practice

1.8   The importance of Codes of Practice in assessing the lawfulness of activities which might interfere with art 8 rights was recently emphasised by the ECt HR in *Perry v United Kingdom*[1] where the failure to comply with Code D issued under the Police and Criminal Evidence Act 1984 (PACE 1984) was held to mean that the interference with the rights of the suspect was not 'in accordance with law.'

Four draft Codes under RIPA 2000, s 71 were published in July 2000. The Interception of Communications Code of Practice (**Interception Code**) was not brought into effect until 1 July 2002 (SI 2002/1693) and the Covert Surveillance Code of Practice (**Surveillance Code**) and Covert Human Intelligence Sources Code of Practice (**CHIS Code**) until 1 August 2002 (SI 2002/1933 and SI 2002/1932). The Surveillance Code replaces that issued under Police Act 1997, Pt III. The Investigation of Electronic Data Code of Practice has not yet come into force. Although RIPA 2000, Pt I, Ch II came into force on 5 January 2004, the relevant Code of Practice is still in draft. In addition, the Retention of Communications Data under Part 11 of the Anti-terrorism, Crime and Security Act 2001 Voluntary Code of Practice came into force on 5 December 2003 (SI 2003/3175). The delay by the Home Office in bringing the Codes into operation has been criticised by the Surveillance Commissioner in his Reports for 2000–01 and 2001–02.

> 'All the public authorities whose conduct of covert surveillance and use of CHIS I am responsible for keeping under review have in my judgement been considerably and unfairly handicapped by the fact that there have not yet been issued under s 71(1) of the 2000 Act codes of practice relating to the exercise and performance of the powers and duties conferred or imposed on public authorities under the Act and the 1997 Act.'[2]

The comments are more than justified in the light of the decision taken to relegate critical issues such as the protection offered to privileged or confidential material from the body of the statute to the Code.

1   [2003] All ER (D) 296 (Jul), (2003) Times, 26 August.
2   2001–02 Report, para 9.1.

1.9   The piecemeal development of the law relating to issues of surveillance is partly explained by the lack of any coherent approach to the issue of privacy in the English legal system. Before considering particular aspects of the legislation involved, it is proposed to note briefly the position in that regard in English law as it was prior to and post 2 October 2000.

What is privacy?

1.10   In America privacy has been described as the 'right to be let alone'.[1] In England, both the Younger Committee on Privacy 1972[2] and the Calcutt Committee on Privacy 1990[3] concluded that the concept could not be satisfactorily defined. More recently, Lord Mustill, agreeing that on a proper construction of the Broadcasting Act 1996, a company could make a complaint of unwarranted infringement of its privacy, accepted that the concept is hard to define but attempted to give a flavour of what it involved.

> 'To my mind the privacy of a human being denotes at the same time the personal "space" in which the individual is free to be itself, and also the carapace, or shell or umbrella, or whatever other metaphor is preferred, which protects that space from intrusion. An infringement of privacy is an affront to the personality, which is damaged both by the violation and by the demonstration that the personal space is not inviolate.'

Such considerations could not apply to a body corporate. He was, however, prepared to give an expanded reading to the concept of privacy bearing in mind that the task of the Broadcasting Standards Commission was not to enforce hard-edged legal rights but rather to uphold general standards of decent behaviour.[4]

The recognition that the concept is essentially context-dependent is integral to an understanding that the 'right' not to be spied upon is but one aspect of the problem of defining privacy.

1   Judge Cooley, as quoted in Warren, S D and Brandei, L D *Right to Privacy* (1890).
2   Cm 5012, paras 57–61.
3   Cm 1102, paras 3.1–3.8.
4   *R v Broadcasting Standards Commission, ex p BBC* [2000] 3 WLR 1327 at para 1340.

Four faces of privacy

1.11   It is submitted that even before 2 October 2000, observations such as those of Lord Nolan in *R v Khan*,[1] to the effect that there is no right of privacy in English law, were potentially misleading. It is noteworthy that none of the other members of the House of Lords in that case were prepared to go so far. Certain aspects of what would normally be thought of as amounting to privacy were at that time protected by statute or by common law. The following are examples.

(1)   The privacy of one's house/personal territory.
      This is a physical concept protected by the law of trespass and in the context of the criminal law by PACE 1984. There can be little doubt that an action against the police for trespass and possibly a prosecution for criminal damage in the case of *Khan* would have been successful.
(2)   Freedom from interference with one's person, including personal space, a form of privacy protected by the law of assault.
      The act must be intentional or reckless (see *Wainwright v Home Office*[2] at **para 1.12**).

(3)   The privacy of one's work or personal information, ie not to be distributed without consent.

The obtaining and use of such information is now protected by the Data Protection Act 1998 (DPA 1998) (previously DPA 1984) (see **Chapter 3**).

(4)   The right not to be spied upon.

This aspect is common both to cases in which the state is involved in surveillance activities and those in which the media use covert photography to publish aspects of a person's private life. A breach of confidence action may be available if the circumstances amount to a confidential relationship (see *Peck v United Kingdom*[3] at **para 1.13** below). The test of what amounts to such a relationship was recently examined by the House of Lords in *Campbell v Mirror Group Newspapers plc*.[4] The underlying question was said to be whether the information that was disclosed was private and not public. If this approach is correct, it must at the very least give ammunition to those who argue that there is now a freestanding right of privacy. Even if there is, it remains to be seen whether the existence of any such right would add substantially to any argument that evidence obtained during the course, for instance, of unauthorised undercover investigations by the media should be excluded. To this extent the observations of Lord Nolan were correct.

1   [1996] 2 Cr App Rep 440.
2   [2003] UKHL 53, [2003] 4 All ER 969
3   (2003) 36 EHRR 41 at p 719.
4   [2004] UKHL 22, [2004] NLJR 733

No tort of invasion of privacy

1.12   In *Wainwright v Home Office*,[1] the facts of which took place before the advent of HRA 1998, the House of Lords upheld the view of the law taken by Megarry V-C in *Malone v Metropolitan Police Comr*.[2] The claimants, a mother and son, went to visit a relative in prison who was suspected of using drugs while in Armley Prison, Leeds. A prison officer told them that they would have to be strip-searched. They reluctantly agreed but found the experience upsetting. During the search of the son, one of the prison officers touched his penis, which was conceded by the Home Office to amount to a battery. The judge further ruled that requiring the claimants to remove their clothes was a form of trespass to the person. It was argued on their behalf that there was and always had been in English law in theory a tort of invasion of privacy. In rejecting the argument, the House observed that the creation of a general tort would pre-empt the controversial question of the extent, if any, to which the European Convention on Human Rights required the state to provide remedies for invasions of privacy by persons who were not public authorities. A finding by the ECtHR that there was a breach of art 8 would demonstrate only that there was a gap in the English remedies which had since been filled by HRA 1998, ss 6 and 7. It did not require the courts to provide an alternative remedy which distorted the principles of the common law.

1   [2003] UKHL 53, [2003] 4 All ER 969.
2   [1979] Ch 344.

1.13   In *Peck v United Kingdom*,[1] the facts of which are summarised in **para 2.70**, a local authority had permitted CCTV pictures of the applicant to be disseminated to both the local and national media. In responding to the alleged violation of art 13, the government referred to 'the regime of legal protection' which performed substantially the same function as a law of privacy. They drew attention to the possibility of complaint to various media commissions, of judicial review and of an action for breach of confidence. The government did not suggest that DPA 1984 was relevant no doubt because the definitions in that act were significantly narrower than under DPA 1998. As the relevant activities took place before 2 October 2000, there was no possibility of an action under the HRA 1998. The ECt HR disagreed with the government and found that there had been a violation of both arts 8 and 13. The test of irrationality applied by the domestic courts could not equate to the test of proportionality. The media commissions had no power to award damages or grant an injunction. An action for breach of confidence was unlikely to succeed as it would have been difficult to establish the necessary quality of confidence.

1   (2003) 36 EHRR 41.

Data protection and CCTV

1.14   Data protection is a central feature of certain aspects of surveillance law. CCTV images now fall within the definition of 'personal data' in DPA 1998, which came into force on 1 March 2000. The Act was designed to take into account the European Directive 95/46/EC of 24 October 1995 as well as simplify certain aspects of DPA 1984. In the absence of any specific form of statutory control of CCTV, the DPA 1998 represents the most obvious form of potential redress for those whose images have been wrongly retained or disseminated. In addition, it would also be difficult to understand the principles at the heart of RIPA 2000, Pt I, Ch II without some understanding of the subject. Relevant parts of the 1997 Telecoms Data Protection Directive 97/66/EC are set out in Chapter 7 (see **para 7.5**).

Privacy post 2 October 2000

1.15   HRA 1998, s 6(1) provides:

'It is unlawful for a public authority to act in a way which is incompatible with a Convention right.'

The Convention right that is directly concerned with surveillance is art 8, 'the right to respect for private life'. The interpretation given by the ECt HR to private life is a wide one capable of including professional or business activities.[1] In some circumstances, art 6 considerations, 'the right to a fair trial', may also arise (**Chapter 11**). The scope of both these articles and the implications of any violation are considered in **Chapter 2**.

The effect of HRA 1998, s 6 is to fill the gap identified by Lord Nolan in *Khan* and to create a freestanding right of privacy against the police or any other public authority. It does not create such a right against private detective agencies or those parts of the independent media which specialise in undercover investigations and which do not therefore require the protection provided by RIPA 2000.

1   *Niemitz v Germany* (1992) 16 EHRR 97.

Who may snoop?

1.16   RIPA 2000 is concerned with the activities of public authorities. Those persons who practise covert surveillance on behalf of private investigation agencies or certain sections of the media are not covered by the protective cloak afforded by RIPA 2000. Similarly, overt surveillance in the form of CCTV cameras or speeding cameras is not covered (see **para 1.22**). Nevertheless, the number of agencies who are protected is extensive. RIPA 2000, Sch 1 as amended by SI 2003/3171 lists 43 categories of public authority as relevant authorities for the purposes of using both directed surveillance and CHIS, and a further eight categories entitled only to use directed surveillance. One of the categories entitled to use both forms of surveillance includes any county council or district council. According to the 2001–02 Annual Report of the Chief Surveillance Commissioner, 'in addition to the law enforcement agencies there are about 980 public authorities within my remit' (see **para 8.12**). In his previous Report, he had stated that he could not carry out any meaningful oversight of so many bodies without assistance. In the 2001–02 Report he explained that those comments may have been misunderstood and that the Office of Surveillance Commissioners was properly resourced. Both his findings and those of the Interception Commissioner are referred to in **Chapter 10**.

NCIS and NCS

1.17   Apart from the police, HMCE and the Intelligence Services, the only body entitled to use all forms of surveillance is the National Criminal Intelligence Service (NCIS). Surprisingly the National Crime Squad (NCS) may not apply for an interception warrant but may apply for authorisation under RIPA 2000, Pt I, Ch II and under Pt II. Any application for an interception warrant by the police and NCS is made via the NCIS. The Police Act 1997, s 2(2) states that the function of the NCIS shall be:

'(a)   to gather, store and analyse information in order to provide criminal intelligence,

(b)   to provide criminal intelligence to police forces in Great Britain, the Royal Ulster Constabulary, the National Crime Squad and other law enforcement agencies, and

(c)   to act in support of such police forces, the Royal Ulster Constabulary, the National Crime Squad and other law enforcement agencies carrying out their criminal intelligence activities.'

The NCIS shall be maintained by a body known as the NCIS Service Authority. The Authority consists of 19 members. It has a common core membership of ten members with the NCS Service Authority (see **para 1.19**). Police Act 1997, Sch 1 provides further details as to the membership of both authorities.

1.18   Its website[1] states that it specialises in four business areas:

(1)   the provision of strategic intelligence overviews for national targeting of organised criminality;

(2)   the supply of operational intelligence on the most difficult and dangerous criminal organisations;

(3)   the supply of specialist co-ordinating functions and facilities for UK law enforcement; and

(4)   the publication of intelligence 'know how' products for law enforcement.

In addition, it provides access to specialist facilities for investigators, to target flagging and interception as well as to foreign law enforcement. UK financial disclosures are made to NCIS. It is also responsible for running the Government Technical Assistance Centre (GTAC).

1   www.ncis.gov.uk.

The National Crime Squad (NCS)

1.19   The NCS came into existence in April 1998. It was itself a development of the regional crime squads set up in 1964 to tackle crime committed across police borders. There were originally nine regions covering England and Wales consisting of detective officers seconded from local police forces for up to five years. Their function was proactively to target those responsible for serious criminal offences regionally, nationally and internationally. In 1993 the nine regions were amalgamated into six.

1.20   The Police Act 1997, s 48(2) provides that:

'the function of the National Crime Squad shall be to prevent and detect serious crime which is of relevance to more than one police area in England and Wales.'

It may act in support of any police force in England and Wales in the prevention and detection of serious crime, act in support of NCIS and other law enforcement agencies and it may institute criminal proceedings. It is maintained by a body known as the NCS Service Authority which consists of 17 members and has a structure similar to that of the NCIS.

1.21   The NCS now has an HQ in London with operational units in Bristol and Wakefield. It is staffed by up to 1330 officers and 420 support staff. Its targets are the same as the regional crime squads it replaced. Typically these include drug trafficking, immigration crime, illegal arms dealing, money laundering, counterfeit currency dealing, kidnap and extortion. According to its website,[1] 75% of its operations involve drug trafficking.

1   www.nationalcrimesquad.police.uk.

What is meant by surveillance?

1.22   In view of the narrow scope of the legislation preceding RIPA 2000, it is not surprising that there was no earlier attempt to consider the overall concept of surveillance. In 1985, when what was to become the first of a series of statutes dealing with aspects of the subject was being debated, the Secretary of State explained:

> 'There is a special case for dealing with the interception of communications passing through public communications systems, because somebody has committed such a communication to a carrier over which he has no control and is entitled to believe that except for good reason, his privacy will be safeguarded. Furthermore, legislation on surveillance would pose far more difficult problems.'[1]

Fifteen years later the government faced up to the far more difficult problems.

Surveillance is defined in RIPA 2000, s 48(2) as including the:

'(a)   monitoring, observing or listening to persons, their movements, their conversations or their activities or communications;
(b)   recording anything monitored, observed or listened to in the course of surveillance; and
(c)   surveillance by or with the assistance of a surveillance device.'

This includes directed surveillance and intrusive surveillance, and interception where one party agrees to the interception (see **Chapter 8**). Somewhat confusingly, the Act then excludes certain activities which would otherwise clearly fall within the definition.

1   75 HC Official Report col 255.

Examples of what is not surveillance

1.23   Three forms of conduct which might otherwise come within the definition of surveillance are specifically excluded from the definition.

(a)   Intercepted telephone calls do not come within the definition of surveillance unless one party to the communication has consented to the interception (s 48(4)).
(b)   The activities of a CHIS are excluded by s 48(3)(a) and (b).
(c)   Bugging and burglary under Part III Police Act 1997 or ISA 1994 is excluded by s 48(3)(c).

(see **para 8.4**).

1.24 Certain other activities which would fall within the broad definition of surveillance referred to above are not affected by RIPA 2000 and are not the concern of this book. Commercial espionage is one example; speed cameras are another. Such surveillance is unlikely to result in obtaining private information. As long as the camera is focused at the number plate of the vehicle rather than its occupants, the practice is unlikely to raise any art 8 considerations. In *Brown v Stott*[1] the procedure under the Road Traffic Act 1988, s 172 of obtaining details of the driver of an offending vehicle was held to be compatible with art 6. In addition, certain aspects of the Proceeds of Crime Act 2002, Pt 7 could be interpreted as involving an obligation on professional advisors to monitor the activities or communications of their clients in such a way as would bring them within the definition in s 48(2).[2] If so, such conduct is beyond the scope of this book.

1   [2003] 1 AC 681.
2   See *P v P (ancillary relief: proceeds of crime)* [2003] EWHC 2260 (Fam), [2004] Fam 1.

Why no case law?

1.25 It will become abundantly apparent in the pages that follow that there has been precious little domestic consideration by the courts of the issues raised by covert surveillance activities. Such as there has been, e g the repeated trips to the House of Lords to clarify the meaning of the 'impenetrable' IOCA 1985, s 9 has been notable for the wholly contradictory contentions being advanced by the Crown and the failure by the Court of Appeal to understand the significance of an express overruling of one of its decisions. The forthcoming decision of the House on the equally impenetrable RIPA 2000, s 17 in *A-G's Reference (No 5 of 2002)*[1] is awaited with interest. In none of the previous decisions has the court departed from the narrow question of interpretation to consider the 'menace of surveillance' as the ECt HR was able to do in *Klass v Germany*.[2] In that case, the court was prepared to consider the issue in depth despite the fact that the applicants themselves could not establish that they had been the subjects of surveillance. In the UK, the lack of locus standi in such a case would be likely to prove an insuperable obstacle. The case of *Malone v Metropoiltan Police Comr*,[3] in which Megarry V-C was highly critical of the state of English law regarding intercepted telephone conversations, might not have raised any such issue had it not emerged fortuitously during the course of the trial that details of an intercepted conversation with the applicant had been noted in a police officer's notebook.

1   [2003] EWCA Crim 1632, [2003] 1 WLR 2902.
2   (1978) 2 EHRR 214.
3   (1979) 2 All ER 620.

1.26 The overwhelming requirement for secrecy which underpinned IOCA 1985, s 9 is reinforced by the apparent ousting of the jurisdiction of the courts to consider matters that come within the jurisdiction of the Tribunal.

IOCA 1985, s 7(8) provided that the decisions of the Tribunal 'shall not be subject to appeal or liable to be questioned in any court'. Schedule 1, para 3(2) further provided that the Tribunal 'shall not, except in reports under s 7(4) of this Act, give reasons for any decisions made by them'. The Security Services Act 1989 and ISA 1994 make similar provision. The Police Act 1997 introduced a complaints procedure to a Commissioner and then to the Chief Commissioner, instead of a Tribunal. Section 91(10) stated in similar terms that:

> 'The decisions of the Chief Commissioner or, subject to sections 104 and 106, any other Commissioner (including decisions as to his jurisdiction) shall not be subject to appeal or liable to be questioned in any court.'

The relevant tribunal is now that set up by RIPA 2000, s 65. The prohibition against the giving of reasons remains.[1] The combined effect of these provisions has contributed to the dearth of domestic case law.

1   RIPA 2000, s 68(4).

Jurisdiction

1.27 Surveillance activities are increasingly likely to involve an international dimension. The routing of telecommunications signals may involve many different countries. It is provided by RIPA 2000, s 1(1) that the offence of unlawful interception may only be committed if the interception takes place 'at any place in the United Kingdom'. By s 2(4) the interception takes place in the UK:

> 'if and only if, the modification, interference or monitoring or in the case of a postal item, the interception is effected by conduct within the United Kingdom and the communication is either–
>
> (a)   intercepted in the course of its transmission by means of a public postal service or public telecommunications system; or
> (b)   intercepted in the course of its transmission by means of a private telecommunications system in a case in which the sender or intended recipient of the communication is in the United Kingdom.'

If the interception is of the public telecommunications system, the fact that both the sender and the recipient of the communication is abroad does not prevent an offence being committed in the UK. On the other hand, if the interception takes place abroad, no offence is committed in the UK even if the subject of the intercept resides in the UK. In such circumstances, evidence obtained thereby is admissible.[1]

1   See *R v Governor of Belmarsh Prison, ex p Martin* [1995] 1 WLR 412, *R v Aujla* [1998] 2 Cr App Rep 16 and *R v P* [2002] 1 AC 146.

External communications

1.28 An external communication is one sent or received outside the British Islands.[1] Where the Secretary of State has certified that he considers it necessary to examine specified types of material he may issue a warrant pursuant to RIPA 2000, s 8(4) that does not need to specify either the target or the address (see **para 6.58**).

Interceptions may also be carried out without a warrant where the person in respect of whom communications information is sought is believed to be outside the UK, the interception relates to the use of a public telecommunications system in that other country, the person who provides the service is obliged by the law of the other country to carry out the interception and it is carried out in accordance with regulations made by the Secretary of State[2] (see **Chapter 6**). The Regulation of Investigatory Powers (Conditions for the Lawful Interception of Persons outside the United Kingdom) Regulations 2004, SI 2004/157 prescribes two conditions for the purposes of s 4(1)(d):

'(a)   the interception is carried out for the purposes of a criminal investiga-
        tion;

(b)   the criminal investigation is being carried out in a country or territory
        that is party to an international agreement designated for the purposes of
        section 1(4) of that Act.'

The commencement date for the Regulations is linked to ratification by the UK. According to the Explanatory Note, they will come into force at the same time as the Convention on Mutual Assistance in Criminal Matters.

1   RIPA 2000, s 20.
2   RIPA 2000, s 4(1).

1.29   The Regulation of Investigatory Powers (Designation of an International Agreement) Order 2004, SI 2004/158 has designated the Convention established by the Council in accordance with art 34 of the Treaty on European Union on Mutual Assistance in Criminal Matters (Cm 5229) as an international agreement for the purposes of RIPA 2000, s 1(4). It came into force on 1 April 2004. The Convention sets out a number of procedural guidelines designed to assist cross-border law enforcement. Article 14, entitled 'Covert Investigations', provides:

'1. The requesting and the requested Member State may agree to assist one another in the conduct of investigations into crime by officers acting under covert or false identity (covert investigations).

2. The decision on the request is taken in each individual case by the competent authorities of the requested Member State with due regard to its national law and procedures. The duration of the covert investigation, the detailed condi-tions, and the legal status of the officers concerned during covert investigations shall be agreed between the Member States with due regard to their national law and procedures.

3. Covert investigations shall take place in accordance with the national law and procedures of the Member State on the territory of which the covert investiga-tion takes place. The Member States involved shall co-operate to ensure that the covert investigation is prepared and supervised and to make arrangements for the security of the officers acting under covert or false identity.'

In the Consultation Paper, Cm 4368, it is stated that the requirements of national law would apply to both the requesting and requested state.

'In effect, this would establish a double lock of safeguards. This means that the UK would not agree to requests by other Member States to intercept targets on

UK territory unless the Secretary of State were able to issue a warrant in accordance with the criteria and safeguards in UK national law.'

1.30 Articles 17 to 21 lay down detailed procedures for cross-border requests for interception, the obligations to make the systems provided by designated service providers directly accessible to the competent authorities of other member states and the obligation to notify the requested member state in circumstances where no technical assistance from that member state is required in order to carry out the interception. According to the explanatory notes to the act, the procedure is designed to allow operators of satellite communications systems to use a ground station in one member state to facilitate interception using a 'service provider', in practice a communications service provider (CSP) which is in a business relationship with the satellite operator located in another member state. The 'service provider' and the subject of the interception are required to be in the same member state.

Authorisations for non–intercept surveillance

1.31 Surveillance Code 1.6 provides that authorisations under RIPA 2000 can be given for surveillance both inside and outside the UK. Authorisations for actions outside the UK can only validate them for the purposes of proceedings in the UK. An authorisation under Pt II does not take into account the requirements of the country outside the UK in which the investigation is taking place.

Northern Ireland

1.32 Certain additional powers are provided by RIPA 2000, s 31. The section gives power to the First Minister and Deputy First Minister to make an order under s 30 specifying which authorities with devolved powers in Northern Ireland can authorise conduct under s 28 or s 29. Such powers do not extend to any provision dealing with an excepted matter nor except with the consent of the Secretary of State a reserved matter.[1]

National Security and economic well being are "reserved matters" for the purposes of the Scotland Act 1998 s 29(2) and Northern Ireland Act 1998 s 6(2)(b) and therefore outside the competence of the Scottish Parliament and the Northern Ireland Assembly respectively.

1   See RIPA (Amendment) Order (Northern Ireland) 2002, SR 2002/183 inserting paras 23A–23D in Pt I of Sch 1 and paras 29–40 in Pt II of Sch 1.

Scotland

1.33 The chief constable of a police force maintained under or by virtue of the Police (Scotland) Act 1967, s 1 is an authorising officer for the purposes of the Police Act 1997, s 93(5). Applications for interception warrants in Scotland are governed by RIPA 2000, Pt I, s 6(2)(g).[1] Scotland has its own RIP(S)A 2000 which, subject to s 46 (below), is the relevant act for surveillance operations carried out north of the border. Its provisions are similar to RIPA 2000, Pt II. Surveillance Code 1.7 provides that where the conduct authorised is likely to take place in Scotland authorisations should be granted under RIP(S)A 2000 unless the authorisation is being obtained by those public authorities listed in RIPA 2000, s 46(3).

Section 46(2) provides that Pt II is the relevant part for the purposes of authorisation where it:

> '(a) is granted or renewed on the grounds that it is necessary in the interests of national security or in the interests of the economic well-being of the United Kingdom.'

Section 46(2)(b)–(d) make similar provision where the authorisation concerns the activities of one of the authorities set out in s 46(3). They are the Intelligence Services, Her Majesty's Forces, the Ministry of Defence, the Ministry of Defence Police, HMCE and the British Transport Police.

Section 46(2)(e) makes similar provision in a case where the conduct is treated as surveillance under s 48(4), e g participant monitoring.

SI 2000/2418 specifies 13 other public authorities as relevant public authorities 'for all parts of the UK'. Examples are NCIS, the Commissioners of Inland Revenue and the Department of the Environment. The effect of inclusion is that authorisations may be granted or renewed under ss 28 and 29 by or in relation to that authority even where all the conduct to be authorised is likely to take place in Scotland.

RIPA 2000, s 76 provides that where an authorisation under the relevant Scottish legislation has the effect of permitting conduct to which Pt II applies and:

> '(c) circumstances arise by virtue of which some or all of the conduct so described can for the time being be carried out only outwith Scotland,
> section 27 of this Act shall have effect for the purpose of making lawful the carrying out outwith Scotland of the conduct so described'.

1   614 HL Official Report col 943.

Is domestic legislation compatible with the Convention?

1.34   It is not intended here to examine the detail of any of the statutes referred to above which are the subject of consideration elsewhere. It may, however, be helpful to highlight three areas of concern which to a greater or lesser extent are common to all the legislation:

(1)   the lack of judicial authorisation;
(2)   subsequent notification to the target; and
(3)   licensed fishing expeditions.

1.35   Both (1) and (2) were the subject of recommendations in the 1981 Royal Commission on Criminal Procedure. The Commission recommended that authorisation for all forms of surveillance should be in the form of a warrant issued by the magistrates court, and that a person subject to surveillance should normally be notified after the event (see **para 6.13**). The recommendations were not taken up by the government. In IOCA 1985 the chosen procedure was that of executive authorisation by the Secretary of State. The Security Service Act 1989 and the Intelligence Services Act 1996 followed suit. In *Christie v UK* the system of executive authorisation coupled with supervision by the Tribunal and a Commissioner was given a clean bill of health by the Commission. Both the Security Services Act 1996, giving MI5 the power to act in support of the Police, and the Police Act 1997, however, engendered considerable controversy during the course of their respective passages through Parliament (see **paras 4.18** and **5.4**). Part III of the Police Act 1997 is based on a compromise position in which prior authorisation is required in certain sensitive cases. A similar procedure has been adopted for intrusive surveillance under RIPA 2000, Part II. In a third category of case neither a judicial nor an executive warrant is required. This category includes directed surveillance and the use of a CHIS, both of which require only a form of in-house authorisation. Bearing in mind that the ECt HR had already given judgment in the important case of *Teixeira v Portugal*, the decision to relegate the activities of undercover police officers to such an inadequate form of authorisation could well be described as an even more acute example of "dumb insolence" than that described by the Times in 1985 (see **para 1.2**).

Executive warrants

1.36   The power to authorise the tapping of telephones or to 'bug and burgle' has traditionally been that of the Secretary of State. During the debate in Parliament on the Police Act 1997, which was brought about at least in part by the activities of the police in the case of *Khan v DPP*,[1] Lord Browne-Wilkinson stated his concerns with clarity and force.

> 'We have no written Constitution. We do not enjoy specific constitutional rights against the state. Our freedom depends and depends only, on the fact that no Minister, no administrator and no member of the police has any greater power or any greater right than any other citizen to enter our property or to seize our person. In particular, the state and its officers have no power to enter our houses or workplaces or to seize our property. Such conduct is unlawful and the administrative action which has apparently been pursued has been, subject to any explanation given by the Minister, unlawful conduct on the part of the police. That basic freedom which we enjoy because the executive does not have power over us has been established by the common law for over 200 years.[2] It is one of the foundations of our freedoms. Until the passing of the Security Service Act earlier this year – a Bill about which at the time I was not enthusiastic – there was only one exception to immunity from police invasion of our privacy; that is, a search warrant granted by an independent court and not by the executive. In relation to matters of national security we tolerated (with our eyes half-closed because it was such an awkward subject) bugging and entering in the interests of protecting national security. But now, following from the Security Services Act, we are sanctioning the entry onto our premises

for police purposes not under warrant of the court or under any independent warrant, but under administrative action.'[3]

1   [1996] 2 Cr App Rep 440.
2   *Entick v Carrington* (1765) 19 State Tr 1029.
3   Hansard 575 Official Report col 810, 11 November 1996.

Prior approval by Commissioner in Police Act 1997, Pt III

1.37   The end result of the debates on the Police Bill produced a compromise consisting of a system of self-authorisation subject to prior approval by a Commissioner in certain sensitive cases such as those in which the property concerned consist of a dwelling, a bedroom in a hotel or office premises, or where the action is likely to result in any person acquiring knowledge of matters subject to legal privilege, confidential personal information or confidential journalistic material. In *R v Lawrence,*[1] in which the court addressed a series of arguments that the 1997 Act was not 'convention compliant', the court specifically found that the Act provided a sufficient machinery for independent oversight of the workings of the system.

1   [2001] EWCA Crim 1829.

Prior approval where surveillance is intrusive

1.38   Self-authorisation remained the basis of the approach in the Regulation of Investigatory Powers Bill, the first attempt to provide a comprehensive regulatory structure for the various forms of surveillance not covered by Police Act 1997, Pt III. In cases falling within the description of 'intrusive surveillance' the authorisation is subject to approval by a Commissioner. Unhappily, the concept of intrusive surveillance is not consistent with the approach in Police Act 1997, Pt III. RIPA 2000, s 26(3) provides that surveillance is intrusive if and only if it is covert surveillance that:

'(a)   is carried out in relation to anything taking place on any residential premises or in any private vehicle; and
(b)   involves the presence of an individual on the premises or in the vehicle or is carried out by means of a surveillance device.'

Although residential premises are defined by s 48(1) to include hotel accommodation, there is no reference to office premises (as in Police Act 1997). Thus prior authorisation is required if the proposed course involves entering an office to place a bugging device but not if the device is positioned outside the office. Conversely, approval under RIPA 2000 is required if surveillance involves the presence of a person in a private vehicle even if the risk of obtaining private information is non-existent.[1]

1   cf Police Act 1997.

1.39   In *Klass v Germany*[1] the ECt HR affirmed that interference by the executive with an individual's rights should be subject to an effective control which should normally be assured by the judiciary, at least in the last resort, judicial control offering the best guarantees of independence, impartiality and a proper procedure (see **para 2.12**). Having regard to the particular safeguards in the case, the court concluded that the exclusion of judicial control did not exceed what may be deemed necessary in a democratic society. The control to be exercised by the judiciary is not necessarily satisfied by mere involvement in the process of authorisation but should in some circumstances continue and include oversight of the manner in which the activities are carried out.[2]

In *Teixeira de Castro v Portugal*,[3] however, the ECt HR attached considerable significance to the lack of any prior judicial involvement in the sanctioning of the activities of two undercover officers. In such circumstances, it must at least be open to question whether the safeguards provided by RIPA 2000 in this regard are adequate (see **para 8.25**).

1   (1978) 2 EHRR 214.
2   See *Kopp v Switzerland* (1998) 27 EHRR 91.
3   (1998) 28 EHRR 101.

Subsequent notification

1.40   Unless a case is brought to trial, it is improbable that the target of the surveillance in the UK will ever get to know of the fact of surveillance even if there is no risk to any national interest or to any ongoing criminal investigation. The existence of a right to such notification was at the heart of the decision in *Klass v Germany*.[1] The court concluded that the failure to inform an individual a posteriori that he had been subject to surveillance was not in principle incompatible with art 8(2). Having regard to a decision of the Federal Court to the effect that such notification should take place if it could be done without jeopardising the purpose of the restriction, there was no breach of art 13. This case was at the heart of the later decision in *Lambert v France*,[2] where the lack of any effective control was critical to the conclusion that there had been a violation of art 8. As it is not possible for the target of surveillance to have any effective control unless he is made aware of the surveillance, it may be that the decision will eventually have a significant impact on any jurisdiction, such as that in the UK, that imposes a blanket ban on such notification. The position in Switzerland, New Zealand, Australia and Canada is that the citizen has a right to be informed that he has been the subject of surveillance unless such information is thought likely to prejudice ongoing criminal investigation.

1   (1978) 2 EHRR 214.
2   (1998) 30 EHRR 346.

Licensed fishing expeditions

1.41   Unfocused trawling for evidence is discouraged by the courts. Such practices are usually referred to as "fishing expeditions".

Surveillance by its nature is an intelligence-gathering tool which may legitimately be used well before the stage at which the relevant law enforcement agency has any suspicion that a particular individual is involved in crime. The activities of establishments such as GCHQ would become impossible if the law insisted on the pre-existence of reasonable suspicion. Nevertheless, some safeguards against indiscriminate surveillance must exist. In the case of interception of communications, the relevant warrant must name or describe the interception subject or a single set of premises.[1] No such requirement exists in respect of other forms of surveillance. The most invasive forms of surveillance under RIPA 2000, Pt I, Ch II or Pt II, or under the Police Act 1997, Pt III can be authorised without any suspect being named. Of particular concern is that even CHIS can be deployed without reasonable suspicion and in circumstances that do not amount to serious crime.[2] (See **para 8.20**).

In *Jasper v United Kingdom*,[3] Judge Zupancic, in a dissenting judgment, touched on the question of reasonable suspicion.

'For the State to acquire the right to intrude on someone's privacy there must be probable cause, that is, a suspicion sufficiently fortified by specific, articulable and antecedent evidence to be called reasonable. Clearly if the citizen is to have the right to be left alone by the Government any exception to this must be justified in advance of the intrusion itself.'

The ECt HR has itself not gone so far. Nevertheless, if surveillance is not to be used as a form of licensed fishing expedition, courts will need to be astute to ensure that safeguards exist to minimise the risk of indiscriminate and inappropriate surveillance. When such activity is proved to have taken place, consideration should be given to aggravated and even exemplary damages. Two examples may help to illustrate the nature of the problem.

1   RIPA 2000, s 8(1).
2   Compare the approach in *Teixeira de Castro v Portugal* (1998) 28 EHRR 101 (see **Chapter 8**).
3   (2000) 30 EHRR 441.

Superintendent Ali Dizaei[1]

1.42   The ease with which such techniques can be deployed is illustrated by the case of Superintendent Ali Dizaei, who faced a colourful array of allegations including being suspected of taking cocaine, spying for the Iranian Embassy, being involved with prostitutes, helping drug traffickers and being linked to four criminals in money laundering and fraud. At his trial in September 2003, in which the prosecution offered no evidence, it emerged that he had been subjected to 90 days of surveillance, 3,500 telephone calls had been recorded, other conversations had been bugged, and both CCTV and hidden cameras used. This may or may not have been an example of a licensed fishing expedition. What is clear is that it failed to catch any fish.

1   (2003) Times, 16 September, 13 November.

The case of Dr Diggle[1]

1.43   Dr Diggle was a GP who discovered that a secret camera had been set up opposite his home. His next-door neighbour was a retired police inspector who suspected that Dr Diggle's son had thrown eggs at his car. Senior police ordered a round-the-clock surveillance operation that lasted 31 days. The report fails to make clear under what legislation the surveillance was authorised or how it was thought that such action was justified. Nothing came of the surveillance. The police admitted that the operation was unlawful because it had overrun the 28-day period, for which authorisation had been given, by three days. Dr Diggle complained to the Police Complaints Authority, which upheld the complaint and awarded him £50,000 damages.

1   (2003) Times, 31 July.

Tables

1.44

Statistical Annex to the Report of the Interception Commissioner for 2000

Warrants (a) in force, under Interception of Communications Act 1985, on 1 October 2000 and (b) issued during the period 1 January 2000 to 1 October 2000

	Telecommunications		*Letter*		*Total*
	a	b	a	b	
Home Secretary	446	1425	26	49	1474
Scottish Executive	67	237	0	0	237

Warrants (a) in force, under Regulation of Investigatory Powers Act 2000, on 31 December 2000 and (b) issued during the period 2 October 2000 to 31 December 2000

(NB: Under Regulation of Investigatory Powers Act 2000 there is no longer a breakdown of the figures between Telecommunications and Letters)

	a	b
Home Secretary	555	606*
Scottish Executive#	32	55

*This figure includes 472 IOCA warrants that were revalidated as RIPA warrants on the coming into force of Regulation of Investigatory Powers Act 2000 on 2 October 2000.

In July 1998 a new policy was implemented whereby the section 5 power to modify warrants was to be extended to serious crime warrants. The total figures for modifications are as below:

IOCA (1/1/00–1/10/00)   488

RIPA (2/10/00–31/12/00)   234

Scottish Executive

Under RIPA the Secretary of State for Scotland was initially empowered to sign warrants. An Executive Devolution Order dated 13 December 2000 transferred this power back to the Scottish Ministers.

Interception of Communications Act 1985: 1/1/2000–30/9/2000

The First Minister and Deputy First Minister authorised warrants for 235 serious crime cases and two HM Customs cases.

Regulation of Investigatory Powers Act 2000 Part I: 1/10/2000–31/12/2000

The Secretary of State for Scotland and the First Minister authorised warrants for 53 serious crime cases and two HM Customs cases.

The comparative figures for 1999 are 288 warrants signed, comprising 231 serious crime cases, 44 HM Customs cases and 13 for terrorism (following Devolution, no national security cases have been authorised by Scottish Ministers since 1 July 1999).

ANNEX A TO THE REPORT OF THE CHIEF SURVEILLANCE COMMISSIONER 2002–03

AUTHORISATIONS GIVEN UNDER PART III OF THE POLICE ACT 1997 SINCE IMPLEMENTATION

	1999–2000[1]			2000–2001[1]			2001–2002			2002–2003		
	England, Wales and NI	Scotland	Total	England, Wales and NI	Scotland	Total	England, Wales and NI	Scotland	Total	England, Wales and NI	Scotland	Total
Total number of authorisations (not including renewals)	2,401	58	2,459	2,509	58	2,567	2,437	82	2,519	2,424	87	2,511

PRIOR APPROVALS[2]

	1999–2000[1]			2000–2001			2001–2002			2002–2003		
	England, Wales and NI	Scotland	Total	England, Wales and NI	Scotland	Total	England, Wales and NI	Scotland	Total	England, Wales and NI	Scotland	Total
Number of cases requiring approval	311	12	323	367	8	375	299	7	306	281	18	299
Cases requiring prior approval by category												
• Dwelling	198	7	205	238	7	245	204	3	207	190	13	203
• Office	60	1	61	45	–	45	37	2	39	38	2	40
• Hotel bedroom	50	4	54	77	1	78	56	2	58	49	3	52
• Matters subject to legal privilege	1	–	1	4	–	4	1	–	1	2	–	2
• Journalistic material	–	–	–	–	–	–	–	–	–	–	–	–
• Confidential personal information	4	–	4	3	–	3	1	–	1	2	–	2

1   Some minor corrections have been made to some figures previously reported for 1999–2000 and 2000–2001.

ANNEX B

INTRUSIVE SURVEILLANCE AUTHORISATIONS GIVEN UNDER PART II OF THE REGULATION OF INVESTIGATORY POWERS ACT 2000 AND THE REGULATION OF INVESTIGATORY POWERS (SCOTLAND) ACT 2000 SINCE IMPLEMENTATION

	2000–2001[1]			2001–2002			2002–2003		
	England, Wales and NI	Scotland	Total	England, Wales and NI	Scotland	Total	England, Wales and NI	Scotland	Total
Total number of authorisations (not including renewals)	302	10	312	480	13	493	461	14	475
Case by category									
• Private vehicle	112	5	117	178	7	185	173	3	176
• Residential premises	190	5	195	302	6	308	288	12	299

1   Some minor corrections have been made to some figures previously reported for 1999–2000.

Chapter 2

RIPA 2000: the European dimension

Taking account of European jurisprudence

2.1   A court or tribunal determining a question that has arisen in connection with a Convention Right must take into account any judgment, decision, declaration or advisory opinion of the ECt HR.[1] The judgments with which this chapter are concerned revolve round either, or both, of art 6 and art 8 of the European Convention on Human Rights (the Convention). The effect of the taking into account may be significantly different depending on which article is concerned. When *R v Davis, Rowe and Johnson*[2] returned to the Court of Appeal the court attempted to keep separate the questions of fair trial and the safety of the conviction, stating that the effect of any unfairness upon the safety of the conviction will vary according to the nature and degree of the unfairness.[3] Later the same year a differently constituted court concluded that the circumstances in which the Court of Appeal would uphold a conviction after a finding of an unfair trial by the ECt HR were likely to be rare indeed – see *R v Togher*.[4] Somewhat surprisingly, no reference was made to the former case. The matter has now, it is submitted, been put beyond doubt by *R v Forbes*,[5] which approved the approach in *R v Togher* and held that in such circumstances a conviction will be held to be unsafe.[6]

1   Human Rights Act 1998, s 2.
2   [2001] 1 Cr App Rep 8 at p 115.
3   [2001] 1 Cr App Rep 8 at para 65.
4   [2001] 3 All ER 463.
5   [2001] 1 AC 473 at para 24.
6   See also *R v A* [2001] UKHL 25, [2002] 1 AC 45.

2.2   Article 8, the right to a private life, is at the heart of much of the jurisprudence considered in this chapter. Although a breach of art 8 is a factor which may be relevant to the exercise of the discretion to exclude evidence under the Police and Criminal Evidence Act 1984 (PACE 1984), s 78,[1] such a breach, per se, is unlikely to result in the Court of Appeal quashing a conviction. The extent to which such a breach will be relevant to the discretion to exclude evidence has been further considered by the House of Lords in *R v P*,[2] in which Lord Hobhouse commented to the effect that any remedy for a breach of art 8 lies outside the scope of the criminal trial (see **chapter 11**). It will therefore often be of critical importance to consider when an acknowledged violation of art 8 may impact on the fairness of trial guaranteed by art 6.

1   See Lord Nolan in *R v Khan* [1996] 2 Cr App Rep 440.
2   [2002] 1 AC 146.

The European Court of Human Rights

2.3   The ECt HR itself has no power to quash a criminal conviction and has been at pains to point out that rules of admissibility are not its concern. Article 41 of the Convention provides that:

> 'If the Court finds that there has been a violation of the Convention ... and if the internal law of the High Contracting Party concerned allows only partial reparation to be made, the Court shall, if necessary, afford just satisfaction to the injured party.'

The court may take account of non-pecuniary loss, but it will not award aggravated or exemplary damages. The basis of such awards is often difficult to discern and sometimes inconsistent. The court has stated that the principle underlying the provision of just satisfaction for a breach of art 6 is that the applicant should, as far as possible, be put in the position he would have enjoyed had the proceedings complied with the Convention's requirements. The court will only award monetary compensation where it is satisfied that the loss or damage complained of was actually caused by the violation it has found.[1] Although a violation of art 6 may result in relatively modest sums of compensation being awarded,[2] it is more likely to result in no award of compensation but a statement that the finding of a violation is sufficient just satisfaction.[3] Occasionally the court will add that it is inappropriate to speculate as to the outcome of the trial in other circumstances[4].

1   See *Edwards and Lewis v United Kingdom* (2003) 15 BHRC 189 at para 63.
2   See *Funke v France* (1993) 16 EHRR 297 (£5,000 for unlawful search) and *Teixeira de Castro v Portugal* (1999) 28 EHRR 101 (£30,000 for pecuniary and non-pecuniary damage resulting from six years' wrongful incarceration).
3   See *Atlan v United Kingdom* (2000) 34 EHRR 33 and *Rowe and Davis v United Kingdom* (2000) 30 EHRR 1.
4   See *Allan v United Kingdom* (2002) 36 EHRR 12, *Edwards and Lewis v United Kingdom* (2003) 15 BHRC 189 and *Foucher v France* (1997) 25 EHRR 234 (see **para 2.20**).

2.4   In so far as art 8 is concerned, the rhetoric of the court to the effect that the guarantees in the Convention are intended to be practical and effective[1] has not been met by its actions. The consequences of a violation of art 8 will usually amount to no more than that a finding of a violation is sufficient just satisfaction.[2]

1   See *Artico v Italy* (1980) 3 EHRR 1 and *Amman v Switzerland* (2000) 30 EHRR 843.
2   See *Khan v United Kingdom* (2001) 31 EHRR 45, *Chalkley v United Kingdom (2003)* Crim LR 51, *Campbell v United Kingdom (1992)* 15 EHRR 137, *Taylor Sabori v United Kingdom (2002)* 36 EHRR 17, *Kopp v Switzerland* (1998) 27 EHRR 91, *Amman v Switzerland* (2000) 30 EHRR 843, *Kruslin v France* (1990) 12 EHRR 547, *A v France* (1993) 17 EHRR 462. Exceptions are *Halford v United Kingdom (1997)* 24 EHRR 523 (£10,000 for unlawful interception of office telephone), *Peck v United*

Kingdom (2003) 36 EHRR 719 (€11,800 for wrongful dissemination of CCTV tape) and *Lambert v France* (1998) 30 EHRR 346 (10,000FF for being deprived of an effective form of control over a lawful interception).

2.5   The purpose of this chapter is not to provide an analysis of the wide embrace of art 8 or the somewhat narrower embrace of art 6. Rather, it is an attempt to examine certain decisions of the ECt HR that are directly concerned with surveillance to understand, first, when art 6 may become engaged and, secondly, how the court has attempted to balance the right to a private life in art 8 on the one hand and on the other the right of the state or other public authority to interfere with that right in order, for example, to combat terrorism or crime. Although art 6 is concerned essentially with issues of procedural fairness in the trial such as disclosure (see **para 2.18**), issues such as search and seizure, which precede the moment of charge, may also fall within its ambit (see **para 2.16**).

2.6   As will be seen, a critical factor in many of the art 8 decisions is the nature and extent of the safeguards against arbitrary invasions of privacy. This factor is of particular relevance when considering the quality of law under art 8(2).[1] In this respect the UK has not been alone in dragging its feet. Inadequate safeguards in French, Spanish and Swiss domestic law have resulted in violations of art 8 in respect of the intercept evidence that was used in the course of criminal proceedings – for example, see *Kruslin v France*,[2] *Lambert v France*,[3] *Valenzuela Contreras v Spain*[4] and *Kopp v Switzerland*.[5] Unhappily, in none of these cases was the relationship between art 6 and art 8 examined. Two cases in which the relationship was considered are *Schenk v Switzerland*[6] and *Khan v United Kingdom*,[7] in both of which the acknowledged violations of art 8 brought about by surveillance activities were held not to have had any impact on the overall fairness of the trial. Both cases are considered in more detail below (see **paras 2.33–2.40**).

1   See *Malone v United Kingdom (1985)* 7 EHRR 14.
2   (1990) 12 EHRR 547.
3   (1998) 30 EHRR 346.
4   (1998)28 EHRR 483.
5   (1998) 27 EHRR 91.
6   (1988) 13 EHRR 242.
7   (2001) 31 EHRR 45.

The menace of surveillance

2.7   The fact that modern surveillance techniques can be used without the target ever becoming aware of the surveillance, and the difficulty of establishing an effective system of control lie behind many of the concerns regarding these particular methods of law enforcement. It is this dilemma that was at the heart of the important case of *Klass v Germany*,[1] which was referred to in some detail by Sir Robert Megarry V-C in the 1979 case of *Malone v Metropolitan Police Comr (No 2)*.[2] In order to understand the reasoning of the ECt HR in this case and others, such as *Huvig v France*,[3] the relevant domestic law is set out in some detail.

1   (1978) 2 EHRR 214.
2   [1979] 2 All ER 620.
3   (1990) 12 EHRR 528.

2.8 *Klass v Germany* concerned a group of five lawyers, including a judge, who claimed that they were being subjected to surveillance measures but were unable to point to any particular examples. The Commission commented that some of the applicants were barristers and therefore it was:

> 'not excluded that they are in fact subject to secret surveillance in consequence of contacts they may have with clients who are suspected of anti-constitutional activities.'

The government denied that any such surveillance had taken place. An unpromising factual background did not prevent the court looking at the issues raised in some detail. The judgment recognised the 'menace of surveillance' and pointed out that if a state instituted secret surveillance in such a manner that it was unchallengeable, art 8 could to a large extent be reduced to a nullity. It was unacceptable that the assurance of the enjoyment of a right guaranteed by the Convention could be removed by the simple fact that the person was kept unaware of its violation.

2.9 The surveillance measures about which complaint was made were enacted in 1968 in a statute called Restrictions on the Secrecy of the Mail, Post and Telecommunications, known as G10. Inevitably, the ultimate decision of the court focused on the particular safeguards afforded to the citizen, which are therefore set out below. They can be seen to be substantially greater than those later included in the Interception of Communications Act 1985 (IOCA 1985). Article 1(1) of G10 provided that the competent authorities might open and inspect mail, read telegraphic messages and listen to, and record, telephone conversations in order, inter alia, to protect against imminent dangers threatening the free democratic constitutional order. Article 1(2) provided important protections for the citizen. Surveillance measures may only be taken:

(i)   where there were factual indications for suspecting a person of planning, committing or having committed certain criminal acts;
(ii) where no other means were likely to succeed; and
(iii) surveillance may only cover suspects or others who are on the basis of clear facts presumed to forward or receive communications to suspect.

By art 1(4) the application may only be made by the head or his substitute of the Agency for the Protection of the Constitution, the Army Security Office or the Federal Intelligence Service. In addition, by art 1(5), the measures may only be ordered by the Ministers of the Interior or of Defence, each of whom must personally take the decision as to their application. Although under art 1(5) the person concerned need not be notified of the restrictions affecting him, in 1970 the Federal Court stated that the competent authority must notify the person concerned as soon as notification could be made without jeopardising the purpose of the restriction.[1]

By art 1(7)(1) implementation of the measures should be supervised by an official qualified for judicial office. By art 1(7)(2) the measures must be discontinued once the required conditions have ceased to exist, and in any event remain in force for a maximum of three months and may be renewed only on fresh application.

By art 1(9) the competent minister must at least once in every six months report to a board consisting of five members of parliament and once every month provide the G10 Commission with an account of the measures he has ordered.

By art 1(9)(2) the G10 Commission consisting of three completely independent members, one of whom was qualified to hold judicial office, were empowered either ex officio or on application by the person believing himself to be under surveillance to decide on both the legality of and the necessity for the measures.

1   *Klass v Germany* (1978) 2 EHRR 214 at para 71.

2.10   The applicants challenged the law on the basis that it contained no absolute requirement to notify persons after surveillance had ceased and that it thereby excluded any remedy before the courts. The court not only rejected the government's preliminary argument that the applicants were not victims, but went on to hold that:

> 'in the mere existence of the legislation itself there is involved, for all those to whom the legislation could be applied, a menace of surveillance; this menace necessarily strikes at freedom of communication between users of the postal and telecommunications services and thereby constitutes an "interference by a public authority" with the exercise of the applicants' right to respect for private and family life and for correspondence.'[1]

1   *Klass v Germany* (1978) 2 EHRR 214 at para 41.

Was art 6 engaged?

2.11   The court pointed out that, prior to any notification of termination of the surveillance, the decision to place someone under surveillance was, if validly secret, incapable of judicial control on the initiative of the person concerned and of necessity must escape the requirements of art 6. Once the person concerned had been notified of the discontinuance of surveillance, he had at his disposal several legal remedies that satisfied the requirements of art 6. In the present case the remedies included seeking a declaration in an administrative court, bringing an action for damages in a civil court, and bringing an action for the destruction or, if appropriate, the restitution of documents.[1]

1   *Klass v Germany* (1978) 2 EHRR 214 at para 75.

Is judicial control necessary?

2.12   In considering whether the domestic legislation was compatible with art 8, the court affirmed that interference by the executive with an individual's rights should be subject to an effective control, which should normally be assured by the judiciary, at least in the last resort, judicial control offering the best guarantees of independence, impartiality and a proper procedure. However, having regard to the particular safeguards in the present case, the exclusion of judicial control did not exceed what may be deemed necessary in a democratic society.[1] The Parliamentary Board and the G10 Commission were independent of the authorities carrying out the surveillance.

An individual believing himself to be under surveillance had the right to complain to the G10 Commission and of having recourse to the Constitutional Court (only if made aware).

1   *Klass v Germany* (1978) 2 EHRR 214 at para 56.

Is subsequent notification to the target necessary?

2.13   As the danger against which a particular surveillance measure has been directed may last for years after its suspension, subsequent notification might well jeopardise the long-term purpose that originally prompted the surveillance. Further subsequent notification might serve to reveal the working practices of the intelligence services. Thus, the failure to inform an individual a posteriori that he had been subject to surveillance was not in principle incompatible with art 8(2).[1] Nor, in view in particular of the judgment of the Federal Court in 1970, was there any violation of art 13. In a country such as the UK, where there is no obligation to inform the target that he has been under surveillance, the only circumstances in which such a person might be in a position effectively to challenge the lawfulness of such activity is if he were to become the subject of a criminal prosecution, as happened in *Malone v United Kingdom*.[2]

1   *Klass v Germany* (1978) 2 EHRR 214 at para 58.
2   (1984) 7 EHRR 14.

2.14   Critical aspects of the domestic law in *Klass* were as follows.

- The case was only concerned with the interception of post and the interception and monitoring of telephone calls.
- Such activity could only take place where there were 'factual indications for suspecting a person of planning, committed or having committed certain serious criminal acts'.
- Fishing expeditions were not permitted.
- Alternative methods must have little or no prospect of success.
- The application for surveillance had to be made by the head of the relevant agency.
- Authority has to be given by the relevant minister personally.
- The measures must be discontinued once the required conditions have ceased to exist.
- The surveillance may remain in force for a maximum of three months unless renewed.
- The target has to be notified of the surveillance as soon as notification can be made without jeopardising the purpose of the operation.
- Implementation of the measures is supervised by an official qualified for judicial office.
- The relevant minister had a duty to report to a board consisting of Members of Parliament once every six months.
- The Commission set up under the Act had jurisdiction to hear complaints from those who believed themselves to be victims of surveillance.
- In those cases where the target was notified that he had been the subject of

surveillance, he could seek a declaration or sue for damages in a civil court or bring an action for the destruction or, if appropriate, the restitution of documents.

2.15   It was in this context that Sir Robert Megarry V-C concluded that:

'Not a single one of these safeguards is to be found as a matter of established law in England and only a few corresponding provisions exist as a matter of administrative procedure … this is not a subject on which it is possible to feel any pride in English law.'[1]

As will be seen in **Chapter 6**, the British government was not persuaded by his comments to introduce any form of statutory control until some six years later, by which time the ECt HR had given its judgment in *Malone v United Kingdom*[2] (see **para 2.55**).

1   [1979] 2 All ER 620.
2   (1984) 7 EHRR 14.

At what stage does art 6 become engaged?

2.16   As identified in *Klass*, art 6 can play no part unless the target becomes aware of the surveillance (see **para 2.11**). In most cases art 6 will not become engaged until the moment of charge. The word has been given an autonomous meaning as:

'the official notification given to an individual by the competent authority of an allegation that he has committed an offence, a definition that also corresponds to the test whether the situation of the suspect has been substantially affected.'[1]

This may be the date of arrest.[2] Once this situation has arisen, however, the manner in which evidence has been obtained may be directly relevant to issues of fair trial under art 6. In *Teixeira de Castro v Portugal*,[3] the activities of the undercover officers forced the court to conclude that 'right from the outset the applicant was definitively deprived of a fair trial'.[4]

1   *Eckle v Germany* (1983) 5 EHRR 1.
2   *Foti v Italy* (1983) 5 EHRR 313.
3   (1998) 28 EHRR 101.
4   See also *Murray v United Kingdom* (1996) 22 EHRR 29 and *Funke v France* (1993) 16 EHRR 297.

Article 6

2.17

'6.1.   In the determination of his civil rights and obligations or of any criminal charge against him, everyone is entitled to a fair and public hearing within a reasonable time by an independent and impartial tribunal established by law. Judgment shall be pronounced publicly but the press and public may be excluded from all or part of the trial in the interests of morals, public order or national security in a democratic society, where the interests of juveniles or the protection of the private life of the parties so require, or to the extent strictly necessary in the opinion of the court in special circumstances where publicity would prejudice the interests of justice.

6.2.   Everyone charged with a criminal offence shall be presumed innocent until proved guilty according to law.

6.3.   Everyone charged with a criminal offence has the following minimum rights:

    (a)   to be informed promptly, in a language which he understands and in detail, of the nature and cause of the allegation against him;

    (b)   to have adequate time and facilities for the preparation of his defence;

    (c)   to defend himself in person or through legal assistance of his own choosing, or if he has not the means to pay for legal assistance, to be given it free when the interests of justice so require;

    (d)   to examine or have examined witnesses against him and to obtain the attendance and examination of witnesses on his behalf under the same conditions as witnesses against him;

    (e)   to have the free assistance of an interpreter if he cannot understand or speak the language used in court.'

Disclosure

2.18   Surveillance operations by their very nature may last for months if not years and generate significant amounts of material. The circumstances in which such material is generated may give rise to difficult issues of public interest immunity (see **para 2.21**). Whether any or all such material is in principle disclosable will depend first on whether the particular operation leads to a charge (see **para 2.16**). Those detained without charge have no right to automatic disclosure of material obtained during a surveillance operation. Although not expressly provided for by the Convention, the right to disclosure is implied by art 6(1) and more particularly art 6(3)(b). Both have been the subject of case law. While some of the cases cited below are not directly concerned with surveillance, they support the proposition that once charged a person has the right to pre-trial disclosure of any material that may help him prove his innocence. The Convention approach is summed up by the concept of 'equality of arms' which was explored in the case *Jespers v Belgium*,[1] in which the applicant, a judge, was convicted of the attempted murder of his wife. He complained that a 'special folder' had not been disclosed to the defence. The Commission held that art 6(3):

'recognises the right of the accused to have at his disposal for the purpose of exonerating himself or obtaining a reduction in his sentence all relevant elements that have been or could be collected by the competent authorities.'[2]

1   (1981) 27 DR 61.
2   (1981) 27 DR 61 at para 58.

2.19   The duty to disclose all material evidence was again emphasised in *Edwards v United Kingdom*,[1] where, during the trial of the applicant for robbery, the police had informed the court that no fingerprints were found at the scene of the crime. In fact, two fingerprints had been found which belonged to the next-door neighbour of the victim. This fact, however, did not become known to the applicant until after the trial. The new evidence was considered by the Court of Appeal, who rejected the appeal on the basis that it would not have affected the assessment made by the jury of the credibility of the main witness. The ECt HR confirmed that it is a requirement of a fair trial that the prosecution should disclose to the defence all material evidence for or against the accused. However, having regard to the fact that the evidence was ultimately disclosed to the defence and considered by the Court of Appeal, the trial as a whole was not unfair.

1   (1992) 15 EHRR 417.

2.20   The duty of disclosure applies equally to less serious offences. In *Foucher v France*,[1] the imposition of unreasonable conditions before permitting disclosure was held to breach art 6. The applicant and his father were charged with having used insulting and threatening words and behaviour towards public service employees including a game warden. The applicant decided to conduct his own case and his mother went to the police court registry to consult the case file and obtain copies of relevant documentation. The documentation included an official report by the game warden, which under French law was good evidence in the absence of proof to the contrary. The prosecutor refused to provide copies on the basis that copies could not be supplied except through a lawyer or an insurance company. When the applicant went to the registry for the same purpose, he met with a similar response. The ECt HR concluded that the applicant had not been afforded equality of arms and that there was a violation of art 6(3) taken together with art 6(1). However, the court was not prepared to speculate as to the outcome of the proceedings had there not been a violation, and it did not award compensation.

1   (1997) 25 EHRR 234.

Public interest immunity

2.21   The ECt HR has recognised that the entitlement to disclosure of relevant evidence is not an absolute right. In any criminal proceedings there may be competing interests such as national security or the need to protect witnesses at risk of reprisals or keep secret police methods of investigation of crime. However, only such measures restricting the rights of the defence which are strictly necessary are permissible under art 6(1). In order to ensure the accused receives a fair trial, any difficulties caused to the defence by a limitation on its rights must be sufficiently counterbalanced by the procedures followed by the judicial authorities. In cases where evidence has been withheld from the defence on public interest immunity (PII) grounds, it is not the role of the ECt HR to decide whether or not such non-disclosure was strictly necessary, since, as a general rule, it is for the national courts to assess the evidence before them. Instead, the court's task is to ascertain whether the decision-making procedure applied in each case complied as far as possible with the requirements of adversarial proceedings and equality of arms and incorporated adequate safeguards to protect the interests of the accused.

2.22   In *Rowe and Davis v United Kingdom*[1] the prosecution took it upon themselves at trial not to disclose that an admitted accessory to the crime in question had received a reward of £10,300 for information given to the police that the applicants were responsible for offences including a murder and robbery. Although the evidence withheld in the trial was made available to the Court of Appeal when the case was referred back by the Criminal Cases Review Commission, it was not disclosed to the defence. In holding that there had been a violation of art 6(1), the court observed that such an ex post facto procedure was inadequate to remedy the unfairness caused at the trial by the absence of any scrutiny of the withheld information by the trial judge. The relevant distinction between this case and *Edwards v United Kingdom*[2] was that in the latter, by the appeal stage, the defence had received most of the missing information. The importance of the material being disclosed to the trial judge was again emphasised in *Dowsett v United Kingdom*,[3] a case in which the prosecution similarly failed to involve the trial judge. Also, in *Atlan v United Kingdom*,[4] the repeated denials by the prosecution of the existence of relevant undisclosed material and their failure to inform the trial judge of the true position were held to be inconsistent with the requirements of art 6(1).

1   (2000) 30 EHRR 1.
2   (1992) 15 EHRR 417.
3   Application 39482/98, [2003] Crim LR 890.
4   (2002) 34 EHRR 833.

2.23   In *Jasper v United Kingdom*,[1] decided on the same day as *Rowe and Davis*, the court was considering a request by the defence for the product of surveillance. At the trial, which preceded the enactment of the Criminal Procedure and Investigations Act 1996 (CPIA 1996), the applicant was convicted of being knowingly concerned in the fraudulent evasion of the prohibition on the importation of cannabis. He had been kept under observation and seen to drive from London to a meat storage depot near Sevenoaks and load a consignment of meat and return to a garage in East London. HMCE raided the garage and discovered that four of the pallets of meat contained quantities of cannabis. At trial his case was that he collected the meat pursuant to instructions received by telephone the previous night. It was not suggested he had been entrapped. Prior to the trial, an ex parte PII application took place in which the defence were notified of that fact but were not informed of the category of material involved. Shortly thereafter, the defence served a written request for particular items of unused material which they suspected existed but had not been disclosed. The request included confirmation as to whether any listening device or intercept had been used and, if so, whether any record existed, whether there existed any other witness statements, whether there were any previous observations, particularly of the meat storage depot, and whether HMCE acted on information received. The prosecution informed the defence that there had been no previous observations on the meat storage depot and there was no information received from an informant, but refused to answer whether any listening device or intercept had been used. The judge refused to order further disclosure. The Court of Appeal agreed with the judge.

1   (2000) 30 EHRR 441.

2.24   On appeal to the ECt HR the defence argued that as far as the PII hearing was concerned the ex parte procedure was unfair as the defence were never informed as to the nature of the material and thus were not able to address the court in any meaningful manner. In contrast to *Edwards v United Kingdom*,[1] the material was not disclosed to the defence even during the appeal proceedings, although it was disclosed to the Court of Appeal. They submitted that in such circumstances 'special counsel' should have been appointed to represent the interests of the applicant. The ECt HR gave detailed consideration to the disclosure regime as it existed prior to the implementation of CPIA 1996. Having recognised that the national court was in certain circumstances entitled to withhold material on public interest grounds, the court somewhat surprisingly held that:

> 'It is not the role of this Court to decide whether or not such non-disclosure was strictly necessary since, as a general rule, it is for the national courts to assess the evidence before them. In any event, in many cases, such as the present, where the evidence in question has never been revealed, it would not be possible for the Court to attempt to weigh the public interest in non-disclosure against that of an accused in having sight of the material.'

In holding by nine votes to eight that the trial as a whole had been fair, the court placed weight on the following, that at the PII hearing:

- the defence had been given an opportunity to outline the defence case to the trial judge;
- the trial judge examined the material in question;
- the defence were thereafter kept informed;
- the material that was not disclosed played no part in the prosecution case whatever;
- the trial judge kept the question of disclosure under assessment at all times;
- it could be assumed the judge applied the principles in *R v Ward*[2] and *R v Davis, Johnson and Rowe*;[3]
- that such principles were consistent with art 6; and
- in so far as the intercept material was concerned, it was not established that such material existed. Further, since neither side was entitled to adduce any such evidence the principle of equality of arms was respected.

The reasoning echoes that of the Commission in *Preston v United Kingdom*.[4] The fact that the undisclosed material formed no part of the prosecution case was also referred to as a reason for finding that the trial had not been unfair in *PG and JH v United Kingdom*.[5] It is respectfully submitted that the point is a statement of the obvious and fails to focus on the real issue namely whether the material may have assisted the defence.

1   (1993) 15 EHRR 417.
2   [1993] 2 All ER 577.
3   [1993] 2 All ER 643.
4   [1997] EHRLR 695.
5   Reports of Judgments and Decisions, 2001 IX p 195.

Special counsel

2.25   Following the judgments of the ECt HR in *Chahal v United Kingdom*[1] and *Tinnelly v United Kingdom*.[2] the UK government introduced legislation making provision for special counsel in certain cases involving national security. The provisions are contained in the Special Immigration Appeals Commission Act 1997. Rule 7 of the Procedure Rules 1998 made thereunder provides as follows:

'(4)   The function of the special advocate is to represent the interest of the appellant by–

(a)   making submissions to the Commission in any proceedings from which the appellant or his representative are excluded;

(b)   cross-examining witnesses at any such proceedings; and

(c)   making written submissions to the Commission.

(5)   Except in accordance with paragraphs (6) to (9) the special advocate may not communicate directly or indirectly with the appellant or his representative on any matter connected with proceedings before the Commission.'

The rules provide further details of the relevant procedure that may apply in such circumstances. A further example of special counsel being appointed is also to be found in the Youth Justice and Criminal Evidence Act 1999, s 38, where an unrepresented defendant seeks to cross-examine a complainant in a rape case.

1   1996) 23 EHRR 413.
2   (1998) 27 EHRR 249.

2.26   In *Jasper v United Kingdom*,[1] the government argued that the judge had been able to determine all issues relating to the disclosure of evidence. The proposed special counsel scheme would give rise to practical difficulties with regard to the duties owed to the accused, the amount of information the special counsel could pass on and the quality of instructions he could expect to receive from the defence. Such difficulties would be particularly acute in cases involving more than one co-accused. The majority rejection of the suggestion that special counsel would have been an appropriate procedure made no reference to these difficulties but repeated that the material never formed part of the prosecution case.[2] For the reasons already explained (see **para 2.24**), it is submitted that such reasoning is unhelpful. The dissenting judgment of six of the judges emphasised that the defence had not been able to participate in any meaningful way in the ex parte procedure and that the procedure could not therefore be said to have been properly adversarial. The position could be contrasted with that in *Edwards v United Kingdom*,[3] where by the time of the appeal the defence had received most of the missing information and could address the court accordingly. Seven of the dissenting judges referred to the requirement that any limitation on the rights of the defence should be sufficiently counterbalanced by the procedures followed by the judicial authorities and could best be met by the appointment of special counsel.

1   (2000) 30 EHRR 441.
2   (2000) 30 EHRR 441, para 55.
3   See **para 2.24**.

2.27   In *Fitt v United Kingdom*,[1] also decided on the same day as *Rowe and Davis*, in which the applicant alleged he had been set up by a participating informer, the court came to the same conclusion. As all but two of the paragraphs in the judgment of the court and most of those in the dissenting judgments follow an identical formula to those in *Jasper v United Kingdom*, it is not proposed to recite them here.

1   (2000) 30 EHRR 480.

Non-disclosure of material relevant to issue decided by the judge

2.28   The reluctance of the court in *Jasper* and *Fitt* to consider the merits of the decision of the national court was not shared by the court in the two cases of *Edwards v United Kingdom* and *Lewis v United Kingdom*,[1] which included two of the dissenting judges in *Jasper*. Following a surveillance and undercover operation, the applicant in the first of those cases had been arrested in a van in the company of an undercover officer. In the van was a briefcase containing 4.8 kg of heroin. During the trial, which took place in 1995, the prosecution made a successful PII application. The applicant's case was that he believed he was taking part in a transaction to sell stolen jewellery and that others concerned, who were not arrested, were undercover officers who had effectively entrapped him into becoming involved in drug dealing. He applied unsuccessfully to exclude the evidence of the main witness on the basis that he had been entrapped. He was convicted of possessing a class A drug with intent to supply. His appeal to the Court of Appeal on the basis of non-disclosure was rejected. On appeal to the ECt HR he contended that he had been entrapped and that the PII procedure was unfair. The court, having recited the importance of aspects of a fair trial in terms similar to *Jasper*, emphasised that the function of the court was to scrutinise the decision-making procedure to ensure that as far as possible it complied with the requirement to provide adversarial proceedings and equality of arms and incorporated adequate safeguards to protect the interests of the accused. As the undisclosed evidence related or may have related to a question of fact decided by the judge, namely whether the applicant had indeed been entrapped into committing the offence, the withholding of evidence may have been determinative of the question of abuse. The government revealed before the ECt HR that that which had not been disclosed included material suggesting that the applicant had been involved in drug dealing prior to the events that led to his arrest. Unlike *Jasper*, the undisclosed material may have formed part of the prosecution case. In those circumstances, the court held unanimously that the procedure followed to determine the question of disclosure did not comply with the requirements of art 6.

1   (2003) 15 BHRC 189.

2.29   In *Lewis v United Kingdom*,[1] the applicant, who had been tried in 1996, had pleaded guilty to three charges of possession of counterfeit notes. His case was that he had been pressed by an acquaintance of a friend to obtain some counterfeit currency as part of a bona fide business transaction. He was subsequently introduced to others, one of whom was later revealed to be an undercover officer. Transcripts of covert recordings revealed that he was actively encouraged to become involved by the undercover officer. The defence applied to stay the proceedings on the grounds of abuse of process. Prior to ruling on the application, a PII application had been made. The judge refused to stay the proceedings or order further disclosure. As a result, the applicant pleaded guilty. The ECt HR assumed that the undisclosed material was adverse to the applicant and was taken into account by the judge and, for the same reasons as in *Edwards*, found a violation of art 6(1).

The court refused to award compensation in either case, commenting that the finding of a violation did not imply that the applicants had been wrongly convicted.

1   (2003) 15 BHRC 189 at p 193. See also *R v H* [2004] UKHL 3, [2004] 1 All ER 1269 (and see para 11.37).

Undercover operations

2.30   Undercover operations involving test purchases of drugs remain controversial because, inter alia, of the ever-present risk of unreliable evidence brought about by entrapment. Such operations have been held to engage art 6, for example in *Teixeira de Castro v Portugal*.[1] In that case two undercover officers were introduced to the applicant, who had no previous convictions, by a third party. The officers said they wished to buy 20 g of heroin and produced a roll of banknotes from the Bank of Portugal. The applicant without hesitation agreed to procure the heroin and, accompanied by the third party, went to the home of another who obtained three sachets from another person and then handed the sachets to the applicant. The court noted that it was not suggested that the officers were acting in the course of an anti-drug operation ordered and supervised by a judge, nor did it appear that the competent authorities had good reason to suspect that the applicant was a drug trafficker. Furthermore, the drugs had to be obtained from a third party who in turn obtained them from another person. The court concluded that the activities of the undercover officers in effect created the offence of which the applicant had been convicted and that the use of the evidence meant that right from the outset he had been definitively deprived of a fair trial in violation of art 6(1). In view of that finding the court did not find it necessary to consider art 8. At the same time it did not suggest that art 8 had no part to play simply because the applicant must have known he was embarking on a course of criminal conduct.[2]

1   (1998) 28 EHRR 101.
2   See *Ludi v Switzerland* (1993) 15 EHRR 173, and para 2.31.

2.31   In *Ludi v Switzerland*,[1] the activities of the undercover officer were not alleged to have amounted to entrapment. Having been released by a German court without trial on a drug trafficking charge, owing to procedural problems arising from the use of an undercover officer, the applicant returned to Switzerland, where, pursuant to a preliminary investigation by a court, his telephone was tapped. The investigation centred on information from the German police that while in custody he had asked a fellow countryman for financial help in purchasing approximately 5 kg of cocaine in Switzerland. Although not provided for by Swiss law, the police also authorised an undercover officer to interact with him. The reports of the telephone interception demonstrated that the applicant on his own initiative offered to obtain drugs for the officer. He was subsequently convicted of several offences linked to drug trafficking. He complained that the interception and the use of an undercover officer amounted to violations of art 8 and that the inability to cross-examine the undercover officer amounted to a violation of art 6. Although the ECt HR upheld the latter complaint, it held that the interception had been necessary in a democratic society and further that the use of an undercover officer in the context of a police investigation into drug trafficking was not, contrary to the opinion of the Commission, an interference with private life. The reason for this conclusion was that the applicant must have known he was engaging in criminal activity and was therefore running the risk of encountering an undercover officer whose task would be to expose him. The contention that art 8 provides no protection for those allegedly involved in crime was not accepted in the later case of *A v France*[2] (see **para 2.61**).

If this reasoning is correct, it would seem to follow that the applicant would also be at risk of forfeiting his right to a fair trial. Indeed, the partly dissenting judgment of Judge Matscher was to the effect that the dismissal by the trial court of the application to call the witness was not open to criticism as the applicant had substantially admitted the acts he was accused of. Although the reasoning of the ECt HR may be unsatisfactory, the judgment of the Federal Court dismissing the public law appeal demonstrates prescience of the later judgment in *Teixeira de Castro:*

> 'Where the undercover agent by means of his contacts merely ascertains conduct which would have taken place in the same or similar fashion even without his intervention, the use of an undercover agent is no doubt unobjectionable. On the other hand, it would not be permissible if the undercover agent were to take the initiative, as it were, and provoke criminal activity which would otherwise not have come about at all.'[3]

1   (1992) 15 EHRR 173.
2   (1993) 17 EHRR 462.
3   (1993) 15 EHRR 173, at para 21.

2.32   In the context of decisions of the ECt HR, both before and since, *Teixeira de Castro* stands alone as a warning as to the circumstances in which certain types of surveillance activity may have a decisive effect on the fairness of a trial guaranteed by art 6. This may be the case even when the reliability or authenticity of the evidence is unchallenged. Perhaps unusually in cases of this sort, there is no suggestion in the judgment that the exchanges between the undercover officers and the applicant were tape-recorded. Certain other features, such as the lack of reasonable suspicion and no prior judicial authorisation, are central to the conclusion that right from the outset the applicant had been deprived of a fair trial. It may be that these features which can be argued differentiate this decision from those cases involving other forms of highly intrusive surveillance, such as the interception of telephone calls, in none of which has art 6 even been considered (see **paras 2.57–2.64**).

When does a violation of art 8 affect the fairness of a trial?

2.33   Allegations of entrapment of a different kind were made in *Schenk v Switzerland,*[1] in which the applicant was convicted of attempted incitement to murder his wife. The main evidence against him came from a hitman ('P') whom he had employed to kill his wife (Mrs S). P had second thoughts and visited Mrs S and told her that he had been hired by her husband to kill her. Two days later Mrs S and P reported the matter to the investigating judge in the Canton of Vaud, who issued letters rogatory to the police in Paris whither P had returned. P was interviewed by the French police and informed them that he would certainly receive a call from the applicant asking for details of the murder. Without any authorisation P set up a cassette recorder and connected it to his telephone. Article 179 bis of the Swiss Cantonal Code made such conduct a criminal offence punishable by imprisonment. If carried out by the police such conduct would have been unlawful without authorisation by a judge. Six days after the matter had been reported to the investigating judge, P, while still in France, received a call from the applicant which he recorded. In it the applicant asked 'Where did it happen?' and on being informed that the body had been taken to a place near Montreux three days earlier, commented that 'it's odd the job's been done and there's been no news yet'. The conversation ended and P immediately took the tape recording to the police in Paris. The police took the recording back to Lausanne, where Mrs S identified S's voice. The applicant was arrested, interviewed and charged by the investigating judge. Approximately two months later a lawyer instructed by him requested an expert examination of the cassette, as in his view the recording was not a faithful and complete reproduction of the telephone conversation. At the conclusion of his enquiries, the investigating judge discharged the applicant on the basis that the statements of P could not be relied upon with absolute confidence. The prosecutor appealed and in his response the applicant filed a statement of defence alleging that P was an agent provocateur and supporting the suggestion that the recording should be played. The applicant was committed for trial.

1   (1988) 13 EHRR 242.

2.34   At trial the applicant changed tack and applied unsuccessfully for the recording to be excluded. His case was that the assignment was merely to obtain information. He was convicted and the court gave a long judgment summarising the evidence and their reasoning. Having considered the expert evidence, the court was satisfied that the recording was an accurate reproduction of the conversation between P and the applicant. The applicant appealed unsuccessfully to the domestic courts of appeal and ultimately to the Commission, which dismissed the complaint based on art 8 concerning the making of the recording on the grounds that the domestic remedies had not been exhausted, but allowed the complaint in regard to the use of the recording based on art 6(1) and (3). During the course of the argument before the ECt HR the government conceded that the recording had been obtained unlawfully in the sense of being contrary to domestic criminal law.

2.35   The court held that art 6 does not lay down any rules on the admissibility of evidence, which is primarily a matter for domestic national law. The court could not:

'exclude as a matter of principle and in the abstract that unlawfully obtained evidence of the present kind might be admissible. It has only to ascertain whether Mr Schenk's trial as a whole was fair.'[1]

The applicant had the opportunity to challenge the authenticity of the recording and to cross-examine the persons allegedly involved in its making. The court attached considerable weight to the fact that the evidence was not the only evidence against the applicant and in order to illustrate the point summarised part of the judgment of the court of first instance rubbishing the utter improbability of the applicant's account. The flavour of the comments are contained in the following extract:

'But there is all the other evidence before the court: the unbelievably elaborate precautions taken by the defendant, the fact that for years the defendant had had to pay an allowance to his wife although her misconduct, which the defendant was aware of but unable to prove, would probably have dictated a different assessment of the position; the fact that the agreement on ancillary matters was about to confirm the situation; the utter improbability of anyone's wanting to send a man who claimed to be a former member of the Foreign Legion and who lacked training culture and ability to Haiti and then to Switzerland in order to obtain relatively innocuous information which was in any event of doubtful relevance for the purposes of the divorce proceedings ...'[2]

The court further concluded that the argument that the use of the recording was a violation of art 8 was subsumed under the decision regarding art 6.

1   (1988) 13 EHRR 242 at para 46.
2   (1988) 13 EHRR 242 at para 48.

2.36   Four judges joined in a dissenting judgment, emphatic that no court should be seen to rely on unlawfully obtained evidence.

'To our very great regret, we cannot share the majority's view since in our opinion, compliance with the law when taking evidence is not an abstract or formalistic requirement. On the contrary, we consider that it is of first importance for the fairness of a criminal trial. No court can, without detriment to the proper administration of justice, rely on evidence which has been obtained not only by unfair means but above all, unlawfully. If it does so, the trial cannot be fair within the meaning of the Convention.'[1]

1   (1988) 13 EHRR 242 at para 53.

Bugging devices

2.37   A case in which there was no other evidence other than unlawfully obtained evidence was *Khan v United Kingdom*.[1] In view of the reasoning in the above case, it might have been expected that the court would have found a violation of art 6. It did not. In *Khan*, both he and his cousin (N) were stopped on arrival at Manchester Airport. N was found to be in possession of £100,000 worth of heroin and was arrested and charged. The applicant was released without charge. Four months later the police installed a listening device on the exterior of an address of another suspect (B) in Sheffield. Authorisation was given by the Chief Constable on the basis that that there were good grounds for suspecting that B was dealing in heroin and that conventional methods of surveillance were unlikely to succeed. At the time it was not expected that applicant would visit the premises. Two weeks later the applicant did visit the premises and while there made statements which were recorded and which amounted to an admission that he had been involved in the importation.

1   (1997) 31 EHRR 45.

2.38   In its judgment the ECt HR referred to the comment in the judgment of the House of Lords that the lack of any statutory system regulating the use of surveillance devices was astonishing. It went on to conclude that that fact meant that the interference could not be considered to be 'in accordance with law' as required by art 8(2). In the light of that conclusion, it was not necessary to determine whether the interference was 'necessary in a democratic society'. It did not, however, follow that there was a violation of art 6. The court noted that, in contrast to the position in *Schenk*, the fixing of the listening device and the recording of the applicant's conversation were not unlawful in the sense of being contrary to domestic criminal law. Moreover, there was no suggestion that the police had acted otherwise than in accordance with Home Office guidelines. In addition, the admissions were made voluntarily, there being no entrapment or inducement. Although the contested evidence was the only evidence against the applicant, the relevance of other evidence depended on the facts of the case. In the present case, the tape recording was acknowledged to be very strong evidence, and where there was no risk of it being unreliable the need for supporting evidence is correspondingly weaker. The applicant did not challenge the authenticity of the recording but challenged its use. Had the domestic courts been of the opinion that the admission of the evidence would have given rise to substantive unfairness, they would have had a discretion to exclude it under PACE 1984, s 78. In the circumstances there was no breach of art 6. However, the system of complaints against the police did not meet the requisite standard of independence to constitute sufficient protection against the abuse of authority. Accordingly, there was a breach of art 13.

2.39   In a strong dissenting judgment Judge Loucaides made the same point as the dissenting judges in *Schenk*:

> 'I cannot accept that a trial can be "fair" as required by Art 6, if a person's guilt for any offence is established through evidence obtained in breach of rights guaranteed by the Convention. It is my opinion that the term "fairness" when examined in the context of the European Convention of Human Rights implies observance of the rule of law and for that matter it presupposes respect of the human rights set out in the Convention. I do not think one can speak of a "fair" trial if it is conducted in breach of the law. It is true that the Convention is not part of the domestic legal system of the United Kingdom but for the purposes in question in issue, it should be treated as such in view of its ratification by that country.'

He went on to state that not only did the use of evidence obtained in such a manner amount to a violation of art 6 but that:

> 'the exclusion of evidence obtained contrary to the protected right to privacy should be considered as an essential corollary of the right, if such right is to be of any value ... It should be recalled here that the court has on many occasions stressed "that the Convention is intended to guarantee not rights that are theoretical or illusory but rights that are practical and effective." The exclusion of such evidence, in my view, becomes even more imperative in cases like the present, where no alternative effective remedy exists against the breach of the relevant right.'

2.40   As noted above (**para 2.35**), in *Schenk* the court stated that it would not exclude 'as a matter of principle and in the abstract' the possibility that unlawfully obtained evidence might be admissible. The phrase tends to recognise that, other than in exceptional circumstances, such evidence would not be admissible. In addition, *Schenk* is not the only case in which the court has laid considerable emphasis on the fact that the conviction was not based mainly on the impugned evidence.[1] Furthermore, the suggestion that the fixing of the bugging device was not contrary to domestic criminal law ignores the fact that, prima facie, it amounted to criminal damage. In any event, the domestic legal framework has been changed by the Police Act 1997, Pt III, which, while not providing a criminal offence, now provides a procedure for authorisation of such activity (see **Chapter 5**). A failure to comply with the appropriate procedure would now be likely to be unlawful by virtue of HRA 1998, s 6. Such unlawfulness would be highly relevant to any decision to exclude (see **Chapter 11**).

1   See also *Doorson v Netherlands* (1996) 22 EHRR 330.

Trickery

2.41   The use of subterfuge or trickery will not generally engage art 6. Where, however, the surveillance technique involves trickery which affects the will of an accused person, effectively depriving him of his privilege against self-incrimination, art 6 may be engaged. In *Allan v United Kingdom*,[1] while the applicant was in custody on a charge of robbery, an anonymous informant told the police that he had been involved in a murder that had taken place in February 1995, two weeks prior to the robbery. The Chief Constable granted authority for an unlimited period for the cell and visiting areas to be bugged. Recordings were made of the applicant's conversations with a friend in the prison visiting area and with his co-accused in the cell they shared, and a police informant was placed in his cell for the purpose of eliciting information from him. He was arrested for the murder and during interviews made no comment. During conversation with the informant it was alleged that the applicant had admitted his presence at the murder scene. No other evidence connected him with the murder. In the Court of Appeal the defence attempted to distinguish *R v Khan* on the basis that in the present case the tapes were not truly covert tapes because the applicant was aware that what he said was being recorded. In the ECt HR it was submitted that he was in a no-win situation, as if he whispered that was said to be incriminating and if his remarks were not incriminating he was said to be tailoring his remarks for the microphone. Further, the recording was much more invasive and protracted than in *Khan* and the evidence obtained was filled with inaccuracies and unreliable. The government accepted that there was at the time no statutory system to regulate the use of covert recording devices by the police and that there was thus a violation of art 8. However, the government argued that the case could not be distinguished from *Khan* except that there was other evidence in the form of the testimony of the informant. In considering art 6, the court was not persuaded that the use of the taped material consisting of conversations with the friend or his co-accused conflicted with the requirements of fairness guaranteed by art 6, as the defence had been entitled to challenge the evidence as being unreliable or unfair in both the trial and the appeal. In considering the evidence of the informant, however, the court observed that the right of the accused to choose whether to speak or to remain silent was at the heart of the notion of a fair procedure. Such freedom of choice was undermined in a case where the accused had elected to remain silent but the authorities had used subterfuge to elicit statements of an incriminating nature. In the present case the admissions allegedly made by the applicant were not spontaneous or unprompted (as in *Khan*), but were induced by persistent questioning by the informant in circumstances which were the functional equivalent of interrogation. The information could be regarded as having been obtained in defiance of the will of the applicant and its use at trial impinged on his right to silence. The court was unanimous in finding a breach of art 6, but somewhat confusingly made no award of just satisfaction as the court refused to speculate on the outcome of the trial in other circumstances. It did, however, make an award for the breach of art 8 (see **para 2.50**).

1   (2002) 36 EHRR 12 p 143.

2.42   In *PG and JH v United Kingdom*,[1] the applicants were suspected of planning an armed robbery. The police installed a bugging device in the home of a third party (B) but failed to obtain the necessary written authorisation. They also applied to British Telecom for itemised billing of B's telephone. The applicants discovered the device and abandoned the premises. No robbery took place. The applicants were arrested and declined to comment during subsequent interviews. The police obtained authorisation to install covert listening devices in the cells being used by the applicants and samples of their speech were recorded. As the main purpose of the recording of the conversations in the police station was to provide voice samples to compare with the other recordings of conversations that had taken place in the house, the ECt HR held that no question of infringing the privilege against self-incrimination arose. Although the court found breaches of art 8 in respect of the bugging of the house and the police station (see **para 2.49**), there was no breach of art 6 because there was no entrapment or inducement in respect of the former and no admissions in respect of the latter which could be seen as akin to a sample of blood or hair. There was no breach of art 8 regarding the metering of calls from B's phone, as lawful authority was to be found in the Telecommunications Act 1984, s 45. In her partly dissenting opinion, Judge Tulkens contrasted the unlawfulness under domestic law that was in issue in *Schenk* with the unlawfulness under the Convention in issue in the present case. In her opinion, what was forbidden under one provision of the Convention (art 8) could not be permitted under another provision (art 6):

> 'In concluding that there has not been a violation of Article 6, the Court renders Article 8 completely ineffective … Will there come a point at which the majority's reasoning will be applied where the evidence has been obtained in breach of other provisions of the Convention, such as Art 3, for example? Where and how should the line be drawn? According to which hierarchy in the guaranteed rights? Ultimately the very notion of fairness in a trial might have a tendency to decline or become subject to shifting goalposts.'

1   Reports of Judgments and Decisions 2001 IX p 195; [2002] Crim LR 308.

Legal advice

2.43 Surveillance activities which threaten to interfere with the lawyer-client relationship may engage both art 6 and art 8. In *Niemietz v Germany*,[1] the court was concerned with the search of a solicitor's office which it was hoped would throw light on the identity of the author of an insulting telefax sent to a judge. No such information was forthcoming and no charges were ever brought. Nevertheless, the court concluded that not only was the interference disproportionate, and therefore a breach of art 8, but that:

> 'where a lawyer is involved, an encroachment on professional secrecy may have repercussions on the proper administration of justice and hence on the rights guaranteed by Art 6 of the Convention.'[2]

1   (1992) 16 EHRR 97.
2   (1992) 16 EHRR 97, at para 37.

2.44 *S v Switzerland*[1] concerned the activities of a suspected terrorist. The activities, which lasted for a period of years, included not only the use of explosives but the writing of graffiti. While in custody almost all his communications with his lawyer were overseen or intercepted by the police. The authorities justified the action on the grounds of the possibility of collusion between lawyers representing other accuseds. The surveillance lasted for over seven months. Some of the letters to his lawyer were intercepted to be used for the purposes of handwriting comparison. S complained that such surveillance prevented any confidential conversation with his lawyer aimed at refuting the evidence collected during the investigation. The applicant was eventually granted bail but failed to appear for his trial. He was convicted in his absence. The ECt HR reminded itself that the Convention is intended to guarantee rights that are practical and effective and held that legal advice provided in such circumstances would lose much of its usefulness. The conduct of the particular lawyer instructed had never been called into question. As no sufficient risk of collusion had been established there was a violation of art 6(3)(c).

1   (1991) 14 EHRR 670.

2.45 In *Foxley v United Kingdom*,[1] the opening, reading and copying to file of letters from a solicitor to a bankrupt by the trustee in bankruptcy after the expiry of a redirection order was held to be an interference with the bankrupt's rights under art 8. As there was no pressing need for such activities, the interference was not necessary in a democratic society. The ECt HR recalled that where a lawyer is involved, an encroachment on professional secrecy may have repercussions on the proper administration of justice and hence on the rights guaranteed by art 6 of the Convention. However, having regard to the finding under art 8, the court considered that it was unnecessary to examine the applicant's complaints under art 6.

1   (2000) 8 BHRC 571.

Article 8

2.46   Article 8 is a qualified right in the sense that once a prima facie interference with the right has been established it is open to the state (or relevant public authority) to justify the interference having regard to the objectives specified in art 8(2). Article 8 states:

> '8.1.   Everyone has the right to respect for his private and family life, his home and correspondence.
>
> 8.2.   There shall be no interference by a public authority with the exercise of this right except such as in accordance with the law and is necessary in a democratic society in the interests of national security, public safety or the economic well-being of the country, for the prevention of disorder or crime, for the protection of health or morals or for the protection of the rights and freedoms of others.'

Before considering the structure of art 8 in greater detail it is proposed to look at examples of the width of art 8. As pointed out in **para 2.4**, the finding of a violation of this article is almost invariably considered to be sufficient just satisfaction.

Examples

2.47   Article 8 has been held to include:

- search and seizure;[1]
- prison staff opening prisoners' correspondence with their legal advisors;[2]
- the stopping of prisoners' letters (although in the case of *Silver v United Kingdom*[3] the stopping of one particular letter to a solicitor was found to be justified since it might relate to the disposal of the proceeds of crime);
- fingerprinting suspects;[4]
- storage of information;[5] and
- photographing detainees in custody.[6]

1   See *Funke v France* (1993) 16 EHRR 297 and *McLeod v United Kingdom* (1998) 27 EHRR 493.
2   See *Campbell v United Kingdom* (1992) 15 EHRR 137.
3   (1983) 5 EHRR 347.
4   See *McVeigh v United Kingdom* (1983) 5 EHRR 71.
5   See *Leander v Sweden* (1987) 9 EHRR 433, *Amman v Switzerland* [2000] 30 EHRR 843 and *Hewitt and Harman v United Kingdom* (1989) 14 EHRR 657.
6   See *Murray v United Kingdom* (1994) 19 EHRR 193.

Does private life include business premises?

2.48   The concept of private life is not restricted to that of a home life and may include activities of a professional or business nature. In *Niemietz v Germany*,[1] the applicant, a lawyer, complained about the search of his business premises on the pretext that the search might reveal information about who was responsible for writing a threatening letter to a judge.

'Respect for private life must also comprise to a certain degree the right to establish and develop relationships with other human beings.'[2]

In the case of:

'a person exercising a liberal profession his work in that context may form part and parcel of his life to such a degree that it becomes impossible to know in what capacity he is acting at a given moment of time.'

The court added that:

'to interpret the words "private life" and "home" as including certain professional or business activities or premises would be consonant with the essential object and purpose of Art 8, namely to protect the individual against arbitrary interference by the public authorities.'[3]

Having regard to the broad terms in which the warrant was drawn and the fact that the search impinged on professional secrecy, the interference was disproportionate. The case was relied on in subsequent cases, such as *Kopp v Switzerland*[4] (a solicitor's office), *Amman v Switzerland*[5] (a business office), and *Halford v United Kingdom*[6] (a designated telephone line in a police station).

1   (1992) 16 EHRR 97.
2   (1992) 16 EHRR 97 at para 29.
3   (1992) 16 EHRR 97 at para 31.
4   (1998) 27 EHRR 91.
5   (2000) 30 EHRR 843.
6   (1997) 24 EHRR 523.

Does a suspect in custody have a right to a private life?

2.49   In the UK the covert recording of a suspect's conversations with others in police cells is a not uncommon form of evidence gathering – see, for example, *R v Bailey and Smith*,[1] *R v Jelen and Katz*,[2] *R v Shaukat Ali*,[3] *R v Roberts*,[4] and *R v Mason*.[5] Only in the latter case was art 8 raised. In *PG and JH v United Kingdom*[6] (see **para 2.42**), the court considered that no material difference arose where the recording device was operated without the knowledge or consent of the individual concerned on police premises. Thus the fact that the recording of a suspect's voice in a police cell was for comparison purposes rather than to rely on the contents of conversations did not prevent an interference with art 8.

'There are a number of elements relevant to a consideration of whether a person's private life is concerned by measures effected outside a person's home or private premises. Since there are occasions when people knowingly or intentionally involve themselves in activities which are or may be recorded or reported in a public manner, a person's reasonable expectation as to privacy may be a significant, although not conclusive, factor. A person who walks down the street will inevitably be visible to any member of the public who is also present. Monitoring by technological means of the same public scene (for example a security guard viewing through closed circuit television) is of a similar character. Private life considerations may arise, however, once any systematic or permanent record comes into existence of such material from the public domain. It is for this reason that files gathered by the security services on a particular individual fall within Art 8 even where the information has not been gathered by any intrusive or covert method.'[7]

1   (1993) 97 Cr App Rep 365.
2   (1990) 90 Cr App Rep 456.
3   (1991) Times, 19 February.
4   [1997] Crim LR 222.
5   [2002] 2 Cr App Rep 32.
6   [2002] Crim LR 308, [2002] EHRLR 262, Reports of Judgments and Decisions 2001 IX p 195.
7   Reports of Judgments and Decisions, 2001 IX at para 57.

2.50   In *Allan v United Kingdom*[1] (see **para 2.41**) the government accepted that the use of audio and video recording devices in the applicant's cell, the prison visiting area and on a fellow prisoner amounted to an interference with private life. In view of the fact that the applicant's case was that he was aware of the presence of the devices, the concession could be described as a generous one. As there was no statutory system to regulate the use of such devices, the measures were not in accordance with law and there was thus a breach of art 8. In considering just satisfaction, the court commented that there had been several violations of art 8 and that the applicant had no effective remedy under domestic law. He must 'thereby have suffered some feelings of frustration and invasion of privacy which is not sufficiently compensated by a finding of a violation', and he was awarded €1,642 (£1,200) compensation. As has been seen, the court made no award for the violation of art 6 brought about by the undermining of his right to silence.

1   (2002) 36 EHRR 12 p 143.

To a private individual in a public setting

2.51   In *Friedl v Austria*[1] the applicant had been filmed by the police during a public demonstration and the Commission held that art 8 had not been infringed on the basis that the individuals in the photographs remained anonymous and that the personal data and photographs taken were not entered into a data processing system.[2] However, the questioning that took place on the same occasion and the recording of personal data constituted an interference with the right guaranteed by art 8(1). In these particular circumstances both the questioning and the retention of the data were necessary and there was thus no violation of art 8. Even where the individual is identifiable, it has been held that mere monitoring of an individual in a public setting was not a breach of art 8. In *Peck v United Kingdom*,[3] where the ECt HR distinguished between the use of photographic equipment to monitor a person in a town centre, which was not an interference with art 8 rights and the recording and subsequent dissemination of that material, which was an interference with art 8 rights (see **Chapter 3**). In such circumstances a person's reasonable expectation of privacy may be relevant but not decisive.[4]

1   Series A 305, (1995) 21 EHRR 83.
2   Series A 305, 21 EHRR 83 at para 50.
3   (2003) 36 EHRR 41 (p 719) at para 57.
4   See *PG and JH v United Kingdom* (**para 2.50**).

The five hurdles

2.52   To come within art 8(2), the interference must be in accordance with law and be necessary in a democratic society. These two concepts can conveniently be subdivided to form five separate hurdles. The question of what is in accordance with law involves three of those hurdles:

(1)   Was there a legal basis for the interference in question?
(2)   If so, was the law accessible?
(3)   Was it foreseeable? (This question has a special meaning in the context of surveillance – see **para 2.56**.

The question of 'necessity' involves two further hurdles:
(4)   Did the interference pursue a legitimate aim? (see **para 2.68.**)
(5)   Was it proportionate? (see **para 2.69.**)

Each case must be considered on its own facts so that it should be recognised that the height of the hurdle, particularly when considering proportionality, may vary. Only if the state or relevant public authority is able to 'jump all hurdles' can it rely on art 8(2). Thus, if there is no legal basis for the interference there is no need to consider whether it is 'necessary in a democratic society'.[1]

1   *Khan v United Kingdom* (1997) *31 EHRR 45.*

The first hurdle

2.53   The first requirement of art 8(2) is that there must be a legal basis for the action in question.[1] Although the courts have always understood the term 'law' in its substantive sense and not its formal one,[2] Home Office circulars and other forms of guidance are insufficient.[3]

The failure by successive British governments to appreciate the significance of the judgments in *Klass* and *Malone* (see **para 2.55**) and to introduce a statutory basis for surveillance activities by the police and others has resulted in numerous adverse findings by the ECt HR.[4]

1   *Klass v Germany* (1978) 2 EHRR 214; *Malone v United Kingdom (1985)* 7 EHRR 14.
2   See *Huvig v France* (1990) 12 EHRR 528 and *Kopp v Switzerland* (1998) 27 EHRR 91.
3   See *Khan v United Kingdom* (1997) 31 EHRR 45,
4   *Halford v United Kingdom (1997)* 24 EHRR 523, *Hewitson v United Kingdom (2003)* 37 EHRR 31 p 687, *PG and JH v United Kingdom [2002] EHRLR 262,* [2002] Crim LR 308 (see above **para 2.42**), *Allan v United Kingdom (2002)* 36 EHRR 12 (see above **para 2.41**), *Chalkley v United Kingdom* [2003] Crim LR 51 (admissibility decision), *Taylor Sabori v United Kingdom (2002)* 36 EHRR 17 p 248, *Armstrong v United Kingdom* (2002) Times, 31 October, 36 EHRR 30 p 515.

The second hurdle

2.54   The relevant law must be accessible to those likely to be affected. In *Silver v United Kingdom,*[1] it was held that publication of the Prison Act 1952 and the Prison Rules made thereunder met this criterion but that unpublished orders and instructions to officials did not.

1   (1983) 5 EHRR 347.

The third hurdle

2.55 The relevant law must be sufficiently precise to enable citizens to be aware of the circumstances in which it applies. In *Malone v United Kingdom* it was stated that the law:

> 'must indicate the scope of any such discretion conferred on the competent authority and the manner of its exercise with sufficient clarity having regard to the legitimate aim of the measure in question to give the individual adequate protection against arbitrary interference.'[1]

The applicant was an antiques dealer who was prosecuted for handling stolen goods. During his trial in 1978, it emerged that his telephone had been tapped by the police pursuant to a warrant issued by the Home Secretary. Following his acquittal, he brought civil proceedings to obtain a declaration that the tapping had been unlawful even if done pursuant to a warrant of the Secretary of State. At the time no statutory power existed which entitled the Secretary of State or anyone else to intercept letters or telephone calls. Although the civil action was unsuccessful, Megarry V-C, in his judgment dated 28 February 1979, commented that in comparing the state of English law with that of Germany as disclosed in *Klass*:

> 'Not a single one of the safeguards is to be found as a matter of established law in England, and only a few corresponding provisions exist as a matter of administrative procedure. In this respect English law compares most unfavourably with West German law.'

1   (1985) 7 EHRR 14 at para 68.

2.56 No doubt encouraged by the comments of Megarry V-C, the applicant then made a claim against the UK government alleging breaches of art 8 and 13. The court held that there had been a breach of art 8 because English law did not satisfy the qualitative test necessary to meet the 'in accordance with law' criterion.

> 'The Court would reiterate its opinion that the phrase "in accordance with law" does not merely refer back to domestic law but also relates to the quality of the law, requiring it to be compatible with the rule of law, which is expressly mentioned in the preamble to the Convention. The phrase thus implies – and this follows from the object and purpose of Art 8 – that there must be a measure of legal protection in domestic law against arbitrary interferences by public authorities with the rights safeguarded by paragraph 1. Especially where a power of the executive is exercised in secret, the risks of arbitrariness are evident. Undoubtedly, as the Government rightly suggested, the requirements of the Convention, notably in regard to forseeability, cannot be exactly the same in the special context of interception of communications for the purposes of police investigations as they are where the object of the relevant law is to place restrictions on the conduct of individuals. In particular, the requirement of forseeability cannot mean that an individual should be enabled to foresee when the authorities are likely to intercept his communications so that he can adapt his conduct accordingly. Nevertheless, the law must be sufficiently clear in its terms to give citizens an adequate indication as to the circumstances in which

and the conditions on which public authorities are empowered to resort to this secret and potentially dangerous interference with the right to respect for private life and correspondence.'[1]

The court also considered that, for similar reasons, the process of metering, which involved the use of a device to register the numbers dialled on a particular phone as well as the time and duration of the call, was in breach of art 8.

For reasons that are unclear, the court did not consider it necessary to rule on art 13. The judgment does not record what, if any, compensation was awarded.

1   (1984) 7 EHRR 14 at para 67.

2.57   The importance of the quality of law test can be illustrated by a series of cases concerning interception. In each case it was accepted that there was a legal basis for such interference but that the domestic law failed to give citizens an adequate indication as to the circumstances in and conditions on which public authorities were empowered to take any such secret measures. As will be seen, English law was not unique in its failure to anticipate the importance of the quality of law in such a sensitive area. The first four cases concern France, which, since the Act of 17 July 1970,[1] has recognised the right to private life. Article 22 of this Act was incorporated in art 9 of the Code Civil. As the Act did not define private life, the exact nature of the right has been described as 'problematic'.[2] The Act also added an art 368 to the Criminal Code:

'Anyone who wilfully intrudes on the privacy of others:

1.   By listening to, recording or transmitting by means of any device words spoken by a person in a private place, without that person's consent;

2.   ...shall be liable to imprisonment for not less than two months and not more than one year and a fine ... or to only one of these two measures.'

1   Loi No 70–643 du 17 Juillet 1970.
2   B Edelman case note under Cour de Cassation 1 ch civ, 3 Decembre 1980, 'affaire du pullover rouge' (1981) Dalloz 221.

2.58   In *Huvig v France,*[1] the court undertook an interesting analysis into the state of French law both at the time of the judgment in 1990 and at the time of the suspected offences in 1974. During the course of an investigation into suspected tax evasion an investigating judge had issued a warrant requiring the police to monitor the telephones of the applicants over a period of less than two days. During the trial, which did not take place until 1982, the applicants raised a plea of nullity on the basis of the unlawfulness of the tapping. The court rejected the plea on the basis, inter alia, that art 81 of the 1958 Code of Criminal Procedure permitted the investigating judge to 'take all investigative measures which he deems useful for establishing the truth'. The appeal to the Court of Cassation was also unsuccessful. On appeal to the ECt HR the court recognised that although French criminal law adopts the principle that any kind of evidence is admissible there was no statutory authority empowering investigating judges to order telephone tapping or the taking of photographs or fingerprints, shadowing or surveillance, requisitions, confrontation of witnesses or reconstruction of crimes. It also noted the existence of the offence under art 368 of the Criminal Code.

1   (1990) 12 EHRR 528.

2.59   The court then conducted a detailed examination of the case law, noting that practically all of the safeguards laid down by the courts post-dated the interception complained of by the applicants. In concluding that there had been a breach of art 8, the court stated:

> 'Above all, the system does not for the time being afford adequate safeguards against various possible abuses. For example the categories of people liable to have their telephones tapped by judicial order and the nature of the offences which may give rise to such an order are nowhere defined. Nothing obliges a judge to set a limit on the duration of telephone tapping. Similarly unspecified are the procedure for drawing up summary reports containing intercepted conversations; the precautions to be taken in order to communicate the recordings intact and in their entirety for possible inspection by the judge and by the defence; and the circumstances in which recordings may or must be erased or the tapes destroyed, in particular where an accused has been discharged by an investigating judge or acquitted by a court.'[1]

1   (1990) 12 EHRR 528 at para 34

2.60   *Kruslin v France*[1] was a murder case decided by the same court on the same day as *Huvig* and containing many identically worded paragraphs (including that quoted above). The case concerned evidence of an intercepted telephone call which was said to be a decisive piece of the evidence against the applicant in respect of two offences of robbery and one of murder. In this respect the case was significantly different from *Huvig*, in which the telephone tapping evidence did not 'serve as the basis for the prosecution'. The applicant argued that art 368 of the Criminal Code prohibited telephone tapping in principle and that there had been a violation of art 8 of the Convention. For reasons that are unclear, although he appealed to the Court of Cassation on the basis that the evidence was inadmissible, he did not pursue a complaint based on art 6. Although the ECt HR agreed that there had been a violation of art 8 on the basis that the applicant did not enjoy the minimum protection to which citizens are entitled, his claim for compensation of FF1m, in respect of his 15-year sentence, was rejected. Somewhat unsatisfactorily, no reasons were given. No reference was made to the case of *Schenk*, decided two years previously, and there was only a passing reference to art 6.

1   (1990) 12 EHRR 547.

2.61   In *A v France*,[1] the applicant was charged with conspiracy to murder. She was a cardiologist. A third party (G) who was himself also charged, had gone to the police to tell them that he had been hired by the applicant to kill a man (V). G volunteered to phone the applicant in circumstances which permitted the police to telephone tap the applicant and record the conversation. A chief superintendent (B) agreed to the proposed course but did not reveal to his superiors what he had done. Such conduct was prima facie a criminal offence pursuant to art 368 (see **para 2.57**). The applicant was subsequently acquitted but claimed damages in separate proceedings for a violation of her art 8 rights. As with *Kruslin*, despite the fact that the unlawfully obtained evidence was used as the basis for a prosecution, a violation of art 6 was not alleged. The government accepted that the interference was not in accordance with law, as no law permitted B to make the recording, but argued that:

(a)   the conversation concerned only the applicant's plans to kill V and therefore did not concern her private life; and

(b)   art 8 did not protect conversations in circumstances where one party consented to the recording in question.

The Commission took the view that it was irrelevant that one of the two speakers may agree to, or even co-operate in, the interception or recording of the conversation concerned. The recording of a private conversation without the knowledge of one of the participants was an interference in their private life.[1] Furthermore, a telephone conversation did not cease to be private merely because its content concerned matters of public interest. If the field protected by art 8 were limited to those aspects of private life in which the public authorities have no interest art 8 would be largely divested of its substance. The court found that the contested recording had no basis in domestic law and agreed with the Commission that there had been a breach of art 8. The court considered that although the applicant may have sustained non-pecuniary damage, the judgment constituted sufficient just satisfaction. No reference was made to the comments in the earlier case of *Ludi v Switzerland*[2] (see **para 2.31**) that art 8 provides no protection for those allegedly involved in crime.

1   (1993) 17 EHRR 462 at para 34.
2   (1992) 15 EHRR 173.

2.62   The shortcomings in French law exposed in *Huvig* and *Kruslin* resulted in a revision of the Criminal Code in 1991, the effect of which was to entitle the investigating judge to order telephone tapping subject to a number of preconditions designed to minimise the risk of abuse.

Article 100 provides that:

'In the case of serious crime or other major offence attracting a sentence of at least two years' imprisonment, the investigating judge may, when necessary for the investigation, order the interception, recording and transcription of tel-ecommunications messages. Such operations shall be carried out under his authority and supervision. Decisions to intercept shall be in writing. They shall not constitute judicial decisions and no appeal shall lie against them.'

Article 100–1 provides that:

'Decisions made pursuant to Art 100 shall contain all the information necessary for identifying the link to be monitored, the offence that justifies the intercep-tion and the duration of the interception.'

Article 100–2 provides that:

'Such decisions shall be valid for a maximum duration of four months. Their validity may be extended only subject to the same procedural requirements and maximum duration.'

Article 100–3 provides for the giving of instructions to an authorised network operator or provider of telecommunications services.

Article 100–4 provides that:

'The investigating judge or the senior detective acting on his instructions shall draw up a report on each of the interception and recording operations. This report shall give the date, and time of the beginning and end of each operation.'

Article 100–5 provides for the transcription of messages.

Article 100–6 provides that:

'The Public Prosecutor or Principal Public Prosecutor shall ensure that the recordings are destroyed when prosecution becomes time barred. A full report of the destruction shall be drawn up.'

The concept of effective control

2.63   These additional provisions were considered in the potentially highly significant case of *Lambert v France*[1] and declared to satisfy the quality of law test.[2] During the course of an investigation into large scale illicit furniture dealing, an investigating judge had issued a warrant to intercept the phone of a third party ('B'). The period of the interceptions was extended in all to six months and as a result of the interceptions the applicant was charged with handling the proceeds of aggravated theft. The applicant applied to the Court of Appeal for a ruling that the extensions were invalid on the basis that they had been ordered by standard-form written instructions without any reference to the offences which justified the tapping. No separate complaint was made under art 6. Both the Court of Appeal and the Court of Cassation ruled that he had no locus standi to challenge the manner in which the interception of a third party's telephone line was extended. The ECt HR disagreed, stating that such a conclusion could lead to decisions whereby a very large number of people were deprived of the protection of art 8, namely all those who have conversations on a telephone line other than their own. The court unanimously concluded that in the circumstances the applicant did not have available to him the 'effective control' to which citizens are entitled under the rule of law, and awarded him FF10,000. The implication of the judgment is that a citizen is entitled to challenge the use of interception in order to restrict the interference in question to what was necessary in a democratic society. Thus, having succeeded in jumping the third hurdle, the state appears to have fallen at the final hurdle (see below), not on the basis that the interference was not necessary but simply that the target had not been permitted to challenge its use. The fact that had he been able to mount such a challenge he would have stood no chance of success was not considered relevant. The effect of the case for legal systems, such as that in the UK whose citizens are unlikely ever to be informed of the fact of interception let alone to raise any meaningful complaint, has yet to be considered.

1   (2000) 30 EHRR 346.
2   (2000) 30 EHRR 346 at para 28.

2.64   Actual interference with the telephone lines of the applicant's law firm was established in *Kopp v Switzerland*.[1] An investigation had been opened by the Swiss authorities (Federal Public Prosecutor) in order to identify the person working at the Federal Department of Justice and Peace who might have been responsible for having disclosed official secrets. The Prosecutor applied to be allowed to tap the phones of two informants (X and Y) and also those of the applicant and his wife. The applicant was monitored as a third party not as a suspect. The relevant domestic law was Federal Criminal Procedure Act, s 66, which provided that:

> 'third parties may also be monitored if specific facts give rise to the presumption that they are receiving or imparting information intended for the accused or suspect or sent by him.'

An order sanctioning such tapping was made by the President of the Indictments Division but expressly mentioned that lawyers' conversations were not to be taken into account. The ECt HR remarked on the fact that the domestic legislation prohibited the monitoring of a lawyer's telephone when he was neither suspected nor accused. The law was intended to protect the professional relations between a lawyer and his clients. However, it failed to state clearly how, under what circumstances and by whom the distinction was to be drawn between matters specifically connected with a lawyer's work under instructions from a party to those proceedings and those relating to activity other than that of counsel.[2] Above all, the court found it astonishing that this task should be assigned to an official of the Post Office legal department, who was a member of the executive, without supervision by an independent judge.[3] The astonishment did not translate into a decision to award any form of compensation to the applicant.

1   (1998) 27 EHRR 91.
2   (1998) 27 EHRR 91 at para 73.
3   (1998) 27 EHRR 91 at para 74.

2.65   Actual interference with a telephone call and the creation of a 'card' was also established by the applicant in *Amman v Switzerland*.[1] The applicant was a businessman who imported depilatory appliances into Switzerland. A telephone call from a customer in the Soviet Embassy in Berne, ordering a 'Perma Tweez' depilatory device, was intercepted by the Federal Public Prosecutor's Office. Shortly afterwards the Office drew up a card on the applicant for its national security card index. The card identified him as a contact with the Russian Embassy. Nine years later the applicant learnt of the existence of the card and asked to see it. On seeing it he filed for compensation for the unlawful entry of his particulars on the card. The representative for the state informed the court that where someone at the former Soviet embassy was under surveillance, on every telephone call both parties to the conversation were identified, a card drawn up on them and a telephone monitoring report made. The Federal Court found that as it was not immediately clear that the 'Perma Tweez' appliance was a harmless device the authorities had acted correctly.

The ECt HR held[2] that the relevant Swiss law provided no indication as to the persons concerned by such measures, the circumstances in which they might be ordered, the means to be employed or the procedures to be observed, and was thus insufficiently clear to satisfy the requirements of art 8. Further, the court noted that the primary object of the Federal Criminal Procedure Act was the surveillance of persons suspected or accused of a crime or major offence, or even third parties presumed to be receiving information from or sending it to such persons. The Act did not regulate in detail the case of persons monitored fortuitously as necessary participants in a telephone conversation recorded pursuant to these provisions. In particular, the Act did not specify the precautions which should be taken with regard to those persons.

1   (2000) 30 EHRR 843.
2   (2000) 30 EHRR 843 at para 58.

2.66 Similar observations were made with regard to the storage of the card, in particular that the relevant directive did not specify the conditions in which the cards may be created, the procedures to be followed, the information which may be stored or comments that may be forbidden. The directive did not give adequate protection against interference by the authorities with the applicant's art 8 rights. Both the creation and the storage of the card were found to violate art 8,[1] but not art 13 as the applicant was entitled to complain to the Federal Court once he became aware of the existence of the card.

1   (2000) 30 EHRR 843 at para 76.

2.67 For a particularly clear example of the importance of the quality of law see *Valenzuela Contreras v Spain*,[1] where, notwithstanding that the investigating judge anticipated most of the concerns expressed five years later in *Huvig v France* and *Kruslin v France*, the court held that the telephone tapping was not in accordance with law as there were in fact at the time no laws governing the categories of people liable to have their phones tapped nor controls on the duration of or procedure for such activity.

1   (1998) 28 EHRR 483.

The fourth hurdle: is there a legitimate aim?

2.68 This is the first part of the necessity test. The interference must be consistent with the purposes set out in art 8(2); for example, in the interests of national security[1] or public safety or the economic well-being of the country[2] or for the prevention of disorder or crime,[3] or for the protection of health or morals[4] or the protection of the rights and freedoms of others.[5]

In *Sunday Times v United Kingdom*,[6] the court held that while the word necessary did not mean 'indispensable', it did not have the flexibility of such expressions as admissible, ordinary, useful, reasonable or desirable. Rather, it implies a pressing social need.

1   See *Leander v Sweden* (1987) 9 EHRR 433.
2   See *Funke v France (1993)* 16 EHRR 297 and *Mialle v France* (1993) 16 EHRR 332.
3   *Klass v Germany (1978)* 2 EHRR 214 and *Huvig v France* (1990) 12 EHRR 528.
4   *Erickson v Sweden* (1989) 12 EHRR 183.
5   *Ohlson v Sweden* (1988) 11 EHRR 259.
6   (1979) 2 EHRR 245.

The fifth hurdle: proportionality

2.69 The height of this hurdle is fact dependent. Was there a reasonable relationship between the means used and the objective sought to be achieved? Restrictions on rights must be strictly proportionate to any legitimate aim. There must be a reasonable relationship between the goal pursued and the means used. The decision should not be based on arbitrary or unfair considerations.[1]

In *McLeod v United Kingdom*,[2] police officers entered the applicant's home in her absence in order to assist her ex-husband to remove property. They were relying on a common law power of entry to prevent a breach of the peace. The ECt HR accepted that the officers' actions were in accordance with the law and that the prevention of crime was a legitimate aim. However, their actions were not necessary in a democratic society as they ought to have checked the court order themselves. Had they done so they would have discovered that the applicant was not obliged to surrender the property at that time.

In *Mialle v France*,[3] the wholesale and indiscriminate seizure of nearly 15,000 documents as part of an investigation into suspected tax evasion held to be too lax was full of loopholes and disproportionate and in breach of art 8.[4]

1   See *Niemietz v Germany* (1992) 16 EHRR 97.
2   (1998) 27 EHRR 493.
3   (1996) 23 EHRR 491.
4   See, to similar effect, *Cremieux v France* (1993) 16 EHRR 357.

Peck v United Kingdom

2.70   Most UK cases have not considered proportionality as the initial hurdle of lawfulness has not been overcome. A case which did is *Peck v United Kingdom*,[1] the facts of which arose before incorporation of the Convention (and the government accepted that there was no general right to privacy but referred to 'the regime of legal protection'). In this case the applicant had been captured on CCTV walking around Brentwood town centre on an evening in August 1995, carrying a large knife in the process of attempting to commit suicide. As a result of the CCTV coverage the police were alerted to the situation and were able to recover the knife and prevent the applicant causing any harm to himself.

1   (2003) 36 EHRR 41.

2.71   The CCTV footage was owned by the local council, who released it to the local press as an example of the success of CCTV in preventing crime (and enabling the police to respond to incidents). A photograph of the applicant was used in publicity material. At all times his face was not specifically masked. The footage was subsequently provided at no cost to the BBC and Anglia TV and to a commercial news agency, who subsequently published the material. Before publication by the BBC the council had asked the producers of the programme to ensure that the faces of all persons were masked. Although the BBC made some attempt to do so, the masking was inadequate.

2.72   Some months later when he learnt of the publication, the applicant made a number of appearances in the media to protest about the publication of photographs from the CCTV footage. His complaint to both the Broadcasting Standards Commission (regarding the BBC programme) and to the Independent Television Commission were upheld. His complaint to the Press Complaints Commission was rejected on the basis that the events in question took place in a town high street open to public view. It did not consider that the article in the local newspaper implied that the applicant had committed a crime.

2.73 He instituted judicial review proceedings against the local council but was unsuccessful. The High Court was sympathetic to the applicant but held that in view of the Criminal Justice and Public Order Act 1994, s 163, the council were empowered to provide CCTV equipment in order to promote the prevention of crime and that the council had power to distribute the footage by virtue of Local Government Act 1972, s 111. The decision to do so could not be considered irrational.

2.74 In the ECt HR the applicant contended that both art 8 and art 13 had been violated. The government contended that his art 8 rights had not been engaged as the incident had taken place in public. Disclosure of those actions simply distributed a public event to a wider public. The applicant did not take issue about the fact of having been filmed but merely with the disclosure by the council of the CCTV material. He maintained that Convention jurisprudence accepts that the occurrence of an event in a public place was only one element in the overall assessment of whether there was an interference with private life. Other relevant factors, including the use made of the material obtained and the extent to which it was made available to the public.

2.75 The court considered that it was significant that the applicant was not in the street participating in a public event and he was not a public figure. It was late at night and he was in a state of some distress. Although the suicide attempt was not filmed, footage of the immediate aftermath was recorded and disclosed by the council direct to the public in its CCTV news. In addition, it was disclosed to the media. As a result, the relevant moment was viewed to an extent which far exceeded any exposure to a passer by and to a degree surpassing that which the applicant could possibly have foreseen. His identity was not adequately, or in some cases at all, masked in the photographs and footage so published and broadcast. It was a serious interference with his private life.

2.76 The court considered that the disclosure did have a basis in law and was, with appropriate advice, foreseeable. It also pursued the legitimate aim of public safety, the prevention of disorder and crime and the protection of the rights of others. However, the court noted that the council had other options open to it. It could have identified him through enquiries of the police and then sought his consent. It could have masked the images itself or taken more care in ensuring that the media did so, including asking for written undertakings. Although a consent-based system of disclosure could undermine the effectiveness of the CCTV system, the relevant footage in the present case concerned one individual. The insufficiency of the safeguards were such that the disclosure was disproportionate and an interference with his private life contrary to art 8.

2.77   In considering art 13, the government submitted that the breach of confidence remedy was the most relevant, suggesting that he would have been entitled to bring such an action if he had been filmed 'in circumstances giving rise to an expectation of privacy on his part'. However, the court considered to be particularly noteworthy the fact that the government had not claimed that the applicant had failed to exhaust his domestic remedies. The court considered that the applicant did not have an actionable remedy in breach of confidence as he would have had difficulty in establishing that the footage disclosed the necessary quality of confidence about it or that the information had been 'imparted in circumstances importing an obligation of confidence'. Furthermore, once the material was in the public domain its republication was not actionable, which would have significantly reduced its effectiveness. The procedure of judicial review did not entitle the High Court to consider the issue of proportionality and could not therefore provide an effective remedy. The media commissions had no power to award damages and were similarly ineffective. There was thus a violation of art 13. The court awarded the applicant €11,800 in respect of non-pecuniary loss.

A summary of factors relevant to an assessment of the quality of law

2.78   In considering whether domestic legislation is compatible with art 8 the most significant of the hurdles is likely to be the third. A summary of the relevant factors include the following:

- Are the categories of people liable to be the subject of surveillance clearly defined?
- Is the category of offence which would entitle the authority to use such techniques clearly defined?
- Is the duration of any such surveillance subject to adequate control?
- Is there a sufficiently clear procedure for limiting intrusion of privacy of third parties?
- Is there a clearly defined procedure for the provision of reports of such surveillance?
- Is there a clearly defined procedure for ensuring the integrity of the product of surveillance?
- Are there clearly defined procedures for identifying what material should be retained for inspection by the defence and the judge?
- Are there clearly defined procedures for identifying legally privileged material?
- Is the assessment of what may amount to such material carried out by an independent person?
- Are there clearly defined procedures for the treatment of any such material?
- Are there clearly defined procedures for the destruction of material considered irrelevant?
- Are there clearly defined procedures for the destruction of material where the accused has been discharged or acquitted?

- Does the person affected by the surveillance measure have the possibility of effective control?

The effect of the above is that the law should be as precise as possible. The ECt HR has, however, recognised that some discretion must be left to the authorities:

'A law which confers a discretion must indicate the scope of that discretion. However, the Court has already recognised the impossibility of attaining absolute certainty in the framing of laws and the risk that the search for certainty may entail excessive rigidity.'[1]

1   *Silver v United Kingdom* (1983) 5 EHRR 347.

Summary of relevance of art 6

2.79   Since the compass of a case before the ECt HR is delimited by the Commission's decision on admissibility, it is by no means surprising that in some cases there is no consideration of art 6. Nevertheless, the lack of any consistent or comprehensive consideration by the ECt HR of the relationship between art 6 and art 8 in cases such as *Kruslin* makes it difficult to form any useful test for assessing whether in any given case a violation of art 8 may have an impact on the fairness of the trial. It is submitted that the approach in the dissenting judgments in *Schenk* and *Khan* fail to have regard to the seriousness of the violation. To exclude evidence merely on the basis that it has been obtained in breach of art 8 is unrealistic. To date, there is no sign of the court articulating a 'significant and substantial breach' approach to art 8 similar to that developed by the UK courts when considering breaches of PACE 1984. Until some future case attempts to grapple with this critical question in a more convincing manner than heretofore, the following is an attempt to summarise the present position:

- surveillance that threatens the client–lawyer relationship is likely to engage art 6;
- surveillance that involves the use of undercover officers is likely to engage art 6; and
- where the product of surveillance is used in the course of a trial art 6 may be engaged.

Chapter 3

The data protection regime

The Data Protection Act 1998 (DPA 1998)

3.1   In the absence of any broadly based tort of invasion of privacy or any specific statutory system of control of CCTV, DPA 1998 represents the only form of legal control on the use of CCTV. It was passed to give effect to EC Directive 95/46/EC and came into force on 1 March 2000. One of the effects of DPA 1998 was to extend the scheme of protection from exclusively computerised data to personal data held in manual files. According to the Information Commissioner:

> 'Data protection law stands in the way of a surveillance society where government and commercial bodies know everything about everybody. It helps to prevent the growing problems of identity theft and the buying and selling of personal information'[1]

The regime of data protection is also of considerable importance to other law enforcement activities such as the communications data regime of RIPA 2000, Pt I, Ch II (see **Chapter 7**) and is at the heart of employment monitoring (see **para 3.56**). The purpose of this chapter is to examine the main principles of DPA 1998 and how those principles affect the use of CCTV for surveillance purposes and for monitoring in the workplace. It is also to examine how the police retain and disclose personal information, other than in the context of a specific investigation, in which case the guiding principles are likely to be those in the Criminal Procedure and Investigations Act 1996 (CPIA 1996).[2]

1   'Further Guidance on the DPA' 14 January 2004.
2   See in particular para 5 of the Code of Practice issued thereunder.

CCTV

3.2   As an extension of its Crime Reduction Programme, the government announced in July 1998 an extension of funding for CCTV systems. A sum of £153m was made available over a period of three years. Although there is some agreement that the UK is now the most spied upon country in the world, the actual number of CCTV cameras is unclear. In *The Times*, 8 November 2003, it was stated that there are more than 2,500,000 representing about 10% of the world's total. According to the November 2003 edition of the *National Geographic Magazine*, there are now over four million such cameras in Britain. In London, it is said to be possible to be caught on CCTV 300 times per day.

Codes of practice

3.3 As with PACE 1984, CPIA 1996 and RIPA 2000, codes of practice play an important part in clarifying the principles behind the legislation. In the course of this chapter, particular reference will be made to the code produced by the Association of Chief Police Officers (ACPO) and two codes issued by the Information Commissioner, namely that on CCTV in July 2000 and that on 'monitoring at work' in June 2003. Both codes are issued pursuant to DPA 1998, s 51(3) and are intended as guidance on good practice. Whereas the ECt HR has accorded the status of law to the codes issued under PACE 1984, s 67,[1] the status of the codes issued under DPA 1998 is altogether different. In her first annual report in June 2001, the Commissioner wrote:

'Codes of Practice do not add to the regulatory burden, nor go beyond the requirements of the law already in place. Their aim is further to explain the interpretation which this Office (as regulator) is taking of the requirements of the DPA 1998.'

1   See *Perry v United Kingdom* [2003] All ER (D) 296 (Jul), (2003) Times, 20 August.

The CCTV Code

3.4 This is expressly stated not to apply to:

- targeted and intrusive surveillance activities which are covered by provisions of RIPA 2000;
- use of surveillance techniques by employers to monitor their employees' compliance with their contracts of employment (see separate code at **para 3.6**);
- security equipment (including cameras) installed in homes by individuals for home security purposes; and
- use of cameras and similar equipment by the broadcast media for the purposes of journalism, or for artistic or literary purposes.

Certain public authorities have also published their own codes on the use of CCTV such as the British Standards Institute (Closed Circuit Television – Management and Operation – Code of Practice 99/703319) and the Local Government Information Unit (A Watching Brief – A Code of Practice for CCTV).

3.5 The Information Commissioner has also produced a 'CCTV Small User Checklist' highlighting the requirements of DPA 1998. As a result of the Court of

Appeal decision in *Durant v Financial Services Authority*,[1] a Guidance Note has been published explaining that small retailers who only have a couple of cameras that have no remote facility and just record on tape whatever the cameras pick up would not be covered by the Act. On the other hand if the cameras were used to check whether a member of staff was doing his job properly then their use would be covered by the Act.

1   [2003] EWCA Civ 1746, [2003] All ER (D) 124 (Dec).

The 'Monitoring at Work' Code of Practice

3.6   This states that the basic legal requirement on each employer is to comply with DPA 1998 itself. The code does not impose new legal obligations. It sets out the Information Commissioner's recommendations as to how the legal requirements of the Act can be met. Employers may have alternative ways of meeting these require-ments, but if they do nothing they risk breaking the law. Any enforcement action would be based on a failure to meet the requirements of the Act itself. However, relevant parts of the code are likely to be cited by the Commissioner in connection with any enforcement action that arises in relation to the processing of personal information in the employment context.

The ACPO Code

3.7   In addition, reference will also be made to the ACPO Code for Data Protection 2002 edition (ACPO Code). The code is produced by a group of Force Data Protection Officers representing police forces throughout the UK and was endorsed by the Information Commissioner under DPA 1998, s 51(4)(b). Its purpose is to establish procedures and safeguards to promote the maintenance of good practice and compliance with the DPA 1998.

Peck v UK

3.8   Before attempting to summarise the principles embodied in the Act, it is proposed to look briefly at certain aspects of the decision of the ECt HR in *Peck v United Kingdom*,[1] a case directly concerned with the use of material obtained by means of CCTV. The facts of this case are set out in the previous chapter at **para 2.70**. In the course of the judgment the ECt HR highlighted three factors in determining whether there was a breach of art 8.

(1)   Monitoring of the actions of an individual in a public place by the use of photographic equipment that does not record the visual data does not as such give rise to an interference with the individual's private life.

(2)   The recording of the data and the systematic or permanent nature of the record may give rise to such considerations even if the event takes place in public.

(3)   The dissemination of the material to an extent which far exceeded any exposure to a passer by or to a security observation and to a degree surpassing

that which the applicant could possibly have foreseen when he walked through the town centre gave rise to a serious interference with his rights under art 8.

Although the government invited the court to consider the UK regime of legal protection for privacy, it did not invite the court to consider DPA 1998.

1   (2003) 36 EHRR 41.

3.9   Notwithstanding the view of the ECt HR that the use of a camera in a public place is unlikely to give rise to an interference with private life, para 1.4 of the Covert Surveillance Code of Practice (Surveillance Code) issued under RIPA 2000 recognises that the use of CCTV to monitor an individual for the purposes of a specific investigation may require authorisation under that Act.

The data protection regime

3.10   All 'processing' of personal data, including disclosure of communications data, whether under RIPA 2000 or any other statutory or common law regime, must comply with the requirements of DPA 1998. Although the police, like other data controllers, have to comply with all the data protection principles, the statutory exemption for law enforcement purposes (see **para 3.46**) nullifies much of the protection provided by the regime.

DPA 1998, s 1(1) defines processing as obtaining, recording or holding the information or data or carrying out any operation or set of operations on the information or data including:

*   organisation, adaptation or alteration;
*   retrieval, consultation or use;
*   disclosure by transmitting it or disseminating it or otherwise making it available; and
*   alignment, combination, blocking erasure or destruction.

According to the glossary to the CCTV Code of Practice, the definition is:

> 'wide enough to cover the simple recording and holding of images for a limited period of time even if no further reference is made to those images. It is also wide enough to cover real time transmission of the images. Thus if images of individuals passing in front of a camera are shown in real time on a monitor, this constitutes "transmission, dissemination or otherwise making available". Thus even the least sophisticated capturing and use of images falls within the definition of processing in the 1998 Act.'

Definitions

3.11   DPA 1998, s 1(1) provides that:

"data" means information which–

(a)   is being processed by means of equipment operating automatically in response to instructions given for that purpose,

(b)   is recorded with the intention that it should be processed by means of such equipment,

(c)   is recorded as part of a relevant filing system or with the intention that it should form part of a relevant filing system [see **para 3.12**],

(d)   does not fall within (a), (b), or (c) but forms part of an accessible record as defined by section 68; or

(e)   is recorded information held by a public authority and does not fall within any of paragraphs (a)–(d).'

DPA 1998, s 68 gives a comprehensive catalogue of records including health records, educational records and records kept by local authorities. Both the latter terms are themselves the subject of further definition in DPA 1998, Sch 11 and 12 respectively.

What is a relevant filing system?

3.12   Relevant filing system:

'means any set of information relating to individuals to the extent that although the information is not processed by means of equipment operating automatically in response to instructions given for that purpose, the set is structured, either by reference to individuals or by reference to criteria to individuals, in such a way that specific information relating to a particular individual is readily accessible.'[1]

In *Durant v Financial Services Authority*,[2] the Court of Appeal stated that it was clear from the provisions that the intention was to provide, as near as possible, the same standard or sophistication of accessibility to personal data in manual filing systems as to computerised records. It went on to hold that Parliament intended to apply the Act to manual records:

'only if they are of sufficient sophistication to provide the same or similar ready accessibility as a computerized filing system. That requires a system so referenced or indexed that it enables the data controller's employee responsible to identify at the outset of his search with reasonable certainty and speed the file or files in which the specific data relating to the person requesting the information is located …'

It should be noted that the significance of this aspect of the decision will disappear on 1 January 2005 when the Freedom of Information Act 2000 will extend DPA 1998 to all personal information regardless of whether it is held in a 'relevant filing system'.

1   DPA 1998, s 1(1).
2   [2003] EWCA Civ 1746, [2003] All ER (D) 124 (Dec).

What is personal data?

3.13   Personal data is defined by DPA 1998, s 1(1) as:

'data which relate to a living individual who can be identified–

(a)   from those data, or

(b)   from those data and other information which is in the possession of or is likely to come into the possession of the data controller,

and includes any expression of opinion about the individual and any indication of the intentions of the data controller or any other person in respect of the individual'.

The provisions of the DPA 1998 are based on the EC Directive 95/46/EC, art 2(a) of which states:

"Personal data" shall mean any information relating to an identified or identifiable natural person; an identifiable person is one who can be identified directly or indirectly, in particular by reference to an identification number or to one or more factors specific to his physical, physiological, mental, economic, cultural or social identity.'

3.14   In *Durant* the Court of Appeal gave a restrictive interpretation to the phrase and described personal data as:

'information that affects [the individual's] privacy, whether in his personal or family life, business or professional capacity.'

Two requirements were emphasised. It:

'must be biographical in a significant sense ... going beyond the recording of ... involvement in a matter or an event that has no personal connotations ...'

and the information:

'must have the data subject as its focus.'

As a result, there was no obligation on the Financial Services Authority (FSA) to disclose records of complaints made by Mr Durant against Barclays Bank and the FSA.

The approach of the Court of Appeal is significantly narrower than that of the Information Commissioner, whose guidance suggests that the test should be 'whether a data controller can form a connection between the data and the individual'.[1] No reference to the Commissioner or his guidance was made in the Court of Appeal.

1   'DPA 1998 Legal Guidance' para 2.2.

3.15   In the glossary to the CCTV Code, the Information Commissioner states that personal data is not limited to circumstances in which the controller can attribute a name to a particular image. If images of a distinguishable individual's features are processed and an individual can be identified from these images, they will amount to personal data. The conclusion is based on the definition in the EC Directive and, notwithstanding *Durant*, it is submitted, remains accurate.

What is sensitive personal data?

3.16 Sensitive personal data is defined by DPA 1998, s 2 to mean information as to:
'(a) the racial or ethnic origin of the data subject,
(b) his political opinions,
(c) his religious beliefs or other beliefs of a similar nature,
(d) whether he is a member of a trade union,
(e) his physical or mental health or condition,
(f) his sexual life,
(g) the commission or alleged commission of any offence, or
(h) any proceedings for any offence committed or alleged to have been committed, the disposal of such proceedings or the sentence of any court in such proceedings.'

In view of (g) and (h), CCTV schemes set up in order to reduce crime are likely to concern the processing of sensitive personal data and will need to ensure that at least one of the paragraphs of DPA 1998, Sch 3 is satisfied (see **para 3.20** below).

What is a data subject?

3.17 Data subject means an individual who is the subject of personal data.

What is a data controller?

3.18 A data controller is a person who (either alone or jointly or in common with other persons) determines the purposes for which, and the manner in which, any personal data are or are to be processed. Where the police and a local authority and local retailers enter into an agreement to prevent or detect crime or protect public safety, all three parties will be acting as data controllers.

The data protection principles

3.19 The eight principles are set out in DPA 1998, Sch 1, Pt I.

The first principle

3.20 To be processed fairly and lawfully and only if at least one of the specified conditions in DPA 1998, Sch 2 is met and in the case of sensitive personal data one of the conditions in DPA 1998, Sch 3 is also met.

The relevant conditions of DPA 1998, Sch 2 are processing:

(a) with consent of the data subject;
(b) necessary for contractual purposes;

(c)   necessary for compliance with a legal obligation other than one imposed by contract;

(d)   necessary to protect the vital interests of the subject;

(e)   necessary for the administration of justice or the exercise of any function conferred under any enactment, the functions of the Crown, a Minister of the Crown or a government department or any other function of a public nature exercised in the public interest; and

(f)   necessary for the legitimate interests of the data controller or third parties, providing these are not outweighed by the interests of the data subject.

The DPA 1998, Sch 3 conditions are processing:

(a)   with the explicit consent of the subject;

(b)   necessary for the purpose of exercising or performing a legal right or obligation in the context of employment;

(c)   necessary to protect the vital interests of the data subject or another in cases where consent cannot be obtained;

(d)   of political, philosophical, religious or trade union data in connection with its legitimate interests by non-profit making bodies;

(e)   of information already made public as a result of steps deliberately taken by the data subject;

(f)   necessary for the purpose of any legal proceedings, obtaining legal advice or establishing, exercising or defending legal rights;

(g)   necessary for the administration of justice, the performance of statutory functions, exercise of any function of the Crown, Ministers or government departments;

(h)   of medical data by medical professionals or others owing an obligation of confidence to the data subject; and

(j)   ethnic monitoring.

3.21   It will be noted that (c) and (g) are similar to but slightly more restrictive than (d) and (e) in Sch 2.

As noted in **para 3.16**, CCTV that is designed to reduce crime needs to satisfy one of the conditions in Sch 3. It is suggested in the glossary to the CCTV Code that it may be that the use of such information by a public authority in order to meet the objectives of the Crime and Disorder Act 1998 would satisfy the statutory function in (g) (see **para 3.22**).

The CCTV Code also draws attention to the importance of the siting of the cameras because the way in which images are captured will need to comply with the First Data Protection Principle. If domestic areas such as gardens border the areas intended to be covered by the CCTV equipment, the owners of such areas should be consulted.

DPA 1998, Sch 1, Pt II (see **para 3.23**) draws attention to the importance of signs designed to alert members of the public to matters such as the use of CCTV. As will be seen in **Chapter 7**, Communications Service Suppliers (CSPs) may disclose personal data only if:

(a)   the person consents; or
(b)   there is a legal requirement to make the disclosure; or
(c)   there is an overriding public interest.

Examples of statutory functions

3.22   The use of CCTV in town centres by a local authority or the police is likely to come within the objectives of the Crime and Disorder Act 1998 and thus fall within (g) of Sch 3, the performance of a statutory function. Section 115 of that Act provides the power for anyone involved in a crime and disorder strategy under the Act to disclose information to a relevant authority, namely the police, local authority, probation committee or health authority. See also Criminal Justice and Public Order Act 1994 (CJPOA 1994), s 163, which specifically empowers local authorities to provide CCTV in order to promote the prevention of crime or the welfare of the victims of crime. No specific provision is made as to how to deal with data obtained thereby.

The Local Government Act 1972, s 111(1) empowers local councils to distribute CCTV footage to the media in the discharge of their functions under the CJPOA 1994, s 163.

Signs

3.23   DPA 1998, Sch 1, Pt II details other matters that should be taken into account in determining whether personal data are processed fairly, including whether the person from whom the data is obtained has been deceived. Data are to be treated as obtained fairly if the information is obtained from a person who is authorised by any enactment to supply it or is required to supply it by any enactment or convention or other instrument imposing an international obligation on the UK. In order to process fairly, the following information should be provided to individuals at the point of obtaining their images:

(a)   the identity of the data controller;
(b)   the identity of a representative, if any, nominated by the data controller for the purposes of the Act;
(c)   the purpose for which the data are intended to be processed; and
(d)   any other information which is necessary, having regard to the specific circumstances in which the data are or are to be processed, to enable processing in respect of the individual to be fair.[1]

1   See DPA 1998, Sch 1, Pt II, para 2(3).

When may covert processing be appropriate?

3.24   Because fair processing requires that individuals are made aware that they are entering an area where their images may be captured, eg by the use of signs, it follows that the use of covert processing is prima facie a breach of the fairness requirement of the first data protection principle. However, see **para 3.45** and **3.46** for the exemptions provided by DPA 1998, s 28(1) and 29(1).

The second principle

3.25   This principle is likely to be of particular relevance in considering issues of data sharing. Unless the disclosure can properly be considered to be compatible with the purpose for which the data were obtained, DPA 1998 effectively precludes data sharing.

Personal data shall be obtained only for specified and lawful purposes and not be processed in any manner incompatible with those purposes. A data controller should notify the Commissioner of the purposes for which the data is held and the categories of people to whom the data may be disclosed. Paragraph 5.1 of the ACPO Code emphasises that personal information can only lawfully be disclosed to individuals and organisations mentioned in the notified purpose; unless the person to whom disclosure is to be made is the subject of an exemption under the Act or is authorised by other legislation.

The requirement of compatibility may be particularly significant when considering disclosure to a third party, e g by a local authority or police to the media. In such a case regard should be had to the purpose for which the third party may process the data. The glossary to the CCTV Code gives the example of a local authority that discloses to the media pictures of drunken individuals in a town centre, which might be justified in the context of crime prevention but not for inclusion in a humorous video. The glossary further points out that if disclosure is to take place, the images of unrelated third parties will need to be disguised.

Criminal records under the Police Act 1997, Pt V

3.26   Any person is entitled to apply to the Criminal Records Bureau for a basic criminal conviction certificate, provided they are the subject of the certificate and provide two forms of identity or fingerprints in case of doubt.[1] Police Act 1997, s 113 created a system of certification for sensitive areas of employment involving vulnerable groups and those involved in the administration of justice. In such a case the certificate known as a disclosure will include details of all past convictions including spent convictions, and cautions, but is only available to employers or organisations that would be entitled to ask an exempted question. An exempted question is one to which the Rehabilitation of Offenders Act 1974, s 4(2)(a) or (b) has been excluded by an order of the Secretary of State.

The Police Act 1997, ss 115 and 116 provide for enhanced criminal certificates (ECRC)[2], which allow for disclosure of acquittals and the results of ongoing or inconclusive police investigations as well as uncorroborated allegations from informants. Such certificates are confined to those seeking employment with children or vulnerable adults, the appointment of the judiciary and certain sensitive areas of licensing.

1   Police Act 1997, ss 112(1) and 118(2).
2   See *X v Chief Constable of West Midlands Police* [2004] EWMC 61 (admin) where a social worker successfully challenged the issue of a ECRC.

In what circumstances might the use of information lawfully obtained by the police amount to a breach of confidence?

3.27 Where the police take a photograph of a suspected criminal pursuant to the provisions of PACE 1984, a duty of confidence could arise so that the subsequent wrongful disclosure to third parties might be actionable. However, where the photograph was distributed to shopkeepers as part of a shop watch scheme, such dissemination was plainly lawful.[1] Even absenting any duty of confidence, the police should where possible obtain the offender's version of events before releasing personal information. In *R v Chief Constable of North Wales Police, ex p Thorpe*[2] it was held that the police should disclose the identity of former paedophile offenders in their area to members of the public only when there was a pressing need to do so.

1   See *Hellewell v Chief Constable of Derbyshire* [1995] 1 WLR 804.
2   [1999] QB 396

The third principle

3.28 Personal data shall be adequate, relevant and not excessive in relation to those purposes. CCTV equipment should be properly maintained. Cameras installed to record acts of vandalism or theft in a car park should not overlook private gardens. The code provides that if images from nearby properties might be recorded, the owners of those properties should be consulted.

Paragraph 7.2 of the ACPO Code states that all criminal intelligence will be graded using a standard evaluation system, which gives an indication of the quality of the information, the reliability of the source of the information and provides guidance on the subsequent dissemination of the information. Police officers, support staff and special constables originating information must ensure that the intelligence is adequate, unambiguous and professionally worded. Opinions should be clearly distinguished from matters of fact.

The fourth principle

3.29 Personal data shall be accurate and kept up to date. Paragraph 7.5 of the ACPO Code points out that the failure to update or create records of court results may result in an unsuitable person obtaining employment with children or vulnerable persons. The code provides that details of at least 90% of all persons arrested/ reported must be entered onto the Police National Computer within 24 hours. Details of all persons granted police bail must be entered within 24 hours. Results of all court cases, or other disposal of cases, must be entered within 72 hours of the information coming into the possession of the police.

The glossary to the CCTV Code provides that if the information may be used as evidence in court the controller should ensure the clarity of the images by replacing tapes on a regular basis to avoid degradation. Any references to time and date should be accurate. Attention is also drawn to the possible evidential difficulties that can arise as a result of digital enhancement.

The fifth principle

3.30 Personal data should not to be kept for longer than is necessary for the specified purpose. The glossary to the CCTV Code recommends that tapes that have recorded images relevant to any legal proceedings should be kept until the conclusion of those proceedings. Where there are no such relevant images the tape may be erased after a very short period.

Paragraph 8.2 of the ACPO Code suggests that account should be taken of the individual concerned and their circumstances with regard to the information recorded. For example, if the information relates to a convicted person, the seriousness and nature of the offences and/or whether there are reasonable grounds for believing that he is an active criminal or likely to reoffend should be considered. More difficult is information which might form the basis of mere suspicion, eg that the subject is an associate of a known criminal. In practice, the exemption provided by DPA 1998, s 29(1) (see **para 3.46**) is likely to provide the police with ample protection.

The fifth principle is relevant to retention under Anti Terrorism, Crime and Security Act 2001 (see **para 3.64**).

General rules for criminal record weeding on police systems

3.31 Paragraph 8.4 of the ACPO Code states that the general rule is that any record will be deleted where the subject has not been convicted of a recordable offence for a period of ten years from the date of their last conviction. A recordable offence is one punishable with imprisonment, or certain miscellaneous offences such as soliciting or having a bladed article in a public place, included in SI 1985/1941 as amended by SI 1989/694 issued under PACE 1984.

Exceptions to the general rule

3.32 To the general rule there is set out a significant list of exceptions, including cases in which there is an impending prosecution or in which the subject is shown on the Police National Computer as wanted or missing or the record contains a total of six months' or more imprisonment, in which case the record will be kept until the death of the subject or until he reaches 100 years of age. In the event that the subject did not receive six months' imprisonment but was convicted of certain offences of violence, the record will be kept for a similar period.[1]

1   ACPO Code 8.4.5–8.4.6.

Retention of records of cautions and police reprimands

3.33 If there are cautions but no convictions on the record and no further cautions have been recorded for a period of five years the record will be deleted except where the caution is accompanied by an 'offends against vulnerable person' information marker. Records containing police reprimands or final warnings will be dealt with in a similar way. If no such reprimands or final warnings have been recorded for five years the record will be deleted on the subject becoming 18.[1]

1   ACPO Code 8.4.8–8.4.9.

Retention of records of acquittals or discontinued cases

3.34   With two exceptions, details of acquittals or of cases discontinued without caution should not be retained beyond 42 days after notification. The two exceptions are acquittals for an offence of unlawful sexual intercourse by a male with a female under 16, which should be deleted when the male reaches 24, and offences of handling where details may be retained for one year from the date of charging pursuant to the Theft Act 1968, s 27(3). Paragraph 8.4.14 of the ACPO Code forms a further discretionary exception in cases where the subject is acquitted of a sexual offence, provided identity was not an issue. In such a case an officer not below the rank of superintendent must give authorisation for continued retention.[1]

1   ACPO Code 8.4.12.

Criminal intelligence

3.35   Paragraph 8.5 of the ACPO Code states that the need to retain or remove such information can only be judged from the nature of the information and whether it is necessary, lawful, proportional and relevant to its purpose. Regard should be taken of the requirements of CPIA 1996 and RIPA 2000. In some cases it is recognised that information will have to be retained for long periods. All intelligence reports will be reviewed on a regular basis and considered for deletion subject to a maximum of 12 months. Para 12 of the CCTV Code (under the heading "Standards") provides that information obtained for the purposes of crime prevention or detection should not be retained for any other purposes. In comparison to MI5 practice where information is retained ad infinitum (see para 4.15).

Accountability

3.36   Surveillance operations will invariably throw up a substantial amount of random and irrelevant information. Although the fifth principle makes it clear that personal data should not be kept for any longer than necessary, there appears to be little possibility of effective accountability. In the absence of the Information Commissioner being given the power to conduct random inspections in the manner of the Surveillance Commissioner under RIPA 2000, s 62(1), data controllers such as the police have little incentive to comply with that principle.

The sixth principle

3.37   Personal data should be processed in accordance with the data subject's rights. The rights include the right to be provided, in appropriate cases, with a copy of the information constituting the personal data held about them and the right to prevent processing which is likely to cause damage or distress.[1]

1   See 'subject access rights' in **para 3.40** and 'other rights given to subjects' in **para 3.44**. Also see 'rights in relation to automated decision-taking', DPA 1998, s 12.

The seventh principle

3.38   Personal data should be kept secure. Consideration should be given to the harm that might result from unauthorised or unlawful processing or accidental loss. The nature of the data to be protected must also be considered.

Paragraph 10 of the ACPO Code recognises the value of criminal intelligence and refers to the ACPO Community Security Policy, which sets out common standards for safeguarding sensitive information. All police information systems should take specific measures to preserve the confidentiality, integrity, availability and non-repudiation of information.

The eighth principle

3.39   Personal data should not be transferred to countries outside the European Economic Area without adequate protection. Images should not be put on the Internet or on a website.

Subject access rights: DPA 1998, Pt II

3.40   DPA 1998, ss 7 and 8 collectively provide that upon making a request in writing (which includes transmission by electronic means) an individual is entitled to be informed if the data controller is processing information on them and to have access to personal data held on them. Where such access would necessarily involve disclosure of third-party information the data subject may not be entitled to the information (see **para 3.42**). Such information should be supplied in permanent form and within not more than 40 days. The information should not be tampered with before being supplied. In addition, the subject is entitled to any information as to the source of data. The controller may charge a fee for dealing with subject access.

In *Durant* the court pointed out that the purpose of DPA 1998, ss 7 and 8 is to enable an individual to check whether the data controller's processing of their personal data unlawfully infringes their privacy and if so to take such steps as the Act provides to protect it (see **para 3.44**).

> 'It is not an automatic key to any information, readily accessible or not, of matters in which he may be named or involved. Nor is it to assist him, for example, to obtain discovery of documents that may assist him in litigation or complaints against third parties.'

3.41   Paragraph 9.3 of the ACPO Code states that it is important to establish the identity of the person making the request and that therefore chief officers will usually request identification such as a driving licence before complying with the request. Once a completed application form is received together with the appropriate fee the police must respond within 40 days.

Paragraph 9.5 of the ACPO Code makes provision for further information being required. In respect of CCTV material, for example, it would be necessary to provide details of dates, times and locations to enable the data to be located.

The access rights are subject to the exemptions in DPA 1998, ss 28 and 29 (see **paras 3.45–3.46**).

Third-party information

3.42 Where compliance with a subject access request may reveal data relating to a third party the controller is only obliged to comply where either the third party has consented to the disclosure or where it is reasonable in all the circumstances to comply without the consent of the third party. Relevant factors may include any duty of confidentiality, any steps taken to try to seek consent, whether the third party is capable of giving consent and whether he has expressly refused consent.

As an example of when it would not be reasonable to provide information, para 9.6 of the ACPO Code gives that of a request the answer to which would provide details of a complainant or witness.

Detailed guidance on the subject is given in the CCTV Code, including the suggestion of editing of the tape to disguise or blur images of third parties.

Where a subject access request is refused the code suggests that the following should be documented:

(a) the identity of the individual making the request;
(b) the date of the request;
(c) the reason for refusal; and
(d) the name and signature of the manager or designated member of staff making the decision.

Money laundering

3.43 In certain circumstances, the right of subject access may conflict with the obligation not to tip off an individual about whom a Suspicious Transaction Report (STR) has been made. The Proceeds of Crime Act 2002, s 333 replaces the previous tipping off provisions in the Criminal Justice Act 1988, s 93D and the Drug Trafficking Act 1994. In April 2002 various government departments involved in co-ordinating the UK's anti-money laundering legislation issued Guidance Notes designed to address the problem. Paragraph 19 of the Notes concludes that:

> 'where disclosure of a particular STR would constitute a tipping off offence, the section 29 exemption [see **para 3.46**] will apply, and where disclosure of an STR would not constitute a tipping off offence the section 29 exemption will

not be available in respect of the money laundering element. However it must be emphasized that each request for information must be considered on its merits ...'

Other rights given to a data subject

3.44 Data subjects:

- are entitled to serve a written 'data subject notice' on data controllers requiring them not to begin or to cease processing personal data relating to them. In the event of a dispute upon application by the subject a court may order the data controller to take such steps as are necessary to comply with the notice;[1]
- may by written notice require data controllers to refrain from processing personal data relating to them for the purpose of direct marketing;[2]
- are entitled to require a data controller, eg an employer, to ensure that no decision which significantly affects them is based solely on the processing of their personal data by automatic means. Subjects also have the right to be informed of the logic of any automated decision process taken concerning them;[3]
- have the right to compensation where the subject suffers damage as a result of processing in contravention of the Act;[4]
- have the right to take action to rectify, block, erase or destroy data relating to them which is inaccurate or contains an expression of opinion that the court finds is based on inaccurate data;[5]
- have the right to request an assessment by the Commissioner as to whether or not personal data is being processed in accordance with the Act.[6]

1   DPA 1998, s 10.
2   DPA 1998, s 11.
3   DPA 1998, s 12.
4   DPA 1998, s 13.
5   DPA 1998, s 14.
6   DPA 1998, s 42.

The national security exemption

3.45 DPA 1998, s 28(1) provides that:

'personal data are exempt from any of the provisions of–

(a)   the data protection principles,
(b)   Parts II, III and V, and[1]
(c)   section 55,
if the exemption from that provision is required for the purpose of safeguard-ing national security.[2]'

By DPA 1998, s 28(2) a certificate signed by a minister that exemption is required shall, subject to s 28(4), be conclusive evidence of that fact.

Section 28(4) provides for appeal to the Information Tribunal by any person affected by such a certificate.

In *Baker v Secretary of State for the Home Department*[3] the Data Protection Tribunal (as it then was) found that there were no reasonable grounds for the issue of a certificate by the Secretary of State refusing to disclose whether MI5 held any information on the subject pursuant to s 7(1)(a). The non-committal response was an example of 'neither confirm nor deny' (NCND). The Tribunal concluded that the blanket exemption purportedly permitted M15 to give a NCND reply to every request, and if the certificate was issued on reasonable grounds the person affected by it had no means of challenging such response under the Act. At its most extreme, the respondent's submission meant that the Tribunal effectively had no power to consider individual cases under s 28(4). Since not every bit of personal information held by M15 related to national security or might impact on it if released, a blanket exemption must be excessive. In the circumstances the Tribunal concluded that the terms of the certificate were too wide and allowed the appeal.

According to Justice,[4] MI5 has not registered under DPA 1998, on the grounds that its files are held for national security purposes and therefore exempt. Both Justice and the then Data Protection Registrar make the point that MI5 should not be able to rely on its exemption in areas of traditional policing.

1   For Pt II see **para 3.40**, Pt III deals with compulsory notification by data controllers to the Commissioner Pt V deals with procedures for enforcement of the data protection principles.
2   'Safeguarding national security' is not defined, see **para 4.9–4.11**.
3   [2001] UKHRR 1275
4   'Under Surveillance' 1998.

The prevention or detection of crime exemption: DPA 1998, s 29(1)

3.46   The use of covert surveillance is prima facie a breach of the first data protection principle.

DPA 1998, s 29(1), however, provides a specific exemption:

'Personal data processed for any of the following purposes–

(a)   the prevention or detection of crime,
(b)   the apprehension or prosecution of offenders, or
(c)   the assessment or collection of any tax or duty or of any imposition of a similar nature,

are exempt from the first data protection principle (except to the extent to which it requires compliance with the conditions in Schedules 2 and 3) and section 7 [subject access] in any case to the extent to which the application of those provisions to the data would be likely to prejudice any of the matters mentioned in this subsection.'

The effect of the section is that the police do not have to comply with the fair and lawful processing provisions (other than in relation to sensitive personal data), the subject access request provisions or the restrictions on disclosure provisions if to do so would be likely to prejudice the prevention or detection of crime or the apprehension or prosecution of offenders.

Paragraph 9.6 of the ACPO Code gives an example of information being held on an intelligence system to the effect that a data subject is believed to be supplying drugs within the local community. The entry states that covert observations are being undertaken on the individual. Consideration might then be given to applying for a search warrant. Disclosure of this information would be likely to prejudice the policing purpose and therefore the decision may be made for it to be withheld. However, once any warrant has been executed, the exemption would no longer apply.

According to evidence given by the Director General of the NCIS to a House of Lords Committee in 1998, all 44 subject requests since 1995 had been denied.[1]

1   Hansard HL 25.02.98 Col 341.

3.47   Where a financial institution is in doubt as to whether disclosure would be likely to prejudice an investigation, para 24 of the Guidance Notes for the Financial Sector suggest that advice should be sought from the NCIS. Paragraph 25 observes that:

'It should be noted that where an institution withholds a piece of information in reliance on the DPA s 29 exemption, it is not obliged to tell the individual that any information has been withheld. It can simply leave out that piece of information and make no reference to it when responding to the individual who has made the request.'[1]

1   Notes published by The Financial Crime Branch, HM Treasury, April 2002.

3.48   The application of the exemption in practice is problematic. Although it should not act as a blanket exemption (see *Equifax v Data Protection Registrar*,[1]) identification of the kind of criminal intelligence that in any particular case falls within its compass may prove difficult.

1   (June 1991, unreported)

3.49   In the context of the siting of CCTV cameras, the CCTV Code provides that:

'11. In exceptional and limited cases, if it is assessed that the use of signs would not be appropriate, the user of the scheme must ensure that they have:

(a)   identified specific criminal activity;
(b)   identified the need to use surveillance to obtain evidence of that criminal activity;
(c)   assessed whether the use of signs would prejudice success in obtaining such evidence;
(d)   assessed how long the covert monitoring should take place to ensure that it is not carried out for longer than necessary;
(e)   documented (a)–(d) above.

12. Information so obtained must only be obtained for prevention or detection of criminal activity, or the apprehension and prosecution of offenders. It should not be retained and used for any other purpose. If the equipment used has a sound recording facility, this should not be used to record conversations between members of the public (First and Third Data Protection Principles).'

In the context of communications data (see **Chapter 7**), CSPs have hitherto been protected by DPA 1998, s 29 and Telecommunications Act 1984, s 45.[1]

1   RIPA 2000, Pt I, Ch II, in force 5 January 2004.

The legal proceedings exemption

3.50   Section 35 of DPA 1998 provides exemption from the non-disclosure provisions (only) where disclosure is required by or under any enactment, by any rule of law or by order of the court, or for the purpose of legal proceedings or obtaining legal advice.

Grounds for disclosure (to third parties) under DPA 1998

3.51   For more details, see **paras 3.25–3.27**.

Enforcement

3.52   The Information Commissioner has the power to serve an enforcement notice on the data controller where there has been a contravention of one of the data protection principles. The notice will specify what the controller must do, eg to refrain from disclosing CCTV images to the media. The Annual Reports of the Commissioner indicate that in practice few such notices are served, the Commissioner preferring to pursue a 'softly softly' approach.

Compensation

3.53   Under DPA 1998, s 13 individuals who suffer damage or, if the processing involves personal data, distress as a result of any contravention of the Act are entitled to go to court to seek compensation in certain circumstances. Section 13(3) provides the equivalent of a due diligence defence. This right is in addition to an individual's right under DPA 1998, s 42(1) to request the Information Commissioner to make an assessment as to whether processing is likely or unlikely to comply with the Act.

Paragraph 11 of the ACPO Code provides guidance on how complaints against the police in relation to data protection issues will be dealt with.

In her Legal Guidance on the DPA 1998, the Commissioner gave a realistic but unhelpful assessment on the question of quantum:

'There are no guidelines as to appropriate levels of compensation for a claim under the Act and the Commissioner is not routinely advised of the outcome of cases where individuals have made a successful claim for compensation under the Act. The judge hearing the case has discretion in these matters and would have to take into consideration many factors including the seriousness of the breach and the effect upon the claimant, particularly when considering damages for distress.'

The criminal offence

3.54   DPA 1998, s 55(1) creates the offence of unlawfully obtaining, disclosing or procuring the disclosure of personal information. No offence is committed where it can be shown that the disclosure or procuring was necessary for the purpose of preventing or detecting crime, or required or authorised by any enactment or rule of law or order of the court, or where the individual acted in the reasonable belief that he had in law the right to procure or disclose the data, or that the data controller would have consented to such a course, or that in the particular circumstances it was justified as being in the public interest.

The offence is subject to a maximum fine on summary conviction of £5,000 or an unlimited fine on indictment.

3.55   The offence appears to have been created as a direct result of intrusive searches in 1992/3 into the affairs of several government ministers and other celebrity figures, which subsequently became the subject of newspaper articles. Information was obtained from banks and other organisations by deception and the information was used by the media to illustrate the ease with which the information could be obtained.

Employment monitoring

3.56   Most information that is processed by an organisation in the context of employment will fall within the scope of the 'Monitoring at Work' Code. This includes all automated and computerised information and some information held on paper in a relevant filing system.[1] Examples are sickness records, trade union membership, details of salaries, bank accounts and emails about an incident involving a named worker.

Monitoring of employees in order to check performance is a necessary if not inevitable aspect of working life. Reasonable monitoring of which the employee is aware is unlikely to be considered unfair. Although art 8 considerations are relevant in the workplace, the degree of privacy which an employee is entitled to expect is less than in the home. Unreasonable or excessive monitoring may undermine respect for correspondence or interfere with the relationship of mutual trust and confidence between employer and employee.

1   See restrictive definition in *Durant v Financial Services Authority* [2003] EWCA Civ 1746.

The 'Monitoring at Work' Code

3.57 The Code is primarily directed at employers, especially larger organisations using or planning some form of systematic monitoring of all workers as a matter of routine by, for example, using electronic devices to scan all email messages, keeping recordings of telephone calls, or by using CCTV to check that workers are complying with health and safety rules. Where the monitoring involves interception, the employer will also need to have regard to the Lawful Business Practice Regulations made under RIPA 2000 (see **para 6.42**). Before embarking on any such monitoring, the code advises the employer to carry out an impact assessment in order to satisfy himself that the proposed course is proportionate. The code provides detailed guidance on how to make such an assessment, including the consideration of less intrusive forms of monitoring such as spot checks or an audit. Account should be taken of whether and how employees will be notified about the monitoring arrangements. It emphasises that there are limitations as to how far consent can be relied on to justify the processing of personal data. Consent must be freely given, which may not be the case in the employment environment.

Disclosure of personal information: Code 3.2.6–3.2.9

3.58 The employer should keep to a minimum those who have access to personal information. Those persons should be subject to confidentiality and security requirements and be properly trained. Personal information collected through monitoring should not be used for other purposes unless it is clearly in the individual's interests to do so or it reveals activity that no employer could reasonably be expected to ignore. He should ensure that the right of access of workers to information about them which is kept or obtained through monitoring is not compromised.

Electronic communications: Code 3.3.1–3.3.8

3.59 The employer should set out clearly to workers the circumstances in which they may or may not use the employer's telephone systems, including mobile phones, the email system and Internet access for private communications.

He should ensure that, where monitoring involves the interception of a communication, it is not outlawed by RIPA 2000. Although accessing emails that have been opened does not amount to interception, opening of unopened emails, especially ones that clearly show they are private or personal, should be avoided. Where it is necessary to check the email accounts of workers in their absence they should be made aware of the fact.

Code 3.3.5 advises the employer to ensure that those making calls to or receiving calls from workers are aware of any monitoring and the purpose behind it.

Video monitoring in the workplace: Code 3.4.1–3.4.2

3.60   Where possible any video or audio monitoring should be targeted at areas of particular risk and confined to areas where expectations of privacy are low. Continuous video or audio monitoring of particular individuals is only likely to be justified in rare circumstances. Clear warnings should be given both to employees and to customers as to the reasons why the monitoring is being carried out.

Covert monitoring in the workplace: Code 3.5.1–3.5.4

3.61   Senior management should normally authorise any covert monitoring. They should satisfy themselves that there are grounds for suspecting criminal activity or equivalent malpractice and that notifying individuals about the monitoring would prejudice its prevention or detection. Such monitoring should cease once the investigation has been completed. Where a private investigator is employed the terms of the contract should be consistent with data protection principles.

In-vehicle monitoring: Code 3.6.1–3.6.2

3.62   Tracking devices allocated to specific vehicles to monitor the movements of the vehicle will fall within the scope of the Act. Where private use is allowed, covert monitoring will rarely be justified.

Monitoring through information from third parties: Code 3.7.1–3.7.2

3.63   Employers need to take special care when wishing to make use of information held by third parties such as credit reference agencies or electoral roll information. Where an employer needs to know about a worker's criminal convictions, disclosure must be obtained via the Criminal Records Bureau (see **para 3.26**). A worker's financial circumstances should not be monitored unless there are firm grounds to conclude that financial difficulties would pose a significant risk to the employer. Workers should be told what information sources are to be used to carry out checks on them and why the checks are to be carried out, unless to do so would prejudice the prevention or detection of crime. Credit reference agencies that are used to carry out checks on customers should not be used to monitor workers.

Anti-terrorism[1]

3.64   The Anti-terrorism, Crime and Security Act 2001, Pt 11 has introduced a scheme whereby CSPs may retain data for periods in excess of that allowed by the fifth data protection principle. The Voluntary Code issued under the Act "explains" that if necessary the s 28 DPA exemption could be relied on to exempt such data from the fifth principle enabling it to be retained in accordance with the Code (see para 7.31). The Information Commissioner commented that:

'The provisions could have a significant impact on the privacy of individuals whose data are retained. If there is a demonstrable and pressing need for these provisions, an appropriate balance must be struck between personal privacy and the legitimate needs of the law enforcement community. There are particular concerns that leaving matters to a voluntary code of practice, or to agreements, may pose difficulties for data protection and human rights compliance. Although recent events have prompted these measures to be brought forward, law enforcement agencies will make use of them on a day to day basis for a variety of matters. Careful consideration must be given to ensure that the provisions are appropriate to addressing these more routine needs.'

1   See **Chapter 7**.

Chapter 4

The intelligence services

Introduction

4.1 This chapter is concerned with the activities of the intelligence services, namely the Security Service (MI5), the Secret Intelligence Service (MI6) and the Government Communications Headquarters (GCHQ), all of which are entitled in certain circumstances to enter on and interfere with property pursuant to the Intelligence Services Act 1994 (ISA 1994), to intercept communications pursuant to RIPA 2000, Pt I, to acquire and disclose communications data within RIPA 2000, Pt I, Ch II, to use the three forms of surveillance in RIPA 2000, Pt II, and have the power to require disclosure under RIPA 2000, Pt III. This chapter will consider the functions of each of the intelligence services and identify the circumstances in which each is entitled to enter on and interfere with property.[1] In Parliament, the phrase used was 'bug and burgle' and will be adopted hereafter. It will also highlight other relevant powers provided by RIPA 2000 that are considered separately in **Chapters 6–9**.

1   ISA 1994, s 5(2).

4.2 The two commissioners tasked with oversight of their respective service under the Security Service Act 1989, s 4 and ISA 1994, s 8 have been amalgamated by RIPA 2000 (see ss 59(8), 82(2), and Sch 5, and **Chapter 10**).

Similarly, the investigation of complaints against any of the intelligence services is now dealt with by the single Investigatory Powers Tribunal set up by RIPA 2000, s 65 (see **Chapter 10**).

The functions of MI5

4.3 Prior to the Security Services Act 1989, members of MI5 had no special powers conferred on them and were effectively in a position no different from private citizens. Their activities were governed by the Directive to the Director General, issued by the Home Secretary Sir David Maxwell Fife on 24 September 1952:

'(i)   In your appointment as Director General of the Security Service you will be responsible to the Home Secretary personally. The Security Service is not however a part of the Home Office. On appropriate occasion you will have the right of direct access to the Prime Minister.

(ii)   The Security Service is part of the Defence Forces of the Country. Its task is the Defence of the Realm as a whole, from external and internal dangers arising from attempts at espionage and sabotage or from actions of persons and organisations whether directed from within or without the country which may be judged to be subversive of the state.

(iii)   You will take special care to see that the work of the Security Service is strictly limited to what is necessary for the purposes of this task.

(iv)   It is essential that the Security Service should be kept absolutely free from any political bias or influence and nothing should be done that might lend colour to any suggestion that it is concerned with the interests of any particular section of the community, or with any other matter than the Defence of the Realm as a whole.

(v)   No enquiry is to be carried out on behalf of any Government Department unless you are satisfied that an important public interest bearing on the Defence of the Realm, as defined in paragraph (ii) is at stake.

(vi)   You and your staff will maintain the well established convention whereby Ministers do not concern themselves with the detailed information which may be obtained by the Security Service in particular cases, but are furnished with such information only as may be necessary for the determination of any issue on which guidance is sought.'

The Denning Report 1963[1]

4.4   Having heard a considerable body of evidence during the inquiry into what was known as the Profumo affair, Lord Denning found that the Directive correctly identified the principles on which MI5 acted.

'No one can understand the role of the Security Service in the Profumo affair unless he realises the cardinal principle that their operations are to be used for one purpose only, the Defence of the Realm. They are not to be used so as to pry into any man's private conduct or business affairs: or even into his political opinions, except in so far as they are subversive, that is, they would contemplate the overthrow of the government by unlawful means.'[2]

1   Cmnd 2152, Ch XVII.
2   Cmnd 2152, Ch XVII, para 230.

4.5   Lord Denning confirmed that MI5 had no special powers of arrest or search such as the police have.

'They cannot enter premises without the consent of the householder even if they suspect a spy is there.'

The lack of any proper statutory basis does not, however, seem to have prevented M15 using interception techniques as noted by the Birkett Committee in 1953 (see **para 6.10**).

4.6   A further 25 years elapsed before Home Secretary Douglas Hurd announced that the government would introduce legislation:

> 'to ensure that the Service can continue to serve the nation well. Few people argue about the need for a Security Service or the need for them to work without their activities being the subject of intensive discussion and debate. But in recent years there has been some concern that people who wish to complain about the Security Service actions against them have the means to do so.'

At that time the media had revealed that applicants for employment with the BBC were routinely screened by MI5. Considerable concern was expressed at the fact that those who were refused employment or dismissed from employment had no means of redress. A further factor was no doubt the forthcoming airing of the inadequacies of the UK system in the European Commission in the case of *Hewitt and Harman*.[1]

1   *Hewitt and Harman v United Kingdom (1989)* 14 EHRR 657.

Hewitt and Harman v UK

4.7   The applicants, Hewitt and Harman, now Trade Secretary and Solicitor-General respectively, were at the time General Secretary and Legal Officer of the National Council for Civil Liberties (now Liberty). They complained that they had been subject to secret surveillance by MI5. In particular, they complained that their telephones had been tapped and that records classifying them as 'communist sympathisers' and 'subversives' had been maintained by MI5. That information had come to light as a result of information supplied by a former intelligence officer of MI5. According to her, the security service file would include the fullest possible personal particulars a photograph, usually taken from a passport application; data from surveillance by the local police special branch; press reports relating to the individual's activities and political views; references to the subject in telephone or mail intercepts operating against other individuals or organisations; and references to the subject in agents' reports. The government neither confirmed nor denied the allegations.

The Commission concluded that the Directive, although published, did not constitute legally enforceable rules nor provide a framework which indicated with the requisite degree of certainty the scope and manner of the exercise of discretion by the authorities. There was therefore a breach of art 8. As the Commission had not been informed of the existence of an effective remedy under the law of the UK, there was also a breach of art 13. The case was subsequently settled by the UK government, who informed the Commission that the activities of MI5 had been put on a statutory basis by the Security Service Act 1989, which came into force on 18 December of that year.

The Security Service Act 1989

4.8 Most of the Security Service Act 1989 (the 1989 Act) has now been replaced by ISA 1994, eg the powers governing the authorisation of a property warrant (see **para 4.27**).

All that remains of the 1989 Act are ss 1 and 2. The effect of s 1 is to confirm that 'there shall continue to be a Security Service'.

Section 1(2) provides that its function:

> 'shall be the protection of national security and, in particular, its protection against threats from espionage, terrorism and sabotage, from the activities of agents of foreign powers and from actions intended to overthrow or undermine parliamentary democracy by political, industrial or violent means.'

The reference to espionage and agents of foreign powers is potentially wide enough to include the Secret Intelligence Services (MI6). Any possible ambiguity has been resolved by ISA 1994, where it is stated that the function of MI6 is directed specifically at the actions or intentions of persons outside the British Isles (see **para 4.23**).

The meaning of national security

4.9 National security is not otherwise defined. In the second reading in the House of Commons the Home Secretary stated:

> 'By its very nature, the phrase refers and can only refer to matters relating to the survival or well being of the nation as a whole, and not to party political or sectional interests.'[1]

The lack of any precise definition is not a breach of the quality of law aspect of art 8. In *Esbester v United Kingdom*,[2] the Commission accepted that the phrase 'the interests of national security' is not susceptible of precise definition (referred to by the Security Service Commissioner in his 1993 Report).

1   143 HC Official Report col 1113.
2   (1993) 18 EHRR CD 72.

The role of the court in considering issues of national security

4.10 This issue has recently been the subject of some difference of emphasis in two decisions of the House of Lords. The first was *Secretary of State for the Home Department v Rehman*,[1] in which the House gave the phrase a wide interpretation in holding that the interests of national security were not confined to direct threats to national security. In the course of his judgment, Lord Slynn stated that he accepted that reciprocal co-operation between the UK and other states in combating international terrorism is capable of promoting the UK's national security and that such co-operation itself is capable of fostering such security by the UK taking action against supporters within the UK of terrorism directed against other states. Lord Hoffman stressed the limited function of the courts in such cases.

> 'The question of whether something is "in the interests" of national security is not a question of law. It is a matter of judgement and policy. Under the constitution of the UK and most other countries, decisions as to whether something is in the interests of national security are not a matter for judicial decision. They are entrusted to the executive.'

1   [2001] UKHL 47, [2003] 1 AC 153.

4.11   In *R v Shayler*[1] the main question turned on the interpretation of the Official Secrets Act 1989, s 1. In deciding that question, Lord Hope gave detailed consideration to the role of the proportionality test in deciding issues of national security.[2] In doing so, he quoted with approval the following comments of Professor Feldman:

> 'In some cases, then no balancing of rights against security will be permitted. Even where non-absolute rights are in issue, the careful balancing required by the doctrine of proportionality should become a major check on the acceptability of claims to the shield of national security, both in relation to the existence of threats to national security and their significance in relation to the interference with rights in the particular case. There will be some cases in which the national security considerations are so sensitive and important that the courts will still decline to intervene, but the doctrine of proportionality should be able to operate (giving appropriate but not unquestioning weight to national security) whenever the court is not satisfied that it ought to treat the particular type of national security consideration as being of such overriding sensitivity and importance as to make the decision in respect of it essentially non-justiciable.'[3]

1   [2001] UKHL 11, [2003] 1 AC 247.
2   [2001] UKHL 11, [2003] 1 AC 247 at paras 67–79.
3   Feldman, *Proportionality and The Human Rights Act 1998*, 1999.

The economic well-being of the UK

4.12   The Security Service Act 1989, s 1(3) adds the safeguarding of 'the economic well-being of the United Kingdom against threats posed by the actions or intentions of persons outside the British Islands'. As with national security, the phrase 'economic well-being' is not defined. It does not need to be substantial. It is capable of including the well-being of any UK-based company, eg the obtaining of an order from abroad. Examples given by the Home Secretary were threats to a commodity such as oil or the use by foreign powers of covert intelligence methods to obtain scientific or technical secrets.[1]

Serious crime was added and inserted as s 1(4) by the Security Service Act 1996 (see **para 4.16**).

1   145 HC Official Report col 221.

4.13   National security and economic well-being are 'reserved matters' for the purposes of the Scotland Act 1998, s 29(2)(b), and are therefore outside the legislative competence of the Scottish Parliament. They are also 'excepted matters' for the purposes of the Northern Ireland Act 1998, s 6(2)(b), and are therefore outside the competence of the Northern Ireland Assembly.

The Director General of the Security Service: Security Service Act 1989, s 2

4.14   His responsibility is to ensure the efficiency of the service. Two aspects of that responsibility are:

(1)   to ensure that no information is obtained or disclosed by the service except so far as is necessary for the discharge of its functions, or for the prevention or detection of serious crime or for the purpose of any criminal proceedings; and

(2)   to ensure that the service maintains a politically neutral stance.[1]

Information in the possession of the service should not be disclosed for use in determining whether anyone should be employed or continue to be employed.[2]

1   Security Service Act 1989, s 2(2) (as amended by RIPA 2000 and ISA 1994).
2   Security Service Act 1989, s 2(3).

4.15   In his second report, May 1992, the Security Service Commissioner dealt with the issue of retention of records. At para 18 he stated:

'The Service's general policy is to retain records indefinitely in case they are of relevance at any time in the future to the Service's work. In the past, espionage investigations have been seriously hampered because the Service's earlier practice had not prohibited destruction. Reconstruction of a number of files was attempted but this was not satisfactory. Since then the Service has changed its policy and, save in exceptional cases, files are retained. The Service instituted its present general policy on retention of records on the basis that they are the key to their work and they cannot accurately predict when files will ever be needed again. In my opinion as a general policy this is acceptable.'

The following paragraph details the system of colour coding, namely green, amber or red, applied to the file to denote the extent to which new information may or may not be added. It is finally microfilmed and transferred to the Research Index.

In his 1997 report,[1] the Commissioner confirmed that files and documents have to be retained in case a complaint is made to the Tribunal.

1   At para 33.

The Security Service Act 1996

4.16   This highly controversial Act adds the prevention and detection of 'serious crime' to the list of functions of the Security Service. The additional functions became the Security Service Act 1989, s 1(4), which was itself the subject of further amendment by the Police Act 1997.[1]

'It shall also be the function of the Service to act in support of the activities of police forces, the National Criminal Intelligence Service [NCIS], the National Crime Squad [NCS] and other law enforcement agencies in the prevention and detection of serious crime.'

Serious crime is not defined, but Security Service Act 1996, s 2 replaces the original s 5(3) of ISA 1994 and provides that a warrant issued under s 1(4) 'may not relate to property in the British Islands unless it authorises the taking of action in relation to conduct within subsection (3B)'.

Conduct is within subsection (3B) if either:

'(a)   it involves the use of violence, results in substantial financial gain or is conduct by a large number of persons in pursuit of a common purpose; or

(b)   the offence or one of the offences is an offence which a person who has attained the age of 21 and has no previous convictions could reasonably expect to be sentenced to imprisonment for a term of three years or more.'

As the two subsections are disjunctive, it follows that common assault or a public demonstration in the street is capable of amounting to serious crime.

1   Police Act 1997, s 134(1) and Sch 9, para 60.

The confusion of function between MI5 and other law enforcement agencies

4.17   The Security Service Act 1996 provides no guidance as to the manner in which it is intended that MI5 should act in support of the other agencies. The potential confusion in the system of complaints was a focus of concern from Baroness Hilton who, as she explained, had 34 years of experience in the police force.

'MI5 does not have a system of clear accountability. Of necessity, it is a secret organisation, its budget is secret, its members and resources are secret. It is accorded special privileges by the courts: for example its internal paperwork is protected from disclosure and its members can be given anonymity as witnesses. So its proceedings are not open. It has no public complaints system … In contrast the Police Service is subject to an elaborate open complaints system which is often widely criticised for being insufficiently independent and accountable … If there is a joint operation between MI5 and the Police Service which goes wrong, if the wrong house is entered, if an innocent person's telephone is bugged, how will the complaint be investigated?'[1]

In her reply, Baroness Blatch was unable to answer the specific question, merely asserting that there were appropriate mechanisms in place.[2]

1   Hansard HL vol 572, col 401, 14 May 1996.
2   Hansard HL, vol 572, col 427, 14 May 1996.

No judicial warrant required by MI5 to sanction entry on private property

4.18 According to the annotators of Current Law Statutes, this was shocking because for the first time a national security service was to be engaged in everyday policing. In giving authority to the service to interfere with property on the basis of an executive warrant, the government failed to acknowledge the fundamental constitutional principle established in *Entick v Carrington*.[1] Lord Browne-Wilkinson drew attention to the problem:

> 'Those who know better than I do say that the addition of the security service into the fight against it [serious crime] is a good thing. In that case I am for it. What I am not for is the carry over of powers, which are unhappily necessary in the context of national security, into a policing function enabling a member of the executive to sanction entry onto private property without prior judicial warrant.'[2]

1   (1765) 19 State TR 1029.
2   573 HL Official Report col 1044.

4.19 In reply Baroness Blatch explained:

> 'There must be grave doubts about whether the authorisation of this type of warrant is an appropriate function for the judiciary. There is an important distinction between property warrants now issued under the Intelligence Services Act and search warrants issued under PACE which are authorised by the judiciary. Search warrants are overt and are normally disclosed to the subject of the warrant at the time of their execution. Property warrants, by contrast, are covert and will not be disclosed at the time of their execution. The only way in which the subject of a warrant could become aware of its existence would be in the course of any subsequent court proceedings. Given that property warrants will often be issued for the purpose of intelligence gathering rather than the collection of evidence there is a good chance that these warrants will never be disclosed to their subject ... judges would be involved in the covert development of operations. This may be seen as a threat to their impartiality by placing them firmly in the law enforcement camp.'[1]

1   573 HL Official Report col 1049.

4.20 Justice make the point that MI5 should exercise their powers under the same safeguards as the police. Otherwise:

> 'there are obvious dangers in two agencies having different powers and operating to different procedures when tackling the same threat of serious crime. For example MI5 could be tasked to undertake activities which could not legally be undertaken by the police. In addition those affected are faced with a lottery of deciding between two separate and unsatisfactory complaints procedures without any information as to which one it was appropriate to pursue in the particular circumstances.'[1]

1   From Justice report 'Under Surveillance'. See comments of Secret Service Commissioner at para 20 of his 1997 Report. See generally 269 HC Official Report col 215; 271 HC Official Report col 1016; 569 HL Official Report col 723; 572 HL Official Report cols 394 and 1491; 573 HL Official Report col 1025; and 574 HL Official Report col 76.

4.21 Paragraph 6 of the Security Service Commissioner's Report for 1996 states:

'The 1996 Act will enable the Security Service to use, in the fight against serious crime, the skills and expertise that it has built up over many years. Counter-terrorism work will still remain the Service's top priority but it is clearly sensible that the Service should be able to make a contribution to the efforts that are made to combat other forms of serious crime. This does not mean that the Security Service will become another police force or that it will be patrolling the streets or arresting people.'

He explained that it was intended that the service would be co-ordinated by the NCIS.

4.22 In commenting on the additional function in his report for 1998, the same Commissioner stated at para 8:

'The additional role is a supporting one and the primary responsibility for tackling serious crime remains with the police and other law enforcement agencies. Consequently this does not mean that the Security Service has usurped the functions of the police force and indeed the 1996 Act specifically ensures that the Security Service does not act independently under this function. The Service therefore collaborates with the police to combat serious crime as it has for many years to combat terrorism.'

The Intelligence Services Act 1994 (ISA 1994)

4.23 This Act came into force on 15 December 1994. It gives statutory recognition to MI6 and GCHQ and harmonises the system for obtaining warrants by all three services.

MI6 originated in 1909 as the foreign section of the Secret Service Bureau under Sir Mansfield Cumming. By 1922 the section had become a separate service with the title SIS, latterly known as MI6.

The functions of MI6 are widely defined by ISA 1994, s 1(1) as:

'(a)   to obtain and provide information relating to the actions or intentions of persons outside the British Islands, and
(b)   to perform other tasks relating to the actions or intentions of such persons.'

British Islands are defined as the UK, the Channel Islands and the Isle of Man.[1]

Section 1(2) provides that the functions of MI6 shall be exercisable only:
'(a)   in the interests of national security with particular reference to the defence and foreign policies of Her Majesty's Government in the United Kingdom; or
(b)   in the interests of the economic well-being of the United Kingdom; or
(c)   in support of the prevention or detection of serious crime.'

National security, etc are not defined in the Act (see **para 4.9** for national security, **para 4.12** for economic well-being of the UK and **para 4.16** for serious crime).

1   See Interpretation Act 1978, s 5 and Sch 1.

The Chief of the Intelligence Service

4.24   His functions are described by ISA 1994, s 2 in similar terms to those of the Director General of the Secret Service (see **para 4.14**), but include wider circumstances in which disclosure of information may be permitted, eg in the interests of national security. As with the Director General, disclosure is not permitted in the economic well-being of the UK.

Section 2(3) gives two examples of disclosure of information that shall be regarded as necessary, eg if it consists of disclosure subject to and in accordance with the Public Records Act 1958 or is disclosure to the Comptroller and Auditor General. The Lord Chancellor stated that:

> 'the purpose of the provision is solely to enable the services to place their records, if and when appropriate, in the Public Record Office.'[1]

1   130 HC Official Report col 1075

GCHQ

4.25   The predecessor of GCHQ was the Government Code and Cipher School based at Bletchley Park, best known for its work decrypting German messages during the 1939–45 war. GCHQ was founded in 1946 and has been based at Cheltenham since 1952.

ISA 1994, s 3 for the first time gave it statutory recognition. Its functions are:

'(a)   to monitor or interfere with electromagnetic, acoustic and other emissions and any equipment producing such emissions and to obtain and provide information derived from or related to such emissions or equipment and from encrypted material; and

(b)   to provide advice and assistance about–
  (i) languages, including terminology used for technical matters, and
  (ii) cryptography and other matters relating to the protection of information and other material,
to the armed forces of the Crown, to Her Majesty's Government in the United Kingdom or to a Northern Ireland Department or to any other organisation which is determined for the purposes of this section in such manner as may be specified by the Prime Minister.'

The purposes of GCHQ are described in terms identical to the purposes of MI6, with the exception that, in relation to economic well-being, the persons being monitored must be outside the British Islands. Both receive directions from the Joint Intelligence Committee.

The director of GCHQ

4.26   ISA 1994, s 4(2) provides that the director shall be responsible for the efficiency of GCHQ and shall ensure that no information is obtained or disclosed except so far as is necessary for the discharge of its functions or for the purpose of any criminal proceedings. Disclosure in accordance with the Public Records Act 1958 or to the Comptroller and Auditor General is permitted in the same circumstances as at **para 4.24**.

In common with the duties of the Director General of MI5 and the Chief of MI6, to ensure neutrality of their Service, he shall ensure the neutrality of the GCHQ.

Property warrants

4.27   Applications for warrants for entry onto or interference with property (property warrants) on behalf of MI5, MI6 and GCHQ are made to the Secretary of State. Section 3 of the 1989 Act was repealed by ISA 1994, s 6(6)(b), thus harmonising the issue of all warrants involving these services.

ISA 1994, s 5(1) provides that 'no entry on or interference with property or wireless telegraphy shall be unlawful if it is authorised under this section'. The section goes further than the 1989 Act in permitting interference with wireless telegraphy, e g by jamming radio signals.

ISA 1994, s 5(2) gives the Secretary of State a very wide power to authorise 'such action as is specified' in respect of the property. This is potentially significantly wider than the installation of bugging equipment and could extend to the search and seizure of property.

The same section states that the Secretary of State may not grant a warrant unless he:

(a)   thinks it necessary for the action to be taken on the ground that it is likely to be of substantial value in assisting the respective service in carrying out its function; and

(b)   is satisfied that the taking of the action is proportionate to what the action seeks to achieve; and

(c)   is satisfied that satisfactory arrangements are in force with respect to the disclosure of information obtained by virtue of the warrant and that any information obtained will be subject to those arrangements.

The matters to be taken into account in considering whether the requirements of (a) and (b) are satisfied in the case of any warrant shall include whether what is thought necessary could reasonably be achieved by other means.[1]

1   See ISA 1994, s 5(2A) and see generally the Covert Surveillance Code 6.32–6.36 and RIPA 2000.

4.28   A warrant authorising the taking of action by M15 in support of the prevention or detection of serious crime may not relate to property in the British Islands unless it authorises the taking of action in relation to serious crime[1] (see **para 4.16**).

This is an important qualification, as otherwise the responsibilities of MI5 in particular might encroach on those of the police whose bugging and burglary powers are provided by the Police Act 1997, Part III, the provisions of which are significantly tighter:

(a)   MI5 warrant authorisation is by the Secretary of State with no involvement of a High Court Judge; and

(b)   there are no safeguards covering legally privileged, confidential or journalistic material.

In addition, ISA 1994, s 5(4) provides that MI5 may apply for a warrant:

'to take such action as is specified in the warrant on behalf of the Intelligence Service or GCHQ and where such a warrant is issued, the functions of the Security Service shall include the carrying out of the action specified, whether or not it would otherwise be within its functions'.

ISA 1994, s 5(5) restricts the actions to those which could legitimately be authorised in respect of M16 or GCHQ.

1   ISA 1994, s 5(3A) and (3B)

The process of authorisation

4.29   Neither the 1989 Act nor ISA 1994 provides guidance on the procedure to be adopted. Paragraphs 4 and 5 of the First Report by the Secret Service Commissioner throw some light on the subject.

'The application for a property warrant under s 3 of the Act contains a description of the case, the name of the person or organisation, the property involved, and details of the operational plan ... When an application arrives at the Home Office ... it is processed by the warrants unit. It is scrutinised on arrival at Grade 7 level, to ensure that the application is in order and that the application satisfies ss 1 and 3 of the Act. This includes checking that satisfactory arrangements are in force regarding the disclosure of information obtained under the warrant and that these arrangements will be applied. If there is any doubt on any of these scores the application is referred back to the Service. If the application is approved at that level, it is referred, through Grade 5 level to the Permanent Under Secretary, or in his absence a Deputy Under Secretary, normally the head of the Police department. It is only after it has been approved by him that it is put before the Home Secretary for his personal approval.'[1]

1   March 1991

Warrants procedure and duration

4.30   Warrants under ISA 1994, s 5 shall not be issued except by the Secretary of State or, in an urgent case where he has expressly authorised its issue and a statement of the fact is endorsed thereon, by a senior official of his department.[1]

Warrants will cease to have effect after six months, except in a case of urgency in which it will cease to have effect at the end of the period ending with the second working day following that day.[2]

'Urgency' is not defined, but see the Surveillance Code (**para 4.41**).

A warrant may be renewed for a further six months.[3]

The Secretary of State shall cancel a warrant if he is satisfied that the action authorised by it is no longer necessary.[4]

1   ISA 1994, s 6(1)(b).
2   ISA 1994, s 6(2).
3   ISA 1994, s 6(3).
4   ISA 1994, s 6(4).

Authorisation of acts outside the British Islands

4.31   Under ISA 1994, s 7 the Secretary of State may authorise MI6 to carry out acts outside the British Islands which are necessary for the proper discharge of its functions. Before granting an authorisation he must be satisfied that arrangements are in force to ensure that nothing is done beyond that which is necessary and that the nature and consequence of any action is reasonable in the circumstances. In addition, he must also be satisfied that satisfactory arrangements are in force under ISA 1994, s 2(2)(a) with respect to disclosure of any information obtained as a result.

The Anti-terrorism, Crime and Security Act 2001, s 116 has added GCHQ to the list of agencies entitled to seek authorisation under ISA 1994, s 7. In addition, the section allows both M16 and GCHQ to carry out authorised acts in the UK, but only where the intention relates to apparatus believed to be located abroad.

Examples of s 7 authorisations

4.32   The section provides for authorisation to be given in respect of particular acts, acts of a description specified in the authorisation (class authorisation) or acts carried out in the course of an operation so specified. According to the 1995 Report of the Commissioner:

'It is intended that class authorisations would be sought only for relatively minor infractions of the law not involving significant risks to persons or property ... Examples of the type of act which might be covered by a class authorisation under s 7 are the obtaining of documents which might involve theft or trespass on property for the purpose of planting a listening device or payment to an agent which might involve bribery.'

The Intelligence and Security Committee (ISC)

4.33   In addition to the respective commissioners, oversight of the activities of all three agencies is provided by the ISC. This was established by ISA 1994, s 10. Its function is to examine the expenditure, administration and policy of MI5, MI6 and

GCHQ. It has a cross-party membership of nine, appointed by the Prime Minister after consultation with the Leader of the Opposition. It has to provide an annual report which, subject to deletions of material prejudicial to the continuing discharge of the functions of either service or GCHQ, is laid before Parliament.

Interpretation

4.34 ISA 1994, s 11(1A) applies RIPA 2000, s 81(5) as it applies for the purposes of Ch I of Pt I, s 81(5)(b) provides that 'detecting crime' shall not include a reference to gathering evidence for use in any legal proceedings.

This has further been amended by the Anti-terrorism, Crime and Security Act 2001, s 116 in order to align the definitions of the prevention and detection of crime which presently apply to M15 and M16 so that both now operate under the same definition.

The Regulation of Investigatory Powers Act 2000 (RIPA 2000)

4.35 The powers of the Intelligence Services to obtain an interception warrant under IOCA 1985 have been replaced by RIPA 2000, Pt I, and the power to obtain a property warrant under ISA 1994, s 5 have been significantly supplemented by the powers in RIPA 2000, Pt I, Ch II, Pt II and Pt III. RIPA 2000, s 42(4) entitles MI5 in certain circumstances to act on behalf of MI6 or GCHQ in making an application for directed surveillance, CHIS or intrusive surveillance. This is permissible only in respect of something which either service is entitled to do other than in support of the prevention or detection of serious crime.

RIPA 2000, Pt I, Ch I: interception

4.36 RIPA 2000, s 6(2) provides that the Director General of the Security Service, the Chief of the Intelligence Service and the Director of GCHQ may apply for an interception warrant (see s 6(2)(a), (b) and (c)).

For criteria and procedure see **Chapter 6**.

RIPA 2000, Pt I, Ch II: access to communications data

4.37 The combination of RIPA 2000, ss 22(3) and 25(1)(f) provide that any of the Intelligence Services is a relevant public authority for the purposes of Ch II.

For criteria and procedure see **Chapter 7**.

RIPA 2000, Pt II: directed surveillance and CHIS

4.38 The Intelligence Services, which include MI5, MI6 and GCHQ, are relevant public authorities for the purposes of RIPA 2000, ss 28–30 (see Sch 1) and can therefore self-authorise. Such authorisation may be, in the case of MI5, by General Duties 3, or any other officer at level 3; in the case of MI6, Grade 6 or equivalent; and in the case of GCHQ, at level GC8 (SI 2003/3171).

RIPA 2000, s 30(2)(b) provides that the Secretary of State may also authorise directed surveillance or CHIS but only where combined with an authorisation for intrusive surveillance.

For criteria and procedure see **Chapter 8**.

RIPA 2000, Pt II: intrusive surveillance

4.39   RIPA 2000, s 41 provides that intrusive surveillance by any of the three Intelligence Services may be authorised by the Secretary of State (and only the Secretary of State – see s 44(1)). Such authorisation does not require approval by a Surveillance Commissioner.

Authorisation of intrusive surveillance by MI6 or GCHQ relating to any premises or vehicle in the British Isles will only be permitted on grounds of national security or in the interests of the economic well-being of the UK.[1]

Such warrants will normally last for six months, but may be renewed before the end of that time[2] (see also Code 5.31). This is longer than the equivalent period when not granted by the Secretary of State.

For criteria and procedure see **Chapter 8** and Surveillance Code 5.25 onwards.

1   RIPA 2000, s 42(3).
2   RIPA 2000, s 44(4).

Combined authorisations

4.40   RIPA 2000, s 42(1) provides that authorisation to any of the Intelligence Services is by way of warrant. By s 42(2) the warrant may combine an authorisation under Pt II with a property warrant under ISA 1994, s 5, provided that the relevant requirements under both Acts are satisfied.

Urgent situations

4.41   As with property warrants under ISA 1994 (see **para 4.27**), provision is made in cases of urgency for the issue, but not the renewal, of a warrant for intrusive surveillance by a senior official. Such a course will only be permitted where the Secretary of State has himself expressly authorised the issue of a warrant in that case.[1] Such a warrant, if not renewed by the Secretary of State, will cease to have effect at the end of the second working day following the day of its issue.

Urgency is not defined in the Act, but the Surveillance Code 4.13 and 5.13 provide that a case is not normally to be regarded as urgent unless the time that would elapse before the authorising officer was available to grant the authorisation would, in the judgment of the person giving the authorisation, be likely to endanger life or jeopardise the investigation or operation for which the authorisation was being given. An authorisation is not to be regarded as urgent where the need for an authorisation has been neglected or the urgency is of the authorising officer's own making.

1   RIPA 2000, s 44(2)(b).

Statistics

4.42   No details of the number of warrants issued to the Intelligence Services has been made available in the reports of either the Secret Service Commissioner or the Intelligence Services Commissioner. In para 14 of the First Report, the Commissioner, the Rt Hon Lord Justice Stuart Smith, gave the following explanation:

> 'I have carefully considered whether I should publish the number of warrants that have been issued, renewed and cancelled since the Act came into force. I have come to the conclusion that it is not in the public interest that I should do so. This is in contrast with the practice adopted by the Commissioner for Interception of Communications Act 1985. The reason why I have felt unable to publish this information is because of the comparatively small number of warrants issued under the 1989 Act and the fact that the purposes for which they can be granted is more restricted than under the 1985 Act in that they do not include the prevention or detection of crime.'

Although that situation has been changed by the Security Service Act 1996, the Commissioner has not changed his approach. At para 8 of the 1997 Report he explained that in his opinion:

> 'particulars of the actual numbers would assist the operation of agencies hostile to the state if they were able to estimate even approximately the extent of the Security Service's work in fulfilling its functions.'

The present Intelligence Services Commissioner, Lord Justice Simon Brown, has adopted a similar approach.[1]

1   See para 30 of the 2002 Report.

Chapter 5

The Police Act 1997, Pt III

Introduction

5.1   The Police Act 1997 came into force on 22 February 1999. It is concerned only with activities by the police, including the National Criminal Intelligence Service (NCIS), the National Crime Squad (NCS) and HM Customs and Excise (HMCE). The original Code of Practice issued under the Police Act 1997, s 101 has now been superseded by the Covert Surveillance Code of Practice (Surveillance Code) issued under RIPA 2000, s 71(5), which came into force on 1 August 2002.[1] Chapter 6 of that Code refers specifically to Police Act 1997 and Intelligence Services Act 1994 (ISA 1994) authorisations.

1   SI 1933/2002.

5.2   In *R v Khan*[1] (see para 2.37) the focal point of the argument on behalf of the appellant was that there was no legal framework to regulate the installation and use by the police of listening devices. This was in contrast to the use of such devices by MI5 which was regulated by the Security Service Act 1989. It was submitted that the 1984 Guidelines were not sufficiently accessible, and that there was a breach of art 8. Although the House of Lords agreed that a breach of art 8 might be relevant to the determination of the discretionary power under s 78, it concluded that the evidence was both admissible as a matter of law and in the exercise of the discretion. At the time the 1984 Guidelines were the only form of control. The House described the lack of a statutory system for regulating the use of surveillance devices as "astonishing". The relevant parts were set out in the judgment and are included below.

1   [1997] AC 558.

The 1984 Guidelines on the use of equipment in police surveillance operations

5.3

'4.   In each case in which the covert use of a listening device is requested the authorising officer should satisfy himself that the following criteria are met:

(a) the investigation concerns serious crime;

(b) normal methods of investigation must have been tried and failed, or must, from the nature of things, be unlikely to succeed if tried;

(c) there must be good reason to think that use of the equipment would lead to an arrest and a conviction, or where appropriate, to the prevention of acts of terrorism;

(d) use of the equipment must be operationally feasible.

5.   In judging how far the seriousness of the crime under investigation justifies the use of particular surveillance techniques, authorising officers should satisfy themselves that the degree of intrusion into the privacy of those affected by the surveillance is commensurate with the seriousness of the offence. Where the targets of surveillance might reasonably assume a high degree of privacy, for instance in their homes, listening devices should be used only for the investigation of major organised conspiracies and of other particularly serious offences, especially crimes of violence.

6.   The covert use in operations of listening, recording and transmitting equipment (for example microphones, tape recorders and tracking equipment) requires the personal authority of the chief officer.

7.   An Assistant Chief Constable may give authorisation where the relevant equipment was to be–

(a) knowingly carried by a person other than a police officer who is party to a conversation which is to be recorded or transmitted;

(b) carried by a police officer whose identity is known to at least one other non–police party to a conversation which is to be recorded or transmitted;

(c) installed in premises, with the consent of the lawful occupier, to record or transmit a conversation in circumstances where at least one of the parties to the conversation will know of the surveillance;

(d) used, with the consent of one of the parties concerned, to record a telephone conversation;

(e) used with the consent, in the case of a vehicle, of the owner (though not necessarily the driver) to track a vehicle, package or person.'

Paragraph 10 provided that:

'It is accepted that there may be circumstances in which material obtained through the use of equipment by the police for surveillance as a necessary part of a criminal investigation could appropriately be used in evidence at subsequent court proceedings.'

Parliamentary history

5.4   Despite some agreement between the government and the Labour opposition that the main aims of the Bill were desirable, there were strongly voiced opinions, particularly in the House of Lords, that the methods of surveillance being proposed in Pt III were unacceptable. In introducing the second reading on 11 November 1996, Baroness Blatch referred to the 1984 Home Office Guidelines, which she stated had imposed a tightly controlled system which:

> 'has served us well and I know that chief officers take their responsibilities very seriously. The courts recognise and accept evidence obtained in this way. But there is a strong case ... for putting the authorisation system on a statutory footing. This will establish greater clarity in the way this crucial activity is controlled.'[1]

Somewhat surprisingly, no reference was made to the decision in *R v Khan*, decided only four months earlier.

1   HL Official Report vol 575, col 792.

5.5   Lord Browne-Wilkinson, in terms similar to his concerns regarding the Security Service Act 1996 (see **Chapter 4**), voiced the opinion that the previous practice was unlawful.

> 'Our freedom depends, and depends only, on the fact that no Minister, no administrator and no member of the police has any greater power or any greater right than any other citizen to enter our property or to seize our person. In particular the state and its officers have no power to enter our houses or workplaces or to seize our property. Such conduct is unlawful and the administrative action which is apparently being pursued has been, subject to any explanation given by the Minister, unlawful conduct by the police.'[1]

He went on to point out that what would be authorised under the Bill was:

> 'the taking of such action in respect of such property, as the chief constable may consider necessary.'

In his view, that action might involve not only the placing of bugs but also the searching of property and the removal of documents and other things found there. He expressed further concern that the definition of serious crime, as the activity of a large number of people acting together, would entitle the police to bug the home of a protester against the Newbury bypass. If such action revealed material suggesting that the protester had telephoned his solicitor, the police might obtain authority to enter and bug the solicitor's office. Such concerns led him to conclude that in each case there should be prior judicial authority.[2]

1   HL Official Report vol 575, col 810.
2   HL Official Report vol 575, col 812.

5.6   In reply Baroness Blatch said that the government had considered prior judicial authorisation but ruled it out in terms similar to those she had used in respect of the Security Service Act 1996 (**para 4.19**).

'We do not believe that it is right to involve judges at the early intelligence gathering stage as regards the prevention of crime as well as the investigation of crimes that have already taken place. There is the danger of the judiciary becoming too closely involved in the investigative process and of its impartiality being called into question. There is a distinct difference between sensitive surveillance and the requirement for search warrants. Warrants come at a much later stage, when police can show to a judge evidence to suggest that crime has been committed ... Intrusive surveillance is used at an intelligence gathering stage and may never produce evidence sufficient for prosecution. It may also be important to conceal that it has ever taken place.'[1]

1   HL Official Report vol 575, col 837.

5.7   In the weeks that followed there was a considerable amount of public debate. When the matter came back to the House on 20 January 1997, there had been a rethink by the government on certain aspects of the Bill including a limited concession that there should be a procedure of immediate notification to the Commissioner of any intrusive surveillance.

A Labour amendment, proposing prior judicial authorisation in respect of any entry onto or interference with premises, except in cases where it was not reasonably practical, was debated at the same time as a Liberal amendment proposing that there should be prior judicial authorisation by a circuit judge in all cases. Lord Rogers informed the House that *The Times*, the *Daily Telegraph*, the *Guardian*, the *Observer*, the *Daily Mail*, the *Financial Times* and *The Economist* all advocated prior judicial authorisation. Somewhat confusingly, both amendments were carried by a significant majority.

5.8   During the course of the debate, two previous Home Secretaries, Lord Callaghan and Lord Carr, expressed astonishment at the figure of 2,100 authorisations having been given in 1995, stating that they had no recollection during their terms in office of being asked by the police, as opposed to the Intelligence Services, to grant such warrants. In supporting both amendments, Lord Callaghan asked why, if the Intelligence Services were required to secure warrants, should not the police be expected to do the same?

In her reply Baroness Blatch stressed that under the proposed system, as under that which had existed previously, chief officers of police were accountable and could be called to give evidence in court. Such could not be the case if a judge had to give prior authorisation.

Lords Hutchinson and Alexander expressed concerns that in almost all cases the subjects of the surveillance would never know that their privacy had been invaded. Lord Alexander pointed out that in the United States, Australia, New Zealand, France and Germany there could be no invasion of property without a prior judicial warrant.

5.9   The Bill came before the House of Commons for the second reading on 12 February 1997. During his introduction, the Home Secretary, Michael Howard, was asked about the third limb of the definition of serious crime by Tony Benn, who pointed out that 'conduct by a large number of persons in pursuit of a common purpose' would entitle a Labour Home Secretary to bug any Conservative party office. The Home Secretary responded by referring to the activities of neo-Nazi youths disrupting a major football match and drew attention to the obligation of the chief officer to make a judgment about proportionality. On the issue of approval, he confirmed that the prior approval of a commissioner would be required where there were reasonable grounds for thinking that the operation could affect legal, medical or journalistic privilege or when the operation involved intrusion into residential dwellings, offices or hotel bedrooms. He also made clear that the test to be applied by the commissioner was not the test appropriate to judicial review, as had originally been proposed, but a test based on whether he was satisfied that there were reasonable grounds for believing that the authorisation fulfilled the requirements of clause 92. The Shadow Home Secretary, Jack Straw, supported the amended Bill, provoking a comment from the floor that the official opposition had not done its job. Similarly, the Liberal Democrats gave the Bill their qualified support, noting that it was illogical that there was in existence a proper authorisation procedure should the Intelligence Services need to carry out such activities. The qualification was based on their proposed amendment that the bugging of private places should always require prior judicial authorisation. The amendment was defeated by a substantial majority and the Bill was given a second reading.

What type of surveillance is covered?

5.10   The Police Act 1997 introduced a scheme whereby, for the first time, the police and HMCE (as opposed to Intelligence Services) and NCIS and NCS were required to apply for prior authorisation before embarking on covert 'surveillance' involving entry onto or interference with property or wireless telegraphy without the consent of the owner. Interference with wireless telegraphy might include jamming of a private telecommunications system used by those under suspicion. Authorisations under the Police Act 1997, Pt III may not be necessary where the public authority is acting with the consent of a person able to give permission in respect of the relevant property. It follows that the bugging of prison visiting areas or the cells at a police station or police vehicles is not covered by Pt III, as such activities would be with the consent of the owner[1] (although consideration should still be given to the need to obtain authorisation under RIPA 2000, Pt II[2]).

1   See *R v McLeod* [2002] EWCA Crim 989, [2002] All ER (D) 61 (May) and *R v Mason* [2002] 2 Cr App Rep 628.
2   See Covert Surveillance Code 6.4 (see **Chapter 8**).

Are there geographical limits to the extent of the authorisation?

5.11   An authorisation may only apply to the 'relevant area', which is limited to the area for which the particular police force is maintained. This may be of considerable importance where the police are dealing with cases such as those involving widespread drug dealing or car theft. Surveillance Code 6.5 does provide an exception in that an authorising officer may authorise the taking of action outside the relevant area solely for the purpose of maintaining or retrieving any device, apparatus or equipment. Where the authorisation concerns the NCIS the relevant area is the whole of the UK and where it concerns the NCS it is England and Wales. In practice, where the police require authorisation outside their own area, they have to use the machinery of the NCIS or NCS.

What are the criteria for authorisation?

5.12   In contrast to the equivalent provisions of ISA 1994, the only ground for authorisation is the prevention or detection of serious crime. The Police Act 1997, s 93(2) as amended by s 75(4) RIPA 2000, provides that such action may be taken:

'where the authorising officer believes–

(a)   that it is necessary for the action specified to be taken for the purpose of preventing or detecting serious crime, and
(b)   that the taking of the action is proportionate to what the action seeks to achieve.'

Section 93(2B) is inserted and states that in considering sub-s 5(2) consideration should be given to whether or not what is thought necessary to achieve could be achieved by other means.

Although the section does not use the phrase 'reasonably believe', where the authorisation requires the approval of a Commissioner, s 97(5) provides that the authorising officer will have to demonstrate that his belief was held on reasonable grounds. In the committee stage of the Bill, Lord Mackay explained that:

'the whole structure of the clause requires authorising officers to proceed on a reasonable basis. If they fail to do so and complaints are made, the Commissioner will undoubtedly intervene; equally in the absence of any complaint, he will deal with such a matter in the reports he is required to make.'[1]

This somewhat disingenuous explanation fails to recognise that it is unlikely that the target of the surveillance will ever get to know of its existence.

The Surveillance Code 6.8 directs the attention of the authorising officer to particular sensitivities in the local community and of similar activities being undertaken by other public authorities which could impact on the deployment.

The fact that, under the Police Act 1997, s 93(2B), the authorising officer has to be satisfied that what is sought cannot be achieved by other means, would seem to suggest that in most cases the officer will first have to consider the use of directed or even intrusive surveillance that falls to be authorised under the terms of RIPA 2000 before going on to consider the arguably more intrusive activities under Pt III. If this has been happening, one would expect to see a significant fall in the number of property interference authorisations. In fact, totals have remained similar.

1   HL vol 576 col 232, 26 November 1996

Combined authorisations

5.13 The Surveillance Code recognises that a single authorisation may permit an authorisation under Police Act 1997, Pt III and an authorisation under RIPA 2000, Pt II.[1] In such a case the provisions applicable in the case of each must be considered separately.[2] In a situation involving office premises this would require prior authorisation by a Commissioner to bug and burgle but no form of prior or subsequent authorisation where the activity involved the use of long-range equipment.

1   See RIPA 2000, s 33(5)(b).
2   Covert Surveillance Code 2.12.

Collateral intrusion

5.14 Surveillance Code 2.10 makes it clear that the general rules on authorisations apply to applications under Pt III. Of particular significance is Surveillance Code 2.6, which enjoins the authorising officer to take into account the risk of intrusion into the privacy of persons other than those who are directly the subjects of the investigation. When powers are exercised, steps should be taken to minimise collateral intrusion.

This was an aspect that concerned those applying for authorisation in *R v Lawrence*,[1] in which the police sought to bug offices and vehicles being used by the two main targets. It was anticipated that apart from their respective wives the only other persons likely to be affected were criminal associates of the two main targets.[2] It was submitted, on behalf of certain less involved defendants, that the authorisations disclosed that insufficient consideration had been given to their position. In rejecting the argument, the court commented:

> 'As a general proposition if and insofar as the police apply for authorisation of "eavesdropping" surveillance, it is virtually inevitable that it will pick up conversations conducted between the individuals targeted and others unaware of the relevant device. Equally, if premises or a car are the subject of such surveillance, casual visitors or passengers will inevitably have their privacy breached in respect of conversations picked up by the device. The best that can usually be done to consider the position of such persons is to speculate in an informed manner as to their number, the likely nature of their business and content of their conversation and to make a decision accordingly.'[3]

1   [2001] EWCA Crim 1829, [2002] Crim LR 584.
2   [2001] EWCA Crim 1829.
3   [2001] EWCA Crim 1829.

Is it necessary that any target be reasonably suspected of committing or having committed a serious offence before authorisation can be given?

5.15 No, no offence need have been committed. There is no requirement to name a target or have any reasonable suspicion as to any person. Where the identity is known his name should be included in the application.[1]

1   See Covert Surveillance Code 6.12 (**para 5.18**).

What is serious crime?

5.16 Serious crime is defined by the Police Act 1997, s 93(4) as:

'if, and only if,–

(a)   it involves the use of violence, results in substantial financial gain or is conduct by a large number of persons in pursuit of a common purpose, or

(b)   the offence or one of the offences is an offence for which a person who has attained the age of twenty-one and has no previous convictions could reasonably be expected to be sentenced to imprisonment for a term of three years or more.'

The definition follows that in IOCA 1985, s 10(3) and ISA 1994, s 5(3)(b).

If the matter involves HMCE it must also be an assigned matter within the Customs and Excise Management Act 1979, s 1(1).

The procedure under Pt III

Who may apply for authorisation?

5.17 The application for authorisation should be made in writing by an officer of any rank, providing he is a member of the relevant police force.

What information should be included in the application?

5.18 Surveillance Code 6.12 provides that the application should specify:

- the identity of those to be targeted (where known);
- the property which the entry or interference will affect;
- the identity of individuals and/or categories of people, where known, who are likely to be affected by collateral intrusion;
- details of the offence planned or committed;
- details of the intrusive surveillance involved;
- how the authorisation criteria have been met; and

- any action which may be necessary to retrieve any equipment used in the surveillance.

In case of a renewal under the Police Act 1997, s 95(3) the application should include the results obtained so far, or a full explanation of the failure to obtain any results, and whether an authorisation was given or refused, by whom and the date.

In addition, in urgent cases, the authorisation should record the reason why the case was considered so urgent that an oral authorisation was given.

Who may authorise?

5.19   The authorising officer should be a chief constable of the police force by whom the application is made, including Scotland, or where appropriate, the Commissioner or Assistant Commissioner of the Metropolitan Police, the Chief Constable or Deputy Chief Constable of the RUC, the Director General of the NCIS or the NCS, or the designated HMCE officer.[1] These agencies have now been extended by RIPA 2000, s 75(6) to include the Chief constable of the Ministry of Defence Police and of the British Transport Police, and the Provost Marshals of the Royal Naval Police, the Royal Military Police and the Royal Air Force Police.

1   Police Act 1997, s 93(5).

Urgent applications

5.20   Provision is made in the Police Act 1997, s 94 for authorisations to be given by officers of lesser rank where it is not reasonably practicable for the authorising officer or, where appropriate, the designated deputy to consider the application. Where the case is urgent, authorisation may be given by an assistant chief constable of any force in the UK, by a commander in the Metropolitan Police or the City of London Police, a person designated for this purpose by the Director General of the NCIS or the NCS, or a Customs Officer designated for this purpose by the Commissioners of Customs and Excise. Such authorisations must always be in writing[1] and last only 72 hours (see **para 5.21**). Oral authorisation may be given in an urgent case only by the senior authorising officer.

Although para 6 of the Surveillance Code gives no further guidance on the meaning of 'urgent', both para 4.13 and 5.13 do so in identical terms:

'A case is not normally to be regarded as urgent unless the time that would elapse before the authorising officer was available to grant the authorisation would, in the judgement of the person giving the authorisation be likely to endanger life or jeopardise the investigation or operation for which the authorisation was being given. An authorisation is not to be regarded as urgent where the need for an authorisation has been neglected or the urgency is of the authorising officers own making.'

1   Police Act 1997, s 95(1).

How long may authorisation last?

5.21   Unless the matter is one of urgency, the authorisation should be in writing[1] and will normally last for three months.[2] Where the authorisation is given orally or in the absence of the authorising officer by virtue of Police Act 1997, s 94, it shall lapse after 72 hours unless renewed.[3] Provision is made for a further extension of up to three months where the authorising officer considers it necessary.[4] Any renewal should be recorded on the authorisation record[5] and Commissioners must be notified of renewals.[6] There appears to be no limit to the number of such renewals. In *R v Lawrence*,[7] a case involving allegations of VAT fraud, 36 successive authorisations were permitted, lasting a total of 17 months. It was apparent that surveillance had been continuing for a considerable time before the commencement of the authorisations, but the prosecution did not rely on any evidence obtained during the earlier period. It was submitted that the police had no interest in 'preventing or detecting' a fraud on the Revenue and that the renewed authorisations were given in respect of other serious crimes.[8] Alternatively, it was submitted that after the arrest of one of the conspirators the police were no longer involved in 'preventing or detecting' VAT fraud but simply gathering evidence in relation to it and conniving in the loss of vast amounts of VAT. In refusing to accept that such surveillance was unjustified, the Court of Appeal stated that where police are in possession of intelligence which gives rise to suspicion of involvement in serious crime, such persons are a paradigm case for intrusive surveillance under the Police Act 1997, s 93(2) for the 'prevention or detection' of serious crime, in a situation where this cannot be achieved by other means. The fact that while investigating one serious crime another is discovered did not mean that the continued use of listening devices was disproportionate. On a true analysis of the situation, the applications and authorisations over the relevant period were made for the purpose of detecting the extent of and the parties to the new VAT fraud.

1   Police Act 1997, s 95(1)
2   Police Act 1997, s 95(2)(b); Covert Surveillance Code 6.18.
3   See Covert Surveillance Code 6.19.
4   Police Act 1997, s 95(3).
5   Covert Surveillance Code 6.20.
6   Covert Surveillance Code 6.21.
7   [2001] EWCA Crim 1829, [2002] Crim LR 584.
8   Police Act 1997, s 93(2).

5.22   Such long-term surveillance is likely to be exceptional. It is submitted that the courts should be careful to ensure that such surveillance does not become a form of licensed fishing expedition. It should be noted that the failure of the domestic legislation to impose a time limit was one of the considerations that caused the ECt HR to conclude that there had been a violation of art 8 in *Valanzuela Contreras v Spain*.[1]

1   (1998) 28 EHRR 483.

Who has to be notified?

5.23   In all cases, notification of the granting, renewing or cancelling of any authorisation should be given to a Commissioner.[1] The notification should specify whether approval of a Commissioner is required[2] and, where prior approval has not been obtained, the grounds upon which it believed to be a case of urgency.[3]

1   Police Act 1997, s 96(1). See Covert Surveillance Code 6.15.
2   Police Act 1997, s 96(3)(a).
3   Police Act 1997, s 96(3)(b).

When is prior approval of a Commissioner required?

5.24   In any case other than one of urgency (see **para 5.20**), where the authorisation relates to property that is used wholly or mainly as a dwelling or as a bedroom in a hotel or constitutes office premises or where knowledge of matters subject to legal privilege, confidential personal or journalistic information is likely to result, prior approval of a Commissioner is required.[1] The authorisation is of no effect until such approval has been given and received,[2] unless the person giving the authorisation believes the case is one of urgency.[3]

Surveillance Code 6.31 defines office premises as any building or part of a building whose sole or principal use is as an office or for office purposes (which means purposes of administration, clerical work, handling money and telephone or telegraph operation).

A Commissioner shall only approve an authorisation if he is satisfied that there are reasonable grounds for believing the matters specified in the Police Act 1997, s 93(2).[4] This approach represents a significant change to that based on the judicial review test that was part of the original bill. He shall, as soon as reasonably practical, give notice of his decision to approve or refuse the authorisation to the person giving the authorisation.[5]

1   Police Act 1997, s 97(2).
2   Police Act 1997, s 97(1).
3   See Covert Surveillance Code 6.30.
4   Police Act 1997, s 97(5).
5   Police Act 1997, s 97(4).

Meaning of legal privilege, etc.

5.25   Matters subject to legal privilege are defined by the Police Act 1997, s 98 in terms almost identical to PACE 1984, s 10. They are any communication between a legal adviser and his client (or representative) made in connection with giving legal advice, or made in connection with, or in contemplation of, legal proceedings and for the purpose of those proceedings, and extends to items enclosed in communications of the above kind.

Confidential personal information is defined by s 99 as personal information which a person has acquired or created in the course of any trade or business, profession or other occupation or for the purposes of any paid or unpaid office and which he holds in confidence. Personal information means information concerning an individual who can be identified from it, and relating to his physical or mental health, or to spiritual counselling. Information is held in confidence if it is held subject to an express or implied undertaking to hold it in confidence, or to a restriction on disclosure or an obligation of secrecy contained in any enactment.

Confidential journalistic material means material that has been acquired or created for the purpose of journalism which is in, and has always been in, the possession of the person who created it, and which is held subject to an undertaking, restriction or obligation, as is mentioned in s 99. Section 98(5) states that no privilege attracts if the communication or item is in the possession of someone not entitled to possession or if it is held with the intention of furthering a criminal purpose.

5.26   Surveillance Code 3.6 advises that:

'In general, an application for surveillance which is likely to result in the acquisition of legally privileged information should only be made in exceptional and compelling circumstances. Full regard should be had to the particular proportionality issues such surveillance raises.'

The Code sets out additional safeguards such as the need for reasons being given in the application why such surveillance is considered necessary and an assessment of the likelihood that such material may be acquired. Where such material is acquired and retained, the matter should be reported to the relevant Commissioner. It is recommended that in cases of doubt advice should be sought from a legal adviser to the relevant public authority.[1] Similar considerations should also be given to authorisations that involve confidential personal information and confidential journalistic material.[2]

1   See generally Covert Surveillance Code 3.3–3.9.
2   Covert Surveillance Code 3.10–3.12.

5.27   According to the most recent Annual Report of the Chief Surveillance Commissioner, of the total prior approvals in 1999–2000 only one concerned matters subject to legal privilege, four concerned confidential personal information and none concerned journalistic material. In 2000–01, four concerned matters of legal privilege, three concerned confidential information and none concerned journalistic material. In 2001–02 one approval concerned legal privilege, one concerned personal information and none concerned journalistic material. In 2002–03 two approvals concerned legal privilege, two concerned confidential information and again none concerned journalistic material.

Reviews

5.28   Surveillance Code 6.23 provides that authorising officers should regularly review authorisations to assess the need for the entry onto, or interference with, wireless telegraphy to continue. Such reviews should take place at least once a month. This is of particular importance where the authorised conduct provides access to confidential information or involves collateral intrusion. A record of any such review should be included on the authorisation record.

Who are the Commissioners?

5.29 The Commissioners consist of a Chief Commissioner and such number of other Commissioners as the Prime Minister thinks fit. The Chief Commissioner is Sir Andrew Leggatt. At present there are six Commissioners assisted by three Assistant Commissioners. The persons appointed shall all hold or have held high judicial office, and hold office for a period of three years but may be reappointed. A Commissioner once appointed may only be removed by a resolution of both Houses of Parliament or by the Prime Minister in the event of bankruptcy, disqualification as a company director or conviction of an offence resulting in a sentence of imprisonment.[1]

1   Police Act 1997, s 91(7).

5.30 The function of a Commissioner is to consider whether the criteria for authorisations in certain sensitive cases have been established.[1] Such responsibility, as he had to deal with complaints under the Police Act 1997, s 102, has now been transferred to the Investigatory Powers Tribunal set up by RIPA 2000, s 65.

The Chief Commissioner still has responsibility for dealing with appeals by the police against the refusal or quashing of an authorisation under the Police Act 1997, s 104 but his responsibility for hearing appeals from a Commissioner has now been replaced by the Tribunal procedure established by RIPA 2000, s 65. He also has to provide an annual report.

1   Police Act 1997, s 97.

5.31 The Police Act 1997, s 91(10) provides that the decisions of the Chief Commissioner or, subject to ss 104 and 106, any other Commissioner, including decisions as to his jurisdiction, 'shall not be subject to appeal or liable to be questioned in any court'. Similar wording appeared in IOCA 1985, s 7(8), Security Service Act 1989, s 5(4) and ISA 1994, s 9(4).

The words 'including decisions as to his jurisdiction' were included as a result of the decision of the House of Lords in *Anisminic v Foreign Compensation Commission.*[1]

Despite the apparently wide effect of the provision, it is submitted that the section does not have the effect of ousting PACE 1984, s 78. It is concerned with challenges to the decisions of Commissioners, the machinery for such challenges being found in the Police Act 1997, s 104. Such decisions are concerned with whether the application satisfies the minimum criteria required and not with the fairness of admitting such surveillance as evidence in a criminal trial. In *R v Templar,*[2] the court stated that the subsection did not preclude an inquiry into whether the relevant decision of the Commissioner had been obtained by deception or by other reprehensible conduct which might found an argument under PACE 1984, s 78.

1   [1969] 2 AC 147.
2   [2003] EWCA Crim 3186, [2003] All ER (D) 191 (Nov).

The quashing of authorisations

5.32   If satisfied that there were no reasonable grounds for believing the matters set out in the Police Act 1997, s 93(2), a Commissioner may quash an authorisation. Similarly, in a case in which he considers or is satisfied there were reasonable grounds for believing that the property is used as a dwelling or a bedroom in a hotel or office premises, or that the action is likely to result in acquiring knowledge of matters subject to legal privilege, confidential personal information or confidential journalistic material, he may quash the authorisation if it has been granted without the approval of a Commissioner.[1] If at any time after an authorisation has been granted, the Commissioner is satisfied that there were no reasonable grounds for believing the matters specified in s 93(2) he may cancel the authorisation.[2] In either case, he may order that the authorisation may remain effective for so long as it takes to retrieve anything that has been left on the property concerned. Similarly, in either case he shall notify both the authorising officer and the Chief Commissioner of his decision.

1   Police Act 1997, s 103(1) and (2).
2   Police Act 1997, s 103(4).

5.33   According to the 1999–2000 Report of the Chief Surveillance Commissioner there were 322 authorisations notified to a Commissioner for approval. None was refused. According to the 2000–01 Report, in 97% of cases the authorising officer has been informed of the Commissioner's decision within 16 hours of the receipt by him of all the necessary information. In that year, of the 371 authorisations for property interference and the 285 authorisations for intrusive surveillance notified to the Commissioner, only one was refused. The reason for the refusal was that the authorised surveillance had been started before the authority had been notified. Seven authorisations for property interference were quashed, in four of which the Commissioner was not satisfied that the investigation concerned serious crime. In the year 2001–02 there were 306 authorisations requiring prior approval, only two of which were quashed. In 2002–03, there were 299 authorisations, with three being quashed. One related to the authorisation of interference outside the specific police force area, the second failed to meet the test of necessity and the third gave insufficient detail to persuade the Commissioner that it complied with the legislation.

The destruction of records

5.34   Where he quashes or cancels the authorisation, the Commissioner may order the destruction of any records relating to information obtained by virtue of the authorisation.[1] The present position is somewhat unsatisfactory, as records that are required for pending criminal or civil proceedings are exempt from an order to destroy them. This creates the possibility that material which has been wrongfully obtained may be preserved and put in evidence in a future trial. In such circumstances a defendant would have a strong argument for exclusion under PACE 1984, s 78.

1   Police Act 1997, s 103(3) and (5).

Appeals by authorising officers

5.35 Where a Commissioner refuses to approve an authorisation, or cancels an authorisation already in existence, the Police Act 1997, s 104 provides machinery by which the authorising officer may appeal to the Chief Commissioner. The machinery also provides for an appeal against a decision ordering the destruction of records and a decision refusing to make an order permitting the retrieval of equipment left on the property. The authorising officer must appeal within seven days of being notified of the decision of the Commissioner. Although the Chief Commissioner is obliged to inform both the authorising officer and the Commissioner of the result of any appeal, he shall not give reasons for his decision.[1]

1   Police Act 1997, s 105(2).

The authorisation record

5.36   A record should be created which includes:

- the time and date of any authorisation;
- whether the authorisation is in written or oral form;
- the time and date it was notified to the Commissioner;
- the time and date when the Commissioner notified his approval;
- every occasion when entry onto or interference with property has occurred;
- the result of reviews of any authorisation;
- the date of any renewal; and
- the time and date when any instruction was given to cease the interference.[1]

1   See Covert Surveillance Code 6.27.

Complaints

5.37   The complaints procedure established by the Police Act 1997 has been abolished by RIPA 2000, Sch 5. RIPA 2000, s 65 establishes a new Investigatory Powers Tribunal made up of senior members of the judiciary. Section 65(5)(f) specifically provides that the Tribunal is the appropriate forum for complaints arising from the Police Act 1997, Pt III (for details of procedure, etc see **Chapter 10**).[1]

1   In most cases this is a farce as the target will not get to hear about the surveillance. See comments by
     Lords Hutchinson, Hansard HL vol 577 col 408.

Conclusions

5.38   In *R v Lawrence*[1] it was submitted that the interference was not in accordance with law and thus in violation of art 8. The two principal points argued were inspired by comparisons with RIPA 2000. First, it was pointed out that advance authorisation under the Police Act 1997 was not required where the surveillance took place in a vehicle. In contrast, RIPA 2000, s 26(3) includes anything taking place in any private vehicle. Second, RIPA 2000, s 65(8) has placed all complaints under the Police Act 1997 under the new Investigatory Powers Tribunal, which places upon all persons involved in granting authorisations a duty of disclosure to the Tribunal as well as providing a right for legal representation. It was submitted that the absence of such provisions in the Police Act 1997 made the Act defective. The court did not agree. The fact that RIPA 2000 provides that authorisations for intrusive surveillance should only become effective on approval by a Commissioner and that tighter provisions had been introduced for disclosure to the Tribunal did not suggest that the Police Act 1997, Pt III was incompatible with art 8. The court considered the overall scheme of the Act and rejected the submission that any part of it was not Convention compliant.

1   [2001] EWCA Crim 584, [2001] EWCA Crim 1829.

5.39   Even though there is now a statutory basis for interference with property, with respect to their Lordships, it is questionable whether the law is sufficiently clear and detailed to comply with the quality of law test in art 8 (see **paras 2.55–2.66**). The Act is wholly unspecific as to the extent of powers permitted to police. Although the phrase 'bug and burgle' has been used in this chapter, the phrase used in s 93(1) is 'Such action … as he may specify'. As was pointed out in the House of Lords, such action could be interpreted so widely as to allow the police without obtaining a judicial warrant to search a house and seize property, thus effectively bypassing PACE 1984. Other questions remain unanswered:

- are officers entitled to cause damage?
- are they entitled to use the electricity of the homeowner, particularly if he is not the target?
- in what manner may wireless telegraphy be interfered with?
- are police entitled to return to the property on a daily basis, eg to check the equipment is working correctly?
- what instructions should be included regarding the retrieval of any device?
- do the officers using the equipment need to be named?
- who may listen to the product?

In granting such intrusive powers, it is submitted that the extent of those powers should have been more clearly specified within the statute.

Chapter 6

Interception

Introduction

6.1 In outline, RIPA 2000 consists of powers to authorise five different forms of surveillance activity and the power to order the production of a key to enable the product of interception to be intelligible:

(a) Pt I, Ch I: interception;
(b) Pt I, Ch II: acquisition and disclosure of communications data;
(c) Pt II: directed surveillance;
(d) Pt II: covert human intelligence sources (CHIS);
(e) Pt II: intrusive surveillance of residential premises or vehicles; and
(f) Pt III: encryption.

This chapter deals only with (a), which came into force on 2 October 2000. The accompanying Interception of Communications Code of Practice (Interception Code) did not come into force until 1 July 2002.

The meaning of interception

6.2 The Interception of Communications Act 1985 (IOCA 1985) did not define interception. The definition is to be found in RIPA 2000, s 2(2), which provides that a:

> 'person intercepts a communication in the course of its transmission by means of a telecommunication system if, and only if, he–
>
> (a) so modifies or interferes with the system, or its operation,
> (b) so monitors transmissions made by means of the system, or
> (c) so monitors transmissions made by wireless telegraphy to or from apparatus comprised in the system,

as to make some or all of the contents of the communication available, while being transmitted, to a person other than the sender or intended recipient of the communication.'

What is not interception

6.3   There follow three examples of what does *not* amount to interception.

RIPA 2000, s 2(3) excludes from the provisions of the Act the interception of any communication which is broadcast for general reception. Lord Bassam explained:

> 'In our view, broadcasting for general reception implies that the transmission is intended to be received by anyone who wants to receive it. The question arises of whether pager messages and mobile telephone base stations fall within this category. We believe the answer is no. A paging message has to be addressed to a particular number or group of persons whose pager is programmed with that address number ... The same is true for mobile telephones.'[1]

1   615 HL Official Report col 267.

6.4   RIPA 2000, s 2(4) provides an important reminder of the limited jurisdiction of the domestic legal system. Although the menace at which this part of the Act is directed is by its nature international, the effect of s 2(4) is to limit the relevant conduct to that within the UK. Thus, even though the effect of the interception may be to prejudice British subjects, the conduct will not come within the jurisdiction of the British courts unless the 'interceptor' is in the UK at the moment of interception and the communication is of the public postal service or telecommunications system or, if of a private system, either the sender or intended recipient is in the UK.

Lord Bassam in responding to a proposed amendment by Lord Lucas explained:

> 'Amendment No 16 would criminalise interception carried out in another country which had an effect in the UK. The criminal law must be precise and this test is imprecise. An important question is: where does the interception of a wireless communication have effect? It is almost impossible to answer that question and interception currently is not prohibited by IOCA 1985. To do so would make a criminal of anyone anywhere in the world who undertook the interception of a communication in the UK. We have no evidence that it is necessary to extend the scope of the offence worldwide. Generally, criminal law is limited to the jurisdiction of this country.'[1]

1   613 HL Official Report col 1430, 12 June 2000.

6.5   RIPA 2000, s 2(5) excludes conduct that takes place in relation only to so much of the communication as consists of traffic data, which is covered by the regime in Pt I, Ch II (see **Chapter 7**). Traffic data is defined in RIPA 2000, s 2(9) in identical terms to s 21(6) as meaning:

> '(a)   any data identifying or purporting to identify any person, apparatus or location to or from which the communication is or may be transmitted,

(b)   any data identifying or selecting, or purporting to identify or select, apparatus through which, or by means of which, the communication is or may be transmitted,

(c)   any data comprising signals for the actuation of apparatus used for the purposes of a telecommunication system for effecting (in whole or in part) the transmission of any communication, and

(d)   any data identifying the data or other data as data comprised in or attached to a particular communication,

but that expression includes data identifying a computer file or computer program access to which is obtained, or which is run, by means of the communication to the extent only that the file or program is identified by reference to the apparatus in which it is stored.'

The definition covers, for example, subscriber information under (a) and routing information under (b). Section 2(9)(c) must be read with s 2(10) (which operates on s 2(5)) and addresses what is commonly known as dial-through fraud. It covers data entered by a user seeking to arrange for a telephone call to be accepted and routed by a telecommunications system.[1]

According to the explanatory note, (d) catches the data which is found at the beginning of each packet in a packet switched network, which indicates which communications data attaches to which communication. The tailpiece of the definition puts beyond doubt that in relation to Internet communications, traffic data stops at the apparatus within which files or programs are stored, so the traffic data may identify a server but not a website or page (further explanation given at **para 7.7**).

1   See *Morgans v DPP* [2001] 1 AC 315, [2000] 2 All ER 522.

In the course of transmission

6.6   The definition makes it clear that the RIPA 2000, like IOCA 1985, is concerned only with interceptions in the course of transmission. Lord Bassam explained:

'The course of transmission begins where a postal service or telecommunications system first begins to transmit a communication. In a telephone, the sound waves from the human voice first begin to be in the course of their transmission by means of a telecommunication when they are received by the microphone in the handset. They continue to be in the course of their transmission until they are emitted by the speaker.'[1]

In *R v Hardy*,[2] it was submitted on behalf of the defence that recordings of conversations between the defendant and an undercover officer fell within RIPA 2000, s 2(2) and therefore fell to be excluded under s 17. The court, however, ruled that as the contents of the calls were **not made available whilst being transmitted to any third party the case was not one of telephone tapping.** While it was surveillance which required authorisation, which was correctly given, it was not interception. Some doubt on the correctness of this conclusion is expressed in the commentary to this case in Criminal Law Review.[3]

1   613 HL Official Report col 1435, 12 June 2000.

2   [2003] 1 Cr App Rep 494.

3   [2003] Crim LR 394. See also *R v Hammond, McIntosh and Gray* [2002] EWCA Crim 1423 and *R v E* [2004] EWCA Crim 1243.

Stored communications

6.7 By RIPA 2000, s 2(7) and (8), the course of transmission includes the time when the system is storing the information for later collection by the recipient; for example, an email awaiting downloading by the recipient. Interception Code 2.15 points out that stored communications may also be accessed by means of a production order under PACE 1984 or a search warrant.

The background to RIPA 2000, Pt I

6.8 Until 1937, telephone interception occurred without warrant. In that year the Home Secretary and the Postmaster General decided that it was undesirable that records of telephone conversations should be made by Post Office servants and disclosed to the police and that such practices should in future require a warrant signed by the Secretary of State.

1951 guidelines

6.9 In September 1951, the Home Office issued guidelines to the Metropolitan Police and HMCE which laid out the conditions which must be satisfied before a warrant for interception could be authorised by the Secretary of State:

- the offence must be really serious;
- normal methods of investigation must have been tried and failed or must by the nature of things be unlikely to succeed if tried; and
- there must be good reason to think that an interception would result in a conviction.

Serious crime was not defined, but in a letter to the police the Home Office explained that the phrase meant offences for which a man with no previous record could reasonably be expected to be sentenced to three years' imprisonment, or offences of lesser gravity in which a large number of people were involved. A separate letter to HMCE defined serious crime as:

> 'involving a substantial and continuing fraud which would seriously damage the revenue or the economy of the country if it went unchecked.'

The Birkett Report[1]

6.10   The report was produced as a result of an inquiry into the interception of communications by the committee of Privy Councillors. The committee summarised the state of the law as they saw it:

'(a)   The power to intercept letters has been exercised from the earliest times, and has been recognised in successive Acts of Parliament.

(b)   The power extends to telegrams.

(c)   It is difficult to resist the view that if there is a lawful power to intercept communications in the form of letters or telegrams then it is wide enough to cover telephone communications as well.'

The grounds on which the Secretary of State would issue a warrant to the police and HMCE were as set out in the 1951 guidelines.

The grounds on which he would issue a warrant to the Security Service were that:

(a)   there must be a major subversive or espionage activity that is likely to injure the national interest;

(b)   the product of the interception must be of direct use in compiling information that is necessary to the Security Service in carrying out the tasks laid upon it by the state; and

(c)   normal methods of investigation must have been tried and failed or must by the nature of things be unlikely to succeed if tried.

The Committee was told that the Home Office insisted that the power to intercept should be used for investigation purposes only on the basis that if used in court the practices would become widely known and their efficacy diminished. The Committee, however, concluded that there was no reason why in a proper case evidence should not be tendered, the question of admissibility being decided by the court. It further concluded that the powers of interception should continue to be used subject to the safeguards referred to in the report.

1   October 1957, Cmnd 283.

The White Paper 1980[1]

6.11   As has been seen in **Chapter 2**, the Court of Appeal in *Malone v Metropolitan Police Comr*[2] drew attention to serious shortcomings in English law in so far as it concerned telephone tapping. Megarry V-C commented that:

'It is impossible to read the judgment in the *Klass* case without it becoming abundantly clear that a system which has no legal safeguards whatever has small chance of satisfying the requirement of that court, whatever administrative procedures there may be'.

In response to the judgment the government produced a White Paper in 1980. It reported that since 1957 the 'essential features of *Birkett* are closely followed'. The police, HMCE and the Security Service may request authority but three conditions must be satisfied:

(1)   the offence must be really serious (defined as an offence for which a man with no previous record could reasonably be expected to be sentenced to three years' imprisonment);

(2)   normal methods of investigation must have been tried and failed or must by the nature of things be unlikely to succeed; and

(3)   there must be good reason to think that an interception would be likely to lead to an arrest and a conviction.

On 1 April 1980, on the publication of the White Paper, the Home Secretary announced in Parliament that after careful consideration the government had decided not to introduce legislation as the interception of communications was a practice that depended for its effectiveness on being carried out in secret. He went on to add that if the power to intercept were to be regulated by statute, then the courts would have power to inquire into the matter and to do so, if not in public, then at least in the presence of the complainant. He concluded by stating that the government thought it would be desirable for a continuous independent check to be carried out and proposed to invite a senior member of the judiciary to do so.[3]

1   Cmnd 7873
2   [1979] Ch 344.
3   See *Malone v United Kingdom* (1984) 7 EHRR 14 at para 37.

The Diplock Report 1981[1]

6.12   Lord Diplock was appointed to carry out such checks and in 1981 he provided a report to the government. In considering the effectiveness of the procedures he listed the following matters:

●   that the public interest which will be served by obtaining the information which it is hoped will result from the interception of communications is of sufficient importance to justify this step;

●   that the interception applied for offers a reasonable prospect of providing the information sought;

●   that other methods of obtaining it, such as surveillance or the use of informants, have been tried and failed or from the nature of the case are not feasible;

●   that the interception stops as soon as it has ceased to provide information of the kind sought or it has become apparent that it is unlikely to provide it;

●   that all products of interception not directly relevant to the purpose for which the warrant was granted are speedily destroyed; and

●   that such material as is directly relevant to that purpose is given no wider circulation than is essential for carrying it out.

Applying those tests he concluded that:

'the interception of communications, particularly telephone conversations, remains an effective, indeed essential, weapon in the armoury of those authorities responsible for the maintenance of law and order and the safety of the realm. Major crime has become more highly organised, international trafficking in drugs brings enormous profits, and terrorism has become a world wide problem: and all this has made it more necessary for the members of criminal gangs in each of these categories to communicate with one another by telephone about their activities and plans.'

1   Cmnd 8191.

The Royal Commission on Criminal Procedure 1981[1]

6.13   Chapter 3 of this report made recommendations regarding the use of all forms of surveillance devices by the police, which can be seen to have been commendably far-sighted. It recommended that the use of such devices (including the interception of letters and telephone communications) should be regulated by statute. It suggested that each occasion for the use of a device should require specific authority in the form of a warrant issued by a magistrates' court. The authorisation should be specific, limited in place and duration and should contain the reasons for the intrusion.

> 'At the hearing of the application the interests of the person subject to surveillance should be represented by the Official Solicitor or a similar body. Unless judicial authority to the contrary is obtained, the person subjected to the surveillance should be told of the surveillance after the event as is the requirement in a number of other countries ... The proposals would enable the police to use the evidence obtained by surveillance in court which they are at present unwilling to do in relation to telephone tapping.'

The recommendations were ignored.

1   Cmnd 8092.

The White Paper 1985[1]

6.14   As a result of the decision of the ECt HR in *Malone v United Kingdom*,[2] the government produced another White Paper that conceded that changes were required. It introduced proposals for a statutory framework covering the authorisation of interception, its use and the storage of the product, as well as independent oversight by a commissioner and the setting up of an independent tribunal.

The Bill, when published, was described by *The Times* (6 March 1985) as an act of 'dumb insolence' in which the minimum action possible was taken to comply with the letter of rulings under international agreements.

1   Cmnd 9438.
2   (1984) 7 EHRR 14.

The Interception of Communications Act 1985 (IOCA 1985)

6.15   This Act placed the interception of communications sent by post or by means of a public telecommunications system on a statutory basis for the first time. The following is a summary of its main effects.

It created an offence of unlawful interception, but only where the communication was by post or by means of a public telecommunications system. Despite the Telecommunications Act 1984, the effect of which was to break up the state monopoly that existed at the time, it was not anticipated that private systems would have the impact they have had. Specific exception was provided where the interceptor reasonably believed that the person to whom, or the person by whom, the communication was sent had consented to the interception. This might include the situation where a member of a family had been kidnapped or where he was being blackmailed. Similarly, exception was made for the case of an interception made for purposes connected with the provision of postal or telecommunications services, eg where an engineer needs to discover whether a line is being used before he starts work on it.

6.16   IOCA 1985 also:

(a)   established a framework controlling the issue, renewal, modification and cancellation of warrants;

(b)   authorised interceptions of communications sent by post or by means of a public telecommunications system;

(c)   established the principle that such warrants should be issued by the Secretary of State rather than by a judge;

(d)   specified that the purposes for which such warrants might be issued were limited to:

    (i)   the interests of national security (not defined)

    (ii)   the prevention or detection of serious crime (see **para 6.18**); and

    (iii)   the safeguarding of the economic well-being of the UK (see **para 6.19**);

(e)   limited the extent to which the product of interceptions could be disclosed, copied or retained, requiring arrangements to be made to keep each of these to the minimum;

(f)   created the office of Interception Commissioner whose function was to keep under review the way in which the power to issue warrants was exercised as well as the operation of the safeguards in the Act (see **para 6.21**); and

(g)   set up a tribunal to investigate complaints. The tribunal was to apply judicial review principles and its decision could not be appealed or be subject to any question in any court.

Disclosure under IOCA 1985

6.17   The limited disclosure of the product of interception referred to at (e) above included the curiously drafted IOCA 1985, s 9, which was ultimately decided by the House of Lords to amount to a prohibition against the use of such evidence in any court or tribunal. The process of clarification has been a somewhat tortuous one. In *Morgans v DPP*[1] Lord Steyn admitted that the earlier restrictive interpretation he had given to s 9 in the course of his Court of Appeal judgment in *R v Effick*[2] was mistaken. The interpretation was based on the fact that the Act contained no express provision making it clear that any evidence obtained as a result of an interception will be inadmissible. Having regard to the fact that the language of s 9 was, however, capable of such an interpretation, and to the later decision of *R v Preston*,[3] which destroyed the foundation of the reasoning in *Effick*, Lord Steyn was fully persuaded that his earlier interpretation was wrong.

1   [2001] 1 AC 315 at p 320, [2000] 2 WLR 386.
2   (1992) 95 Cr App Rep 427.
3   [1994] 2 AC 130, [1993] 3 WLR 891.

Definition of serious crime

6.18   IOCA 1985, s 10(3) provided that an offence will be regarded as serious crime if, and only if, it is an offence involving the use of violence; or resulting in substantial financial gain; or is conduct involving a large number of persons in pursuit of a common purpose; or alternatively an offence for which a person who has attained the age of 21 and has no previous convictions could reasonably be expected to be sentenced to a term of imprisonment for a term of three years or more.

Definition of economic well-being of the UK

6.19   There is no definition of this phrase. The Lord President of the Council stated that it was concerned with the interception that is necessary for the effective protection of the country's economic interests at the international level:

'It is an important part of our foreign policy to protect the country from adverse developments overseas which may not necessarily affect our national security so directly as to justify interception on that ground but which may have damaging consequences for our economic well-being.'

He was not able to give examples, even hypothetical ones:

'I am strongly advised that to do so in an area as sensitive as this would in itself be damaging … If I refer in a general way to a threat to the supply from abroad of a commodity on which our economy is particularly dependent, I hope your Lordships will accept that I have gone as far as I can by way of offering an example.'[1]

IOCA 1985, s 2(4) provided that a warrant:

'shall not be considered necessary as mentioned in subsection (2)(c) above unless the information which it is considered necessary to acquire is information relating to the acts or intentions of persons outside the British Islands.'

Both the terms 'interests of national security' and 'economic well-being' were the subject of consideration by the Commission in *Christie v United Kingdom*.[2] The Commission attached significance to the fact that the Reports of the Interception Commissioner had elaborated on both terms by reference in the former to the definition given by Lord Harris and by reference in the latter to the limitation that it relates to persons outside the British Islands. The Commission concluded that it was consistent with the requirement of forseeability that terms which are on their face general and unlimited are explained by administrative or executive statements and instructions, since it is the provision of sufficiently precise guidance to enable individuals to regulate their conduct, rather than the source of that guidance, which is of relevance.

1   464 HL Official Report col 879.
2   (1993) 78-A DR 119.

Proportionality

6.20   In considering whether a warrant was necessary, account must be given to whether the material could be acquired by other means.[1]

1   IOCA 1985, s 2(3).

Scrutiny

6.21   IOCA 1985 also provided for the appointment of an Interception Commissioner who holds, or has held, high judicial office. His function was to oversee the exercise of the Secretary of State's power to issue warrants. It also set up a tribunal whose function was to determine complaints by members of the public who believe they may have been victims of unlawful interception. It could not investigate an interception which was not authorised by warrant. It has now been superseded by the Investigatory Powers Tribunal set up by RIPA 2000, s 65 (see **Chapter 10**).

6.22   Since 1985 there have been challenges to IOCA 1985 in the ECt HR, none of which have been successful. In *Christie v United Kingdom*[1] the applicant was General Secretary of the Scottish Trades Union Congress. The case concerned the alleged interception by GCHQ of telexes to the applicant from East European trade unions. The Commission held that the scope and manner of the exercise of the powers to intercept and make use of the product were indicated with the required degree of clarity to comply with art 8.

In *Preston v United Kingdom*[2] the product of interceptions had been destroyed pursuant to IOCA 1985, s 6. It was held that there was no breach of the equality of arms principle under art 6.

1   (1993) 18 EHRR 188, 78A DR 119.
2   [1997] EHRLR 695.

Table of interception warrants issued under IOCA 1985

6.23   See **para 1.44** for the figures from 2000 Interception Commissioners Report.

In line with established practice based on para 121 of the Birkett Report, no figures are published regarding the number of warrants issued by the Foreign Secretary or the Secretary of State for Northern Ireland.

According to the Report of the Commissioner for the year to end of 2000 the great majority of warrants issued remain related to the prevention and detection of serious crime. The position remains the same under RIPA 2000, see Report of the Commissioner for 2002.

Deficiencies of IOCA 1985

6.24   In 1994, the House of Lords ruled that the public telecommunications system ends at the service provider's cable socket in the wall.[1] This meant that the interception of cordless phones was not subject to the controls of IOCA 1985. In the same year, the Court of Appeal held that an interception takes place:

> 'when, and at the place where, the electrical impulse or signal which is passing along the telephone line is intercepted in fact.'[2]

Mobile phones which do not require to use any network of cables were therefore not covered by IOCA 1985. Similarly, emails which do not pass through a public telecommunication network could not be lawfully intercepted.

1   *R v Effick* (1994) 99 Cr App Rep 312.
2   See *R v Ahmed* [1995] Crim LR 246.

Internal office systems

6.25   In *Halford v United Kingdom*,[1] the ECt HR held that IOCA 1985 did not apply to interception on an internal office telephone system. The combination of adverse rulings from the ECt HR and the technical advances since 1985 made it inevitable that the government would need to act. In June 1999 the Home Office issued a Consultation Paper[2] setting out the position of the government and inviting responses, particularly from providers of communications services. The paper pointed out that there are perfectly respectable reasons for allowing employers to record telephone conversations in the workplace, for instance to provide evidence of commercial transactions or to counter fraud. It also recognised that forms of 'dynamic metering' as well as itemised billing can be of tremendous investigative value. The subject of metering had formed the basis of an adverse ruling in *Malone v United Kingdom*[3] that, although lawful in terms of domestic practice, there were no legal rules concerning the scope and manner of exercise of the discretion.[4]

1   (1997) 24 EHRR 523.
2   Cm 4368.
3   (1984) 7 EHRR 14.
4   See now the Wireless Telegraphy Act 1984 (see **para 6.32**).

The Consultation Paper, Cm 4368

6.26   According to the Paper,[1] the intention of the government was to provide a single legal framework which dealt with all interceptions in the UK, regardless of the means of communication, how it is licensed or at what point on the route of communication it is intercepted. It was not proposed that the 'warranted interception regime' would affect the recording or monitoring of communications in the course of lawful business practice where the system operator had taken reasonable steps to inform the parties to the communication that it may occur. Such practices were already subject to a 'privacy of messages' condition within their operating licence.

1   Cm 4368 at **para 4.1**.

What is a CSP?

6.27   The Paper also indicated that the government would take into account the effects on Communications Service Providers (CSPs), defined as:

'any person providing publicly available communications services or authorised to provide telecommunications systems or networks for the conveyance of publicly available telecommunications services.'

Although the phrase is used in the Interception Code,[1] it is not used in RIPA 2000. See, for example, RIPA 2000, s 11(4), which provides that the warrant may be served on:

'(a)   a person who provides a postal service,
(b)   a person who provides a public telecommunications service, or
(c)   a person not falling within paragraph (b) who has control of the whole or any part of a telecommunications system ...'

In chapter II and its draft code, the expression used is "a postal or telecommunications operator" which is defined in s 25(1) as a person who provides a postal service or telecommunications service. A telecommunications service is defined in s 2(1) to mean any service that consists in the provision of, access to, and facilities for making use of, any telecommunications system (whether or not one provided by the person providing the service).The 2003 Consultation Paper "Access to Communications Data" again refers to CSPs. Both this chapter and **Chapter 7** will use the phrase CSP to accommodate both providers and operators.

All such providers would be required to take reasonable steps to ensure that their system was capable of being intercepted, as well as providing reasonable assistance to affect warranted intercepts. The Paper emphasised that such requirements already applied in countries such as France, Germany, the Netherlands, Sweden, the USA, Canada and Australia. Such requirements ought therefore not to place UK-based CSPs at a disadvantage. The government would try to minimise any additional burdens on the industry.

1   See Interception Code 2.7, 2.9, 2.10, 4.7, 4.15, 5.9, 5.14.

6.28   The Paper confirmed that consideration had been given to the possibility of either judicial warranting or a procedure based on that of the Police Act 1997, Pt III, but that the government was not persuaded of the need to depart from the current procedure of Secretary of State authorisation. The main reason for this view was that:

'there would remain the need for the Executive to issue warrants applied for on national security or economic well-being grounds'.

In Parliament, the Minister Charles Clarke stated:

'I maintain the view that authorising interception involves particularly sensitive decisions that are properly a matter for the executive. The warrant issuing process is a key part of the line of accountability from the law enforcement and intelligence agencies to the Secretary of State and then to Parliament ... I do not believe that judges can reasonably be expected to make decisions on what is or is not in the interests of national security, or that they are appropriately accountable.'[1]

The explanation given by the government in 'The Interception of Communications in the UK' (Cm 4368) that judges would be inappropriate because of the need to deal with cases of national security and economic well-being has been dismissed as 'wholly spurious'.[2]

1　HC Official Report col 587, 8 May 2000.
2　Akdeniz, Taylor and Walker in [2001] Crim LR 78.

6.29 Significant changes to the form of the warrant were also proposed. Under IOCA 1985 the law required the warrant to specify the telephone number or the address. Although the system was satisfactory in 1985, technological advances since then meant that one person might have access to many different types of communication. The government therefore proposed that a single warrant should authorise interception of all specified communications addresses relating to the person named on the face of it. The warrant application would detail the background of the case and the grounds on which the warrant was sought. It would also specify each of the communications addresses which the person is believed to be using, together with the reasons why it was necessary to intercept each of them. Attached to the application would be the warrant itself as well as a schedule listing each of the addresses. If the application was approved the Secretary of State would sign the warrant. The schedule, but not the warrant, could be modified thereafter.

6.30 Under the IOCA 1985 system, each time the person intercepted changed his address the warrant would have to go back to the Secretary of State for modification. It was therefore proposed that, once the Secretary of State had given his authorisation, modifications should thereafter be carried out on his behalf by senior officials. It was also proposed that the duration of warrants be extended from two to three months and that thereafter serious crime warrants could be renewed for a period of three months and national security and economic well-being warrants for six months. No changes were proposed for the procedure for cancelling warrants.

6.31 It was also proposed that a code of practice should be issued which would clarify the procedures involved, particularly where the intercepted material might fall into the sensitive category, such as legally privileged material.

The Paper acknowledged that there was a difference of opinion as to the value of IOCA 1985, s 9 preventing the use of the product of any intercept as evidence in court. The Inquiry into Legislation Against Terrorism chaired by Lord Lloyd had recommended that the law be amended so as to allow the prosecution to adduce intercept material in evidence in cases affecting national security. It was recognised also that such evidence was used in many European countries and its use had been approved by the ECt HR.[1] The counter-argument, which remained the position of the government, was that exposure of interception capabilities would educate criminals and terrorists who would then use greater counter-interception measures than they were at present. This would mean that any advantage of repealing s 9 would be shortlived.

1　See *Valenzuela Contreras v Spain* (1998) 28 EHRR 483 and *Lambert v France* (1998) 30 EHRR 346.

6.32   The Paper also referred to the provision of communications data (such as metering (see **para 6.37**), an aspect not covered by IOCA 1985). A statutory basis for disclosure of such material was provided by a new Telecommunications Act 1984, s 45, which allows disclosure on the broad grounds of prevention or detection of crime or for the purposes of criminal proceedings.[1] The government was now of the view that it was right for the police to have access to communications data when necessary to prevent or detect crime, but only where this level of intrusion was justified, taking into account the lower level of intrusion that access to such data involved. The criteria for justifying such intrusion would be less than for interception of communications:

- for the prevention or detection of crime;
- for the apprehension or prosecution of offenders;
- in the interests of national security;
- for the purpose of safeguarding the economic interests of the UK;
- for the urgent prevention of injury or damage to health;
- for the assessment or collection of any tax or duty or any imposition of a similar nature.

CSPs would be required to provide the specified material within a reasonable period.

1   See also Data Protection Act 1998, s 29.

RIPA 2000, Pt I, Ch I

6.33   RIPA 2000, Pt I, Ch I replaces IOCA 1985 and provides a regulatory structure for the interception of communications in the course of their transmission by a public or private telecommunications system. It makes it unlawful to intercept either intentionally and without authorisation under the Act.[1] In the case of a private system, the person who has the right to control the operation or use of the system or any person acting with that person's consent is excluded from criminal liability.[2]

In the House of Lords Lord Bassam explained that:

'the Bill extends this [IOCA] to make unlawful also interception on a private system attached to a public system; for example, an office or hotel network, or the telephones in a domestic household. This extension seeks to implement the requirement of Art 5 of the European Telecommunications Directive.'[3]

The maximum penalty on summary conviction is the statutory maximum, currently a £5,000 fine and two years' imprisonment or an unlimited fine or both on indictment.

1   RIPA 2000, s 1(1) and (2)(a).
2   RIPA 2000, s 1(2)(b) and (6).
3   613 HL Official Report col 1425, 17 June 2000.

6.34   The difference between RIPA 2000, s 1(2)(a) and s 1(2)(b) is that whereas the interception on a private line without the consent of the person with the right to control the line might involve an offence, where the intercept is made by or with the consent of the controller of the line, no question of a criminal offence arises because such conduct is 'excluded from criminal liability'. In *A–G's Reference (No 5 of 2002)*[1] the interception of specific telephone extensions in a police station took place with the consent of the relevant chief constable. The defence maintained that the system was a public system and that the information obtained thereby was inadmissible. Although the facts of the case took place before the enactment of RIPA 2000, the Court of Appeal considered the impact of s 17 and concluded that in such a case the court would need to decide firstly whether the interception concerned a private line and, if it did, to decide if it had taken place with the consent of the person with the right to control the line.

1   [2003] EWCA Crim 1632, [2003] Crim LR 793.

The tort of unlawful interception of a private telecommunications system

6.35   RIPA 2000, s 1(3) creates a tort where a communication is sent by a private telecommunications system and is intercepted by the person who has control of the system, but that person does not have lawful authority to do so. It is actionable at the instance of either sender or recipient. Where an employee believes that his employer has unlawfully intercepted a telephone conversation with a third party, either the third party or the employee may sue.

Lord Bassam explained:

'One of the key drivers for this legislation is that such interception should be in accordance with the law. It must be within the legal framework and for a lawful purpose. Hence also the lawful business practice regulations, which will govern the actions of businesses in this context and of any public authorities which monitor calls to the switchboard or the communications of the staff. These will contain the stipulation that businesses have reasonable grounds to believe that all parties to any communication are aware that monitoring may take place.'[1]

1   613 HL Official Report col 1416 (see SI 2000/2699 at **para 6.42**).

What sort of systems are covered?

6.36   RIPA 2000, s 2(1) defines a telecommunications system in wide terms as:

'any system (including the apparatus comprised in it) which exists (whether wholly or partly in the United Kingdom or elsewhere) for the purpose of facilitating the transmission of communications by any means involving the use of electrical or electro-magnetic energy.'

The definition makes it clear that mobile phones, emails and pagers are included.

What is metering?

6.37   In *Malone v United Kingdom*,[1] the defendant suspected that his telephone had been 'metered' to enable the police to obtain details of about 20 people whose premises had been searched. The process involves the use of a device (a meter check printer) which registers the numbers dialled on a particular telephone and the time and duration of each call. In making such records, the operator makes use only of signals sent to itself as the provider of the telephone service and does not monitor or intercept telephone conversations at all. The ECt HR concluded that the release of such information to the police without the consent of the subscriber amounted to an interference with a right guaranteed by art 8.[2]

1   (1984) 7 EHRR 14.
2   (1984) 7 EHRR 14 at para 84.

6.38   Although the distinction between a communication and mere metering may appear clear, it may in practice create difficult problems. In *Morgans v DPP*,[1] the prosecution argued that the information on which they relied to establish the offence of fraudulent use of a telecommunications system contrary to Telecommunications Act 1984, s 42 amounted to metering. During the course of the investigation a logger had been placed on the defendant's telephone line, which listed the time and date on which the telephone was being used, the duration of calls and the digits dialled before or after connection to another line. If the information which had been intercepted by the logging device had been confined to the recording of the numbers dialled at that stage it could be described as metering information. However, as Lord Hope explained, the evidence went significantly further:

> 'The numbers he dialled after making the connection were in an entirely different category. At this stage he was communicating with the networks to which he had been connected. The numbers he dialled resulted in the transmission of signals to those networks. They produced the same kind of computer generated response from them as he would have achieved if they had been programmed to respond to the human voice.'

Lord Hope rejected the prosecution argument and held that the information relied on in the trial was a communication for the purposes of the Act.

1   [2001] 1 AC 315 at p 332.

Does it matter if the information is brought about by metering?

6.39   The answer to this question is Yes. Such information is described in RIPA 2000 as 'traffic data' (see **para 6.5**). RIPA 2000, s 2(5) specifically states that references to an interception of a communication:

'do not include references to–

(a)   any conduct that takes place in relation only to so much of the communication as consists in any traffic data comprised in or attached to a communication (whether by the sender or otherwise) for the purposes of any postal service or telecommunication system by means of which it is being or may be transmitted [eg address or telephone number]; or

(b)   any such conduct, in connection with conduct falling within paragraph (a) as gives a person who is neither the sender nor the intended recipient only so much access to a communication as is necessary for the purpose of identifying traffic data so comprised or attached'.

Lawful authority

6.40   An intercept will not give rise to criminal or civil liability if carried out under lawful authority.[1] In addition to interceptions carried out under warrant (see **para 6.46**) the following are also lawful.

- Where the interceptor reasonably believes that both the sender and the intended recipient have agreed to the interception, eg where a person uses an answerphone to record a message.[2]

- Where one party consents to the interception, and surveillance by means of that interception has been authorised under RIPA 2000, Pt II.[3] In effect, such conduct is treated as a form of directed surveillance subject to RIPA 2000, s 26(4)(b) and 48(4) (see **Chapter 8**). According to the explanatory notes, this situation might arise where a kidnapper is telephoning relatives of a hostage and the police wish to record the call in order to identify or trace the kidnapper. In *R v Hardy*,[4] the conduct of an undercover officer covertly recording conversations with the defendant was considered in the context of authorisations that had been granted for CHIS and directed surveillance. The court held that such conduct did not amount to interception because the contents of the calls were not made available while being transmitted to a third party. Even if that had not been the case it would have amounted to directed surveillance.

- Where the interception is by a CSP for the purposes of providing or operating a postal or telecommunications service or where any enactment relating to the use of the service is to be enforced. This might occur, for example, where the postal provider needs to open a letter to determine the address of the sender because the recipient's address is unknown.[5]

- Where the interception is authorised by a designated person and is undertaken for purposes connected with certain parts of the Wireless Telegraphy Act 1949. Section 5 of that Act, dealing with misleading messages, is amended by RIPA 2000, s 73 and makes provision for interception under the authority of the Secretary of State. For the meaning of 'a designated person' see, Wireless Telegraphy Act 1949, s 5(12).[6]

- Where an existing statutory power is used to obtain stored communications (s 1(5)(c)).

    This covers circumstances where a person has been arrested in possession of a pager and the police have reason to believe that the messages sent previously to the pager may be of assistance to their case. In such a case they could apply for a production order under PACE 1984, Sch 1.[7]

1   RIPA 2000, s 1(5).
2   RIPA 2000, s 3(1).
3   RIPA 2000, s 3(2) and Interception Code 10.4.
4   [2003] 1 Cr App Rep 494.
5   RIPA 2000, s 3(3) and Interception Code 10.5.
6   RIPA 2000, s 3(4).
7   See *R (on the application of NTL) v Ipswich Crown Court* [2002] EWHC 1585 (Admin), [2003] QB 131, [2002] Crim LR 972.

Power to provide for lawful interception without the need for a warrant

6.41   RIPA 2000, s 4(1) permits interceptions where the subject of the interception is believed to be outside the UK, the interception relates to the use of a public telecommunications service in that other country, the CSP is obliged by the law of that other country to carry out or facilitate that interception, and it is carried out in accordance with regulations made by the Secretary of State (SI 2004/157). This subsection applies only where the subject is in the country whose competent authorities issued the interception warrant. It will allow the UK to comply with art 17 of the Convention on Mutual Assistance in Criminal Matters between the Member States of the European Union. Article 17 is intended to allow operators of satellite communications systems to use a ground station in one member state to facilitate interception using a CSP which is in a business relationship with the satellite operator located in another member state. The CSP and the subject of the interception are required to be in the same member state.

The Telecommunications (Lawful Business Practice) Regulations, SI 2000/2699

6.42   RIPA 2000, s 4(2) provides for interception to be authorised by regulations made by the Secretary of State in relation to business communications. The regulations are subject to art 5 of Directive 97/66/EC (**para 7.5**).

The relevant regulations came into force on 24 October 2000. They authorise certain interceptions which would otherwise be prohibited by RIPA 2000, s 1. The interception has to be by or with the consent of the person carrying on a business (which includes the activities of government departments, public authorities and others exercising statutory functions) for the purposes relevant to that person's business and using that business's own telecommunications system. In addition, the controller must make all reasonable efforts to inform potential users that interceptions may be made.[1]

Such interceptions may be authorised for monitoring or recording of communications:

- to establish the existence of facts, to ascertain compliance with regulatory practices or to ascertain or demonstrate standards which are or ought to be achieved (quality control and training);
- in the interests of national security;
- to prevent or detect crime;
- to investigate or detect unauthorised use of telecommunication systems; or
- where the recording or monitoring is undertaken in order to secure the effective operation of the system.

1   SI 2000/2699 reg 3(2)(c)

6.43 Interceptions may also be authorised for monitoring received communications to determine whether they are business or personal communications or for monitoring communications made to anonymous telephone helplines.[1]

1   SI 2000/2699 reg 3(1)(b) and (c)

6.44 Interception may also be authorised where the interception is carried out in the exercise of powers conferred by Police Act 1952, s 47 or similar legislation in Scotland or Northern Ireland[1] or in relation to any hospital where high security psychiatric services are provided in accordance with any direction under the National Health Service Act 1977, s 17.[2] RIPA 200, s 4(6) makes equivalent provision for state hospitals in Scotland.

1   RIPA 2000, s 4(4).
2   RIPA 2000, s 4(5).

6.45 It should be noted that in all the above examples where interception takes place under RIPA 2000, ss 3 or 4, there is no prohibition on the evidential use of any material obtained thereby. Such material may, however, be excluded under PACE 1984, s 78 or under common law.[1]

1   See Interception Code 10.

Warrants

6.46 In rejecting the suggestion that the UK should follow the example of most European jurisdictions and require judicial authorisation for interception warrants, the Home Secretary Jack Straw replied:

> 'If one looks at the practice in other countries it does not necessarily follow that just because a judicial warrant is required there is a greater safeguard for the individual. Indeed I suggest that in quite a number of other countries, the fact that a judicial warrant is required lessens the protection that is offered to people because the judicial warrant acts as a fig leaf for people's human rights and not as a serious safeguard.'[1]

The executive authorisation procedure was approved in *Christie v United Kingdom.*[2]

1   Hansard HC Official Report col 770, 6 March 2000.
2   (1993) 78-A DR 119.

What criteria must be satisfied?

6.47 By RIPA 2000, s 5(2) the Secretary of State must believe that:

(a)   the warrant is necessary; and
(b)   the conduct authorised is proportionate.

RIPA 2000, s 5(3) provides that a warrant is necessary if it is necessary:

(a)   in the interests of national security;
(b)   for the purpose of preventing or detecting serious crime;
(c)   for the purpose of safeguarding the economic well-being of the UK; or

(d) for the purpose of giving effect to the provisions of any international mutual assistance agreement in circumstances equivalent to (b).

RIPA 2000, s 5(3)(a)–(c) replicate the equivalent s 2(a)–(c) of IOCA 1985.

6.48 Serious crime is defined in RIPA 2000, s 81(2) in the same way as in Police Act 1997, Pt III. By virtue of RIPA 2000, s 81(5)(b), preventing or detecting serious crime does not extend to gathering evidence for the purpose of a prosecution, so that intercepted material should normally be destroyed by virtue of RIPA 2000, s 15(3) prior to any trial.[1]

1   Interception Code 6.8.

6.49 Neither national security nor the economic well-being of the UK are defined, although RIPA 2000, s 5(5) provides that in order for s 5(3)(c) to be satisfied the information must relate to the acts or intentions of persons outside the British Islands. On 21 March 2000, Mr Clarke in Standing Committee stated that the government intended that 'safeguarding the economic well-being of the UK' should provide a higher test than in the interests of 'the economic well-being of the UK', which is the test for authorising other forms of surveillance under the Act.

Interception Code 4.4 confirms that the Secretary of State will not issue a warrant on s 5(3)(c) grounds if this direct link between the economic well-being of the UK and state security is not established. Any application for a warrant on such grounds should explain how the two are linked.

The explanatory note confirms that it would not be sufficient for the Secretary of State to consider that a warrant might be useful in supplementing other material, or that the information that it could produce would be interesting. It also points out that the limitation provided by s 5(5) is not found in the Convention.

Proportionality

6.50 The conduct authorised should be proportionate to what is sought to be achieved by that conduct. RIPA 2000, s 5(4) specifically enjoins the Secretary of State to consider whether the information sought could reasonably be obtained by other means. The test is less stringent than that for obtaining access to sensitive material under PACE 1984, Sch 1, where the judge must be satisfied that other methods of obtaining the material have been tried without success or have not been tried because it appeared they were bound to fail.

Interception Code 2.5 provides further guidance on the question of proportionality.

> 'Then, if the interception is necessary, the Secretary of State must also believe that it is proportionate to what is sought to be achieved by carrying it out. This involves balancing the intrusiveness of the interference against the need for it in operational terms. Interception of communications will not be proportionate if it is excessive in the circumstances of the case or if the information which is sought could reasonably be obtained by other means. Further, all interception should be carefully managed to meet the objective in question and must not be arbitrary or unfair'.

What conduct may be authorised?

6.51 The warrant may authorise any conduct designed to secure the required interception, or the making of a request for international mutual assistance, or the provision of such assistance to the competent authorities of a country outside the UK.[1]

RIPA 2000, s 5(1)(d) provides for disclosure of the product of any authorised interception. Such disclosure is restricted by the safeguards in RIPA 2000, s 15.

RIPA 2000, s 5(6) provides that the conduct authorised shall be taken to include all such conduct (including the interception of communications not identified by the warrant) as it is necessary to undertake in order to do what is expressly authorised or required by the warrant. This includes obtaining related communications data and conduct by any person pursuant to a requirement imposed by or on behalf of the person to whom the warrant is addressed to provide assistance with giving effect to the warrant.[2]

1   RIPA 2000, s 5(1)(a)–(c).
2   See RIPA 2000, s 11(4), **para 6.72**.

Who may apply for warrants?

6.52   RIPA 2000, s 6(2) provides a list of those who may apply for an interception warrant:[1]

'Those persons are–

(a)   the Director General of the Security Service;
(b)   the Chief of the Secret Intelligence Service;
(c)   the Director of GCHQ;
(d)   the Director General of the National Criminal Intelligence Service;
(e)   the Commissioner of the Metropolitan Police;
(f)   the Chief Constable of the Royal Ulster Constabulary;
(g)   the chief constable of any police force maintained under section 1 of the Police (Scotland) Act 1967;
(h)   the Commissioner of Customs and Excise;
(i)   the Chief of Defence Intelligence;
(j)   a person who for purposes of any international mutual assistance agreement, is the competent authority of a country or territory outside the United Kingdom.'

The list does not include chief constables of police forces in England and Wales, who must make application through the NCIS. Other agencies with investigative powers should do likewise.[2]

1   See also Interception Code 2.1.
2   613 HL Official Report col 1476.

Who may issue warrants?

6.53   RIPA 2000, s 7(1) provides that a warrant may be issued by the Secretary of State, or in cases of urgency (in which authorisation is required within 24 hours[1]) or mutual assistance within s 7(2), by a senior official. In an urgent case a warrant may only be signed by a senior official if the Secretary of State has expressly authorised the issue of a warrant in that case and it must contain a statement that the case is urgent and that the Secretary of State has expressly authorised it.[2] A senior official means a member of the Senior Civil Service or a member of the Senior Management Structure of Her Majesty's Diplomatic Service.[3] A warrant issued by a senior official will be limited in duration to five working days.[4]

The Interception Code 4.6 has the heading 'Urgent Authorisation of a Section 8(1) Warrant' and Code 5.7 has the heading 'Urgent Authorisation of a Section 8(4) Warrant'. Although the former, but not the latter, details the duration of the warrant, the procedure in each case is identical.

1   Interception Code 4.6
2   RIPA 2000, s 7(4)(a).
3   RIPA 2000, s 81(1).
4   RIPA 2000, s 9(1).

Mutual assistance agreements

6.54   A warrant for the purposes of assistance under a mutual assistance agreement may be signed by a senior official without the express authorisation of the Secretary of State, but a senior official can issue such a warrant only if it appears that the subject of the interception is outside the UK,[1] or the interception to which the warrant relates is to take place in relation only to premises outside the UK.[2] In such a case, the warrant should state which of the two conditions apply[3] along with a statement of the purpose of the warrant.[4]

This procedure is designed to allow the UK to comply with the requirements of art 16 of the Convention on Mutual Assistance in Criminal Matters (eg where the UK is requested to issue an interception warrant to the operator of a satellite ground station in the UK for the purpose of intercepting a satellite telephone being used on the territory of another member state). Article 16 enables such warrants to be issued by the requested member state 'without further formality' provided the competent authorities of the requesting member state have already issued an interception order against the subject of the interception. Since no decision is being made on the merits of the case, and the purpose of the warrant is solely to require the satellite operator to provide technical assistance to the other member state, it is considered appropriate for these warrants to be issued by senior officials rather than the Secretary of State (see also **para 1.29**).

1   RIPA 2000, s 7(2)(b)(i).
2   RIPA 2000, s 7(2)(b)(ii).
3   RIPA 2000, s 7(5).
4   RIPA 2000, s 7(4)(b).

Contents of warrants

6.55 A warrant must be addressed to the person by whom, or on whose behalf, the application was made.[1]

As noted above, the Consultation Paper, Cm 4368, drew attention to defects in the IOCA 1985 warranting procedure. In particular, as a result of advances in technology, it was pointed out that the subject of the interception may have access to several different types of communication or may simply change his telephone number. Each time such a change took place a fresh warrant had to be applied for, resulting in a number of different warrants being issued and possibly renewed in respect of the same person. As a result a new statutory regime was set up by RIPA 2000, s 8(1) requiring either the subject of the interception or a single set of premises to be described in the warrant. Section 8(2) provides for a schedule setting out the addresses, numbers, apparatus or other factors that are to be used for identifying the communications that may be intercepted. Section 8(3) somewhat obviously states that such communications are likely to be or include communications from, or intended for, the subject of the interception, or communications originating on, or intended for, transmission to the premises described. The advantage of such a procedure is that in cases of urgency modifications to the scheduled part of a warrant may be made without the authority of the Secretary of State. This may, for example, include the person to whom the warrant is addressed or his subordinate.[2]

1 RIPA 2000, s 7(3)(a).
2 RIPA 2000, s 10(8) (see **para 6.67**).

The content of a s 8(1) application

6.56 Interception Code 4.2 details the content of an application for a s 8(1) warrant. It should include:

(a) the background to the operation in question;
(b) the person or premises to which the application relates (and how the person or premises feature in the operation);
(c) a description of the communications to be intercepted, details of the CSP (see RIPA 2000, s 11(4), **para 6.72**) and an assessment of the feasibility of the interception operation where this is relevant;
(d) a description of the conduct to be authorised as considered necessary in order to carry out the interception, where appropriate;
(e) an explanation of why the interception is considered necessary under the provisions of RIPA 2000, s 5(3);
(f) a consideration of why the conduct to be authorised by the warrant is proportionate to what is sought to be achieved by that conduct;
(g) a consideration of any unusual degree of collateral intrusion and why that intrusion is justified in the circumstances (in particular, where the communication in question might affect religious, medical or journalistic confidentiality or legal privilege, this must be specified in the application);
(h) where an application is urgent, supporting justification should be provided;

(i)   an assurance that all material intercepted will be handled in accordance with the safeguards required by RIPA 2000, s 15.

The format of a s 8(1) warrant

6.57   Interception Code 4.7 refers to two sections of the warrant, namely the warrant instrument which each CSP will receive and the schedule or set of schedules. Only the schedule relevant to the communications that can be intercepted by the specified CSP will be provided to that CSP.

Interception Code 4.8 states that the warrant instrument should include the name or description of the intercept subject or set of premises, the warrant number and the names of persons who may subsequently modify the scheduled part.

Interception Code 4.9 sets out the contents of the scheduled part, namely the name of the CSP or other person who is to take action, the warrant number and a means of identifying the communications to be intercepted.[1]

1   RIPA 2000, s 8(2).

The certified warrant procedure

6.58   The above conditions do not apply to a certified warrant granted pursuant to RIPA 2000, s 8(4). The procedure is a descendant of the Official Secrets Act 1920, s 4, which was replaced by IOCA 1985, s 3(2). In his 1986 report, Lord Lloyd[1] drew attention to the problem that could be created by IOCA 1985, s 3(3), which provided that the material specified shall not include an address in the UK except in the case of counter-terrorism. In cases involving subversion it had become the practice to apply for a separate warrant under s 3(1), known as an overlapping warrant, in addition to a warrant under s 3(2). He concluded that it was obviously a sound practice and recommended that where it was desired to intercept communications to or from an individual residing in the British Islands as a separate target:

'then in all cases other than counter-terrorism there should be a separate warrant under s 3(1) even though the communications may already be covered by a warrant under s 3(2)'.

1   1986 Report of the Interception Commissioner, at para 36.

The certified warrant

6.59   RIPA 2000, s 8(4) describes another form of warrant which can only come into existence where:

(a)   the conduct consists of the interception of external communications in the course of their transmission. (An external communication is one that is sent or received outside the British Islands[1] but Interception Code 5.1 points out that communications that are both sent and received in the UK but pass outside the UK en route are not to be regarded as external);

(b)   the conduct falls within RIPA 2000, s 5(6) (the scope of necessary conduct); and

(c)   the Secretary of State certifies the description of the intercepted material and that he considers the examination of such material necessary for one of the reasons mentioned in RIPA 2000, s 5(3)(a)–(c) (not (d)) (see **para 6.47**).

Interception Code 5.4 emphasises that in considering RIPA 2000, s 5(3)(c) the Secretary of State will not issue a warrant unless the direct link between the economic well-being of the UK and state security has been established. The effect of this subsection is to require the Secretary of State to authorise a certificate describing the intercepted material which falls properly within the purpose and may therefore be read, looked at or listened to by any person. No other intercepted material may be so examined. How the person responsible for putting the warrant into effect is to determine the nature of the material without reading, looking at or listening to it is not clear.

Postal items are not included in RIPA 2000, s 8(5)(a).

1   RIPA 2000, s 20.

The content of a s 8(4) application

6.60   Interception Code 5.2 provides that each application for a s 8(4) warrant should contain similar details as a s 8(1) application, but in addition should contain:

(a)   the description of the conduct to be authorised, which must be restricted to the interception of external communications;

(b)   the certificate that will regulate the examination of intercepted material;

(c)   an assurance that the intercepted material will be read, looked at or listened to only so far as it is certified and it meets the conditions of RIPA 2000, s 16(2)–(6); and

(d)   an assurance that all material intercepted will be handled in accordance with the safeguards required by RIPA 2000, ss 15 and 16.

Unlike a s 8(1) application, it is not necessary to include details of the person or premises.[1]

1   RIPA 2000, s 8(4).

The s 8(4) certificate

6.61   RIPA 2000, s 8(6) provides that only the Secretary of State may issue a s 8(4) warrant.

Interception Code 5.6 provides that a s 8(4) warrant should be accompanied by a certificate in which the Secretary of State certifies that he considers examination of the intercepted material to be necessary for one or more of the RIPA 2000, s 5(3) purposes. The Secretary of State has a duty to ensure that arrangements are in force for securing that only that material which has been certified as necessary for examination for a s 5(3) purpose, and which meets the conditions set out in RIPA

2000, s 16(2)–(6), is in fact read, looked at or listened to. The Interception Commissioner is under a duty to review the adequacy of those arrangements.

Format of a s 8(4) warrant

6.62 Interception Code 5.9 provides that each warrant is addressed to the person who submitted the application. This person may then serve a copy upon such CSPs as he believes will be able to assist in implementing the interception.

The warrant should include a description of the communications to be intercepted, the warrant reference number and the names of those who may subsequently modify the scheduled part of the warrant in an urgent case (if authorised in accordance with RIPA 2000, s 10(8)). The CSP will not receive a copy of the certificate provided for by Interception Code 5.6.

Extra safeguards provided by RIPA 2000, s 16

6.63 The section provides extra safeguards in the case of warrants to which RIPA 2000, s 8(4) applies. Material intercepted under a s 8(4) warrant should only be examined if it has been certified as necessary to be examined in the interests of national security, for the purpose of preventing or detecting serious crime or for the purpose of safeguarding the economic well-being of the UK, and it does not have as its purpose the identification of material contained in communications sent by or intended for an individual who is known to be in the British Islands and has not been selected by reference to such an individual.

Limited exceptions are provided by RIPA 2000, s 8(3)–(6).

Duration of warrants

6.64 RIPA 2000, s 9(1) provides that a warrant shall cease to have effect at the end of the relevant period (three months under s 9(6)(c) or two months under IOCA 1985, s 4(6)) unless the warrant was issued under s 7(2)(a) by a senior official, in which case it is the period ending on the fifth working day following the day of the warrant's issue.

Cancellation

6.65 RIPA 2000, s 9(3) provides that the Secretary of State shall cancel an interception warrant if he is satisfied that the warrant is no longer necessary on grounds falling within RIPA 2000, s 5(3). Interception Code 4.16 asserts that intercepting agencies will therefore need to keep their warrants under continuous review.

RIPA 2000, s 9(4) requires the Secretary of State to cancel a warrant where the warrant or renewal instrument was issued under the hand of a senior official on the basis that the subject of the interception was outside the UK, but the Secretary of

State is satisfied that the subject is now in the UK. For the interception to continue in such circumstances, a new warrant will need to be issued by the Secretary of State himself. In practice, cancellation instruments will be signed by a senior official on behalf of the Secretary of State. The cancellation instrument will be addressed to the person to whom the warrant was issued. A copy of the cancellation instrument should be sent to those CSPs who have given effect to the warrant during the preceding 12 months.

Renewal

6.66   RIPA 2000, s 9(1)(b) provides that a warrant may be renewed at any time before the expiry of the relevant period by the Secretary of State if he believes that the warrant continues to be necessary on the grounds set out in RIPA 2000, s 5(3). In the case of a warrant issued under RIPA 2000, s 7(2)(b) (interception outside the UK) it may be renewed by a senior official but in such a case the renewal instrument must contain a statement that the interception subject or the premises to which the interception relates is outside the UK.[1] In either case the applicant should give an assessment of the value of interceptions to the operation to date and explain why he considers that interception continues to be necessary.[2]

If the warrant is renewed by the Secretary of State on the grounds of national security or economic well-being the period is six months, and if renewed on the grounds of the prevention or detection of serious crime the period is three months.

1   RIPA 2000, s 9(5)(a) and (b).
2   See Interception Code 4.13 and 5.12.

Modification of warrants and certificates

6.67   The unscheduled part of a warrant may be modified by the Secretary of State or, in an urgent case in which the Secretary of State has expressly authorised the modification and a statement to that effect is endorsed on the modifying instrument, by a senior official.[1] Where modified by a senior official, the modification ceases to have effect after five working days following the day of issue, unless renewed by the Secretary of State.[2]

1   RIPA 2000, s 10(1) and (5).
2   See Interception Code 4.10 and 5.10.

6.68   The scheduled part of the warrant may be modified by the Secretary of State, and in an urgent case where expressly provided for in the warrant, by the person to whom the warrant is addressed or a person holding any such position subordinate to that person as may be identified in the provisions of the warrant.[1] On the basis that the greater includes the lesser, it would appear that a senior official may also modify the scheduled part. If so, it would follow that the restriction in s 10(5) does not apply and that such a modification can take place without being referred personally to the Secretary of State. This approach would appear to be supported by Interception

Code 4.11, albeit that the note to the Code appears to confuse the senior official with the person to whom the warrant is addressed.

1   RIPA 2000, s 10(8) and Interception Code 4.12.

6.69   The certificate of a s 8(4) warrant may be modified by the Secretary of State or, in an urgent case, by a senior official who is either expressly authorised to do so by the terms of the certificate or is authorised by the Secretary of State to do so and that fact is endorsed on the modifying instrument.[1] Where a senior official is responsible for the modification, it will cease to have effect after five working days following the day of issue unless it is endorsed by the Secretary of State.

1   RIPA 2000, s 10(7).

6.70   The Secretary of State is obliged to modify the warrant if he considers that any factor set out in the schedule is no longer relevant or if he considers that the material certified by a s 8(4) certificate includes material the examination of which is no longer necessary within RIPA 2000, s 5(3).[1]

1   See RIPA 2000, s 10(2) and (3).

Implementation of warrants

6.71   RIPA 2000, s 11 sets out the procedure for implementation of the warrant and the role of different people within the process. Although the person to whom the warrant is addressed, in practice the intercepting agency, may give effect to it, it is likely that he will require the assistance of a CSP. Section 11(2) provides that the person to whom the warrant is addressed may serve a copy of the warrant (or make arrangements to do so) on such persons as he considers able to provide such assistance (the CSP). The copy may omit one or more of the schedules. In most cases the CSP will only need to see the front of the warrant and the relevant schedule.

Interception Code 2.8 provides that, in addition to the above, the intercepting agency should also provide the CSP with a covering document specifying any other details regarding the means of interception and delivery as may be necessary. Contact details with respect to the intercepting agency will either be provided in this covering document or will be available in the handbook provided to all postal and telecommunications operators who maintain an intercept capability.

6.72   Where a copy of an interception warrant has been served, the recipient is placed under a duty to take reasonable steps to enforce the warrant,[1] which include steps that would have been reasonably practicable for the person to have taken had they complied with the obligation to maintain an intercept capability under RIPA 2000, s 12. The duty to provide assistance is enforceable by civil proceedings[2] and the knowing failure to comply may amount to a criminal offence.[3] The CSP may disclose the product of any authorised interception to the person to whom the warrant is addressed.[4]

1   RIPA 2000, s 11(4) and (5).
2   RIPA 2000, s 11(8).
3   RIPA 2000, s 11(7).
4   RIPA 2000, s 11(9).

Maintenance of intercept capability

6.73   RIPA 2000, s 12 permits the Secretary of State to require that providers of public communications services maintain a reasonable intercept capability. A public telecommunications service is defined in RIPA 2000, s 2 to mean any such service 'which is offered or provided to, or to a substantial section of, the public in any one or more parts of the UK'. It is to be contrasted with the definition in IOCA 1985, s 10, which referred to 'a telecommunications service provided by means of a public telecommunications system'.

The Secretary of State may, by order, set out the obligations on CSPs that appear to him to be reasonable, but before doing so must consult as required by s 12(9).

6.74   The Regulation of Investigatory Powers (Maintenance of Interception Capability) Order 2002, SI 2002/1931, came into force on 1 August 2002. It provides that the obligations in Pt II of its Schedule shall not apply to CSPs who do not intend to provide a public telecommunications service to more than 10,000 persons in any one or more parts of the UK, or who only provide or intend to provide a public telecommunications service in relation to the provision of banking, insurance, investment or other financial services.

Part I of the Schedule details the obligations of any public postal service to intercept and retain specified items or items sent by identified persons where the carrier keeps records of who sent which item and to maintain a system of opening, copying and resealing any item carried for less than £1. The service is to comply with the above obligations in such a way that the chance of the interception subject becoming aware of any interception is minimised.

Part II obliges CSPs to provide a mechanism for implementing interceptions within one working day of being informed that the interception has been appropriately authorised. The schedule sets out further specific responsibilities relating to both the way in which the intercept is to be carried out and simultaneously handed over as agreed with the person on whose application the warrant was issued, and a continuing duty to ensure that the reliability of the interception capability is at least equal to the reliability of the public telecommunications service carrying the communication which is being intercepted. The obligations are to be complied with in the same way and for the same reasons as those in Pt I.

6.75   RIPA 2000, s 12(5) provides for the person served with a notice under s 12(2) to refer the notice to the Technical Advisory Board (TAB), established under s 13, which must then report on the technical requirements and the financial consequences of the notice to the Secretary of State, who may then either withdraw or confirm the notice. Interception Code 2.9 states that details of how to submit a notice to the TAB will be provided either before or at the time the notice is served. Where a notice has been so referred the person on whom it was served does not have to comply with it unless and until it is confirmed under s 12(6)(c).

The obligation to comply with the notice is enforceable by civil proceedings for an injunction or for specific performance of a statutory duty.[1]

1   RIPA 2000, s 12(7).

The Technical Advisory Board

6.76   The section was inserted as a result of an opposition amendment in the House of Lords.[1] As stated above, the TAB must be consulted before the Secretary of State makes an order under RIPA 2000, s 12(1). The Technical Advisory Board Order 2001, SI 2001/3734, came into force on 22 November 2001. It provides that the TAB shall consist of 13 persons: a chairman and six persons representing each of the intercepting agency and the CSP.

1   615 HL Official Report col 290.

Grants for interception costs

6.77   Considerable concern was expressed in Parliament at the potential expense of providing adequate intercept capability. RIPA 2000, s 14 requires the Secretary of State to ensure that there are arrangements to secure that CSPs receive such a contribution as is fair in each case to the costs of providing an intercept capability or in the provision of assistance in respect of individual warrants.

General safeguards regarding the use of intercepted material

6.78   RIPA 2000, s 15 has the effect of restricting the use of intercepted material to the minimum necessary for the authorised purposes. It extends the safeguards originally found in IOCA 1985, s 6. RIPA 2000, s 82(6) contains a transitional provision applying the provisions of ss 15 and 16 to warrants and certificates under IOCA 1985. It imposes an obligation on the Secretary of State to ensure that detailed safeguards are drawn up by each of the intercepting agencies. According to the Report of the Interception Commissioner for 2002, this has been done.

RIPA 2000, s 15(3) requires that all copies of any intercepted material and related communications data be destroyed as soon as it is no longer necessary to retain it for any of the authorised purposes. If it is retained, Interception Code 6.8 states that it should be reviewed at appropriate intervals to confirm that the justification for its retention is still valid.

6.79   The authorised purposes are widely defined and set out in s 15(4):

(a)   if it continues to be or is likely to become necessary for any of the purposes set out in s 5(3);

(b)   if it is necessary for facilitating the carrying out of the functions of the Secretary of State under Chapter I of Part I of the Act;

(c)   if it is necessary for facilitating the carrying out of any of the functions of the Interception Commissioner or the tribunal;

(d)   if it is necessary to ensure that a person conducting a criminal prosecution has the information he needs to determine what is required of him by his duty to secure the fairness of the prosecution;

(e)   if it is necessary for the performance of any duty imposed by the Public Records Acts.

The duty under (d) represents a significant departure from the previous IOCA 1985 regime, and the failure to comply with the duty could have significant consequences in any related criminal proceedings (see **Chapter 11**).[1] Because the authorised purpose for the issue of an interception warrant in RIPA 2000, s 5(3)(b) is for the purpose of 'preventing or detecting serious crime' as opposed to gathering evidence, it is probable that much intercepted material will not survive to the prosecution stage.

1   See Interception Code 7.7.

Dissemination generally

6.80   Interception Code 6.4 adds further guidance as to how the principle of minimum disclosure should be enforced.

> 'This obligation applies equally to disclosure to additional persons within an agency, and to disclosure outside the agency. It is enforced by prohibiting disclosure to persons who do not hold the required security clearance and also by the need to know principle: intercepted material must not be disclosed to any person unless the person's duties, which must relate to one of the authorised purposes, are such that he needs to know about the material to carry out his duties. In the same way only so much of the material may be disclosed as the recipient needs; for example if a summary of the material will suffice, no more than that should be disclosed.'

Interception Code 6.9 states that each intercepting agency should maintain a distribution list of persons who may have access to intercepted material, which should be kept up to date.

The Interception Code lays down further detailed requirements designed to ensure that any copying is kept to a minimum[1] and that there are arrangements for storage designed to minimise the risk of loss or theft.[2]

1   Interception Code 6.6.
2   Interception Code 6.7.

Exclusion of matters from criminal proceedings

6.81   See **paras 11.18–28**.

Offence for unauthorised disclosures

6.82   RIPA 2000, s 19(4) creates an offence of unlawful disclosure punishable on summary conviction by six months' imprisonment and on indictment by five years' imprisonment. A defence is provided by RIPA 2000, s 19(5) where the person can show that he could not reasonably be expected after first becoming aware of the matter disclosed to take steps to prevent the disclosure. Similarly, defences are provided where the disclosure was made to or by a professional legal adviser in the context of advice about the effects of Pt I, eg where a CSP seeks advice on the implementation of a warrant,[1] or that it was made by a legal adviser in connection with any legal proceedings and for the purpose of those proceedings,[2] or that it was made to the Commissioner or authorised by him or by the terms of the warrant.[3] The offence can only be committed by a person on whom the duty to keep secret the matters specified in RIPA 2000, s 19(3) is laid. These include every person holding office under the Crown, every police officer, every member of NCIS and NCS, as well as employees of CSPs. Such persons must keep secret the existence and contents of the warrant and any s 8(4) certificate, the details of the issue of the warrant, the existence and contents of any requirement to provide assistance with giving effect to the warrant, the steps taken in pursuance of the warrant, and everything in the intercepted material together with any related communications data.

1   RIPA 2000, s 19(6).
2   RIPA 2000, s 19(7).
3   RIPA 2000, s 19(9).

Chapter 7

Communications data

Introduction

7.1 In *Malone v United Kingdom*,[1] the ECt HR distinguished metering and interception but did not accept that the former did not give rise to an issue under art 8.

> 'The records of metering contain information, in particular the numbers called, which is an integral element in the communications made by telephone. Consequently, release of that information to the police without the consent of the subscriber also amounts, in the opinion of the Court, to an interference with the rights guaranteed by Art 8.'

As there were no legal rules concerning the scope and manner of exercise of the discretion, the interference was not in accordance with law. Metering is not the only form of data with which this chapter is concerned. Every time someone uses a mobile phone, sends an email or logs onto the Internet, he increases the volume of data available for inspection by others. All such data is communications data. In the summer of 2002 the government produced a draft order allowing a wide variety of public authorities access to such data. It was widely criticised as a 'Snoopers' Charter' and withdrawn to be replaced by what is now SI 2003/3172, which came into force on 5 January 2004 at the same time as RIPA 2000, Pt I, Ch II. The purpose of this Chapter is to regulate access to communications data rather than to extend it. Unlike Chapter 1 no criminal offence such as deliberately misusing access to such data is created.

1   (1984) 7 EHRR 14.

Codes of Practice

7.2 The Accessing Communications Data Draft Code of Practice (Draft Code) provides guidance on the procedures that must be followed before access to communications data can take place. Draft Code 7.5 provides that communications data must be handled securely and emphasises that the requirements of the Data Protection Act 1998 (DPA 1998) and its data protection principles should be adhered to.

Neither RIPA 2000, Pt I, Ch II nor the Draft Code dealt with the contentious issue of the retention of communications data. The subject is now dealt with in the Anti-terrorism, Crime and Security Act 2001 (ATCSA 2001), Part 11 and the Retention of Communications Data Under Part 11: Anti-terrorism, Crime and Security Act 2001 Voluntary Code Of Practice (Voluntary Code) issued thereunder (see **para 7.31**), which came into force on 5 December 2003.

The Consultation Paper

7.3   In March 2003 the Home Office published a Consultation Paper entitled 'Access to Communications Data. Respecting Privacy and Protecting the Public from Crime'. Many of examples below of the different types of communications data are taken from this Paper. In the course of the Paper, reference is made to communications service providers (CSPs) (see **para 6.27**).

The Consultation Paper was designed to explain why so many public authorities might require to access communications data. In the Forward the Home Secretary accepted that the original draft Order published in the summer of 2002 was too permissive and that a more restrictive approach was necessary. The preferred option was to reduce drastically the number of authorities allowed to access the full range of communications data and to apply a range of additional restrictions and safeguards to the remainder.

Relevance of Data Protection Act 1998 (DPA 1998)

7.4   All CSPs are data controllers and therefore subject to the principles enshrined in DPA 1998 (see **Chapter 3**).

Prior to the coming into force of RIPA 2000, Ch II, a public authority could request communications data from the relevant CSP under DPA 1998 and Telecommunications Act 1984, s 45. But there was no machinery for enforcement for failing to disclose. CSPs could, and did, turn down requests for data if in doubt about the necessity or proportionality of the request.

The fact that the disclosure falls within the exemptions in DPA 1998, ss 28, 29 or 35 does not create immunity from other legal duties such as the common law duty of confidence. The Consultation Paper makes the point that under DPA 1998 it is the CSP who would be liable to legal action. Unless the CSP is a public authority, it cannot be sued under the Human Rights Act 1998 (HRA 1998) for breach of a Convention right.

The limitation effectively means that the right to check intelligence information in the hands of the police is illusory.[1]

Disclosure by the police to third parties such as individuals or the press is permitted only if it falls within the exemptions in DPA 1998.

1   See 1998 Justice report 'Under Surveillance' p 94.

The Telecommunications Data Protection Directive 97/66/EC

7.5   The Directive was adopted in December 1997. It is directly relevant to both aspects of Part 1, art 6 being of particular significance in the context of Chapter II.

Article 5, 'Confidentiality of the communications', states:

'1.   Member states shall ensure via national regulations the confidentiality of communications made by means of a public telecommunications network and publicly available telecommunications services. In particular they shall prohibit listening, tapping, storage or other kinds of interception or surveillance of communications, by other than users without the consent of the users concerned, except where legally authorised in accordance with Art 14(1).

2.   Paragraph 1 shall not affect any legally authorised recording of communications in the course of lawful business practice for the purpose of providing evidence of a commercial transaction or of any other business communication.'

Article 14 permits member states to adopt legislation to restrict the obligations imposed under art 5 (and art 6, below) when such restriction is necessary to safeguard national security, defence, public security, the prevention, investigation, detection and prosecution of criminal offences or of unauthorised use of telecommunications systems.

Article 6, 'Traffic and billing data', states:

'1.   Traffic data relating to subscribers and users processed to establish calls and stored by the provider of a public telecommunications network and/or publicly available telecommunications service must be erased or made anonymous upon termination of the call without prejudice to the provisions of paragraphs 2, 3 and 4.

2.   For the purpose of subscriber billing and interconnection payments, data indicated in the Annex may be processed. Such processing is permissible only up to the end of the period during which the bill may be lawfully challenged or payment may be pursued.

3.   For the purpose of marketing its own telecommunications services, the provider of a publicly available telecommunications service may process the data referred to in paragraph 2, if the subscriber has given his consent.

4.   Processing of traffic and billing data must be restricted to persons acting under the authority of providers of the public telecommunications networks and/or publicly available telecommunications services handling, billing or traffic management, customer enquiries, fraud detection

and marketing the providers own telecommunications services and it must be restricted to what is necessary for the purposes of such activities.

5. Paragraphs 1, 2, 3 and 4 shall apply without prejudice to the possibility for competent authorities to be informed of billing or traffic data in conformity with applicable legislation in view of settling disputes, in particular interconnection or billing disputes.'

What is communications data?

7.6   RIPA 2000, Pt I, Ch II creates a regulatory framework for access to, and disclosure of, communications data. Such data include telephone metering, which records not only the date, time and length of calls but can also involve a form of dynamic metering that can pinpoint the location of a mobile phone when it is in use. It is said that in an urban context such information is accurate to within 50 metres. It does not include the contents of the communication itself, such as speech, correspondence, music or images. By implication, so-called communications data may reveal as much as the content of the call.[1] If the data fall within RIPA 2000, s 21 they may be obtained by a process of self-authorisation by any of the bodies listed in RIPA 2000, s 25.

According to RIPA 2000, s 21(4), communications data falls into one of three categories:

(1)   traffic data;
(2)   service use information; and
(3)   subscriber information.

At present, data available are likely to be kept for billing purposes and then destroyed.

Section 21 only permits the obtaining and disclosure of information not retention. A scheme for retention of data is provided by ATCSA 2001, Pt 11 (see **para 7.31**).

1   See *Amman v Switzerland* (2000) 30 EHRR 843, where the point at issue was whether the applicant was a contact of the Soviet Embassy.

What is traffic data?

7.7   By RIPA 2000, s 21(4)(a) communications data shall include:

'any traffic data comprised in or attached to a communication (whether by the sender of otherwise) for the purposes of any postal service or telecommunications system by means of which it is being or may be transmitted'.

Traffic data is further defined in s 21(6) in terms identical to those in s 2(9).

According to the Home Office Consultation Paper (see **para 7.2**), traffic data includes:

(i)   information identifying the sender and recipient of a communication;

(ii) information identifying any location of a communication, such as mobile phone cell site location data;

(iii) routing information identifying or selecting any apparatus, such as equipment, machinery or cable, through which a communication is transmitted, for example dynamic IP address allocation, web postings and email headers. The subject line of an email is considered content;

(iv) information written on the outside of a postal item;

(v) call detail records for specific calls, such as calling line identity;

(vi) web browsing information (to the extent that only the host machine or domain name (website name) is disclosed). Data identifying 'www.homeoffice.gov.uk' would be traffic data whereas data identifying 'www.homeoffice.gov.uk/kbsearch?=ripa+traffic=data' would be content;

(vii) online tracking of communications; and

(viii) signalling information and dialling sequences that affects the routing of a communication (but not the delivery of information) in the investigation of dial-through fraud.

7.8   In explaining the effect on the Internet, Lord Bassam confirmed that:

'the tailpiece of the new definition puts beyond doubt I think that in relation to Internet communications, traffic data stop at the apparatus within which files or programs are stored. To clarify the noble Lord's point, traffic data may identify a server but not a website or page.'[1]

1   615 Official Report col 330, 12 July 2000.

What is service use information?

7.9   By RIPA 2000, s 21(4)(b) service use information is:

'any information which includes none of the contents of a communication (apart from any information falling within paragraph (a)) and is about the use made by any person:

(i)   of any postal service or telecommunications service; or

(ii)   in connection with the provision to or use by any person of any part of a telecommunications service or any part of a telecommunications system.'

According to the Consultation Paper, service use data includes:

(i) itemised telephone call records (numbers called);

(ii) itemised connection records;

(iii) itemised timing and duration of service usage (calls and or connections);

(iv) information about the connection, disconnection and reconnection of services;

(v) information about the provision and use of forwarding/redirection services (by postal and telecommunications service providers);

(vi) information about the provision of conference calling, call messaging, call waiting and call barring telecommunications services; and

(vii) records of postal items, such as records of registered, recorded or special delivery postal items, records of parcel consignment, delivery and collection.

What is subscriber information?

7.10 By RIPA 2000, s 21(4)(c) subscriber information is:

'any information not falling within paragraph (a) or (b) that is held or obtained in relation to persons to whom he provides the service by a person providing a postal service or telecommunications service.'

According to the Consultation Paper, subscriber information includes:

(i) service user information (known as subscriber checks or reverse look-ups) such as 'who is the subscriber of phone number 01234 56789' or 'who is the subscriber of email account xyz@anyisp.co.uk';

(ii) service users' account information, including payment method;

(iii) addresses for installation and billing; and

(iv) abstract personal records provided by a subscriber to a service provider (such as demographic information or sign up data (to the extent that password or personalised service access information is not disclosed).

Lord Bassam informed the House of Lords that in the first three months of 2000 96.8% of the communications data requests by HMCE had been for subscriber details and 2.9% for itemised billing inquiries.

There is a significant difference between telephone data and Internet data. Historically, only the former has proved a useful form of evidence. In the House of Lords the Earl of Northesk adverted to the indiscriminate nature of certain categories of Internet data:

'The Internet is a packet-switching system which for technical reasons that are way beyond my understanding of the subject, means that it is only possible to tap anything by tapping everything. In effect the Bill as drafted is in breach of the data protection principles.'[1]

1   613 HL Official Report col 906, 25 May 2000.

Single points of contact

7.11 Under the present procedure (under DPA 1998), the public authorities listed in RIPA 2000 each have an accredited single point of contact (SPOC) through whom all requests are routed. This ensures that CSPs do not receive requests from many different individuals within the same organisation and that requests are of a consistent standard and only for data that the CSP can properly provide. Accreditation is achieved through participation on a training course developed jointly by the Association of Chief Police Officers (ACPO) and CSPs.

Other means of obtaining data?

7.12 Certain public authorities, such as the police, HMCE and the Legal Services Directorate of the DTI, may apply for a production order under PACE 1984, Sch 1 and use this procedure to obtain access to communications data.

In addition, specific powers of access are made available by:

- the Social Security Fraud Act 2001, s 1;
- the Charities Act 1993;
- the Criminal Justice Act 1987 (SFO);
- the Environmental Protection Act 1990;
- the Financial Services and Markets Act 2000; and
- the Health and Safety at Work Act 1974.

Who is responsible under RIPA 2000?

7.13   The purpose of RIPA 2000, Pt I, Ch II is to introduce a single statutory framework for the requisition of communications data.

Under RIPA 2000 the liability for taking proper account of the principles of necessity and proportionality is that of the public authority seeking access, rather than the CSP. Section 22(4) obliges the CSP to comply with the requirements of any notice. Such compliance is limited to that which it is reasonably practicable for him to do. Representatives of the industry have expressed considerable concern at the prospect of the procedure being used by criminals to access data for their own purposes. Draft Code 5.12 advises that the notice should contain contact details so that the veracity of the notice may be checked. It is submitted that a CSP would be entitled to refuse to act on a notice unless properly satisfied. Should a CSP disclose data on the basis of a notice without having taken sufficient care to verify its authenticity, it would itself be responsible to the data subject.

Who may apply to have access to such data under RIPA 2000?

7.14   RIPA 2000, s 25(1) lists the following public authorities:

- any police force;
- the National Criminal Intelligence Service (NCIS);
- the National Crime Squad (NCS);
- HMCE;
- the Security Service (M15);
- the Inland Revenue;
- the Secret Intelligence Service (M16); and
- GCHQ.

In addition, the following have been added by SI 2003/3172:

- the Financial Services Authority;
- the Scottish Crime Squad;
- the Atomic Energy Authority;
- the Department of Trade and Industry;
- the Police Ombudsman for Northern Ireland;

- a National Health Service Trust;
- the Welsh, Scottish and Northern Ireland Ambulance Service Trusts;
- the Department of Transport;
- any fire authority;
- a council constituted under the Local Government (Scotland) Act 1994, s 2; and
- a joint board under the Fire Services Act 1947, s 36 or Local Government (Scotland) Act 1973, s 147.

On what grounds may such data be obtained?

7.15   RIPA 2000, s 22(1) provides that if the person designated (see **para 7.18**) believes that it is necessary he may authorise any conduct to which Ch II applies.

It will only be necessary if the grounds fall within s 22(2), as follows:

'(a)   in the interests of national security;
(b)   for the purpose of preventing or detecting crime or of preventing disorder;
(c)   in the interests of the economic well-being of the United Kingdom;
(d)   in the interests of public safety;
(e)   for the purpose of protecting public health;
(f)   for the purpose of assessing or collecting any tax, duty, levy or other imposition, contribution, or charge payable to a government department;
(g)   for the purpose, in an emergency, of preventing death or injury or any damage to a person's physical or mental health; or
(h)   for any purpose (not falling within paragraphs (a) to (g)) which is specified for the purposes of this subsection by an order made by the Secretary of State.'

National security is not defined (see **para 4.9**).

By RIPA 2000, s 81(5) detecting crime shall be taken to include:
'(a)   establishing by whom, for what purpose, by what means and generally in what circumstances any crime was committed; and
(b)   the apprehension of the person by whom the crime was committed;

and any reference in this Act to preventing or detecting serious crime shall be construed accordingly, except that in Chapter I of Part I, it shall not include a reference to gathering evidence for use in any legal proceedings.'

It would seem to follow that in so far as RIPA 2000, Pt I Ch II is concerned, detecting crime includes gathering evidence for legal proceedings.

If the grounds do not fall within (a)–(d) or (g) above then only subscriber data may be obtained.[1]

---

1   SI 2003/3172.

Economic well-being

7.16 In the interests of the economic well-being of the UK imposes a lower test than the equivalent in RIPA 2000, s 5(3)(c).[1] Draft Code 4.2 states that the concept of economic well-being needs also to be related to the question of state security. It refers to Directive 97/66/EC (see **para 7.5**) where state security should be interpreted in the same way as national security, which is used elsewhere in RIPA 2000 (but not defined). A designated person will not grant an authorisation under RIPA 2000, s 22(2)(c) unless this link is established. Any application should state how, on the facts of the case, the economic well-being of the UK is related to state security.

Mr Clarke explained that clause 21(2)(f) (now RIPA 2000, s 22(2)(f)), relating to the collection of any tax, duty, levy or other imposition, reflected DPA 1998, s 9(4), which was used by agencies such as HMCE to investigate the shadow economy.

> 'An example of when such a provision is used is when flyers promising cheap cigarettes or tobacco and giving a telephone number to call are pushed through letter boxes. An investigation at that stage may very well not be a criminal investigation but merely to ascertain whether the supplier had a tax liability.'

In dealing with s 22(2)(h), the 'for any purpose' clause, he said:

> 'I should like to make two points. First, we are dealing with a new area of legislation and despite all the effort that my colleagues and others have put into the Bill we are not absolutely certain that the existing purposes cover every-thing that may be required. It is possible that the purposes will have to be extended in the future, especially if other Government Departments apply to be subject to those provisions rather than relying on the DPA. However I stress that the Government have absolutely no plans to do that at present. My second point should reassure anyone who believes that s-s (2) gives the Government a blank cheque. It does not since any new purpose would, of course, be limited by Art 8 of the ECHR: that imposes a serious restriction.'

Apart from s 22(2)(g) the grounds are the same as those for directed surveillance under RIPA 2000, s 28 and the use of CHIS under s 29.

1   Hansard HC vol 349 8.05.00 col 597 and 598.

Proportionality

7.17 RIPA 2000, s 22(5) provides that the person designated shall not grant an authorisation unless he believes that the conduct authorised is proportionate to what is sought to be achieved by obtaining the data. Draft Code 4.4 provides that:

> 'Proportionality is a crucial concept … This means that even if a particular case which interferes with a Convention right is aimed at pursuing a legitimate aim … this will not justify the interference if the means used to achieve the aim are excessive in the circumstances. Any interference with a Convention right should be carefully designed to meet the objective in question and must not be arbitrary or unfair.'

There is no express requirement in RIPA 2000, Pt I, Ch II or the Draft Code that other means of obtaining the information should have been tried and failed or by their nature be unlikely to succeed (compare Interception Code 2.5).

Who may be a designated person?

7.18   A designated person is one holding such office as is specified in an Order of the Secretary of State.[1]

According to Draft Code 3.2, the person authorising data under RIPA 2000, s 21(4)(a) or (b) should be of the rank of superintendent or equivalent and, if under s 21(4)(c), of inspector or equivalent.

1   RIPA 2000, s 25(2). See SI 2003/3172.

Contents of the application

7.19   The application form is subject to examination by the Commissioner and both the applicant and designated person may be required to justify their decisions.

Applications must be made on a standard form (paper or electronic), which must be retained by the public authority.

The contents of the application are set out in Draft Code 5.6, as follows:

- the name (or designation) of the officer requesting the communications data;
- the operation and person (if known) to which the requested data relates;
- a description, in as much detail as possible, of the communications data requested (there will also be a need to identify whether it is communications data under section 21(4)(a), (b) or (c) of RIPA 2000);
- the reason why obtaining the requested data is considered to be necessary;
- an explanation of why obtaining the data constitutes conduct proportionate to what it seeks to achieve, and where appropriate a consideration of issues of collateral intrusion; and
- the timescale within which the communications data is required. Where the timescale is any greater than routine, the reasoning for this must be included.

An application for an authorisation or a notice on RIPA 2000, s 22(2)(c) grounds should explain how the economic well-being of the UK is related to state security.

The fact of approval or denial, the identity of the officer approving or denying, and the date should be subsequently recorded on the application.[1]

1   Draft Code 5.7.

Who obtains the data?

7.20   In most cases the CSP will obtain the data. RIPA 2000, s 22(4) provides for service of a notice requiring the CSP:

(a)   if he is not in possession, to obtain the data; or

(b)   in any case, to disclose all of the data in his possession.

RIPA 2000, s 22(3) permits the designated person to grant an authorisation to a person in the same public authority to engage in any conduct to which Ch II applies. Draft Code 5.2 illustrates when a s 22(3) authorisation may be appropriate, e g:

● where the CSP is not capable of collecting or retrieving the data;

● where it is believed the investigation may be prejudiced if the CSP is asked to collect the data itself; or

● there is a prior agreement in place between the relevant public authority and the postal or telecommunications operator (CSP) as to the appropriate mechanisms for disclosure of data.

Draft Code 5.4 adopts the practice under the DPA 1998 of having a SPOC within each public authority in order to provide for an efficient regime, since the SPOC will deal with the CSP on a regular basis. It will also help the public authority to regulate itself. The Draft Code points out that the SPOC will be able to advise the designated person on whether an authorisation or a notice is appropriate (see **para 7.11**).

The form of the authorisation or notice

7.21   A RIPA 2000, s 22(3) authorisation must:

● be in writing, or if not in writing in a manner that produces a record of its having been produced;

● describe the conduct authorised and the communications data in relation to which it is authorised;

● specify why the proposed action is necessary; and

● specify the rank of the person granting the authorisation.

Draft Code 5.10 suggests that the authorisation should also include a unique reference number.

7.22   Where the procedure of notice under RIPA 2000, s 22(4) is adopted, the notice should include all the above matters and should, in addition, specify the manner in which any disclosure required by the notice is to be made.

The notice shall not require disclosure to any person other than the person giving the notice or such other person as is specified in the notice (who must be of the same rank as the person giving the notice[1]).

Draft Code 5.12 states that in addition to a unique reference number, the notice should also contain, where appropriate, an indication of any urgency, a statement that the data is sought under RIPA 2000, Ch II, ie an explanation that compliance is a legal requirement, and contact details so that the veracity of the notice may be checked.

This last detail is of critical importance in ensuring that data does not fall into the wrong hands, which could result in expensive litigation from the point of view of the CSP (see **para 7.13**).

In the debate in the House of Commons, Oliver Heald raised the concerns of those in the industry. He cited an email from Philip Virgo:

> 'Most of the City Institutions do not appear particularly concerned by the Human Rights issues. Their main concern is over the uncertainty as to who will have what rights of access to their data and communications and the risk of criminal access under guise of a warrant or via the law enforcement agencies themselves.'[2]

1   RIPA 2000, s 22(3)(b).
2   HC Official Report vol 349 col 593, 8 May 2000.

Subsequent disclosure

7.23   This matter was referred to by Harry Cohen in the House of Commons:

> 'If I am correct the authorisation process in Chapter II would be irrelevant to the protection of privacy because communications data could be volunteered to or demanded by other bodies at a later stage. An official could legitimately authorise collections of communications data and keep proper records only for them subsequently to be used for another purpose. If that is true, the relevant commissioner who examined the authorisation process, would not know of such disclosures, nor would the telecommunications operator or the public. To put it bluntly, the whole authorisation process and all the protection afforded by Chapter II could be reduced to a meaningless sham, because there would be no record of subsequent disclosures as part of the authorisation process.'[1]

In his response, Mr Clarke declined to accept the views of Philip Virgo as expressed by Oliver Heald. On the question of disclosure, the government took the view that the second of the data protection principles covered the situation:

> 'personal data shall be obtained only for one or more specified purposes and shall not be further processed in any manner incompatible with that purpose or those purposes.'[2]

He added that he perceived the merit of explaining the relevant data protection principles in the Draft Code.

A similar point was made in the House of Lords by the Earl of Northesk:

> 'The single biggest barrier to the development of e-commerce from consumers and traders alike revolves around confidence in and trust of the security of transactions online. This applies as much to protections from an over-mighty state as it does from criminal elements.'[3]

1   HC Official Report vol 349 col 595, 8 May 2000.
2   HC Official Report vol 349 col 598, 8 May 2000.
3   HL Official Report vol 613 col 904, 25 May 2000.

Urgent applications

7.24   Such applications may be approved orally where the circumstances fall within RIPA 2000, s 22(2)(g) (preventing death or injury). The fact of an oral application and approval must be recorded by the applicant and designated person as soon as possible.[1]

1   See Draft Code 5.14.

The duration of the notice or authorisation

7.25   RIPA 2000, s 23(4) provides that the duration is one month from the date on which the authorisation is granted or the notice given.

Renewal

7.26   RIPA 2000, s 23(5) provides for renewal of both authorisations under RIPA 2000, s 22(3) and notices under s 22(4) at any time before the end of the one month which shall be by grant or giving of a further authorisation or notice. There is no limit on the number of renewals.

Cancellation

7.27   RIPA 2000, s 23(8) requires a notice to be cancelled by the designated person if it is no longer necessary or if the conduct required by the notice is no longer proportionate.

Provision is made by s 23(9) for the Secretary of State to make regulations to provide for cancellation where the person who issued the notice is no longer available.

For reasons that are unclear, there is no equivalent provision for cancellation of an authorisation. Draft Code 6.6, however, suggests that as matter of good practice authorisations should be cancelled in accordance with the same procedure.

Retention of records

7.28

- Draft Code 7.1 provides that applications, authorisations and notices for communications data must be retained by the relevant public authority until it has been audited by the Commissioner. A record of the dates on which the authorisation or notice is given and cancelled should also be kept. Applications should be retained thereafter for the benefit of the Investigatory Powers tribunal.

- Draft Code 7.2 provides for records to be made of errors in the authorisation procedure, together with any report or explanation, which should be sent to the Commissioner as soon as possible.
- Draft Code 7.4 draws attention to the requirement under the Criminal Procedure and Investigations Act 1996 to retain material which might undermine the case for the prosecution.

Oversight

7.29 RIPA 2000, s 57(2)(b) provides for the Interception Commissioner to keep under review the exercise and performance of the powers and duties conferred or imposed under Ch II. Any person using the powers conferred by Ch II has a duty to comply with any request by the Commissioner to provide information (see Draft Code 8.1).

Section 65(5) provides for complaints concerning conduct under Ch II to be heard by the Tribunal (see **Chapter 10**).

Arrangements for payments

7.30 RIPA 2000, s 24 provides for payments to be made to the CSPs by the government as an appropriate contribution towards the costs of complying with RIPA 2000, s 22(4) notices. According to the Explanatory Memorandum accompanying the draft of SI 2003/3172,[1] agreements for cost recovery are currently in place that have been reached independently of the government.

1   September 2003.

Anti-terrorism, Crime and Security Act 2001 (ATCSA 2001), Pt 11

7.31 Part 11 of ATCSA 2001 allows for the introduction of a voluntary scheme of data retention. Under the scheme CSPs may elect to retain data for extended periods of time, for the purpose of safeguarding national security or the detection of crime or prosecution of offenders, which may relate directly or indirectly to national security. Under ATCSA 2001 s 104 if the voluntary scheme has not worked the Secretary of State can require CSPs to retain data for extended periods.

Part 11 came into force on 14 December 2001. As noted in **para 7.2** the Voluntary Code issued under s 102(1) of ATCSA 2001 came into force on 5 December 2003 (SI 2003/3175). In the foreword to the Voluntary Code, the government state that the object is not to enlarge the fields of data which CSPs may or must retain, but to encourage them to retain data for longer than they would otherwise need to do for their own commercial purposes.

Voluntary Code 9 states that:

'As indicated, the Secretary of State considers the retention of data in accordance with Appendix A to be necessary for the purpose of national security and accordingly retention for those periods should comply with the fifth data protection principle. However, because the purpose of retention is to safeguard national security were it to be suggested that retention in accordance with this Code did not comply with the fifth principle, the national security exemption in s 28 of the Data Protection Act 1998 could be relied on to exempt such data from the fifth principle so enabling it to be retained in accordance with the Code. If necessary the Secretary of State would issue a certificate under s 28(2) confirming the same.'

Voluntary Code App A provides for differing periods depending on the nature of the data. Subscriber details, contact information and the identity of services subscribed to may be retained for 12 months from the end of subscription/last change. Other data, such as email data, may only be retained for six months.

Do the data subject access provisions apply?

7.32   Voluntary Code 10 states that the access provisions (see **Chapter 3**) continue to apply. Somewhat surprisingly, it adds that:

'subscribers should be notified where their personal data will be retained for the purpose of the Act, as well as for the CSP's business purposes, and that it may be disclosed to relevant public authorities as set out in paragraph 27 of the Code. Every effort should be made to ensure that this is brought to the attention of the subscriber, for example this could be added to billing information or sent by way of a text message or email.'

The Code advises that CSPs should notify the Information Commissioner that they are processing for the following purpose:

'National Security. Retention of communications data for the purpose of safeguarding national security or for the purposes of prevention or detection of crime or the prosecution of offenders which may relate directly or indirectly to national security.'

Chapter 8

Covert surveillance

Introduction

8.1

'Powers of secret surveillance of citizens, characterising as they did the police state, were tolerable under the Convention only so far as strictly necessary for safeguarding democratic institutions.'[1]

RIPA 2000, Pt II, which came into force on 25 September 2000, concerns three types of activity:

(1)   directed surveillance;
(2)   intrusive surveillance; and
(3)   the use of covert human intelligence sources (CHIS).

Each has its own procedure for authorisations dependent not only on the nature of the surveillance but on who is making the application, all of which are different from the regime under the Police Act 1997, Pt III. According to para 2.4 of the Report of the Chief Surveillance Commissioner for 2000–01, there are approximately 950 public authorities entitled to carry out covert surveillance under RIPA 2000 (see **para 8.12**). Commissioners who may have to scrutinise applications for authorisation for intrusive surveillance at the same time as applications for a property warrant under the Police Act 1997, Pt III will have to take account of different criteria (see below).

Unlike RIPA 2000, Pt I, Pt II creates no offence of unauthorised surveillance. The purpose of authorisation is to legitimise activities that would otherwise be unlawful under HRA 1998, s 6.

1   *Klass v Germany* (1978) 2 EHRR 214.

The codes

8.2   Two relevant codes have been issued pursuant to RIPA 2000, s 71, namely the Covert Surveillance Code (Surveillance Code) and the Covert Human Intelligence

Sources Code (CHIS Code). The codes did not come into effect until 1 August 2002, some 674 days after RIPA 2000 came into force, a delay that caused the Chief Surveillance Commissioner to air his misgivings.[1] RIPA 2000, s 72(1) provides that a person exercising or performing any power or duty under, inter alia, Pt II shall have regard to the provisions of every code of practice in force under s 71. Such a code shall be admissible in evidence in any criminal or civil proceedings. The Surveillance Code provides guidance on both directed and intrusive surveillance as well as the 'bugging and burglary' powers of the Intelligence Services Act 1994 (ISA 1994), s 5 and the Police Act 1997, Pt III. The code replaces that issued in 1999 pursuant to s 101(3) of the Police Act 1997. The CHIS Code provides guidance to the police, the Intelligence Services and any other public authority entitled to use CHIS. CHIS Code 1.3 points out that a member of the public who volunteers information to the police would not generally be regarded as a source.

1   See para 14.3 of the 2000–01 Report and again at para 9.2 of the 2001–02 Report (see **para 1.8**).

What is surveillance?

8.3   In order to understand where RIPA 2000, Pt I ends and Pt II begins, it may be helpful to turn to the definition section at the end of Pt II to see what Pt II means by 'surveillance'.

RIPA 2000, s 48(2) states that, subject to s 48(3), surveillance includes:

'(a)   monitoring, observing or listening to persons, their movements, their conversations or their other activities or communications;

(b)   recording anything monitored, observed or listened to in the course of surveillance; and

(c)   surveillance by or with the assistance of a surveillance device'.

Subject to s 48(3) and (4) (see **para 8.4**), all forms of covert surveillance which do not involve 'bugging and burglary' now fall to be considered under the provisions of Pt II.

Section 48(4) provides that an interception that takes place with the consent of the sender or recipient and where there is no warrant amounts to surveillance for the purposes of Pt II. RIPA 2000, s 26(4)(b) makes it clear that such surveillance is not intrusive surveillance. RIPA 2000, s 3(2) specifically includes such interception as being lawful in the absence of a warrant. The corollary is that warranted intercepts and other forms of lawful interception do not amount to surveillance.

What is not surveillance?

8.4   General observation duties would not normally amount to surveillance. An example is given in Surveillance Code 1.3 where HMCE or trading standards officers covertly observe and then visit a shop as part of their enforcement duties. Such activities would neither be intrusive or directed surveillance. Specific exception is also made by RIPA 2000, s 48(3), which provides that the following activities which would normally be described as surveillance do not amount to surveillance for the purposes of Pt II:

'(a)   any conduct of a covert human intelligence source for obtaining or recording (whether or not using a surveillance device) any information which is disclosed in the presence of the source;

(b)   the use of a covert human intelligence source for so obtaining or recording information; or

(c)   any such entry on or interference with property or wireless telegraphy as would be unlawful unless authorised under–

(i) section 5 Intelligence Services Act 1994 (warrants for the intelligence services) or

(ii) Part III Police Act 1997 (powers of the police and customs officers).'

The purpose of s 48(3)(a) and (b) is to prevent any such conduct being treated as either directed or intrusive surveillance and therefore requires authorisation as a CHIS.

Covert surveillance

8.5   A central feature of each type of activity is that it is covert, as defined by RIPA 2000, s 26(9):

'(a)   surveillance is covert if, and only if, it is carried out in a manner that is calculated to ensure that persons who are subject to the surveillance are unaware that it is or may be taking place;

(b)   a purpose is covert, in relation to the establishment or maintenance of a personal relationship, if and only if the relationship is conducted in a manner that is calculated to ensure that one of the parties to the relationship is unaware of the purpose; and

(c)   a relationship is used covertly and information obtained as mentioned in subsection (8)(c) is disclosed covertly, if and only if it is used or, as the case may be, disclosed in a manner that is calculated to ensure that one of the parties to the relationship is unaware of the use or disclosure in question.'

RIPA 2000, s 26(8)(c) refers to the definition of a CHIS. The combination of s 26(8)(c) and (9)(c) has been identified as creating a significant evidential problem (see **para 8.16**).

What is directed surveillance?

8.6   Directed surveillance is:

(a)   covert;

(b)   non-intrusive;

(c)   carried out for the purposes of a specific investigation or operation; and

(d)   undertaken in such a manner as is likely to result in the obtaining of private information about a person (whether or not one specifically identified for the purposes of the investigation or operation).[1]

It is not restricted to an intention to gain private information. An authorisation is required whenever there is a real possibility that the proposed surveillance is likely to result in the obtaining of private information about any person. Private information includes any information relating to a person's private or family life (s 26(10)).

Specific exception is made by RIPA 2000, s 26(2)(c) to surveillance which is an immediate response to events or circumstances, the nature of which is such that it would not be reasonably practicable to seek authorisation.

An example is given in Surveillance Code 4.4 of a police officer who would not need authorisation to conceal himself and observe a suspicious person that he came across in the course of a patrol.

1   RIPA 2000, s 26(2).

8.7   Although the Chief Surveillance Commissioner is not obliged to specify the number of non-intrusive authorisations in any given year, he was able to provide figures for directed surveillance for 2001–02 in respect of NCIS, NCS, the Scottish Drugs Enforcement Agency (SDEA), HMCE and UK police forces. The total for that year was 27,800, of which 4,800 were current at the end of the year. In the following year, the figures were 26,400, of which 4,300 were current at the end of the year. No figures are available for the other public authorities who carry out directed surveillance.

What is intrusive surveillance?

8.8   To be intrusive the surveillance must:

(a)   be covert;
(b)   be carried out in relation to anything taking place on residential premises or in a private vehicle (see **paras 8.10** and **8.11**);
(c)   involve the presence of an individual on the premises or in the vehicle; or
(d)   be carried out by means of a surveillance device.[1]

If the device is not on the premises or in the vehicle, the surveillance is to be considered non-intrusive unless it consistently provides information of the same quality and detail as might be expected to be obtained from a device actually present on the premises or in the vehicle.[2]

The use of the word 'same' rather than 'similar' is likely to exclude all but the most sophisticated equipment with the result that surveillance of unoccupied residential premises will usually fall to be authorised as directed rather than intrusive surveillance.

The use of such devices is commonplace in surveillance activity and likely to raise difficult if not impossible questions which have to be answered before the giving of the authorisation as to what quality or detail might normally be expected to be obtained from the device in question. When tested in the cauldron of the ECt HR, it is difficult to see how such an imprecise provision could satisfy the quality of law test in art 8 (see **para 2.55**).

1   RIPA 2000, s 26(3).
2   RIPA 2000, s 26(5).

Two exceptions to intrusive surveillance

8.9   Two exceptions to what might otherwise fall within the description of intrusive surveillance are provided by RIPA 2000, s 26(4), where:

(1)   the surveillance is carried out by means only of a device designed or adapted principally for the purpose of providing information about the location of a vehicle (a tracking device); or

(2)   the surveillance consists of the interception of communications where there is no interception warrant and where the communication is sent or intended for a person who has consented to the interception.[1]

Such conduct is treated as directed surveillance.

1   RIPA 2000, s 26(4)(b).

Meaning of residential premises

8.10   Residential premises are defined in RIPA 2000, s 48(1) as any premises as are, for the time being, occupied or used by any person, however temporarily, for residential purposes or otherwise as living accommodation (including hotel or prison accommodation that is so occupied or used). Section 48(7)(b) excludes:

> 'so much of any premises as constitutes any common area to which he has or is allowed access in connection with his use or occupation of any accommodation.'

Police cells are not referred to but Surveillance Code 5.4 suggests that the bugging of a police cell is intrusive. Where the observations include residential premises or private vehicles there will be little difficulty in classifying the operation as intrusive. On the other hand, surveillance involving such activities as using a covert camera in a hedgerow focused on an open field or recording conversations in office premises or business vehicles will not be intrusive. These were two examples given by the Chief Surveillance Commissioner in his 2000–01 Report.

The exclusion of office premises from the concept of intrusive surveillance appears to be ignoring the approach of the ECt HR in such cases as *Niemietz v Germany*[1] (see **Chapter 2**) and contradicts the basis of Police Act 1997, Pt III authorisations, which require prior authorisation.[2]

1   (1992) 16 EHRR 97.
2   See Police Act 1997, s 97(2)(a)(ii) and Surveillance Code 6.30. Note that para 4.8 of that code recognises that covert surveillance of office premises does amount to directed surveillance.

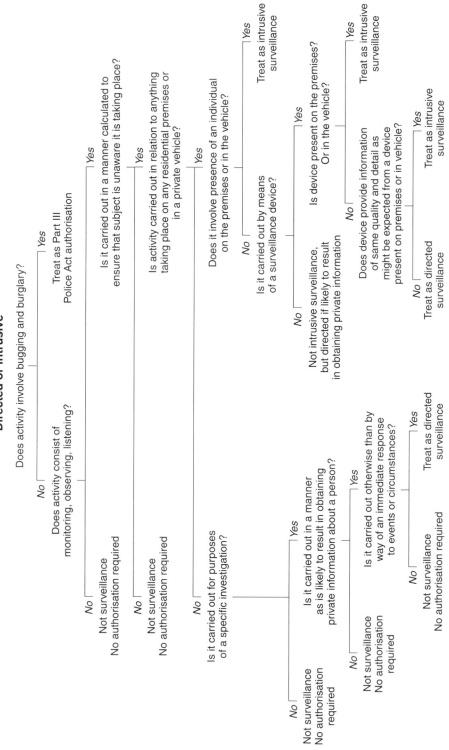

Directed or Intrusive

Does activity involve bugging and burglary?

- No → Does activity consist of monitoring, observing, listening?
- Yes → Treat as Part III Police Act authorisation

Does activity consist of monitoring, observing, listening?

- No → Not surveillance No authorisation required
- Yes → Is it carried out in a manner calculated to ensure that subject is unaware it is taking place?

Is it carried out in a manner calculated to ensure that subject is unaware it is taking place?

- No → Not surveillance No authorisation required
- Yes → Is activity carried out in relation to anything taking place on any residential premises or in a private vehicle?

Is activity carried out in relation to anything taking place on any residential premises or in a private vehicle?

- No → Is it carried out for purposes of a specific investigation?
- Yes → Does it involve presence of an individual on the premises or in the vehicle?

Is it carried out for purposes of a specific investigation?

- No → Not surveillance No authorisation required
- Yes → Is it carried out in a manner as is likely to result in obtaining private information about a person?

Is it carried out in a manner as is likely to result in obtaining private information about a person?

- No → Not surveillance No authorisation required
- Yes → Is it carried out otherwise than by way of an immediate response to events or circumstances?

Is it carried out otherwise than by way of an immediate response to events or circumstances?

- No → Not surveillance No authorisation required
- Yes → Treat as directed surveillance

Does it involve presence of an individual on the premises or in the vehicle?

- No → Is it carried out by means of a surveillance device?
- Yes → Treat as intrusive surveillance

Is it carried out by means of a surveillance device?

- No → Not intrusive surveillance, but directed if likely to result in obtaining private information
- Yes → Is device present on the premises? Or in the vehicle?

Is device present on the premises? Or in the vehicle?

- No → Does device provide information of same quality and detail as might be expected from a device present on premises or in vehicle?
- Yes → Treat as intrusive surveillance

Does device provide information of same quality and detail as might be expected from a device present on premises or in vehicle?

- No → Treat as directed surveillance
- Yes → Treat as intrusive surveillance

Meaning of private vehicle

8.11 A private vehicle is defined in RIPA 2000, s 48(1) as any vehicle which is used primarily for the purposes of the person who owns it or has the right to use it. The section makes it clear that a vehicle is not to be considered private if the right to use it depends on payment for a particular journey.[1] Whereas a taxi would not fall within the description of a private vehicle, a hire car might well.

1   RIPA 2000, s 48(7) and Surveillance Code 5.5.

Who is protected?

8.12 The categories of bodies whose use of directed surveillance techniques or CHIS are covered by RIPA 2000 are extremely wide. There are 23 such categories.[1] According to the Chief Surveillance Commissioner, the total number of such authorities exceeds 950. It includes not only the police, NCIS, NCS, the Serious Fraud Office, the Intelligence Services, the armed forces, HMCE and the DSS, but also the Departments of Health and Trade and Industry, the Environment Agency, the Inland Revenue, the Financial Services Authority, the Personal Investment Authority, the Food Standards Agency, the Board for Agricultural Produce, the Post Office, all local authorities, the Department for Environment, Food and Rural Affairs and the BBC. In addition, health authorities and NHS Trusts can authorise directed surveillance but not the use of CHIS. In the Report of the Chief Surveillance Commissioner for 2001–02, the total number of authorities is explained. It includes 52 police forces, a total of 409 local authorities and 466 NHS Trusts or Health Authorities. In addition, there are 85 authorities in Scotland who are entitled to use covert surveillance in Scotland. Newspapers that indulge in snooping activities are not covered by RIPA 2000, Sch 1.

In para 8.14.11 of the same report the Chief Commissioner also referred to the fact that by virtue of the definition of local authority in the Local Government Act 1999, s 1(2), a local authority meant:

> 'A county council, a district council, a London Borough Council, a parish Council or a meeting of a parish which does not have a separate parish council.'

He went on to comment that he had not identified any parish council that had required to use directed surveillance or CHIS and recommended that parish councils be removed from RIPA 2000, Sch 1. SI 2003/3171, which has replaced the previous SI 2000/2417, has taken note of his concerns as well as adding a further seven authorities to Sch 1.

1   See RIPA 2000, Sch 1.

8.13 RIPA 2000, Sch 1 does not refer to intrusive surveillance as covered by RIPA 2000, s 32 but it is clear from s 32(6) that the only bodies entitled to use intrusive techniques are the police, police forces associated with the three armed services, the British Transport Police, NCIS, NCS and HMCE. The authorities entitled to use these powers are the same as those entitled to 'bug and burgle' under the amended Police Act 1997, Pt II. The Intelligence Services are not mentioned in s 32(6).

However, s 42(3) makes it clear that the Secretary of State may authorise intrusive surveillance on application by the Intelligence Services or GCHQ but only if the authorisation relates to the interests of national security or the economic well-being of the UK, but not for the prevention or detection of serious crime. The Serious Fraud Office has no power to use intrusive surveillance.

Criteria for authorisation of directed surveillance

8.14   RIPA 2000, s 28(2) provides that an authorisation shall not be granted unless the authorising officer believes it is both necessary and proportionate. What may be considered necessary is very wide, eg the interests of national security, the prevention or detection of crime or disorder, the interests of public safety, the protection of public health, the assessment and collection of tax, etc, or any other purpose which the Secretary of State may order.[1] The latter two categories are potentially controversial as they are not covered by art 8(2).

There is no further definition of proportionate. In particular, there is no requirement in RIPA 2000, s 28 to consider whether the information could be obtained by other means.[2] Surveillance Code 2.5, however, does state that the activity will not be proportionate if the information could reasonably be obtained by other, less intrusive, means.

1   RIPA 2000, s 28(3)(g).
2   cf RIPA 2000, s 32.

Criteria for authorisation of intrusive surveillance

8.15   RIPA 2000, s 32(2) provides that no authorisation shall be granted unless the authorising officer believes that it is both necessary and proportionate.

What is necessary is restricted to the interests of national security, the prevention or detection of serious crime or the interests of the economic well-being of the UK.[1] Even this is wider than the equivalent provisions under the Police Act 1997, s 93(2) which does not encompass national security or economic well-being. The grounds are the same as those for an interception warrant under RIPA 2000, s 5(3), although that section refers to 'safeguarding the economic well-being of the United Kingdom'. It might perhaps be argued that the latter is a slightly higher test than the former. Serious crime is defined by RIPA 2000, s 81(3) in terms identical to the Police Act 1997. National security and economic well-being are explained but not defined in **Chapter 4** (see **paras 4.9–4.12**).

In considering whether intrusive surveillance is proportionate, matters to be taken into account shall include whether the information could reasonably be obtained by other means.[2]

1   RIPA 2000, s 32(3).
2   RIPA 2000, s 32(4).

What is a CHIS?

8.16   Under RIPA 2000, s 26(8) a person is a CHIS if:

'(a)   he establishes or maintains a personal or other relationship with a person for the covert purpose of facilitating the doing of anything within paragraph (b) or (c);

(b)   he covertly uses such a relationship to obtain information or to provide access to any information to another person; or

(c)   he covertly discloses information obtained by the use of such a relationship or as a consequence of the existence of such a relationship.'

For the definition of covert see **para 8.5**.

It is pointed out in *Archbold News*[1] that the combination of the definition in s 26(8)(c) and (9)(c) has created a significant evidential problem, since the disclosure of the information obtained by a CHIS in the course of a trial would breach the basis of the authorisation.

1   Simon McKay, *Archbold News*, Issue 2, 8 March 2004.

8.17   No attempt is made by RIPA 2000 to delimit the extent of the activities of the CHIS. In particular, it fails to deal adequately (or at all) with the conduct of participating informants, defined by the 1999 ACPO Code of Practice (ACPO Code) as persons 'engaged in a course of action which without authority could lead or could have led to his/her arrest and prosecution'.

CHIS Code 2.10 recognises the problem but states somewhat blandly:

'In a very limited range of circumstances an authorisation under Part II may, by virtue of sections 26(7) and 27 of the 2000 Act render lawful conduct which would otherwise be criminal, if it is incidental to any conduct falling within section 26(8) of the 2000 Act which the source is authorised to undertake. This would depend on the circumstances of each individual case and consideration should always be given to seeking advice from the legal adviser within the relevant public authority when such activity is contemplated. A source that acts beyond the limits recognised by the law will be at risk from prosecution. The need to protect the source cannot alter this principle'.

Tasking

8.18   Tasking is the assignment given to the source. It should cover in broad terms the nature of the source's task. Authorisation for the use or conduct of a source is required prior to any tasking where such tasking requires the source to establish or maintain a personal or other relationship.[1] Where the source is tasked merely to find out purely factual information, such as the layout of commercial premises, an authorisation may not be required. It is for the authority to determine if authorisation is required.[2] Where the source meets the subject of an investigation and unforeseen events take place, a record should be made as soon as practicable. If the existing authorisation is insufficient it should either be updated or a new authorisation be obtained.[3] Where it is intended to task the source in a new way, consideration should be given to referring the proposed tasking to the authorising officer.[4]

1   CHIS Code 4.26.
2   CHIS Code 4.29.
3   CHIS Code 4.31.
4   CHIS Code 4.32.

Criteria for authorisation of a CHIS

8.19   In *Teixeira de Castro v Portugal*,[1] the ECt HR made it clear that the use of undercover officers must be restricted and safeguards put in place even in cases concerning the fight against drug trafficking.

RIPA 2000, s 29(2)(b) provides that no authorisation shall be granted unless the authorising officer believes that it is both necessary and proportionate.

Section 29(3) defines what is necessary in identical terms to s 28(3) (see **para 8.14**). It need not be serious crime but can be any form of crime, however trivial.

Although, as with RIPA 2000, s 28, there is no further definition of what might be proportionate, CHIS Code 2.5 provides that the use of a source will not be proportionate if it is excessive in the circumstances of the case or if the information which is sought could reasonably be obtained by other means.

Finally, the authorising officer must believe that arrangements exist that satisfy the requirements of s 29(5) as to the security and welfare of the source (see **para 8.21**).

1   (1998) 28 EHRR 101.

8.20   It is submitted that the aspect of proportionality is central to the attempt by Parliament to restrict the use of undercover officers as required by *Teixeira de Castro* (see **para 8.19**) and should not be watered down or interpreted as placing a lighter burden on those public authorities seeking to use such powers than was the case under the previous ACPO Code issued to all UK police authorities and HMCE (see **para 11.44**). In *R v Looseley*[1] Lord Hoffman noted that under that Code, undercover officers would be used only in connection with national security or serious crime and that the authorising officer must be satisfied that the desired result could not be reasonably achieved by other means.[2] It is ironic that a statute that was said by the Home Secretary to represent a 'significant step forward for the protection of human rights in this country' has had the effect of greatly increasing the potential for the use of CHIS without at the same time introducing any compensatory safeguards such as prior approval by a Commissioner (see **para 8.30**). It is submitted that the failure to take heed of the warnings in *Teixeira de Castro* is likely to result in a successful challenge to the ECt HR.

1   [2002] 1 Cr App Rep 360.
2   [2002] 1 Cr App Rep 360 at para 64.

Records relating to the source

8.21 RIPA 2000, s 29(2)(c) provides that one of the conditions for the deployment of a CHIS is that there are in existence arrangements for the source's welfare (see **para 8.19**). Section 29(5)(b) provides that a specific person within the authority should have general oversight of the use made of the source and either that person or another person should be responsible for maintaining a record of the use made of the source. The Regulation of Investigatory Powers (Source Records) Regulations 2000, SI 2000/2725, states that the records should include the following:

(a) the identity of the source;

(b) the identity, where known, used by the source;

(c) any relevant investigating authority other than the authority maintaining the records;

(d) the means by which the source is referred to within each relevant investigating authority;

(e) any other significant information connected with the security and welfare of the source;

(f) any confirmation made by a person granting or renewing an authorisation for the conduct or use of a source that the information referred to in paragraph (d) has been considered and that any identified risks to the security and welfare of the source have, where appropriate, been properly explained to and understood by the source;

(g) the date when, and the circumstances in which, the source was recruited;

(h) the identities of the persons who, in relation to the source, are discharging or have discharged the functions mentioned in RIPA 2000, s 29(5)(a)–(c) or in any order made by the Secretary of State under s 29(2)(c);

(i) the periods during which those persons have discharged those responsibilities;

(j) the tasks given to the source and the demands made of him in relation to his activities as a source;

(k) all contacts or communications between the source and a person acting on behalf of any relevant investigating authority;

(l) the information obtained by each relevant investigating authority by the conduct or use of the source;

(m) any dissemination by that authority of information obtained in that way; and

(n) in the case of a source who is not an undercover operative, every payment, benefit or reward and every offer of payment, benefit or reward that is made or provided by or on behalf of any relevant investigating authority in respect of the source's activities for the benefit of that or any other relevant investigating authority.

Juvenile sources

8.22 The Regulation of Investigatory Powers (Juveniles) Order 2000, SI 2000/2793, which came into force on 6 November 2000, prohibits the use of sources under the age of 16 to provide information about the relationship between the source and his parent or guardian. In other circumstances, the use of sources under 16 is dependent on there being an appropriate adult present at any meeting with any relevant investigating authority. Restrictions are also imposed on the use of any source under the age of 18. In particular, a person in the investigating authority must make a risk assessment in order to assess the nature and magnitude of any risk of physical injury or psychological distress involved in the proposed course of action, and the person granting the authorisation must be satisfied that the risks are justified and that the source understands the risk and that he has given consideration to the particular relationship, if any, between the source and the target of the authorisation.

The relevance of reasonable suspicion

8.23   None of the powers discussed above require that the target of the surveillance be reasonably suspected of having committed an offence. All that is required is that the conduct falls within the description of being both necessary and proportionate. The fact that the powers may be used for the purposes of the prevention of crime underlines that no crime needs to have been committed. As will be seen below, the codes specify that the application for authorisation requires details of the target only where one is known.[1] Such potential vagueness could have the effect of permitting generalised trawling expeditions unless a rigorous approach is adopted to the issue of proportionality. Where the invasion of privacy is likely to be greatest, eg where one or more CHIS are involved, it is submitted that the test of proportionality is unlikely to be satisfied unless the public authority reasonably suspects the target to have committed, or be about to commit, the offence in question. In *Teixeira de Castro v Portugal*[2] the lack of any reasonable suspicion on behalf of the competent authorities was a critical factor in the conclusion of the ECt HR that the actions of the officers went beyond those of undercover officers.

In *R v Looseley*,[3] although it was pointed out that having grounds for suspicion of a particular individual is not always essential, the circumstances when the use of undercover officers would be appropriate in the absence of such reasonable suspicion are limited. Lord Nicholls stated:

> 'Sometimes suspicion may be centred on a particular place, such as a public house.'[4]

Lord Hoffman gave the example of a decoy (human or inanimate) being used in the course of the detection of crime that has been prevalent in a particular place[5] (see also *Williams v DPP*[6]).

1   See **paras 8.25–8.27**.
2   (1998) 28 EHRR 101.
3   [2002] 1 Cr App Rep 360.
4   [2002] 1 Cr App Rep 360 at para 27.
5   [2002] 1 Cr App Rep 360 at para 65.
6   (1993) 98 Cr App Rep 209.

Collateral intrusion

8.24   Although the concept is not specifically referred to in RIPA 2000, Surveillance Code 2.6 enjoins the authorising officer to take into account the risk of intrusion into the privacy of persons other than those directly the subject of the investigation. An application for authorisation should include an assessment of the risk of such intrusion. Surveillance Code 2.9 refers to the need to be aware of the local sensitivities in the community and of similar activities being taken by other authorities such as NCIS, NCS or HMCE.

Authorisation: procedural requirements

8.25   Under RIPA 2000, s 30 directed surveillance and the use of CHIS can be self-authorised. The Regulation of Investigatory Powers (Prescription of Offices, Ranks and Positions) Order 2003, SI 2003/3171, sets out the prescribed offices in relation to each of the public authorities entitled to use the powers. This means, for example, that in the case of the police, NCIS or NCS, authorisation is by a superintendent, and in the case of HMCE, an officer of band 9 level. If the authorisation is combined with an authorisation by the Secretary of State for the carrying out of intrusive surveillance, the Secretary of State is also entitled to grant authorisation for directed surveillance or the use of a CHIS.[1] The Secretary of State cannot authorise directed surveillance or the use of a CHIS on its own. It is submitted that the process of self-authorisation of such highly intrusive activities as those of a CHIS is liable to violate art 6. In *Teixeira de Castro v Portugal*,[2] a critical factor in finding that there had been an unfair trial was that, unlike the case of *Ludi v Switzerland*,[3] the undercover officers were not taking part in an operation ordered and supervised by a judge.

1   RIPA 2000, s 30(2).
2   (1998) 28 EHRR 101.
3   (1992) 15 EHRR 173.

8.26   Where the surveillance is intrusive, the authorisation can only be given by the senior authorising officer, such as the chief constable of every police force, the Commissioner of the Metropolitan Police, the respective Provost Marshals of the armed services police or the designated HMCE officer.[1] In cases of urgency provision is made for authorisations to be considered by the designated deputy of a senior authorising officer,[2] or by the person entitled to act for any senior authorising officer[3] (see **para 8.36**). Any such authorisation is ineffective until approved by a Commissioner (see **para 8.30**).

For a definition of 'urgent' see Surveillance Code 5.13 (**para 8.36**).

1   RIPA 2000, s 32(6).
2   RIPA 2000, s 34(6).
3   RIPA 2000, s 34(4).

Information to be included in the application for directed surveillance

8.27   Surveillance Code 4.16 sets out what information is required in applications for authorisation for directed surveillance, e g the nature of the surveillance and why it is necessary and proportionate, the identities, where known, of those to be subject to surveillance, what information it is desired to obtain, details of collateral intrusion, details of any confidential information likely to be obtained, the level of authority required and a subsequent record of whether authorisation is granted and if so when and by whom.

Information to be included in the application for CHIS

8.28 CHIS Code 4.14 sets out the information required, which is similar to the above. In addition, the application should state the purpose for which the source will be tasked or deployed (eg in relation to organised serious crime, espionage, a series of racially motivated crimes, etc), where a specific investigation is involved, the nature of that operation, and the nature of what the source will be tasked to do. The examples of organised serious crime or espionage given in the CHIS Code is at odds with RIPA 2000, which entitles a relevant public authority to use a CHIS to investigate any criminal offence, however trivial.

Information to be included in the application for intrusive surveillance

8.29 Surveillance Code 5.16 provides that applications for intrusive surveillance should specify:

'•   the reasons why the authorisation is necessary in the particular case and on the grounds (eg for the purpose of preventing or detecting serious crime) listed in section 32(3) of the 2000 Act;
•   the reasons why the surveillance is considered proportionate to what it seeks to achieve;
•   the nature of the surveillance;
•   the residential premises or private vehicle in relation to which the surveillance will take place;
•   the identities, where known, of those to be the subject of the surveillance;
•   an explanation of the information which it is desired to obtain as a result of the surveillance;
•   details of any potential collateral intrusion and why the intrusion is justified;
•   details of any confidential information that is likely to be obtained as a consequence of the surveillance.
•   A subsequent record should be made of whether authority was given or refused, by whom and the time and date.'

In addition, in urgent cases the authorisation should record why the case was urgent and why it could not be considered by the senior authorising officer or the designated deputy.

When is prior approval of a Commissioner required?

8.30   Where the surveillance is intrusive the system of authorisation requires an element of independence and checks that is similar to that of the Police Act 1997, ie prior approval by a Commissioner. RIPA 2000, s 36(2) provides that, unless the case is one of urgency,[1] the authorisation shall not take effect until it has been approved by a Commissioner and written notice of the approval has been received by the person who granted the authorisation.[2]

Section 36(4) provides that the Commissioner shall only give his approval if satisfied that there are reasonable grounds for believing that the authorisation is both necessary and proportionate (not a judicial review test). He should consider whether the information that is sought could reasonably be obtained by other means.

Where the person granting the authorisation believes the case is urgent and gives notice to the Surveillance Commissioner under RIPA 2000, s 35(3)(b), the authorisation shall have effect from the time of its grant.

1   See RIPA 2000, s 36(3).
2   See Surveillance Code 5.19.

8.31   According to the 2000–01 Report of the Surveillance Commissioner, in the six months of that year during which RIPA 2000, Pt II was in force 285 authorisations for intrusive surveillance were submitted for prior approval. In only one case was approval declined. This was a case where the authorised surveillance had started before the authorisation was notified to the Commissioner.

In 2001–02, there were 493 authorisations of intrusive surveillance, one of which was quashed by a Commissioner, and in 2002–03 there were 475 such authorisations, one of which was quashed by a Commissioner (see table at **para 1.44**).

Participant monitoring

8.32   The activities of undercover officers who are wired in such a way as to record conversations with members of the public who may or may not be suspected of committing criminal offences have the potential to be highly intrusive. RIPA 2000, s 26(4)(b) provides, however, that surveillance consisting of the interception of a communication as falls within RIPA 2000, s 48(4) is not intrusive. Section 48(4) provides that an interception which is consented to by either the sender or the recipient where no warrant is in existence amounts to surveillance. As the undercover officer in the above example consents to the interception, it follows that such activity amounts neither to interception under RIPA 2000, Pt I nor intrusive surveillance under Pt II. According to CHIS Code 4.40, such interception is to be treated as directed surveillance. CHIS Code 4.41 asserts that a source, whether or not wearing a surveillance device and invited into residential premises or a private vehicle, does not require additional authorisation to record any activity taking place therein in his presence. If a surveillance device is to be used other than in the presence of the source an intrusive surveillance authorisation or an authorisation for a property warrant should be obtained.[1]

1   CHIS Code 4.42.

8.33 Such activities have been the subject of consideration both in Canada and by the ECt HR. In Canada, a leading case is *R v Duarte*,[1] in which an informant had been wired up to record conversations between himself and the suspect. The Canadian Code required a warrant for the use of electronic surveillance devices generally, but none was needed for a consent operation. As a preliminary matter, the court concluded that a person's privacy is intruded on in an unreasonable manner whenever the state, without prior showing of reasonable cause before a neutral judicial officer, arrogates to itself the right to record surreptitiously communications that the originator expects will not be intercepted by anyone other than the intended recipient. Having observed that the Canadian Code placed no restriction on participant surveillance, La Forest J stated:

> 'I am unable to see any logic to this distinction between third party electronic surveillance and participant surveillance. The question whether unauthorised electronic surveillance of private communications violates a reasonable expectation of privacy cannot, in my view, turn on the location of the hidden microphone. Whether the microphone is hidden in the wall or concealed on the body of a participant to the conversation, the assessment whether the surreptitious recording trenches on a reasonable expectation of privacy must turn on whether the person whose words were recorded spoke in circumstances in which it was reasonable for that person to expect that his or her words would only be heard by the person he or she was addressing.'[2]

The reasonable expectation of privacy was also at the heart of the judgment of the ECt HR in *Lambert v France*[3] (see **Chapter 2**).

It is submitted that such a highly intrusive form of surveillance should fall within the protection of the intrusive surveillance regime and that the lack of adequate safeguards in the present system is likely to breach art 8.

1   (1990) 53 CCC 3(d) 1.
2   1990) 53 CCC at p 13.
3   (1998) 30 EHRR 346.

Confidential information

8.34 Unlike PACE 1984 and the Police Act 1997, Pt III, RIPA 2000 provides no special protection for confidential information, including matters subject to legal privilege. The subject is, however, dealt with in detail in the respective codes. Both the Surveillance Code and CHIS Code 3.1 recognise that particular care should be taken in circumstances where the target might reasonably expect a high degree of privacy or where confidential information is involved. Where it is likely that knowledge of confidential information will be acquired, the use of surveillance is subject to higher authorisation.[1] CHIS Code 3.5 recognises that legally privileged information is particularly sensitive and extremely unlikely to be admissible as evidence in criminal proceedings. Moreover, the mere fact that such surveillance has taken place may lead to any related criminal proceedings being stayed as an abuse of process. The CHIS Code reflects the view taken by Newman J in *R v Sutherland*.[2]

1   See Annex A of the Surveillance Code and **para 8.35**.
2   (30 January 2002, unreported) see **para 11.48**.

Annex A of the Surveillance Code

8.35   Annex A is concerned with levels of authorisation where knowledge of confidential information is likely to be acquired or when a vulnerable individual or juvenile is to be used as a source.

It also provides that in the case of the police, the authorisation level required is that of the chief constable instead of a superintendent. The authorisation level in the case of MI5 is the Deputy Director General and in the case of the MI6, a Director. No separate approval by a Commissioner is required, as under the Police Act 1997, s 97(2)(b), let alone approval by a judge as under PACE.

Under the Police Act 1997 and RIPA 2000 applications are made by one side to an authorising officer without the possibility of representations such as are an integral part of the Sch 1 procedure under PACE 1984.

Urgent situations

8.36   As noted in **para 8.30**, in cases of intrusive surveillance provision is made for a lower category of authorising officer in cases where it is not reasonably practical having regard to the urgency of the case for the authorisation to be considered either by the senior authorising officer or the 'designated deputy'. The designated deputy in relation to a chief constable means the person designated to act under the Police Act 1996, s 12(4).[1] In such a case the application may be considered by any person entitled under s 12(4) to consider the application. RIPA 2000, s 34(4) provides a list of those who may grant authorisation in the absence of the senior authorising officer.

Surveillance Code 5.14 points out that the consideration of an authorisation by the senior authorising officer is only to be regarded as not reasonably practicable if he is on annual leave, is absent from his office and his home, or for some other reason not able to obtain access to a secure telephone or fax machine. Pressure of work is not sufficient reason.

Similar powers are provided to the Intelligence Services. In an urgent case, where application has been made for authorisation of intrusive surveillance and the Secretary of State has himself expressly authorised the issue of a warrant in that case, the warrant may be issued (but not renewed) under the hand of a senior official.[2]

Despite the fact that both sections are concerned only with situations that can be described as urgent, the word is not defined within RIPA 2000.

For assistance it is necessary to turn to Surveillance Code 4.13 or 5.13 and CHIS Code 4.11, which deal with the subject in identical terms.

> 'A case is not normally to be regarded as urgent unless the time that would elapse before the authorising officer was available would in the judgement of the person giving the authorisation be likely to endanger life or jeopardise the investigation for which the authorisation was being given. An authorisation is not to be regarded as urgent where the need for an authorisation has been neglected or the urgency is of the authorising officer's own making.'

No specific exceptions are made in cases of directed surveillance or CHIS.

1   RIPA 2000, s 34(6).
2   RIPA 2000, s 44(2).

Combined authorisations

8.37 A single authorisation may combine two or more different authorisations under RIPA 2000, Pt II or an authorisation under Pt II with one under Police Act 1997, Pt III or a warrant under ISA 1994, s 5. The provisions need to be considered separately so that any intrusive surveillance undertaken by the police would still require authorisation by a chief constable and approval by a Commissioner.[1] Similar powers are provided to the Intelligence Services (see **para 8.40**).

1   RIPA 2000, s 33(5).

Quashing of police and HMCE authorisations

8.38 Where an ordinary Surveillance Commissioner is satisfied that there were no reasonable grounds for believing that the authorisation was both necessary and proportionate, he may quash the authorisation with effect from the time it was granted.[1] Similarly, if after the authorisation has been granted he is satisfied that such reasonable grounds for belief no longer exist, he may cancel the authorisation. If a Commissioner is satisfied that there were no reasonable grounds for believing that the case was one of urgency he may quash any authorisation which has been granted on that basis. Where he makes any such order, he may also order the destruction of any records relating to the authorisation. No such order shall be made if the records are required for pending criminal or civil proceedings.[2] No order for the destruction of records shall take effect until the period for appealing has passed and any such appeal has been dismissed by the Chief Surveillance Commissioner.[3]

1   RIPA 2000, s 37(2).
2   RIPA 2000, s 37(7).
3   RIPA 2000, s 37(9).

Appeals against decisions by Surveillance Commissioners

8.39 Any senior authorising officer or designated deputy may appeal to the Chief Surveillance Commissioner against any refusal by a Commissioner to approve an authorisation for intrusive surveillance, any decision to quash or cancel such an authorisation, or any decision to make an order for the destruction of records.[1] Such an appeal must be brought within seven days of the decision appealed against being reported to the appellant.[2] If satisfied that there were reasons for believing that the original action was necessary and proportionate and that the urgency procedure has not been abused, the Chief Surveillance Commissioner shall allow the appeal.[3] He may modify the decision if he considers there were grounds for the action taken by the Commissioner but that such action should have taken effect at a different time.[4] He shall also quash any order for the destruction of records.[5] Having determined an appeal, the Chief Surveillance Commissioner shall give notice of his determination both to the appellant and to the Commissioner whose decision was appealed against.

1   RIPA 2000, s 38(1).
2   RIPA 2000, s 38(3).
3   RIPA 2000, s 38(4).
4   RIPA 2000, s 38(5).
5   RIPA 2000, s 38(6).

Intelligence Services authorisations

8.40   The Intelligence Services are a relevant public authority for the purposes both of directed surveillance and CHIS. As such, each service may self-authorise. Where the application concerns intrusive surveillance the authorisation is the responsibility of the Secretary of State and is made by issue of a warrant in line with ISA 1994, s 5.[1] An authorisation by the Secretary of State does not require approval by a Commissioner. A single warrant may combine an authorisation under RIPA 2000, Pt II and under ISA 1994, s 5, but the respective criteria for authorisation remain separate.[2] Authorisation to GCHQ and MI6 can only be on the basis of national security or the economic well-being of the UK.[3] MI5 can act on behalf of MI6 or GCHQ in respect of Pt II provided that the conduct relates to activities which the relevant service has the power to do otherwise than in support of the prevention or detection of crime.[4]

1   RIPA 2000, s 42(1).
2   RIPA 2000, s 42(2).
3   RIPA 2000, s 42(3).
4   RIPA 2000, s 42(4).

The Ministry of Defence and armed forces

8.41   The Secretary of State has similar responsibilities under RIPA 2000, s 41 in respect of an application made by an official of the Ministry of Defence, a member of the armed forces or any individual holding an office, rank or position with any such public authority as may be designated as an authority whose activities may require the carrying out of intrusive surveillance.

In respect of authorisations granted to the Ministry of Defence or a member of the armed forces, RIPA 2000, s 41(2) provides that such authorisation may only be granted in the interests of national security, or for the purpose of preventing or detecting serious crime. For these purposes, the armed forces do not include membership of the armed services police.[1] Such persons are treated as being a member of a police force[2] and are therefore governed by the procedure in RIPA 2000, ss 33–40.

Procedures for Secretary of State authorisations are covered in Surveillance Code 5.25 onwards.

1   RIPA 2000, s 41(7).
2   See RIPA 2000, s 81(1).

Duration of authorisation, RIPA 2000, s 43

8.42   In respect of both directed surveillance and intrusive surveillance, the period is three months,[1] but 12 months in the case of a CHIS.[2] This longer period was justified by the minister by reference to the nature of the conduct involved.[3] Three months is also the duration of a warrant issued under Police Act 1997, s 95(2)(b). In the case of the Intelligence Services the warrant shall cease to have effect six months after the day it was issued.[4] The longer period is explained by the need to provide consistency with the provisions of ISA 1994. CHIS Code 4.19 underlines the importance of regular reviews to assess the need for the use of a source to continue. Surveillance Code 4.21 also stresses the importance of regular reviews, particularly where access to confidential information or collateral intrusion is involved. The results should be recorded on the central record of authorisation. In either case, where the authorising officer is satisfied that the criteria for authorisation no longer exist he must cancel the warrant.

1   RIPA 2000, s 43(3)(c).
2   RIPA 2000, s 43(3)(b).
3   See 614 HL Official Report col 950.
4   RIPA 2000, s 44(4)(a).

Other procedural requirements

8.43   Authorisations must be in writing except in urgent cases.[1]

The person who is designated for the purposes of RIPA 2000, s 28 or 29 to grant an authorisation shall do so only on application by a member of the same force service or squad.[2] Similarly, an application for intrusive surveillance may only be granted by a senior authorising officer of the same force service or squad.[3] Where the application is for authorisation of intrusive surveillance, the applicant must belong to the force, service or squad operating in the area in which the residential premises are situated.[4]

1   Surveillance Code 5.10 and CHIS Code 4.10.
2   RIPA 2000, s 33(1).
3   RIPA 2000, s 33(3)(a).
4   RIPA 2000, s 33(3)(b).

Cancellation of authorisations

8.44 RIPA 2000, s 45 imposes a requirement on the person who granted or renewed the authorisation to cancel it if he is satisfied that the relevant requirements are no longer satisfied. Where the authorisation was granted in a case of urgency by the person entitled to act for the senior authorising officer or that person's deputy, either that person or the senior authorising officer shall cancel the authorisation.[1] The Surveillance Commissioners must be notified where police, NCIS, NCS or HMCE authorisations are cancelled.

1   See Surveillance Code 4.28 and 5.41.

Record keeping

8.45 RIPA 2000, s 35 provides for the giving of notices to an ordinary Surveillance Commissioner of authorisation (or cancellation of authorisation) of intrusive surveillance. The notification should include the grounds on which the authorising officer believes the matters set out in s 32(2)(a) and (b) are satisfied, the nature of the authorised conduct, including details of the relevant residential premises or vehicle, the identity, where known, of the target, and details of any collateral intrusion. Renewals should also be notified together with the reasons therefore and details of how long it is considered necessary for the authorisation to continue. Cancellation should be notified together with the reasons for cancellation, details of the outcome of the authorised investigation, and what arrangements have been made for the storage or destruction of material obtained thereby.[1]

In urgent cases the notification must specify the grounds on which the case is believed to be one of urgency.[2]

1   Regulation of Investigatory Powers (Notification of Authorisations etc) Order 2000, SI 2000/2563.
2   Surveillance Code 5.23.

8.46 Notification to a Commissioner of directed surveillance or CHIS is not required. However, Surveillance Code 2.14 and CHIS Code 2.13 provide that a centrally retrievable record of all authorisations should be held by every public authority and sets out the type of information which should be included. The record should be made available to the relevant Commissioner and should be retained for three years from the ending of the authorisation or for longer if the product could be relevant to future criminal or civil proceedings. In addition, the relevant authority should also maintain, inter alia, a copy of the application and a copy of the authorisation as well as any renewals thereof.[1] Thereafter, each public authority must ensure that arrangements are in place for the handling, storage and destruction of material obtained through the use of covert surveillance.[2]

Additional requirements should be taken into account where the authorisation concerns a CHIS[3] (see **para 8.21**).

RIPA 2000, s 29(5)(e) provides that records that disclose the identity of the source will not be available 'except to the extent that there is a need for access to them to be made available to those persons' (see *R v H*).[4]

1   Covert Surveillance Code 2.15.
2   Covert Surveillance Code 2.18.
3   Covert Surveillance Code 2.14.
4   [2004] UKHL 3, [2004] 1 All ER 1269.

8.47   Some differences between Police Act 1997, Pt III and RIPA 2000, Pt II are as follows.

- Categories of public authority who may use respective powers are considerably wider under RIPA 2000, Pt II.
- RIPA 2000 triggering criteria for intrusive surveillance are wider than under Police Act 1997, Pt III, in that Pt II permits intrusive surveillance on grounds of the interests of national security as well as the economic well-being of the UK.
- RIPA 2000 triggering criteria for directed surveillance or the use of CHIS are much wider than under the Police Act 1997, Pt III.
- Confidential information: There are no distinct procedures in RIPA 2000, but see Surveillance Code 3.2–3.5.
- Under RIPA 2000 office premises are not afforded specific protection in cases of intrusive surveillance.
- RIPA 2000 adds protection to the presence of an individual in a private vehicle.
- A function of a Commissioner under the Police Act 1997 was to investigate complaints. Under RIPA 2000 complaints are dealt with by the Investigatory Powers Tribunal.

Scrutiny[1]

8.48   The Chief Surveillance Commissioner oversees both the Police Act 1997, Pt III and RIPA 2000, Pt II.

1   See in general **Chapter 10**.

Chapter 9

RIPA 2000, Pt III: investigation of electronic data protected by encryption

9.1 RIPA 2000, Pt III is not yet in force. Despite the importance attached to this aspect of the Bill in Parliament, no timetable has yet been announced. A Preliminary Draft Code was issued at the time of the passage of the Bill through Parliament but has not yet been put out for proper public consultation. The Preliminary Draft Code was criticised as having failed to deal with the potential problems of abuse, the lack of any provision for remedies, or a realisation of the need for disciplinary codes of conduct and offences to provide a basis for action when abuse is discovered.[1]

1   Comments on Preliminary Draft Code by Dr B R Gladman, 11 July 2000, www.cyber-rights.org/reports/p3copcom.pdf.

9.2 The encrypting of computer data has significant advantages both for the law-abiding and for the criminal. It can be used to provide a variety of security services for commercial transactions. Integrity services can guarantee that data has not been accidentally or deliberately corrupted; authentication services guarantee that the originator or recipient of material is the person he claims to be; and confidentiality services ensure that data cannot be read by anyone other than the intended recipient.

Used properly, it can ensure that funds are transferred securely by replacing information like credit card details or account numbers in such away that they cannot be used fraudulently. Used by criminals, it can render the product of lawful interception totally valueless.

What is a key?

9.3 RIPA 2000, s 56 (1) defines a key in relation to any electronic data as any:

'key, code, password, algorithm or other data the use of which (with or without other keys)–

(a)   allows access to the electronic data, or

(b)   facilitates the putting of data into an intelligible form.'

Digital encryption keys are classified according to how many bits they have. In a report published in May 1999, entitled 'Encryption and Law Enforcement', an example of the problems caused by a readily available 128-bit key is given.

'Using a brute force approach – with a billion computers that are able to try a billion keys per second (which is far beyond anything available at present) – it would still take the decrypter 10,000,000,000,000 years to try all the possible combinations. That is something like a thousand times the age of the universe.'

The purpose of Pt III

9.4   Part III is concerned with protected information, which is defined as:

'any electronic data which, without the key to the data–

(a)   cannot, or cannot readily, be accessed, or
(b)   cannot, or cannot readily, be put into an intelligible form.'[1]

In order to ensure that such material that has been lawfully intercepted or obtained by other lawful means can be used for law enforcement purposes, it may be necessary to decrypt/decipher the material. In such circumstances the relevant agency, eg the police, HMCE or Intelligence Services may by notice impose a disclosure requirement on the person believed to be in possession of the key (often a Communications Service Supplier (CSP)). The effect of such a requirement is that the CSP is obliged to disclose the information in an intelligible form or to disclose the key(s). Failure to do so may result in a fine or up to two years' imprisonment.

1   RIPA 2000, s 56(1).

Who may impose a disclosure requirement?

9.5   Two preconditions must be met:

(a)   the person must be legitimately in possession of the protected information (s 49(1)); and
(b)   he must have the appropriate permission under s 49(2).

The power to require disclosure is, by RIPA 2000, s 49(1) closely linked to the power to obtain the information in the first place, so as to ensure that the power is not used for speculative purposes.

RIPA 2000, s 49(1)(a) refers to the statutory power to seize and retain, etc under PACE 1984, Pt II or to authorise interference with property under the Police Act 1997, Pt III. Section 49(1)(b) refers to material obtained through interception and s 49(1)(c) to communications data obtained under Pt I, Ch II and to any information obtained as a result of directed or intrusive surveillance or the use of a CHIS under Pt II. Section 49(1)(d) refers to material obtained other than under a warrant, e g under the Customs and Excise Management Act 1979. Section 49(1)(e) refers to material which has, for example, been voluntarily handed over.

Lord Bassam explained that:

> 'The Bill does not permit the power to be used for speculative fishing for keys. The Government believe section 49(1)(a) to (e) is needed for cases where there are reasonable grounds for anticipating that, for example, a suspected criminal is using encryption to protect material, and reasonable grounds for believing that the location of the relevant key to that material is known. In such circumstances, the futuristic element allows an agency to apply for the power to serve a section 49 decryption notice at the same time as an application is made to use the underlying power to lawfully obtain the material in question.'[1]

1   614 HL Official Report, col 959, 28 June 2000.

9.6   The person making the requirement must have the 'appropriate permission' under RIPA 2000, Sch 2. The general rule is that permission to serve a notice may only be granted by a circuit judge or the equivalent in Scotland or Northern Ireland. However, there are a number of exceptions set out in Sch 2, paras 2–5. Paragraph 2 provides appropriate permission in relation to a statutory power that is exercised in accordance with a warrant issued by the Secretary of State, e g under RIPA 2000, Pt I or by a judge under PACE 1984 or an authorisation under the Police Act 1997, Pt III. In such circumstances, if the warrant or authorisation gives explicit permission for the notice to be given, no application to a circuit judge is necessary. Similarly, para 3 provides for appropriate permission in relation to data obtained by the Intelligence Services under a statutory power but without a warrant, e g as a result of directed surveillance. In such a case, if the Secretary of State has given written permission, no application to a circuit judge is necessary. Paragraph 4 provides for appropriate permission in relation to data obtained under a statutory power but without a warrant other than by the Intelligence Services, e g under RIPA 2000, Pt I, Ch I or under Pt II or under PACE 1984, s 19. The effect of this paragraph is that senior officers of police, HMCE, and the armed forces may authorise the service of a written notice.

However, where material is obtained by other agencies, application to a circuit judge is required. Paragraph 5 provides for appropriate permission in relation to information obtained without the use of statutory powers, e g where material has been voluntarily handed over to either the Intelligence Services, HMCE or the police. Paragraph 6 imposes further conditions as to persons entitled to impose a disclosure requirement under s 49. For example, in the case of the police, the officer concerned must be of, or above, the rank of superintendent or have the authority of an officer of such a rank. Where information has come into the possession of the police by means of the powers of stop and search under the Terrorism Act 2000 or the Prevention of Terrorism (Temporary Provisions) Act 1989, those able to authorise the serving of a notice must be of or above the rank specified in s 44 and s 13A respectively. In the case of the latter, this is a commander of the Metropolitan Police area or assistant chief constable for any other area.

Other conditions attaching to the grant of permission

9.7 RIPA 2000, Sch 1, para 7 provides that permission, once granted, will continue to have effect until such time as it expires in accordance with any limitation on its duration that was contained in its terms or is withdrawn by the person who granted it.

Paragraph 8 provides that a permission granted by the Secretary of State must be granted under his hand except in urgent cases where he has expressly authorised the grant of the permission, when it may be granted by a senior official.

In what circumstances may a disclosure requirement be made?

9.8 Where a person with the 'appropriate permission' believes on reasonable grounds that:

(a)   the key to the relevant protected information is in the possession of the person on whom the notice is to be served;

(b)   serving such a notice is necessary in the interests of national security, for the purpose of preventing or detecting crime, in the interests of the economic well-being of the UK, or for the exercise of statutory power or duty;

(c)   imposing a disclosure requirement is proportionate; and

(d)   an intelligible version of the protected information cannot reasonably be obtained by other means,[1]

he may impose a disclosure requirement in respect of that information.

1   RIPA 2000, s 49(2).

What form should the notice take?

9.9 The notice must be in writing and must specify the information to which the notice relates, how disclosure is to be made, why such disclosure is necessary, the rank or position held by both the person giving the notice and the person who granted permission, and the time by which the notice is to be complied with. It must also set out the disclosure that is required by the notice and the form in which it is to be made.[1] Disclosure may only be required to the person giving the notice or a person specified in the notice.[2]

1   RIPA 2000, s 49(4).
2   RIPA 2000, s 49(8).

On whom should the notice be served?

9.10 The notice should be served on the person who is believed to be in possession of the key. Where a body corporate or firm is involved, it should be served on a senior officer unless there are special circumstances which would defeat the purpose of the notice, eg where the senior officer is a suspect.[1] A senior officer is defined by RIPA 2000, s 49(10) as a director, manager, secretary or other similar officer.

[1]RIPA 2000, s 49(5)–(7).

What is the effect of a notice imposing a disclosure requirement?

9.11 The service of a notice will entitle the person served to use any key in his possession to obtain access to the information in order either to make disclosure of the information in an intelligible form or to disclose the key to the information.[1] Where the person served is not in possession of the information or cannot access the information without use of a key which is not in his possession, or the notice states that it can be complied with only by disclosure of a key, that person must disclose any key to the information that is in his possession at a relevant time.[2] Relevant time means the time of the giving of the notice or any subsequent time before which the requirement must be complied with.[3] The person served need only provide those keys which suffice to access the information and render it intelligible and may choose which keys to provide to achieve that end.[4] If the person served has been in possession of the key, but is no longer in possession, he is required to disclose all such information as will facilitate the discovery of the key.[5]

1   RIPA 2000, s 50(2).
2   RIPA 2000, s 50(3).
3   RIPA 2000, s 50(10).
4   RIPA 2000, s 50(4)–(6).
5   RIPA 2000, s 50(8) and (9).

In what circumstances may a key alone be required?

9.12 As has been seen, the person served will usually be able to satisfy a disclosure requirement by disclosing the protected information in an intelligible form. In certain circumstances a notice may direct that only the disclosure of a key will amount to compliance: 'a s 51(1) direction'. Such a direction requires the permission of either the chief officer of police, the Commissioners of Customs and Excise or, in the case of the armed services, a person of or above the rank of brigadier or its equivalent. RIPA 2000, s 51(4) provides that such a direction may not be given unless the person giving the direction believes:

'(a)   that there are special circumstances of the case which mean that the purposes for which it was believed necessary to impose the requirement in question would be defeated, in whole or in part, if the direction were not given; and

(b)   that the giving of the direction is proportionate to what is sought to be achieved by prohibiting any compliance with the requirement in question otherwise than by disclosure of the key itself.'

In considering proportionality, regard should be given to the sort of other information that is also protected by the key in question and any potential adverse impact on the business concerned.[1]

1   RIPA 2000, s 51(5).

Notification requirements

9.13   Where a s 51(1) direction is given by a member of the armed services otherwise than in connection with activities in Northern Ireland, notification must be given within seven days to the Intelligence Services Commissioner. In all other cases notice must be given to the Chief Surveillance Commissioner.[1]

1   RIPA 2000, s 51(6) and (7).

Arrangements for payment

9.14   RIPA 2000, s 52 places a duty on the Secretary of State to pay an appropriate contribution to the costs of complying with notices. Such costs are likely to be substantial.

Failure to comply with a notice

9.15   Knowingly failing to make the disclosure required is an offence punishable on indictment by a fine or up to two years' imprisonment.[1]

RIPA 2000, s 53(2) deems any person who can be shown to have been in possession of a relevant key to have continued to be in possession of that key at all subsequent times, unless it is shown that the key was not in his possession after the giving of the notice and before the time he was required to disclose it. Section 53(3) makes it clear that the burden on a defendant in such circumstances is an evidential rather than a legal one.[2] Section 53(4) provides a defence where the person served can show that it was not reasonably practicable to comply with the disclosure requirement in the time allowed but that he did so as soon as practicable.

1   RIPA 2000, s 53(5).
2   See also 615 HL Official Report col 423.

Tipping-off

9.16   RIPA 2000, s 54(4) creates an offence where the recipient of a notice which explicitly contains a secrecy requirement tips off another person that a notice has been served or reveals its contents. The offence is one of strict liability, except in so far as the recipient of the notice is able to bring himself within one of the exceptions set out below (**para 9.17**). The offence is punishable on indictment by a fine or up to five years' imprisonment.

A secrecy requirement may only be included where it is reasonable in order to maintain the effectiveness of any investigation or operation or of investigatory techniques generally or in the interests of the safety or well-being of any person.[1] Such a requirement must be authorised by the person giving permission.[2]

1   RIPA 2000, s 54(3).
2   RIPA 2000, s 54(2).

Specific defences to tipping off

9.17

- RIPA 2000, s 54(5) provides a defence where the tipping-off occurred entirely as the result of software designed to give an automatic warning that a key had been compromised and where in addition the defendant was unable to prevent this from taking place.
- RIPA 2000, s 54(6) and (7) provide a defence where a disclosure is made to or by a legal adviser as part of advice about the effect of the provisions of the Act given to a client or his representative, or where a disclosure was made by a legal adviser in connection with any proceedings before a court or tribunal. Where a legal adviser tips off his client with a view to furthering any criminal purpose, the defence will not apply.[1] These provisions are similar to those under RIPA 2000, s 19(6)–(8) relating to interception warrants.
- RIPA 2000, s 54(9) provides a defence where the disclosure was made to a relevant Commissioner or was authorised by a Commissioner, or by the terms of the notice, or by the person who gave the notice or the person in possession of the information to which the notice relates. The effect of the subsection is to ensure that persons within an organisation may be informed about a notice in order to give effect to it without falling foul of the tipping-off offence.
- RIPA 2000, s 54(10) provides a defence to a person other than the person to whom the notice was given if he can show that he neither knew nor had reasonable grounds for suspecting that the notice contained a secrecy requirement.

1   RIPA 2000, s 54(8).

Safeguards

9.18   RIPA 2000, s 55 imposes duties on all those whose officers or employees are involved with the giving of s 49 notices. This includes the Secretary of State, every other minister in charge of a government department, every chief police officer and the Commissioners of Customs and Excise. Section 55(2) places an onus on those identified to ensure that:

(a)   any material disclosed is used only for the purpose for which it may be required;

(b)   the uses to which the material is put are reasonable;

(c)   the use and retention of any material is proportionate;

(d)   the material is shared with the minimum number of people;

(e)   the keys are stored in a secure manner; and

(f)   all records of a key are destroyed as soon as the key is no longer needed.

These arrangements are to be overseen by the Interception Commissioner by virtue of RIPA 2000, s 57(2)(d), or the Intelligence Services Commissioner by virtue of s 59(2), or the Chief Surveillance Commissioner by virtue of s 62(1).

Right to damages

9.19   Unlike most aspects of RIPA 2000 and the Police Act 1997, for which the only form of redress available is the Investigatory Powers Tribunal, RIPA 2000, s 55(4) specifically provides for access to a court for damages.

Such a course of action may be available to a 'relevant person', who is defined as a person who has made a disclosure pursuant to a s 49 notice or a person whose protected information or key has been disclosed pursuant to such a notice.[1] Such an action would lie against any of those with duties under s 55(1) for breach of any duty imposed under s 55(2), or against any person whatever for contravention of arrangements made under that subsection.

1   RIPA 2000, s 55(5).

Chapter 10

Scrutiny: the Commissioners and the Tribunal

The Commissioners

10.1 The Commissioners are critical to the functioning of the whole of the surveillance regime under not only RIPA 2000 but also the Intelligence Services Act 1994 (ISA 1994) and the Police Act 1997, Pt III.

RIPA 2000 provides for the appointment of four Commissioners:

(1) an Interception Commissioner, who replaces the Commissioner appointed under IOCA 1985, s 8;

(2) an Intelligence Services Commissioner, who replaces the two separate Commissioners appointed under Security Services Act 1989, s 4 and ISA 1994, s 8;

(3) an Investigatory Powers Commissioner for Northern Ireland; and

(4) a Chief Surveillance Commissioner, who, in addition to his remaining functions under the Police Act 1997 to keep under review the performance of functions under that Act, is tasked with specific responsibilities to oversee RIPA 2000, Pts II and III.

10.2 In explaining why the government had decided not to amalgamate the Commissioners into a single unified Commission, the Parliamentary Secretary for the Lord Chancellor's Department Jane Kennedy stated:

'There are strong arguments for retaining separately in statute the identity of some commissioners' who are experts in their respective fields regularly visiting those agencies whose activities they oversee … Amalgamating commissioners functions would risk obscuring the lines of accountability and compromising their expertise. The system proposed in the Bill is designed to ensure that the need to know principle is strictly observed and that details about particular individuals are shared to the minimum extent possible.'[1]

1   Vol 349, HC Official Report col 532, 8 May 2000.

Interception Commissioner

10.3   RIPA 2000, s 57 provides for an Interception Commissioner, who is or has been a High Court judge, who may hold office 'in accordance with the terms of his appointment'.[1] Lord Lloyd was the first Commissioner, 1986–91, his successors being Lord Bingham, 1992–93, Lord Nolan, 1994–2000, and Lord Justice Swinton-Thomas, 2001 to present. His functions are to keep under review:

'(a)   the exercise and performance by the Secretary of State of the powers and duties conferred or imposed on him by or under sections 1 to 11;

(b)   the exercise and performance, by the persons on whom they are conferred or imposed, of the powers and duties conferred or imposed by or under Chapter II of Part I;

(c)   the exercise and performance by the Secretary of State in relation to information obtained under Part I of the powers and duties conferred or imposed on him by or under Part III; and

(d)   the adequacy of any arrangements by virtue of which–

  (i) the duty which is imposed on the Secretary of State by section 15, and

  (ii) so far as applicable to information obtained under Part I, the duties imposed by section 55,

are sought to be discharged.'[2]

RIPA 2000, s 55, which refers to the duty to make arrangements regarding the uses to which a key may be put, is not yet in force. As none of Pt III is in force, s 57(2)(c) and (d)(ii) above have no present application.

By s 57(3) he shall also give the Tribunal such assistance as it may require.

1   RIPA 2000, s 57(5).
2   RIPA 2000, s 57(2).

Annual reports

10.4   RIPA 2000, s 58(4) makes specific requirement in terms identical to IOCA 1985, s 8(6) for the provision by the Commissioner of an annual report to the Prime Minister. The report is then laid before Parliament. If it appears to the Prime Minister that publication of any matter would be contrary to the public interest on the grounds of national security, the prevention or detection of serious crime, the economic well-being of the UK or the continued discharge of the functions of any of the public authorities whose activities are the subject of review by the Commissioner, he may exclude such matter from the report laid before Parliament.[1] Where he does so, a statement to this effect should accompany the report. In practice, each report contains an annex including such material.

Certain areas, such as the extent and duration of external warrants, have never been the subject matter of comment in any annual report.

1   RIPA 2000, s 58(7).

The number of warrants

10.5   In para 121 of the Birkett Report the Committee expressed the opinion that it would be wrong for figures to be disclosed at regular or irregular intervals:

'It would greatly aid the operation of agencies hostile to the state if they were able to estimate even approximately the extent of the interceptions of communications for interceptions purposes.'

The 1985 White Paper did, however, set out the number of warrants outstanding on 31 December 1984. Of the total of 411, 295 had been signed by the Home Secretary, 98 by the Foreign and Commonwealth Secretary and 18 by the Secretary of State for Scotland.

In his first report as Interception Commissioner, Lord Lloyd in 1986 accepted that there might be security implications if a detailed breakdown of the figures for the number of warrants was published, but saw no reason for not publishing a total figure:

'for the simple reason that the total includes not only warrants issued in the interests of national security but also warrants issued for the prevention of serious crime.'

Such figures do not include warrants issued by the Foreign Office or the Northern Ireland Office, nor do they reveal the extent of interception in circumstances which do not require a warrant, such as participant monitoring.

The process of scrutiny

10.6   Lord Diplock, in his 1981 report on Interception of Communications in Great Britain, Cmnd 8191, set out the following criteria by which the practices of the police, Customs and the Security Service should be judged:

- '● that the public interest which will be served by obtaining the information which it is hoped will result from the interception of communications is of sufficient importance to justify the step;
- ● that the interception applied for offers a reasonable prospect of providing the information sought;
- ● that other methods of obtaining it such as surveillance or the use of informants have been tried and failed or from the nature of the case are not feasible;
- ● that the interception stops as soon as it has ceased to provide information of the kind sought or it has become apparent that it is unlikely to provide it;
- ● that all products of interception not directly relevant to the purpose for which the warrant was granted are speedily destroyed; and
- ● that such material as is directly relevant to that purpose is given no wider circulation than is essential for carrying it out.'

In applying those criteria he was satisfied that the procedures at the time, albeit not controlled by statute, were working satisfactorily. He gave no figures for interceptions but did point out that there was a significant difference between police and HMCE interceptions on the one hand and those of the Security Service on the other. Whereas the information obtained by the former was intended to lead to apprehension and prosecution of the perpetrators of major crime, the information obtained by the Security Service, who had no independent executive powers of law enforcement, was obtained to gather intelligence about subversive or terrorist groups. As such, warrants issued on behalf of the Security Service tend to remain in force longer than in the case of other authorities.

10.7   In detailing his practice in the 1986 Report, Lord Lloyd explained that he adopted that first described by Lord Diplock and then followed by Lord Bridge of Harwich in selecting warrants at random, except in the case of warrants concerning counter-subversion, all of which he examined:

> 'I have then discussed these warrants in detail with the officers concerned, have inspected the files and asked for any explanation that I have thought necessary. I can say at once that I have not come across a single case in which the information supplied to the Secretary of State has been incomplete or inaccurate, whether on the issue of a warrant or renewal. Nor have I come across a single case where the Secretary of State has not been justified in regarding the issue of a warrant as necessary in the interests of national security or for the other purposes mentioned in s 2(2) of the Act.'

10.8   In considering the warrants issued on the grounds of counter-subversion, having acknowledged that there are persons on the fringe of subversion which may make it difficult to draw the line, he said:

> 'In these cases my duty is to apply the principles of judicial review. Although it is not spelt out in the Act, I cannot suppose that Parliament intended different principles to apply to the Commissioner and to the Tribunal.'

Applying that test, he was satisfied that in every such case the Home Secretary had been justified in issuing the warrant. Individual cases were considered in greater detail in the Annex to the report.

10.9   Lord Lloyd detailed his findings under the headings of unlawful interception; procedure for issuing warrants; the application, renewal and modification of warrants; the issue of warrants in practice; the prevention and detection of serious crime; national security; economic well-being; warrants under s 3(2) of IOCA 1985 (external warrants); interception in practice; postal warrants; and safeguards. He concluded that he was satisfied that there were adequate arrangements for ensuring that the dissemination of intercepted material was no wider than necessary. He described the quota system, then imposed by the Secretary of State, as a most useful discipline.

The system ended on 1 January 1993 (see Report of 1994 at para 7). His overall impression was of the high value of the intelligence obtained from interception and of the care taken by all concerned to observe not only the letter but also the spirit of IOCA 1985.

Postal warrant procedure

10.10   In describing the procedure for postal warrants, Lord Lloyd explained how letters were taken out of the post, opened, photographed and resealed and then returned to the ordinary course of post and delivered at the usual time:

> 'Neither the sorting officer, nor the delivery officer knows or could know whether a letter has been intercepted or not. All developing is done centrally. Only one print is made of each negative. The print is then dispatched by special courier to the Security Service or other agency requesting interception. The negative is normally destroyed within 6 months and always destroyed within 12 months.'

Telephone interception procedure

10.11   In describing the procedure for interception, he explained that once British Telecom had checked that the warrant was in order, they would effect the interception. Thereafter, all calls on the intercepted line were recorded on tape until the warrant was cancelled. If the interception was at the request of HMCE, a Customs officer would be listening simultaneously in a room to which not more than a dozen officers have access.

> 'If the call is between members of the public the officer ceases to listen and makes no note of the conversation whatsoever. If the conversation appears to be relevant, he makes a note of the gist of the conversation together with the time. If it is very important he may make a verbatim note and check his note against the tape. The tape is made available by BT. He will also listen to tapes of communications intercepted during the preceding night, or at any time when his desk has been empty. The tapes are always returned to BT usually within 24 hours and are erased at once. The officer who has listened to the conversation communicates by direct telephone line with the officer in charge of the operation, who makes such use of the intelligence as he needs. No note or copy of the intercepted conversation comes into existence, other than the original record made by the listening officer. That record is destroyed by shredding, within a year.'

10.12   The procedure for the police is similar. In the case of the Criminal Intelligence Branch (then C11), some 16 officers were engaged in listening from time to time. The manuscript notes of relevant conversations may be typed, in which case the originals were destroyed within three to four days. The original typed version was then kept on file and access limited to two or three investigating officers. These officers may make notes in a special notebook but may not remove the original. At the conclusion of the investigation the transcript was destroyed.

In the case of the Security Service, although the procedure is similar, transcribers' reports are retained indefinitely within the Service. Disclosure to parties outside the Service will only take place in exceptional circumstances, such as where the subject matter relates to terrorism.[1]

---

1   See paras 45–48 of the 1986 Report.

10.13　Subsequent Commissioners' Reports have not been as detailed but have consistently addressed the issue of such errors as have arisen and suggested improvements. The procedure of interception is described only by Lord Lloyd in his first report.

The Intelligence Services Commissioner

10.14　RIPA 2000, s 59(1) provides for the appointment of an Intelligence Services Commissioner, who combines the functions of the Security Service Commissioner and the Intelligence Services Commissioner. He shall, like the Interception Commissioner, be a past or present High Court judge. The present incumbent is Lord Justice Simon Brown. It is his duty to keep under review:

(a)　the exercise by the Secretary of State of his powers under ss 5 to 7 of ISA 1994 (to issue property warrants);

(b)　the exercise and performance by the Secretary of State, in connection with or in relation to:

　(i)　the activities of the Intelligence Services, and

　(ii)　the activities in places other than Northern Ireland of the officials of the Ministry of Defence and of Her Majesty's Forces,

of the powers and duties conferred on him by Pts II and III of RIPA 2000;

(c)　the exercise and performance by members of the Intelligence Services of the powers and duties conferred or imposed on them by or under Pts II and III of RIPA 2000

(d)　the exercise and performance in places other than Northern Ireland by officials of the Ministry of Defence and by members of Her Majesty's Forces, of the powers and duties conferred or imposed on such officials or members of Her Majesty's Forces by or under Pts II and III; and

(e)　the adequacy of the arrangements by virtue of which the duty imposed by RIPA 2000, s 55 is sought to be discharged:

　(i)　in relation to the members of the Intelligence Services; and

　(ii)　in connection with any of their activities in places other than Northern Ireland, in relation to officials of the Ministry of Defence and members of Her Majesty's forces.

By RIPA 2000, s 59(3) he shall give the Tribunal such assistance as it may require and by s 60(2) he shall provide a report to the Prime Minister in circumstances identical to those of the Interception Commissioner (see **para 10.4**). Otherwise he has no powers to deal with breaches.

Reports of the Intelligence Services Commissioner

10.15　In his report for 2000 (published October 2001) he stated:

'In issuing warrants the Secretary of State is dependent on the accuracy of the information contained in the application and the candour of those applying for it. This is essentially a question of the integrity and quality of the personnel involved in the warranty process both in the agencies and the government departments concerned. I regard one of my functions to check these matters so far as I can and as a result I am satisfied that the applications made properly reflected the position at the time of the submission and that the Secretaries of State have properly exercised their powers under the Acts.'[1]

Paragraph 29 of the 2001 and 2002 reports are in almost identical terms. Of more concern is the number of complaints investigated by the Tribunal. In 2000 only three of the 22 complaints received were investigated. By the following year, of the total of 102 received during the period 2 October 2000 to 31 December 2001, 71 had been investigated. In the following year 130 complaints were received and 67 investigated. In no case has the Tribunal upheld a complaint.

1   See para 29 of the 2000 Report.

The Investigatory Powers Commissioner for Northern Ireland

10.16   RIPA 2000, s 61(1) provides for the appointment of the Investigatory Powers Commissioner for Northern Ireland after consultation with the First Minister and the Deputy First Minister for Northern Ireland.

It shall be his duty to keep under review the exercise and performance in Northern Ireland of the powers or duties under RIPA 2000, Pt II.[1]

He shall give the Tribunal all such assistance as it may require and provide an annual report to the First Minister and Deputy First Minister.

1   RIPA 2000, s 61(2).

Additional functions of the Chief Surveillance Commissioner

10.17   Under the Police Act 1997, the Chief Commissioner had to deal with complaints by members of the public under s 102, as well as appeals by authorising officers against the decision of a Commissioner under s 104.

The former function has been abolished by RIPA 2000, s 70 but the latter remains.

By Police Act 1997, s 107(3) he has also to provide an annual report.

By RIPA 2000, s 62(1) the Chief Surveillance Commissioner shall in addition keep under review so far as they are not to be kept under review by the other Commissioners:

(a)   the exercise and performance, by the persons on whom they are conferred or imposed, of the powers and duties conferred or imposed under RIPA 2000, Pt II;

(b)   the exercise and performance by any person other than a judicial authority of the powers and duties conferred or imposed, otherwise than with the permission of such an authority, by or under RIPA 2000, Pt III; and

(c)   the adequacy of the arrangements by virtue of which the duties imposed by RIPA 2000, s 55 are sought to be discharged in relation to persons whose conduct is subject to review under para (b).

As RIPA 2000, Pt III is not in force, (b) and (c) are of no relevance at present.

The present Chief Surveillance Commissioner is Lord Justice Leggatt.

The Investigatory Powers Tribunal

History

10.18   RIPA 2000, s 65(1) provides for the creation of an all-embracing tribunal, which came into existence on 2 October 2000. The Investigatory Powers Tribunal replaces the three separate tribunals set up under IOCA 1985, s 7, Security Services Act 1989, s 5, ISA 1994, s 9, and the complaints system set up under Police Act 1997, s 102, all of which are formally abolished by RIPA 2000, s 70.

10.19   The new Tribunal is made up of members of the legal profession of at least ten years' standing. At present there are seven. Its President is Lord Justice Mummery and its Vice-President is Mr Justice Burton. A Registrar has also been appointed.[1]

In their previous incarnations, the respective tribunals allowed any person who believed that he had been a victim of the relevant service to complain to the tribunal and unless it considered the matter to be frivolous or vexatious it was obliged to investigate. If it concluded that there had been a contravention by the Secretary of State, the tribunal had to make a formal report to the Prime Minister and could quash the warrant, order the destruction of copies of any (intercepted) material and order compensation to the complainant. If it concluded that there had been no contravention of the terms of the relevant Act it would give notice to the applicant stating there had been no contravention. It is a matter of record that no complaints have been upheld under Police Act 1997, s 102 nor by any of the tribunals.

1   See RIPA 2000, Sch 3.

10.20   In his annual report for 1997, Lord Nolan explained the procedure of the Interception of Communications Tribunal in some detail. He explained that if there was no warrant in existence or if there was no contravention of the powers for the issuing of a warrant, IOCA 1985 specifically prevents the Tribunal from disclosing whether or not a warrant is or was in existence.

IOCA 1985, Sch 1, para 4(2) provided that:

'The Tribunal shall not except in reports under s 7(4) of the Act give reasons for any decision made by them.'

In cases where there is no warrant or no contravention of s 7(7) the Act provided that the:

'Tribunal shall give notice to the applicant stating that there has been no contravention of sections 2–5 in relation to the warrant or the certificate.'

He pointed out that the provisions were intentionally unhelpful.

'If the Tribunal were able to tell a complainant that he or she had or had not been the subject of a legitimate interception, silence or any equivocal answer on another occasion might be interpreted as an implication that interception had taken place. Furthermore a positive answer would allow criminals or terrorists to know whether they were subject to interception or not, leading to effective action to avoid detection.'[1]

1   See para 30 of the 1997 Report.

10.21

'Since the Tribunal was established in 1986 it has considered 568 complaints, 5 further cases were under consideration on 31st December 1997. It is a published fact (as set out in the Annual Reports) that the Tribunal has never found there to have been a contravention of the provisions of the Act. This has led to a measure of suspicion as to the effectiveness of the Tribunal's work. The fact is that investigation by the Tribunal has revealed that in only 8 of the 568 cases was interception being carried out by a Government agency and in each of the 8 cases the interception was authorised by a valid warrant issued by the Secretary of State. In these circumstances it is hardly surprising that no contravention of the Act by Government agencies has been found to exist.'[1]

1   See para 31 of the 1997 Report.

Jurisdiction

10.22   The jurisdiction of the Tribunal is as set out in RIPA 2000, s 65(2):

'(a)   to be the only appropriate tribunal for the purpose of section 7 of the Human Rights Act 1998 in relation to any proceedings under subsection (1)(a) of that section (proceedings for actions incompatible with Convention rights) which fall within subsection (3) of this section;

(b)   to consider and determine any complaints made to them which in accordance with subsection (4) are complaints for which the Tribunal is the appropriate forum [see **paras 10.23–24**];

(c)   to consider and determine any reference to them by any person that he has suffered detriment as a consequence of any prohibition or restriction, by virtue of section 17, on his relying in, or for the purpose of any civil proceeding on any matter; and

(d)   to hear and determine any other such proceedings falling within subsection (3) as may be allocated to them in accordance with provision made by the Secretary of State by order [see also s 66].'

10.23   RIPA 2000, s 65(3) refers to proceedings against the Intelligence Services or persons acting on their behalf, proceedings under RIPA 2000, s 55(4) for loss or damage from misuse of a key (not in force), or proceedings relating to the taking place in challengeable circumstances of conduct falling within s 65(5), ie conduct by any of the Intelligence Services, interception under Pt I, conduct to which Ch II of Pt I applies, and all forms of surveillance under Pt II, the giving of notice under s 49, or any disclosure or use of a key to protected information as well as any entry onto or interference with property under the Police Act 1997, Pt III.

10.24   The Tribunal is also the appropriate forum for any complaint by a person who is aggrieved by any such conduct (within RIPA 2000, s 65(5)) which he believes to have taken place in challengeable circumstances or to have been carried out by or on behalf of any of the Intelligence Services.[1]

1   RIPA 2000, s 65(4).

When does conduct take place in challengeable circumstances?

10.25   RIPA 2000, s 65(7) provides that conduct takes place in challengeable circumstances if:

(a)   it takes place with the authority or purported authority of an interception warrant under RIPA 2000, Pt I (or IOCA 1985), an authorisation or notice under Ch II of Pt I, an authorisation under Pt II (or its Scottish equivalent), a permission for the purposes of Sch 2 (not in force), a notice under s 49 (not in force) or an authorisation under the Police Act 1997, Pt III; or

(b)   the circumstances are such that (whether or not there is such authority) it would not have been appropriate for the conduct to take place without it, or at least without proper consideration having been given to whether such authority should be sought.

As an example of clear drafting, s 65(7)(b) leaves a lot to be desired. The purpose is clear. As the complainant will be unlikely to know if authorisation has been given, let alone be able to prove it, s 65(7)(b) allows him to pursue his complaint regardless.

Conduct which takes place with the permission of a judicial authority (including a magistrate) does not take place in challengeable circumstances.

The exercise of the Tribunal's jurisdiction

10.26   The following is a summary of the main features of the exercise of its jurisdiction.

●   To hear/consider and determine matters set out in RIPA 2000, s 65(2) (see **para 10.22**). But the Tribunal is not obliged to hear a complaint made under s 65(2)(b) which it considers frivolous or vexatious nor any complaint made thereunder unless it is made within 12 months of the conduct to which it relates.

●   RIPA 2000, s 67(2) provides that where the Tribunal is hearing proceedings by virtue of HRA 1998, s 7 it shall apply the same principles for making its determination as would be applied by a court on application for judicial review. It is open to question whether such a test satisfies art 13.[1]

●   Where the Tribunal is hearing a complaint from a person who is aggrieved by conduct which he believes to have been carried out in challengeable circumstances it must first investigate if any person has engaged in any such conduct and if so under what authority and only then to determine the complaint by applying the principles of judicial review.[2]

- As was the case with the respective tribunals which it replaced, the Tribunal may make such award of compensation or other order as it sees fit including the quashing or cancelling of any warrant or authorisation and order the destruction of any records of information obtained pursuant to a warrant or authorisation or which is held by any public authority in relation to any person.[3]

- Orders or other decisions of the Tribunal shall not be subject to appeal or liable to be questioned in any court.[4] Despite similar ouster clauses in IOCA 1985, s 7(8), Security Service Act 1989, s 5(4) and ISA 1994, s 9(4), no challenge, let alone a successful one, appears to have been mounted to the width of the prohibition.

1   See *Chahal v United Kingdom* (1996) 23 EHRR 413, *Tinnelly v United Kingdom* (1998) 27 EHRR 249 and *Smith and Grady v United Kingdom* (1999) 29 EHRR 493, *Vilvarajah v United Kingdom* (1991) 14 EHRR 248, *Soering v United Kingdom* (1989) 11 EHRR 439.
2   RIPA 2000, s 67(3).
3   RIPA 2000, s 67(7).
4   RIPA 2000, s 67(8).

Procedure

10.27

- By RIPA 2000, s 68(1) the Tribunal shall be entitled to determine its own procedure. It may require the relevant Commissioner to give such assistance as it sees fit[1] (so far it has not done so). In any event, the relevant Commissioner should be kept informed of any determination made by the Tribunal.[2]

- By s 68(4), where the Tribunal makes a determination, it shall give notice to the complainant that either they have made a determination in his favour or that no determination has been made in his favour (NCND, see **para 10.34**).

- By s 68(5), where the Tribunal make a determination in favour of a complainant, it shall also make a report to the Prime Minister.

- Section 68(6) imposes on 14 categories of person who may broadly be described as being entitled to take action under the Act an obligation to disclose or provide to the Tribunal all such documents and information as the Tribunal may require.

1   RIPA 2000, s 68(2).
2   RIPA 2000, s 68(3).

Tribunal Rules

10.28   The Investigatory Powers Tribunal Rules 2000, SI 2000/2665 came, into force on 2 October 2000. They are divided into two parts. Part I contains the first six Rules.

Part I of the Rules

Rule 4 provides that the jurisdiction of the Tribunal may be exercised at any place in the UK by any two or more members of the Tribunal.

Rule 5 provides that certain powers, eg to require a Commissioner to provide assistance, may be exercised by one member of the Tribunal.

Rule 6(1) provides that the Tribunal shall carry out its functions in such a way as to secure that information is not disclosed to an extent or in a manner that is contrary to the public interest or prejudicial to national security, the prevention or detection of serious crime, the economic well-being of the UK or the continued discharge of the functions of any of the Intelligence Services.

10.29 Rule 6(2) specifically states that, subject to the consent of the relevant person, the Tribunal may not disclose to the complainant or any other person:

(a)   the fact that the Tribunal has held or proposes to hold an oral hearing;
(b)   any information or document disclosed or provided to the Tribunal or the identity of any witness at that hearing;
(c)   any information or document disclosed pursuant to RIPA 2000, s 68(6);
(d)   any information or opinion provided by a Commissioner pursuant to s 68(2); or
(e)   the fact that any information, document, identity or opinion has been disclosed.

Rule 6(3) allows disclosure of all the above subject to the relevant consent.

10.30 In the past, the practice of the respective tribunals has been largely governed by schedules to the Acts. The schedule to IOCA 1985 and the Security Service Act 1989 are to all intents identical and provided a similar prohibition against disclosure of any document to any complainant without consent.

In practice, the Tribunal has not given any reasons. In view of the wording of RIPA 2000, s 69(4)(d), which gives the power to the Tribunal to limit disclosure of particular matters and which refers to the duty to give reasons, such a blanket approach may not be appropriate and may need to be reconsidered.

Part II of the Rules

10.31 Rule 9 provides that the Tribunal is under no duty to hold oral hearings but may do so where appropriate.

Rule 9(6) provides that the proceedings shall be conducted in private.

Rule 10 provides that the complainant has the right to be legally represented.

Rule 11 provides that the Tribunal may receive evidence in any form, including hearsay evidence, but has no power to compel any person to give oral evidence. In this respect, the Interception Code 9.1, which states 'the Tribunal has full powers to investigate and decide any case within its jurisdiction', is incorrect.

10.32 RIPA 2000, s 69(2)(g) refers to the rules prescribing the practice and procedure to be followed by the Tribunal, including questions of admissibility of evidence and the mode and burden of proof. The burden of proof has not been dealt with in the Rules.

In the matter of Application No IPT/01/62 and IPT/01/77 (23 January 2003)

10.33 The case concerned two sets of proceedings and complaints based on allegations of interception of communications by the Intelligence Services, and in one of the cases also by a police force. Having heard the argument, the Tribunal concluded that it should sit in public in order to decide the preliminary legal issues and not in private as stated in Rule 9(6). The complainants invited the Tribunal to give directions for the conduct of the claims to the effect that:

(a)   there be an oral hearing;
(b)   the hearing be in public;
(c)   there be mutual disclosure and inspection between the parties;
(d)   evidence on behalf of the complainants be heard in the presence of the respondents, and vice versa;
(e)   any opinion of a Commissioner be disclosed to the parties;
(f)   each party be at liberty to derogate from any of the above in relation to a particular piece of evidence; and
(g)   the Tribunal to give reasons for its final determination.

NCND

10.34   Paragraph 10.20 above explains the reasons for the policy of 'neither confirm nor deny' (NCND). The complainants did not challenge the NCND policy as such but contended that it did not justify the scale of departure in RIPA 2000 and the Rules from the Convention and common law requirements of a fair trial. In particular, it was contended that certain of the Rules were ultra vires the enabling power in RIPA 2000, s 69. The offending Rules were:

- Rule 6(2) to (5) regarding disclosure;
- Rules 9 and 6(2)(a) so far as they prevented the Tribunal from conducting its proceedings in public and adopting an adversarial procedure;
- Rule 11(3) regarding the compellability of unwilling source evidence; and
- Rule 13 regarding the lack of any statement of reasons for an unsuccessful complainant.

The conclusions of the Tribunal were that:

- art 6 applies to the activities of the Tribunal;
- the Rules are not incompatible with art 8;
- the Rules protecting information from being disclosed are for the maintenance of the NCND policy and were a proportionate interference with art 10(2); and
- the Secretary of State had power to make all the Rules with the exception of Rule 9(6).

In so far as the complaints regarding other Rules were concerned, having regard to the NCND policy, neither the disclosure rules nor the discretionary nature of the oral hearings amounted to an interference with art 6. Rule 13, regarding the giving of reasons for a determination, was also, having regard to the NCND policy, both necessary and justifiable but did not prevent reasons being given during a preliminary hearing.

Is the Tribunal procedure art 8 compliant?

10.35   In *Esbester v United Kingdom*,[1] the applicant alleged that information relating to his private life had been kept on secret files by one or other of the Intelligence Services and that the use of such information in the context of negative vetting procedures amounted to a violation of art 8. He also complained that the Tribunal did not offer adequate or effective protection against abuse because, inter alia, it was prevented from giving reasons for its decisions. In rejecting the complaint as manifestly ill-founded, the Commission held that the state could legitimately fear that the efficacy of surveillance procedures might be jeopardised if information were divulged to the person concerned.[2] It noted that the Tribunal consisted of lawyers of ten years' experience who acted in an independent capacity. In the absence of any evidence that the system was not functioning as required by domestic law, the Commission found that the framework of safeguards achieved a compromise between the requirements of defending a democratic society and the rights of the individual which was compatible with the provisions of the Convention.

1   Application No 18601/91, (1993) 18 EHRR CD 72.
2   See *Klass v Germany* (1978) 2 EHRR 214.

Chapter 11

Evidence and admissibility

Introduction

11.1 RIPA 2000, Pt I, Ch I has a complicated regime characterised by a general rule of non-disclosure and inadmissibility subject to a substantial list of exceptions. RIPA 2000, Pt I, Ch II, Pt II and Pt III, in common with the Police Act 1997, Pt III, start from the premise that all relevant material is admissible, subject to the discretion to exclude under PACE 1984, s 78. In certain cases the distinction between interception and the use of devices under RIPA 2000, Pt II may be hard to draw. Where, for instance, sophisticated surveillance devices are used which enable law enforcement agencies to overhear/record the details of a telephone conversation in the same manner as if the conversation had been intercepted, should the procedure be that under RIPA 2000 Pt I or Pt II?[1] Surveillance Code 4.32 states that the use of such devices should not be ruled out simply because they may pick up both ends of a telephone conversation. However, where the sole purpose is to overhear speech an application should be made for a warrant under RIPA 2000, s 5.

The first part of this chapter considers the obligation to disclose the product of surveillance and the second part the discretion to exclude such material. Although both Pts I and II of RIPA 2000 have been in force since 2 October 2000, reference is also made to the equivalent provisions of IOCA 1985 in order to understand the background from which certain relevant aspects of RIPA 2000 emerged.

1   See *R v Hammond, McIntosh and Gray* [2002] EWCA Crim 1423, a decision under IOCA 1985, *R v E* [2004] EWCA Crim 1243, and *R v Hardy* [2003] 1 Cr App Rep 494, [2003] Crim LR 394 (see **para 6.6**).

The duty to disclose

11.2 It is intended here only to provide a summary of certain aspects of the disclosure regime that have particular relevance to surveillance, including in particular the duty to retain material. The Criminal Procedure and Investigations Act 1996

(CPIA 1996), s 3 obliges the prosecutor to disclose material which has not previously been disclosed and which in his opinion might undermine the case against the accused. Such an obligation arises when the defendant is charged. The two exceptions to this duty are set out in CPIA 1996, s 3(6), public interest immunity, and s 3(7), where disclosure is prohibited by RIPA 2000, s 17. Prior to the stage of charging, material may come into existence a substantial part of which will not be relevant to any criminal prosecution and will not therefore fall within the normal regime of disclosure covered by CPIA 1996. In what circumstances is there any obligation to retain such material? Are there special rules for the product of interception?

The destruction of the product of interception under IOCA 1985

11.3 IOCA 1985, s 6 provided that the Secretary of State shall make arrangements to ensure the minimum disclosure of any intercepted material. IOCA 1985, s 6(3) provided that:

> 'The requirements of this subsection are satisfied in relation to any intercepted material if each copy made of any intercepted material is destroyed as soon as its retention is no longer necessary as mentioned in s 2(2) above.'

IOCA 1985, s 2(2) set out the three purposes for which the Secretary of State might issue a warrant, which included, at s 2(2)(b), 'for the purpose of preventing or detecting serious crime'.

As explained in *R v Preston* (see **para 11.4**), preventing and detecting crime did not include the prosecution of crime. A similar requirement is made by RIPA 2000, s 15 (see **para 11.7**).

Prevention and detection of serious crime

11.4 In *R v Preston*[1] the defence sought disclosure of the contents of telephone intercepts which it was thought would establish that one of the defendants had acted under duress. The House of Lords held that the prohibition in IOCA 1985, s 9 was insufficient reason for refusing to disclose information which might assist a defendant. The appropriate test was one of materiality not admissibility. However, in determining the true meaning of the prohibition in s 9, it was necessary to have regard to the duty to destroy such material in IOCA 1985, ss 6(3) and 2(2). Lord Mustill, who gave the leading judgment, explained his reasons for concluding that prevention and detection in IOCA 1985, s 2(2)(b) did not include the prosecution of crime.

> 'To my mind the expression "preventing and detecting" calls up only two stages of the fight against crime. First, the forestalling of potential crimes

which have not yet been committed. Second, the seeking out of crimes not so forestalled, which have already been committed. There as it seems to me the purpose ends.'

If there was no duty to retain intercepted material, it followed that there would be no material available for disclosure. Thus, even if such material might have assisted the defence, the obligation to destroy it once it was no longer necessary for the prevention or detection of crime trumped any obligation to the defence.

'The need for surveillance and the need to keep it secret are undeniable. So also is the need to protect to the feasible maximum the privacy of those whose conversations are overheard without their consent. Hence sections 2 and 6. These policies are in flat contradiction to current opinions on the transparency of the trial process. Something has to give way, and the history, structure and terms of the statute leave me in little doubt that this must be the duty to give complete disclosure of unused materials. The result is a vulnerable compromise, but it may be the best that can be achieved.'

1   [1994] 2 AC 130, [1993] 4 All ER 638, 98 Cr App Rep 405, at p 430.

11.5   It should be emphasised that Lord Mustill was referring to the product of interception which it was admitted by the prosecution had been obtained by means of a warrant. To the extent that such an admission ought not to have been made at all, the facts of the case are unlikely to be repeated.

11.6   RIPA 2000, s 81(5) has extended the definition of detecting crime to include:

'(a)   establishing by whom, for what purpose, by what means and generally in what circumstances any crime was committed; and

(b)   the apprehension of the person by whom any crime was committed;

and any reference in this Act to preventing and detecting serious crime shall be construed accordingly, except that, in Chapter I of Part I, it shall not include a reference to gathering evidence for use in any legal proceedings.'

This definition has been applied to the Security Service Act 1989 and the Police Act 1997, Pt III as it applies for the purposes of the provisions of RIPA 2000 not contained in Pt I, Ch I, but to the Intelligence Services Act 1994 (ISA 1994) as it applies for the purposes of RIPA 2000, Pt I, Ch I.[1] The functions of the respective services now expressly include the purpose of any criminal proceedings as well as the prevention and detection of crime.[2]

The effect of the amendments is to ensure a consistency of approach to issues such as the obtaining and disclosure of information.

1   See RIPA 2000, s 82(1) and Sch 4, paras 4, 6 and 8.
2   See Security Service Act 1989, s 2(2)(a), ISA 1994, ss 2(2)(a)(iv) and 4(2)(a) and Police Act 1997, s 93(2) as amended by RIPA 2000, s 82(1).

Is there a duty to destroy intercept material under RIPA 2000, Pt I?

11.7   RIPA 2000, s 15(3) provides for the destruction of any intercept material or related communications data as soon as it is no longer necessary for any of the authorised purposes. Authorised purposes are defined in RIPA 2000, s 15(4) and include not only national security, the prevention and detection (but not prosecution) of serious crime and the economic well-being of the UK, but also any of the functions of the Secretary of State, the Interceptions Commissioner and the Tribunal for enabling prosecuting counsel to secure the fairness of a prosecution and the Public Record Office to perform its duty. Related communications data is defined in RIPA 2000, s 20 to mean 'so much of any communications data (within RIPA 2000, Pt I, Ch II) as is obtained by or in connection with the interception and relates to the communication or to the sender or recipient or intended recipient of the communication'. Although the categories of authorised purposes which would justify retention of intercept material appear wider than the similar provisions in IOCA 1985, the difference may be more apparent than real. In particular, as noted below (see **para 11.35**), the extension of authorised purposes to considerations of a future trial is likely to prove little more than a meaningless gesture.

The destruction of other surveillance product (post IOCA 1985)

11.8   Surveillance Code 2.18 and CHIS Code 2.19 provide that:

> 'Each public authority must ensure that arrangements are in place for the handling, storage and destruction of material obtained through the use of covert surveillance. Authorising officers must ensure compliance with the appropriate data protection requirements and any relevant codes of practice produced by individual authorities relating to the handling and storage of material.'

There is a duty imposed on the respective heads of the Intelligence Services to ensure that there are arrangements in existence for securing that no information is obtained or disclosed by the service except so far as is necessary for the proper discharge of its functions.[1] The Surveillance Code 2.19 and the CHIS Code 2.20 interpret the obligation of obtaining and disclosure as including storage of information:

> 'The heads of these agencies are responsible for ensuring that arrangements exist for securing that no information is stored by the authorities except as is necessary for the proper discharge of their functions.'

1   See the Security Service Act 1989, s 2(2)(a) and ISA 1994, ss 2(2)(a) and 4(2)(a).

11.9   Given that, by RIPA 2000, s 81(5), these functions now include the purposes of criminal proceedings, it is submitted that any matter that may be relevant to any criminal prosecution should be retained as per the regime of CPIA 1996.[1] Surveillance Code 2.16 and CHIS Code 2.17 endorse this view:

> 'Where the product of surveillance could be relevant to pending or future criminal or civil proceedings it should be retained in accordance with established disclosure requirements for a suitable further period commensurate to any subsequent review.'

1   See the Code of Practice, para 5 issued under the CPIA 1996 (**para 11.10**).

Retention of the product of surveillance other than by way of interception

11.10   The Code of Practice issued under CPIA 1996, Pt II (CPIA Code) states in para 5.1 that the investigator must retain material obtained in a criminal investigation which may be relevant to the investigation. If material has been seized under the provisions of PACE 1984, the duty of retention is subject to PACE1984, s 22. CPIA Code 5.6 makes it clear that such material should be retained until a decision is taken as to whether to institute proceedings against a person, in which case it should be kept until the person is acquitted or convicted. An investigation is widely defined in CPIA Code 2.1 to include:

- investigations into crimes which have been committed;
- investigations whose purpose is to ascertain whether a crime has been committed with a view to the possible institution of criminal proceedings; and
- investigations which begin in the belief that a crime may be committed, for example when the police keep premises or individuals under observation for a period of time, with a view to the possible institution of criminal proceedings.

Retention of the application and the warrant/authorisation under RIPA 2000, Pt I, Ch I

11.11   A copy of the application and any application for renewal, and any refusal thereof, as well as the warrant itself, together with any renewal and schedule modifications, must be retained by the intercepting agency for scrutiny by the Interception Commissioner.[1]

1   See Interception Code 4.18 for s 8(1) warrants and 5.17 for s 8(4) warrants.

The centrally retrievable record of authorisations under RIPA 2000, Pt II

11.12   Surveillance Code 2.14 provides that:

'A centrally retrievable record of all authorisations should be held by each public authority and regularly updated whenever an authorisation is granted, renewed or cancelled. The record should be made available to the relevant Commissioner or an Inspector from the Office of Surveillance Commissioners upon request. These records should be retained for a period of at least three years from the ending of the authorisation and should contain the following information:

- the type of authorisation;
- the date the authorisation was given;
- name and rank/grade of the authorising officer;
- the unique reference number (URN) of the investigation or operation;

- the title of the investigation or operation, including a brief description and names of suspects, if known;
- whether the urgency provisions were used, and if so why;
- if the authorisation is renewed when it was renewed and who authorised the renewal, including the name and rank/grade of the authorising officer;
- whether the investigation or operation is likely to result in obtaining confidential information as defined in this code of practice; and
- the date the authorisation was cancelled.'

11.13 Surveillance Code 2.15 sets out the material which should be maintained but which need not form part of the centrally retrievable record. This includes:

- a copy of the application and a copy of the authorisation, together with any supplementary documentation and notification of approval given by the authorising officer;
- a record of the period over which the surveillance has taken place;
- the frequency of reviews prescribed by the authorising officer;
- a record of the result of each review of the authorisation;
- a copy of the renewal of an authorisation, together with the supporting documentation submitted when the renewal was requested; and
- the date and time when any instruction was given by the authorising officer.

Records relating to the use of a CHIS

11.14 Proper records must be kept of the authorisation and use of a source[1] **(para 8.21)**. In addition, CHIS Code 2.15 states that records or copies of the following should be kept by the relevant authority:

- a copy of the authorisation, together with any supplementary documentation and notification of the approval given by the authorising officer;
- a copy of any renewal of an authorisation, together with the supporting documentation submitted when the renewal was requested;
- the reason why the person renewing the authorisation considered it necessary to do so;
- any authorisation which was granted or renewed orally (in an urgent case) and the reason why the case was considered urgent;
- any risk assessment made in relation to the source;
- the circumstances in which tasks were given to the source;
- the value of the source to the investigating authority;
- a record of the results of any reviews of the authorisation;
- the reasons, if any, for renewing an authorisation;
- the reasons for cancelling an authorisation; and
- the date and time when any instruction was given by the authorising officer to cease being a source.

1   RIPA s 29(2)(c).

Authorisation record under ISA 1994, s 5 and the Police Act 1997, Part III

11.15 Surveillance Code 6.27 provides for the matters which should be included in the record of authorisation under the above as follows:

- the time and date when an authorisation is given;
- whether the authorisation is in written or oral form;
- the time and date when it was notified to a Surveillance Commissioner;
- the time and date when the Surveillance Commissioner notified his approval;
- every occasion when entry onto or interference with property or wireless telegraphy has occurred;
- the result of periodic reviews of the authorisation;
- the date of every renewal; and
- the time and date when the authorising officer gave any instruction to cease the interference.

Retention of communications data under RIPA 2000, Pt I, Ch II

11.16 There is no duty of retention by CSPs under RIPA 2000. For duties of retention of communications data under the Anti-terrorism, Crime and Security Act 2001 see **Chapter 7**. Once such material has been obtained by a law enforcement agency the CPIA principles apply.

Is there a duty of retention where no proceedings are taken or the person is acquitted?

11.17 Material gathered during a surveillance operation will often include personal data which will fall within the scope of the Data Protection Act 1998 (DPA 1998). As such, the data should not be retained any longer than necessary (see **Chapter 3**). Where no proceedings are instituted, Ch 8, para 2 of the ACPO Code of Practice for Data Protection (ACPO Code) gives general advice about the criteria to be considered. It is pointed out that the failure to remove data when their purpose has been served will result in inaccurate, irrelevant, excessive and out-of-date data being held, all of which would be breaches of the data protection principles. In some cases it will be necessary for further enquiries to be made and/or views of the officer responsible for the initial record to be sought before a decision to remove the information can be properly taken. When the person is acquitted, ACPO Code 8.4.12 suggests that details of acquittals or of cases discontinued without caution should not be retained beyond 42 days. An exception is made in cases of an offence of unlawful sexual intercourse by a male with a female under the age of 16, where such details must be retained. Details will be deleted when a male reaches the age of 24.[1] The disclosure of the fact of a person having been charged with a sexual offence is likely to be deemed unlawful if the case against him was discontinued.[2]

1   Sexual Offences Act 1956, s 6(3).
2   See *R v Chief Constable of West Midlands Police* (2004) EWHC 61 (admin).

The prohibition against disclosure of the product of interception

11.18   IOCA 1985, s 9 has been repealed by RIPA 2000 but the paramount importance of secrecy which underpinned it is common to RIPA 2000, s 17, which has replaced it. It would be difficult to understand the latter without some under-standing of the problems caused by the former, described by Lord Mustill as 'impenetrable' in *R v Preston*.[1] Indeed, in *A-G's Reference (No 5 of 2002)*,[2] the court confirmed that s 17 should be considered in the light of s 9. The paragraphs that follow (see **paras 11.19–11.26**) attempt to highlight certain areas likely to be relevant in construing the latter, and assume some familiarity with the background to the whole of this 'short but difficult statute'.[3]

1   (1994) 98 Cr App Rep 405 at 431.
2   [2003] EWCA Crim 1632, [2003] 1 WLR 2902.
3   (1994) 98 Cr App Rep 405 at 416 (see **para 11.22**).

11.19

IOCA 1985, s 9 provided that:
> '(1)   In any proceedings before any court or tribunal no evidence shall be adduced and no question in cross-examination shall be asked which (in either case) tends to suggest–
>   (a)   that an offence under section 1 above has been or is to be committed by any of the persons mentioned in subsection (2) below; or
>   (b)   that a warrant has been or is to be issued to any of those persons.
> (2)   The persons referred to in subsection (1) above are–
>   (a)   any person holding office under the Crown;
>   (b)   the Post Office and any person engaged in the business of the Post Office; and
>   (c)   any public telecommunications operator and any person engaged in the running of a public telecommunications system.'

In *R v Sargent*,[1] the victim of an arson attack was a telephone engineer who put a tester on the telephone of his ex-wife, suspecting that she might be involved. In doing so, he committed an offence under IOCA 1985, s 1(1). The intercept produced a record of a conversation between the ex-wife and the defendant which formed the basis of the prosecution case against him. The prosecution argued successfully in the Court of Appeal that the victim was acting without authority and therefore did not fall within s 9(2)(c). The House of Lords overruled the Court of Appeal and concluded that he had been so engaged. Although the underlying purpose of the prohibition was to protect information as to the authorisation and carrying out of official intercepts, it extended also to unauthorised activity. It reflected the public interest that the circumstances in which the activities of those involved in serious crime came to the notice of the police should not be capable of being explored at a trial.

Of particular note is the fact that the section did not expressly prevent disclosure of the contents of an intercept.

So impenetrable was s 9 that it has resulted in at least seven journeys to the Court of Appeal at least and four to the House of Lords.

1   [2001] UKHL 54, [2003] 1 AC 347.

The exceptions to the prohibition

11.20   IOCA 1985, s 9(3) provided that s 9(1) did not apply–

'(a)   in relation to proceedings for a relevant offence or proceedings before the Tribunal; or

(b)   where evidence is adduced or the question in cross-examination is asked for the purpose of establishing the fairness or unfairness of a dismissal on grounds of an offence under section 1 above or conduct from which such an offence might be inferred; and paragraph (a) of that subsection shall not apply where a person has been convicted of the offence under that section.'

A relevant offence was defined to include specific offences under the Telegraph Acts and the Official Secrets Acts, perjury, attempted perjury or contempt of court committed in the course of any such offence.

The importance of being private

11.21   As IOCA 1985, s 1 was concerned only with communications by means of a public telecommunications system, it followed that there was no prohibition against the use of evidence obtained by means of the interception of a private system. Considerable ingenuity has been expended by the prosecution in attempting to establish that the particular system was private and the evidence admissible on the one hand, and by the defence trying to establish the opposite on the other.[1] Although RIPA 2000, s 1 has created the offence of interception of a communication in the course of its transmission by means of a private telecommunications system, the distinction between public and private will still be of relevance if, for instance, it is suggested that the interception took place with the consent of the person with the right to control the system. Thus, decisions under IOCA 1985, s 1 may still be relevant. Until recently it does not seem to have been appreciated that the mere process of enquiry might itself contravene the terms of s 9(1).[2]

1   See *R v Effick* (1992) 95 Cr App Rep 427, *R v Allan* [2001] EWCA Crim 1027 (6 April 2001, unreported) and *R v Goodman* [2002] EWCA Crim 903 (4 March 2002, unreported).
2   See *A-G's Reference (No 5 of 2002)* [2003] EWCA Crim 1632, [2003] Crim LR 793.

11.22   The first case in which the public/private issue was raised was *R v Effick*,[1] where the prosecution sought to introduce the contents of telephone conversations made on a cordless telephone to establish that the defendants had been involved in the supply of controlled drugs. The police had obtained no warrant for the interceptions. The trial judge ruled that the calls had been intercepted when they were passing between the cordless telephone and the base unit and that the cordless telephone was not part of the public telecommunications network. He admitted the evidence. In the Court of Appeal, it was generously assumed in the appellant's favour that the calls made on a cordless telephone were part of the public telecommunications system. The Crown contended that such evidence was admissible so long as no question was asked tending to suggest an offence or the existence of a warrant. Lord Steyn concluded:

> 'The express terms of section 9 do not provide that no evidence obtained as a result of an interception may be admitted. The forbidden territory is drawn in a much narrower fashion. And there is a logical reason for the narrow exclusionary provision. That is the reflection that it cannot be in the public interest to allow those involved in espionage or serious crime to discover at a public trial the basis on which their activities had come to the notice of the police, the Customs and Excise or the Security Services such as, for example, by questions designed to find out who provided the information which led to the issue of the warrant. So interpreted section 9(1) makes sense. And it would make no sense to stretch that language to become a comprehensive exclusion of all evidence obtained as a result of any interception.'

1   (1992) 95 Cr App Rep 427.

11.23   The following year the House again had occasion to consider IOCA 1985, s 9. In *R v Preston*,[1] the appellants were arrested as a result of intensive police surveillance and charged with conspiracy to import drugs. The prosecution sought to prove the conspiracy by means of a large number of telephone calls. The defence appealed on the grounds, inter alia, that the judge's ruling to admit evidence of the telephone conversations without requiring the prosecution to disclose details of the intercepted calls was a material irregularity. Although in *R v Effick* the Crown had adopted the stance that such evidence was admissible, in the present appeal they maintained that the judgment in *Effick* was wrong, that counsel had been wrongly instructed and that the judgment should be overruled. Lord Mustill agreed with the suggestion that it should be overruled and dismissed the appeal.[2]

1   [1994] 98 Cr App Rep 405.
2   See **para 11.4**.

11.24   Eight years after his observations in *R v Effick*, and 'aided by the incisive arguments of counsel', Lord Steyn was fully persuaded that his interpretation was wrong.[1] He gave three reasons for his conversion. First, the language of the section was 'at least capable of amounting to a general provision that any evidence obtained as a result of any interception will be inadmissible.' The second factor was that in practice, as explained by Lord Woolf in *R v Preston*:[2]

'To lay the groundwork for material to be admissible in evidence the manner in which the material has been obtained will normally have to be given in evidence in court.'

The third factor was that the invariable practice before the passing of the Act was that intercepted material was not used in evidence.

1   See *Morgans v DPP* [2001] 1 AC 315.
2   (1992) 95 Cr App Rep 355.

11.25   In *R v Effick*,[1] the House of Lords reversed the Court of Appeal on the facts and upheld the decision of the trial judge that no communication was being made by means of a public telecommunications system. Lord Oliver, who gave the leading judgment, identified what he saw as the mischief at which the Act was aimed.

'It set out, as it seems to me, to achieve three objects, viz:– first to protect the integrity of that system of communication which is under public, and not under individual, control by creating a specific offence of interception of communications through the public system; secondly, to provide for the authorisation of such limited exceptions, under proper safeguards, as are necessitated by the requirements of national security and the prevention of serious crime; and, thirdly, to ensure that the use of material acquired by resort to these exceptional procedures is strictly limited to the purposes for which it has been acquired and is not used for any other purpose. It was not an Act designed nor does it purport to confer any general protection against eaves-dropping or intrusion on the privacy of individuals or provide for any general authorisation for telephone tapping on private premises. And there is a logic in this. The individual who connects his own private apparatus to the public system has means at his disposal to protect his own private apparatus from interference. What he cannot protect himself from is interference with the public system without which his private apparatus is useless. Hence the necessity for statutory protection of that system.'[2]

This final comment is at odds with the earlier disavowal of privacy being the impetus behind the legislation. It is respectfully submitted that the earlier comment is closer to the reality of the situation, which is that the main impetus is not privacy but secrecy. The House expressly approved the decision in *R v Ahmed*,[3] in which Evans LJ ruled that:

'The interception of a communication takes place where the electrical impulse or signal which is passing along the telephone line is intercepted in fact.'

1   (1994) 99 Cr App Rep 312.
2   (1994) 99 Cr App Rep 312 at p 320.
3   [1995] Crim LR 246.

11.26

Three subsequent cases interpreted the House of Lords decision in *R v Preston* to overrule *R v Effick* as referring only to warranted intercepts: *R v Rasool*,[1] *R v Owen*[2] and *Morgans v DPP QBD*. Thus in all non-warrant cases intercept evidence would be admissible. The latter case was a non-warrant case. When it got to the House of Lords, the House did its best to resolve the confusion that still hung over the meaning of IOCA 1985, s 9. The police, who suspected the appellant of gaining unauthorised access to various computer systems, intercepted his telephone line without obtaining a warrant. The prosecution continued to rely on *R v Effick* as authority for the proposition that intercepted material obtained other than by virtue of a warrant was admissible. They argued that the purpose of s 9 was to prevent the giving of information as to the authorisation of intercepts. Lord Hope, who gave the leading judgment, accepted the argument of the appellant that it would be quite extraordinary if material which had been obtained without any of the safeguards provided by the authorisation process was admissible. He went on to say:

> 'evidence of material obtained by interception by the persons mentioned in s 9(2) of the 1985 Act of communications of the kind described in s 1 of that Act, except for the purposes described in s 1(3), will always be inadmissible. It is not possible to say that s 9(1) of the Act provides for this in express language. But in the context of the Act as a whole, the prohibitions which it contains lead inexorably to that result. So I would hold that it has that effect by necessary implication.'[3]

Thus, even if it were to be suggested that the interception was consensual, as had happened in the case of *R v Rasool*, the evidence would still be inadmissible. This was because the issue as to whether the interception was under a warrant or if it was not whether it was consensual could not be made the subject of evidence.

1   [1997] 1 WLR 1092.
2   [1999] 1 WLR 949.
3   [2001] 1 AC 315 at 338.

The prohibition of the disclosure of the product of interception under RIPA 2000

11.27   RIPA 2000, s 17 provides:

> '(1)   Subject to section 18, no evidence shall be adduced, question asked, assertion or disclosure made or other thing done in, for the purposes of or in connection with any legal proceedings which (in any manner)–
>   (a)   discloses, in circumstances from which its origin in anything falling within subsection (2) may be inferred, any of the contents of an intercepted communication or any related communication data; or
>   (b)   tends (apart from any such disclosure) to suggest that anything falling within subsection (2) has or may have occurred or be going to occur.
> (2)   The following fall within this subsection–
>   (a)   conduct by a person falling within subsection (3) that was or would be an offence under section 1(1) or (2) of this Act or under section 1 of the Interception of Communications Act 1985;
>   (b)   a breach by the Secretary of State of his duty under section 1(4) of this Act;

    (c) the issue of an interception warrant or of a warrant under the Interception of Communications Act 1985;

    (d) the making of an application by any person for an interception warrant, or for a warrant under that Act;

    (e) the imposition of any requirement on any person to provide assistance with giving effect to an interception warrant.'

Section 17(3) refers to:

    '(a) any person to whom a warrant under this Chapter may be addressed;

    (b) any person holding office under the Crown;

    (c) any member of the NCIS;

    (d) any member of the NCS;

    (e) any person employed by or for the purposes of a police force;

    (f) any person providing a postal service or employed for the purposes of any business of providing such a service;

    (g) any person providing a public telecommunications service or employed for the purposes of any business of providing such a service.'

For the offences created by IOCA 1985, s 1 and RIPA 2000, s 1 see **paras 6.15** and **6.33** respectively.

11.28   If Parliament intended to clarify the confusion caused by the impenetrable IOCA 1985, s 9, it has signally failed to do so. It is noteworthy that there is still no outright prohibition against disclosing the contents of an intercept. Only if the disclosure will lead to the consequences in RIPA 2000, s 1(1)(a) is such disclosure prohibited. As under previous legislation, ie IOCA 1985, however, it is difficult to envisage a situation in which the contents could be disclosed without some reference to provenance (see **para 11.24**). According to Interception Code 7.3, the general rule is that neither the possibility of interception, nor intercepted material itself, plays any part in legal proceedings. The rule means that the material cannot be used by prosecution or defence, thus preserving equality of arms under art 6. As will be seen, the general rule is subject to a list of exceptions in s 18 which is significantly longer than under IOCA 1985 (see **para 11.29**).

When is interception evidence admissible under RIPA 2000?

11.29   The following is a summary of the exceptions in RIPA 2000, s 18:

(a)   any proceedings for a relevant offence (a relevant offence is defined in s 18(12) to include an offence under any provision of RIPA 2000 or IOCA 1985 as well as offences under certain Telegraphy Acts, the Official Secrets Acts and offences of perjury or contempt of court arising out of any of the above);

(b)   any civil proceedings by the Secretary of State to enforce an interception warrant;

(c)   any proceedings before the Tribunal (or appeal therefrom);

(d)   any proceedings before the Special Immigration Appeals Commission;

(e)   any proceedings before the Proscribed Organisations Appeal Commission;

(f) any legal proceedings for unfair dismissal arising out of an offence under RIPA 2000, ss 1(1) or (2), 11(7) or 19 or IOCA 1985, s 1;[1]

(g) where the interception was lawful in relation to any stored communication in the exercise of any statutory power, eg obtaining access to stored data on a pager found on an arrested person which may be authorised under PACE 1984, Sch 1;[2]

(h) where the interceptor has reasonable grounds for believing that both the sender and recipient of the communication have consented;[3]

(i) where only the sender or the recipient has consented and there is an authorisation under RIPA 2000, Pt II;[4]

(j) where interception is undertaken by or on behalf of the provider of the postal service or CSP for purposes connected with the provision of that service;[5]

(k) where the interception is authorised under the Wireless Telegraphy Act 1949, s 5 for purposes connected with the issue of licences or the prevention or detection of interference with wireless telegraphy;[6]

(l) where the interception is carried out for the purpose of obtaining information about the communications of a person who is or is reasonably believed to be outside the UK, the interception relates to a public telecommunications system in that country, the CSP is obliged to facilitate that interception and it is carried out in accordance with regulations made by the Secretary of State;[7]

(m) where the interception is effected by a person carrying on a business for the purposes of monitoring or keeping a record of business transactions,[8] including for these purposes any government department or public authority (see Directive 97/66/EC, art 5, which exempts from its prohibition 'any legally authorised recording of communications in the course of lawful business practice.' See **para 6.42**);

(n) where the interception takes place in a prison and is authorised under rules made under Prison Act 1952, s 47 or its equivalent in Scotland or Northern Ireland;

(o) where the interception takes place in a high security hospital and is authorised under the National Health Service Act 1977, s 17 or its equivalent in Scotland;

(p) where disclosure is to a person conducting a criminal prosecution to enable that person to secure the fairness of the prosecution;[9] and

(q) where the disclosure is to a relevant judge in a case in which that judge has ordered disclosure to be made to him alone.[10]

Not included in the above is any reference to RIPA 2000, s 1(6), where the interception is of a private system by the person with the right to control the system. This was a point argued in *A-G's Reference (No 5 of 2002)* (at para 82). According to the Court of Appeal (at para 92), s 17 does not prevent the introduction into evidence of the contents of an intercept made by the person with the right to control the line (see **para 11.33**). In this case, no directed surveillance authorisation required.

1   RIPA 2000, s 18(3).
2   RIPA 2000, s 18(4).
3   RIPA 2000, s 18(4) (see Code 10.3).
4   RIPA 2000, s 18(4) (see **para 11.30**).
5   RIPA 2000, s 3(3).
6   RIPA 2000, s 3(4).

7   See SI 2004/157.
8   See SI 2000/2699.
9   RIPA 2000, s 18(7)(a) (see **para 11.35**).
10   RIPA 2000, s 18(7)(b) (see **para 11.36**).

Where one party has consented (RIPA 2000, s 18(4))

11.30   Of particular significance in the context of criminal investigations is where one party has consented to the interception. The fact that such activity is deemed not to amount to interception does not mean that it is uncontrolled. By virtue of RIPA 2000, ss 26(4)(b) and 48(4) it is to be considered as directed surveillance and authorised accordingly. Chapter 4 of the Surveillance Code and Ch 2 of the CHIS Code provide guidance.

The practice is often referred to as participant monitoring.[1] On the one hand it may permit banks or other businesses routinely to record telephone conversations with customers and on the other it may be used to permit undercover officers or informant to record conversations with suspects. The latter offends against the concept of a reasonable expectation of privacy and is inconsistent with the principle that it is the person whose privacy is infringed who should be afforded safeguards. The subject was considered by the Canadian Supreme Court in the case of *R v Duarte*[2] in which the accused was charged with drug trafficking. The police, without authorisation, had set up an informant in an apartment which was equipped with audio-visual recording equipment. The court held that there was no logical reason to distinguish third-party electronic surveillance where neither of the participants consent and surveillance where one party consents.

> 'The rationale for regulating the power of the state to record communications that their originator expects will not be intercepted by anyone other than the person intended by the originator to receive them has nothing to do with protecting individuals from the threat that the person to whom they talk will divulge communications that are meant to be private. Rather, the regulation of electronic surveillance protects against the more insidious danger inherent in allowing the state in its unfettered discretion to record and transmit our words. It is unacceptable in a free society that agents of the state be free to use this technology at their sole discretion.'

1   See **para 8.32**.
2   (1990) 53 CCC (3d).

11.31   The predecessor of RIPA 2000, s 18(4), IOCA 1985, s 1(2)(b), was the subject of the appeal in *R v Rasool*,[1] in which the Court of Appeal held that the overruling of *Effick* had no effect on consensual interceptions and concluded that evidence that had been recorded by a police informant was admissible. The case was itself overruled in *Morgans v DPP*[2] by the House of Lords which held that consensual interceptions were also caught by the prohibition in IOCA 1985, s 9(1)(a). Thus the issue of whether the interception was under a warrant or if not whether it was consensual could not be made the subject of evidence. Does the same prohibition apply to s 17? Apparently not (see s 18(5) and **para 11.32**). Where the prosecution claim that the evidence is admissible for any reason unconnected with a warrant, such evidence should be disclosed to the defence. If the defence object to admissibility the issue of lawfulness will need to be decided by the judge. A decision that the interception was lawful does not prevent the defence then submitting that the evidence should be excluded under PACE 1984, s 78. The Interception Code 10.2 states that:

> 'For lawful interception which takes place without a warrant pursuant to sections 3 or 4 of the Act or pursuant to some other statutory power, there is no prohibition in the Act on the evidential use of any material that is obtained as a result. The matter may still, however, be regulated by the exclusionary rules of evidence to be found in the common law, s 78 PACE 1984 and/or pursuant to the Human Rights Act 1998.'

1   [1997] 1 WLR 1092.
2   [2001] 1 AC 315.

Where prosecution seek to adduce intercept evidence, may the defence challenge the basis of authorisation (if any)?

11.32   Although RIPA 2000, s 17 may appear wider than IOCA 1985, s 9, appearances may be deceptive. RIPA 2000, s 18(5) provides that where any disclosure is proposed to be or has been made on the grounds that it is authorised by s 18(4) (see **para 11.30**), s 17(1) shall not prohibit the doing of anything in, or for the purpose of, so much of any legal proceedings as relates to the question whether that disclosure is or was so authorised. Thus, should disclosure be made by the prosecution on the basis, for example, that one party consented to the interception, it seems that the defence may challenge the basis of the authorisation.[1] To this extent it seems that *Morgans v DPP*[2] has been statutorily overruled.

1   RIPA 2000, s 18(5).
2   [2001] 1 AC 315 at 337.

May enquiry into the public/private character of a telecommunications system breach RIPA 2000, s 17?

11.33   In *A-G's Reference (No 5 of 2002)*,[1] the facts arose before RIPA 2000 came into force, but the trial took place afterwards. The case concerned an allegation of corruption involving three police officers who provided confidential information to a known criminal. During the course of the investigation in 1996 the relevant chief constable gave his consent in writing for an interception to take place on a number of specific telephone extensions at a police station. At trial the prosecution maintained that the extensions were part of the internal system which was made up of a network of Private Automated Branch Exchanges (PABX). The defence wished to assert that the interceptions took place on a public communications system. The judge ruled that the effect of RIPA 2000, s 17 was that the defence were not entitled to assert that the interception had taken place on the public side of the system. The defence therefore submitted that to admit evidence designed to show that the interceptions had taken place on the private telecommunications system without permitting the defence to prove the contrary would have such an adverse effect on the fairness of the proceedings that the judge ought not to admit it under PACE 1984, s 78. The judge accepted the submissions. The prosecution appealed. It was held, allowing the appeal, that the relevant statute was RIPA 2000, s 17 as it applies to offences created by IOCA 1985. In none of the cases decided under IOCA 1985 had it been argued that evidence on the question of whether the transmission was by means of a public telecommunications system was inadmissible. Evidence that the system is public does not in any way disclose the contents of the communications and so is not prohibited by RIPA 2000, s 17(1)(a). There was no possible conduct that was or would be an offence under RIPA 2000, s 1(1) or (2) because those sections were not in force at the time of the relevant events. There was no relevant distinction between IOCA 1985, s 9 and RIPA 2000, s 17. The judge was wrong to rule that the defence were prevented from adducing evidence that the system was a public system. If no question of an offence can arise because the circumstances in which the interception took place are 'excluded from criminal liability' under RIPA 2000, s 1(6), then s 17 does not prevent the introduction into evidence of the contents of an intercept made by a person with the right to control the line.

There would normally be two issues for the court to decide before admitting evidence of an intercept: whether the interception was on a private line, and if so, whether it was made by or with the consent of the person with the right to control the line.

1   [2003] Crim LR 793, 12 June 2003.

11.34   A critical aspect of the judgment is the conclusion that RIPA 2000, s 17(2)(a) did not apply to the facts of the case. It is, with respect, questionable whether this is correct. Section 17(2)(a) refers to conduct by a police officer that was or would be an offence under RIPA 2000, s 1(1) or (2) or under IOCA 1985, s 1(1). While it is true, as the court stated (at para 67), that neither RIPA 2000, s 1(1) or (2) were in force at the time, the same does not apply to IOCA 1985, s 1, which provides that:

'subject to the following provisions of this section, a person who intentionally intercepts a communication in the course of its transmission by post or by means of a public telecommunications system shall be guilty of an offence.'

It was not suggested that the exceptions in IOCA 1985, s 1(2) or (3) applied.

Any question designed to show that the interception in the present case was of a public telecommunications system was bound to suggest the commission of an offence by the police officer concerned. The failure to see any relevant distinction between the two is, to the present writer, inexplicable. The fact that the point has not been taken in the past, on which the court also relied, is to say the least an unconvincing form of reasoning. As permission has been given to appeal to the House of Lords the position will hopefully be clarified.

Disclosure of intercept material to the prosecutor

11.35   Should any information survive the destruction requirement referred to above (see **para 11.7**), RIPA 2000, s 18(7)(a) permits disclosure of any information that continues to be available to prosecuting counsel to enable him to secure the fairness of any prosecution. Interception Code 7.7 confirms that:

> 'The exception does not mean that intercepted material should be retained against a remote possibility that it might be relevant to future proceedings ...'

Where the material has been destroyed in accordance with RIPA 2000, s 15(3), the Code somewhat obviously advises that:

> 'there is no need to consider disclosure to a prosecutor if in fact no intercepted material remains in existence.'

Neither RIPA 2000 nor the Interception Code identifies who is responsible for overseeing the destruction of unnecessary material. The unreality of the present position that now appears to exist as a result of RIPA 2000, s 18(7)(a) was clearly foreseen by Lord Mustill in *R v Preston*.[1] Having commented on the psychological difficulties of the decision maker in reconciling his duty to keep material secret with a duty to help the accused at trial, he said:

> 'The practical difficulties are equally great. The decision maker has to decide whether what he hears may be helpful to a defendant not yet identified not yet charged in relation to offences not yet determined, and perhaps not even committed, who may raise defences which under current practice can be concealed until the trial is well under way.'

1   [1994] 2 AC 130, 98 Cr App Rep 405.

The prosecution is aware of its duty. Disclosure to the relevant judge (RIPA 2000, s 18(7)(b))

11.36   Under this subsection the prosecutor, having seen material under s 18(7)(a), may in exceptional circumstances invite the judge to make an order for disclosure to him alone.[1] Interception Code 7.12 states that this is an exceptional procedure as normally the prosecutor's functions under s 18(7)(a) will not fall to be reviewed by the judge. In order to do so, the judge will need to see the intercepted material. The 'Catch 22' nature of this procedure is the subject of comment by *Mirfield*.[2] Interception Code 7.13 provides that the judge, having considered the intercepted material, may direct the prosecution to make an admission of fact in such a manner as not to reveal the fact of interception.

> 'This is likely to be a very unusual step. The Act only allows it where the judge considers it essential in the interests of justice.'

Although the Interception Code stresses the exceptional nature of this course of action, no guidance is given as to what might amount to exceptional circumstances. It is submitted that the situation would certainly cover the facts of a case such as *R v*

Preston[3] if the contents of the intercept did indeed lend support to the suggestion of duress. It is, however, difficult to understand how such an admission could be made without revealing the fact of the interception or how, even if that difficulty could be overcome, a mere admission by the prosecution would enable a jury to determine whether the duress was of such a degree to amount to a defence.

1   RIPA 2000, s 18(7)(b).
2   [2003] Crim LR 97.
3   [1994] 2 AC 130.

Disclosure of material other than the product of intercepts

11.37   All material obtained under RIPA 2000, Pt 1, Ch II, Pt II or Pt III and Police Act 1997, Pt III is disclosable in the usual way subject to public interest immunity (PII). The Criminal Justice Act 2003, s 32 requires primary disclosure of any previously undisclosed material which might reasonably be considered capable of undermining the case for the prosecution against the accused or of assisting the case for the accused. In general, the fact of surveillance and the content of that which has been captured of a particular defendant's conversations, if any, should be revealed to the defence at an early stage. Lord Hobhouse in *R v P*[1] said:

'Where surveillance evidence is concerned the use of the evidence comes at a price. If the fairness of the trial is to be preserved the defendant must be permitted to probe the evidence and question the witnesses who come to court to provide the proof. This means that disclosure has to be made and the secrecy of the means and extent of the surveillance has to be sacrificed.'

The very fact that there has been extensive surveillance which has not resulted in anything incriminating is in itself a matter of which the defence are entitled to be informed.[2] However, if the material does not weaken the prosecution case or strengthen that of the defendant there is no need to disclose it.

1   [2001] 1 AC 146.
2   See observations of Newman J in *R v Sutherland* (29 January 2002, unreported) at para 11.

11.38   In *R v Hardy*,[1] the defence sought disclosure of the authorisations for surveillance, including the recording of telephone calls. The authorisations were granted by an assistant chief constable of the NCS and authorised both directed surveillance and the use of CHIS 'to utilise tape recording equipment to effect independent corroboration'. It was contended by the defence that unless they saw those documents they could not properly investigate whether the surveillance had been lawful. The authorisations set out in quite a detailed manner the information which led to them being granted. That information included information relating to the progress of the inquiry and to the means by which the inquiry was being carried out. The Crown applied ex parte to withhold the information. The judge acceded to the application. The Crown nevertheless provided a bundle of redacted authorisations. The Court of Appeal stated that the judge had been wrong not to order disclosure at least of the parts of the authorisations which did not attract PII, as they were relevant to the application under PACE 1984, s 78, but dismissed the argument that full disclosure of the authorisations was required.

1   [2003] 1 Cr App Rep 494, [2003] Crim LR 394.

11.39   *R v P* was referred to in *R v Lawrence*,[1] where the defence sought disclosure of authorisations under the Police Act 1997, Pt III together with details of related intelligence, including notes of meetings and oral discussions between the officers applying for authorisation and the authorising officers. The case concerned a VAT fraud, during the investigation of which NCS obtained some 36 successive authorisations by way of original application, monthly renewal and review in relation to the installation and continuance of three probes. The prosecution disclosed the applications for authorisation and the authorisations granted to deploy and retain the probes between April 1999 and September 2000. Some of the applications contained deletions relating to sensitive material which had been approved by the judge during a PII hearing. The prosecution refused to disclose authorisations prior to April 1999 on the basis that they were not relevant. The defence argued that full disclosure was necessary to explore the fundamental legality of the authorisations for intrusive surveillance and also to enable them to present their case in its best light.[2] The court considered the pre-1999 material and confirmed that it would not have assisted the defence. It added that the defence had no right to probe surveillance evidence on other earlier occasions which were not relied on by the prosecution. In so far as the post-1999 material was concerned it stated:

> 'Given that the structure of the 1997 Act is to provide for authorisation to be given by an authorising officer on the basis of his belief as to the matters set out in s 93(2) and that in connection with authorisations by persons other than Commissioners such persons are bound to have regard to the Code in the performance of their functions (see s 101(1) and (8)), it seems to us that prima facie at least, the matters appearing on the face of the applications and authorisations under the signature of the relevant officers fall to be taken at face value as the grounds for the authorisation. On that basis, unless there is a challenge on substantial grounds to the bona fides of the applying or authorising officer, such notes of meetings or oral discussions should not in the ordinary way be regarded as relevant or subject to disclosure by either side for the purpose of questioning or interpreting the text of the application and authorisation.'[3]

As, on the facts, the challenge to the lawfulness of the authorisations was based simply upon the argument over the length of time usually to be considered as appropriate for the continuation of surveillance, the court concluded that no further disclosure was required.

1   [2001] EWCA Crim 1829, [2002] Crim LR 584..
2   See *R v Agar* (1989) 90 Cr App Rep 318.
3   [2002] Crim LR 584 at para 95.

Public interest immunity (PII)

11.40   The impact of the ECt HR on the domestic procedures surrounding applications by the prosecution for PII has been set out in **Chapter 2 (paras 2.21–**

2.29). In summary, it can be stated that the approach of the Court of Appeal, as developed in cases such as *R v Ward*,[1] *R v Davis, Rowe and Johnson*[2] and *R v Keane*,[3] has been held to be compatible with art 6 in so far as category one and two applications are concerned. In category three applications, consideration may have to be given to the instructing of special counsel.[4] The decision has been considered by the House of Lords in *R v H*,[5] a case in which the appellants were charged with conspiracy to supply a class A drug. The prosecution case was based on observations which began some seven weeks before their arrest. It was alleged that on that date a package, later found to contain 2 kg of heroin, was taken to H's timber yard, put by H into a white van with a quantity of timber and taken to C's business premises where C appeared to inspect it. A preliminary hearing was held during the course of which counsel for H indicated that he wished to mount a challenge to the legality and propriety of the police operation and the integrity of the police surveillance evidence. He indicated that he intended to apply to stay the prosecution as an abuse of process on the grounds of serious executive misconduct and or to seek to exclude the evidence under PACE 1984, s 78. He sought disclosure of the original police observation logs, as well as applications and authorisations under RIPA 2000 and supporting material. Counsel on behalf of the co-defendant made a similar application and added that he intended to apply to dismiss the charge under the Crime and Disorder Act 1998, s 52(6). It was submitted by both counsel that as the judge would be asked to stay or dismiss the case, the decision of *Edwards and Lewis v United Kingdom* required him to appoint special counsel to safeguard the interests of the defendants at any PII hearing held in the absence of the defence. The judge agreed. On appeal to the Court of Appeal, the court held that the judge's decision was premature. The House of Lords agreed with the Court of Appeal and examined the regime of disclosure and PII in the context of art 6.

1   [1993] 1 WLR 619.
2   (1993) 97 Cr App Rep 110.
3   [1994] 1 WLR 746.
4   See *Edwards and Lewis v United Kingdom* (2003) 15 BHRC 189.
5   [2004] UKHL 3, [2004] 1 All ER 1269.

11.41

'When any issue of derogation from the golden rule of full disclosure comes before it, the court must address a series of questions.

(1)   What is the material which the prosecution seek to withhold? This must be considered by the court in detail.

(2)   Is the material such as may weaken the prosecution case or strengthen that of the defence? If No, disclosure should not be ordered. If Yes, full disclosure should (subject to (3), (4) and (5) below) be ordered.

(3)   Is there a real risk of serious prejudice to an important public interest (and, if so, what) if full disclosure of the material is ordered? If No, full disclosure should be ordered.

(4)   If the answer to (2) and (3) is Yes, can the defendant's interest be protected without the disclosure or disclosure be ordered to an extent or

in a way which will give adequate protection to the public interest in question and also afford adequate protection to the interests of the defence?

This question requires the court to consider, with specific reference to the material which the prosecution seek to withhold and the facts of the case and the defence as disclosed, whether the prosecution should formally admit what the defence seek to establish or whether disclosure short of full disclosure may be ordered. This may be done in appropriate cases by the preparation of summaries or extracts of evidence, or the provision of documents in an edited or anonymised form, provided the documents supplied are in each instance approved by the judge. In appropriate cases the appointment of special counsel may be a necessary step to ensure that the contentions of the prosecution are tested and the interests of the defendant protected. In cases of exceptional difficulty, the court may require the appointment of special counsel to ensure a correct answer to questions (2) and (3) as well as (4).

(5)   Do the measures proposed in answer to (4) represent the minimum derogation necessary to protect the public interest in question? If No, the court should order such greater disclosure as will represent the minimum derogation from the golden rule of full disclosure.

(6)   If limited disclosure is ordered pursuant to (4) or (5), may the effect be to render the trial process, viewed as a whole, unfair to the defendant? If Yes, then fuller disclosure should be ordered even if this leads to or may lead the prosecution to discontinue the proceedings so as to avoid having to make disclosure.

(7)   If the answer to (6) when first given is No, does that remain the correct answer as the trial unfolds, evidence is adduced and the defence is advanced? It is important that the answer to (6) should not be treated as a final, once for all answer but as provisional answer which the court must keep under review.'[1]

The decision of *R v Smith*[2] was overruled.

1   *R v H* [2004] UKHL 3, [2004] 1 All ER 1269 at para 37.
2   [2001] 1 WLR 1031.

The admissibility of evidence

11.42   As has been noted in **para 11.27**, RIPA 2000, s 17 provides that certain forms of intercept evidence are inadmissible. The following paragraphs are not concerned with s 17. They concern RIPA 2000, Pt I Ch II, Pt II and Pt III and Police Act 1997, Pt III. Neither Act provides a specific mechanism for deciding on questions of admissibility. Surveillance Code 1.8 asserts that:

'Material obtained through covert surveillance may be used in evidence in criminal proceedings. The proper authorisation of surveillance should ensure the admissibility of such evidence under the common law, section 78 of the Police and Criminal Evidence Act 1984 and the Human Rights Act 1998.'

Although the Police Act 1997 and RIPA 2000 have now filled in the statutory gap which resulted in the series of adverse decisions based on violations of art 8 (see **para 2.53**), it is submitted that the observations in the Surveillance Code are wide of the mark. Except in relation to interception, RIPA 2000 provides for no sanction for unauthorised surveillance activities. Proper authorisation may prevent the activities of a public authority being unlawful by virtue of HRA 1998, s 6 and therefore forestall any argument that evidence is inadmissible for want of proper authorisation.[1] Surveillance Code 1.8 fails to take into account that violations of either or both art 8 and art 6 may still arise, eg because aspects of the Act are not compliant or because of the manner in which the powers have been exercised give rise to an abuse of process, or to such unfairness that the evidence should be excluded under PACE 1984, s 78.

1   See *Khan v United Kingdom* (2000) 31 EHRR 45.

11.43   For example, authorisations under RIPA 2000, Pt II for directed or intrusive surveillance or the use of a CHIS may be given despite the absence of any reasonable suspicion that the target(s) has/have committed or is/are about to commit a criminal offence. As has been seen, a critical factor in the ECt HR concluding that the surveillance measures in issue in the case of *Klass*[1] were necessary in a democratic society was the fact that they were confined to situations in which there were 'factual indications for suspecting a person of committing certain serious acts'. Even then, the surveillance may only cover the specific suspect or his presumed 'contact persons'. Similarly, in *Teixeira de Castro*,[2] the fact that the applicant was not suspected of drug trafficking before the involvement of undercover officers was highly relevant to the conclusion that there had been a violation of art 6.

In *R v Looseley*,[3] Lord Hoffman stated that:

> 'the only proper purpose of police participation is to obtain evidence of criminal acts which they suspect someone is about to commit or in which he is already engaged.'[4]

In such circumstances, it might well be argued that, notwithstanding authorisation, the activity of the undercover officer was in breach of arts 6 and/or 8 or amounted to incitement such as to found an argument for a stay or for exclusion under PACE 1984, s 78.

1   (1978) 2 EHRR 214.
2   (1998) 28 EHRR 101.
3   [2002] 1 Cr App Rep 360.
4   [2002] 1 Cr App Rep 360 at para 56.

11.44   The facts of both *Looseley* and the *A-G's Reference* took place before RIPA 2000 came into force. The activities of the undercover officers in each case were covered by the Undercover Operations Code of Practice. The relevant parts provided as follows.

'2.1. Responsibility for authorisations for the deployment of undercover officers rests with the authorising officer as described below.

2.2. Before giving authorisation for the deployment of undercover officers, the authorising officer must be satisfied that:

- the deployment of undercover officers is likely to be of value in connection with national security, in the prevention or detection of serious crime, in the maintenance of public order or community safety, or in the case of a significant public interest;
- the desired result of the deployment cannot reasonably be achieved by other means (see Note 2A);
- the risks of collateral intrusion have been properly considered.

NOTE 2A

It is not necessary for all other means to have been tried and failed but that in all the circumstances such other means would not be practicable or would be unlikely to achieve what the action seeks to achieve within reasonable time or to the necessary evidential standard.'

Human Rights Act 1998, s 6

11.45   HRA 1998, s 6 states:

'(1)   It is unlawful for a public authority to act in a way which is incompatible with a Convention Right.
(2)   Subsection (1) does not apply to an act if–
    (a)   as a result of one or more provisions of primary legislation, the authority could not have acted differently; or
    (b)   in the case of one or more provisions of, or made under, primary legislation which cannot be read or given effect to in a way which is compatible with the Convention Rights, the authority was acting so as to give effect to or enforce those provisions.'

A court is a public authority. In certain circumstances it could be argued that by admitting unlawfully obtained evidence the court was not acting compatibly with the Convention. This point was referred to by Newman J in *R v Sutherland*:[1]

'Since the advent of the Human Rights Act, the Court has a duty to not to act in contravention of a Convention right. If the Court relieves a party to proceedings from the consequences of a flagrant breach of a fundamental right against the opposing party in the proceedings, which right is recognised by the Convention and the breach takes place in the context of the very proceedings before the Court, it is not difficult for it to be seen that the Court could be regarded as acting in those proceedings in a way which is incompatible with the Convention.'

1   (29 January 2002, unreported) at para 79.

The significance of a breach of art 6

11.46   As has been seen in **Chapter 2**, certain forms of surveillance, notably those involving undercover police operations and those in which there is a risk of confidential information being obtained, are particularly likely to involve art 6 considerations. A conviction following a trial in which art 6 has been violated is likely to be deemed unsafe by the Court of Appeal.[1] Where a court concludes that evidence has been obtained in circumstances which flout an aspect of art 6, it may stay the proceedings as an abuse of process or exclude the evidence under PACE 1984, s 78.[2] A similar approach might be taken where a court concludes that the particular surveillance activity amounts to a deliberate circumvention of protections provided by domestic law, e g PACE 1984. This might occur where, for example, the police adopt the expedient of covert recording of conversations in police cells without any attempt having been made to conduct interviews in accordance with PACE 1984 Code C (see **para 11.57**).

1   See *R v Togher* [2001] 1 Cr App Rep 457, *R v Forbes* [2001] 1 AC 473, *R v A (No 2)* [2001] UKHL 25, [2002] 1 AC 45.
2   See *R v Looseley* [2002] 1 Cr App Rep 360 and *R v Sutherland* (29 January 2002, unreported).

Abuse of process

11.47   Abuse of process is a creature of common law and not statute. Therefore HRA 1998, s 3, which obliges a court to interpret legislation compatibly with the Convention, does not apply. The duty to take account of any judgment, etc of the ECt HR or the Commission under s 2(1) does apply.

In *R v Looseley*,[1] the House of Lords commented that in a case involving the commission of an offence by an accused at the instigation of undercover police officers there was no appreciable difference between the requirements of art 6 or the Strasbourg jurisprudence on art 6 and English law as it had developed in recent years. Having confirmed that the decision of *R v Sang*[2] had been overtaken by developments both statutory and of the common law, Lord Nicholls stated that the grant of a stay rather than exclusion of evidence at the trial should normally be regarded as the appropriate response.[3] The criteria for a stay are distinct from those appropriate to an application to exclude evidence under PACE 1984, s 78, although there may be occasions when an application under s 78 may include factors relevant to an application to stay. According to Lord Hoffman (at para 40), the basis of a stay was not so much to prevent an abuse of process but to prevent abuse of executive power. The comments echo those of Lord Steyn in *R v Latif and Shahzad*,[4] who spoke of 'an affront to the public conscience'. In that case, having regard to the seriousness of the offence allegedly committed by the defendants, the conduct of an investigating officer in importing the large quantity of heroin, about which the case was concerned, into the UK was held not to be so unworthy or shameful that it was an affront to the public conscience to allow the prosecution to proceed.

1   [2002] 1 Cr App Rep 360.
2   [1979] 69 Cr App Rep 282.
3   [2002] 1 Cr App Rep 29 at para 16.
4   [1996] 2 Cr App Rep 92.

11.48   Although both *Looseley* and *Latif and Shahzad* concerned allegations of entrapment, the discretion to stay for abuse of process may be appropriate in other circumstances. In *R v Sutherland*,[1] the defendants were charged with murder. Prior to the arrests there had been extensive surveillance of domestic addresses resulting in 700 hours of tape recording, the lawfulness of which the judge was not asked to rule on. During the course of the investigation, the police deliberately placed a microphone in the exercise yard at both Grantham and Sleaford police stations in order to intercept and record privileged conversations taking place between a solicitor and one or more suspects held at the police station. Authorisations under RIPA 2000 for directed surveillance 'in the communal passage area of the cell complex' area had been granted by a superintendent but did not include the exercise yards. The police knew that detained persons and solicitors frequently consulted in the exercise yards. The application stated that the equipment would not pick up conversations of persons in the same cell and therefore would not constitute intrusive surveillance.

'This action is highly unlikely to result in the acquisition of confidential material.'

Rejecting an application for PII, which he described as 'misconceived', the judge ordered that all the covert surveillance tapes made at the two police stations be disclosed. On a total of 14 out of 74 of the tapes was an annotation:

'On instructions of the SIO this tape is not considered appropriate for transcription. No secondary listening and/or transcription has been completed on this tape as it would appear that it may contain inadvertent recording of matter subject to legal privilege.'

The judge found that once the first-hand listeners knew the device was picking up privileged conversations they continued to listen. At no point was the tape turned off. The judge also rejected the evidence of senior officers that they did not know of the use of the exercise yard as a place where privileged conversations took place. He found that there had been violations of art 6 as well as of PACE 1984, s 58. He stated that the right of silence was meaningless if police officers, having cautioned a suspect, simply wait for him to go out in the hope that they could listen to that which he declined to mention in implementation of his right. Having deliberately obtained confidential information in the course of an inquiry, the police had compromised the trial process. There could be no proper trial of the issue of how one defendant had become the main prosecution witness. Further, wrongly obtained confidential material could be disclosed to the relevant defendant but not to others. The lack of equality of arms could not be cured by the prosecution. In the circumstances, the flagrant breaches of the law meant that no fair trial could take place and the indictment was stayed.

1   (29 January 2002, unreported).

11.49   The fact that the application in the above case was for directed surveillance of the communal passage area outside the cells rather than the cells themselves, if nothing else, underlines the need to scrutinise the reality of the situation in the particular police station with some care. Although the judge did not criticise the distinction made in the present case between the cells and the communal passage area, he made it clear that he did not accept the reasons given for having not included any independent assessment of the exercise yard. The judgment made no reference to the Surveillance Code of Practice for the very good reason that it did not come into force until 1 August 2002. Had it been in force, Surveillance Code 5.4 identifies both prison and police cells as residential premises but 'not any common area to which the person is allowed access'.

Is PACE 1984, s 78 concerned only with procedural fairness?

11.50   The Court of Appeal has only rarely attempted to elucidate the basis for the discretionary power to exclude evidence, no doubt mindful of the observation of Hodgson J in *R v Samuel*[1] that because of the infinite variety of circumstances it was undesirable to attempt any general guidance as to how the judge's discretion under PACE 1984, s 78 should be exercised, although the propriety of the way in which the evidence was obtained was something the court was specifically enjoined to take into account. Despite such sentiments, it is surprising that neither the House of Lords nor the Court of Appeal has made it clear prior to the decision in *R v Looseley*[2] (see **para 11.47**) that the decision in *R v Sang*[3] was legislatively reversed by s 78 in respect of the admissibility of unfairly obtained evidence. Perhaps the nearest the court came to recognising the impact of s 78 is to be found in *R v Smurthwaite and Gill:*[4]

> 'Thus the fact that the evidence has been obtained by entrapment, or by agent provocateur, or by a trick does not of itself require the judge to exclude it. If, however, he considers that in all the circumstances the obtaining of the evidence in that way would have the effect described in the statute he will exclude it.'

1   [1988] QB 615.
2   [2002] 1 Cr App Rep 360 at para 11.
3   [1980] AC 402.
4   (1993) 98 Cr App Rep 437.

11.51   In *R v Shannon*,[1] Potter LJ stated in relation to PACE 1984, s 78 that:

> 'the ultimate question is not the broad one: is the bringing of proceedings fair (in the sense of appropriate) in entrapment cases? It is whether the fairness of the proceedings will be adversely affected by admitting the evidence of the agent provocateur or evidence which is available as a result of his action or activities. So, for instance, if there is good reason to question the credibility of the evidence given by an agent provocateur, or which casts doubt on the reliability of other evidence procured or resulting from his actions, and that question is not susceptible of being fairly or properly resolved in the course of the proceedings from available admissible and "untainted" evidence then the judge may readily conclude that such evidence should be excluded. If on the other hand, the unfairness complained of is no more than a visceral reaction to that it is in principle unfair as a matter of policy or wrong as a matter of law, for a person to be prosecuted for a crime which he would not have committed without the incitement or encouragement of others, then that is not itself sufficient, unless the behaviour of the police (or someone acting on behalf of or

in league with the police) and/or the prosecuting authority has been such as to justify a stay on the grounds of abuse of process.'

1   [2001] 1 Cr App Rep 12 at para 39.

11.52   These comments were referred to by Lord Hoffman in *Looseley*.[1] Without disapproving them, he recognised that there may be circumstances in which an application to exclude under s 78 may in substance be a belated application for a stay. Lord Nicholls also agreed that the phrase 'fairness of the proceedings' is directed:

> 'primarily at matters going to fairness in the actual conduct of the trial; for instance the reliability of evidence and the defendant's ability to test its reliability. But, rightly, the courts have been unwilling to limit the scope of this wide and comprehensive expression strictly to procedural fairness.'

He went on to cite approvingly the decision in *R v Smurthwaite and Gill*.[2] A breach of art 8 is clearly capable of being a relevant factor, although on the facts in *Looseley* the House dismissed the suggestion that the actions of the undercover officer in persistently telephoning the defendant amounted to an infringement of his rights.

> 'The policeman did not invade his privacy any more than a customer who walks into a shop.'[3]

1   [2002] 1 Cr App Rep 360 at para 43.
2   (1993) 98 Cr App Rep 437.
3   [2002] 1 Cr App Rep 360 at para 79.

Significance of a breach of art 8

11.53   The numerous decisions in which the UK has been found to have breached art 8 as a result of surveillance carried out under non-statutory guidelines have been referred to elsewhere (see **para 2.53**). As has been noted, the ECt HR has not accepted the argument in many of the dissenting judgments that the use of such evidence in a criminal trial must amount also to a violation of art 6. In each case, the 1984 Guidelines had been complied with, a fact to which importance was attached in *Khan v United Kingdom*.[1] Having regard to the previous case law of the ECt HR (see **para 2.40**), it might have been anticipated, nevertheless, that a finding of unfairness would follow from the use of evidence obtained in breach of a Convention right and that the decision to the contrary is questionable for the reasons set out in **Chapter 2**. Not only did the court in that case ignore its own previous case law, it failed to acknowledge the significance of a breach of the Convention right as opposed to domestic law.[2]

1   (2000) 31 EHRR 45
2   On this point, see the commentary to the case in the *Criminal Law Review* by Professor Ashworth, [2000] Crim LR 684.

11.54   In *R v Khan*,[1] decided before HRA 1998 came into force, the House of Lords accepted that a violation of art 8 may be relevant to the discretion to exclude under PACE 1984, s 78:

'Its significance, however, will normally be determined not so much by its apparent unlawfulness or irregularity as upon its effect, taken as a whole, upon the fairness of the proceedings.'

It might have been thought that the advent of HRA 1998 would have added significant strength to the argument for exclusion. In *R v P*,[2] the House was invited to consider the appeal on the basis that the Act was in force even though the relevant conduct preceded 2 October 2000. The case concerned intercepted conversations which had been properly authorised outside the UK. The prosecution sought to use the recordings of the intercepts in evidence, which were therefore disclosed to the defence. It was conceded that the circumstances in which the evidence was obtained did not involve a breach of art 8. The defence therefore contended that the use of the intercepts in the UK was a breach of art 8. The House accepted that the use of intercept evidence could amount to an interference for the purposes of art 8 but that in the present case, distinguishing *Amman v Switzerland*,[3] the information had not been used for any purpose other than that for which it had been obtained, namely the prosecution of drug traffickers. In the circumstances, there had been no breach of art 8. Even if the evidence had been unlawfully obtained, there would not have been a breach of art 6. The House referred extensively to the decision in *Khan v United Kingdom* as support for the proposition that any remedy for a breach of art 8 lies outside the scope of the criminal trial and that art 13 does not require a remedy for a breach of art 8 to be given within that trial. It was a cogent factor in favour of admission that one of the parties to the relevant conversation was going to be a witness at the trial and give evidence of what was said during it. The tape recordings and transcripts, the accuracy of which was not disputed, were the best evidence. The fairness of the trial required that the evidence be admissible.

As the House had found no breach of art 8, it did not need to consider the impact of HRA 1998. For the same reason, the observations about the significance of a breach of art 8 could be described as being obiter. Should a situation arise in the future in which a court concluded that there had been a violation of art 8, it is clear that it would have to have regard to HRA 1998, s 6 (see observations of Newman J at **para 11.45**).

1   [1997] 1 AC 558.
2   [2002] 1 AC 146.
3   (2000) 30 EHRR 843.

11.55   The proper approach in a case where it is alleged that authorisations granted under RIPA 2000 were inadequate and/or in breach of the Convention was considered in *R v Hardy*.[1] Although the court agreed with the trial judge that the authorisations were properly given, it stated that even had that not been the case the application for a stay on the grounds of abuse of process was misdirected. If the surveillance undertaken by the police or some part of it was illegal, then the proper remedy was to apply for the judge to exclude it under PACE 1984, s 78. Its legality would be very material to the question of fairness. The very fact that the court had power to refuse to admit evidence that would render the trial unfair meant that the proceedings were not arguably an abuse of process.

1   [2003] 1 Cr App Rep 494.

Surveillance in prisons/police cells

11.56   The covert recording of a suspect's conversations with others in police cells is a not uncommon form of evidence gathering in the UK and is clearly capable of engaging art 8.[1] Where such surveillance involves eavesdropping on conversations with lawyers, art 6 may be engaged.[2] Surveillance Code 5.4 extends the definition of 'residential premises' in RIPA 2000, s 48(1) to include not only prison cells but also those at a police station. Thus any such activities should be authorised as intrusive surveillance.

Examples of pre-RIPA 2000 decisions include, *R v Jelen and Katz,*[3] *R v Shaukat Ali,*[4] *R v Bailey and Smith,*[5] *R v Roberts,*[6] *R v Bailey*[7] and *R v Mason.*[8] Objection has in the past been taken on the basis that such activities were nothing more than a means of evading the constraints of PACE 1984 or that they amounted to a form of entrapment. In *Jelen and Katz* the police, knowing they had insufficient evidence to arrest a suspect, used a co-defendant covertly to record a conversation with the suspect. Having noted that the suspect had not been arrested and that Code C under PACE 1984 did not therefore apply, the court went on to state that:

> 'The provisions of the Code governing the detention, treatment and questioning of persons by police officers are for the protection of those who are vulnerable because they are in the custody of the police. They are not intended to confine police investigation of crime to conduct which might be regarded as sporting to those under investigation.'

In *R v Shaukat Ali*, where the police without authorisation of any sort bugged conversations between the defendant and his family after he had been charged, the suggestion that such activity might be a violation of art 8 received short shrift:

> 'We do not recognise Art 8 as of relevance to the considerations we must give to the issue of admissibility in this case.'

Both judgments were referred to in *R v Bailey and Smith*, a case in which, having obtained the appropriate authorisation to install a bug in a remand cell, the investigating officer enlisted the support of the custody officer to enact a charade designed to increase the chances of the defendants incriminating themselves. The court took an equally pragmatic view of conduct of the sort complained of:

> 'Where as here very serious crimes have been committed and committed by men who have not shrunk from trickery and a good deal worse – and there has never been the least suggestion that their covertly taped confessions were oppressively obtained or other than wholly reliable, it seems to us hardly surprising that the trial judge exercised his undoubted discretion as he did.'

1   See *PG and JH v United Kingdom* [2002] Crim LR 308 and *Allan v United Kingdom* (2002) 36 EHRR 12, 13 BHRC 652 (**Chapter 2**). See generally David Ormerod *Police Cells and Unwanted Bugs*, Journal of Criminal Law, Feb 2003, p37.

2   *S v Switzerland* (1991) 14 EHRR 670, *Brennan v United Kingdom* (2001) 34 EHRR 507. But compare *La Rose v Metropolitan Police Comr* [2002] Crim LR 215.

3   (1989) 90 Cr App Rep 456.

4   (1991) Times, 16 February.

5   (1993) 97 Cr App Rep 365.

6   [1997] Crim LR 222.
7   [2001] EWCA Crim 733.
8   [2002] 2 Cr App Rep 32.

11.57   In *R v Mason*, it was contended that covert surveillance in the police station
was against the spirit of the PACE 1984 Codes and in breach of art 8. The appellants
were alleged to have been involved in a series of burglaries and robberies. During the
currency of these activities some had been arrested but then released on account of
lack of evidence. The police decided to arrest three of the appellants and then place
them in a cell in which covert audio equipment was installed. On the basis of
information he had received, the chief constable gave authority for the operation to
go ahead pursuant to the Guidelines on the Use of Equipment in Police Surveillance.
The guidelines provided that the investigation must concern serious crime; normal
methods of investigation must have been tried and failed or must from the nature of
things be unlikely to succeed if tried; there must be good reason to think that the use
of the equipment would be likely to lead to an arrest; and it must be operationally
feasible. The tapes and those subsequently authorised played a fundamental role in
the case for the prosecution against the appellants. The defence contended that the
use of such equipment was premature, was contrary to the spirit of PACE 1984 and
that there were breaches of art 8 and art 6, and the evidence should be excluded
under either s 76 or s 78 of PACE 1984. During the course of the voir dire, the police
accepted that forensic tests and further identification parades were anticipated at the
time the authorisation was given. The judge admitted the evidence. The court held,
agreeing with the judge and distinguishing *R v Sutherland*,[1] that it was not suggested
that the chief constable gave his authority otherwise than in good faith. Although the
court was far from satisfied that the guidelines were intended to apply to those in
custody in police cells, this was a situation in which the police were responding
reasonably and proportionately to a serious threat to law and order. It was not
contrary to the spirit of PACE 1984 for there to be covert taping. Although the lack of
any domestic legislation at the time meant there was a violation of art 8, it did not
follow that the evidence should be excluded.[2] Nor was there a violation of art 6. The
appellants were not tricked into saying what they did even though they were placed
in a position where they were likely to do so. The reliability and quality of the tapes
did not distinguish the case from *Khan v United Kingdom*.[3] They were very much
questions for the jury. See also, to similar effect, *R v Arif*.[4]

1   (29 January 2002, unreported).
2   See *PG and JH v United Kingdom* Reports of Judgments and Decisions 2001 IX at p 195.
3   (2000) 31 EHRR 45.
4   (3 July 2000, unreported), No 1999 04609/W5.

11.58   *R v Mason* was relied on in *R v McLeod*,[1] a case in which the police covertly
recorded a conversation involving the appellant while he was in a police van being
escorted to an identification parade. During the conversation, the appellant admitted
possession of a gun prior to the altercation with the victim of an attempted murder.
Permission had been given by the Deputy Assistant Commissioner of Police to place
covert audio and visual recording devices in the vehicle pursuant to the same
guidelines. Although it was conceded that there was a breach of art 8, the court held
that:

'the question was whether the admission of having the gun in his possession was reliable and whether it was fair to allow the admission of the conversation under s 78. It was clearly reliable. It was also fair as the matter had been properly considered on the basis of the Guidelines. The only basis for finding a violation was the lack of any statutory framework.'

1   [2002] EWCA Crim 989.

Significant and substantial breaches

11.59   The concept of the significant and substantial breach has been fundamental to the approach of the courts to breaches of PACE 1984.[1] Is such an approach likely to prove helpful in the context of the Police Act 1997, Pt III and RIPA 2000? Despite the fact that both statutes have been in force for some time, neither has yet begun to generate the volume of appellate activity that followed hard on the heels of the coming into force of PACE 1984. The ECt HR's own attitude to violations of art 8 is an unpromising starting point as it fails to make any attempt to distinguish a significant violation from a less serious one. This is particularly important in the context of art 8 on account of the width of the interests it aims to protect. This problem lies also at the heart of the dissenting judgments referred to in **Chapter 2**, which assume that a breach of art 8, however irrelevant to the fairness of the trial in question, must of necessity impact on art 6. The failure of the ECt HR to grapple with this point, and the observations in *R v P*[2] to the effect that the remedy for a breach of art 8 lies outside the criminal trial, appear initially at least to have had the effect of reducing the significance to be attached to a breach of art 8. As already noted, the consequence of failing to comply with RIPA 2000 or the Police Act 1997, Pt III is that the public authority is at risk of being found to have acted unlawfully within HRA 1998, s 6. It remains to be seen whether when significant or substantial violations of the Police Act 1997/RIPA 2000/art 8 have been established, the courts will follow the lead given by Newman J in *R v Sutherland* and put HRA 1998, s 6 to work.

1   See *R v Keenan* (1989) 90 Cr App Rep 1, *R v Absolam* (1988) 88 Cr App Rep 332 and *R v Walsh* (1989) 91 Cr App Rep 161.
2   [2002] 1 AC 146.

Appendix 1

REGULATION OF INVESTIGATORY POWERS ACT 2000

2000 CHAPTER 23

An Act to make provision for and about the interception of communications, the acquisition and disclosure of data relating to communications, the carrying out of surveillance, the use of covert human intelligence sources and the acquisition of the means by which electronic data protected by encryption or passwords may be decrypted or accessed; to provide for Commissioners and a tribunal with functions and jurisdiction in relation to those matters, to entries on and interferences with property or with wireless telegraphy and to the carrying out of their functions by the Security Service, the Secret Intelligence Service and the Government Communications Headquarters; and for connected purposes.

[28th July 2000]

BE IT ENACTED by the Queen's most Excellent Majesty, by and with the advice and consent of the Lords Spiritual and Temporal, and Commons, in this present Parliament assembled, and by the authority of the same, as follows:–

PART I
COMMUNICATIONS

CHAPTER I
INTERCEPTION

Unlawful and authorised interception

1 Unlawful interception

(1) It shall be an offence for a person intentionally and without lawful authority to intercept, at any place in the United Kingdom, any communication in the course of its transmission by means of–

> (a) a public postal service; or

> (b) a public telecommunication system.

(2) It shall be an offence for a person–

> (a) intentionally and without lawful authority, and

> (b) otherwise than in circumstances in which his conduct is excluded by subsection (6) from criminal liability under this subsection,

to intercept, at any place in the United Kingdom, any communication in the course of its transmission by means of a private telecommunication system.

(3) Any interception of a communication which is carried out at any place in the United Kingdom by, or with the express or implied consent of, a person having the right to control the operation or the use of a private telecommunication system shall be actionable at the suit or instance of the sender or recipient, or intended recipient, of the communication if it is without lawful authority and is either–

> (a) an interception of that communication in the course of its transmission by means of that private system; or

(b)   an interception of that communication in the course of its transmission, by means of a public telecommunication system, to or from apparatus comprised in that private telecommunication system.

(4) Where the United Kingdom is a party to an international agreement which–

(a)   relates to the provision of mutual assistance in connection with, or in the form of, the interception of communications,

(b)   requires the issue of a warrant, order or equivalent instrument in cases in which assistance is given, and

(c)   is designated for the purposes of this subsection by an order made by the Secretary of State,

it shall be the duty of the Secretary of State to secure that no request for assistance in accordance with the agreement is made on behalf of a person in the United Kingdom to the competent authorities of a country or territory outside the United Kingdom except with lawful authority.

(5) Conduct has lawful authority for the purposes of this section if, and only if–

(a)   it is authorised by or under section 3 or 4;

(b)   it takes place in accordance with a warrant under section 5 ("an interception warrant"); or

(c)   it is in exercise, in relation to any stored communication, of any statutory power that is exercised (apart from this section) for the purpose of obtaining information or of taking possession of any document or other property;

and conduct (whether or not prohibited by this section) which has lawful authority for the purposes of this section by virtue of paragraph (a) or (b) shall also be taken to be lawful for all other purposes.

(6) The circumstances in which a person makes an interception of a communication in the course of its transmission by means of a private telecommunication system are such that his conduct is excluded from criminal liability under subsection (2) if–

(a)   he is a person with a right to control the operation or the use of the system; or

(b)   he has the express or implied consent of such a person to make the interception.

(7) A person who is guilty of an offence under subsection (1) or (2) shall be liable–

(a)   on conviction on indictment, to imprisonment for a term not exceeding two years or to a fine, or to both;

(b)   on summary conviction, to a fine not exceeding the statutory maximum.

(8) No proceedings for any offence which is an offence by virtue of this section shall be instituted–

(a)   in England and Wales, except by or with the consent of the Director of Public Prosecutions;

(b)   in Northern Ireland, except by or with the consent of the Director of Public Prosecutions for Northern Ireland.

Notes

Initial Commencement

To be appointed

> To be appointed: see s 83(2).

Appointment

> Sub-ss (1), (2), (4)–(8): Appointment: 2 October 2000: see SI 2000/2543, art 3.
> Sub-s (3): Appointment: 24 October 2000: see SI 2000/2543, art 4.

Subordinate Legislation

> Regulation of Investigatory Powers (Designation of an International Agreement) Order 2004, SI 2004/158 (made under sub-s (4)(c)).

2 Meaning and location of "interception" etc

(1) In this Act–

"postal service" means any service which–

> (a)   consists in the following, or in any one or more of them, namely, the collection, sorting, conveyance, distribution and delivery (whether in the United Kingdom or elsewhere) of postal items; and

> (b)   is offered or provided as a service the main purpose of which, or one of the main purposes of which, is to make available, or to facilitate, a means of transmission from place to place of postal items containing communications;

"private telecommunication system" means any telecommunication system which, without itself being a public telecommunication system, is a system in relation to which the following conditions are satisfied–

> (a)   it is attached, directly or indirectly and whether or not for the purposes of the communication in question, to a public telecommunication system; and

> (b)   there is apparatus comprised in the system which is both located in the United Kingdom and used (with or without other apparatus) for making the attachment to the public telecommunication system;

"public postal service" means any postal service which is offered or provided to, or to a substantial section of, the public in any one or more parts of the United Kingdom;

"public telecommunications service" means any telecommunications service which is offered or provided to, or to a substantial section of, the public in any one or more parts of the United Kingdom;

"public telecommunication system" means any such parts of a telecommunication system by means of which any public telecommunications service is provided as are located in the United Kingdom;

"telecommunications service" means any service that consists in the provision of access to, and of facilities for making use of, any telecommunication system (whether or not one provided by the person providing the service); and

"telecommunication system" means any system (including the apparatus comprised in it) which exists (whether wholly or partly in the United Kingdom or elsewhere) for the purpose of facilitating the transmission of communications by any means involving the use of electrical or electro-magnetic energy.

(2) For the purposes of this Act, but subject to the following provisions of this section, a person intercepts a communication in the course of its transmission by means of a telecommunication system if, and only if, he—

    (a)   so modifies or interferes with the system, or its operation,

    (b)   so monitors transmissions made by means of the system, or

    (c)   so monitors transmissions made by wireless telegraphy to or from apparatus comprised in the system,

as to make some or all of the contents of the communication available, while being transmitted, to a person other than the sender or intended recipient of the communication.

(3) References in this Act to the interception of a communication do not include references to the interception of any communication broadcast for general reception.

(4) For the purposes of this Act the interception of a communication takes place in the United Kingdom if, and only if, the modification, interference or monitoring or, in the case of a postal item, the interception is effected by conduct within the United Kingdom and the communication is either—

    (a)   intercepted in the course of its transmission by means of a public postal service or public telecommunication system; or

    (b)   intercepted in the course of its transmission by means of a private telecommunication system in a case in which the sender or intended recipient of the communication is in the United Kingdom.

(5) References in this Act to the interception of a communication in the course of its transmission by means of a postal service or telecommunication system do not include references to—

    (a)   any conduct that takes place in relation only to so much of the communication as consists in any traffic data comprised in or attached to a communication (whether by the sender or otherwise) for the purposes of any postal service or telecommunication system by means of which it is being or may be transmitted; or

    (b)   any such conduct, in connection with conduct falling within paragraph (a), as gives a person who is neither the sender nor the intended recipient only so much access to a communication as is necessary for the purpose of identifying traffic data so comprised or attached.

(6) For the purposes of this section references to the modification of a telecommunication system include references to the attachment of any apparatus to, or other modification of or interference with—

    (a)   any part of the system; or

    (b)   any wireless telegraphy apparatus used for making transmissions to or from apparatus comprised in the system.

(7) For the purposes of this section the times while a communication is being transmitted by means of a telecommunication system shall be taken to include any time when the system by means of which the communication is being, or has been, transmitted is used for storing it in a manner that enables the intended recipient to collect it or otherwise to have access to it.

(8) For the purposes of this section the cases in which any contents of a communication are to be taken to be made available to a person while being transmitted shall include any case in which any of the contents of the communication, while being transmitted, are diverted or recorded so as to be available to a person subsequently.

(9) In this section "traffic data", in relation to any communication, means–

(a) any data identifying, or purporting to identify, any person, apparatus or location to or from which the communication is or may be transmitted,

(b) any data identifying or selecting, or purporting to identify or select, apparatus through which, or by means of which, the communication is or may be transmitted,

(c) any data comprising signals for the actuation of apparatus used for the purposes of a telecommunication system for effecting (in whole or in part) the transmission of any communication, and

(d) any data identifying the data or other data as data comprised in or attached to a particular communication,

but that expression includes data identifying a computer file or computer program access to which is obtained, or which is run, by means of the communication to the extent only that the file or program is identified by reference to the apparatus in which it is stored.

(10) In this section–

(a) references, in relation to traffic data comprising signals for the actuation of apparatus, to a telecommunication system by means of which a communication is being or may be transmitted include references to any telecommunication system in which that apparatus is comprised; and

(b) references to traffic data being attached to a communication include references to the data and the communication being logically associated with each other;

and in this section "data", in relation to a postal item, means anything written on the outside of the item.

(11) In this section "postal item" means any letter, postcard or other such thing in writing as may be used by the sender for imparting information to the recipient, or any packet or parcel.

Notes

Initial Commencement

To be appointed
To be appointed: see s 83(2).

Appointment
Appointment: 2 October 2000: see SI 2000/2543, art 3.

---

3 Lawful interception without an interception warrant

(1) Conduct by any person consisting in the interception of a communication is authorised by this section if the communication is one which, or which that person has reasonable grounds for believing, is both–

(a) a communication sent by a person who has consented to the interception; and

(b)   a communication the intended recipient of which has so consented.

(2) Conduct by any person consisting in the interception of a communication is authorised by this section if–

(a)   the communication is one sent by, or intended for, a person who has consented to the interception; and

(b)   surveillance by means of that interception has been authorised under Part II.

(3) Conduct consisting in the interception of a communication is authorised by this section if–

(a)   it is conduct by or on behalf of a person who provides a postal service or a telecommunications service; and

(b)   it takes place for purposes connected with the provision or operation of that service or with the enforcement, in relation to that service, of any enactment relating to the use of postal services or telecommunications services.

(4) Conduct by any person consisting in the interception of a communication in the course of its transmission by means of wireless telegraphy is authorised by this section if it takes place–

(a)   with the authority of a designated person under section 5 of the Wireless Telegraphy Act 1949 (misleading messages and interception and disclosure of wireless telegraphy messages); and

(b)   for purposes connected with anything falling within subsection (5).

(5) Each of the following falls within this subsection–

(a)   the issue of licences under the Wireless Telegraphy Act 1949;

(b)   the prevention or detection of anything which constitutes interference with wireless telegraphy; and

(c)   the enforcement of any enactment contained in that Act or of any enactment not so contained that relates to such interference.

Notes

Initial Commencement

To be appointed
    To be appointed: see s 83(2).

Appointment
    Appointment: 2 October 2000: see SI 2000/2543, art 3.

---

4 Power to provide for lawful interception

(1) Conduct by any person ("the interceptor") consisting in the interception of a communication in the course of its transmission by means of a telecommunication system is authorised by this section if–

(a)   the interception is carried out for the purpose of obtaining information about the communications of a person who, or who the interceptor has reasonable grounds for believing, is in a country or territory outside the United Kingdom;

(b)   the interception relates to the use of a telecommunications service provided to persons in that country or territory which is either–

  (i)   a public telecommunications service; or

  (ii)   a telecommunications service that would be a public telecommunications service if the persons to whom it is offered or provided were members of the public in a part of the United Kingdom;

(c)   the person who provides that service (whether the interceptor or another person) is required by the law of that country or territory to carry out, secure or facilitate the interception in question;

(d)   the situation is one in relation to which such further conditions as may be prescribed by regulations made by the Secretary of State are required to be satisfied before conduct may be treated as authorised by virtue of this subsection; and

(e)   the conditions so prescribed are satisfied in relation to that situation.

(2) Subject to subsection (3), the Secretary of State may by regulations authorise any such conduct described in the regulations as appears to him to constitute a legitimate practice reasonably required for the purpose, in connection with the carrying on of any business, of monitoring or keeping a record of–

(a)   communications by means of which transactions are entered into in the course of that business; or

(b)   other communications relating to that business or taking place in the course of its being carried on.

(3) Nothing in any regulations under subsection (2) shall authorise the interception of any communication except in the course of its transmission using apparatus or services provided by or to the person carrying on the business for use wholly or partly in connection with that business.

(4) Conduct taking place in a prison is authorised by this section if it is conduct in exercise of any power conferred by or under any rules made under section 47 of the Prison Act 1952, section 39 of the Prisons (Scotland) Act 1989 or section 13 of the Prison Act (Northern Ireland) 1953 (prison rules).

(5) Conduct taking place in any hospital premises where high security psychiatric services are provided is authorised by this section if it is conduct in pursuance of, and in accordance with, any direction given under section 17 of the National Health Service Act 1977 (directions as to the carrying out of their functions by health bodies) to the body providing those services at those premises.

(6) Conduct taking place in a state hospital is authorised by this section if it is conduct in pursuance of, and in accordance with, any direction given to the State Hospitals Board for Scotland under section 2(5) of the National Health Service (Scotland) Act 1978 (regulations and directions as to the exercise of their functions by health boards) as applied by Article 5(1) of and the Schedule to The State Hospitals Board for Scotland Order 1995 (which applies certain provisions of that Act of 1978 to the State Hospitals Board).

(7) In this section references to a business include references to any activities of a government department, of any public authority or of any person or office holder on whom functions are conferred by or under any enactment.

(8) In this section–

"government department" includes any part of the Scottish Administration, a Northern Ireland department and the National Assembly for Wales;

"high security psychiatric services" has the same meaning as in the National Health Service Act 1977;

"hospital premises" has the same meaning as in section 4(3) of that Act; and

"state hospital" has the same meaning as in the National Health Service (Scotland) Act 1978.

(9) In this section "prison" means–

(a) any prison, young offender institution, young offenders centre or remand centre which is under the general superintendence of, or is provided by, the Secretary of State under the Prison Act 1952 or the Prison Act (Northern Ireland) 1953, or

(b) any prison, young offender institution or remand centre which is under the general superintendence of the Scottish Ministers under the Prisons (Scotland) Act 1989,

and includes any contracted out prison, within the meaning of Part IV of the Criminal Justice Act 1991 or section 106(4) of the Criminal Justice and Public Order Act 1994, and any legalised police cells within the meaning of section 14 of the Prisons (Scotland) Act 1989.

Notes

Initial Commencement

To be appointed
To be appointed: see s 83(2).

Appointment
Appointment: 2 October 2000: see SI 2000/2543, art 3.

Subordinate Legislation
Telecommunications (Lawful Business Practice) (Interception of Communications) Regulations 2000, SI 2000/2699 (made under sub-s (2)).

Regulation of Investigatory Powers (Conditions for the Lawful Interception of Persons outside the United Kingdom) Regulations 2004, SI 2004/157 (made under sub-s (1)(d)).

5 Interception with a warrant

(1) Subject to the following provisions of this Chapter, the Secretary of State may issue a warrant authorising or requiring the person to whom it is addressed, by any such conduct as may be described in the warrant, to secure any one or more of the following–

(a) the interception in the course of their transmission by means of a postal service or telecommunication system of the communications described in the warrant;

(b) the making, in accordance with an international mutual assistance agreement, of a request for the provision of such assistance in connection with, or in the form of, an interception of communications as may be so described;

(c) the provision, in accordance with an international mutual assistance agreement, to the competent authorities of a country or territory outside the United Kingdom of any such assistance in connection with, or in the form of, an interception of communications as may be so described;

(d)   the disclosure, in such manner as may be so described, of intercepted material obtained by any interception authorised or required by the warrant, and of related communications data.

(2)   The Secretary of State shall not issue an interception warrant unless he believes–

(a)   that the warrant is necessary on grounds falling within subsection (3); and

(b)   that the conduct authorised by the warrant is proportionate to what is sought to be achieved by that conduct.

(3)   Subject to the following provisions of this section, a warrant is necessary on grounds falling within this subsection if it is necessary–

(a)   in the interests of national security;

(b)   for the purpose of preventing or detecting serious crime;

(c)   for the purpose of safeguarding the economic well-being of the United Kingdom; or

(d)   for the purpose, in circumstances appearing to the Secretary of State to be equivalent to those in which he would issue a warrant by virtue of paragraph (b), of giving effect to the provisions of any international mutual assistance agreement.

(4)   The matters to be taken into account in considering whether the requirements of subsection (2) are satisfied in the case of any warrant shall include whether the information which it is thought necessary to obtain under the warrant could reasonably be obtained by other means.

(5)   A warrant shall not be considered necessary on the ground falling within subsection (3)(c) unless the information which it is thought necessary to obtain is information relating to the acts or intentions of persons outside the British Islands.

(6)   The conduct authorised by an interception warrant shall be taken to include–

(a)   all such conduct (including the interception of communications not identified by the warrant) as it is necessary to undertake in order to do what is expressly authorised or required by the warrant;

(b)   conduct for obtaining related communications data; and

(c)   conduct by any person which is conduct in pursuance of a requirement imposed by or on behalf of the person to whom the warrant is addressed to be provided with assistance with giving effect to the warrant.

Notes

Initial Commencement

To be appointed

To be appointed: see s 83(2).

Appointment

Appointment: 2 October 2000: see SI 2000/2543, art 3.

Transfer of Functions

Functions under this section: certain functions under this section are transferred, in so far as they are exercisable in or as regards Scotland, to the Scottish Ministers, by the Scotland Act 1998 (Transfer of Functions to the Scottish Ministers etc) (No 2) Order 2000, SI 2000/3253, arts 2, 3, Sch 1, para 2 (as amended by SI 2003/2617, art 4(a)), Sch 2.

Functions under this section: certain functions under this section are transferred, in so far as they are exercisable in or as regards Scotland, to the Scottish Ministers, by the Scotland Act 1998 (Transfer of Functions to the Scottish Ministers etc) (No 2) Order 2003, SI 2003/2617, arts 2, 3, Sch 1, para 1, Sch 2.

Interception warrants

6 Application for issue of an interception warrant

(1) An interception warrant shall not be issued except on an application made by or on behalf of a person specified in subsection (2).

(2) Those persons are–

   (a)   the Director-General of the Security Service;

   (b)   the Chief of the Secret Intelligence Service;

   (c)   the Director of GCHQ;

   (d)   the Director General of the National Criminal Intelligence Service;

   (e)   the Commissioner of Police of the Metropolis;

   (f)   the [Chief Constable of the Police Service of Northern Ireland];

   (g)   the chief constable of any police force maintained under or by virtue of section 1 of the Police (Scotland) Act 1967;

   (h)   the Commissioners of Customs and Excise;

   (i)   the Chief of Defence Intelligence;

   (j)   a person who, for the purposes of any international mutual assistance agreement, is the competent authority of a country or territory outside the United Kingdom.

(3) An application for the issue of an interception warrant shall not be made on behalf of a person specified in subsection (2) except by a person holding office under the Crown.

Notes

Initial Commencement

To be appointed

To be appointed: see s 83(2).

Appointment

Appointment: 2 October 2000: see SI 2000/2543, art 3.

Amendment

Sub-s (2): in para (f) words "Chief Constable of the Police Service of Northern Ireland" in square brackets substituted by the Police (Northern Ireland) Act 2000, s 78(2)(a).

Date in force: 4 November 2001: see the Police (Northern Ireland) Act 2000 (Commencement No 3 and Transitional Provisions) Order 2001, SR 2001/396, art 2, Schedule.

7 Issue of warrants

(1) An interception warrant shall not be issued except–

    (a)   under the hand of the Secretary of State [or, in the case of a warrant issued by the Scottish Ministers (by virtue of provision made under section 63 of the Scotland Act 1998), a member of the Scottish Executive]; or

    (b)   in a case falling within subsection (2)[(a) or (b)], under the hand of a senior official[; or

    (c)   in a case falling within subsection (2)(aa), under the hand of a member of the staff of the Scottish Administration who is a member of the Senior Civil Service and who is designated by the Scottish Ministers as a person under whose hand a warrant may be issued in such a case].

(2) Those cases are–

    (a)   an urgent case in which the Secretary of State has himself expressly authorised the issue of the warrant in that case; and

    [(aa) an urgent case in which the Scottish Ministers have themselves (by virtue of provision made under section 63 of the Scotland Act 1998) expressly authorised the use of the warrant in that case and a statement of that fact is endorsed on the warrant; and]

    (b)   a case in which the warrant is for the purposes of a request for assistance made under an international mutual assistance agreement by the competent authorities of a country or territory outside the United Kingdom and either–

        (i)   it appears that the interception subject is outside the United Kingdom; or

        (ii)   the interception to which the warrant relates is to take place in relation only to premises outside the United Kingdom.

(3) An interception warrant–

    (a)   must be addressed to the person falling within section 6(2) by whom, or on whose behalf, the application for the warrant was made; and

    (b)   in the case of a warrant issued under the hand of a senior official, must contain, according to whatever is applicable–

        (i)   one of the statements set out in subsection (4); and

        (ii)   if it contains the statement set out in subsection (4)(b), one of the statements set out in subsection (5).

(4) The statements referred to in subsection (3)(b)(i) are–

    (a)   a statement that the case is an urgent case in which the Secretary of State has himself expressly authorised the issue of the warrant;

    (b)   a statement that the warrant is issued for the purposes of a request for assistance made under an international mutual assistance agreement by the competent authorities of a country or territory outside the United Kingdom.

(5) The statements referred to in subsection (3)(b)(ii) are–

    (a)   a statement that the interception subject appears to be outside the United Kingdom;

    (b)   a statement that the interception to which the warrant relates is to take place in relation only to premises outside the United Kingdom.

Notes

Initial Commencement

To be appointed
> To be appointed: see s 83(2).

Appointment
> Appointment: 2 October 2000: see SI 2000/2543, art 3.

Amendment
> Sub-s (1): in para (a) words from "or, in the case" to "the Scottish Executive" in square brackets inserted by SI 2000/3253, art 4(1), Sch 3, Pt II, paras 3, 4(a).

> Date in force: 15 December 2000: see SI 2000/3253, art 1(1).

> Sub-s (1): in para (b) words "(a) or (b)" in square brackets inserted by SI 2000/3253, art 4(1), Sch 3, Pt II, paras 3, 4(b).

> Date in force: 15 December 2000: see SI 2000/3253, art 1(1).

> Sub-s (1): para (c) and word "; or" immediately preceding it inserted by SI 2000/3253, art 4(1), Sch 3, Pt II, paras 3, 4(c).

> Date in force: 15 December 2000: see SI 2000/3253, art 1(1).

> Sub-s (2): para (aa) inserted by SI 2000/3253, art 4(1), Sch 3, Pt II, paras 3, 4(d).

> Date in force: 15 December 2000: see SI 2000/3253, art 1(1).

8 Contents of warrants

(1) An interception warrant must name or describe either–

    (a)   one person as the interception subject; or

    (b)   a single set of premises as the premises in relation to which the interception to which the warrant relates is to take place.

(2) The provisions of an interception warrant describing communications the interception of which is authorised or required by the warrant must comprise one or more schedules setting out the addresses, numbers, apparatus or other factors, or combination of factors, that are to be used for identifying the communications that may be or are to be intercepted.

(3) Any factor or combination of factors set out in accordance with subsection (2) must be one that identifies communications which are likely to be or to include–

    (a)   communications from, or intended for, the person named or described in the warrant in accordance with subsection (1); or

    (b)   communications originating on, or intended for transmission to, the premises so named or described.

(4) Subsections (1) and (2) shall not apply to an interception warrant if–

    (a)   the description of communications to which the warrant relates confines the conduct authorised or required by the warrant to conduct falling within subsection (5); and

    (b)   at the time of the issue of the warrant, a certificate applicable to the warrant has been issued by the Secretary of State certifying–

        (i)   the descriptions of intercepted material the examination of which he considers necessary; and

        (ii)   that he considers the examination of material of those descriptions necessary as mentioned in section 5(3)(a), (b) or (c).

(5) Conduct falls within this subsection if it consists in–

(a)   the interception of external communications in the course of their transmission by means of a telecommunication system; and

(b)   any conduct authorised in relation to any such interception by section 5(6).

(6) A certificate for the purposes of subsection (4) shall not be issued except under the hand of the Secretary of State.

Notes

Initial Commencement

To be appointed
To be appointed: see s 83(2).

Appointment
Appointment: 2 October 2000: see SI 2000/2543, art 3.

9 Duration, cancellation and renewal of warrants

(1) An interception warrant–

(a)   shall cease to have effect at the end of the relevant period; but

(b)   may be renewed, at any time before the end of that period, by an instrument under the hand of the Secretary of State [or, in the case of a warrant issued by the Scottish Ministers (by virtue of provision made under section 63 of the Scotland Act 1998), a member of the Scottish Executive] or, in a case falling within section 7(2)(b), under the hand of a senior official.

(2) An interception warrant shall not be renewed under subsection (1) unless the Secretary of State believes that the warrant continues to be necessary on grounds falling within section 5(3).

(3) The Secretary of State shall cancel an interception warrant if he is satisfied that the warrant is no longer necessary on grounds falling within section 5(3).

(4) The Secretary of State shall cancel an interception warrant if, at any time before the end of the relevant period, he is satisfied in a case in which–

(a)   the warrant is one which was issued containing the statement set out in section 7(5)(a) or has been renewed by an instrument containing the statement set out in subsection (5)(b)(i) of this section, and

(b)   the latest renewal (if any) of the warrant is not a renewal by an instrument under the hand of the Secretary of State,

that the person named or described in the warrant as the interception subject is in the United Kingdom.

(5) An instrument under the hand of a senior official that renews an interception warrant must contain–

(a)   a statement that the renewal is for the purposes of a request for assistance made under an international mutual assistance agreement by the competent authorities of a country or territory outside the United Kingdom; and

(b)   whichever of the following statements is applicable–

(i)   a statement that the interception subject appears to be outside the United Kingdom;

(ii) a statement that the interception to which the warrant relates is to take place in relation only to premises outside the United Kingdom.

(6) In this section "the relevant period"–

(a) in relation to an unrenewed warrant issued in a case falling within section 7(2)(a) under the hand of a senior official, means the period ending with the fifth working day following the day of the warrant's issue;

(b) in relation to a renewed warrant the latest renewal of which was by an instrument endorsed under the hand of the Secretary of State with a statement that the renewal is believed to be necessary on grounds falling within section 5(3)(a) or (c), means the period of six months beginning with the day of the warrant's renewal; and

(c) in all other cases, means the period of three months beginning with the day of the warrant's issue or, in the case of a warrant that has been renewed, of its latest renewal.

Notes

Initial Commencement

To be appointed

To be appointed: see s 83(2).

Appointment

Appointment: 2 October 2000: see SI 2000/2543, art 3.

Amendment

Sub-s (1): in para (b) words from "or, in the case" to "the Scottish Executive" in square brackets inserted by SI 2000/3253, art 4(1), Sch 3, Pt II, paras 3, 5.

Date in force: 15 December 2000: see SI 2000/3253, art 1(1).

Transfer of Functions

Functions under this section: certain functions under sub-ss (1)(b), (3) are transferred, in so far as they are exercisable in or as regards Scotland, to the Scottish Ministers, by the Scotland Act 1998 (Transfer of Functions to the Scottish Ministers etc) (No 2) Order 2000, SI 2000/3253, arts 2, 3, Sch 1, para 3 (as amended by SI 2003/2617, art 4(b)), Sch 2.

Functions under this section: certain functions under sub-ss (1)(b), (3) are transferred, in so far as they are exercisable in or as regards Scotland, to the Scottish Ministers, by the Scotland Act 1998 (Transfer of Functions to the Scottish Ministers etc) (No 2) Order 2003, SI 2003/2617, arts 2, 3, Sch 1, para 2, Sch 2.

10 Modification of warrants and certificates

(1) The Secretary of State may at any time–

(a) modify the provisions of an interception warrant; or

(b) modify a section 8(4) certificate so as to include in the certified material any material the examination of which he considers to be necessary as mentioned in section 5(3)(a), (b) or (c).

(2) If at any time the Secretary of State considers that any factor set out in a schedule to an interception warrant is no longer relevant for identifying communications which, in the case of that warrant, are likely to be or to include communications falling within section 8(3)(a) or (b), it shall be his duty to modify the warrant by the deletion of that factor.

(3) If at any time the Secretary of State considers that the material certified by a section 8(4) certificate includes any material the examination of which is no longer necessary as mentioned in any of paragraphs (a) to (c) of section 5(3), he shall modify the certificate so as to exclude that material from the certified material.

(4) Subject to subsections (5) to (8), a warrant or certificate shall not be modified under this section except by an instrument under the hand of the Secretary of State or of a senior official.

[(4A) Subject to subsections (5A), (6) and (8), a warrant issued by the Scottish Ministers (by virtue of provision made under section 63 of the Scotland Act 1998) shall not be modified under this section except by an instrument under the hand of a member of the Scottish Executive or a member of the staff of the Scottish Administration who is a member of the Senior Civil Service and is designated by the Scottish Ministers as a person under whose hand an instrument may be issued in such a case (in this section referred to as "a designated official")]

(5) Unscheduled parts of an interception warrant shall not be modified under the hand of a senior official except in an urgent case in which–

    (a)   the Secretary of State has himself expressly authorised the modification; and

    (b)   a statement of that fact is endorsed on the modifying instrument.

[(5A) Unscheduled parts of an interception warrant issued by the Scottish Ministers shall not be modified under the hand of a designated official except in an urgent case in which–

    (a)   they have themselves (by virtue of provision made under section 63 of the Scotland Act 1998) expressly authorised the modification; and

    (b)   a statement of that fact is endorsed on the modifying instrument.]

(6) Subsection (4) [or (4A)] shall not authorise the making under the hand of either–

    (a)   the person to whom the warrant is addressed, or

    (b)   any person holding a position subordinate to that person,

of any modification of any scheduled parts of an interception warrant.

(7) A section 8(4) certificate shall not be modified under the hand of a senior official except in an urgent case in which–

    (a)   the official in question holds a position in respect of which he is expressly authorised by provisions contained in the certificate to modify the certificate on the Secretary of State's behalf; or

    (b)   the Secretary of State has himself expressly authorised the modification and a statement of that fact is endorsed on the modifying instrument.

(8) Where modifications in accordance with this subsection are expressly authorised by provision contained in the warrant, the scheduled parts of an interception warrant may, in an urgent case, be modified by an instrument under the hand of–

    (a)   the person to whom the warrant is addressed; or

    (b)   a person holding any such position subordinate to that person as may be identified in the provisions of the warrant.

(9) Where–

    (a)   a warrant or certificate is modified by an instrument under the hand of a person other than the Secretary of State [or, as the case may be, the Scottish Ministers (by virtue of provision made under section 63 of the Scotland Act 1998)], and

(b)   a statement for the purposes of subsection (5)(b)[, (5A)(b)] or (7)(b) is endorsed on the instrument, or the modification is made under subsection (8),

that modification shall cease to have effect at the end of the fifth working day following the day of the instrument's issue.

(10)   For the purposes of this section–

(a)   the scheduled parts of an interception warrant are any provisions of the warrant that are contained in a schedule of identifying factors comprised in the warrant for the purposes of section 8(2); and

(b)   the modifications that are modifications of the scheduled parts of an interception warrant include the insertion of an additional such schedule in the warrant;

and references in this section to unscheduled parts of an interception warrant, and to their modification, shall be construed accordingly.

Notes

Initial Commencement

To be appointed
To be appointed: see s 83(2).

Appointment
Appointment: 2 October 2000: see SI 2000/2543, art 3.

Amendment
Sub-s (4A): inserted by SI 2000/3253, art 4(1), Sch 3, Pt II, paras 3, 6(a).

Date in force: 15 December 2000: see SI 2000/3253, art 1(1).

Sub-s (5A): inserted by SI 2000/3253, art 4(1), Sch 3, Pt II, paras 3, 6(b).

Date in force: 15 December 2000: see SI 2000/3253, art 1(1).

Sub-s (6): words "or (4A)" in square brackets inserted by SI 2000/3253, art 4(1), Sch 3, Pt II, paras 3, 6(c).

Date in force: 15 December 2000: see SI 2000/3253, art 1(1).

Sub-s (9): in para (a) words from "or, as the case" to "the Scotland Act 1998)" in square brackets inserted by SI 2000/3253, art 4(1), Sch 3, Pt II, paras 3, 6(d)(i).

Date in force: 15 December 2000: see SI 2000/3253, art 1(1).

Sub-s (9): in para (b) words ", (5A)(b)" in square brackets inserted by SI 2000/3253, art 4(1), Sch 3, Pt II, paras 3, 6(d)(ii).

Date in force: 15 December 2000: see SI 2000/3253, art 1(1).

Transfer of Functions
Functions under this section: certain functions under sub-ss (1)(a), (2) are transferred, in so far as they are exercisable in or as regards Scotland, to the Scottish Ministers, by the Scotland Act 1998 (Transfer of Functions to the Scottish Ministers etc) (No 2) Order 2000, SI 2000/3253, arts 2, 3, Sch 1, para 3 (as amended by SI 2003/2617, art 4(b)), Sch 2.

Functions under this section: certain functions under sub-ss (1)(a), (2) are transferred, in so far as they are exercisable in or as regards Scotland, to the Scottish Ministers, by the Scotland Act 1998 (Transfer of Functions to the Scottish Ministers etc) (No 2) Order 2003, SI 2003/2617, arts 2, 3, Sch 1, para 2, Sch 2.

11 Implementation of warrants

(1)   Effect may be given to an interception warrant either–

(a)   by the person to whom it is addressed; or

(b)   by that person acting through, or together with, such other persons as he may require (whether under subsection (2) or otherwise) to provide him with assistance with giving effect to the warrant.

(2) For the purpose of requiring any person to provide assistance in relation to an interception warrant the person to whom it is addressed may–

(a)   serve a copy of the warrant on such persons as he considers may be able to provide such assistance; or

(b)   make arrangements under which a copy of it is to be or may be so served.

(3) The copy of an interception warrant that is served on any person under subsection (2) may, to the extent authorised–

(a)   by the person to whom the warrant is addressed, or

(b)   by the arrangements made by him for the purposes of that subsection,

omit any one or more of the schedules to the warrant.

(4) Where a copy of an interception warrant has been served by or on behalf of the person to whom it is addressed on–

(a)   a person who provides a postal service,

(b)   a person who provides a public telecommunications service, or

(c)   a person not falling within paragraph (b) who has control of the whole or any part of a telecommunication system located wholly or partly in the United Kingdom,

it shall (subject to subsection (5)) be the duty of that person to take all such steps for giving effect to the warrant as are notified to him by or on behalf of the person to whom the warrant is addressed.

(5) A person who is under a duty by virtue of subsection (4) to take steps for giving effect to a warrant shall not be required to take any steps which it is not reasonably practicable for him to take.

(6) For the purposes of subsection (5) the steps which it is reasonably practicable for a person to take in a case in which obligations have been imposed on him by or under section 12 shall include every step which it would have been reasonably practicable for him to take had he complied with all the obligations so imposed on him.

(7) A person who knowingly fails to comply with his duty under subsection (4) shall be guilty of an offence and liable–

(a)   on conviction on indictment, to imprisonment for a term not exceeding two years or to a fine, or to both;

(b)   on summary conviction, to imprisonment for a term not exceeding six months or to a fine not exceeding the statutory maximum, or to both.

(8) A person's duty under subsection (4) to take steps for giving effect to a warrant shall be enforceable by civil proceedings by the Secretary of State for an injunction, or for specific performance of a statutory duty under section 45 of the Court of Session Act 1988, or for any other appropriate relief.

(9) For the purposes of this Act the provision of assistance with giving effect to an interception warrant includes any disclosure to the person to whom the warrant is addressed, or to persons acting on his behalf, of intercepted material obtained by any interception authorised or required by the warrant, and of any related communications data.

Notes

Initial Commencement

To be appointed
>To be appointed: see s 83(2).

Appointment
>Appointment: 2 October 2000: see SI 2000/2543, art 3.

Interception capability and costs

12 Maintenance of interception capability

(1) The Secretary of State may by order provide for the imposition by him on persons who–

    (a)   are providing public postal services or public telecommunications services, or

    (b)   are proposing to do so,

of such obligations as it appears to him reasonable to impose for the purpose of securing that it is and remains practicable for requirements to provide assistance in relation to interception warrants to be imposed and complied with.

(2) The Secretary of State's power to impose the obligations provided for by an order under this section shall be exercisable by the giving, in accordance with the order, of a notice requiring the person who is to be subject to the obligations to take all such steps as may be specified or described in the notice.

(3) Subject to subsection (11), the only steps that may be specified or described in a notice given to a person under subsection (2) are steps appearing to the Secretary of State to be necessary for securing that that person has the practical capability of providing any assistance which he may be required to provide in relation to relevant interception warrants.

(4) A person shall not be liable to have an obligation imposed on him in accordance with an order under this section by reason only that he provides, or is proposing to provide, to members of the public a telecommunications service the provision of which is or, as the case may be, will be no more than–

    (a)   the means by which he provides a service which is not a telecommunications service; or

    (b)   necessarily incidental to the provision by him of a service which is not a telecommunications service.

(5) Where a notice is given to any person under subsection (2) and otherwise than by virtue of subsection (6)(c), that person may, before the end of such period as may be specified in an order under this section, refer the notice to the Technical Advisory Board.

(6) Where a notice given to any person under subsection (2) is referred to the Technical Advisory Board under subsection (5)–

    (a)   there shall be no requirement for that person to comply, except in pursuance of a notice under paragraph (c)(ii), with any obligations imposed by the notice;

    (b)   the Board shall consider the technical requirements and the financial consequences, for the person making the reference, of the notice referred

to them and shall report their conclusions on those matters to that
person and to the Secretary of State; and

(c)   the Secretary of State, after considering any report of the Board relating
to the notice, may either–

   (i)   withdraw the notice; or

   (ii)   give a further notice under subsection (2) confirming its effect, with
   or without modifications.

(7) It shall be the duty of a person to whom a notice is given under subsection (2) to
comply with the notice; and that duty shall be enforceable by civil proceedings by the
Secretary of State for an injunction, or for specific performance of a statutory duty
under section 45 of the Court of Session Act 1988, or for any other appropriate relief.

(8) A notice for the purposes of subsection (2) must specify such period as appears
to the Secretary of State to be reasonable as the period within which the steps
specified or described in the notice are to be taken.

(9) Before making an order under this section the Secretary of State shall consult
with–

(a)   such persons appearing to him to be likely to be subject to the obligations
for which it provides,

(b)   the Technical Advisory Board,

(c)   such persons representing persons falling within paragraph (a), and

(d)   such persons with statutory functions in relation to persons falling
within that paragraph,

as he considers appropriate.

(10) The Secretary of State shall not make an order under this section unless a draft
of the order has been laid before Parliament and approved by a resolution of each
House.

(11) For the purposes of this section the question whether a person has the practical
capability of providing assistance in relation to relevant interception warrants shall
include the question whether all such arrangements have been made as the Secretary
of State considers necessary–

(a)   with respect to the disclosure of intercepted material;

(b)   for the purpose of ensuring that security and confidentiality are maintained in relation to, and to matters connected with, the provision of any
such assistance; and

(c)   for the purpose of facilitating the carrying out of any functions in
relation to this Chapter of the Interception of Communications Commissioner;

but before determining for the purposes of the making of any order, or the imposition
of any obligation, under this section what arrangements he considers necessary for
the purpose mentioned in paragraph (c) the Secretary of State shall consult that
Commissioner.

(12) In this section "relevant interception warrant"–

(a)   in relation to a person providing a public postal service, means an
interception warrant relating to the interception of communications in
the course of their transmission by means of that service; and

(b)　in relation to a person providing a public telecommunications service, means an interception warrant relating to the interception of communications in the course of their transmission by means of a telecommunication system used for the purposes of that service.

Notes

Initial Commencement

To be appointed

> To be appointed: see s 83(2).

Appointment

> Appointment: 2 October 2000: see SI 2000/2543, art 3.

Subordinate Legislation

> Regulation of Investigatory Powers (Maintenance of Interception Capability) Order 2002, SI 2002/1931 (made under sub-ss (1), (2), (5)).

13　Technical Advisory Board

(1)　There shall be a Technical Advisory Board consisting of such number of persons appointed by the Secretary of State as he may by order provide.

(2)　The order providing for the membership of the Technical Advisory Board must also make provision which is calculated to ensure–

(a)　that the membership of the Technical Advisory Board includes persons likely effectively to represent the interests of the persons on whom obligations may be imposed under section 12;

(b)　that the membership of the Board includes persons likely effectively to represent the interests of the persons by or on whose behalf applications for interception warrants may be made;

(c)　that such other persons (if any) as the Secretary of State thinks fit may be appointed to be members of the Board; and

(d)　that the Board is so constituted as to produce a balance between the representation of the interests mentioned in paragraph (a) and the representation of those mentioned in paragraph (b).

(3)　The Secretary of State shall not make an order under this section unless a draft of the order has been laid before Parliament and approved by a resolution of each House.

Notes

Initial Commencement

To be appointed

> To be appointed: see s 83(2).

Appointment

> Appointment: 2 October 2000: see SI 2000/2543, art 3.

Subordinate Legislation

> Regulation of Investigatory Powers (Technical Advisory Board) Order 2001, SI 2001/3734 (made under sub-ss (1), (2)).

14 Grants for interception costs

(1) It shall be the duty of the Secretary of State to ensure that such arrangements are in force as are necessary for securing that a person who provides–

(a)   a postal service, or

(b)   a telecommunications service,

receives such contribution as is, in the circumstances of that person's case, a fair contribution towards the costs incurred, or likely to be incurred, by that person in consequence of the matters mentioned in subsection (2).

(2) Those matters are–

(a)   in relation to a person providing a postal service, the issue of interception warrants relating to communications transmitted by means of that postal service;

(b)   in relation to a person providing a telecommunications service, the issue of interception warrants relating to communications transmitted by means of a telecommunication system used for the purposes of that service;

(c)   in relation to each description of person, the imposition on that person of obligations provided for by an order under section 12.

(3) For the purpose of complying with his duty under this section, the Secretary of State may make arrangements for payments to be made out of money provided by Parliament.

Notes

Initial Commencement

To be appointed

> To be appointed: see s 83(2).

Appointment

> Appointment: 2 October 2000: see SI 2000/2543, art 3.

Restrictions on use of intercepted material etc

15 General safeguards

(1) Subject to subsection (6), it shall be the duty of the Secretary of State to ensure, in relation to all interception warrants, that such arrangements are in force as he considers necessary for securing–

(a)   that the requirements of subsections (2) and (3) are satisfied in relation to the intercepted material and any related communications data; and

(b)   in the case of warrants in relation to which there are section 8(4) certificates, that the requirements of section 16 are also satisfied.

(2) The requirements of this subsection are satisfied in relation to the intercepted material and any related communications data if each of the following–

(a)   the number of persons to whom any of the material or data is disclosed or otherwise made available,

(b)   the extent to which any of the material or data is disclosed or otherwise made available,

(c)   the extent to which any of the material or data is copied, and

(d)   the number of copies that are made,

is limited to the minimum that is necessary for the authorised purposes.

(3) The requirements of this subsection are satisfied in relation to the intercepted material and any related communications data if each copy made of any of the material or data (if not destroyed earlier) is destroyed as soon as there are no longer any grounds for retaining it as necessary for any of the authorised purposes.

(4) For the purposes of this section something is necessary for the authorised purposes if, and only if–

(a)   it continues to be, or is likely to become, necessary as mentioned in section 5(3);

(b)   it is necessary for facilitating the carrying out of any of the functions under this Chapter of the Secretary of State;

(c)   it is necessary for facilitating the carrying out of any functions in relation to this Part of the Interception of Communications Commissioner or of the Tribunal;

(d)   it is necessary to ensure that a person conducting a criminal prosecution has the information he needs to determine what is required of him by his duty to secure the fairness of the prosecution; or

(e)   it is necessary for the performance of any duty imposed on any person by the Public Records Act 1958 or the Public Records Act (Northern Ireland) 1923.

(5) The arrangements for the time being in force under this section for securing that the requirements of subsection (2) are satisfied in relation to the intercepted material or any related communications data must include such arrangements as the Secretary of State considers necessary for securing that every copy of the material or data that is made is stored, for so long as it is retained, in a secure manner.

(6) Arrangements in relation to interception warrants which are made for the purposes of subsection (1)–

(a)   shall not be required to secure that the requirements of subsections (2) and (3) are satisfied in so far as they relate to any of the intercepted material or related communications data, or any copy of any such material or data, possession of which has been surrendered to any authorities of a country or territory outside the United Kingdom; but

(b)   shall be required to secure, in the case of every such warrant, that possession of the intercepted material and data and of copies of the material or data is surrendered to authorities of a country or territory outside the United Kingdom only if the requirements of subsection (7) are satisfied.

(7) The requirements of this subsection are satisfied in the case of a warrant if it appears to the Secretary of State–

(a)   that requirements corresponding to those of subsections (2) and (3) will apply, to such extent (if any) as the Secretary of State thinks fit, in relation to any of the intercepted material or related communications data possession of which, or of any copy of which, is surrendered to the authorities in question; and

(b)   that restrictions are in force which would prevent, to such extent (if any) as the Secretary of State thinks fit, the doing of anything in, for the purposes of or in connection with any proceedings outside the United Kingdom which would result in such a disclosure as, by virtue of section 17, could not be made in the United Kingdom.

(8) In this section "copy", in relation to intercepted material or related communications data, means any of the following (whether or not in documentary form)–

(a) any copy, extract or summary of the material or data which identifies itself as the product of an interception, and

(b) any record referring to an interception which is a record of the identities of the persons to or by whom the intercepted material was sent, or to whom the communications data relates,

and "copied" shall be construed accordingly.

Notes

Initial Commencement

To be appointed

To be appointed: see s 83(2).

Appointment

Appointment: 2 October 2000: see SI 2000/2543, art 3.

Transfer of Functions

Functions under this section: certain functions under sub-s (1) are transferred, in so far as they are exercisable in or as regards Scotland, to the Scottish Ministers, by the Scotland Act 1998 (Transfer of Functions to the Scottish Ministers etc) (No 2) Order 2000, SI 2000/3253, arts 2, 3, Sch 1, para 3 (as amended by SI 2003/2617, art 4(b)), Sch 2.

Functions under this section: certain functions under sub-s (1) are transferred, in so far as they are exercisable in or as regards Scotland, to the Scottish Ministers, by the Scotland Act 1998 (Transfer of Functions to the Scottish Ministers etc) (No 2) Order 2003, SI 2003/2617, arts 2, 3, Sch 1, para 2, Sch 2.

16 Extra safeguards in the case of certificated warrants

(1) For the purposes of section 15 the requirements of this section, in the case of a warrant in relation to which there is a section 8(4) certificate, are that the intercepted material is read, looked at or listened to by the persons to whom it becomes available by virtue of the warrant to the extent only that it–

(a) has been certified as material the examination of which is necessary as mentioned in section 5(3)(a), (b) or (c); and

(b) falls within subsection (2).

(2) Subject to subsections (3) and (4), intercepted material falls within this subsection so far only as it is selected to be read, looked at or listened to otherwise than according to a factor which–

(a) is referable to an individual who is known to be for the time being in the British Islands; and

(b) has as its purpose, or one of its purposes, the identification of material contained in communications sent by him, or intended for him.

(3) Intercepted material falls within subsection (2), notwithstanding that it is selected by reference to any such factor as is mentioned in paragraph (a) and (b) of that subsection, if–

(a) it is certified by the Secretary of State for the purposes of section 8(4) that the examination of material selected according to factors referable to the individual in question is necessary as mentioned in subsection 5(3)(a), (b) or (c); and

(b)   the material relates only to communications sent during a period of not more than three months specified in the certificate.

(4) Intercepted material also falls within subsection (2), notwithstanding that it is selected by reference to any such factor as is mentioned in paragraph (a) and (b) of that subsection, if–

(a)   the person to whom the warrant is addressed believes, on reasonable grounds, that the circumstances are such that the material would fall within that subsection; or

(b)   the conditions set out in subsection (5) below are satisfied in relation to the selection of the material.

(5) Those conditions are satisfied in relation to the selection of intercepted material if–

(a)   it has appeared to the person to whom the warrant is addressed that there has been such a relevant change of circumstances as, but for subsection (4)(b), would prevent the intercepted material from falling within subsection (2);

(b)   since it first so appeared, a written authorisation to read, look at or listen to the material has been given by a senior official; and

(c)   the selection is made before the end of the first working day after the day on which it first so appeared to that person.

(6) References in this section to its appearing that there has been a relevant change of circumstances are references to its appearing either–

(a)   that the individual in question has entered the British Islands; or

(b)   that a belief by the person to whom the warrant is addressed in the individual's presence outside the British Islands was in fact mistaken.

Notes

Initial Commencement

To be appointed
>   To be appointed: see s 83(2).

Appointment
>   Appointment: 2 October 2000: see SI 2000/2543, art 3.

17 Exclusion of matters from legal proceedings

(1) Subject to section 18, no evidence shall be adduced, question asked, assertion or disclosure made or other thing done in, for the purposes of or in connection with any legal proceedings which (in any manner)–

(a)   discloses, in circumstances from which its origin in anything falling within subsection (2) may be inferred, any of the contents of an intercepted communication or any related communications data; or

(b)   tends (apart from any such disclosure) to suggest that anything falling within subsection (2) has or may have occurred or be going to occur.

(2) The following fall within this subsection–

(a) conduct by a person falling within subsection (3) that was or would be an offence under section 1(1) or (2) of this Act or under section 1 of the Interception of Communications Act 1985;

(b) a breach by the Secretary of State of his duty under section 1(4) of this Act;

(c) the issue of an interception warrant or of a warrant under the Interception of Communications Act 1985;

(d) the making of an application by any person for an interception warrant, or for a warrant under that Act;

(e) the imposition of any requirement on any person to provide assistance with giving effect to an interception warrant.

(3) The persons referred to in subsection (2)(a) are–

(a) any person to whom a warrant under this Chapter may be addressed;

(b) any person holding office under the Crown;

(c) any member of the National Criminal Intelligence Service;

(d) any member of the National Crime Squad;

(e) any person employed by or for the purposes of a police force;

(f) any person providing a postal service or employed for the purposes of any business of providing such a service; and

(g) any person providing a public telecommunications service or employed for the purposes of any business of providing such a service.

(4) In this section "intercepted communication" means any communication intercepted in the course of its transmission by means of a postal service or telecommunication system.

Notes

Initial Commencement

To be appointed
> To be appointed: see s 83(2).

Appointment
> Appointment: 2 October 2000: see SI 2000/2543, art 3.

---

18 Exceptions to section 17

(1) Section 17(1) shall not apply in relation to–

(a) any proceedings for a relevant offence;

(b) any civil proceedings under section 11(8);

(c) any proceedings before the Tribunal;

(d) any proceedings on an appeal or review for which provision is made by an order under section 67(8);

(e) any proceedings before the Special Immigration Appeals Commission or any proceedings arising out of proceedings before that Commission; or

(f)   any proceedings before the Proscribed Organisations Appeal Commission or any proceedings arising out of proceedings before that Commission.

(2) Subsection (1) shall not, by virtue of paragraph (e) or (f), authorise the disclosure of anything–

(a)   in the case of any proceedings falling within paragraph (e), to–

(i)   the appellant to the Special Immigration Appeals Commission; or

(ii)   any person who for the purposes of any proceedings so falling (but otherwise than by virtue of an appointment under section 6 of the Special Immigration Appeals Commission Act 1997) represents that appellant;

or

(b)   in the case of proceedings falling within paragraph (f), to–

(i)   the applicant to the Proscribed Organisations Appeal Commission;

(ii)   the organisation concerned (if different);

(iii) any person designated under paragraph 6 of Schedule 3 to the Terrorism Act 2000 to conduct proceedings so falling on behalf of that organisation; or

(iv)   any person who for the purposes of any proceedings so falling (but otherwise than by virtue of an appointment under paragraph 7 of that Schedule) represents that applicant or that organisation.

(3) Section 17(1) shall not prohibit anything done in, for the purposes of, or in connection with, so much of any legal proceedings as relates to the fairness or unfairness of a dismissal on the grounds of any conduct constituting an offence under section 1(1) or (2), 11(7) or 19 of this Act, or section 1 of the Interception of Communications Act 1985.

(4) Section 17(1)(a) shall not prohibit the disclosure of any of the contents of a communication if the interception of that communication was lawful by virtue of section 1(5)(c), 3 or 4.

(5) Where any disclosure is proposed to be or has been made on the grounds that it is authorised by subsection (4), section 17(1) shall not prohibit the doing of anything in, or for the purposes of, so much of any legal proceedings as relates to the question whether that disclosure is or was so authorised.

(6) Section 17(1)(b) shall not prohibit the doing of anything that discloses any conduct of a person for which he has been convicted of an offence under section 1(1) or (2), 11(7) or 19 of this Act, or section 1 of the Interception of Communications Act 1985.

(7) Nothing in section 17(1) shall prohibit any such disclosure of any information that continues to be available for disclosure as is confined to–

(a)   a disclosure to a person conducting a criminal prosecution for the purpose only of enabling that person to determine what is required of him by his duty to secure the fairness of the prosecution; or

(b)   a disclosure to a relevant judge in a case in which that judge has ordered the disclosure to be made to him alone.

(8) A relevant judge shall not order a disclosure under subsection (7)(b) except where he is satisfied that the exceptional circumstances of the case make the disclosure essential in the interests of justice.

(9) Subject to subsection (10), where in any criminal proceedings–

(a)   a relevant judge does order a disclosure under subsection (7)(b), and

(b)   in consequence of that disclosure he is of the opinion that there are exceptional circumstances requiring him to do so,

he may direct the person conducting the prosecution to make for the purposes of the proceedings any such admission of fact as that judge thinks essential in the interests of justice.

(10) Nothing in any direction under subsection (9) shall authorise or require anything to be done in contravention of section 17(1).

(11) In this section "a relevant judge" means–

(a)   any judge of the High Court or of the Crown Court or any Circuit judge;

(b)   any judge of the High Court of Justiciary or any sheriff;

(c)   in relation to a court-martial, the judge advocate appointed in relation to that court-martial under section 84B of the Army Act 1955, section 84B of the Air Force Act 1955 or section 53B of the Naval Discipline Act 1957; or

(d)   any person holding any such judicial office as entitles him to exercise the jurisdiction of a judge falling within paragraph (a) or (b).

(12) In this section "relevant offence" means–

(a)   an offence under any provision of this Act;

(b)   an offence under section 1 of the Interception of Communications Act 1985;

(c)   an offence under section 5 of the Wireless Telegraphy Act 1949;

(d)   an offence under … [section 83 or 84 of the Postal Services Act 2000];

(e)   *an offence under section 45 of the Telecommunications Act 1984;*

(f)   an offence under section 4 of the Official Secrets Act 1989 relating to any such information, document or article as is mentioned in subsection (3)(a) of that section;

(g)   an offence under section 1 or 2 of the Official Secrets Act 1911 relating to any sketch, plan, model, article, note, document or information which incorporates or relates to the contents of any intercepted communication or any related communications data or tends to suggest as mentioned in section 17(1)(b) of this Act;

(h)   perjury committed in the course of any proceedings mentioned in subsection (1) or (3) of this section;

(i)   attempting or conspiring to commit, or aiding, abetting, counselling or procuring the commission of, an offence falling within any of the preceding paragraphs; and

(j)   contempt of court committed in the course of, or in relation to, any proceedings mentioned in subsection (1) or (3) of this section.

(13) In subsection (12) "intercepted communication" has the same meaning as in section 17.

Notes

Initial Commencement

To be appointed

To be appointed: see s 83(2).

Appointment

Appointment: 2 October 2000: see SI 2000/2543, art 3.

Amendment

Sub-s (12): in para (d) words omitted repealed by SI 2001/1149, art 3(2), Sch 2.

Date in force: 26 March 2001: see SI 2001/1149, art 1(2).

Sub-s (12): in para (d) words "section 83 or 84 of the Postal Services Act 2000" in square brackets substituted by SI 2001/1149, art 3(1), Sch 1, para 135(1), (2).

Date in force: 26 March 2001: see SI 2001/1149, art 1(2).

Sub-s (12): para (e) repealed by the Communications Act 2003, s 406(7), Sch 19(1).

Date in force: to be appointed: see the Communications Act 2003, s 411(2).

19 Offence for unauthorised disclosures

(1) Where an interception warrant has been issued or renewed, it shall be the duty of every person falling within subsection (2) to keep secret all the matters mentioned in subsection (3).

(2) The persons falling within this subsection are–

- (a)　the persons specified in section 6(2);

- (b)　every person holding office under the Crown;

- (c)　every member of the National Criminal Intelligence Service;

- (d)　every member of the National Crime Squad;

- (e)　every person employed by or for the purposes of a police force;

- (f)　persons providing postal services or employed for the purposes of any business of providing such a service;

- (g)　persons providing public telecommunications services or employed for the purposes of any business of providing such a service;

- (h)　persons having control of the whole or any part of a telecommunication system located wholly or partly in the United Kingdom.

(3) Those matters are–

- (a)　the existence and contents of the warrant and of any section 8(4) certificate in relation to the warrant;

- (b)　the details of the issue of the warrant and of any renewal or modification of the warrant or of any such certificate;

- (c)　the existence and contents of any requirement to provide assistance with giving effect to the warrant;

- (d)　the steps taken in pursuance of the warrant or of any such requirement; and

- (e)　everything in the intercepted material, together with any related communications data.

(4) A person who makes a disclosure to another of anything that he is required to keep secret under this section shall be guilty of an offence and liable–

(a) on conviction on indictment, to imprisonment for a term not exceeding five years or to a fine, or to both;

(b) on summary conviction, to imprisonment for a term not exceeding six months or to a fine not exceeding the statutory maximum, or to both.

(5) In proceedings against any person for an offence under this section in respect of any disclosure, it shall be a defence for that person to show that he could not reasonably have been expected, after first becoming aware of the matter disclosed, to take steps to prevent the disclosure.

(6) In proceedings against any person for an offence under this section in respect of any disclosure, it shall be a defence for that person to show that–

(a) the disclosure was made by or to a professional legal adviser in connection with the giving, by the adviser to any client of his, of advice about the effect of provisions of this Chapter; and

(b) the person to whom or, as the case may be, by whom it was made was the client or a representative of the client.

(7) In proceedings against any person for an offence under this section in respect of any disclosure, it shall be a defence for that person to show that the disclosure was made by a legal adviser–

(a) in contemplation of, or in connection with, any legal proceedings; and

(b) for the purposes of those proceedings.

(8) Neither subsection (6) nor subsection (7) applies in the case of a disclosure made with a view to furthering any criminal purpose.

(9) In proceedings against any person for an offence under this section in respect of any disclosure, it shall be a defence for that person to show that the disclosure was confined to a disclosure made to the Interception of Communications Commissioner or authorised–

(a) by that Commissioner;

(b) by the warrant or the person to whom the warrant is or was addressed;

(c) by the terms of the requirement to provide assistance; or

(d) by section 11(9).

Notes

Initial Commencement

To be appointed
To be appointed: see s 83(2).

Appointment
Appointment: 2 October 2000: see SI 2000/2543, art 3.

Interpretation of Chapter I

20 Interpretation of Chapter I

In this Chapter–

"certified", in relation to a section 8(4) certificate, means of a description certified by the certificate as a description of material the examination of which the Secretary of State considers necessary;

"external communication" means a communication sent or received outside the British Islands;

"intercepted material", in relation to an interception warrant, means the contents of any communications intercepted by an interception to which the warrant relates;

"the interception subject", in relation to an interception warrant, means the person about whose communications information is sought by the interception to which the warrant relates;

"international mutual assistance agreement" means an international agreement designated for the purposes of section 1(4);

"related communications data", in relation to a communication intercepted in the course of its transmission by means of a postal service or telecommunication system, means so much of any communications data (within the meaning of Chapter II of this Part) as–

(a)   is obtained by, or in connection with, the interception; and

(b)   relates to the communication or to the sender or recipient, or intended recipient, of the communication;

"section 8(4) certificate" means any certificate issued for the purposes of section 8(4).

Notes

Initial Commencement

To be appointed

To be appointed: see s 83(2).

Appointment

Appointment: 2 October 2000: see SI 2000/2543, art 3.

CHAPTER II
ACQUISITION AND DISCLOSURE OF COMMUNICATIONS DATA

21 Lawful acquisition and disclosure of communications data

(1) This Chapter applies to–

(a)   any conduct in relation to a postal service or telecommunication system for obtaining communications data, other than conduct consisting in the interception of communications in the course of their transmission by means of such a service or system; and

(b)   the disclosure to any person of communications data.

(2) Conduct to which this Chapter applies shall be lawful for all purposes if–

(a)   it is conduct in which any person is authorised or required to engage by an authorisation or notice granted or given under this Chapter; and

(b)   the conduct is in accordance with, or in pursuance of, the authorisation or requirement.

(3) A person shall not be subject to any civil liability in respect of any conduct of his which–

(a)   is incidental to any conduct that is lawful by virtue of subsection (2); and

(b)   is not itself conduct an authorisation or warrant for which is capable of being granted under a relevant enactment and might reasonably have been expected to have been sought in the case in question.

(4)   In this Chapter "communications data" means any of the following–

(a)   any traffic data comprised in or attached to a communication (whether by the sender or otherwise) for the purposes of any postal service or telecommunication system by means of which it is being or may be transmitted;

(b)   any information which includes none of the contents of a communication (apart from any information falling within paragraph (a)) and is about the use made by any person–

(i)   of any postal service or telecommunications service; or

(ii)   in connection with the provision to or use by any person of any telecommunications service, of any part of a telecommunication system;

(c)   any information not falling within paragraph (a) or (b) that is held or obtained, in relation to persons to whom he provides the service, by a person providing a postal service or telecommunications service.

(5)   In this section "relevant enactment" means–

(a)   an enactment contained in this Act;

(b)   section 5 of the Intelligence Services Act 1994 (warrants for the intelligence services); or

(c)   an enactment contained in Part III of the Police Act 1997 (powers of the police and of customs officers).

(6)   In this section "traffic data", in relation to any communication, means–

(a)   any data identifying, or purporting to identify, any person, apparatus or location to or from which the communication is or may be transmitted,

(b)   any data identifying or selecting, or purporting to identify or select, apparatus through which, or by means of which, the communication is or may be transmitted,

(c)   any data comprising signals for the actuation of apparatus used for the purposes of a telecommunication system for effecting (in whole or in part) the transmission of any communication, and

(d)   any data identifying the data or other data as data comprised in or attached to a particular communication,

but that expression includes data identifying a computer file or computer program access to which is obtained, or which is run, by means of the communication to the extent only that the file or program is identified by reference to the apparatus in which it is stored.

(7)   In this section–

(a)   references, in relation to traffic data comprising signals for the actuation of apparatus, to a telecommunication system by means of which a communication is being or may be transmitted include references to any telecommunication system in which that apparatus is comprised; and

    (b)   references to traffic data being attached to a communication include references to the data and the communication being logically associated with each other;

and in this section "data", in relation to a postal item, means anything written on the outside of the item.

Notes

Initial Commencement

To be appointed
    To be appointed: see s 83(2).

Appointment
    Sub-ss (1)–(3), (5)–(7): Appointment: 5 January 2004: see SI 2003/3140, art 2(a).
    Sub-s (4): Appointment (for certain purposes): 2 October 2000: see SI 2000/2543, art 3.
    Sub-s (4): Appointment (for remaining purposes): 5 January 2004: see SI 2003/3140, art 2(a).

---

22 Obtaining and disclosing communications data

(1) This section applies where a person designated for the purposes of this Chapter believes that it is necessary on grounds falling within subsection (2) to obtain any communications data.

(2) It is necessary on grounds falling within this subsection to obtain communications data if it is necessary–

    (a)   in the interests of national security;

    (b)   for the purpose of preventing or detecting crime or of preventing disorder;

    (c)   in the interests of the economic well-being of the United Kingdom;

    (d)   in the interests of public safety;

    (e)   for the purpose of protecting public health;

    (f)   for the purpose of assessing or collecting any tax, duty, levy or other imposition, contribution or charge payable to a government department;

    (g)   for the purpose, in an emergency, of preventing death or injury or any damage to a person's physical or mental health, or of mitigating any injury or damage to a person's physical or mental health; or

    (h)   for any purpose (not falling within paragraphs (a) to (g)) which is specified for the purposes of this subsection by an order made by the Secretary of State.

(3) Subject to subsection (5), the designated person may grant an authorisation for persons holding offices, ranks or positions with the same relevant public authority as the designated person to engage in any conduct to which this Chapter applies.

(4) Subject to subsection (5), where it appears to the designated person that a postal or telecommunications operator is or may be in possession of, or be capable of obtaining, any communications data, the designated person may, by notice to the postal or telecommunications operator, require the operator–

    (a)   if the operator is not already in possession of the data, to obtain the data; and

    (b)   in any case, to disclose all of the data in his possession or subsequently obtained by him.

(5) The designated person shall not grant an authorisation under subsection (3), or give a notice under subsection (4), unless he believes that obtaining the data in question by the conduct authorised or required by the authorisation or notice is proportionate to what is sought to be achieved by so obtaining the data.

(6) It shall be the duty of the postal or telecommunications operator to comply with the requirements of any notice given to him under subsection (4).

(7) A person who is under a duty by virtue of subsection (6) shall not be required to do anything in pursuance of that duty which it is not reasonably practicable for him to do.

(8) The duty imposed by subsection (6) shall be enforceable by civil proceedings by the Secretary of State for an injunction, or for specific performance of a statutory duty under section 45 of the Court of Session Act 1988, or for any other appropriate relief.

(9) The Secretary of State shall not make an order under subsection (2)(h) unless a draft of the order has been laid before Parliament and approved by a resolution of each House.

Notes

Initial Commencement

To be appointed
>To be appointed: see s 83(2).

Appointment
>Appointment: 5 January 2004: see SI 2003/3140, art 2(a).

23 Form and duration of authorisations and notices

(1) An authorisation under section 22(3)–

    (a)   must be granted in writing or (if not in writing) in a manner that produces a record of its having been granted;

    (b)   must describe the conduct to which this Chapter applies that is author-ised and the communications data in relation to which it is authorised;

    (c)   must specify the matters falling within section 22(2) by reference to which it is granted; and

    (d)   must specify the office, rank or position held by the person granting the authorisation.

(2) A notice under section 22(4) requiring communications data to be disclosed or to be obtained and disclosed–

    (a)   must be given in writing or (if not in writing) must be given in a manner that produces a record of its having been given;

    (b)   must describe the communications data to be obtained or disclosed under the notice;

    (c)   must specify the matters falling within section 22(2) by reference to which the notice is given;

    (d)   must specify the office, rank or position held by the person giving it; and

(e)   must specify the manner in which any disclosure required by the notice is to be made.

(3) A notice under section 22(4) shall not require the disclosure of data to any person other than–

(a)   the person giving the notice; or

(b)   such other person as may be specified in or otherwise identified by, or in accordance with, the provisions of the notice;

but the provisions of the notice shall not specify or otherwise identify a person for the purposes of paragraph (b) unless he holds an office, rank or position with the same relevant public authority as the person giving the notice.

(4) An authorisation under section 22(3) or notice under section 22(4)–

(a)   shall not authorise or require any data to be obtained after the end of the period of one month beginning with the date on which the authorisation is granted or the notice given; and

(b)   in the case of a notice, shall not authorise or require any disclosure after the end of that period of any data not in the possession of, or obtained by, the postal or telecommunications operator at a time during that period.

(5) An authorisation under section 22(3) or notice under section 22(4) may be renewed at any time before the end of the period of one month applying (in accordance with subsection (4) or subsection (7)) to that authorisation or notice.

(6) A renewal of an authorisation under section 22(3) or of a notice under section 22(4) shall be by the grant or giving, in accordance with this section, of a further authorisation or notice.

(7) Subsection (4) shall have effect in relation to a renewed authorisation or renewal notice as if the period of one month mentioned in that subsection did not begin until the end of the period of one month applicable to the authorisation or notice that is current at the time of the renewal.

(8) Where a person who has given a notice under subsection (4) of section 22 is satisfied–

(a)   that it is no longer necessary on grounds falling within subsection (2) of that section for the requirements of the notice to be complied with, or

(b)   that the conduct required by the notice is no longer proportionate to what is sought to be achieved by obtaining communications data to which the notice relates,

he shall cancel the notice.

(9) The Secretary of State may by regulations provide for the person by whom any duty imposed by subsection (8) is to be performed in a case in which it would otherwise fall on a person who is no longer available to perform it; and regulations under this subsection may provide for the person on whom the duty is to fall to be a person appointed in accordance with the regulations.

Notes

Initial Commencement

To be appointed

To be appointed: see s 83(2).

Appointment

> Appointment: 5 January 2004: see SI 2003/3140, art 2(a).

24 Arrangements for payments

(1) It shall be the duty of the Secretary of State to ensure that such arrangements are in force as he thinks appropriate for requiring or authorising, in such cases as he thinks fit, the making to postal and telecommunications operators of appropriate contributions towards the costs incurred by them in complying with notices under section 22(4).

(2) For the purpose of complying with his duty under this section, the Secretary of State may make arrangements for payments to be made out of money provided by Parliament.

Notes

Initial Commencement

To be appointed

> To be appointed: see s 83(2).

Appointment

> Appointment: 5 January 2004: see SI 2003/3140, art 2(a).

25 Interpretation of Chapter II

(1) In this Chapter–

> "communications data" has the meaning given by section 21(4);

> "designated" shall be construed in accordance with subsection (2);

> "postal or telecommunications operator" means a person who provides a postal service or telecommunications service;

> "relevant public authority" means (subject to subsection (4)) any of the following–

> (a) a police force;

> (b) the National Criminal Intelligence Service;

> (c) the National Crime Squad;

> (d) the Commissioners of Customs and Excise;

> (e) the Commissioners of Inland Revenue;

> (f) any of the intelligence services;

> (g) any such public authority not falling within paragraphs (a) to (f) as may be specified for the purposes of this subsection by an order made by the Secretary of State.

(2) Subject to subsection (3), the persons designated for the purposes of this Chapter are the individuals holding such offices, ranks or positions with relevant public authorities as are prescribed for the purposes of this subsection by an order made by the Secretary of State.

(3) The Secretary of State may by order impose restrictions–

    (a)   on the authorisations and notices under this Chapter that may be granted or given by any individual holding an office, rank or position with a specified public authority; and

    (b)   on the circumstances in which, or the purposes for which, such authorisations may be granted or notices given by any such individual.

(4) The Secretary of State may by order remove any person from the list of persons who are for the time being relevant public authorities for the purposes of this Chapter.

(5) The Secretary of State shall not make an order under this section that adds any person to the list of persons who are for the time being relevant public authorities for the purposes of this Chapter unless a draft of the order has been laid before Parliament and approved by a resolution of each House.

Notes

Initial Commencement

To be appointed

To be appointed: see s 83(2).

Appointment

Appointment: 5 January 2004: see SI 2003/3140, art 2(a).

Subordinate Legislation

Regulation of Investigatory Powers (Communications Data) Order 2003, SI 2003/3172 (made under sub-ss (1)(g), (2), (3)).

PART II
SURVEILLANCE AND COVERT HUMAN INTELLIGENCE SOURCES
Introductory

26 Conduct to which Part II applies

(1) This Part applies to the following conduct–

    (a)   directed surveillance;

    (b)   intrusive surveillance; and

    (c)   the conduct and use of covert human intelligence sources.

(2) Subject to subsection (6), surveillance is directed for the purposes of this Part if it is covert but not intrusive and is undertaken–

    (a)   for the purposes of a specific investigation or a specific operation;

    (b)   in such a manner as is likely to result in the obtaining of private information about a person (whether or not one specifically identified for the purposes of the investigation or operation); and

    (c)   otherwise than by way of an immediate response to events or circumstances the nature of which is such that it would not be reasonably practicable for an authorisation under this Part to be sought for the carrying out of the surveillance.

(3) Subject to subsections (4) to (6), surveillance is intrusive for the purposes of this Part if, and only if, it is covert surveillance that–

    (a)   is carried out in relation to anything taking place on any residential premises or in any private vehicle; and

    (b)   involves the presence of an individual on the premises or in the vehicle or is carried out by means of a surveillance device.

(4) For the purposes of this Part surveillance is not intrusive to the extent that–

    (a)   it is carried out by means only of a surveillance device designed or adapted principally for the purpose of providing information about the location of a vehicle; or

    (b)   it is surveillance consisting in any such interception of a communication as falls within section 48(4).

(5) For the purposes of this Part surveillance which–

    (a)   is carried out by means of a surveillance device in relation to anything taking place on any residential premises or in any private vehicle, but

    (b)   is carried out without that device being present on the premises or in the vehicle,

is not intrusive unless the device is such that it consistently provides information of the same quality and detail as might be expected to be obtained from a device actually present on the premises or in the vehicle.

(6) For the purposes of this Part surveillance which–

    (a)   is carried out by means of apparatus designed or adapted for the purpose of detecting the installation or use in any residential or other premises of a television receiver (within the meaning of *section 1 of the Wireless Telegraphy Act 1949*) [Part 4 of the Communications Act 2003], and

    (b)   is carried out from outside those premises exclusively for that purpose,

is neither directed nor intrusive.

(7) In this Part–

    (a)   references to the conduct of a covert human intelligence source are references to any conduct of such a source which falls within any of paragraphs (a) to (c) of subsection (8), or is incidental to anything falling within any of those paragraphs; and

    (b)   references to the use of a covert human intelligence source are references to inducing, asking or assisting a person to engage in the conduct of such a source, or to obtain information by means of the conduct of such a source.

(8) For the purposes of this Part a person is a covert human intelligence source if–

    (a)   he establishes or maintains a personal or other relationship with a person for the covert purpose of facilitating the doing of anything falling within paragraph (b) or (c);

    (b)   he covertly uses such a relationship to obtain information or to provide access to any information to another person; or

    (c)   he covertly discloses information obtained by the use of such a relation-ship, or as a consequence of the existence of such a relationship.

(9) For the purposes of this section–

    (a)   surveillance is covert if, and only if, it is carried out in a manner that is calculated to ensure that persons who are subject to the surveillance are unaware that it is or may be taking place;

(b)   a purpose is covert, in relation to the establishment or maintenance of a personal or other relationship, if and only if the relationship is conducted in a manner that is calculated to ensure that one of the parties to the relationship is unaware of the purpose; and

(c)   a relationship is used covertly, and information obtained as mentioned in subsection (8)(c) is disclosed covertly, if and only if it is used or, as the case may be, disclosed in a manner that is calculated to ensure that one of the parties to the relationship is unaware of the use or disclosure in question.

(10) In this section "private information", in relation to a person, includes any information relating to his private or family life.

(11) References in this section, in relation to a vehicle, to the presence of a surveillance device in the vehicle include references to its being located on or under the vehicle and also include references to its being attached to it.

Notes

Initial Commencement

To be appointed

To be appointed: see s 83(2).

Appointment

Appointment: 25 September 2000: see SI 2000/2543, art 2.

Amendment

Sub-s (6): in para (a) words "section 1 of the Wireless Telegraphy Act 1949)" in italics repealed and subsequent words in square brackets substituted by the Communications Act 2003, s 406(1), Sch 17, para 161(1), (2).

Date in force: to be appointed: see the Communications Act 2003, s 411(2).

Authorisation of surveillance and human intelligence sources

27 Lawful surveillance etc

(1) Conduct to which this Part applies shall be lawful for all purposes if–

(a)   an authorisation under this Part confers an entitlement to engage in that conduct on the person whose conduct it is; and

(b)   his conduct is in accordance with the authorisation.

(2) A person shall not be subject to any civil liability in respect of any conduct of his which–

(a)   is incidental to any conduct that is lawful by virtue of subsection (1); and

(b)   is not itself conduct an authorisation or warrant for which is capable of being granted under a relevant enactment and might reasonably have been expected to have been sought in the case in question.

(3) The conduct that may be authorised under this Part includes conduct outside the United Kingdom.

(4) In this section "relevant enactment" means–

(a)   an enactment contained in this Act;

(b)   section 5 of the Intelligence Services Act 1994 (warrants for the intelligence services); or

(c)   an enactment contained in Part III of the Police Act 1997 (powers of the police and of customs officers).

Notes

Initial Commencement

To be appointed

To be appointed: see s 83(2).

Appointment

Appointment: 25 September 2000: see SI 2000/2543, art 2.

---

28 Authorisation of directed surveillance

(1) Subject to the following provisions of this Part, the persons designated for the purposes of this section shall each have power to grant authorisations for the carrying out of directed surveillance.

(2) A person shall not grant an authorisation for the carrying out of directed surveillance unless he believes–

(a)   that the authorisation is necessary on grounds falling within subsection (3); and

(b)   that the authorised surveillance is proportionate to what is sought to be achieved by carrying it out.

(3) An authorisation is necessary on grounds falling within this subsection if it is necessary–

(a)   in the interests of national security;

(b)   for the purpose of preventing or detecting crime or of preventing disorder;

(c)   in the interests of the economic well-being of the United Kingdom;

(d)   in the interests of public safety;

(e)   for the purpose of protecting public health;

(f)   for the purpose of assessing or collecting any tax, duty, levy or other imposition, contribution or charge payable to a government department; or

(g)   for any purpose (not falling within paragraphs (a) to (f)) which is specified for the purposes of this subsection by an order made by the Secretary of State.

(4) The conduct that is authorised by an authorisation for the carrying out of directed surveillance is any conduct that–

(a)   consists in the carrying out of directed surveillance of any such description as is specified in the authorisation; and

(b)   is carried out in the circumstances described in the authorisation and for the purposes of the investigation or operation specified or described in the authorisation.

(5) The Secretary of State shall not make an order under subsection (3)(g) unless a draft of the order has been laid before Parliament and approved by a resolution of each House.

Notes

Initial Commencement

To be appointed
> To be appointed: see s 83(2).

Appointment
> Appointment: 25 September 2000: see SI 2000/2543, art 2.

---

29 Authorisation of covert human intelligence sources

(1) Subject to the following provisions of this Part, the persons designated for the purposes of this section shall each have power to grant authorisations for the conduct or the use of a covert human intelligence source.

(2) A person shall not grant an authorisation for the conduct or the use of a covert human intelligence source unless he believes–

> (a) that the authorisation is necessary on grounds falling within subsection (3);
>
> (b) that the authorised conduct or use is proportionate to what is sought to be achieved by that conduct or use; and
>
> (c) that arrangements exist for the source's case that satisfy the requirements of subsection (5) and such other requirements as may be imposed by order made by the Secretary of State.

(3) An authorisation is necessary on grounds falling within this subsection if it is necessary–

> (a) in the interests of national security;
>
> (b) for the purpose of preventing or detecting crime or of preventing disorder;
>
> (c) in the interests of the economic well-being of the United Kingdom;
>
> (d) in the interests of public safety;
>
> (e) for the purpose of protecting public health;
>
> (f) for the purpose of assessing or collecting any tax, duty, levy or other imposition, contribution or charge payable to a government department; or
>
> (g) for any purpose (not falling within paragraphs (a) to (f)) which is specified for the purposes of this subsection by an order made by the Secretary of State.

(4) The conduct that is authorised by an authorisation for the conduct or the use of a covert human intelligence source is any conduct that–

> (a) is comprised in any such activities involving conduct of a covert human intelligence source, or the use of a covert human intelligence source, as are specified or described in the authorisation;
>
> (b) consists in conduct by or in relation to the person who is so specified or

described as the person to whose actions as a covert human intelligence source the authorisation relates; and

(c)   is carried out for the purposes of, or in connection with, the investigation or operation so specified or described.

(5)   For the purposes of this Part there are arrangements for the source's case that satisfy the requirements of this subsection if such arrangements are in force as are necessary for ensuring–

(a)   that there will at all times be a person holding an office, rank or position with the relevant investigating authority who will have day-to-day responsibility for dealing with the source on behalf of that authority, and for the source's security and welfare;

(b)   that there will at all times be another person holding an office, rank or position with the relevant investigating authority who will have general oversight of the use made of the source;

(c)   that there will at all times be a person holding an office, rank or position with the relevant investigating authority who will have responsibility for maintaining a record of the use made of the source;

(d)   that the records relating to the source that are maintained by the relevant investigating authority will always contain particulars of all such matters (if any) as may be specified for the purposes of this paragraph in regulations made by the Secretary of State; and

(e)   that records maintained by the relevant investigating authority that disclose the identity of the source will not be available to persons except to the extent that there is a need for access to them to be made available to those persons.

(6)   The Secretary of State shall not make an order under subsection (3)(g) unless a draft of the order has been laid before Parliament and approved by a resolution of each House.

(7)   The Secretary of State may by order–

(a)   prohibit the authorisation under this section of any such conduct or uses of covert human intelligence sources as may be described in the order; and

(b)   impose requirements, in addition to those provided for by subsection (2), that must be satisfied before an authorisation is granted under this section for any such conduct or uses of covert human intelligence sources as may be so described.

(8)   In this section "relevant investigating authority", in relation to an authorisation for the conduct or the use of an individual as a covert human intelligence source, means (subject to subsection (9)) the public authority for whose benefit the activities of that individual as such a source are to take place.

(9)   In the case of any authorisation for the conduct or the use of a covert human intelligence source whose activities are to be for the benefit of more than one public authority, the references in subsection (5) to the relevant investigating authority are references to one of them (whether or not the same one in the case of each reference).

Notes

Initial Commencement

To be appointed

To be appointed: see s 83(2).

Appointment

Appointment: 25 September 2000: see SI 2000/2543, art 2.

Subordinate Legislation

Regulation of Investigatory Powers (Source Records) Regulations 2000, SI 2000/2725 (made under sub-s (5)(d)).

Regulation of Investigatory Powers (Juveniles) Order 2000, SI 2000/2793 (made under sub-ss (2)(c), (7)(a), (b)).

30 Persons entitled to grant authorisations under ss 28 and 29

(1) Subject to subsection (3), the persons designated for the purposes of sections 28 and 29 are the individuals holding such offices, ranks or positions with relevant public authorities as are prescribed for the purposes of this subsection by an order under this section.

(2) For the purposes of the grant of an authorisation that combines–

    (a)   an authorisation under section 28 or 29, and

    (b)   an authorisation by the Secretary of State for the carrying out of intrusive surveillance,

the Secretary of State himself shall be a person designated for the purposes of that section.

(3) An order under this section may impose restrictions–

    (a)   on the authorisations under sections 28 and 29 that may be granted by any individual holding an office, rank or position with a specified public authority; and

    (b)   on the circumstances in which, or the purposes for which, such authorisations may be granted by any such individual.

(4) A public authority is a relevant public authority for the purposes of this section–

    (a)   in relation to section 28 if it is specified in Part I or II of Schedule 1; and

    (b)   in relation to section 29 if it is specified in Part I of that Schedule.

(5) An order under this section may amend Schedule 1 by–

    (a)   adding a public authority to Part I or II of that Schedule;

    (b)   removing a public authority from that Schedule;

    (c)   moving a public authority from one Part of that Schedule to the other;

    (d)   making any change consequential on any change in the name of a public authority specified in that Schedule.

(6) Without prejudice to section 31, the power to make an order under this section shall be exercisable by the Secretary of State.

(7) The Secretary of State shall not make an order under subsection (5) containing any provision for–

    (a)   adding any public authority to Part I or II of that Schedule, or

    (b)   moving any public authority from Part II to Part I of that Schedule,

unless a draft of the order has been laid before Parliament and approved by a resolution of each House.

Notes

Initial Commencement

To be appointed

> To be appointed: see s 83(2).

Appointment

> Appointment: 25 September 2000: see SI 2000/2543, art 2.

Subordinate Legislation

> Regulation of Investigatory Powers (Prescription of Offices, Ranks and Positions) Order 2000, SI 2000/2417 (made under sub-ss (1), (3)).
> Regulation of Investigatory Powers (Prescription of Offices, Ranks and Positions) (Amendment) Order 2002, SI 2002/1298 (made under sub-ss (1), (3)).

31 Orders under s 30 for Northern Ireland

(1) Subject to subsections (2) and (3), the power to make an order under section 30 for the purposes of the grant of authorisations for conduct in Northern Ireland shall be exercisable by the Office of the First Minister and deputy First Minister in Northern Ireland (concurrently with being exercisable by the Secretary of State).

(2) The power of the Office of the First Minister and deputy First Minister to make an order under section 30 by virtue of subsection (1) or (3) of that section shall not be exercisable in relation to any public authority other than–

    (a)   the Food Standards Agency;

    (b)   ...

    (c)   an authority added to Schedule 1 by an order made by that Office;

    (d)   an authority added to that Schedule by an order made by the Secretary of State which it would (apart from that order) have been within the powers of that Office to add to that Schedule for the purposes mentioned in subsection (1) of this section.

(3) The power of the Office of the First Minister and deputy First Minister to make an order under section 30–

    (a)   shall not include power to make any provision dealing with an excepted matter;

    (b)   shall not include power, except with the consent of the Secretary of State, to make any provision dealing with a reserved matter.

(4) The power of the Office of the First Minister and deputy First Minister to make an order under section 30 shall be exercisable by statutory rule for the purposes of the Statutory Rules (Northern Ireland) Order 1979.

(5) A statutory rule containing an order under section 30 which makes provision by virtue of subsection (5) of that section for–

    (a)   adding any public authority to Part I or II of Schedule 1, or

    (b)   moving any public authority from Part II to Part I of that Schedule,

shall be subject to affirmative resolution (within the meaning of section 41(4) of the Interpretation Act (Northern Ireland) 1954).

(6) A statutory rule containing an order under section 30 (other than one to which subsection (5) of this section applies) shall be subject to negative resolution (within the meaning of section 41(6) of the Interpretation Act (Northern Ireland) 1954).

(7) An order under section 30 made by the Office of the First Minister and deputy First Minister may–

(a)   make different provision for different cases;

(b)   contain such incidental, supplemental, consequential and transitional provision as that Office thinks fit.

(8) The reference in subsection (2) to an addition to Schedule 1 being within the powers of the Office of the First Minister and deputy First Minister includes a reference to its being within the powers exercisable by that Office with the consent for the purposes of subsection (3)(b) of the Secretary of State.

(9) In this section "excepted matter" and "reserved matter" have the same meanings as in the Northern Ireland Act 1998; and, in relation to those matters, section 98(2) of that Act (meaning of "deals with") applies for the purposes of this section as it applies for the purposes of that Act.

Notes

Initial Commencement

To be appointed
> To be appointed: see s 83(2).

Appointment
> Appointment: 25 September 2000: see SI 2000/2543, art 2.

Amendment
> Sub-s (2): para (b) repealed by SI 2001/3686, reg 6(17)(a).
> Date in force: 15 November 2001: see SI 2001/3686, reg 1(1).

32 Authorisation of intrusive surveillance

(1) Subject to the following provisions of this Part, the Secretary of State and each of the senior authorising officers shall have power to grant authorisations for the carrying out of intrusive surveillance.

(2) Neither the Secretary of State nor any senior authorising officer shall grant an authorisation for the carrying out of intrusive surveillance unless he believes–

(a)   that the authorisation is necessary on grounds falling within subsection (3); and

(b)   that the authorised surveillance is proportionate to what is sought to be achieved by carrying it out.

(3) Subject to the following provisions of this section, an authorisation is necessary on grounds falling within this subsection if it is necessary–

(a)   in the interests of national security;

(b)   for the purpose of preventing or detecting serious crime; or

(c)   in the interests of the economic well-being of the United Kingdom.

[(3A) In the case of an authorisation granted by the chairman of the OFT, the authorisation is necessary on grounds falling within subsection (3) only if it is necessary for the purpose of preventing or detecting an offence under section 188 of the Enterprise Act 2002 (cartel offence).]

(4) The matters to be taken into account in considering whether the requirements of subsection (2) are satisfied in the case of any authorisation shall include whether the information which it is thought necessary to obtain by the authorised conduct could reasonably be obtained by other means.

(5) The conduct that is authorised by an authorisation for the carrying out of intrusive surveillance is any conduct that–

> (a) consists in the carrying out of intrusive surveillance of any such description as is specified in the authorisation;
>
> (b) is carried out in relation to the residential premises specified or described in the authorisation or in relation to the private vehicle so specified or described; and
>
> (c) is carried out for the purposes of, or in connection with, the investigation or operation so specified or described.

(6) For the purposes of this section the senior authorising officers are–

> (a) the chief constable of every police force maintained under section 2 of the Police Act 1996 (police forces in England and Wales outside London);
>
> (b) the Commissioner of Police of the Metropolis and every Assistant Commissioner of Police of the Metropolis;
>
> (c) the Commissioner of Police for the City of London;
>
> (d) the chief constable of every police force maintained under or by virtue of section 1 of the Police (Scotland) Act 1967 (police forces for areas in Scotland);
>
> (e) the [Chief Constable of the Police Service of Northern Ireland] and the Deputy Chief Constable of the [Police Service of Northern Ireland];
>
> (f) the Chief Constable of the Ministry of Defence Police;
>
> (g) the Provost Marshal of the Royal Navy Regulating Branch;
>
> (h) the Provost Marshal of the Royal Military Police;
>
> (i) the Provost Marshal of the Royal Air Force Police;
>
> (j) the Chief Constable of the British Transport Police;
>
> (k) the Director General of the National Criminal Intelligence Service;
>
> (l) the Director General of the National Crime Squad and any person holding the rank of assistant chief constable in that Squad who is designated for the purposes of this paragraph by that Director General;
>   …
>
> (m) any customs officer designated for the purposes of this paragraph by the Commissioners of Customs and Excise[; and
>
> (n) the chairman of the OFT].

Notes

Initial Commencement

To be appointed
> To be appointed: see s 83(2).

Appointment

Appointment: 25 September 2000: see SI 2000/2543, art 2.

Amendment

Sub-s (3A): inserted by the Enterprise Act 2002, s 199(1), (2)(a).

Date in force: 20 June 2003: see SI 2003/1397, art 2(1), Schedule; for transitional and transitory provisions see the Enterprise Act 2002, s 276, Sch 24, paras 2–6.

Sub-s (6): in para (e) words "Chief Constable of the Police Service of Northern Ireland" and "Police Service of Northern Ireland" in square brackets substituted by the Police (Northern Ireland) Act 2000, s 78(2)(a), (b).

Date in force: 4 November 2001: see the Police (Northern Ireland) Act 2000 (Commencement No 3 and Transitional Provisions) Order 2001, SR 2001/396, art 2, Schedule.

Sub-s (6): in para (l) word omitted repealed by the Enterprise Act 2002, s 278(2), Sch 26.

Date in force: 20 June 2003: see SI 2003/1397, art 2(1), Schedule; for transitional and transitory provisions and savings see the Enterprise Act 2002, s 276, Sch 24, paras 2–6.

Sub-s (6): para (n) and word "; and" immediately preceding it inserted by the Enterprise Act 2002, s 199(1), (2)(b).

Date in force: 20 June 2003: see SI 2003/1397, art 2(1), Schedule; for transitional and transitory provisions see the Enterprise Act 2002, s 276, Sch 24, paras 2–6.

Transfer of Functions

Functions under this section: certain functions under this section are transferred, in so far as they are exercisable in or as regards Scotland, to the Scottish Ministers, by the Scotland Act 1998 (Transfer of Functions to the Scottish Ministers etc) (No 2) Order 2000, SI 2000/3253, arts 2, 3, Sch 1, para 4, Sch 2.

See Further

See further, in relation to reference to the British Transport Police: the Railways and Transport Safety Act 2003, Sch 5, para 4(1).

Police and customs authorisations

33 Rules for grant of authorisations

(1) A person who is a designated person for the purposes of section 28 or 29 by reference to his office, rank or position with a police force, the National Criminal Intelligence Service or the National Crime Squad shall not grant an authorisation under that section except on an application made by a member of the same force, Service or Squad.

(2) A person who is designated for the purposes of section 28 or 29 by reference to his office, rank or position with the Commissioners of Customs and Excise shall not grant an authorisation under that section except on an application made by a customs officer.

(3) A person who is a senior authorising officer by reference to a police force, the National Criminal Intelligence Service or the National Crime Squad shall not grant an authorisation for the carrying out of intrusive surveillance except–

  (a) on an application made by a member of the same force, Service or Squad; and

  (b) in the case of an authorisation for the carrying out of intrusive surveillance in relation to any residential premises, where those premises are in the area of operation of that force, Service or Squad.

(4) A person who is a senior authorising officer by virtue of a designation by the Commissioners of Customs and Excise shall not grant an authorisation for the carrying out of intrusive surveillance except on an application made by a customs officer.

[(4A) The chairman of the OFT shall not grant an authorisation for the carrying out of intrusive surveillance except on an application made by an officer of the OFT.]

(5) A single authorisation may combine both–

(a)   an authorisation granted under this Part by, or on the application of, an individual who is a member of a police force, the National Criminal Intelligence Service or the National Crime Squad, or who is a customs officer [or the chairman or an officer of the OFT]; and

(b)   an authorisation given by, or on the application of, that individual under Part III of the Police Act 1997;

but the provisions of this Act or that Act that are applicable in the case of each of the authorisations shall apply separately in relation to the part of the combined authorisation to which they are applicable.

(6) For the purposes of this section–

(a)   the area of operation of a police force maintained under section 2 of the Police Act 1996, of the metropolitan police force, of the City of London police force or of a police force maintained under or by virtue of section 1 of the Police (Scotland) Act 1967 is the area for which that force is maintained;

(b)   the area of operation of the [Police Service of Northern Ireland] is Northern Ireland;

(c)   residential premises are in the area of operation of the Ministry of Defence Police if they are premises where the members of that police force, under section 2 of the Ministry of Defence Police Act 1987, have the powers and privileges of a constable;

(d)   residential premises are in the area of operation of the Royal Navy Regulating Branch, the Royal Military Police or the Royal Air Force Police if they are premises owned or occupied by, or used for residential purposes by, a person subject to service discipline;

(e)   the area of operation of the British Transport Police and also of the National Criminal Intelligence Service is the United Kingdom;

(f)   the area of operation of the National Crime Squad is England and Wales;

and references in this section to the United Kingdom or to any part or area of the United Kingdom include any adjacent waters within the seaward limits of the territorial waters of the United Kingdom.

(7) For the purposes of this section a person is subject to service discipline–

(a)   in relation to the Royal Navy Regulating Branch, if he is subject to the Naval Discipline Act 1957 or is a civilian to whom Parts I and II of that Act for the time being apply by virtue of section 118 of that Act ;

(b)   in relation to the Royal Military Police, if he is subject to military law or is a civilian to whom Part II of the Army Act 1955 for the time being applies by virtue of section 209 of that Act; and

(c)   in relation to the Royal Air Force Police, if he is subject to air-force law or is a civilian to whom Part II of the Air Force Act 1955 for the time being applies by virtue of section 209 of that Act.

Notes

Initial Commencement

To be appointed

To be appointed: see s 83(2).

Appointment

Appointment: 25 September 2000: see SI 2000/2543, art 2.

Amendment

Sub-s (4A): inserted by the Enterprise Act 2002, s 199(1), (3).

Date in force: 20 June 2003: see SI 2003/1397, art 2(1), Schedule; for transitional and transitory provisions see the Enterprise Act 2002, s 276, Sch 24, paras 2–6.

Sub-s (5): in para (a) words "or the chairman or an officer of the OFT" in square brackets inserted by the Enterprise Act 2002, s 199(1), (4).

Date in force: 20 June 2003: see SI 2003/1397, art 2(1), Schedule; for transitional and transitory provisions see the Enterprise Act 2002, s 276, Sch 24, paras 2–6.

Sub-s (6): in para (b) words "Police Service of Northern Ireland" in square brackets substituted by the Police (Northern Ireland) Act 2000, s 78(2)(f).

Date in force: 4 November 2001: see the Police (Northern Ireland) Act 2000 (Commencement No 3 and Transitional Provisions) Order 2001, SR 2001/396, art 2, Schedule.

See Further

See further, in relation to reference to the British Transport Police: the Railways and Transport Safety Act 2003, Sch 5, para 4(1).

34 Grant of authorisations in the senior officer's absence

(1) This section applies in the case of an application for an authorisation for the carrying out of intrusive surveillance where–

  (a) the application is one made by a member of a police force, of the National Criminal Intelligence Service or of the National Crime Squad or by [an officer of the OFT or] a customs officer; and

  (b) the case is urgent.

(2) If–

  (a) it is not reasonably practicable, having regard to the urgency of the case, for the application to be considered by any person who is a senior authorising officer by reference to the force, Service or Squad in question or, as the case may be, [as chairman of the OFT or] by virtue of a designation by the Commissioners of Customs and Excise, and

  (b) it also not reasonably practicable, having regard to the urgency of the case, for the application to be considered by a person (if there is one) who is entitled, as a designated deputy of a senior authorising officer, to exercise the functions in relation to that application of such an officer,

the application may be made to and considered by any person who is entitled under subsection (4) to act for any senior authorising officer who would have been entitled to consider the application.

(3) A person who considers an application under subsection (1) shall have the same power to grant an authorisation as the person for whom he is entitled to act.

(4) For the purposes of this section–

  (a) a person is entitled to act for the chief constable of a police force maintained under section 2 of the Police Act 1996 if he holds the rank of assistant chief constable in that force;

  (b) a person is entitled to act for the Commissioner of Police of the Metropolis, or for an Assistant Commissioner of Police of the Metropolis, if he holds the rank of commander in the metropolitan police force;

(c)   a person is entitled to act for the Commissioner of Police for the City of London if he holds the rank of commander in the City of London police force;

(d)   a person is entitled to act for the chief constable of a police force maintained under or by virtue of section 1 of the Police (Scotland) Act 1967 if he holds the rank of assistant chief constable in that force;

(e)   a person is entitled to act for the [Chief Constable of the Police Service of Northern Ireland], or for the Deputy Chief Constable of the [Police Service of Northern Ireland], if he holds the rank of assistant chief constable in the [Police Service of Northern Ireland];

(f)   a person is entitled to act for the Chief Constable of the Ministry of Defence Police if he holds the rank of deputy or assistant chief constable in that force;

(g)   a person is entitled to act for the Provost Marshal of the Royal Navy Regulating Branch if he holds the position of assistant Provost Marshal in that Branch;

(h)   a person is entitled to act for the Provost Marshal of the Royal Military Police or the Provost Marshal of the Royal Air Force Police if he holds the position of deputy Provost Marshal in the police force in question;

(i)   a person is entitled to act for the Chief Constable of the British Transport Police if he holds the rank of deputy or assistant chief constable in that force;

(j)   a person is entitled to act for the Director General of the National Criminal Intelligence Service if he is a person designated for the purposes of this paragraph by that Director General;

(k)   a person is entitled to act for the Director General of the National Crime Squad if he is designated for the purposes of this paragraph by that Director General as a person entitled so to act in an urgent case;

(l)   a person is entitled to act for a person who is a senior authorising officer by virtue of a designation by the Commissioners of Customs and Excise, if he is designated for the purposes of this paragraph by those Commissioners as a person entitled so to act in an urgent case;

[(m)   a person is entitled to act for the chairman of the OFT if he is an officer of the OFT designated by it for the purposes of this paragraph as a person entitled so to act in an urgent case].

(5) A police member of the National Criminal Intelligence Service or the National Crime Squad appointed under section 9(1)(b) or 55(1)(b) of the Police Act 1997 (police members) may not be designated under subsection (4)(j) or (k) unless he holds the rank of assistant chief constable in that Service or Squad.

(6) In this section "designated deputy"–

(a)   in relation to a chief constable, means a person holding the rank of assistant chief constable who is designated to act under section 12(4) of the Police Act 1996 or section 5(4) of the Police (Scotland) Act 1967;

(b)   in relation to the Commissioner of Police for the City of London, means a person authorised to act under section 25 of the City of London Police Act 1839;

(c)   in relation to the Director General of the National Criminal Intelligence

Service or the Director General of the National Crime Squad, means a person designated to act under section 8 or, as the case may be, section 54 of the Police Act 1997.

Notes

Initial Commencement

To be appointed

To be appointed: see s 83(2).

Appointment

Appointment: 25 September 2000: see SI 2000/2543, art 2.

Amendment

Sub-s (1): in para (a) words "an officer of the OFT or" in square brackets inserted by the Enterprise Act 2002, s 199(1), (5)(a).

Date in force: 20 June 2003: see SI 2003/1397, art 2(1), Schedule; for transitional and transitory provisions see the Enterprise Act 2002, s 276, Sch 24, paras 2–6.

Sub-s (2): in para (a) words "as chairman of the OFT or" in square brackets inserted by the Enterprise Act 2002, s 199(1), (5)(b).

Date in force: 20 June 2003: see SI 2003/1397, art 2(1), Schedule; for transitional and transitory provisions see the Enterprise Act 2002, s 276, Sch 24, paras 2–6.

Sub-s (4): in para (e) words "Chief Constable of the Police Service of Northern Ireland" in square brackets and words "Police Service of Northern Ireland" in square brackets in both places they occur substituted by the Police (Northern Ireland) Act 2000, s 78(2)(a), (b).

Date in force: 4 November 2001: see the Police (Northern Ireland) Act 2000 (Commencement No 3 and Transitional Provisions) Order 2001, SR 2001/396, art 2, Schedule.

Sub-s (4): para (m) inserted by the Enterprise Act 2002, s 199(1), (5)(c).

Date in force: 20 June 2003: see SI 2003/1397, art 2(1), Schedule; for transitional and transitory provisions see the Enterprise Act 2002, s 276, Sch 24, paras 2–6.

See Further

See further, in relation to reference to the British Transport Police: the Railways and Transport Safety Act 2003, Sch 5, para 4(1).

35 Notification of authorisations for intrusive surveillance

(1) Where a person grants or cancels a police[, customs or OFT] authorisation for the carrying out of intrusive surveillance, he shall give notice that he has done so to an ordinary Surveillance Commissioner.

(2) A notice given for the purposes of subsection (1)–

(a)   must be given in writing as soon as reasonably practicable after the grant or, as the case may be, cancellation of the authorisation to which it relates;

(b)   must be given in accordance with any such arrangements made for the purposes of this paragraph by the Chief Surveillance Commissioner as are for the time being in force; and

(c)   must specify such matters as the Secretary of State may by order prescribe.

(3) A notice under this section of the grant of an authorisation shall, as the case may be, either–

(a)   state that the approval of a Surveillance Commissioner is required by section 36 before the grant of the authorisation will take effect; or

(b)   state that the case is one of urgency and set out the grounds on which the case is believed to be one of urgency.

(4) Where a notice for the purposes of subsection (1) of the grant of an authorisation has been received by an ordinary Surveillance Commissioner, he shall, as soon as practicable–

(a)   scrutinise the authorisation; and

(b)   in a case where notice has been given in accordance with subsection (3)(a), decide whether or not to approve the authorisation.

(5) Subject to subsection (6), the Secretary of State shall not make an order under subsection (2)(c) unless a draft of the order has been laid before Parliament and approved by a resolution of each House.

(6) Subsection (5) does not apply in the case of the order made on the first occasion on which the Secretary of State exercises his power to make an order under subsection (2)(c).

(7) The order made on that occasion shall cease to have effect at the end of the period of forty days beginning with the day on which it was made unless, before the end of that period, it has been approved by a resolution of each House of Parliament.

(8) For the purposes of subsection (7)–

(a)   the order's ceasing to have effect shall be without prejudice to anything previously done or to the making of a new order; and

(b)   in reckoning the period of forty days no account shall be taken of any period during which Parliament is dissolved or prorogued or during which both Houses are adjourned for more than four days.

(9) Any notice that is required by any provision of this section to be given in writing may be given, instead, by being transmitted by electronic means.

(10) In this section references to a police[, customs or OFT] authorisation are references to an authorisation granted by–

(a)   a person who is a senior authorising officer by reference to a police force, the National Criminal Intelligence Service or the National Crime Squad;

(b)   a person who is a senior authorising officer by virtue of a designation by the Commissioners of Customs and Excise; …

[(ba) the chairman of the OFT; or]

(c)   a person who for the purposes of section 34 is entitled to act for a person falling within paragraph (a) or for a person falling within paragraph (b) [or for a person falling within paragraph (ba)].

Notes

Initial Commencement

To be appointed

To be appointed: see s 83(2).

Appointment

Appointment: 25 September 2000: see SI 2000/2543, art 2.

Amendment

Sub-s (1): words ", customs or OFT" in square brackets substituted by the Enterprise Act 2002, s 199(1), (6)(a).

Date in force: 20 June 2003: see SI 2003/1397, art 2(1), Schedule; for transitional and transitory provisions and savings see the Enterprise Act 2002, s 276, Sch 24, paras 2–6.

Sub-s (10): words ", customs or OFT" in square brackets substituted by the Enterprise Act 2002, s 199(1), (6)(a).

Date in force: 20 June 2003: see SI 2003/1397, art 2(1), Schedule; for transitional and transitory provisions and savings see the Enterprise Act 2002, s 276, Sch 24, paras 2–6.

Sub-s (10): in para (b) word omitted repealed by the Enterprise Act 2002, s 278(2), Sch 26.

Date in force: 20 June 2003: see SI 2003/1397, art 2(1), Schedule; for transitional and transitory provisions and savings see the Enterprise Act 2002, s 276, Sch 24, paras 2–6.

Sub-s (10): para (ba) inserted by the Enterprise Act 2002, s 199(1), (6)(b).

Date in force: 20 June 2003: see SI 2003/1397, art 2(1), Schedule; for transitional and transitory provisions see the Enterprise Act 2002, s 276, Sch 24, paras 2–6.

Sub-s (10): in para (c) words "or for a person falling within paragraph (ba)" in square brackets inserted by the Enterprise Act 2002, s 199(1), (6)(c).

Date in force: 20 June 2003: see SI 2003/1397, art 2(1), Schedule; for transitional and transitory provisions see the Enterprise Act 2002, s 276, Sch 24, paras 2–6.

Subordinate Legislation

Regulation of Investigatory Powers (Notification of Authorisations etc) Order 2000, SI 2000/2563 (made under sub-s (2)(c)).

36 Approval required for authorisations to take effect

(1) This section applies where an authorisation for the carrying out of intrusive surveillance has been granted on the application of–

(a)   a member of a police force;

(b)   a member of the National Criminal Intelligence Service;

(c)   a member of the National Crime Squad; ...

(d)   a customs officer[; or

(e)   an officer of the OFT].

(2) Subject to subsection (3), the authorisation shall not take effect until such time (if any) as–

(a)   the grant of the authorisation has been approved by an ordinary Surveillance Commissioner; and

(b)   written notice of the Commissioner's decision to approve the grant of the authorisation has been given, in accordance with subsection (4), to the person who granted the authorisation.

(3) Where the person who grants the authorisation–

(a)   believes that the case is one of urgency, and

(b)   gives notice in accordance with section 35(3)(b),

subsection (2) shall not apply to the authorisation, and the authorisation shall have effect from the time of its grant.

(4) Where subsection (2) applies to the authorisation–

(a)   a Surveillance Commissioner shall give his approval under this section to the authorisation if, and only if, he is satisfied that there are reasonable grounds for believing that the requirements of section 32(2)(a) and (b) are satisfied in the case of the authorisation; and

(b)   a Surveillance Commissioner who makes a decision as to whether or not the authorisation should be approved shall, as soon as reasonably practicable after making that decision, give written notice of his decision to the person who granted the authorisation.

(5) If an ordinary Surveillance Commissioner decides not to approve an authorisation to which subsection (2) applies, he shall make a report of his findings to the most senior relevant person.

(6) In this section "the most senior relevant person" means–

(a) where the authorisation was granted by the senior authorising officer with any police force who is not someone's deputy, that senior authorising officer;

(b) where the authorisation was granted by the Director General of the National Criminal Intelligence Service or the Director General of the National Crime Squad, that Director General;

(c) where the authorisation was granted by a senior authorising officer with a police force who is someone's deputy, the senior authorising officer whose deputy granted the authorisation;

(d) where the authorisation was granted by the designated deputy of the Director General of the National Criminal Intelligence Service or a person entitled to act for him by virtue of section 34(4)(j), that Director General;

(e) where the authorisation was granted by the designated deputy of the Director General of the National Crime Squad or by a person designated by that Director General for the purposes of section 32(6)(l) or 34(4)(k), that Director General;

(f) where the authorisation was granted by a person entitled to act for a senior authorising officer under section 34(4)(a) to (i), the senior authorising officer in the force in question who is not someone's deputy; ...

(g) where the authorisation was granted by a customs officer, the customs officer for the time being designated for the purposes of this paragraph by a written notice given to the Chief Surveillance Commissioner by the Commissioners of Customs and Excise[; and

(h) where the authorisation was granted by the chairman of the OFT or a person entitled to act for him by virtue of section 34(4)(m), that chairman].

(7) The references in subsection (6) to a person's deputy are references to the following–

(a) in relation to–

(i) a chief constable of a police force maintained under section 2 of the Police Act 1996,

(ii) the Commissioner of Police for the City of London, or

(iii) a chief constable of a police force maintained under or by virtue of section 1 of the Police (Scotland) Act 1967,

to his designated deputy;

(b) in relation to the Commissioner of Police of the Metropolis, to an Assistant Commissioner of Police of the Metropolis; and

(c)   in relation to the [Chief Constable of the Police Service of Northern Ireland], to the Deputy Chief Constable of the [Police Service of Northern Ireland];

and in this subsection and that subsection "designated deputy" has the same meaning as in section 34.

(8) Any notice that is required by any provision of this section to be given in writing may be given, instead, by being transmitted by electronic means.

Notes

Initial Commencement

To be appointed

> To be appointed: see s 83(2).

Appointment

> Appointment: 25 September 2000: see SI 2000/2543, art 2.

Amendment

> Sub-s (1): in para (c) word omitted repealed by the Enterprise Act 2002, s 278(2), Sch 26.
>
> Date in force: 20 June 2003: see SI 2003/1397, art 2(1), Schedule; for transitional and transitory provisions and savings see the Enterprise Act 2002, s 276, Sch 24, paras 2–6.
>
> Sub-s (1): para (e) and word "; or" immediately preceding it inserted by the Enterprise Act 2002, s 199(1), (7)(a).
>
> Date in force: 20 June 2003: see SI 2003/1397, art 2(1), Schedule; for transitional and transitory provisions see the Enterprise Act 2002, s 276, Sch 24, paras 2–6.
>
> Sub-s (6): in para (f) word omitted repealed by the Enterprise Act 2002, s 278(2), Sch 26.
>
> Date in force: 20 June 2003: see SI 2003/1397, art 2(1), Schedule; for transitional and transitory provisions and savings see the Enterprise Act 2002, s 276, Sch 24, paras 2–6.
>
> Sub-s (6): para (h) and word "; and" immediately preceding it inserted by the Enterprise Act 2002, s 199(1), (7)(b).
>
> Date in force: 20 June 2003: see SI 2003/1397, art 2(1), Schedule; for transitional and transitory provisions see the Enterprise Act 2002, s 276, Sch 24, paras 2–6.
>
> Sub-s (7): in para (c) words "Chief Constable of the Police Service of Northern Ireland" and "Police Service of Northern Ireland" in square brackets substituted by the Police (Northern Ireland) Act 2000, s 78(2)(a), (b).
>
> Date in force: 4 November 2001: see the Police (Northern Ireland) Act 2000 (Commencement No 3 and Transitional Provisions) Order 2001, SR 2001/396, art 2, Schedule.

37 Quashing of police and customs authorisations etc

(1) This section applies where an authorisation for the carrying out of intrusive surveillance has been granted on the application of–

(a)   a member of a police force;

(b)   a member of the National Criminal Intelligence Service;

(c)   a member of the National Crime Squad; ...

(d)   a customs officer[; or

(e)   an officer of the OFT].

(2) Where an ordinary Surveillance Commissioner is at any time satisfied that, at the time when the authorisation was granted or at any time when it was renewed, there were no reasonable grounds for believing that the requirements of section 32(2)(a) and (b) were satisfied, he may quash the authorisation with effect, as he thinks fit, from the time of the grant of the authorisation or from the time of any renewal of the authorisation.

(3) If an ordinary Surveillance Commissioner is satisfied at any time while the authorisation is in force that there are no longer any reasonable grounds for believing that the requirements of section 32(2)(a) and (b) are satisfied in relation to the authorisation, he may cancel the authorisation with effect from such time as appears to him to be the time from which those requirements ceased to be so satisfied.

(4) Where, in the case of any authorisation of which notice has been given in accordance with section 35(3)(b), an ordinary Surveillance Commissioner is at any time satisfied that, at the time of the grant or renewal of the authorisation to which that notice related, there were no reasonable grounds for believing that the case was one of urgency, he may quash the authorisation with effect, as he thinks fit, from the time of the grant of the authorisation or from the time of any renewal of the authorisation

(5) Subject to subsection (7), where an ordinary Surveillance Commissioner quashes an authorisation under this section, he may order the destruction of any records relating wholly or partly to information obtained by the authorised conduct after the time from which his decision takes effect.

(6) Subject to subsection (7), where–

(a) an authorisation has ceased to have effect (otherwise than by virtue of subsection (2) or (4)), and

(b) an ordinary Surveillance Commissioner is satisfied that there was a time while the authorisation was in force when there were no reasonable grounds for believing that the requirements of section 32(2)(a) and (b) continued to be satisfied in relation to the authorisation,

he may order the destruction of any records relating, wholly or partly, to information obtained at such a time by the authorised conduct.

(7) No order shall be made under this section for the destruction of any records required for pending criminal or civil proceedings.

(8) Where an ordinary Surveillance Commissioner exercises a power conferred by this section, he shall, as soon as reasonably practicable, make a report of his exercise of that power, and of his reasons for doing so–

(a) to the most senior relevant person (within the meaning of section 36); and

(b) to the Chief Surveillance Commissioner.

(9) Where an order for the destruction of records is made under this section, the order shall not become operative until such time (if any) as–

(a) the period for appealing against the decision to make the order has expired; and

(b) any appeal brought within that period has been dismissed by the Chief Surveillance Commissioner.

(10) No notice shall be required to be given under section 35(1) in the case of a cancellation under subsection (3) of this section.

Notes

Initial Commencement

To be appointed

To be appointed: see s 83(2).

Appointment

Appointment: 25 September 2000: see SI 2000/2543, art 2.

Amendment

Sub-s (1): in para (c) word omitted repealed by the Enterprise Act 2002, s 278(2), Sch 26.

Date in force: 20 June 2003: see SI 2003/1397, art 2(1), Schedule; for transitional and transitory provisions and savings see the Enterprise Act 2002, s 276, Sch 24, paras 2–6.

Sub-s (1): para (e) and word "; or" immediately preceding it inserted by the Enterprise Act 2002, s 199(1), (8).

Date in force: 20 June 2003: see SI 2003/1397, art 2(1), Schedule; for transitional and transitory provisions see the Enterprise Act 2002, s 276, Sch 24, paras 2–6.

---

38 Appeals against decisions by Surveillance Commissioners

(1) Any senior authorising officer may appeal to the Chief Surveillance Commissioner against any of the following–

> (a)   any refusal of an ordinary Surveillance Commissioner to approve an authorisation for the carrying out of intrusive surveillance;
>
> (b)   any decision of such a Commissioner to quash or cancel such an authorisation;
>
> (c)   any decision of such a Commissioner to make an order under section 37 for the destruction of records.

(2) In the case of an authorisation granted by the designated deputy of a senior authorising office or by a person who for the purposes of section 34 is entitled to act for a senior authorising officer, that designated deputy or person shall also be entitled to appeal under this section.

(3) An appeal under this section must be brought within the period of seven days beginning with the day on which the refusal or decision appealed against is reported to the appellant.

(4) Subject to subsection (5), the Chief Surveillance Commissioner, on an appeal under this section, shall allow the appeal if–

> (a)   he is satisfied that there were reasonable grounds for believing that the requirements of section 32(2)(a) and (b) were satisfied in relation to the authorisation at the time in question; and
>
> (b)   he is not satisfied that the authorisation is one of which notice was given in accordance with section 35(3)(b) without there being any reasonable grounds for believing that the case was one of urgency.

(5) If, on an appeal falling within subsection (1)(b), the Chief Surveillance Commissioner–

> (a)   is satisfied that grounds exist which justify the quashing or cancellation under section 37 of the authorisation in question, but
>
> (b)   considers that the authorisation should have been quashed or cancelled from a different time from that from which it was quashed or cancelled by the ordinary Surveillance Commissioner against whose decision the appeal is brought,

he may modify that Commissioner's decision to quash or cancel the authorisation, and any related decision for the destruction of records, so as to give effect to the decision under section 37 that he considers should have been made.

(6) Where, on an appeal under this section against a decision to quash or cancel an authorisation, the Chief Surveillance Commissioner allows the appeal he shall also quash any related order for the destruction of records relating to information obtained by the authorised conduct.

(7) In this section "designated deputy" has the same meaning as in section 34.

Notes

Initial Commencement

To be appointed
> To be appointed: see s 83(2).

Appointment
> Appointment: 25 September 2000: see SI 2000/2543, art 2.

39 Appeals to the Chief Surveillance Commissioner: supplementary

(1) Where the Chief Surveillance Commissioner has determined an appeal under section 38, he shall give notice of his determination to both–

>   (a)   the person by whom the appeal was brought; and

>   (b)   the ordinary Surveillance Commissioner whose decision was appealed against.

(2) Where the determination of the Chief Surveillance Commissioner on an appeal under section 38 is a determination to dismiss the appeal, the Chief Surveillance Commissioner shall make a report of his findings–

>   (a)   to the persons mentioned in subsection (1); and

>   (b)   to the Prime Minister.

(3) Subsections (3) and (4) of section 107 of the Police Act 1997 (reports to be laid before Parliament and exclusion of matters from the report) apply in relation to any report to the Prime Minister under subsection (2) of this section as they apply in relation to any report under subsection (2) of that section.

(4) Subject to subsection (2) of this section, the Chief Surveillance Commissioner shall not give any reasons for any determination of his on an appeal under section 38.

Notes

Initial Commencement

To be appointed
> To be appointed: see s 83(2).

Appointment
> Appointment: 25 September 2000: see SI 2000/2543, art 2.

40 Information to be provided to Surveillance Commissioners

It shall be the duty of–

>   (a)   every member of a police force,

>   (b)   every member of the National Criminal Intelligence Service,

>   (c)   every member of the National Crime Squad, and

(d)   every customs officer, [and

(e)   every officer of the OFT,]

to comply with any request of a Surveillance Commissioner for documents or information required by that Commissioner for the purpose of enabling him to carry out the functions of such a Commissioner under sections 35 to 39.

Notes

Initial Commencement

To be appointed

To be appointed: see s 83(2).

Appointment

Appointment: 25 September 2000: see SI 2000/2543, art 2.

Amendment

Para (e) and word "and" immediately preceding it inserted by the Enterprise Act 2002, s 199(1), (9).

Date in force: 20 June 2003: see SI 2003/1397, art 2(1), Schedule; for transitional and transitory provisions see the Enterprise Act 2002, s 276, Sch 24, paras 2–6.

Other authorisations

41 Secretary of State authorisations

(1) The Secretary of State shall not grant an authorisation for the carrying out of intrusive surveillance except on an application made by–

(a)   a member of any of the intelligence services;

(b)   an official of the Ministry of Defence;

(c)   a member of Her Majesty's forces;

(d)   an individual holding an office, rank or position with any such public authority as may be designated for the purposes of this section as an authority whose activities may require the carrying out of intrusive surveillance.

(2) Section 32 shall have effect in relation to the grant of an authorisation by the Secretary of State on the application of an official of the Ministry of Defence, or of a member of Her Majesty's forces, as if the only matters mentioned in subsection (3) of that section were–

(a)   the interests of national security; and

(b)   the purpose of preventing or detecting serious crime.

(3) The designation of any public authority for the purposes of this section shall be by order made by the Secretary of State.

(4) The Secretary of State may by order provide, in relation to any public authority, that an application for an authorisation for the carrying out of intrusive surveillance may be made by an individual holding an office, rank or position with that authority only where his office, rank or position is one prescribed by the order.

(5) The Secretary of State may by order impose restrictions–

(a)   on the authorisations for the carrying out of intrusive surveillance that may be granted on the application of an individual holding an office, rank or position with any public authority designated for the purposes of this section; and

(b)   on the circumstances in which, or the purposes for which, such authorisations may be granted on such an application.

(6) The Secretary of State shall not make a designation under subsection (3) unless a draft of the order containing the designation has been laid before Parliament and approved by a resolution of each House.

(7) References in this section to a member of Her Majesty's forces do not include references to any member of Her Majesty's forces who is a member of a police force by virtue of his service with the Royal Navy Regulating Branch, the Royal Military Police or the Royal Air Force Police.

Notes

Initial Commencement

To be appointed

To be appointed: see s 83(2).

Appointment

Appointment: 25 September 2000: see SI 2000/2543, art 2.

Subordinate Legislation

Regulation of Investigatory Powers (Designation of Public Authorities for the Purposes of Intrusive Surveillance) Order 2001, SI 2001/1126 (made under sub-ss (3), (4)).

Regulation of Investigatory Powers (Intrusive Surveillance) Order 2003, SI 2003/3174 (made under sub-ss (3), (4)).

---

42 Intelligence services authorisations

(1) The grant by the Secretary of State [or, the Scottish Ministers (by virtue of provision under section 63 of the Scotland Act 1998)] on the application of a member of one of the intelligence services of any authorisation under this Part must be made by the issue of a warrant.

(2) A single warrant issued by the Secretary of State [or, the Scottish Ministers (by virtue of provision under section 63 of the Scotland Act 1998)] may combine both–

(a)   an authorisation under this Part; and

(b)   an intelligence services warrant;

but the provisions of this Act or the Intelligence Services Act 1994 that are applicable in the case of the authorisation under this Part or the intelligence services warrant shall apply separately in relation to the part of the combined warrant to which they are applicable.

(3) Intrusive surveillance in relation to any premises or vehicle in the British Islands shall be capable of being authorised by a warrant issued under this Part on the application of a member of the Secret Intelligence Service or GCHQ only if the authorisation contained in the warrant is one satisfying the requirements of section 32(2)(a) otherwise than in connection with any functions of that intelligence service in support of the prevention or detection of serious crime.

(4) Subject to subsection (5), the functions of the Security Service shall include acting on behalf of the Secret Intelligence Service or GCHQ in relation to–

(a)   the application for and grant of any authorisation under this Part in connection with any matter within the functions of the Secret Intelligence Service or GCHQ; and

(b)   the carrying out, in connection with any such matter, of any conduct authorised by such an authorisation.

(5) Nothing in subsection (4) shall authorise the doing of anything by one intelligence service on behalf of another unless–

(a)   it is something which either the other service or a member of the other service has power to do; and

(b)   it is done otherwise than in connection with functions of the other service in support of the prevention or detection of serious crime.

(6) In this section "intelligence services warrant" means a warrant under section 5 of the Intelligence Services Act 1994.

Notes

Initial Commencement

To be appointed

To be appointed: see s 83(2).

Appointment

Appointment: 25 September 2000: see SI 2000/2543, art 2.

Amendment

Sub-s (1): words from "or, the Scottish Ministers" to "the Scotland Act 1998)" in square brackets inserted by SI 2000/3253, art 4(1), Sch 3, Pt II, paras 3, 7(a).

Date in force: 15 December 2000: see SI 2000/3253, art 1(1).

Sub-s (2): words from "or, the Scottish Ministers" to "the Scotland Act 1998)" in square brackets inserted by SI 2000/3253, art 4(1), Sch 3, Pt II, paras 3, 7(b).

Date in force: 15 December 2000: see SI 2000/3253, art 1(1).

Transfer of Functions

Functions under this section: certain functions under this section are transferred, in so far as they are exercisable in or as regards Scotland, to the Scottish Ministers, by the Scotland Act 1998 (Transfer of Functions to the Scottish Ministers etc) (No 2) Order 2000, SI 2000/3253, arts 2, 3, Sch 1, para 4, Sch 2.

Grant, renewal and duration of authorisations

43 General rules about grant, renewal and duration

(1) An authorisation under this Part–

(a)   may be granted or renewed orally in any urgent case in which the entitlement to act of the person granting or renewing it is not confined to urgent cases; and

(b)   in any other case, must be in writing.

(2) A single authorisation may combine two or more different authorisations under this Part; but the provisions of this Act that are applicable in the case of each of the authorisations shall apply separately in relation to the part of the combined authorisation to which they are applicable.

(3) Subject to subsections (4) and (8), an authorisation under this Part shall cease to have effect at the end of the following period–

(a)   in the case of an authorisation which–

> > > (i)   has not been renewed and was granted either orally or by a person whose entitlement to act is confined to urgent cases, or
> > >
> > > (ii) was last renewed either orally or by such a person,
> >
> > the period of seventy-two hours beginning with the time when the grant of the authorisation or, as the case may be, its latest renewal takes effect;

> (b)   in a case not falling within paragraph (a) in which the authorisation is for the conduct or the use of a covert human intelligence source, the period of twelve months beginning with the day on which the grant of the authorisation or, as the case may be, its latest renewal takes effect; and

> (c)   in any case not falling within paragraph (a) or (b), the period of three months beginning with the day on which the grant of the authorisation or, as the case may be, its latest renewal takes effect.

(4) Subject to subsection (6), an authorisation under this Part may be renewed, at any time before the time at which it ceases to have effect, by any person who would be entitled to grant a new authorisation in the same terms.

(5) Sections 28 to 41 shall have effect in relation to the renewal of an authorisation under this Part as if references to the grant of an authorisation included references to its renewal.

(6) A person shall not renew an authorisation for the conduct or the use of a covert human intelligence source, unless he–

> (a)   is satisfied that a review has been carried out of the matters mentioned in subsection (7); and

> (b)   has, for the purpose of deciding whether he should renew the authorisation, considered the results of that review.

(7) The matters mentioned in subsection (6) are–

> (a)   the use made of the source in the period since the grant or, as the case may be, latest renewal of the authorisation; and

> (b)   the tasks given to the source during that period and the information obtained from the conduct or the use of the source.

(8) The Secretary of State may by order provide in relation to authorisations of such descriptions as may be specified in the order that subsection (3) is to have effect as if the period at the end of which an authorisation of a description so specified is to cease to have effect were such period shorter than that provided for by that subsection as may be fixed by or determined in accordance with that order.

(9) References in this section to the time at which, or the day on which, the grant or renewal of an authorisation takes effect are references–

> (a)   in the case of the grant of an authorisation to which paragraph (c) does not apply, to the time at which or, as the case may be, day on which the authorisation is granted;

> (b)   in the case of the renewal of an authorisation to which paragraph (c) does not apply, to the time at which or, as the case may be, day on which the authorisation would have ceased to have effect but for the renewal; and

> (c)   in the case of any grant or renewal that takes effect under subsection (2) of section 36 at a time or on a day later than that given by paragraph (a) or (b), to the time at which or, as the case may be, day on which the grant or renewal takes effect in accordance with that subsection.

(10) In relation to any authorisation granted by a member of any of the intelligence services, and in relation to any authorisation contained in a warrant issued by the Secretary of State on the application of a member of any of the intelligence services, this section has effect subject to the provisions of section 44.

Notes

Initial Commencement

To be appointed

> To be appointed: see s 83(2).

Appointment

> Appointment: 25 September 2000: see SI 2000/2543, art 2.

Subordinate Legislation

> Regulation of Investigatory Powers (Juveniles) Order 2000, SI 2000/2793 (made under sub-s (8)).

---

44 Special rules for intelligence services authorisations

(1) Subject to subsection (2), a warrant containing an authorisation for the carrying out of intrusive surveillance–

    (a)   shall not be issued on the application of a member of any of the intelligence services, and

    (b)   if so issued shall not be renewed,

except under the hand of the Secretary of State [or, in the case of a warrant issued by the Scottish Ministers (by virtue of provision made under section 63 of the Scotland Act 1998), a member of the Scottish Executive].

(2) In an urgent case in which–

    (a)   an application for a warrant containing an authorisation for the carrying out of intrusive surveillance has been made by a member of any of the intelligence services, and

    (b)   the Secretary of State has himself [or the Scottish Ministers (by virtue of provision made under section 63 of the Scotland Act 1998) have themselves] expressly authorised the issue of the warrant in that case,

the warrant may be issued (but not renewed) under the hand of a senior official [or, as the case may be, a member of the staff of the Scottish Administration who is a member of the Senior Civil Service and is designated by the Scottish Ministers as a person under whose hand a warrant may be issued in such a case (in this section referred to as "a designated official")].

(3) Subject to subsection (6), a warrant containing an authorisation for the carrying out of intrusive surveillance which–

    (a)   was issued, on the application of a member of any of the intelligence services, under the hand of a senior official [or, as the case may be, a designated official], and

    (b)   has not been renewed under the hand of the Secretary of State [or, in the case of a warrant issued by the Scottish Ministers (by virtue of provision made under section 63 of the Scotland Act 1998), a member of the Scottish Executive],

shall cease to have effect at the end of the second working day following the day of the issue of the warrant, instead of at the time provided for by section 43(3).

(4) Subject to subsections (3) and (6), where any warrant for the carrying out of intrusive surveillance which is issued or was last renewed on the application of a member of any of the intelligence services, the warrant (unless renewed or, as the case may be, renewed again) shall cease to have effect at the following time, instead of at the time provided for by section 43(3), namely–

    (a)   in the case of a warrant that has not been renewed, at the end of the period of six months beginning with the day on which it was issued; and

    (b)   in any other case, at the end of the period of six months beginning with the day on which it would have ceased to have effect if not renewed again.

(5) Subject to subsection (6), where–

    (a)   an authorisation for the carrying out of directed surveillance is granted by a member of any of the intelligence services, and

    (b)   the authorisation is renewed by an instrument endorsed under the hand of the person renewing the authorisation with a statement that the renewal is believed to be necessary on grounds falling within section 32(3)(a) or (c),

the authorisation (unless renewed again) shall cease to have effect at the end of the period of six months beginning with the day on which it would have ceased to have effect but for the renewal, instead of at the time provided for by section 43(3).

(6) The Secretary of State may by order provide in relation to authorisations of such descriptions as may be specified in the order that subsection (3), (4) or (5) is to have effect as if the period at the end of which an authorisation of a description so specified is to cease to have effect were such period shorter than that provided for by that subsection as may be fixed by or determined in accordance with that order.

(7) Notwithstanding anything in section 43(2), in a case in which there is a combined warrant containing both–

    (a)   an authorisation for the carrying out of intrusive surveillance, and

    (b)   an authorisation for the carrying out of directed surveillance,

the reference in subsection (4) of this section to a warrant for the carrying out of intrusive surveillance is a reference to the warrant so far as it confers both authorisations.

Notes

Initial Commencement

To be appointed

    To be appointed: see s 83(2).

Appointment

    Appointment: 25 September 2000: see SI 2000/2543, art 2.

Amendment

    Sub-s (1): words from "or, in the case" to "the Scottish Executive" in square brackets inserted by SI 2000/3253, art 4(1), Sch 3, Pt II, paras 3, 8(a).

    Date in force: 15 December 2000: see SI 2000/3253, art 1(1).

    Sub-s (2): in para (b) words from "or the Scottish Ministers" to "the Scotland Act 1998) have themselves" in square brackets inserted by SI 2000/3253, art 4(1), Sch 3, Pt II, paras 3, 8(b)(i).

    Date in force: 15 December 2000: see SI 2000/3253, art 1(1).

    Sub-s (2): words from "or, as the case" to ""a designated official")" in square brackets inserted by SI 2000/3253, art 4(1), Sch 3, Pt II, paras 3, 8(b)(ii).

Date in force: 15 December 2000: see SI 2000/3253, art 1(1).

Sub-s (3): in para (a) words "or, as the case may be, a designated official" in square brackets inserted by SI 2000/3253, art 4(1), Sch 3, Pt II, paras 3, 8(c)(i).

Date in force: 15 December 2000: see SI 2000/3253, art 1(1).

Sub-s (3): in para (b) words from "or, in the case" to "the Scottish Executive" in square brackets inserted by SI 2000/3253, art 4(1), Sch 3, Pt II, paras 3, 8(c)(ii).

Date in force: 15 December 2000: see SI 2000/3253, art 1(1).

Transfer of Functions

Functions under this section: certain functions under sub-ss (1), (2)(b) are transferred, in so far as they are exercisable in or as regards Scotland, to the Scottish Ministers, by the Scotland Act 1998 (Transfer of Functions to the Scottish Ministers etc) (No 2) Order 2000, SI 2000/3253, arts 2, 3, Sch 1, para 5, Sch 2.

---

45 Cancellation of authorisations

(1) The person who granted or, as the case may be, last renewed an authorisation under this Part shall cancel it if–

    (a)   he is satisfied that the authorisation is one in relation to which the requirements of section 28(2)(a) and (b), 29(2)(a) and (b) or, as the case may be, 32(2)(a) and (b) are no longer satisfied; or

    (b)   in the case of an authorisation under section 29, he is satisfied that arrangements for the source's case that satisfy the requirements mentioned in subsection (2)(c) of that section no longer exist.

(2) Where an authorisation under this Part was granted or, as the case may be, last renewed–

    (a)   by a person entitled to act for any other person, or

    (b)   by the deputy of any other person,

that other person shall cancel the authorisation if he is satisfied as to either of the matters mentioned in subsection (1).

(3) Where an authorisation under this Part was granted or, as the case may be, last renewed by a person whose deputy had power to grant it, that deputy shall cancel the authorisation if he is satisfied as to either of the matters mentioned in subsection (1).

(4) The Secretary of State may by regulations provide for the person by whom any duty imposed by this section is to be performed in a case in which it would otherwise fall on a person who is no longer available to perform it.

(5) Regulations under subsection (4) may provide for the person on whom the duty is to fall to be a person appointed in accordance with the regulations.

(6) The references in this section to a person's deputy are references to the following–

    (a)   in relation to–

       (i)   a chief constable of a police force maintained under section 2 of the Police Act 1996,

       (ii)   the Commissioner of Police for the City of London, or

       (iii)   a chief constable of a police force maintained under or by virtue of section 1 of the Police (Scotland) Act 1967,

    to his designated deputy;

    (b)   in relation to the Commissioner of Police of the Metropolis, to an Assistant Commissioner of Police of the Metropolis;

(c)   in relation to the [Chief Constable of the Police Service of Northern Ireland], to the Deputy Chief Constable of the [Police Service of Northern Ireland];

(d)   in relation to the Director General of the National Criminal Intelligence Service, to his designated deputy; and

(e)   in relation to the Director General of the National Crime Squad, to any person designated by him for the purposes of section 32(6)(l) or to his designated deputy.

(7) In this section "designated deputy" has the same meaning as in section 34.

Notes

Initial Commencement

To be appointed
To be appointed: see s 83(2).

Appointment
Appointment: 25 September 2000: see SI 2000/2543, art 2.

Amendment
Sub-s (6): in para (c) words "Chief Constable of the Police Service of Northern Ireland" and "Police Service of Northern Ireland" in square brackets substituted by the Police (Northern Ireland) Act 2000, s 78(2)(a), (b).

Date in force: 4 November 2001: see the Police (Northern Ireland) Act 2000 (Commencement No 3 and Transitional Provisions) Order 2001, SR 2001/396, art 2, Schedule.

Transfer of Functions
Functions under this section: certain functions under sub-s (1) are transferred, in so far as they are exercisable in or as regards Scotland, to the Scottish Ministers, by the Scotland Act 1998 (Transfer of Functions to the Scottish Ministers etc) (No 2) Order 2000, SI 2000/3253, arts 2, 3, Sch 1, para 5, Sch 2.

Subordinate Legislation
Regulation of Investigatory Powers (Cancellation of Authorisations) Regulations 2000, SI 2000/2794 (made under sub-ss (4), (5)).

Scotland

46 Restrictions on authorisations extending to Scotland

(1) No person shall grant or renew an authorisation under this Part for the carrying out of any conduct if it appears to him–

(a)   that the authorisation is not one for which this Part is the relevant statutory provision for all parts of the United Kingdom; and

(b)   that all the conduct authorised by the grant or, as the case may be, renewal of the authorisation is likely to take place in Scotland.

(2) In relation to any authorisation, this Part is the relevant statutory provision for all parts of the United Kingdom in so far as it–

(a)   is granted or renewed on the grounds that it is necessary in the interests of national security or in the interests of the economic well-being of the United Kingdom;

(b)   is granted or renewed by or on the application of a person holding any office, rank or position with any of the public authorities specified in subsection (3);

(c)   authorises conduct of a person holding an office, rank or position with any of the public authorities so specified;

(d)   authorises conduct of an individual acting as a covert human intelligence source for the benefit of any of the public authorities so specified; or

(e)   authorises conduct that is surveillance by virtue of section 48(4).

(3) The public authorities mentioned in subsection (2) are–

(a)   each of the intelligence services;

(b)   Her Majesty's forces;

(c)   the Ministry of Defence;

(d)   the Ministry of Defence Police;

[(da) the OFT;]

(e)   the Commissioners of Customs and Excise; and

(f)   the British Transport Police.

(4) For the purposes of so much of this Part as has effect in relation to any other public authority by virtue of–

(a)   the fact that it is a public authority for the time being specified in Schedule 1, or

(b)   an order under subsection (1)(d) of section 41 designating that authority for the purposes of that section,

the authorities specified in subsection (3) of this section shall be treated as including that authority to the extent that the Secretary of State by order directs that the authority is a relevant public authority or, as the case may be, is a designated authority for all parts of the United Kingdom.

Notes

Initial Commencement

To be appointed

>   To be appointed: see s 83(2).

Appointment

>   Appointment: 25 September 2000: see SI 2000/2543, art 2.

Amendment

>   Sub-s (3): para (da) inserted by the Enterprise Act 2002, s 199(1), (10).

>   Date in force: 20 June 2003: see SI 2003/1397, art 2(1), Schedule; for transitional and transitory provisions see the Enterprise Act 2002, s 276, Sch 24, paras 2–6.

See Further

>   See further, in relation to reference to the British Transport Police Force: the Railways and Transport Safety Act 2003, Sch 5, para 4(1).

Subordinate Legislation

>   Regulation of Investigatory Powers (Authorisations Extending to Scotland) Order 2000, SI 2000/2418 (made under sub-s (4)).

Supplemental provision for Part II

47 Power to extend or modify authorisation provisions

(1) The Secretary of State may by order do one or both of the following–

(a) apply this Part, with such modifications as he thinks fit, to any such surveillance that is neither directed nor intrusive as may be described in the order;

(b) provide for any description of directed surveillance to be treated for the purposes of this Part as intrusive surveillance.

(2) No order shall be made under this section unless a draft of it has been laid before Parliament and approved by a resolution of each House.

Notes

Initial Commencement

To be appointed

To be appointed: see s 83(2).

Appointment

Appointment: 25 September 2000: see SI 2000/2543, art 2.

Subordinate Legislation

Regulation of Investigatory Powers (British Broadcasting Corporation) Order 2001, SI 2001/1057 (made under sub-s (1)).

---

48 Interpretation of Part II

(1) **In this Part–**

"covert human intelligence source" shall be construed in accordance with section 26(8);

"directed" and "intrusive", in relation to surveillance, shall be construed in accordance with section 26(2) to (6);

["OFT" means the Office of Fair Trading;]

"private vehicle" means (subject to subsection (7)(a)) any vehicle which is used primarily for the private purposes of the person who owns it or of a person otherwise having the right to use it;

"residential premises" means (subject to subsection (7)(b)) so much of any premises as is for the time being occupied or used by any person, however temporarily, for residential purposes or otherwise as living accommodation (including hotel or prison accommodation that is so occupied or used);

"senior authorising officer" means a person who by virtue of subsection (6) of section 32 is a senior authorising officer for the purposes of that section;

"surveillance" shall be construed in accordance with subsections (2) to (4);

"surveillance device" means any apparatus designed or adapted for use in surveillance.

(2) Subject to subsection (3), in this Part "surveillance" includes–

(a) monitoring, observing or listening to persons, their movements, their conversations or their other activities or communications;

(b) recording anything monitored, observed or listened to in the course of surveillance; and

(c) surveillance by or with the assistance of a surveillance device.

(3) References in this Part to surveillance do not include references to–

    (a)   any conduct of a covert human intelligence source for obtaining or recording (whether or not using a surveillance device) any information which is disclosed in the presence of the source;

    (b)   the use of a covert human intelligence source for so obtaining or recording information; or

    (c)   any such entry on or interference with property or with wireless telegraphy as would be unlawful unless authorised under–

        (i)   section 5 of the Intelligence Services Act 1994 (warrants for the intelligence services); or

        (ii)   Part III of the Police Act 1997 (powers of the police and of customs officers).

(4) References in this Part to surveillance include references to the interception of a communication in the course of its transmission by means of a postal service or telecommunication system if, and only if–

    (a)   the communication is one sent by or intended for a person who has consented to the interception of communications sent by or to him; and

    (b)   there is no interception warrant authorising the interception.

(5) References in this Part to an individual holding an office or position with a public authority include references to any member, official or employee of that authority.

(6) For the purposes of this Part the activities of a covert human intelligence source which are to be taken as activities for the benefit of a particular public authority include any conduct of his as such a source which is in response to inducements or requests made by or on behalf of that authority.

(7) In subsection (1)–

    (a)   the reference to a person having the right to use a vehicle does not, in relation to a motor vehicle, include a reference to a person whose right to use the vehicle derives only from his having paid, or undertaken to pay, for the use of the vehicle and its driver for a particular journey; and

    (b)   the reference to premises occupied or used by any person for residential purposes or otherwise as living accommodation does not include a reference to so much of any premises as constitutes any common area to which he has or is allowed access in connection with his use or occupation of any accommodation.

(8) In this section–

"premises" includes any vehicle or moveable structure and any other place whatever, whether or not occupied as land;

"vehicle" includes any vessel, aircraft or hovercraft.

Notes

Initial Commencement

To be appointed

    To be appointed: see s 83(2).

Appointment

    Appointment: 25 September 2000: see SI 2000/2543, art 2.

Amendment

Sub-s (1): definition "OFT" inserted by the Enterprise Act 2002, s 199(1), (11).

Date in force: 20 June 2003: see SI 2003/1397, art 2(1), Schedule; for transitional and transitory provisions see the Enterprise Act 2002, s 276, Sch 24, paras 2–6.

PART III
INVESTIGATION OF ELECTRONIC DATA PROTECTED BY ENCRYPTION ETC

Power to require disclosure

49 Notices requiring disclosure

(1) This section applies where any protected information–

    (a)   has come into the possession of any person by means of the exercise of a statutory power to seize, detain, inspect, search or otherwise to interfere with documents or other property, or is likely to do so;

    (b)   has come into the possession of any person by means of the exercise of any statutory power to intercept communications, or is likely to do so;

    (c)   has come into the possession of any person by means of the exercise of any power conferred by an authorisation under section 22(3) or under Part II, or as a result of the giving of a notice under section 22(4), or is likely to do so;

    (d)   has come into the possession of any person as a result of having been provided or disclosed in pursuance of any statutory duty (whether or not one arising as a result of a request for information), or is likely to do so; or

    (e)   has, by any other lawful means not involving the exercise of statutory powers, come into the possession of any of the intelligence services, the police or the customs and excise, or is likely so to come into the possession of any of those services, the police or the customs and excise.

(2) If any person with the appropriate permission under Schedule 2 believes, on reasonable grounds–

    (a)   that a key to the protected information is in the possession of any person,

    (b)   that the imposition of a disclosure requirement in respect of the protected information is–

        (i)   necessary on grounds falling within subsection (3), or

        (ii)   necessary for the purpose of securing the effective exercise or proper performance by any public authority of any statutory power or statutory duty,

    (c)   that the imposition of such a requirement is proportionate to what is sought to be achieved by its imposition, and

    (d)   that it is not reasonably practicable for the person with the appropriate permission to obtain possession of the protected information in an intelligible form without the giving of a notice under this section,

the person with that permission may, by notice to the person whom he believes to have possession of the key, impose a disclosure requirement in respect of the protected information.

(3) A disclosure requirement in respect of any protected information is necessary on grounds falling within this subsection if it is necessary–

    (a)   in the interests of national security;

    (b)   for the purpose of preventing or detecting crime; or

    (c)   in the interests of the economic well-being of the United Kingdom.

(4) A notice under this section imposing a disclosure requirement in respect of any protected information–

    (a)   must be given in writing or (if not in writing) must be given in a manner that produces a record of its having been given;

    (b)   must describe the protected information to which the notice relates;

    (c)   must specify the matters falling within subsection (2)(b)(i) or (ii) by reference to which the notice is given;

    (d)   must specify the office, rank or position held by the person giving it;

    (e)   must specify the office, rank or position of the person who for the purposes of Schedule 2 granted permission for the giving of the notice or (if the person giving the notice was entitled to give it without another person's permission) must set out the circumstances in which that entitlement arose;

    (f)   must specify the time by which the notice is to be complied with; and

    (g)   must set out the disclosure that is required by the notice and the form and manner in which it is to be made;

and the time specified for the purposes of paragraph (f) must allow a period for compliance which is reasonable in all the circumstances.

(5) Where it appears to a person with the appropriate permission–

    (a)   that more than one person is in possession of the key to any protected information,

    (b)   that any of those persons is in possession of that key in his capacity as an officer or employee of any body corporate, and

    (c)   that another of those persons is the body corporate itself or another officer or employee of the body corporate,

a notice under this section shall not be given, by reference to his possession of the key, to any officer or employee of the body corporate unless he is a senior officer of the body corporate or it appears to the person giving the notice that there is no senior officer of the body corporate and (in the case of an employee) no more senior employee of the body corporate to whom it is reasonably practicable to give the notice.

(6) Where it appears to a person with the appropriate permission–

    (a)   that more than one person is in possession of the key to any protected information,

    (b)   that any of those persons is in possession of that key in his capacity as an employee of a firm, and

    (c)   that another of those persons is the firm itself or a partner of the firm,

a notice under this section shall not be given, by reference to his possession of the key, to any employee of the firm unless it appears to the person giving the notice that there is neither a partner of the firm nor a more senior employee of the firm to whom it is reasonably practicable to give the notice.

(7) Subsections (5) and (6) shall not apply to the extent that there are special circumstances of the case that mean that the purposes for which the notice is given would be defeated, in whole or in part, if the notice were given to the person to whom it would otherwise be required to be given by those subsections.

(8) A notice under this section shall not require the making of any disclosure to any person other than–

    (a)   the person giving the notice; or

    (b)   such other person as may be specified in or otherwise identified by, or in accordance with, the provisions of the notice.

(9) A notice under this section shall not require the disclosure of any key which–

    (a)   is intended to be used for the purpose only of generating electronic signatures; and

    (b)   has not in fact been used for any other purpose.

(10) In this section "senior officer", in relation to a body corporate, means a director, manager, secretary or other similar officer of the body corporate; and for this purpose "director", in relation to a body corporate whose affairs are managed by its members, means a member of the body corporate.

(11) Schedule 2 (definition of the appropriate permission) shall have effect.

Notes

Initial Commencement

To be appointed
> To be appointed: see s 83(2).

50 Effect of notice imposing disclosure requirement

(1) Subject to the following provisions of this section, the effect of a section 49 notice imposing a disclosure requirement in respect of any protected information on a person who is in possession at a relevant time of both the protected information and a means of obtaining access to the information and of disclosing it in an intelligible form is that he–

    (a)   shall be entitled to use any key in his possession to obtain access to the information or to put it into an intelligible form; and

    (b)   shall be required, in accordance with the notice imposing the requirement, to make a disclosure of the information in an intelligible form.

(2) A person subject to a requirement under subsection (1)(b) to make a disclosure of any information in an intelligible form shall be taken to have complied with that requirement if–

    (a)   he makes, instead, a disclosure of any key to the protected information that is in his possession; and

    (b)   that disclosure is made, in accordance with the notice imposing the requirement, to the person to whom, and by the time by which, he was required to provide the information in that form.

(3) Where, in a case in which a disclosure requirement in respect of any protected information is imposed on any person by a section 49 notice–

    (a)   that person is not in possession of the information,

    (b)   that person is incapable, without the use of a key that is not in his possession, of obtaining access to the information and of disclosing it in an intelligible form, or

    (c)   the notice states, in pursuance of a direction under section 51, that it can be complied with only by the disclosure of a key to the information,

the effect of imposing that disclosure requirement on that person is that he shall be required, in accordance with the notice imposing the requirement, to make a disclosure of any key to the protected information that is in his possession at a relevant time.

(4) Subsections (5) to (7) apply where a person ("the person given notice")–

    (a)   is entitled or obliged to disclose a key to protected information for the purpose of complying with any disclosure requirement imposed by a section 49 notice; and

    (b)   is in possession of more than one key to that information.

(5) It shall not be necessary, for the purpose of complying with the requirement, for the person given notice to make a disclosure of any keys in addition to those the disclosure of which is, alone, sufficient to enable the person to whom they are disclosed to obtain access to the information and to put it into an intelligible form.

(6) Where–

    (a)   subsection (5) allows the person given notice to comply with a requirement without disclosing all of the keys in his possession, and

    (b)   there are different keys, or combinations of keys, in the possession of that person the disclosure of which would, under that subsection, constitute compliance,

the person given notice may select which of the keys, or combination of keys, to disclose for the purpose of complying with that requirement in accordance with that subsection.

(7) Subject to subsections (5) and (6), the person given notice shall not be taken to have complied with the disclosure requirement by the disclosure of a key unless he has disclosed every key to the protected information that is in his possession at a relevant time.

(8) Where, in a case in which a disclosure requirement in respect of any protected information is imposed on any person by a section 49 notice–

    (a)   that person has been in possession of the key to that information but is no longer in possession of it,

    (b)   if he had continued to have the key in his possession, he would have been required by virtue of the giving of the notice to disclose it, and

    (c)   he is in possession, at a relevant time, of information to which subsection (9) applies,

the effect of imposing that disclosure requirement on that person is that he shall be required, in accordance with the notice imposing the requirement, to disclose all such information to which subsection (9) applies as is in his possession and as he may be required, in accordance with that notice, to disclose by the person to whom he would have been required to disclose the key.

(9) This subsection applies to any information that would facilitate the obtaining or discovery of the key or the putting of the protected information into an intelligible form.

(10) In this section "relevant time", in relation to a disclosure requirement imposed by a section 49 notice, means the time of the giving of the notice or any subsequent time before the time by which the requirement falls to be complied with.

Notes

Initial Commencement

To be appointed
>   To be appointed: see s 83(2).

---

51 Cases in which key required

(1) A section 49 notice imposing a disclosure requirement in respect of any protected information shall not contain a statement for the purposes of section 50(3)(c) unless–

>   (a)   the person who for the purposes of Schedule 2 granted the permission for the giving of the notice in relation to that information, or
>
>   (b)   any person whose permission for the giving of a such a notice in relation to that information would constitute the appropriate permission under that Schedule,

has given a direction that the requirement can be complied with only by the disclosure of the key itself.

(2) A direction for the purposes of subsection (1) by the police, the customs and excise or a member of Her Majesty's forces shall not be given–

>   (a)   in the case of a direction by the police or by a member of Her Majesty's forces who is a member of a police force, except by or with the permission of a chief officer of police;
>
>   (b)   in the case of a direction by the customs and excise, except by or with the permission of the Commissioners of Customs and Excise; or
>
>   (c)   in the case of a direction by a member of Her Majesty's forces who is not a member of a police force, except by or with the permission of a person of or above the rank of brigadier or its equivalent.

(3) A permission given for the purposes of subsection (2) by a chief officer of police, the Commissioners of Customs and Excise or a person of or above any such rank as is mentioned in paragraph (c) of that subsection must be given expressly in relation to the direction in question.

(4) A person shall not give a direction for the purposes of subsection (1) unless he believes–

>   (a)   that there are special circumstances of the case which mean that the purposes for which it was believed necessary to impose the requirement in question would be defeated, in whole or in part, if the direction were not given; and
>
>   (b)   that the giving of the direction is proportionate to what is sought to be achieved by prohibiting any compliance with the requirement in question otherwise than by the disclosure of the key itself.

(5) The matters to be taken into account in considering whether the requirement of subsection (4)(b) is satisfied in the case of any direction shall include–

    (a)   the extent and nature of any protected information, in addition to the protected information in respect of which the disclosure requirement is imposed, to which the key is also a key; and

    (b)   any adverse effect that the giving of the direction might have on a business carried on by the person on whom the disclosure requirement is imposed.

(6) Where a direction for the purposes of subsection (1) is given by a chief officer of police, by the Commissioners of Customs and Excise or by a member of Her Majesty's forces, the person giving the direction shall give a notification that he has done so–

    (a)   in a case where the direction is given–

        (i)   by a member of Her Majesty's forces who is not a member of a police force, and

        (ii)   otherwise than in connection with activities of members of Her Majesty's forces in Northern Ireland,

    to the Intelligences Services Commissioner; and

    (b)   in any other case, to the Chief Surveillance Commissioner.

(7) A notification under subsection (6)–

    (a)   must be given not more than seven days after the day of the giving of the direction to which it relates; and

    (b)   may be given either in writing or by being transmitted to the Commissioner in question by electronic means.

Notes

Initial Commencement

To be appointed
    To be appointed: see s 83(2).

Contributions to costs

52 Arrangements for payments for disclosure

(1) It shall be the duty of the Secretary of State to ensure that such arrangements are in force as he thinks appropriate for requiring or authorising, in such cases as he thinks fit, the making to persons to whom section 49 notices are given of appropriate contributions towards the costs incurred by them in complying with such notices.

(2) For the purpose of complying with his duty under this section, the Secretary of State may make arrangements for payments to be made out of money provided by Parliament.

Notes

Initial Commencement

To be appointed
    To be appointed: see s 83(2).

Offences

53 Failure to comply with a notice

(1) A person to whom a section 49 notice has been given is guilty of an offence if he knowingly fails, in accordance with the notice, to make the disclosure required by virtue of the giving of the notice.

(2) In proceedings against any person for an offence under this section, if it is shown that that person was in possession of a key to any protected information at any time before the time of the giving of the section 49 notice, that person shall be taken for the purposes of those proceedings to have continued to be in possession of that key at all subsequent times, unless it is shown that the key was not in his possession after the giving of the notice and before the time by which he was required to disclose it.

(3) For the purposes of this section a person shall be taken to have shown that he was not in possession of a key to protected information at a particular time if–

(a) sufficient evidence of that fact is adduced to raise an issue with respect to it; and

(b) the contrary is not proved beyond a reasonable doubt.

(4) In proceedings against any person for an offence under this section it shall be a defence for that person to show–

(a) that it was not reasonably practicable for him to make the disclosure required by virtue of the giving of the section 49 notice before the time by which he was required, in accordance with that notice, to make it; but

(b) that he did make that disclosure as soon after that time as it was reasonably practicable for him to do so.

(5) A person guilty of an offence under this section shall be liable–

(a) on conviction on indictment, to imprisonment for a term not exceeding two years or to a fine, or to both;

(b) on summary conviction, to imprisonment for a term not exceeding six months or to a fine not exceeding the statutory maximum, or to both.

Notes

Initial Commencement

To be appointed
To be appointed: see s 83(2).

54 Tipping-off

(1) This section applies where a section 49 notice contains a provision requiring–

(a) the person to whom the notice is given, and

(b) every other person who becomes aware of it or of its contents,

to keep secret the giving of the notice, its contents and the things done in pursuance of it.

(2) A requirement to keep anything secret shall not be included in a section 49 notice except where–

(a) it is included with the consent of the person who for the purposes of Schedule 2 granted the permission for the giving of the notice; or

(b)   the person who gives the notice is himself a person whose permission for the giving of such a notice in relation to the information in question would have constituted appropriate permission under that Schedule.

(3) A section 49 notice shall not contain a requirement to keep anything secret except where the protected information to which it relates

(a)   has come into the possession of the police, the customs and excise or any of the intelligence services, or

(b)   is likely to come into the possession of the police, the customs and excise or any of the intelligence services,

by means which it is reasonable, in order to maintain the effectiveness of any investigation or operation or of investigatory techniques generally, or in the interests of the safety or well-being of any person, to keep secret from a particular person.

(4) A person who makes a disclosure to any other person of anything that he is required by a section 49 notice to keep secret shall be guilty of an offence and liable–

(a)   on conviction on indictment, to imprisonment for a term not exceeding five years or to a fine, or to both;

(b)   on summary conviction, to imprisonment for a term not exceeding six months or to a fine not exceeding the statutory maximum, or to both.

(5) In proceedings against any person for an offence under this section in respect of any disclosure, it shall be a defence for that person to show that–

(a)   the disclosure was effected entirely by the operation of software designed to indicate when a key to protected information has ceased to be secure; and

(b)   that person could not reasonably have been expected to take steps, after being given the notice or (as the case may be) becoming aware of it or of its contents, to prevent the disclosure.

(6) In proceedings against any person for an offence under this section in respect of any disclosure, it shall be a defence for that person to show that–

(a)   the disclosure was made by or to a professional legal adviser in connection with the giving, by the adviser to any client of his, of advice about the effect of provisions of this Part; and

(b)   the person to whom or, as the case may be, by whom it was made was the client or a representative of the client.

(7) In proceedings against any person for an offence under this section in respect of any disclosure, it shall be a defence for that person to show that the disclosure was made by a legal adviser–

(a)   in contemplation of, or in connection with, any legal proceedings; and

(b)   for the purposes of those proceedings.

(8) Neither subsection (6) nor subsection (7) applies in the case of a disclosure made with a view to furthering any criminal purpose.

(9) In proceedings against any person for an offence under this section in respect of any disclosure, it shall be a defence for that person to show that the disclosure was confined to a disclosure made to a relevant Commissioner or authorised–

(a)   by such a Commissioner;

(b)   by the terms of the notice;

(c)   by or on behalf of the person who gave the notice; or

(d)   by or on behalf of a person who–

  (i)   is in lawful possession of the protected information to which the notice relates; and

  (ii)   came into possession of that information as mentioned in section 49(1).

(10) In proceedings for an offence under this section against a person other than the person to whom the notice was given, it shall be a defence for the person against whom the proceedings are brought to show that he neither knew nor had reasonable grounds for suspecting that the notice contained a requirement to keep secret what was disclosed.

(11) In this section "relevant Commissioner" means the Interception of Communications Commissioner, the Intelligence Services Commissioner or any Surveillance Commissioner or Assistant Surveillance Commissioner.

Notes

Initial Commencement

To be appointed

  To be appointed: see s 83(2).

Safeguards

55 General duties of specified authorities

(1) This section applies to–

(a)   the Secretary of State and every other Minister of the Crown in charge of a government department;

(b)   every chief officer of police;

(c)   the Commissioners of Customs and Excise; and

(d)   every person whose officers or employees include persons with duties that involve the giving of section 49 notices.

(2) It shall be the duty of each of the persons to whom this section applies to ensure that such arrangements are in force, in relation to persons under his control who by virtue of this Part obtain possession of keys to protected information, as he considers necessary for securing–

(a)   that a key disclosed in pursuance of a section 49 notice is used for obtaining access to, or putting into an intelligible form, only protected information in relation to which power to give such a notice was exercised or could have been exercised if the key had not already been disclosed;

(b)   that the uses to which a key so disclosed is put are reasonable having regard both to the uses to which the person using the key is entitled to put any protected information to which it relates and to the other circumstances of the case;

(c)   that, having regard to those matters, the use and any retention of the key are proportionate to what is sought to be achieved by its use or retention;

(d)   that the requirements of subsection (3) are satisfied in relation to any key disclosed in pursuance of a section 49 notice;

(e)   that, for the purpose of ensuring that those requirements are satisfied, any key so disclosed is stored, for so long as it is retained, in a secure manner;

(f)   that all records of a key so disclosed (if not destroyed earlier) are destroyed as soon as the key is no longer needed for the purpose of enabling protected information to be put into an intelligible form.

(3) The requirements of this subsection are satisfied in relation to any key disclosed in pursuance of a section 49 notice if–

(a)   the number of persons to whom the key is disclosed or otherwise made available, and

(b)   the number of copies made of the key,

are each limited to the minimum that is necessary for the purpose of enabling protected information to be put into an intelligible form.

(4) Subject to subsection (5), where any relevant person incurs any loss or damage in consequence of–

(a)   any breach by a person to whom this section applies of the duty imposed on him by subsection (2), or

(b)   any contravention by any person whatever of arrangements made in pursuance of that subsection in relation to persons under the control of a person to whom this section applies,

the breach or contravention shall be actionable against the person to whom this section applies at the suit or instance of the relevant person.

(5) A person is a relevant person for the purposes of subsection (4) if he is–

(a)   a person who has made a disclosure in pursuance of a section 49 notice; or

(b)   a person whose protected information or key has been disclosed in pursuance of such a notice;

and loss or damage shall be taken into account for the purposes of that subsection to the extent only that it relates to the disclosure of particular protected information or a particular key which, in the case of a person falling with paragraph (b), must be his information or key.

(6) For the purposes of subsection (5)–

(a)   information belongs to a person if he has any right that would be infringed by an unauthorised disclosure of the information; and

(b)   a key belongs to a person if it is a key to information that belongs to him or he has any right that would be infringed by an unauthorised disclosure of the key.

(7) In any proceedings brought by virtue of subsection (4), it shall be the duty of the court to have regard to any opinion with respect to the matters to which the proceedings relate that is or has been given by a relevant Commissioner.

(8) In this section "relevant Commissioner" means the Interception of Communications Commissioner, the Intelligence Services Commissioner, the Investigatory Powers Commissioner for Northern Ireland or any Surveillance Commissioner or Assistant Surveillance Commissioner.

Notes

Initial Commencement

To be appointed

> To be appointed: see s 83(2).

Interpretation of Part III

56 Interpretation of Part III

(1) In this Part–

"chief officer of police" means any of the following–

(a) the chief constable of a police force maintained under or by virtue of section 2 of the Police Act 1996 or section 1 of the Police (Scotland) Act 1967;

(b) the Commissioner of Police of the Metropolis;

(c) the Commissioner of Police for the City of London;

(d) the [Chief Constable of the Police Service of Northern Ireland];

(e) the Chief Constable of the Ministry of Defence Police;

(f) the Provost Marshal of the Royal Navy Regulating Branch;

(g) the Provost Marshal of the Royal Military Police;

(h) the Provost Marshal of the Royal Air Force Police;

(i) the Chief Constable of the British Transport Police;

(j) the Director General of the National Criminal Intelligence Service;

(k) the Director General of the National Crime Squad;

"the customs and excise" means the Commissioners of Customs and Excise or any customs officer;

"electronic signature" means anything in electronic form which–

(a) is incorporated into, or otherwise logically associated with, any electronic communication or other electronic data;

(b) is generated by the signatory or other source of the communication or data; and

(c) is used for the purpose of facilitating, by means of a link between the signatory or other source and the communication or data, the establishment of the authenticity of the communication or data, the establishment of its integrity, or both;

"key", in relation to any electronic data, means any key, code, password, algorithm or other data the use of which (with or without other keys)–

(a) allows access to the electronic data, or

(b) facilitates the putting of the data into an intelligible form;

"the police" means–

(a) any constable;

(b) the Commissioner of Police of the Metropolis or any Assistant Commissioner of Police of the Metropolis; or

(c)   the Commissioner of Police for the City of London;

"protected information" means any electronic data which, without the key to the data–

(a)   cannot, or cannot readily, be accessed, or

(b)   cannot, or cannot readily, be put into an intelligible form;

"section 49 notice" means a notice under section 49;

"warrant" includes any authorisation, notice or other instrument (however described) conferring a power of the same description as may, in other cases, be conferred by a warrant.

(2) References in this Part to a person's having information (including a key to protected information) in his possession include references–

(a)   to its being in the possession of a person who is under his control so far as that information is concerned;

(b)   to his having an immediate right of access to it, or an immediate right to have it transmitted or otherwise supplied to him; and

(c)   to its being, or being contained in, anything which he or a person under his control is entitled, in exercise of any statutory power and without otherwise taking possession of it, to detain, inspect or search.

(3) References in this Part to something's being intelligible or being put into an intelligible form include references to its being in the condition in which it was before an encryption or similar process was applied to it or, as the case may be, to its being restored to that condition.

(4) In this section–

(a)   references to the authenticity of any communication or data are references to any one or more of the following–

(i)   whether the communication or data comes from a particular person or other source;

(ii)   whether it is accurately timed and dated;

(iii)   whether it is intended to have legal effect;

and

(b)   references to the integrity of any communication or data are references to whether there has been any tampering with or other modification of the communication or data.

Notes

Initial Commencement

To be appointed

To be appointed: see s 83(2).

Amendment

Sub-s (1): in definition "chief officer of police" in para (d) words "Chief Constable of the Police Service of Northern Ireland" in square brackets substituted by the Police (Northern Ireland) Act 2000, s 78(2)(a).

Date in force: 4 November 2001: see the Police (Northern Ireland) Act 2000 (Commencement No 3 and Transitional Provisions) Order 2001, SR 2001/396, art 2, Schedule.

See Further

See further, in relation to reference to the British Transport Police: the Railways and Transport Safety Act 2003, Sch 5, para 4(1).

PART IV
SCRUTINY ETC OF INVESTIGATORY POWERS AND OF THE FUNCTIONS OF THE INTELLIGENCE SERVICES

Commissioners

57 Interception of Communications Commissioner

(1) The Prime Minister shall appoint a Commissioner to be known as the Interception of Communications Commissioner.

(2) Subject to subsection (4), the Interception of Communications Commissioner shall keep under review–

    (a)   the exercise and performance by the Secretary of State of the powers and duties conferred or imposed on him by or under sections 1 to 11;

    [(aa) the exercise and performance by the Scottish Ministers (by virtue of provision made under section 63 of the Scotland Act 1998) of the powers and duties conferred or imposed on them by or under sections 5, 9 and 10;]

    (b)   the exercise and performance, by the persons on whom they are conferred or imposed, of the powers and duties conferred or imposed by or under Chapter II of Part I;

    (c)   the exercise and performance by the Secretary of State in relation to information obtained under Part I of the powers and duties conferred or imposed on him by or under Part III; and

    (d)   the adequacy of the arrangements by virtue of which–

        (i)   the duty which is imposed on the Secretary of State[, or the Scottish Ministers (by virtue of provision under section 63 of the Scotland Act 1998),] by section 15, and

        (ii)   so far as applicable to information obtained under Part I, the duties imposed by section 55,

are sought to be discharged.

(3) The Interception of Communications Commissioner shall give the Tribunal all such assistance (including his opinion as to any issue falling to be determined by the Tribunal) as the Tribunal may require–

    (a)   in connection with the investigation of any matter by the Tribunal; or

    (b)   otherwise for the purposes of the Tribunal's consideration or determination of any matter.

(4) It shall not be the function of the Interception of Communications Commissioner to keep under review the exercise of any power of the Secretary of State to make, amend or revoke any subordinate legislation.

(5) A person shall not be appointed under this section as the Interception of Communications Commissioner unless he holds or has held a high judicial office (within the meaning of the Appellate Jurisdiction Act 1876).

(6) The Interception of Communications Commissioner shall hold office in accordance with the terms of his appointment; and there shall be paid to him out of money provided by Parliament such allowances as the Treasury may determine.

(7) The Secretary of State, after consultation with the Interception of Communications Commissioner, shall—

(a) make such technical facilities available to the Commissioner, and

(b) subject to the approval of the Treasury as to numbers, provide the Commissioner with such staff,

as are sufficient to secure that the Commissioner is able properly to carry out his functions.

(8) On the coming into force of this section the Commissioner holding office as the Commissioner under section 8 of the Interception of Communications Act 1985 shall take and hold office as the Interception of Communications Commissioner as if appointed under this Act—

(a) for the unexpired period of his term of office under that Act; and

(b) otherwise, on the terms of his appointment under that Act.

Notes

Initial Commencement

To be appointed
>To be appointed: see s 83(2).

Appointment
>Sub-ss (1), (2)(a), (d)(i), (3)–(8): Appointment: 2 October 2000: see SI 2000/2543, art 3.
>Sub-s (2)(b): Appointment: 5 January 2004: see SI 2003/3140, art 2(b).

Amendment
>Sub-s (2): para (aa) inserted by SI 2000/3253, art 4(1), Sch 3, Pt II, paras 3, 9(a).
>Date in force: 15 December 2000: see SI 2000/3253, art 1(1).
>Sub-s (2): in para (d)(i) words from ", or the Scottish Ministers" to "the Scotland Act 1998)," in square brackets inserted by SI 2000/3253, art 4(1), Sch 3, Pt II, paras 3, 9(b).
>Date in force: 15 December 2000: see SI 2000/3253, art 1(1).

58 Co-operation with and reports by s 57 Commissioner

(1) It shall be the duty of—

(a) every person holding office under the Crown,

(b) every member of the National Criminal Intelligence Service,

(c) every member of the National Crime Squad,

(d) every person employed by or for the purposes of a police force,

(e) every person required for the purposes of section 11 to provide assistance with giving effect to an interception warrant,

(f) every person on whom an obligation to take any steps has been imposed under section 12,

(g) every person by or to whom an authorisation under section 22(3) has been granted,

(h) every person to whom a notice under section 22(4) has been given,

    (i)   every person to whom a notice under section 49 has been given in relation to any information obtained under Part I, and

    (j)   every person who is or has been employed for the purposes of any business of a person falling within paragraph (e), (f), (h) or (i),

to disclose or provide to the Interception of Communications Commissioner all such documents and information as he may require for the purpose of enabling him to carry out his functions under section 57.

(2) If it at any time appears to the Interception of Communications Commissioner—

    (a)   that there has been a contravention of the provisions of this Act in relation to any matter with which that Commissioner is concerned, and

    (b)   that the contravention has not been the subject of a report made to the Prime Minister by the Tribunal,

he shall make a report to the Prime Minister with respect to that contravention.

(3) If it at any time appears to the Interception of Communications Commissioner that any arrangements by reference to which the duties imposed by sections 15 and 55 have sought to be discharged have proved inadequate in relation to any matter with which the Commissioner is concerned, he shall make a report to the Prime Minister with respect to those arrangements.

(4) As soon as practicable after the end of each calendar year, the Interception of Communications Commissioner shall make a report to the Prime Minister with respect to the carrying out of that Commissioner's functions.

(5) The Interception of Communications Commissioner may also, at any time, make any such other report to the Prime Minister on any matter relating to the carrying out of the Commissioner's functions as the Commissioner thinks fit.

[(5A) The Interception of Communications Commissioner may also, at any time, make any such other report to the First Minister on any matter relating to the carrying out of the Commissioner's functions so far as they relate to the exercise by the Scottish Ministers (by virtue of provision made under section 63 of the Scotland Act 1998) of their powers under sections 5, 9(1)(b) and (3), 10(1)(a) and (2) and 15(1) of this Act, as the Commissioner thinks fit.]

(6) The Prime Minister shall lay before each House of Parliament a copy of every annual report made by the Interception of Communications Commissioner under subsection (4), together with a statement as to whether any matter has been excluded from that copy in pursuance of subsection (7).

[(6A) The Prime Minister shall send a copy of every annual report made by the Interception of Communications Commissioner under subsection (4) which he lays in terms of subsection (6), together with a copy of the statement referred to in subsection (6), to the First Minister who shall forthwith lay that copy report and statement before the Scottish Parliament.]

(7) If it appears to the Prime Minister, after consultation with the Interception of Communications Commissioner [and, if it appears relevant to do so, with the First Minister], that the publication of any matter in an annual report would be contrary to the public interest or prejudicial to—

    (a)   national security,

    (b)   the prevention or detection of serious crime,

    (c)   the economic well-being of the United Kingdom, or

(d)   the continued discharge of the functions of any public authority whose activities include activities that are subject to review by that Commissioner,

the Prime Minister may exclude that matter from the copy of the report as laid before each House of Parliament.

Notes

Initial Commencement

To be appointed

To be appointed: see s 83(2).

Appointment

Sub-ss (1)(a)–(f), (2)–(7): Appointment: 2 October 2000: see SI 2000/2543, art 3.

Sub-s (1)(g), (h): Appointment: 5 January 2004: see SI 2003/3140, art 2(c).

Sub-s (1)(j): Appointment (for certain purposes): 2 October 2000: see SI 2000/2543, art 3.

Sub-s (1)(j): Appointment (for remaining purposes): 5 January 2004: see SI 2003/3140, art 2(c).

Amendment

Sub-s (5A): inserted by SI 2000/3253, art 4(1), Sch 3, Pt II, paras 3, 10(a).

Date in force: 15 December 2000: see SI 2000/3253, art 1(1).

Sub-s (6A): inserted by SI 2000/3253, art 4(1), Sch 3, Pt II, paras 3, 10(b).

Date in force: 15 December 2000: see SI 2000/3253, art 1(1).

Sub-s (7): words "and, if it appears relevant to do so, with the First Minister" in square brackets inserted by SI 2000/3253, art 4(1), Sch 3, Pt II, paras 3, 10(c).

Date in force: 15 December 2000: see SI 2000/3253, art 1(1).

---

59 Intelligence Services Commissioner

(1) The Prime Minister shall appoint a Commissioner to be known as the Intelligence Services Commissioner.

(2) Subject to subsection (4), the Intelligence Services Commissioner shall keep under review, so far as they are not required to be kept under review by the Interception of Communications Commissioner–

(a)   the exercise by the Secretary of State of his powers under sections 5 to 7 of[, or the Scottish Ministers (by virtue of provision made under section 63 of the Scotland Act 1998) of their powers under sections 5 and 6(3) and (4) of,] the Intelligence Services Act 1994 (warrants for interference with wireless telegraphy, entry and interference with property etc);

(b)   the exercise and performance by the Secretary of State, [or the Scottish Ministers (by virtue of provision made under section 63 of the Scotland Act 1998),] in connection with or in relation to–

(i)   the activities of the intelligence services, and

(ii)   the activities in places other than Northern Ireland of the officials of the Ministry of Defence and of members of Her Majesty's forces,

of the powers and duties conferred or imposed on him by Parts II and III of this Act [or on them by Part II of this Act];

(c)   the exercise and performance by members of the intelligence services of the powers and duties conferred or imposed on them by or under Parts II and III of this Act;

(d)   the exercise and performance in places other than Northern Ireland, by officials of the Ministry of Defence and by members of Her Majesty's forces, of the powers and duties conferred or imposed on such officials or members of Her Majesty's forces by or under Parts II and III; and

(e)   the adequacy of the arrangements by virtue of which the duty imposed by section 55 is sought to be discharged–

    (i)   in relation to the members of the intelligence services; and

    (ii)   in connection with any of their activities in places other than Northern Ireland, in relation to officials of the Ministry of Defence and members of Her Majesty's forces.

(3) The Intelligence Services Commissioner shall give the Tribunal all such assistance (including his opinion as to any issue falling to be determined by the Tribunal) as the Tribunal may require–

(a)   in connection with the investigation of any matter by the Tribunal; or

(b)   otherwise for the purposes of the Tribunal's consideration or determination of any matter.

(4) It shall not be the function of the Intelligence Services Commissioner to keep under review the exercise of any power of the Secretary of State to make, amend or revoke any subordinate legislation.

(5) A person shall not be appointed under this section as the Intelligence Services Commissioner unless he holds or has held a high judicial office (within the meaning of the Appellate Jurisdiction Act 1876).

(6) The Intelligence Services Commissioner shall hold office in accordance with the terms of his appointment; and there shall be paid to him out of money provided by Parliament such allowances as the Treasury may determine.

(7) The Secretary of State shall, after consultation with the Intelligence Services Commissioner and subject to the approval of the Treasury as to numbers, provide him with such staff as the Secretary of State considers necessary for the carrying out of the Commissioner's functions.

(8) Section 4 of the Security Service Act 1989 and section 8 of the Intelligence Services Act 1994 (Commissioners for the purposes of those Acts) shall cease to have effect.

(9) On the coming into force of this section the Commissioner holding office as the Commissioner under section 8 of the Intelligence Services Act 1994 shall take and hold office as the Intelligence Services Commissioner as if appointed under this Act–

(a)   for the unexpired period of his term of office under that Act; and

(b)   otherwise, on the terms of his appointment under that Act.

(10) Subsection (7) of section 41 shall apply for the purposes of this section as it applies for the purposes of that section.

Notes

Initial Commencement

To be appointed
    To be appointed: see s 83(2).

Appointment
    Sub-ss (1), (2)(a), (3)–(10): Appointment: 2 October 2000: see SI 2000/2543, art 3.
    Sub-s (2)(b)–(e): Appointment (for certain purposes): 2 October 2000: see SI 2000/2543, art 3.

Amendment

Sub-s (2): in para (a) words from ", or the Scottish Ministers" to "sections 5 and 6(3) and (4) of," in square brackets inserted by SI 2000/3253, art 4(1), Sch 3, Pt II, paras 3, 11(a).

Date in force: 15 December 2000: see SI 2000/3253, art 1(1).

Sub-s (2): in para (b) words from "or the Scottish Ministers" "the Scotland Act 1998)," in square brackets inserted by SI 2000/3253, art 4(1), Sch 3, Pt II, paras 3, 11(b)(i).

Date in force: 15 December 2000: see SI 2000/3253, art 1(1).

Sub-s (2): in para (b) words "or on them by Part II of this Act" in square brackets inserted by SI 2000/3253, art 4(1), Sch 3, Pt II, paras 3, 11(b)(ii).

Date in force: 15 December 2000: see SI 2000/3253, art 1(1).

60 Co-operation with and reports by s 59 Commissioner

(1) It shall be the duty of–

(a) every member of an intelligence service,

(b) every official of the department of the Secretary of State [and every member of staff of the Scottish Administration (by virtue of provision under section 63 of the Scotland Act 1998)], and

(c) every member of Her Majesty's forces,

to disclose or provide to the Intelligence Services Commissioner all such documents and information as he may require for the purpose of enabling him to carry out his functions under section 59.

(2) As soon as practicable after the end of each calendar year, the Intelligence Services Commissioner shall make a report to the Prime Minister with respect to the carrying out of that Commissioner's functions.

(3) The Intelligence Services Commissioner may also, at any time, make any such other report to the Prime Minister on any matter relating to the carrying out of the Commissioner's functions as the Commissioner thinks fit.

[(3A) The Intelligence Services Commissioner may also, at any time, make any such other report to the First Minister on any matter relating to the carrying out of the Commissioner's functions so far as they relate to the exercise by the Scottish Ministers (by virtue of provision made under section 63 of the Scotland Act 1998) of their powers under sections 5 and 6(3) and (4) of the Intelligence Services Act 1994 or under Parts I and II of this Act, as the Commissioner thinks fit.]

(4) The Prime Minister shall lay before each House of Parliament a copy of every annual report made by the Intelligence Services Commissioner under subsection (2), together with a statement as to whether any matter has been excluded from that copy in pursuance of subsection (5).

[(4A) The Prime Minister shall send a copy of every annual report made by the Intelligence Services Commissioner under subsection (2) which he lays in terms of subsection (4), together with a copy of the statement referred to in subsection (4), to the First Minister who shall forthwith lay that copy report and statement before the Scottish Parliament.]

(5) If it appears to the Prime Minister, after consultation with the Intelligence Services Commissioner [and, if it appears relevant to do so, with the First Minister], that the publication of any matter in an annual report would be contrary to the public interest or prejudicial to–

(a) national security,

(b) the prevention or detection of serious crime,

(c)   the economic well-being of the United Kingdom, or

(d)   the continued discharge of the functions of any public authority whose activities include activities that are subject to review by that Commissioner,

the Prime Minister may exclude that matter from the copy of the report as laid before each House of Parliament.

(6) Subsection (7) of section 41 shall apply for the purposes of this section as it applies for the purposes of that section.

Notes

Initial Commencement

To be appointed

To be appointed: see s 83(2).

Appointment

Appointment: 2 October 2000: see SI 2000/2543, art 3.

Amendment

Sub-s (1): in para (b) words from "and every member" to "the Scotland Act 1998)" in square brackets inserted by SI 2000/3253, art 4(1), Sch 3, Pt II, paras 3, 12(a).

Date in force: 15 December 2000: see SI 2000/3253, art 1(1).

Sub-s (3A): inserted by SI 2000/3253, art 4(1), Sch 3, Pt II, paras 3, 12(b).

Date in force: 15 December 2000: see SI 2000/3253, art 1(1).

Sub-s (4A): inserted by SI 2000/3253, art 4(1), Sch 3, Pt II, paras 3, 12(c).

Date in force: 15 December 2000: see SI 2000/3253, art 1(1).

Sub-s (5): words "and, if it appears relevant to do so, with the First Minister" in square brackets inserted by SI 2000/3253, art 4(1), Sch 3, Pt II, paras 3, 12(d).

Date in force: 15 December 2000: see SI 2000/3253, art 1(1).

---

61 Investigatory Powers Commissioner for Northern Ireland

(1) The Prime Minister, after consultation with the First Minister and deputy First Minister in Northern Ireland, shall appoint a Commissioner to be known as the Investigatory Powers Commissioner for Northern Ireland.

(2) The Investigatory Powers Commissioner for Northern Ireland shall keep under review the exercise and performance in Northern Ireland, by the persons on whom they are conferred or imposed, of any powers or duties under Part II which are conferred or imposed by virtue of an order under section 30 made by the Office of the First Minister and deputy First Minister in Northern Ireland.

(3) The Investigatory Powers Commissioner for Northern Ireland shall give the Tribunal all such assistance (including his opinion as to any issue falling to be determined by the Tribunal) as the Tribunal may require–

(a)   in connection with the investigation of any matter by the Tribunal; or

(b)   otherwise for the purposes of the Tribunal's consideration or determination of any matter.

(4) It shall be the duty of–

(a)   every person by whom, or on whose application, there has been given or granted any authorisation the function of giving or granting which is subject to review by the Investigatory Powers Commissioner for Northern Ireland,

(b)   every person who has engaged in conduct with the authority of such an authorisation,

(c)   every person who holds or has held any office, rank or position with the same public authority as a person falling within paragraph (a), and

(d)   every person who holds or has held any office, rank or position with any public authority for whose benefit (within the meaning of Part II) activities which are or may be subject to any such review have been or may be carried out,

to disclose or provide to that Commissioner all such documents and information as he may require for the purpose of enabling him to carry out his functions.

(5) As soon as practicable after the end of each calendar year, the Investigatory Powers Commissioner for Northern Ireland shall make a report to the First Minister and deputy First Minister in Northern Ireland with respect to the carrying out of that Commissioner's functions.

(6) The First Minister and deputy First Minister in Northern Ireland shall lay before the Northern Ireland Assembly a copy of every annual report made by the Investigatory Powers Commissioner for Northern Ireland under subsection (5), together with a statement as to whether any matter has been excluded from that copy in pursuance of subsection (7).

(7) If it appears to the First Minister and deputy First Minister in Northern Ireland, after consultation with the Investigatory Powers Commissioner for Northern Ireland, that the publication of any matter in an annual report would be contrary to the public interest or prejudicial to–

(a)   the prevention or detection of serious crime, or

(b)   the continued discharge of the functions of any public authority whose activities include activities that are subject to review by that Commissioner,

they may exclude that matter from the copy of the report as laid before the Northern Ireland Assembly.

(8) A person shall not be appointed under this section as the Investigatory Powers Commissioner for Northern Ireland unless he holds or has held office in Northern Ireland–

(a)   in any capacity in which he is or was the holder of a high judicial office (within the meaning of the Appellate Jurisdiction Act 1876); or

(b)   as a county court judge.

(9) The Investigatory Powers Commissioner for Northern Ireland shall hold office in accordance with the terms of his appointment; and there shall be paid to him out of the Consolidated Fund of Northern Ireland such allowances as the Department of Finance and Personnel may determine.

(10) The First Minister and deputy First Minister in Northern Ireland shall, after consultation with the Investigatory Powers Commissioner for Northern Ireland, provide him with such staff as they consider necessary for the carrying out of his functions.

Notes

Initial Commencement

To be appointed

To be appointed: see s 83(2).

Appointment

Appointment: 25 September 2000: see SI 2000/2543, art 2.

62   Additional functions of Chief Surveillance Commissioner

(1) The Chief Surveillance Commissioner shall (in addition to his functions under the Police Act 1997) keep under review, so far as they are not required to be kept under review by the Interception of Communications Commissioner, the Intelligence Services Commissioner or the Investigatory Powers Commissioner for Northern Ireland–

(a)   the exercise and performance, by the persons on whom they are con-ferred or imposed, of the powers and duties conferred or imposed by or under Part II;

(b)   the exercise and performance, by any person other than a judicial authority, of the powers and duties conferred or imposed, otherwise than with the permission of such an authority, by or under Part III; and

(c)   the adequacy of the arrangements by virtue of which the duties imposed by section 55 are sought to be discharged in relation to persons whose conduct is subject to review under paragraph (b).

(2) It shall not by virtue of this section be the function of the Chief Surveillance Commissioner to keep under review the exercise of any power of the Secretary of State to make, amend or revoke any subordinate legislation.

(3) In this section "judicial authority" means–

(a)   any judge of the High Court or of the Crown Court or any Circuit Judge;

(b)   any judge of the High Court of Justiciary or any sheriff;

(c)   any justice of the peace;

(d)   any county court judge or resident magistrate in Northern Ireland;

(e)   any person holding any such judicial office as entitles him to exercise the jurisdiction of a judge of the Crown Court or of a justice of the peace.

Notes

Initial Commencement

To be appointed

To be appointed: see s 83(2).

Appointment

Sub-ss (1)(a), (2), (3): Appointment: 25 September 2000: see SI 2000/2543, art 2.

63   Assistant Surveillance Commissioners

(1) The Prime Minister may, after consultation with the Chief Surveillance Com-missioner as to numbers, appoint as Assistant Surveillance Commissioners such number of persons as the Prime Minister considers necessary (in addition to the ordinary Surveillance Commissioners) for the purpose of providing the Chief Surveillance Commissioner with assistance under this section.

(2) A person shall not be appointed as an Assistant Surveillance Commissioner unless he holds or has held office as–

(a)   a judge of the Crown Court or a Circuit judge;

   (b)   a sheriff in Scotland; or

   (c)   a county court judge in Northern Ireland.

(3) The Chief Surveillance Commissioner may–

   (a)   require any ordinary Surveillance Commissioner or any Assistant Sur-
         veillance Commissioner to provide him with assistance in carrying out
         his functions under section 62(1); or

   (b)   require any Assistant Surveillance Commissioner to provide him with
         assistance in carrying out his equivalent functions under any Act of the
         Scottish Parliament in relation to any provisions of such an Act that are
         equivalent to those of Part II of this Act.

(4) The assistance that may be provided under this section includes–

   (a)   the conduct on behalf of the Chief Surveillance Commissioner of the
         review of any matter; and

   (b)   the making of a report to the Chief Surveillance Commissioner about the
         matter reviewed.

(5) Subsections (3) to (8) of section 91 of the Police Act 1997 (Commissioners) apply
in relation to a person appointed under this section as they apply in relation to a
person appointed under that section.

Notes

Initial Commencement

To be appointed
   To be appointed: see s 83(2).

Appointment
   Appointment: 25 September 2000: see SI 2000/2543, art 2.

---

64 Delegation of Commissioners' functions

(1) Anything authorised or required by or under any enactment or any provision of
an Act of the Scottish Parliament to be done by a relevant Commissioner may be
done by any member of the staff of that Commissioner who is authorised for the
purpose (whether generally or specifically) by that Commissioner.

(2) In this section "relevant Commissioner" means the Interception of Communications Commissioner, the Intelligence Services Commissioner, the Investigatory Powers Commissioner for Northern Ireland or any Surveillance Commissioner or
Assistant Surveillance Commissioner.

Notes

Initial Commencement

To be appointed
   To be appointed: see s 83(2).

Appointment
   Appointment: 25 September 2000: see SI 2000/2543, art 2.

The Tribunal

65 The Tribunal

(1) There shall, for the purpose of exercising the jurisdiction conferred on them by this section, be a tribunal consisting of such number of members as Her Majesty may by Letters Patent appoint.

(2) The jurisdiction of the Tribunal shall be–

(a) to be the only appropriate tribunal for the purposes of section 7 of the Human Rights Act 1998 in relation to any proceedings under subsection (1)(a) of that section (proceedings for actions incompatible with Convention rights) which fall within subsection (3) of this section;

(b) to consider and determine any complaints made to them which, in accordance with subsection (4), are complaints for which the Tribunal is the appropriate forum;

(c) to consider and determine any reference to them by any person that he has suffered detriment as a consequence of any prohibition or restriction, by virtue of section 17, on his relying in, or for the purposes of, any civil proceedings on any matter; and

(d) to hear and determine any other such proceedings falling within subsection (3) as may be allocated to them in accordance with provision made by the Secretary of State by order.

(3) Proceedings fall within this subsection if–

(a) they are proceedings against any of the intelligence services;

(b) they are proceedings against any other person in respect of any conduct, or proposed conduct, by or on behalf of any of those services;

(c) they are proceedings brought by virtue of section 55(4); or

(d) they are proceedings relating to the taking place in any challengeable circumstances of any conduct falling within subsection (5).

(4) The Tribunal is the appropriate forum for any complaint if it is a complaint by a person who is aggrieved by any conduct falling within subsection (5) which he believes–

(a) to have taken place in relation to him, to any of his property, to any communications sent by or to him, or intended for him, or to his use of any postal service, telecommunications service or telecommunication system; and

(b) to have taken place in challengeable circumstances or to have been carried out by or on behalf of any of the intelligence services.

(5) Subject to subsection (6), conduct falls within this subsection if (whenever it occurred) it is–

(a) conduct by or on behalf of any of the intelligence services;

(b) conduct for or in connection with the interception of communications in the course of their transmission by means of a postal service or telecommunication system;

(c) conduct to which Chapter II of Part I applies;

[(ca) the carrying out of surveillance by a foreign police or customs officer (within the meaning of section 76A);]

(d)   [other] conduct to which Part II applies;

(e)   the giving of a notice under section 49 or any disclosure or use of a key to protected information;

(f)   any entry on or interference with property or any interference with wireless telegraphy.

(6) For the purposes only of subsection (3), nothing mentioned in paragraph (d) or (f) of subsection (5) shall be treated as falling within that subsection unless it is conduct by or on behalf of a person holding any office, rank or position with–

(a)   any of the intelligence services;

(b)   any of Her Majesty's forces;

(c)   any police force;

(d)   the National Criminal Intelligence Service;

(e)   the National Crime Squad; or

(f)   the Commissioners of Customs and Excise;

and section 48(5) applies for the purposes of this subsection as it applies for the purposes of Part II.

(7) For the purposes of this section conduct takes place in challengeable circumstances if–

(a)   it takes place with the authority, or purported authority, of anything falling within subsection (8); or

(b)   the circumstances are such that (whether or not there is such authority) it would not have been appropriate for the conduct to take place without it, or at least without proper consideration having been given to whether such authority should be sought;

but conduct does not take place in challengeable circumstances to the extent that it is authorised by, or takes place with the permission of, a judicial authority.

[(7A) For the purposes of this section conduct also takes place in challengeable circumstances if it takes place, or purports to take place, under section 76A.]

(8) The following fall within this subsection–

(a)   an interception warrant or a warrant under the Interception of Communications Act 1985;

(b)   an authorisation or notice under Chapter II of Part I of this Act;

(c)   an authorisation under Part II of this Act or under any enactment contained in or made under an Act of the Scottish Parliament which makes provision equivalent to that made by that Part;

(d)   a permission for the purposes of Schedule 2 to this Act;

(e)   a notice under section 49 of this Act; or

(f)   an authorisation under section 93 of the Police Act 1997.

(9) Schedule 3 (which makes further provision in relation to the Tribunal) shall have effect.

(10) In this section–

(a)   references to a key and to protected information shall be construed in accordance with section 56;

(b)   references to the disclosure or use of a key to protected information taking place in relation to a person are references to such a disclosure or use taking place in a case in which that person has had possession of the key or of the protected information; and

(c)   references to the disclosure of a key to protected information include references to the making of any disclosure in an intelligible form (within the meaning of section 56) of protected information by a person who is or has been in possession of the key to that information;

and the reference in paragraph (b) to a person's having possession of a key or of protected information shall be construed in accordance with section 56.

(11)   In this section "judicial authority" means–

(a)   any judge of the High Court or of the Crown Court or any Circuit Judge;

(b)   any judge of the High Court of Justiciary or any sheriff;

(c)   any justice of the peace;

(d)   any county court judge or resident magistrate in Northern Ireland;

(e)   any person holding any such judicial office as entitles him to exercise the jurisdiction of a judge of the Crown Court or of a justice of the peace.

Notes

Initial Commencement

To be appointed

To be appointed: see s 83(2).

Appointment

Sub-ss (1), (2)(a), (b), (3)(a), (b), (d), (4), (5)(a), (b), (d), (f), (6), (7), (8)(a), (c), (f), (9), (11): Appointment: 2 October 2000: see SI 2000/2543, art 3.

Sub-ss (5)(c), (8)(b): Appointment: 5 January 2004: see SI 2003/3140, art 2(d).

Amendment

Sub-s (5): para (ca) inserted by the Crime (International Co-operation) Act 2003, s 91(1), Sch 5, paras 78, 79(a)(i).

Date in force: to be appointed: see the Crime (International Co-operation) Act 2003, s 94(1).

Sub-s (5): in para (d) word "other" in square brackets inserted by the Crime (International Co-operation) Act 2003, s 91(1), Sch 5, paras 78, 79(a)(ii).

Date in force: to be appointed: see the Crime (International Co-operation) Act 2003, s 94(1).

Sub-s (7A): inserted by the Crime (International Co-operation) Act 2003, s 91(1), Sch 5, paras 78, 79(b).

Date in force: to be appointed: see the Crime (International Co-operation) Act 2003, s 94(1).

66 Orders allocating proceedings to the Tribunal

(1)   An order under section 65(2)(d) allocating proceedings to the Tribunal–

(a)   may provide for the Tribunal to exercise jurisdiction in relation to that matter to the exclusion of the jurisdiction of any court or tribunal; but

(b)   if it does so provide, must contain provision conferring a power on the Tribunal, in the circumstances provided for in the order, to remit the proceedings to the court or tribunal which would have had jurisdiction apart from the order.

(2)   In making any provision by an order under section 65(2)(d) the Secretary of State shall have regard, in particular, to–

(a) the need to secure that proceedings allocated to the Tribunal are properly heard and considered; and

(b) the need to secure that information is not disclosed to an extent, or in a manner, that is contrary to the public interest or prejudicial to national security, the prevention or detection of serious crime, the economic well-being of the United Kingdom or the continued discharge of the functions of any of the intelligence services.

(3) The Secretary of State shall not make an order under section 65(2)(d) unless a draft of the order has been laid before Parliament and approved by a resolution of each House.

Notes

Initial Commencement

To be appointed

  To be appointed: see s 83(2).

---

67 Exercise of the Tribunal's jurisdiction

(1) Subject to subsections (4) and (5), it shall be the duty of the Tribunal–

(a) to hear and determine any proceedings brought before them by virtue of section 65(2)(a) or (d); and

(b) to consider and determine any complaint or reference made to them by virtue of section 65(2)(b) or (c).

(2) Where the Tribunal hear any proceedings by virtue of section 65(2)(a), they shall apply the same principles for making their determination in those proceedings as would be applied by a court on an application for judicial review.

(3) Where the Tribunal consider a complaint made to them by virtue of section 65(2)(b), it shall be the duty of the Tribunal–

(a) to investigate whether the persons against whom any allegations are made in the complaint have engaged in relation to–

(i) the complainant,

(ii) any of his property,

(iii) any communications sent by or to him, or intended for him, or

(iv) his use of any postal service, telecommunications service or telecommunication system,

in any conduct falling within section 65(5);

(b) to investigate the authority (if any) for any conduct falling within section 65(5) which they find has been so engaged in; and

(c) in relation to the Tribunal's findings from their investigations, to determine the complaint by applying the same principles as would be applied by a court on an application for judicial review.

(4) The Tribunal shall not be under any duty to hear, consider or determine any proceedings, complaint or reference if it appears to them that the bringing of the proceedings or the making of the complaint or reference is frivolous or vexatious.

(5) Except where the Tribunal, having regard to all the circumstances, are satisfied that it is equitable to do so, they shall not consider or determine any complaint made by virtue of section 65(2)(b) if it is made more than one year after the taking place of the conduct to which it relates.

(6) Subject to any provision made by rules under section 69, where any proceedings have been brought before the Tribunal or any reference made to the Tribunal, they shall have power to make such interim orders, pending their final determination, as they think fit.

(7) Subject to any provision made by rules under section 69, the Tribunal on determining any proceedings, complaint or reference shall have power to make any such award of compensation or other order as they think fit; and, without prejudice to the power to make rules under section 69(2)(h), the other orders that may be made by the Tribunal include–

(a)   an order quashing or cancelling any warrant or authorisation; and

(b)   an order requiring the destruction of any records of information which–

(i)   has been obtained in exercise of any power conferred by a warrant or authorisation; or

(ii)   is held by any public authority in relation to any person.

(8) Except to such extent as the Secretary of State may by order otherwise provide, determinations, awards, orders and other decisions of the Tribunal (including decisions as to whether they have jurisdiction) shall not be subject to appeal or be liable to be questioned in any court.

(9) It shall be the duty of the Secretary of State to secure that there is at all times an order under subsection (8) in force allowing for an appeal to a court against any exercise by the Tribunal of their jurisdiction under section 65(2)(c) or (d).

(10) The provision that may be contained in an order under subsection (8) may include–

(a)   provision for the establishment and membership of a tribunal or body to hear appeals;

(b)   the appointment of persons to that tribunal or body and provision about the remuneration and allowances to be payable to such persons and the expenses of the tribunal;

(c)   the conferring of jurisdiction to hear appeals on any existing court or tribunal; and

(d)   any such provision in relation to an appeal under the order as corresponds to provision that may be made by rules under section 69 in relation to proceedings before the Tribunal, or to complaints or references made to the Tribunal.

(11) The Secretary of State shall not make an order under subsection (8) unless a draft of the order has been laid before Parliament and approved by a resolution of each House.

(12) The Secretary of State shall consult the Scottish Ministers before making any order under subsection (8); and any such order shall be laid before the Scottish Parliament.

Notes

Initial Commencement

To be appointed

> To be appointed. see s 83(2).

Appointment

> Sub-s (1): Appointment (for certain purposes): 2 October 2000: see SI 2000/2543, art 3.
> Sub-ss (2)–(8), (10)–(12): Appointment: 2 October 2000: see SI 2000/2543, art 3.

68 Tribunal procedure

(1) Subject to any rules made under section 69, the Tribunal shall be entitled to determine their own procedure in relation to any proceedings, complaint or reference brought before or made to them.

(2) The Tribunal shall have power–

    (a)   in connection with the investigation of any matter, or

    (b)   otherwise for the purposes of the Tribunal's consideration or determination of any matter,

to require a relevant Commissioner appearing to the Tribunal to have functions in relation to the matter in question to provide the Tribunal with all such assistance (including that Commissioner's opinion as to any issue falling to be determined by the Tribunal) as the Tribunal think fit.

(3) Where the Tribunal hear or consider any proceedings, complaint or reference relating to any matter, they shall secure that every relevant Commissioner appearing to them to have functions in relation to that matter–

    (a)   is aware that the matter is the subject of proceedings, a complaint or a reference brought before or made to the Tribunal; and

    (b)   is kept informed of any determination, award, order or other decision made by the Tribunal with respect to that matter.

(4) Where the Tribunal determine any proceedings, complaint or reference brought before or made to them, they shall give notice to the complainant which (subject to any rules made by virtue of section 69(2)(i)) shall be confined, as the case may be, to either–

    (a)   a statement that they have made a determination in his favour; or

    (b)   a statement that no determination has been made in his favour.

(5) Where–

    (a)   the Tribunal make a determination in favour of any person by whom any proceedings have been brought before the Tribunal or by whom any complaint or reference has been made to the Tribunal, and

    (b)   the determination relates to any act or omission by or on behalf of the Secretary of State or to conduct for which any warrant, authorisation or permission was issued, granted or given by the Secretary of State,

they shall make a report of their findings to the Prime Minister.

(6) It shall be the duty of the persons specified in subsection (7) to disclose or provide to the Tribunal all such documents and information as the Tribunal may require for the purpose of enabling them–

(a)   to exercise the jurisdiction conferred on them by or under section 65; or

(b)   otherwise to exercise or perform any power or duty conferred or imposed on them by or under this Act.

(7) Those persons are–

(a)   every person holding office under the Crown;

(b)   every member of the National Criminal Intelligence Service;

(c)   every member of the National Crime Squad;

(d)   every person employed by or for the purposes of a police force;

(e)   every person required for the purposes of section 11 to provide assistance with giving effect to an interception warrant;

(f)   every person on whom an obligation to take any steps has been imposed under section 12;

(g)   every person by or to whom an authorisation under section 22(3) has been granted;

(h)   every person to whom a notice under section 22(4) has been given;

(i)   every person by whom, or on whose application, there has been granted or given any authorisation under Part II of this Act or under Part III of the Police Act 1997;

(j)   every person who holds or has held any office, rank or position with the same public authority as a person falling within paragraph (i);

(k)   every person who has engaged in any conduct with the authority of an authorisation under section 22 or Part II of this Act or under Part III of the Police Act 1997;

(l)   every person who holds or has held any office, rank or position with a public authority for whose benefit any such authorisation has been or may be given;

(m) every person to whom a notice under section 49 has been given; and

(n)   every person who is or has been employed for the purposes of any business of a person falling within paragraph (e), (f), (h) or (m).

(8) In this section "relevant Commissioner" means the Interception of Communications Commissioner, the Intelligence Services Commissioner, the Investigatory Powers Commissioner for Northern Ireland or any Surveillance Commissioner or Assistant Surveillance Commissioner.

Notes

Initial Commencement

To be appointed
To be appointed: see s 83(2).

Appointment
Sub-ss (1)–(6), (7)(a)–(f), (i)–(l), (8): Appointment: 2 October 2000: see SI 2000/2543, art 3.
Sub-s (7)(g), (h): Appointment: 5 January 2004: see SI 2003/3140, art 2(e).
Sub-s (7)(n): Appointment (for certain purposes): 2 October 2000: see SI 2000/2543, art 3.

69 Tribunal rules

(1) The Secretary of State may make rules regulating–

- (a) the exercise by the Tribunal of the jurisdiction conferred on them by or under section 65; and

- (b) any matters preliminary or incidental to, or arising out of, the hearing or consideration of any proceedings, complaint or reference brought before or made to the Tribunal.

(2) Without prejudice to the generality of subsection (1), rules under this section may–

- (a) enable the jurisdiction of the Tribunal to be exercised at any place in the United Kingdom by any two or more members of the Tribunal designated for the purpose by the President of the Tribunal;

- (b) enable different members of the Tribunal to carry out functions in relation to different complaints at the same time;

- (c) prescribe the form and manner in which proceedings are to be brought before the Tribunal or a complaint or reference is to be made to the Tribunal;

- (d) require persons bringing proceedings or making complaints or references to take such preliminary steps, and to make such disclosures, as may be specified in the rules for the purpose of facilitating a determination of whether–

  - (i)   the bringing of the proceedings, or

  - (ii) the making of the complaint or reference,

  is frivolous or vexatious;

- (e) make provision about the determination of any question as to whether a person by whom–

  - (i)   any proceedings have been brought before the Tribunal, or

  - (ii) any complaint or reference has been made to the Tribunal,

  is a person with a right to bring those proceedings or make that complaint or reference;

- (f) prescribe the forms of hearing or consideration to be adopted by the Tribunal in relation to particular proceedings, complaints or references (including a form that requires any proceedings brought before the Tribunal to be disposed of as if they were a complaint or reference made to the Tribunal);

- (g) prescribe the practice and procedure to be followed on, or in connection with, the hearing or consideration of any proceedings, complaint or reference (including, where applicable, the mode and burden of proof and the admissibility of evidence);

- (h) prescribe orders that may be made by the Tribunal under section 67(6) or (7);

- (i) require information about any determination, award, order or other decision made by the Tribunal in relation to any proceedings, complaint or reference to be provided (in addition to any statement under section 68(4)) to the person who brought the proceedings or made the complaint or reference, or to the person representing his interests.

(3) Rules under this section in relation to the hearing or consideration of any matter by the Tribunal may provide–

(a) for a person who has brought any proceedings before or made any complaint or reference to the Tribunal to have the right to be legally represented;

(b) for the manner in which the interests of a person who has brought any proceedings before or made any complaint or reference to the Tribunal are otherwise to be represented;

(c) for the appointment in accordance with the rules, by such person as may be determined in accordance with the rules, of a person to represent those interests in the case of any proceedings, complaint or reference.

(4) The power to make rules under this section includes power to make rules–

(a) enabling or requiring the Tribunal to hear or consider any proceedings, complaint or reference without the person who brought the proceedings or made the complaint or reference having been given full particulars of the reasons for any conduct which is the subject of the proceedings, complaint or reference;

(b) enabling or requiring the Tribunal to take any steps in exercise of their jurisdiction in the absence of any person (including the person bringing the proceedings or making the complaint or reference and any legal representative of his);

(c) enabling or requiring the Tribunal to give a summary of any evidence taken in his absence to the person by whom the proceedings were brought or, as the case may be, to the person who made the complaint or reference;

(d) enabling or requiring the Tribunal to exercise their jurisdiction, and to exercise and perform the powers and duties conferred or imposed on them (including, in particular, in relation to the giving of reasons), in such manner provided for in the rules as prevents or limits the disclosure of particular matters.

(5) Rules under this section may also include provision–

(a) enabling powers or duties of the Tribunal that relate to matters preliminary or incidental to the hearing or consideration of any proceedings, complaint or reference to be exercised or performed by a single member of the Tribunal; and

(b) conferring on the Tribunal such ancillary powers as the Secretary of State thinks necessary for the purposes of, or in connection with, the exercise of the Tribunal's jurisdiction, or the exercise or performance of any power or duty conferred or imposed on them.

(6) In making rules under this section the Secretary of State shall have regard, in particular, to–

(a) the need to secure that matters which are the subject of proceedings, complaints or references brought before or made to the Tribunal are properly heard and considered; and

(b)   the need to secure that information is not disclosed to an extent, or in a manner, that is contrary to the public interest or prejudicial to national security, the prevention or detection of serious crime, the economic well-being of the United Kingdom or the continued discharge of the functions of any of the intelligence services.

(7) Rules under this section may make provision by the application, with or without modification, of the provision from time to time contained in specified rules of court.

(8) Subject to subsection (9), no rules shall be made under this section unless a draft of them has first been laid before Parliament and approved by a resolution of each House.

(9) Subsection (8) does not apply in the case of the rules made on the first occasion on which the Secretary of State exercises his power to make rules under this section.

(10) The rules made on that occasion shall cease to have effect at the end of the period of forty days beginning with the day on which they were made unless, before the end of that period, they have been approved by a resolution of each House of Parliament.

(11) For the purposes of subsection (10)–

(a)   the rules' ceasing to have effect shall be without prejudice to anything previously done or to the making of new rules; and

(b)   in reckoning the period of forty days no account shall be taken of any period during which Parliament is dissolved or prorogued or during which both Houses are adjourned for more than four days.

(12) The Secretary of State shall consult the Scottish Ministers before making any rules under this section; and any rules so made shall be laid before the Scottish Parliament.

Notes

Initial Commencement

To be appointed
    To be appointed: see s 83(2).

Appointment
    Appointment: 2 October 2000: see SI 2000/2543, art 3.

Subordinate Legislation
    Investigatory Powers Tribunal Rules 2000, SI 2000/2665 (made under sub-s (1)) .

---

70 Abolition of jurisdiction in relation to complaints

(1) The provisions set out in subsection (2) (which provide for the investigation etc of certain complaints) shall not apply in relation to any complaint made after the coming into force of this section.

(2) Those provisions are–

(a)   section 5 of, and Schedules 1 and 2 to, the Security Service Act 1989 (investigation of complaints about the Security Service made to the Tribunal established under that Act);

(b)   section 9 of, and Schedules 1 and 2 to, the Intelligence Services Act 1994 (investigation of complaints about the Secret Intelligence Service or GCHQ made to the Tribunal established under that Act); and

    (c)   section 102 of, and Schedule 7 to, the Police Act 1997 (investigation of complaints made to the Surveillance Commissioners).

Notes

Initial Commencement

To be appointed
> To be appointed: see s 83(2).

Appointment
> Appointment: 2 October 2000: see SI 2000/2543, art 3.

Codes of practice

71 Issue and revision of codes of practice

(1) The Secretary of State shall issue one or more codes of practice relating to the exercise and performance of the powers and duties mentioned in subsection (2).

(2) Those powers and duties are those (excluding any power to make subordinate legislation) that are conferred or imposed otherwise than on the Surveillance Commissioners by or under–

    (a)   Parts I to III of this Act;

    (b)   section 5 of the Intelligence Services Act 1994 (warrants for interference with property or wireless telegraphy for the purposes of the intelligence services); and

    (c)   Part III of the Police Act 1997 (authorisation by the police or customs and excise of interference with property or wireless telegraphy).

(3) Before issuing a code of practice under subsection (1), the Secretary of State shall–

    (a)   prepare and publish a draft of that code; and

    (b)   consider any representations made to him about the draft;

and the Secretary of State may incorporate in the code finally issued any modifications made by him to the draft after its publication.

(4) The Secretary of State shall lay before both Houses of Parliament every draft code of practice prepared and published by him under this section.

(5) A code of practice issued by the Secretary of State under this section shall not be brought into force except in accordance with an order made by the Secretary of State.

(6) An order under subsection (5) may contain such transitional provisions and savings as appear to the Secretary of State to be necessary or expedient in connection with the bringing into force of the code brought into force by that order.

(7) The Secretary of State may from time to time–

    (a)   revise the whole or any part of a code issued under this section; and

    (b)   issue the revised code.

(8) Subsections (3) to (6) shall apply (with appropriate modifications) in relation to the issue of any revised code under this section as they apply in relation to the first issue of such a code.

(9) The Secretary of State shall not make an order containing provision for any of the purposes of this section unless a draft of the order has been laid before Parliament and approved by a resolution of each House.

Notes

Initial Commencement

To be appointed

> To be appointed: see s 83(2).

Appointment

> Appointment (for certain purposes): 25 September 2000: see SI 2000/2543, art 2.
> Appointment (for certain purposes): 2 October 2000: see SI 2000/2543, art 3.
> Appointment (for certain purposes): 13 August 2001: see SI 2001/2727, art 2.

Subordinate Legislation

> Regulation of Investigatory Powers (Interception of Communications: Code of Practice) Order 2002, SI 2002/1693 (made under sub-s (5)).
> Regulation of Investigatory Powers (Covert Human Intelligence Sources: Code of Practice) Order 2002, SI 2002/1932 (made under sub-s (5)).
> Regulation of Investigatory Powers (Covert Surveillance: Code of Practice) Order 2002, SI 2002/1933 (made under sub-s (5)).

72 Effect of codes of practice

(1) A person exercising or performing any power or duty in relation to which provision may be made by a code of practice under section 71 shall, in doing so, have regard to the provisions (so far as they are applicable) of every code of practice for the time being in force under that section.

(2) A failure on the part of any person to comply with any provision of a code of practice for the time being in force under section 71 shall not of itself render him liable to any criminal or civil proceedings.

(3) A code of practice in force at any time under section 71 shall be admissible in evidence in any criminal or civil proceedings.

(4) If any provision of a code of practice issued or revised under section 71 appears to–

    (a)   the court or tribunal conducting any civil or criminal proceedings,

    (b)   the Tribunal,

    (c)   a relevant Commissioner carrying out any of his functions under this Act,

    (d)   a Surveillance Commissioner carrying out his functions under this Act or the Police Act 1997, or

    (e)   any Assistant Surveillance Commissioner carrying out any functions of his under section 63 of this Act,

to be relevant to any question arising in the proceedings, or in connection with the exercise of that jurisdiction or the carrying out of those functions, in relation to a time when it was in force, that provision of the code shall be taken into account in determining that question.

(5) In this section "relevant Commissioner" means the Interception of Communications Commissioner, the Intelligence Services Commissioner or the Investigatory Powers Commissioner for Northern Ireland.

Notes

Initial Commencement

To be appointed

> To be appointed: see s 83(2).

Appointment

> Appointment (for certain purposes): 25 September 2000: see SI 2000/2543, art 2.
> Appointment (for certain purposes): 2 October 2000: see SI 2000/2543, art 3.
> Appointment (for certain purposes): 13 August 2001: see SI 2001/2727, art 2.

PART V
MISCELLANEOUS AND SUPPLEMENTAL
Miscellaneous

73 Conduct in relation to wireless telegraphy

(1) Section 5 of the Wireless Telegraphy Act 1949 (misleading messages and interception and disclosure of wireless telegraphy messages) shall become subsection (1) of that section.

(2) In paragraph (b) of that subsection–

> (a)   for the words from "under the authority of" to "servant of the Crown," there shall be substituted "under the authority of a designated person"; and

> (b)   in sub-paragraph (i), for the words from "which neither" to the end of the sub-paragraph there shall be substituted "of which neither the person using the apparatus nor a person on whose behalf he is acting is an intended recipient,".

(3) In that section, after that subsection there shall be inserted–

"(2) The conduct in relation to which a designated person may give a separate authority for the purposes of this section shall not, except where he believes the conduct to be necessary on grounds falling within subsection (5) of this section, include–

> (a)   any conduct which, if engaged in without lawful authority, constitutes an offence under section 1(1) or (2) of the Regulation of Investigatory Powers Act 2000;

> (b)   any conduct which, if engaged in without lawful authority, is actionable under section 1(3) of that Act;

> (c)   any conduct which is capable of being authorised by an authorisation or notice granted by any person under Chapter II of Part I of that Act (communications data);

> (d)   any conduct which is capable of being authorised by an authorisation granted by any person under Part II of that Act (surveillance etc).

(3) A designated person shall not exercise his power to give a separate authority for the purposes of this section except where he believes–

> (a)   that the giving of his authority is necessary on grounds falling within subsection (4) or (5) of this section; and

(b)   that the conduct authorised by him is proportionate to what is sought to be achieved by that conduct.

(4) A separate authority for the purposes of this section is necessary on grounds falling within this subsection if it is necessary–

(a)   in the interests of national security;

(b)   for the purpose of preventing or detecting crime (within the meaning of the Regulation of Investigatory Powers Act 2000) or of preventing disorder;

(c)   in the interests of the economic well-being of the United Kingdom;

(d)   in the interests of public safety;

(e)   for the purpose of protecting public health;

(f)   for the purpose of assessing or collecting any tax, duty, levy or other imposition, contribution or charge payable to a government department; or

(g)   for any purpose (not falling within paragraphs (a) to (f)) which is specified for the purposes of this subsection by regulations made by the Secretary of State.

(5) A separate authority for the purposes of this section is necessary on grounds falling within this subsection if it is not necessary on grounds falling within subsection (4)(a) or (c) to (g) but is necessary for purposes connected with–

(a)   the issue of licences under this Act;

(b)   the prevention or detection of anything which constitutes interference with wireless telegraphy; or

(c)   the enforcement of any enactment contained in this Act or of any enactment not so contained that relates to such interference.

(6) The matters to be taken into account in considering whether the requirements of subsection (3) of this section are satisfied in the case of the giving of any separate authority for the purposes of this section shall include whether what it is thought necessary to achieve by the authorised conduct could reasonably be achieved by other means.

(7) A separate authority for the purposes of this section must be in writing and under the hand of–

(a)   the Secretary of State;

(b)   one of the Commissioners of Customs and Excise; or

(c)   a person not falling within paragraph (a) or (b) who is designated for the purposes of this subsection by regulations made by the Secretary of State.

(8) A separate authority for the purposes of this section may be general or specific and may be given–

(a)   to such person or persons, or description of persons,

(b)   for such period, and

(c)   subject to such restrictions and limitations,

as the designated person thinks fit.

(9) No regulations shall be made under subsection (4)(g) unless a draft of them has first been laid before Parliament and approved by a resolution of each House.

(10) For the purposes of this section the question whether conduct is capable of being authorised under Chapter II of Part I of the Regulation of Investigatory Powers Act 2000 or under Part II of that Act shall be determined without reference–

    (a)   to whether the person whose conduct it is is a person on whom any power or duty is or may be conferred or imposed by or under Chapter II of Part I or Part II of that Act; or

    (b)   to whether there are grounds for believing that the requirements for the grant of an authorisation or the giving of a notice under Chapter II of Part I or Part II of that Act are satisfied.

(11) References in this section to a separate authority for the purposes of this section are references to any authority for the purposes of this section given otherwise than by way of the issue or renewal of a warrant, authorisation or notice under Part I or II of the Regulation of Investigatory Powers Act 2000.

(12) In this section "designated person" means–

    (a)   the Secretary of State;

    (b)   the Commissioners of Customs and Excise; or

    (c)   any other person designated for the purposes of this section by regulations made by the Secretary of State."

(4) In section 16(2) of that Act (regulations and orders), after "the said powers" there shall be inserted ", other than one containing regulations a draft of which has been approved for the purposes of section 5(9),".

Notes

Initial Commencement

To be appointed

    To be appointed: see s 83(2).

Appointment

    Appointment: 2 October 2000: see SI 2000/2543, art 3.

74 Warrants under the Intelligence Services Act 1994

(1) In subsection (2) of section 5 of the Intelligence Services Act 1994 (the circumstances in which the Secretary of State may issue a warrant authorising interference with property or wireless telegraphy)–

    (a)   in paragraph (a), for "on the ground that it is likely to be of substantial value in" there shall be substituted "for the purpose of"; and

    (b)   for paragraph (b) there shall be substituted–

    "(b)   is satisfied that the taking of the action is proportionate to what the action seeks to achieve;".

(2) After that subsection, there shall be inserted–

"(2A) The matters to be taken into account in considering whether the requirements of subsection (2)(a) and (b) are satisfied in the case of any warrant shall include whether what it is thought necessary to achieve by the conduct authorised by the warrant could reasonably be achieved by other means."

(3) In each of sections 6(1)(b) and 7(5)(b) of that Act (warrants issued under the hand of a senior official of the Secretary of State's department), the words "of his department" shall be omitted.

(4) In section 11 of that Act (interpretation), for paragraph (1)(d) there shall be substituted–

> "(d) "senior official" has the same meaning as in the Regulation of Investigatory Powers Act 2000;".

Notes

Initial Commencement

To be appointed

> To be appointed: see s 83(2).

Appointment

> Appointment: 25 September 2000: see SI 2000/2543, art 2.

---

75 Authorisations under Part III of the Police Act 1997

(1) Section 93 of the Police Act 1997 (authorisations to interfere with property etc) shall be amended as follows.

(2) In subsection (1) (the action that the authorising officer may authorise), for "or" at the end of paragraph (a) there shall be substituted–

> "(ab) the taking of such action falling within subsection (1A), in respect of property outside the relevant area, as he may specify, or".

(3) After that subsection there shall be inserted–

"(1A) The action falling within this subsection is action for maintaining or retrieving any equipment, apparatus or device the placing or use of which in the relevant area has been authorised under this Part or Part II of the Regulation of Investigatory Powers Act 2000 or under any enactment contained in or made under an Act of the Scottish Parliament which makes provision equivalent to that made by Part II of that Act of 2000.

(1B) Subsection (1) applies where the authorising officer is a customs officer with the omission of–

> (a) the words "in the relevant area", in each place where they occur; and
>
> (b) paragraph (ab)."

(4) In subsection (2) (the grounds on which action may be authorised)–

> (a) in paragraph (a), for the words from "on the ground" to "detection of" there shall be substituted "for the purpose of preventing or detecting"; and
>
> (b) for paragraph (b) there shall be substituted–
>
> "(b) that the taking of the action is proportionate to what the action seeks to achieve."

(5) After subsection (2) there shall be inserted–

"(2A) Subsection (2) applies where the authorising officer is the Chief Constable or the Deputy Chief Constable of the Royal Ulster Constabulary as if the reference in subsection (2)(a) to preventing or detecting serious crime included a reference to the interests of national security.

(2B) The matters to be taken into account in considering whether the requirements of subsection (2) are satisfied in the case of any authorisation shall include whether what it is thought necessary to achieve by the authorised action could reasonably be achieved by other means."

(6) In subsection (5) (the meaning of authorising officer)–

(a) after paragraph (e) there shall be inserted–

"(ea) the Chief Constable of the Ministry of Defence Police;

(eb) the Provost Marshal of the Royal Navy Regulating Branch;

(ec) the Provost Marshal of the Royal Military Police;

(ed) the Provost Marshal of the Royal Air Force Police;

(ee) the Chief Constable of the British Transport Police;";

(b) in paragraph (g), after "National Crime Squad" there shall be inserted ", or any person holding the rank of assistant chief constable in that Squad who is designated for the purposes of this paragraph by that Director General"; and

(c) in paragraph (h), for the word "the", in the first place where it occurs, there shall be substituted "any".

(7) In subsection (6) (the meaning of relevant area), after paragraph (c) there shall be inserted–

"(ca) in relation to a person within paragraph (ea), means any place where, under section 2 of the Ministry of Defence Police Act 1987, the members of the Ministry of Defence Police have the powers and privileges of a constable;

(cb) in relation to a person within paragraph (ee), means the United Kingdom;".

(8) After that subsection there shall be inserted–

"(6A) For the purposes of any authorisation by a person within paragraph (eb), (ec) or (ed) of subsection (5) property is in the relevant area or action in respect of wireless telegraphy is taken in the relevant area if, as the case may be–

(a) the property is owned, occupied, in the possession of or being used by a person subject to service discipline; or

(b) the action is taken in relation to the use of wireless telegraphy by such a person.

(6B) For the purposes of this section a person is subject to service discipline–

(a) in relation to the Royal Navy Regulating Branch, if he is subject to the Naval Discipline Act 1957 or is a civilian to whom Parts I and II of that Act for the time being apply by virtue of section 118 of that Act ;

(b) in relation to the Royal Military Police, if he is subject to military law or is a civilian to whom Part II of the Army Act 1955 for the time being applies by virtue of section 209 of that Act; and

(c) in relation to the Royal Air Force Police, if he is subject to air-force law or is a civilian to whom Part II of the Air Force Act 1955 for the time being applies by virtue of section 209 of that Act."

Notes

Initial Commencement

To be appointed

    To be appointed: see s 83(2).

Appointment

    Appointment: 25 September 2000: see SI 2000/2543, art 2.

See Further

    See further, in relation to reference to the British Transport Police: the Railways and Transport Safety Act 2003, Sch 5, para 4(1).

76 Surveillance etc operations beginning in Scotland

(1) Subject to subsection (2), where–

    (a)   an authorisation under the relevant Scottish legislation has the effect of authorising the carrying out in Scotland of the conduct described in the authorisation,

    (b)   the conduct so described is or includes conduct to which Part II of this Act applies, and

    (c)   circumstances arise by virtue of which some or all of the conduct so described can for the time being be carried out only outwith Scotland,

section 27 of this Act shall have effect for the purpose of making lawful the carrying out outwith Scotland of the conduct so described as if the authorisation, so far as is it relates to conduct to which that Part applies, were an authorisation duly granted under that Part.

(2) Where any such circumstances as are mentioned in paragraph (c) of subsection (1) so arise as to give effect outwith Scotland to any authorisation granted under the relevant Scottish legislation, that authorisation shall not authorise any conduct outwith Scotland at any time after the end of the period of three weeks beginning with the time when the circumstances arose.

(3) Subsection (2) is without prejudice to the operation of subsection (1) in relation to any authorisation on the second or any subsequent occasion on which any such circumstances as are mentioned in subsection (1)(c) arise while the authorisation remains in force.

(4) In this section "the relevant Scottish legislation" means an enactment contained in or made under an Act of the Scottish Parliament which makes provision, corresponding to that made by Part II, for the authorisation of conduct to which that Part applies.

Notes

Initial Commencement

To be appointed

    To be appointed: see s 83(2).

Appointment

    Appointment: 25 September 2000: see SI 2000/2543, art 2.

[76A Foreign surveillance operations]

[(1) This section applies where–

(a) a foreign police or customs officer is carrying out relevant surveillance outside the United Kingdom which is lawful under the law of the country or territory in which it is being carried out;

(b) circumstances arise by virtue of which the surveillance can for the time being be carried out only in the United Kingdom; and

(c) it is not reasonably practicable in those circumstances for a United Kingdom officer to carry out the surveillance in the United Kingdom in accordance with an authorisation under Part 2 or the Regulation of Investigatory Powers (Scotland) Act 2000.

(2) "Relevant surveillance" means surveillance which–

(a) is carried out in relation to a person who is suspected of having committed a relevant crime; and

(b) is, for the purposes of Part 2, directed surveillance or intrusive surveillance.

(3) "Relevant crime" means crime which–

(a) falls within Article 40(7) of the Schengen Convention; or

(b) is crime for the purposes of any other international agreement to which the United Kingdom is a party and which is specified for the purposes of this section in an order made by the Secretary of State with the consent of the Scottish Ministers.

(4) Relevant surveillance carried out by the foreign police or customs officer in the United Kingdom during the permitted period is to be lawful for all purposes if–

(a) the condition mentioned in subsection (6) is satisfied;

(b) the officer carries out the surveillance only in places to which members of the public have or are permitted to have access, whether on payment or otherwise; and

(c) conditions specified in any order made by the Secretary of State with the consent of the Scottish Ministers are satisfied in relation to its carrying out;

but no surveillance is lawful by virtue of this subsection if the officer subsequently seeks to stop and question the person in the United Kingdom in relation to the relevant crime.

(5) The officer is not to be subject to any civil liability in respect of any conduct of his which is incidental to any surveillance that is lawful by virtue of subsection (4).

(6) The condition in this subsection is satisfied if, immediately after the officer enters the United Kingdom–

(a) he notifies a person designated by the Director General of the National Criminal Intelligence Service of that fact; and

(b) (if the officer has not done so before) he requests an application to be made for an authorisation under Part 2, or the Regulation of Investigatory Powers (Scotland) Act 2000, for the carrying out of the surveillance.

(7) "The permitted period" means the period of five hours beginning with the time when the officer enters the United Kingdom.

(8) But a person designated by an order made by the Secretary of State may notify the officer that the surveillance is to cease being lawful by virtue of subsection (4) when he gives the notification.

(9) The Secretary of State is not to make an order under subsection (4) unless a draft of the order has been laid before Parliament and approved by a resolution of each House.

(10) In this section references to a foreign police or customs officer are to a police or customs officer who, in relation to a country or territory other than the United Kingdom, is an officer for the purposes of–

(a)   Article 40 of the Schengen Convention; or

(b)   any other international agreement to which the United Kingdom is a party and which is specified for the purposes of this section in an order made by the Secretary of State with the consent of the Scottish Ministers.

(11) In this section–

"the Schengen Convention" means the Convention implementing the Schengen Agreement of 14th June 1985;

"United Kingdom officer" means–

(a)   a member of a police force;

(b)   a member of the National Criminal Intelligence Service;

(c)   a member of the National Crime Squad or of the Scottish Crime Squad (within the meaning of the Regulation of Investigatory Powers (Scotland) Act 2000);

(d)   a customs officer.]

Notes

Amendment

Inserted by the Crime (International Co-operation) Act 2003, s 83; for further effect see s 84 thereof.

Date in force: to be appointed: see the Crime (International Co-operation) Act 2003, s 94(1).

Supplemental

77 Ministerial expenditure etc

There shall be paid out of money provided by Parliament–

(a)   any expenditure incurred by the Secretary of State for or in connection with the carrying out of his functions under this Act; and

(b)   any increase attributable to this Act in the sums which are payable out of money so provided under any other Act.

Notes

Initial Commencement

To be appointed

To be appointed: see s 83(2).

Appointment

Appointment: 25 September 2000: see SI 2000/2543, art 2.

78 Orders, regulations and rules

(1) This section applies to any power of the Secretary of State to make any order, regulations or rules under any provision of this Act.

(2) The powers to which this section applies shall be exercisable by statutory instrument.

(3) A statutory instrument which contains any order made in exercise of a power to which this section applies (other than the power to appoint a day under section 83(2)) but which contains neither–

    (a)   an order a draft of which has been approved for the purposes of section 12(10), 13(3), 22(9), 25(5), 28(5), 29(6), 30(7), 35(5), 41(6), 47(2), 66(3), 67(11) *or 71(9)* [, 71(9) or 76A(9)], nor

    (b)   the order to which section 35(7) applies,

shall be subject to annulment in pursuance of a resolution of either House of Parliament.

(4) A statutory instrument containing any regulations made in exercise of a power to which this section applies shall be subject to annulment in pursuance of a resolution of either House of Parliament.

(5) Any order, regulations or rules made in exercise of a power to which this section applies may–

    (a)   make different provisions for different cases;

    (b)   contain such incidental, supplemental, consequential and transitional provision as the Secretary of State thinks fit.

Notes

Initial Commencement

To be appointed

To be appointed: see s 83(2).

Appointment

Appointment: 25 September 2000: see SI 2000/2543, art 2.

Amendment

Sub-s (3): in para (a) words "or 71(9)" in italics repealed and subsequent words in square brackets substituted by the Crime (International Co-operation) Act 2003, s 91(1), Sch 5, paras 78, 80.

Date in force: to be appointed: see the Crime (International Co-operation) Act 2003, s 94(1).

79 Criminal liability of directors etc

(1) Where an offence under any provision of this Act other than a provision of Part III is committed by a body corporate and is proved to have been committed with the consent or connivance of, or to be attributable to any neglect on the part of–

    (a)   a director, manager, secretary or other similar officer of the body corporate, or

    (b)   any person who was purporting to act in any such capacity, he (as well as the body corporate) shall be guilty of that offence and liable to be proceeded against and punished accordingly.

(2) Where an offence under any provision of this Act other than a provision of Part III–

    (a)   is committed by a Scottish firm, and

    (b)   is proved to have been committed with the consent or connivance of, or to be attributable to any neglect on the part of, a partner of the firm,

he (as well as the firm) shall be guilty of that offence and liable to be proceeded against and punished accordingly.

(3) In this section "director", in relation to a body corporate whose affairs are managed by its members, means a member of the body corporate.

Notes

Initial Commencement

To be appointed
    To be appointed: see s 83(2).

Appointment
    Appointment: 2 October 2000: see SI 2000/2543, art 3.

---

80 General saving for lawful conduct

Nothing in any of the provisions of this Act by virtue of which conduct of any description is or may be authorised by any warrant, authorisation or notice, or by virtue of which information may be obtained in any manner, shall be construed–

    (a)   as making it unlawful to engage in any conduct of that description which is not otherwise unlawful under this Act and would not be unlawful apart from this Act;

    (b)   as otherwise requiring–

        (i)   the issue, grant or giving of such a warrant, authorisation or notice, or

        (ii)   the taking of any step for or towards obtaining the authority of such a warrant, authorisation or notice,

    before any such conduct of that description is engaged in; or

    (c)   as prejudicing any power to obtain information by any means not involving conduct that may be authorised under this Act.

Notes

Initial Commencement

To be appointed
    To be appointed: see s 83(2).

Appointment
    Appointment: 25 September 2000: see SI 2000/2543, art 2.

---

81 General interpretation

(1) In this Act–

"apparatus" includes any equipment, machinery or device and any wire or cable;

"Assistant Commissioner of Police of the Metropolis" includes the Deputy Commissioner of Police of the Metropolis;

"Assistant Surveillance Commissioner" means any person holding office under section 63;

"civil proceedings" means any proceedings in or before any court or tribunal that are not criminal proceedings;

"communication" includes–

    (a)   (except in the definition of "postal service" in section 2(1)) anything transmitted by means of a postal service;

    (b)   anything comprising speech, music, sounds, visual images or data of any description; and

    (c)   signals serving either for the impartation of anything between persons, between a person and a thing or between things or for the actuation or control of any apparatus;

"criminal", in relation to any proceedings or prosecution, shall be construed in accordance with subsection (4);

"customs officer" means an officer commissioned by the Commissioners of Customs and Excise under section 6(3) of the Customs and Excise Management Act 1979;

"document" includes a map, plan, design, drawing, picture or other image;

"enactment" includes–

    (a)   an enactment passed after the passing of this Act; and

    (b)   an enactment contained in Northern Ireland legislation;

"GCHQ" has the same meaning as in the Intelligence Services Act 1994;

"Her Majesty's forces" has the same meaning as in the Army Act 1955;

"intelligence service" means the Security Service, the Secret Intelligence Service or GCHQ;

"interception" and cognate expressions shall be construed (so far as it is applicable) in accordance with section 2;

"interception warrant" means a warrant under section 5;

["justice of the peace" does not include a justice of the peace in Northern Ireland;]

"legal proceedings" means civil or criminal proceedings in or before any court or tribunal;

"modification" includes alterations, additions and omissions, and cognate expressions shall be construed accordingly;

"ordinary Surveillance Commissioner" means a Surveillance Commissioner other than the Chief Surveillance Commissioner;

"person" includes any organisation and any association or combination of persons;

"police force" means any of the following–

(a)   any police force maintained under section 2 of the Police Act 1996 (police forces in England and Wales outside London);

(b)   the metropolitan police force;

(c)   the City of London police force;

(d)   any police force maintained under or by virtue of section 1 of the Police (Scotland) Act 1967

(e)   the [Police Service of Northern Ireland];

(f)   the Ministry of Defence Police;

(g)   the Royal Navy Regulating Branch;

(h)   the Royal Military Police;

(i)   the Royal Air Force Police;

(j)   the British Transport Police;

"postal service" and "public postal service" have the meanings given by section 2(1);

"private telecommunication system", "public telecommunications service" and "public telecommunication system" have the meanings given by section 2(1);

"public authority" means any public authority within the meaning of section 6 of the Human Rights Act 1998 (acts of public authorities) other than a court or tribunal;

"senior official" means, subject to subsection (7), a member of the Senior Civil Service or a member of the Senior Management Structure of Her Majesty's Diplomatic Service;

"statutory", in relation to any power or duty, means conferred or imposed by or under any enactment or subordinate legislation;

"subordinate legislation" means any subordinate legislation (within the meaning of the Interpretation Act 1978) or any statutory rules (within the meaning of the Statutory Rules (Northern Ireland) Order 1979);

"Surveillance Commissioner" means a Commissioner holding office under section 91 of the Police Act 1997 and "Chief Surveillance Commissioner" shall be construed accordingly;

"telecommunication system" and "telecommunications service" have the meanings given by section 2(1);

"the Tribunal" means the tribunal established under section 65;

"wireless telegraphy" has the same meaning as in the Wireless Telegraphy Act 1949 and, in relation to wireless telegraphy, "interfere" has the same meaning as in that Act;

"working day" means any day other than a Saturday, a Sunday, Christmas Day, Good Friday or a day which is a bank holiday under the Banking and Financial Dealings Act 1971 in any part of the United Kingdom.

(2) In this Act–

(a)   references to crime are references to conduct which constitutes one or more criminal offences or is, or corresponds to, any conduct which, if it all took place in any one part of the United Kingdom would constitute one or more criminal offences; and

(b)   references to serious crime are references to crime that satisfies the test in subsection (3)(a) or (b).

(3) Those tests are–

(a)   that the offence or one of the offences that is or would be constituted by the conduct is an offence for which a person who has attained the age of twenty-one [(eighteen in relation to England and Wales)] and has no previous convictions could reasonably be expected to be sentenced to imprisonment for a term of three years or more;

(b)   that the conduct involves the use of violence, results in substantial financial gain or is conduct by a large number of persons in pursuit of a common purpose.

(4) In this Act "criminal proceedings" includes–

(a)   proceedings in the United Kingdom or elsewhere before–

(i)   a court-martial constituted under the Army Act 1955, the Air Force Act 1955 or the Naval Discipline Act 1957; ...

(ii)   ...;

(b)   proceedings before the Courts-Martial Appeal Court; and

(c)   proceedings before a Standing Civilian Court;

and references in this Act to criminal prosecutions shall be construed accordingly.

(5) For the purposes of this Act detecting crime shall be taken to include–

(a)   establishing by whom, for what purpose, by what means and generally in what circumstances any crime was committed; and

(b)   the apprehension of the person by whom any crime was committed;

and any reference in this Act to preventing or detecting serious crime shall be construed accordingly, except that, in Chapter I of Part I, it shall not include a reference to gathering evidence for use in any legal proceedings.

(6) In this Act–

(a)   references to a person holding office under the Crown include references to any servant of the Crown and to any member of Her Majesty's forces; and

(b)   references to a member of a police force, in relation to the Royal Navy Regulating Branch, the Royal Military Police or the Royal Air Force Police, do not include references to any member of that Branch or Force who is not for the time being attached to or serving either with the Branch or Force of which he is a member or with another of those police forces.

(7) If it appears to the Secretary of State that it is necessary to do so in consequence of any changes to the structure or grading of the home civil service or diplomatic service, he may by order make such amendments of the definition of "senior official" in subsection (1) as appear to him appropriate to preserve, so far as practicable, the effect of that definition.

Notes

Initial Commencement

To be appointed

> To be appointed: see s 83(2).

Appointment

> Appointment: 25 September 2000: see SI 2000/2543, art 2.

Amendment

> Sub-s (1): definition relating to "justice of the peace" inserted by the Justice (Northern Ireland) Act 2002, s 10(6), Sch 4, para 40.

> Date in force: to be appointed: see the Justice (Northern Ireland) Act 2002, s 87(1).

> Sub-s (1): in definition "police force" in para (e) words "Police Service of Northern Ireland" in square brackets substituted by the Police (Northern Ireland) Act 2000, s 78(2)(f).

> Date in force: 4 November 2001: see the Police (Northern Ireland) Act 2000 (Commencement No 3 and Transitional Provisions) Order 2001, SR 2001/396, art 2, Schedule.

> Sub-s (3): in para (a) words "(eighteen in relation to England and Wales)" in square brackets inserted by the Criminal Justice and Court Services Act 2000, s 74, Sch 7, Pt II, para 211.

> Date in force: to be appointed: see the Criminal Justice and Court Services Act 2000, s 80(1).

> Sub-s (4): para (a)(ii) and word omitted immediately preceding it repealed by the Armed Forces Act 2001, s 38, Sch 7, Pt 1.

> Date in force: 28 February 2002: see SI 2002/345, art 2.

See Further

> See further, in relation to reference to the British Transport Police: the Railways and Transport Safety Act 2003, Sch 5, para 4(1).

82 Amendments, repeals and savings etc

(1) The enactments specified in Schedule 4 (amendments consequential on the provisions of this Act) shall have effect with the amendments set out in that Schedule.

(2) The enactments mentioned in Schedule 5 are hereby repealed to the extent specified in the third column of that Schedule.

(3) For the avoidance of doubt it is hereby declared that nothing in this Act ... affects any power conferred on [a postal operator (within the meaning of the Postal Services Act 2000)] by or under any enactment to open, detain or delay any postal packet or to deliver any such packet to a person other than the person to whom it is addressed.

(4) Where any warrant under the Interception of Communications Act 1985 is in force under that Act at the time when the repeal by this Act of section 2 of that Act comes into force, the conduct authorised by that warrant shall be deemed for the period which–

   (a)   begins with that time, and

   (b)   ends with the time when that warrant would (without being renewed) have ceased to have effect under that Act,

as if it were conduct authorised by an interception warrant issued in accordance with the requirements of Chapter I of Part I of this Act.

(5) In relation to any such warrant, any certificate issued for the purposes of section 3(2) of the Interception of Communications Act 1985 shall have effect in relation to that period as if it were a certificate issued for the purposes of section 8(4) of this Act.

(6) Sections 15 and 16 of this Act shall have effect as if references to interception warrants and to section 8(4) certificates included references, respectively, to warrants under section 2 of the Interception of Communications Act 1985 and to certificates under section 3(2) of that Act; and references in sections 15 and 16 of this Act to intercepted or certified material shall be construed accordingly.

Notes

Initial Commencement

To be appointed

To be appointed: see s 83(2).

Appointment

Sub-ss (1), (2): Appointment (for certain purposes): 25 September 2000: see SI 2000/2543, art 2.

Sub-ss (1), (2): Appointment (for remaining purposes): 2 October 2000: see SI 2000/2543, art 3.

Sub-ss (3)–(6): Appointment: 2 October 2000: see SI 2000/2543, art 3.

Amendment

Sub-s (3): words omitted repealed by SI 2001/1149, art 3(2), Sch 2.

Date in force: 26 March 2001: see SI 2001/1149, art 1(2).

Sub-s (3): words "a postal operator (within the meaning of the Postal Services Act 2000)" in square brackets substituted by SI 2001/1149, art 3(1), Sch 1, para 135(1), (3).

Date in force: 26 March 2001: see SI 2001/1149, art 1(2).

83 Short title, commencement and extent

(1) This Act may be cited as the Regulation of Investigatory Powers Act 2000.

(2) The provisions of this Act, other than this section, shall come into force on such day as the Secretary of State may by order appoint; and different days may be appointed under this subsection for different purposes.

(3) This Act extends to Northern Ireland.

Notes

Initial Commencement

Royal Assent

Royal Assent: 28 July 2000: see sub-s (2) above.

Subordinate Legislation

Regulation of Investigatory Powers Act 2000 (Commencement No 1 and Transitional Provisions) Order 2000, SI 2000/2543 (made under sub-s (2)).

Regulation of Investigatory Powers Act 2000 (Commencement No 2) Order 2001, SI 2001/2727 (made under sub-s (2)).

Regulation of Investigatory Powers Act 2000 (Commencement No 3) Order 2003, SI 2003/3140 (made under sub-s (2)).

SCHEDULE 1
RELEVANT PUBLIC AUTHORITIES

Section 30

PART I
RELEVANT AUTHORITIES FOR THE PURPOSES OF SS 28 AND 29

Police forces etc

1 Any police force.

[1A The United Kingdom Atomic Energy Authority Constabulary.]

2 The National Criminal Intelligence Service.

3 The National Crime Squad.

4 The Serious Fraud Office.

The intelligence services

5 Any of the intelligence services.

The armed forces

6 Any of Her Majesty's forces.

The revenue departments

7 The Commissioners of Customs and Excise.

8 The Commissioners of Inland Revenue.

Government departments

9 ...

10 The Ministry of Defence.

[10ZA The Office of the Deputy Prime Minister.]

[10A The Department for Environment, Food and Rural Affairs.]

11 ...

12 The Department of Health.

13 The Home Office.

[13A The Northern Ireland Office.]

14 ...

15 The Department of Trade and Industry.

[15A The Department for Transport.]

[15B The Department for Work and Pensions.]

The National Assembly for Wales

16 The National Assembly for Wales.

Local authorities

[17 Any county council or district council in England, a London borough council, the Common Council of the City of London in its capacity as a local authority, the Council of the Isles of Scilly, and any county council or county borough council in Wales.]

[**17A** Any fire authority within the meaning of the Fire Services Act 1947 (read with paragraph 2 of Schedule 11 to the Local Government Act 1985).]

Other bodies

[**17B** The Charity Commission.]

18 The Environment Agency.

19 The Financial Services Authority.

20 The Food Standards Agency.

[**20A** The Gaming Board for Great Britain.

20B The Office of Fair Trading.

20C The Office of the Police Ombudsman for Northern Ireland.

20D The Postal Services Commission.]

21 ...

22 ...

23 [A universal service provider (within the meaning of the Postal Services Act 2000) acting in connection with the provision of a universal postal service (within the meaning of that Act)].

[**23A** The Office of Communications.]

[Northern Ireland authorities

23A The Department of Agriculture and Rural Development.

23B The Department of Enterprise, Trade and Investment.

23C The Department of the Environment.

23D Any district council (within the meaning of section 44 of the Interpretation Act (Northern Ireland) 1954.]

Notes

Initial Commencement

To be appointed

To be appointed: see s 83(2).

Appointment

Appointment: 25 September 2000: see SI 2000/2543, art 2.

Amendment

Para 1A: inserted by SI 2003/3171, art 2(1), (2).
Date in force: 5 January 2004: see SI 2003/3171, art 1(1).
Para 9: repealed by SI 2002/794, art 5(2), Sch 2.
Date in force: 27 March 2002: see SI 2002/794, art 1(2).
Para 10ZA: inserted by SI 2002/2626, art 20, Sch 2, para 24(b).
Date in force: 25 November 2002: see SI 2002/2626, art 1(2).
Para 10A: inserted by SI 2002/794, art 5(1), Sch 1, para 39.
Date in force: 27 March 2002: see SI 2002/794, art 1(2).
Para 11: repealed by SI 2001/2568, art 16, Schedule, para 18(a).
Date in force: 13 August 2001: see SI 2001/2568, art 1(2).
Para 13A: inserted by SI 2003/3171, art 2(1), (3).
Date in force: 5 January 2004: see SI 2003/3171, art 1(1).

Para 14: repealed by SI 2002/1397, art 12, Schedule, Pt I, para 16(a).

Date in force: 27 June 2002: see SI 2002/1397, art 1(2).

Para 15A: substituted (as inserted by SI 2001/2568, art 16, Schedule, para 18(b)) by virtue of SI 2002/2626, art 20, Sch 2, para 24.

Date in force: 25 November 2002: see SI 2002/2626, art 1(2).

Para 15B: inserted by SI 2002/1397, art 12, Schedule, Pt I, para 16(b).

Date in force: 27 June 2002: see SI 2002/1397, art 1(2).

Para 17: substituted by SI 2003/3171, art 2(1), (4).

Date in force: 5 January 2004: see SI 2003/3171, art 1(1).

Para 17A: inserted by SI 2003/3171, art 2(1), (5).

Date in force: 5 January 2004: see SI 2003/3171, art 1(1).

Para 17B: inserted by SI 2003/3171, art 2(1), (6).

Date in force: 5 January 2004: see SI 2003/3171, art 1(1).

Paras 20A–20D: inserted by SI 2003/3171, art 2(1), (7).

Date in force: 5 January 2004: see SI 2003/3171, art 1(1).

Para 21: repealed by SI 2001/3686, reg 6(17)(b).

Date in force: 15 November 2001: see SI 2001/3686, reg 1(1).

Para 22: repealed by SI 2002/1555, art 26.

Date in force: 3 July 2002: see SI 2002/1555, art 1.

Para 23: substituted by SI 2001/1149, art 3(1), Sch 1, para 135(1), (4).

Date in force: 26 March 2001: see SI 2001/1149, art 1(2).

First para 23A: inserted by the Communications Act 2003, s 406(1), Sch 17, para 161(1), (3).

Date in force: to be appointed: see the Communications Act 2003, s 411(2).

Second para 23A, 23B–23D: inserted by the Regulation of Investigatory Powers Act 2000 (Amendment) Order (Northern Ireland) 2002, SR 2002/183, arts 2, 3.

Date in force: 2 July 2002 (being the date after affirmation by resolution of the Assembly): see the Regulation of Investigatory Powers Act 2000 (Amendment) Order (Northern Ireland) 2002, SR 2002/183, art 1.

PART II
RELEVANT AUTHORITIES FOR THE PURPOSES ONLY OF S 28

The Health and Safety Executive

24 The Health and Safety Executive.

NHS bodies in England and Wales

25 A Health Authority established under section 8 of the National Health Service Act 1977.

26 A Special Health Authority established under section 11 of the National Health Service Act 1977.

27 A National Heath Service trust established under section 5 of the National Health Service and Community Care Act 1990.

[27A Local Health Boards in Wales established under section 6 of the National Health Service Reform and Health Care Professions Act 2002.

Her Majesty's Chief Inspector of Schools in England

27B Her Majesty's Chief Inspector of Schools in England.

The Information Commissioner

27C The Information Commissioner.

The Royal Parks Constabulary

27D The Royal Parks Constabulary.]

The Royal Pharmaceutical Society of Great Britain

28 The Royal Pharmaceutical Society of Great Britain.

[Northern Ireland authorities

29 The Department of Health, Social Services and Public Safety.

30 The Department for Regional Development.

31 The Department for Social Development.

32 The Department of Culture, Arts and Leisure.

33 The Foyle, Carlingford and Irish Lights Commission.

34 The Fisheries Conservancy Board for Northern Ireland.

35 A Health and Social Services trust established under Article 10 of the Health and Personal Services (Northern Ireland) Order 1991.

36 A Health and Social Services Board established under Article 16 of the Health and Personal Services (Northern Ireland) Order 1972.

37 The Health and Safety Executive for Northern Ireland.

38 The Northern Ireland Central Services Agency for the Health and Social Services.

39 The Fire Authority for Northern Ireland.

40 The Northern Ireland Housing Executive.]

Notes

Initial Commencement

To be appointed

To be appointed: see s 83(2).

Appointment

Appointment: 25 September 2000: see SI 2000/2543, art 2.

Amendment

Paras 27A–27D: inserted by SI 2003/3171, art 3(1), (2).

Date in force: 5 January 2004: see SI 2003/3171, art 1(1).

Paras 29–40: inserted by the Regulation of Investigatory Powers Act 2000 (Amendment) Order (Northern Ireland) 2002, SR 2002/183, arts 2, 4.

Date in force: 2 July 2002 (being the date after affirmation by resolution of the Assembly): see the Regulation of Investigatory Powers Act 2000 (Amendment) Order (Northern Ireland) 2002, SR 2002/183, art 1.

SCHEDULE 2
PERSONS HAVING THE APPROPRIATE PERMISSION

Section 49

Requirement that appropriate permission is granted by a judge

1 (1) Subject to the following provisions of this Schedule, a person has the appropriate permission in relation to any protected information if, and only if, written permission for the giving of section 49 notices in relation to that information has been granted–

(a)   in England and Wales, by a Circuit judge;

(b)   in Scotland, by a sheriff; or

(c)   in Northern Ireland, by a county court judge.

(2) Nothing in paragraphs 2 to 5 of this Schedule providing for the manner in which a person may be granted the appropriate permission in relation to any protected information without a grant under this paragraph shall be construed as requiring any further permission to be obtained in a case in which permission has been granted under this paragraph.

Data obtained under warrant etc

2 (1) This paragraph applies in the case of protected information falling within section 49(1)(a), (b) or (c) where the statutory power in question is one exercised, or to be exercised, in accordance with–

    (a)   a warrant issued by the Secretary of State or a person holding judicial office; or

    (b)   an authorisation under Part III of the Police Act 1997 (authorisation of otherwise unlawful action in respect of property).

(2) Subject to sub-paragraphs (3) to (5) and paragraph 6(1), a person has the appropriate permission in relation to that protected information (without any grant of permission under paragraph 1) if–

    (a)   the warrant or, as the case may be, the authorisation contained the relevant authority's permission for the giving of section 49 notices in relation to protected information to be obtained under the warrant or authorisation; or

    (b)   since the issue of the warrant or authorisation, written permission has been granted by the relevant authority for the giving of such notices in relation to protected information obtained under the warrant or authorisation.

(3) Only persons holding office under the Crown, the police and customs and excise shall be capable of having the appropriate permission in relation to protected information obtained, or to be obtained, under a warrant issued by the Secretary of State.

(4) Only a person who–

    (a)   was entitled to exercise the power conferred by the warrant, or

    (b)   is of the description of persons on whom the power conferred by the warrant was, or could have been, conferred,

shall be capable of having the appropriate permission in relation to protected information obtained, or to be obtained, under a warrant issued by a person holding judicial office.

(5) Only the police and the customs and excise shall be capable of having the appropriate permission in relation to protected information obtained, or to be obtained, under an authorisation under Part III of the Police Act 1997.

(6) In this paragraph "the relevant authority"–

    (a)   in relation to a warrant issued by the Secretary of State, means the Secretary of State;

    (b)   in relation to a warrant issued by a person holding judicial office, means any person holding any judicial office that would have entitled him to issue the warrant; and

    (c)   in relation to protected information obtained under an authorisation under Part III of the Police Act 1997, means (subject to sub-paragraph (7)) an authorising officer within the meaning of section 93 of that Act.

(7) Section 94 of the Police Act 1997 (power of other persons to grant authorisations in urgent cases) shall apply in relation to–

    (a)   an application for permission for the giving of section 49 notices in relation to protected information obtained, or to be obtained, under an authorisation under Part III of that Act, and

    (b)   the powers of any authorising officer (within the meaning of section 93 of that Act) to grant such a permission,

as it applies in relation to an application for an authorisation under section 93 of that Act and the powers of such an officer under that section.

(8) References in this paragraph to a person holding judicial office are references to–

    (a)   any judge of the Crown Court or of the High Court of Justiciary;

    (b)   any sheriff;

    (c)   any justice of the peace;

    (d)   any resident magistrate in Northern Ireland; or

    (e)   any person holding any such judicial office as entitles him to exercise the jurisdiction of a judge of the Crown Court or of a justice of the peace.

(9) Protected information that comes into a person's possession by means of the exercise of any statutory power which–

    (a)   is exercisable without a warrant, but

    (b)   is so exercisable in the course of, or in connection with, the exercise of another statutory power for which a warrant is required,

shall not be taken, by reason only of the warrant required for the exercise of the power mentioned in paragraph (b), to be information in the case of which this paragraph applies.

Data obtained by the intelligence services under statute but without a warrant

3 (1) This paragraph applies in the case of protected information falling within section 49(1)(a), (b) or (c) which–

    (a)   has come into the possession of any of the intelligence services or is likely to do so; and

    (b)   is not information in the case of which paragraph 2 applies.

(2) Subject to paragraph 6(1), a person has the appropriate permission in relation to that protected information (without any grant of permission under paragraph 1) if written permission for the giving of section 49 notices in relation to that information has been granted by the Secretary of State.

(3) Sub-paragraph (2) applies where the protected information is in the possession, or (as the case may be) is likely to come into the possession, of both–

    (a)   one or more of the intelligence services, and

    (b)   a public authority which is not one of the intelligence services,

as if a grant of permission under paragraph 1 were unnecessary only where the application to the Secretary of State for permission under that sub-paragraph is made by or on behalf of a member of one of the intelligence services.

Data obtained under statute by other persons but without a warrant

4 (1) This paragraph applies–

  (a)   in the case of protected information falling within section 49(1)(a), (b) or (c) which is not information in the case of which paragraph 2 or 3 applies; and

  (b)   in the case of protected information falling within section 49(1)(d) which is not information also falling within section 49(1)(a), (b) or (c) in the case of which paragraph 3 applies.

(2) Subject to paragraph 6, where–

  (a)   the statutory power was exercised, or is likely to be exercised, by the police, the customs and excise or a member of Her Majesty's forces, or

  (b)   the information was provided or disclosed, or is likely to be provided or disclosed, to the police, the customs and excise or a member of Her Majesty's forces, or

  (c)   the information is in the possession of, or is likely to come into the possession of, the police, the customs and excise or a member of Her Majesty's forces,

the police, the customs and excise or, as the case may be, members of Her Majesty's forces have the appropriate permission in relation to the protected information, without any grant of permission under paragraph 1.

(3) In any other case a person shall not have the appropriate permission by virtue of a grant of permission under paragraph 1 unless he is a person falling within sub-paragraph (4).

(4) A person falls within this sub-paragraph if, as the case may be–

  (a)   he is the person who exercised the statutory power or is of the description of persons who would have been entitled to exercise it;

  (b)   he is the person to whom the protected information was provided or disclosed, or is of a description of person the provision or disclosure of the information to whom would have discharged the statutory duty; or

  (c)   he is a person who is likely to be a person falling within paragraph (a) or (b) when the power is exercised or the protected information provided or disclosed.

Data obtained without the exercise of statutory powers

5 (1) This paragraph applies in the case of protected information falling within section 49(1)(e).

(2) Subject to paragraph 6, a person has the appropriate permission in relation to that protected information (without any grant of permission under paragraph 1) if–

  (a)   the information is in the possession of any of the intelligence services, or is likely to come into the possession of any of those services; and

  (b)   written permission for the giving of section 49 notices in relation to that information has been granted by the Secretary of State.

(3) Sub-paragraph (2) applies where the protected information is in the possession, or (as the case may be) is likely to come into the possession, of both–

  (a)   one or more of the intelligence services, and

  (b)   the police or the customs and excise,

as if a grant of permission under paragraph 1 were unnecessary only where the application to the Secretary of State for permission under that sub-paragraph is made by or on behalf of a member of one of the intelligence services.

General requirements relating to the appropriate permission

6 (1) A person does not have the appropriate permission in relation to any protected information unless he is either–

    (a)   a person who has the protected information in his possession or is likely to obtain possession of it; or

    (b)   a person who is authorised (apart from this Act) to act on behalf of such a person.

(2) Subject to sub-paragraph (3), a constable does not by virtue of paragraph 1, 4 or 5 have the appropriate permission in relation to any protected information unless–

    (a)   he is of or above the rank of superintendent; or

    (b)   permission to give a section 49 notice in relation to that information has been granted by a person holding the rank of superintendent, or any higher rank.

(3) In the case of protected information that has come into the police's possession by means of the exercise of powers conferred by–

    (a)   section 44 of the Terrorism Act 2000 (power to stop and search), or

    (b)   section 13A or 13B of the Prevention of Terrorism (Temporary Provisions) Act 1989 (which had effect for similar purposes before the coming into force of section 44 of the Terrorism Act 2000),

the permission required by sub-paragraph (2) shall not be granted by any person below the rank mentioned in section 44(4) of that Act of 2000 or, as the case may be, section 13A(1) of that Act of 1989.

(4) A person commissioned by the Commissioners of Customs and Excise does not by virtue of paragraph 1, 4 or 5 have the appropriate permission in relation to any protected information unless permission to give a section 49 notice in relation to that information has been granted–

    (a)   by those Commissioners themselves; or

    (b)   by an officer of their department of or above such level as they may designate for the purposes of this sub-paragraph.

(5) A member of Her Majesty's forces does not by virtue of paragraph 1, 4 or 5 have the appropriate permission in relation to any protected information unless–

    (a)   he is of or above the rank of lieutenant colonel or its equivalent; or

    (b)   permission to give a section 49 notice in relation to that information has been granted by a person holding the rank of lieutenant colonel or its equivalent, or by a person holding a rank higher than lieutenant colonel or its equivalent.

Duration of permission

7 (1) A permission granted by any person under any provision of this Schedule shall not entitle any person to give a section 49 notice at any time after the permission has ceased to have effect.

(2) Such a permission, once granted, shall continue to have effect (notwithstanding the cancellation, expiry or other discharge of any warrant or authorisation in which it is contained or to which it relates) until such time (if any) as it–

(a)   expires in accordance with any limitation on its duration that was contained in its terms; or

(b)   is withdrawn by the person who granted it or by a person holding any office or other position that would have entitled him to grant it.

Formalities for permissions granted by the Secretary of State

8 A permission for the purposes of any provision of this Schedule shall not be granted by the Secretary of State except–

(a)   under his hand; or

(b)   in an urgent case in which the Secretary of State has expressly authorised the grant of the permission, under the hand of a senior official.

Notes

Initial Commencement

To be appointed

To be appointed: see s 83(2).

SCHEDULE 3
THE TRIBUNAL

Section 65

Membership of the Tribunal

1 (1) A person shall not be appointed as a member of the Tribunal unless he is–

(a)   a person who holds or has held a high judicial office (within the meaning of the Appellate Jurisdiction Act 1876);

(b)   a person who has a ten year general qualification, within the meaning of section 71 of the Courts and Legal Services Act 1990;

(c)   an advocate or solicitor in Scotland of at least ten years' standing; or

(d)   a member of the Bar of Northern Ireland or solicitor of the Supreme Court of Northern Ireland of at least ten years' standing.

(2) Subject to the following provisions of this paragraph, the members of the Tribunal shall hold office during good behaviour.

(3) A member of the Tribunal shall vacate office at the end of the period of five years beginning with the day of his appointment, but shall be eligible for reappointment.

(4) A member of the Tribunal may be relieved of office by Her Majesty at his own request.

(5) A member of the Tribunal may be removed from office by Her Majesty on an Address presented to Her by both Houses of Parliament.

(6) If the Scottish Parliament passes a resolution calling for the removal of a member of the Tribunal, it shall be the duty of the Secretary of State to secure that a motion for the presentation of an Address to Her Majesty for the removal of that member, and the resolution of the Scottish Parliament, are considered by each House of Parliament.

President and Vice-President

2 (1) Her Majesty may by Letters Patent appoint as President or Vice-President of the Tribunal a person who is, or by virtue of those Letters will be, a member of the Tribunal.

(2) A person shall not be appointed President of the Tribunal unless he holds or has held a high judicial office (within the meaning of the Appellate Jurisdiction Act 1876).

(3) If at any time–

(a)   the President of the Tribunal is temporarily unable to carry out any functions conferred on him by this Schedule or any rules under section 69, or

(b)   the office of President of the Tribunal is for the time being vacant,

the Vice-President shall carry out those functions.

(4) A person shall cease to be President or Vice-President of the Tribunal if he ceases to be a member of the Tribunal.

Members of the Tribunal with special responsibilities

3 (1) The President of the Tribunal shall designate one or more members of the Tribunal as the member or members having responsibilities in relation to matters involving the intelligence services.

(2) It shall be the duty of the President of the Tribunal, in exercising any power conferred on him by rules under section 69 to allocate the members of the Tribunal who are to consider or hear any complaint, proceedings, reference or preliminary or incidental matter, to exercise that power in a case in which the complaint, proceedings or reference relates to, or to a matter involving–

(a)   an allegation against any of the intelligence services or any member of any of those services, or

(b)   conduct by or on behalf of any of those services or any member of any of those services,

in such manner as secures that the allocated members consist of, or include, one or more of the members for the time being designated under sub-paragraph (1).

Salaries and expenses

4 (1) The Secretary of State shall pay to the members of the Tribunal out of money provided by Parliament such remuneration and allowances as he may with the approval of the Treasury determine.

(2) Such expenses of the Tribunal as the Secretary of State may with the approval of the Treasury determine shall be defrayed by him out of money provided by Parliament.

Officers

5 (1) The Secretary of State may, after consultation with the Tribunal and with the approval of the Treasury as to numbers, provide the Tribunal with such officers as he thinks necessary for the proper discharge of their functions.

(2) The Tribunal may authorise any officer provided under this paragraph to obtain any documents or information on the Tribunal's behalf.

Parliamentary disqualification

6 In Part II of Schedule 1 to the House of Commons Disqualification Act 1975 and in Part II of Schedule 1 to the Northern Ireland Assembly Disqualification Act 1975 (bodies whose members are disqualified) there shall be inserted (at the appropriate places) the following entry–

"The Tribunal established under section 65 of the Regulation of Investigatory Powers Act 2000".

Notes

Initial Commencement

To be appointed

> To be appointed: see s 83(2).

Appointment

> Appointment: 2 October 2000: see SI 2000/2543, art 3.

SCHEDULE 4
CONSEQUENTIAL AMENDMENTS

Section 82

...

1 ...

2 ...

The Telecommunications Act 1984 (c 12)

3 In section 45 of the Telecommunications Act 1984 (offence of disclosing of messages and use of telecommunication system), for subsections (2) and (3) there shall be substituted–

"(2) Subsection (1) above does not apply to any disclosure made–

(a)   in accordance with the order of any court or for the purposes of any criminal proceedings;

(b)   in accordance with any warrant, authorisation or notice issued, granted or given under any provision of the Regulation of Investigatory Powers Act 2000;

(c)   in compliance with any requirement imposed (apart from that Act) in consequence of the exercise by any person of any statutory power exercisable by him for the purpose of obtaining any document or other information; or

(d)   in pursuance of any duty under that Act of 2000, or under Part III of the Police Act 1997, to provide information or produce any document to the Interception of Communications Commissioner or to the tribunal established under section 65 of that Act of 2000.

(3) In subsection (2) above "criminal proceedings" and "statutory power" have the same meanings as in the Regulation of Investigatory Powers Act 2000."

The Security Service Act 1989 (c 5)

4 (1) In section 1 of the Security Service Act 1989 (functions of the Security Service), after subsection (4) there shall be inserted–

"(5) Section 81(5) of the Regulation of Investigatory Powers Act 2000 (meaning of "prevention" and "detection"), so far as it relates to serious crime, shall apply for the purposes of this Act as it applies for the purposes of the provisions of that Act not contained in Chapter I of Part I."

(2) In section 2(2)(a) of that Act (duty of Director General to secure that information not disclosed except for authorised purposes), for "preventing or detecting" there shall be substituted "the prevention or detection of".

The Official Secrets Act 1989 (c 6)

5   In section 4(3)(a) of the Official Secrets Act 1989 (offence of disclosing interception information), after "1985" there shall be inserted "or under the authority of an interception warrant under section 5 of the Regulation of Investigatory Powers Act 2000".

The Intelligence Services Act 1994 (c 13)

6   In section 11 of the Intelligence Services Act 1994 (interpretation), after subsection (1) there shall be inserted—

"(1A)   Section 81(5) of the Regulation of Investigatory Powers Act 2000 (meaning of "prevention" and "detection"), so far as it relates to serious crime, shall apply for the purposes of this Act as it applies for the purposes of Chapter I of Part I of that Act."

The Criminal Procedure and Investigations Act 1996 (c 25)

7   (1)   In each of sections 3(7), 7(6), 8(6) and 9(9) of the Criminal Procedure and Investigations Act 1996 (exceptions for interceptions from obligations to make disclosures to the defence), for paragraphs (a) and (b) there shall be substituted "it is material the disclosure of which is prohibited by section 17 of the Regulation of Investigatory Powers Act 2000."

(2)   In section 23(6) of that Act (code of practice not to apply to material intercepted under the Interception of Communications Act 1985), after "1985" there shall be inserted "or under the authority of an interception warrant under section 5 of the Regulation of Investigatory Powers Act 2000".

The Police Act 1997 (c 50)

8   (1)   In section 91(9) of the Police Act 1997 (staff for Surveillance Commissioners)—

(a)   after "Chief Commissioner" there shall be inserted "and subject to the approval of the Treasury as to numbers"; and

(b)   after "Commissioners" there shall be inserted "and any Assistant Surveillance Commissioners holding office under section 63 of the Regulation of Investigatory Powers Act 2000".

(2)   In section 93(3) of that Act (persons who may make an application to an authorising officer within section 93(5))—

(a)   in paragraph (a), for "(e)" there shall be substituted "(ea) or (ee)"; and

(b)   after that paragraph there shall be inserted—

"(aa) if the authorising officer is within subsection (5)(eb) to (ed), by a member, as the case may be, of the Royal Navy Regulating Branch, the Royal Military Police or the Royal Air Force Police;".

(3)   In section 94(1) of that Act (circumstances in which authorisations may be given in absence of authorising officer), in paragraph (b), for ", (f), (g) or (h)" there shall be substituted "or (f)", and after that paragraph there shall be inserted

"or

(c)   if the authorising officer is within paragraph (g) of section 93(5), it is also not reasonably practicable for the application to be considered either–

    (i)   by any other person designated for the purposes of that paragraph; or

    (ii)   by the designated deputy of the Director General of the National Crime Squad."

(4) In section 94(2) of that Act (persons who may act in absence of the authorising officer)–

(a)   after paragraph (d), there shall be inserted–

"(da) where the authorising officer is within paragraph (ea) of that subsection, by a person holding the rank of deputy or assistant chief constable in the Ministry of Defence Police;

(db)   where the authorising officer is within paragraph (eb) of that subsection, by a person holding the position of assistant Provost Marshal in the Royal Navy Regulating Branch;

(dc)   where the authorising officer is within paragraph (ec) or (ed) of that subsection, by a person holding the position of deputy Provost Marshal in the Royal Military Police or, as the case may be, in the Royal Air Force Police;

(dd)   where the authorising officer is within paragraph (ee) of that subsection, by a person holding the rank of deputy or assistant chief constable in the British Transport Police;";

(b)   in paragraph (e), the words "or (g)" and "or, as the case may be, of the National Crime Squad" shall be omitted; and

(c)   after that paragraph, there shall be inserted–

"(ea) where the authorising officer is within paragraph (g) of that subsection, by a person designated for the purposes of this paragraph by the Director General of the National Crime Squad as a person entitled to act in an urgent case;".

(5) In section 94(3) of that Act (rank of police members of the National Crime Intelligence Squad and National Crime Squad entitled to act), after "(2)(e)" there shall be inserted "or (2)(ea)".

(6) In section 95 of that Act (authorisations: form and duration etc)–

(a)   in each of subsections (4) and (5), for the words from "the action" onwards there shall be substituted "the authorisation is one in relation to which the requirements of paragraphs (a) and (b) of section 93(2) are no longer satisfied."; and

(b)   in subsection (6), for "or (e)" there shall be substituted ", (e) or (g)".

(7) In section 97 of that Act (authorisations requiring approval), in subsection (6), the words from "(and paragraph 7" onwards shall be omitted, and after that subsection there shall be inserted–

"(6A) The reference in subsection (6) to the authorising officer who gave the authorisation or in whose absence it was given shall be construed, in the case of an authorisation given by or in the absence of a person within paragraph (b), (e) or (g) of section 93(5), as a reference to the Commissioner of Police, Chief Constable or, as the case may be, Director General mentioned in the paragraph concerned."

(8) In section 103(7) of that Act (quashing authorisations), for the words from "and paragraph 7" onwards there shall be substituted "and subsection (6A) of section 97 shall apply for the purposes of this subsection as it applies for the purposes of subsection (6) of that section."

(9) In section 105 of that Act (appeals by authorising officers: supplementary), in subsection (1)(a), the word "and" shall be inserted at the end of sub-paragraph (i), and sub-paragraph (iii) and the word "and" immediately preceding it shall be omitted.

(10) In section 107 of that Act—

    (a)   in subsection (2) (report of Chief Surveillance Commissioner on the discharge of his functions under Part III of that Act)—

        (i)   for "the discharge of functions under this Part" there shall be substituted "the matters with which he is concerned"; and

        (ii)   for "any matter relating to those functions" there shall be substituted "anything relating to any of those matters";

    (b)   in subsection (4) (matters that may be excluded from a report), for "the prevention or detection of serious crime or otherwise" there shall be substituted "any of the purposes for which authorisations may be given or granted under this Part of this Act or Part II of the Regulation of Investigatory Powers Act 2000 or under any enactment contained in or made under an Act of the Scottish Parliament which makes provision equivalent to that made by Part II of that Act of 2000 or"; and

    (c)   after subsection (5) (duty to co-operate with the Chief Surveillance Commissioner) there shall be inserted the subsections set out in sub-paragraph (11).

(11) The subsections inserted after subsection (5) of section 107 of that Act are as follows—

"(5A) It shall be the duty of—

    (a)   every person by whom, or on whose application, there has been given or granted any authorisation the function of giving or granting which is subject to review by the Chief Commissioner,

    (b)   every person who has engaged in conduct with the authority of such an authorisation,

    (c)   every person who holds or has held any office, rank or position with the same public authority as a person falling within paragraph (a),

    (d)   every person who holds or has held any office, rank or position with any public authority for whose benefit (within the meaning of Part II of the Regulation of Investigatory Powers Act 2000) activities which are or may be subject to any such review have been or may be carried out, and

    (e)   every person to whom a notice under section 49 of the Regulation of Investigatory Powers Act 2000 (notices imposing a disclosure requirement in respect of information protected by a key) has been given in relation to any information obtained by conduct to which such an authorisation relates,

to disclose or provide to the Chief Commissioner all such documents and information as he may require for the purpose of enabling him to carry out his functions.

(5B) It shall be the duty of every Commissioner to give the tribunal established under section 65 of the Regulation of Investigatory Powers Act 2000 all such assistance (including his opinion as to any issue falling to be determined by that tribunal) as that tribunal may require—

(a) in connection with the investigation of any matter by that tribunal; or

(b) otherwise for the purposes of that tribunal's consideration or determination of any matter.

(5C) In this section "public authority" means any public authority within the meaning of section 6 of the Human Rights Act 1998 (acts of public authorities) other than a court or tribunal."

(12) In section 108(1) of that Act after "In this Part—" there shall be inserted—

""Assistant Commissioner of Police of the Metropolis" includes the Deputy Commissioner of Police of the Metropolis;".

(13) In Part VII of that Act, before section 134 there shall be inserted—

"133A Meaning of "prevention" and "detection"

Section 81(5) of the Regulation of Investigatory Powers Act 2000 (meaning of "prevention" and "detection") shall apply for the purposes of this Act as it applies for the purposes of the provisions of that Act not contained in Chapter I of Part I."

The Northern Ireland Act 1998 (c 47)

9 In paragraph 17(b) of Schedule 2 to the Northern Ireland Act 1998 (excepted matters), for "the Interception of Communications Act 1985" there shall be substituted "Chapter I of Part I of the Regulation of Investigatory Powers Act 2000".

The Electronic Communications Act 2000 (c 7)

10 In section 4(2) of the Electronic Communications Act 2000 (exception to rules restricting disclosure of information obtained under Part I of that Act), for the word "or" at the end of paragraph (e) there shall be substituted—

"(ea) for the purposes of any proceedings before the tribunal established under section 65 of the Regulation of Investigatory Powers Act 2000; or".

The Financial Services and Markets Act 2000 (c 8)

11 In section 394(7) of the Financial Services and Markets Act 2000 (exclusion of material from material of the Authority to which a person must be allowed access), for paragraphs (a) and (b) there shall be substituted—

"(a) is material the disclosure of which for the purposes of or in connection with any legal proceedings is prohibited by section 17 of the Regulation of Investigatory Powers Act 2000; or"

The Terrorism Act 2000 (c 11)

12 (1) In section 9(2)(d) of the Terrorism Act 2000 (proceedings under the Human Rights Act 1998), for "8" there shall be substituted "7".

(2) In each of paragraphs 6(3) and 7(5) of Schedule 3 to that Act (references to an organisation and representative in paragraphs 5 and 8 of that Schedule), for "paragraphs 5 and 8" there shall be substituted "paragraph 5".

Notes

Initial Commencement

To be appointed

>To be appointed: see s 83(2).

Appointment

>Paras 1–3, 5, 7, 9–12: Appointment: 2 October 2000: see SI 2000/2543, art 3.
>
>Paras 4, 6, 8: Appointment: 25 September 2000: see SI 2000/2543, art 2.

Amendment

>Paras 1, 2: repealed by SI 2001/1149, art 3(2), Sch 2.
>
>Date in force: 26 March 2001: see SI 2001/1149, art 1(2).
>
>Para 3: repealed by the Communications Act 2003, s 406(7), Sch 19(1).
>
>Date in force: to be appointed: see the Communications Act 2003, s 411(2).

See Further

>See further, in relation to reference to the British Transport Police: the Railways and Transport Safety Act 2003, Sch 5, para 4(1).

SCHEDULE 5
REPEALS

Section 82

Chapter	Short title	Extent of repeal
1975 c 24	The House of Commons Disqualification Act 1975.	In Part II of Schedule 1, the words "The Tribunal established under the Interception of Communications Act 1985", "The Tribunal established under the Security Service Act 1989", and "The Tribunal established under section 9 of the Intelligence Services Act 1994".
1975 c 25	The Northern Ireland Assembly Disqualification Act 1975.	In Part II of Schedule 1, the words "The Tribunal established under the Interception of Communications Act 1985", "The Tribunal established under the Security Service Act 1989", and "The Tribunal established under section 9 of the Intelligence Services Act 1994".
1985 c 56	The Interception of Communications Act 1985.	Sections 1 to 10. Section 11(3) to (5). Schedule 1.
1989 c 5	The Security Service Act 1989.	Sections 4 and 5. Schedules 1 and 2.
1989 c 6	The Official Secrets Act 1989.	In Schedule 1, paragraph 3.
1990 c 41	The Courts and Legal Services Act 1990.	In Schedule 10, paragraphs 62 and 74.
1994 c 13	The Intelligence Services Act 1994.	In section 6(1)(b), the words "of his department". In section 7(5)(b), the words "of his department". Sections 8 and 9. In section 11(1), paragraph (b). Schedules 1 and 2.
1997 c 50	The Police Act 1997.	In section 93(6), paragraph (f) and the word "and" immediately preceding it. In section 94(1), the word "or" at the end of paragraph (a). In section 94(2)(e), the words "or (g)" and "or, as the case may be, of the National Crime Squad". In section 94(4)– (a) the words "in his absence", in each place where they occur; and (b) paragraph (d) and the word "and" immediately preceding it. In section 97(6), the words from "(and paragraph 7" onwards. Sections 101 and 102. In section 104– (a) in subsection (1), paragraph (g); (b) in each of subsections (4), (5) and (6), paragraph (b) and the word "or" immediately preceding it; (c) in subsection (8), paragraph (b) and the word "and" immediately preceding it.

		In section 105(1)(a), sub-paragraph (iii) and the word "and" immediately preceding it.
		Section 106.
		Section 107(6).
		Schedule 7.
1997 c 68	The Special Immigration Appeals Commission Act 1997.	Section 5(7).
1998 c 37	The Crime and Disorder Act 1998.	Section 113(1) and (3).
2000 c 11	The Terrorism Act 2000.	In Schedule 3, paragraph 8.

Notes

Initial Commencement

To be appointed

To be appointed: see s 83(2).

Appointment

Appointment (in part): 25 September 2000: see SI 2000/2543, art 2.
Appointment (remainder): 2 October 2000: see SI 2000/2543, art 3.

POLICE ACT 1997

1997 CHAPTER 50

PART III
AUTHORISATION OF ACTION IN RESPECT OF PROPERTY
The Commissioners

91 The Commissioners

(1) The Prime Minister[, after consultation with the Scottish Ministers,] shall appoint for the purposes of this Part–

(a)   a Chief Commissioner, and

(b)   such number of other Commissioners as the Prime Minister thinks fit.

(2) The persons appointed under subsection (1) shall be persons who hold or have held high judicial office within the meaning of the Appellate Jurisdiction Act 1876.

(3) Subject to subsections (4) to (7), each Commissioner shall hold and vacate office in accordance with the terms of his appointment.

(4) Each Commissioner shall be appointed for a term of three years.

(5) A person who ceases to be a Commissioner (otherwise than under subsection (7)) may be reappointed under this section.

[(6) Subject to subsection (7), a Commissioner shall not be removed from office before the end of the term for which he is appointed unless–

(a)   a resolution approving his removal has been passed by each House of Parliament; and

(b)   a resolution approving his removal has been passed by the Scottish Parliament.]

(7) A Commissioner may be removed from office by the Prime Minister if after his appointment–

(a)   a bankruptcy order is made against him or his estate is sequestrated or he makes a composition or arrangement with, or grants a trust deed for, his creditors;

(b)   a disqualification order under the Company Directors Disqualification Act 1986 or Part II of the Companies (Northern Ireland) Order 1989, or an order under section 429(2)(b) of the Insolvency Act 1986 (failure to pay under county court administration order), is made against him [or his disqualification undertaking is accepted under section 7 or 8 of the Company Directors Disqualification Act 1986]; or

(c)   he is convicted in the United Kingdom, the Channel Islands or the Isle of Man of an offence and has passed on him a sentence of imprisonment (whether suspended or not).

(8) The Secretary of State shall pay to each Commissioner[, other than a Commissioner carrying out functions as mentioned in subsection (8A),] such allowances as the Secretary of State considers appropriate.

[(8A) The Scottish Ministers shall pay to any Commissioner who carries out his functions under this Part wholly or mainly in Scotland such allowances as the Scottish Ministers consider appropriate.]

(9) The Secretary of State shall, after consultation with the Chief Commissioner [and subject to the approval of the Treasury as to numbers], provide the Commissioners [and any Assistant Surveillance Commissioners holding office under section 63 of the Regulation of Investigatory Powers Act 2000][, other than any Commissioner carrying out functions as mentioned in subsection (9A),] with such staff as the Secretary of State considers necessary for the discharge of their functions.

[(9A) The Scottish Ministers shall, after consultation with the Chief Commissioner, provide any Commissioner who carries out his functions under this Part wholly or mainly in Scotland with such staff as the Scottish Ministers consider necessary for the discharge of his functions.]

(10) The decisions of the Chief Commissioner or, subject to sections 104 and 106, any other Commissioner (including decisions as to his jurisdiction) shall not be subject to appeal or liable to be questioned in any court.

Notes

Initial Commencement

To be appointed

> To be appointed: see s 135.

Appointment

> Sub-ss (1)–(9): Appointment: 1 September 1997: see SI 1997/1930, art 2(2)(g).

> Sub-s (10): Appointment: 22 February 1999: see SI 1999/151, art 2.

Amendment

> Sub-s (1): words ", after consultation with the Scottish Ministers," in square brackets inserted by SI 1999/1747, art 3, Sch 6, Pt II, para 2(1), (2)(a).

> Date in force: 1 July 1999: see SI 1999/1747, art 1, and SI 1998/3178, art 3.

> Sub-s (6): substituted by SI 1999/1747, art 3, Sch 6, Pt II, para 2(1), (2)(b).

> Date in force: 1 July 1999: see SI 1999/1747, art 1, and SI 1998/3178, art 3.

> Sub-s (7): in para (b) words from "or his disqualification" to "Company Directors Disqualification Act 1986" in square brackets inserted by the Insolvency Act 2000, s 8, Sch 4, Pt II, para 22(1), (2).

> Date in force: 2 April 2001: see SI 2001/766, art 2(1)(a).

> Sub-s (8): words ", other than a Commissioner carrying out functions as mentioned in subsection (8A)," in square brackets inserted by SI 1999/1747, art 3, Sch 6, Pt II, para 2(1), (2)(c).

> Date in force: 1 July 1999: see SI 1999/1747, art 1, and SI 1998/3178, art 3.

> Sub-s (8A): inserted by SI 1999/1747, art 3, Sch 6, Pt II, para 2(1), (2)(d).

> Date in force: 1 July 1999: see SI 1999/1747, art 1, and SI 1998/3178, art 3.

> Sub-s (9): words "and subject to the approval of the Treasury as to numbers" in square brackets inserted by the Regulation of Investigatory Powers Act 2000, s 82(1), Sch 4, para 8(1)(a).

> Date in force: 25 September 2000: see SI 2000/2543, art 2.

> Sub-s (9): words from "and any Assistant" to "the Regulation of Investigatory Powers Act 2000" in square brackets inserted by the Regulation of Investigatory Powers Act 2000, s 82(1), Sch 4, para 8(1)(b).

> Date in force: 25 September 2000: see SI 2000/2543, art 2.

> Sub-s (9): words ", other than any Commissioner carrying out functions as mentioned in subsection (9A)," in square brackets inserted by SI 1999/1747, art 3, Sch 6, Pt II, para 2(1), (2)(f).

> Date in force: 1 July 1999: see SI 1999/1747, art 1, and SI 1998/3178, art 3.

> Sub-s (9A): inserted by SI 1999/1747, art 3, Sch 6, Pt II, para 2(1), (2)(g).

> Date in force: 1 July 1999: see SI 1999/1747, art 1, and SI 1998/3178, art 3.

Authorisations

92 Effect of authorisation under Part III

No entry on or interference with property or with wireless telegraphy shall be unlawful if it is authorised by an authorisation having effect under this Part.

Notes

Initial Commencement

To be appointed
> To be appointed: see s 135.

Appointment
> Appointment: 22 February 1999: see SI 1999/151, art 2.

---

93 Authorisations to interfere with property etc

(1) Where subsection (2) applies, an authorising officer may authorise–

    (a)   the taking of such action, in respect of such property in the relevant area, as he may specify,

    [(ab) the taking of such action falling within subsection (1A), in respect of property outside the relevant area, as he may specify, or]

    (b)   the taking of such action in the relevant area as he may specify, in respect of wireless telegraphy.

[(1A) The action falling within this subsection is action for maintaining or retrieving any equipment, apparatus or device the placing or use of which in the relevant area has been authorised under this Part or Part II of the Regulation of Investigatory Powers Act 2000 or under any enactment contained in or made under an Act of the Scottish Parliament which makes provision equivalent to that made by Part II of that Act of 2000.

(1B) Subsection (1) applies where the authorising officer is a customs officer [or an officer of the Office of Fair Trading] with the omission of–

    (a)   the words "in the relevant area", in each place where they occur; and

    (b)   paragraph (ab).]

(2) This subsection applies where the authorising officer believes–

    (a)   that it is necessary for the action specified to be taken [for the purpose of preventing or detecting] serious crime, and

    [(b)   that the taking of the action is proportionate to what the action seeks to achieve].

[(2A) Subsection (2) applies where the authorising officer is the Chief Constable or the Deputy Chief Constable of the [Police Service of Northern Ireland] as if the reference in subsection (2)(a) to preventing or detecting serious crime included a reference to the interests of national security.

[(2AA) Where the authorising officer is the chairman of the Office of Fair Trading, the only purpose falling within subsection (2)(a) is the purpose of preventing or detecting an offence under section 188 of the Enterprise Act 2002.]

(2B) The matters to be taken into account in considering whether the requirements of subsection (2) are satisfied in the case of any authorisation shall include whether what it is thought necessary to achieve by the authorised action could reasonably be achieved by other means.]

(3) An authorising officer shall not give an authorisation under this section except on an application made–

    (a)   if the authorising officer is within subsection (5)(a) to [(ea) or (ee)], by a member of his police force, [(aa) if the authorising officer is within subsection (5)(eb) to (ed), by a member, as the case may be, of the Royal Navy Regulating Branch, the Royal Military Police or the Royal Air Force Police;]

(b) if the authorising officer is within subsection (5)(f), by a member of the National Criminal Intelligence Service,

(c) if the authorising officer is within subsection (5)(g), by a member of the National Crime Squad, or

(d) if the authorising officer is within subsection (5)(h), by a customs officer[, or

(e) if the authorising officer is within subsection (5)(i), by an officer of the Office of Fair Trading].

(4) For the purposes of subsection (2), conduct which constitutes one or more offences shall be regarded as serious crime if, and only if,–

(a) it involves the use of violence, results in substantial financial gain or is conduct by a large number of persons in pursuit of a common purpose, or

(b) the offence or one of the offences is an offence for which a person who has attained the age of twenty-one [(eighteen in relation to England and Wales)] and has no previous convictions could reasonably be expected to be sentenced to imprisonment for a term of three years or more,

and, where the authorising officer is within subsection (5)(h), it relates to an assigned matter within the meaning of section 1(1) of the Customs and Excise Management Act 1979.

(5) In this section "authorising officer" means–

(a) the chief constable of a police force maintained under section 2 of the Police Act 1996 (maintenance of police forces for areas in England and Wales except London);

(b) the Commissioner, or an Assistant Commissioner, of Police of the Metropolis;

(c) the Commissioner of Police for the City of London;

(d) the chief constable of a police force maintained under or by virtue of section 1 of the Police (Scotland) Act 1967 (maintenance of police forces for areas in Scotland);

(e) the Chief Constable or a Deputy Chief Constable of the [Police Service of Northern Ireland];

[(ea) the Chief Constable of the Ministry of Defence Police;

(eb) the Provost Marshal of the Royal Navy Regulating Branch;

(ec) the Provost Marshal of the Royal Military Police;

(ed) the Provost Marshal of the Royal Air Force Police;

(ee) the Chief Constable of the British Transport Police;]

(f) the Director General of the National Criminal Intelligence Service;

(g) the Director General of the National Crime Squad[, or any person holding the rank of assistant chief constable in that Squad who is designated for the purposes of this paragraph by that Director General]; or

(h)   [any] customs officer designated by the Commissioners of Customs and Excise for the purposes of this paragraph[; or

(i)   the chairman of the Office of Fair Trading].

(6)   In this section "relevant area"–

(a)   in relation to a person within paragraph (a), (b) or (c) of subsection (5), means the area in England and Wales for which his police force is maintained;

(b)   in relation to a person within paragraph (d) of that subsection means the area in Scotland for which his police force is maintained;

(c)   in relation to a person within paragraph (e) of that subsection, means Northern Ireland;

[(ca) in relation to a person within paragraph (ea), means any place where, under section 2 of the Ministry of Defence Police Act 1987, the members of the Ministry of Defence Police have the powers and privileges of a constable;

(cb) in relation to a person within paragraph (ee), means the United Kingdom;]

(d)   in relation to the Director General of the National Criminal Intelligence Service, means the United Kingdom;

(e)   in relation to the Director General of the National Crime Squad, means England and Wales; ...

(f)   ...

and in each case includes the adjacent United Kingdom waters.

[(6A) For the purposes of any authorisation by a person within paragraph (eb), (ec) or (ed) of subsection (5) property is in the relevant area or action in respect of wireless telegraphy is taken in the relevant area if, as the case may be–

(a)   the property is owned, occupied, in the possession of or being used by a person subject to service discipline; or

(b)   the action is taken in relation to the use of wireless telegraphy by such a person.

(6B) For the purposes of this section a person is subject to service discipline–

(a)   in relation to the Royal Navy Regulating Branch, if he is subject to the Naval Discipline Act 1957 or is a civilian to whom Parts I and II of that Act for the time being apply by virtue of section 118 of that Act ;

(b)   in relation to the Royal Military Police, if he is subject to military law or is a civilian to whom Part II of the Army Act 1955 for the time being applies by virtue of section 209 of that Act; and

(c)   in relation to the Royal Air Force Police, if he is subject to air-force law or is a civilian to whom Part II of the Air Force Act 1955 for the time being applies by virtue of section 209 of that Act.]

(7)   The powers conferred by, or by virtue of, this section are additional to any other powers which a person has as a constable either at common law or under or by virtue of any other enactment and are not to be taken to affect any of those other powers.

Notes

Initial Commencement

To be appointed

To be appointed: see s 135.

Appointment

Appointment: 22 February 1999: see SI 1999/151, art 2.

Amendment

Sub-s (1): para (ab) substituted by the Regulation of Investigatory Powers Act 2000, s 75(1), (2).

Date in force: 25 September 2000: see SI 2000/2543, art 2.

Sub-ss (1A), (1B): inserted by the Regulation of Investigatory Powers Act 2000, s 75(1), (3).

Date in force: 25 September 2000: see SI 2000/2543, art 2.

Sub-s (1B): words "or an officer of the Office of Fair Trading" in square brackets inserted by the Enterprise Act 2002, s 200(1), (2)(a).

Date in force: 20 June 2003: see SI 2003/1397, art 2(1), Schedule; for transitional and transitory provisions see the Enterprise Act 2002, s 276, Sch 24, paras 2–6.

Sub-s (2): in para (a) words "for the purpose of preventing or detecting" in square brackets substituted by the Regulation of Investigatory Powers Act 2000, s 75(1), (4)(a).

Date in force: 25 September 2000: see SI 2000/2543, art 2.

Sub-s (2): para (b) substituted by the Regulation of Investigatory Powers Act 2000, s 75(1), (4)(b).

Date in force: 25 September 2000: see SI 2000/2543, art 2.

Sub-ss (2A), (2B): inserted by the Regulation of Investigatory Powers Act 2000, s 75(1), (5).

Date in force: 25 September 2000: see SI 2000/2543, art 2.

Sub-s (2A): words "Police Service of Northern Ireland" in square brackets substituted by the Police (Northern Ireland) Act 2000, s 78(1), Sch 6, para 20(1), (2)(b).

Date in force: 4 November 2001: see the Police (Northern Ireland) Act 2000 (Commencement No 3 and Transitional Provisions) Order 2001, SR 2001/396, art 2, Schedule.

Sub-s (2AA): inserted by the Enterprise Act 2002, s 200(1), (2)(b).

Date in force: 20 June 2003: see SI 2003/1397, art 2(1), Schedule; for transitional and transitory provisions see the Enterprise Act 2002, s 276, Sch 24, paras 2–6.

Sub-s (3): in para (a) words "(ea) or (ee)" in square brackets substituted by the Regulation of Investigatory Powers Act 2000, s 82(1), Sch 4, para 8(2)(a).

Date in force: 25 September 2000: see SI 2000/2543, art 2.

Sub-s (3): para (aa) inserted by the Regulation of Investigatory Powers Act 2000, s 82(1), Sch 4, para 8(2)(b).

Date in force: 25 September 2000: see SI 2000/2543, art 2.

Sub-s (3): para (e) and word ", or" immediately preceding it inserted by the Enterprise Act 2002, s 200(1), (2)(c).

Date in force: 20 June 2003: see SI 2003/1397, art 2(1), Schedule; for transitional and transitory provisions see the Enterprise Act 2002, s 276, Sch 24, paras 2–6.

Sub-s (4): in para (b) words "(eighteen in relation to England and Wales)" in square brackets inserted by the Criminal Justice and Court Services Act 2000, s 74, Sch 7, Pt II, para 149.

Date in force: to be appointed: see the Criminal Justice and Court Services Act 2000, s 80(1).

Sub-s (5): in para (e) words "Police Service of Northern Ireland" in square brackets substituted by the Police (Northern Ireland) Act 2000, s 78(1), Sch 6, para 20(1), (2)(b).

Date in force: 4 November 2001: see the Police (Northern Ireland) Act 2000 (Commencement No 3 and Transitional Provisions) Order 2001, SR 2001/396, art 2, Schedule.

Sub-s (5): paras (ea)–(ee) inserted by the Regulation of Investigatory Powers Act 2000, s 75(1), (6)(a).

Date in force: 25 September 2000: see SI 2000/2543, art 2.

Sub-s (5): in para (g) words from ", or any person" to "that Director General" in square brackets inserted by the Regulation of Investigatory Powers Act 2000, s 75(1), (6)(b).

Date in force: 25 September 2000: see SI 2000/2543, art 2.

Sub-s (5): in para (h) word "any" in square brackets substituted by the Regulation of Investigatory Powers Act 2000, s 75(1), (6)(c).

Date in force: 25 September 2000: see SI 2000/2543, art 2.

Sub-s (5): para (i) and word "; or" immediately preceding it inserted by the Enterprise Act 2002, s 200(1), (2)(d).

Date in force: 20 June 2003: see SI 2003/1397, art 2(1), Schedule; for transitional and transitory provisions see the Enterprise Act 2002, s 276, Sch 24, paras 2–6.

Sub-s (6): paras (ca), (cb) inserted by the Regulation of Investigatory Powers Act 2000, s 75(1), (7).

Date in force: 25 September 2000: see SI 2000/2543, art 2.

Sub-s (6): para (f) and word omitted immediately preceding it repealed by the Regulation of Investigatory Powers Act 2000, s 82(2), Sch 5.

Date in force: 25 September 2000: see SI 2000/2543, art 2.

Sub-ss (6A), (6B): inserted by the Regulation of Investigatory Powers Act 2000, s 75(1), (8).

Date in force: 25 September 2000: see SI 2000/2543, art 2.

See Further

See further, in relation to reference to the British Transport Police: the Railways and Transport Safety Act 2003, s 73(1), Sch 5, para 4(1), (2)(i).

94 Authorisations given in absence of authorising officer

(1) Subsection (2) applies where it is not reasonably practicable for an authorising officer to consider an application for an authorisation under section 93 and–

    (a)   if the authorising officer is within paragraph (b) or (e) of section 93(5), it is also not reasonably practicable for the application to be considered by any of the other persons within the paragraph concerned; …

    (b)   if the authorising officer is within paragraph (a), (c), (d) [or (f)] of section 93(5), it is also not reasonably practicable for the application to be considered by his designated deputy [or

    (c)   if the authorising officer is within paragraph (g) of section 93(5), it is also not reasonably practicable for the application to be considered either–

        (i)   by any other person designated for the purposes of that paragraph; or

        (ii)   by the designated deputy of the Director General of the National Crime Squad].

(2) Where this subsection applies, the powers conferred on the authorising officer by section 93 may, in an urgent case, be exercised–

    (a)   where the authorising officer is within paragraph (a) or (d) of subsection (5) of that section, by a person holding the rank of assistant chief constable in his force;

    (b)   where the authorising officer is within paragraph (b) of that subsection, by a person holding the rank of commander in the metropolitan police force;

    (c)   where the authorising officer is within paragraph (c) of that subsection, by a person holding the rank of commander in the City of London police force;

    (d)   where the authorising officer is within paragraph (e) of that subsection, by a person holding the rank of assistant chief constable in the [Police Service of Northern Ireland];

  [(da) where the authorising officer is within paragraph (ea) of that subsection, by a person holding the rank of deputy or assistant chief constable in the Ministry of Defence Police;

  (db) where the authorising officer is within paragraph (eb) of that subsection, by a person holding the position of assistant Provost Marshal in the Royal Navy Regulating Branch;

(dc)   where the authorising officer is within paragraph (ec) or (ed) of that subsection, by a person holding the position of deputy Provost Marshal in the Royal Military Police or, as the case may be, in the Royal Air Force Police;

(dd)   where the authorising officer is within paragraph (ee) of that subsection, by a person holding the rank of deputy or assistant chief constable in the British Transport Police;]

(e)   where the authorising officer is within paragraph (f) ... of that subsection by a person designated for the purposes of this section by the Director General of the National Criminal Intelligence Service ...;

[(ea)   where the authorising officer is within paragraph (g) of that subsection, by a person designated for the purposes of this paragraph by the Director General of the National Crime Squad as a person entitled to act in an urgent case;]

(f)   where the authorising officer is within paragraph (h) of that subsection, by a customs officer designated by the Commissioners of Customs and Excise for the purposes of this section;

[(g)   where the authorising officer is within paragraph (i) of that subsection, by an officer of the Office of Fair Trading designated by it for the purposes of this section].

(3) A police member of the National Criminal Intelligence Service or the National Crime Squad appointed under section 9(1)(b) or 55(1)(b) may not be designated under subsection (2)(e) [or (2)(ea)] unless [he holds the rank of assistant chief constable in that Service or Squad].

(4) In subsection (1), "designated deputy"–

(a)   in the case of an authorising officer within paragraph (a) or (d) of section 93(5), means the person holding the rank of assistant chief constable designated to act ... under section 12(4) of the Police Act 1996 or, as the case may be, section 5(4) of the Police (Scotland) Act 1967;

(b)   in the case of an authorising officer within paragraph (c) of section 93(5), means the person authorised to act ... under section 25 of the City of London Police Act 1839; ...

(c)   in the case of an authorising officer within paragraph (f) or (g) of section 93(5), means the person designated to act ... under section 8 or 54 [...

(d)   ...].

Notes

Initial Commencement

To be appointed

    To be appointed: see s 135.

Appointment

    Appointment: 22 February 1999: see SI 1999/151, art 2.

Amendment

    Sub-s (1): in para (a) word omitted repealed by the Regulation of Investigatory Powers Act 2000, s 82(2), Sch 5.

    Date in force: 25 September 2000: see SI 2000/2543, art 2.

Sub-s (1): in para (b) words "or (f)" in square brackets substituted by the Regulation of Investigatory Powers Act 2000, s 82(1), Sch 4, para 8(3).

Date in force: 25 September 2000: see SI 2000/2543, art 2.

Sub-s (1): para (c) and word "or" immediately preceding it inserted by the Regulation of Investigatory Powers Act 2000, s 82(1), Sch 4, para 8(3).

Date in force: 25 September 2000: see SI 2000/2543, art 2.

Sub-s (2): in para (d) words "Police Service of Northern Ireland" in square brackets substituted by the Police (Northern Ireland) Act 2000, s 78(1), Sch 6, para 20(1), (2)(b).

Date in force: 4 November 2001: see the Police (Northern Ireland) Act 2000 (Commencement No 3 and Transitional Provisions) Order 2001, SR 2001/396, art 2, Schedule.

Sub-s (2): paras (da)–(dd) inserted by the Regulation of Investigatory Powers Act 2000, s 82(1), Sch 4, para 8(4)(a).

Date in force: 25 September 2000: see SI 2000/2543, art 2.

Sub-s (2): in para (e) first words omitted repealed by the Regulation of Investigatory Powers Act 2000, s 82(1), (2), Sch 4, para 8(4)(b), Sch 5.

Date in force: 25 September 2000: see SI 2000/2543, art 2.

Sub-s (2): in para (e) second words omitted repealed by the Regulation of Investigatory Powers Act 2000, s 82(1), (2), Sch 4, para 8(4)(b), Sch 5.

Date in force: 25 September 2000: see SI 2000/2543, art 2.

Sub-s (2): para (ea) inserted by the Regulation of Investigatory Powers Act 2000, s 82(1), Sch 4, para 8(4)(c).

Date in force: 25 September 2000: see SI 2000/2543, art 2.

Sub-s (2): para (g) inserted by the Enterprise Act 2002, s 200(1), (3).

Date in force: 20 June 2003: see SI 2003/1397, art 2(1), Schedule; for transitional and transitory provisions see the Enterprise Act 2002, s 276, Sch 24, paras 2–6.

Sub-s (3): words "or (2)(ea)" in square brackets inserted by the Regulation of Investigatory Powers Act 2000, s 82(1), Sch 4, para 8(5).

Date in force: 25 September 2000: see SI 2000/2543, art 2.

Sub-s (3): words "he holds the rank of assistant chief constable in that Service or Squad" in square brackets substituted, for paras (a), (b) as originally enacted, by the Crime and Disorder Act 1998, s 113(2).

Date in force: 30 September 1998: see SI 1998/2327, art 2(1)(x).

Sub-s (4): in para (a) words omitted repealed by the Regulation of Investigatory Powers Act 2000, s 82(2), Sch 5.

Date in force: 25 September 2000: see SI 2000/2543, art 2.

Sub-s (4): in para (b) first words omitted repealed by the Regulation of Investigatory Powers Act 2000, s 82(2), Sch 5.

Date in force: 25 September 2000: see SI 2000/2543, art 2.

Sub-s (4): in para (b) second word omitted repealed by the Crime and Disorder Act 1998, ss 113(3), 120(2), Sch 10.

Date in force: 30 September 1998: see SI 1998/2327, art 2(1)(x).

Sub-s (4): in para (c) first words omitted repealed by the Regulation of Investigatory Powers Act 2000, s 82(2), Sch 5.

Date in force: 25 September 2000: see SI 2000/2543, art 2.

Sub-s (4): para (d) inserted by the Crime and Disorder Act 1998, s 113(3).

Date in force: 30 September 1998: see SI 1998/2327, art 2(1)(x).

Sub-s (4): para (d) and word omitted immediately preceding it repealed by the Regulation of Investigatory Powers Act 2000, s 82(2), Sch 5.

Date in force: 25 September 2000: see SI 2000/2543, art 2.

See Further

See further, in relation to reference to the British Transport Police: the Railways and Transport Safety Act 2003, s 73(1), Sch 5, para 4(1), (2)(i).

95 Authorisations: form and duration etc

(1) An authorisation shall be in writing, except that in an urgent case an authorisation (other than one given by virtue of section 94) may be given orally.

(2) An authorisation shall, unless renewed under subsection (3), cease to have effect–

(a)   if given orally or by virtue of section 94, at the end of the period of 72 hours beginning with the time when it took effect;

(b)   in any other case, at the end of the period of three months beginning with the day on which it took effect.

(3) If at any time before an authorisation would cease to have effect the authorising officer who gave the authorisation, or in whose absence it was given, considers it necessary for the authorisation to continue to have effect for the purpose for which it was issued, he may, in writing, renew it for a period of three months beginning with the day on which it would cease to have effect.

(4) A person shall cancel an authorisation given by him if satisfied that [the authorisation is one in relation to which the requirements of paragraphs (a) and (b) of section 93(2) are no longer satisfied].

(5) An authorising officer shall cancel an authorisation given in his absence if satisfied that [the authorisation is one in relation to which the requirements of paragraphs (a) and (b) of section 93(2) are no longer satisfied].

(6) If the authorising officer who gave the authorisation is within paragraph (b)[, (e) or (g)] of section 93(5), the power conferred on that person by subsections (3) and (4) above shall also be exercisable by each of the other persons within the paragraph concerned.

(7) Nothing in this section shall prevent a designated deputy from exercising the powers conferred on an authorising officer within paragraph (a), (c), (d), (f) or (g) of section 93(5) by subsections (3), (4) and (5) above.

Notes

Initial Commencement

To be appointed

To be appointed: see s 135.

Appointment

Appointment: 22 February 1999: see SI 1999/151, art 2.

Amendment

Sub-ss (4), (5): words from "the authorisation is one" to "no longer satisfied" in square brackets substituted by the Regulation of Investigatory Powers Act 2000, s 82(1), Sch 4, para 8(6)(a).

Date in force: 25 September 2000: see SI 2000/2543, art 2.

Sub-s (6): words ", (e) or (g)" in square brackets substituted by the Regulation of Investigatory Powers Act 2000, s 82(1), Sch 4, para 8(6)(b).

Date in force: 25 September 2000: see SI 2000/2543, art 2.

---

96 Notification of authorisations etc

(1) Where a person gives, renews or cancels an authorisation, he shall, as soon as is reasonably practicable and in accordance with arrangements made by the Chief Commissioner, give notice in writing that he has done so to a Commissioner appointed under section 91(1)(b).

(2) Subject to subsection (3), a notice under this section shall specify such matters as the Secretary of State may by order prescribe.

(3) A notice under this section of the giving or renewal of an authorisation shall specify–

(a)   whether section 97 applies to the authorisation or renewal, and

    (b)   where that section does not apply by virtue of subsection (3) of that section, the grounds on which the case is believed to be one of urgency.

(4) Where a notice is given to a Commissioner under this section, he shall, as soon as is reasonably practicable, scrutinise the notice.

(5) An order under subsection (2) shall be made by statutory instrument.

(6) A statutory instrument which contains an order under subsection (2) shall not be made unless a draft has been laid before, and approved by a resolution of, each House of Parliament.

Notes

Initial Commencement

To be appointed
> To be appointed: see s 135.

Appointment
> Appointment (for certain purposes): 1 September 1997: see SI 1997/1930, art 2(2)(h).
> Appointment (for remaining purposes): 22 February 1999: see SI 1999/151, art 2.

Authorisations requiring approval

97 Authorisations requiring approval

(1) An authorisation to which this section applies shall not take effect until–

    (a)   it has been approved in accordance with this section by a Commissioner appointed under section 91(1)(b), and

    (b)   the person who gave the authorisation has been notified under subsection (4).

(2) Subject to subsection (3), this section applies to an authorisation if, at the time it is given, the person who gives it believes–

    (a)   that any of the property specified in the authorisation–

        (i)   is used wholly or mainly as a dwelling or as a bedroom in a hotel, or

        (ii)   constitutes office premises, or

    (b)   that the action authorised by it is likely to result in any person acquiring knowledge of–

        (i)   matters subject to legal privilege,

        (ii)   confidential personal information, or

        (iii)   confidential journalistic material.

(3) This section does not apply to an authorisation where the person who gives it believes that the case is one of urgency.

(4) Where a Commissioner receives a notice under section 96 which specifies that this section applies to the authorisation, he shall as soon as is reasonably practicable–

    (a)   decide whether to approve the authorisation or refuse approval, and

    (b)   give written notice of his decision to the person who gave the authorisation.

(5) A Commissioner shall approve an authorisation if, and only if, he is satisfied that there are reasonable grounds for believing the matters specified in section 93(2).

(6) Where a Commissioner refuses to approve an authorisation, he shall, as soon as is reasonably practicable, make a report of his findings to the authorising officer who gave it or in whose absence it was given …

[(6A) The reference in subsection (6) to the authorising officer who gave the authorisation or in whose absence it was given shall be construed, in the case of an authorisation given by or in the absence of a person within paragraph (b), (e) or (g) of section 93(5), as a reference to the Commissioner of Police, Chief Constable or, as the case may be, Director General mentioned in the paragraph concerned.]

(7) This section shall apply in relation to a renewal of an authorisation as it applies in relation to an authorisation (the references in subsection (2)(a) and (b) to the authorisation being construed as references to the authorisation renewed).

(8) In this section–

> "office premises" has the meaning given in section 1(2) of the Offices, Shops and Railway Premises Act 1963;

> "hotel" means premises used for the reception of guests who desire to sleep in the premises.

Notes

Initial Commencement

To be appointed
> To be appointed: see s 135.

Appointment
> Appointment: 22 February 1999: see SI 1999/151, art 2.

Amendment
> Sub-s (6): words omitted repealed by the Regulation of Investigatory Powers Act 2000, s 82(1), (2), Sch 4, para 8(7), Sch 5.
> Date in force: 25 September 2000: see SI 2000/2543, art 2.
> Sub-s (6A): inserted by the Regulation of Investigatory Powers Act 2000, s 82(1), Sch 4, para 8(7).
> Date in force: 25 September 2000: see SI 2000/2543, art 2.

---

98 Matters subject to legal privilege

(1) Subject to subsection (5) below, in section 97 "matters subject to legal privilege" means matters to which subsection (2), (3) or (4) below applies.

(2) This subsection applies to communications between a professional legal adviser and–

(a)   his client, or

(b)   any person representing his client,

which are made in connection with the giving of legal advice to the client.

(3) This subsection applies to communications–

(a)   between a professional legal adviser and his client or any person representing his client, or

(b)   between a professional legal adviser or his client or any such representative and any other person, which are made in connection with or in contemplation of legal proceedings and for the purposes of such proceedings.

(4) This subsection applies to items enclosed with or referred to in communications of the kind mentioned in subsection (2) or (3) and made–

    (a)   in connection with the giving of legal advice, or

    (b)   in connection with or in contemplation of legal proceedings and for the purposes of such proceedings.

(5) For the purposes of section 97–

    (a)   communications and items are not matters subject to legal privilege when they are in the possession of a person who is not entitled to possession of them, and

    (b)   communications and items held, or oral communications made, with the intention of furthering a criminal purpose are not matters subject to legal privilege.

Notes

Initial Commencement

To be appointed
> To be appointed: see s 135.

Appointment
> Appointment: 22 February 1999: see SI 1999/151, art 2.

---

99 Confidential personal information

(1) In section 97 "confidential personal information" means–

    (a)   personal information which a person has acquired or created in the course of any trade, business, profession or other occupation or for the purposes of any paid or unpaid office, and which he holds in confidence, and

    (b)   communications as a result of which personal information–

        (i)   is acquired or created as mentioned in paragraph (a), and

        (ii) is held in confidence.

(2) For the purposes of this section "personal information" means information concerning an individual (whether living or dead) who can be identified from it and relating–

    (a)   to his physical or mental health, or

    (b)   to spiritual counselling or assistance given or to be given to him.

(3) A person holds information in confidence for the purposes of this section if he holds it subject–

    (a)   to an express or implied undertaking to hold it in confidence, or

    (b)   to a restriction on disclosure or an obligation of secrecy contained in any enactment (including an enactment contained in an Act passed after this Act).

Notes

Initial Commencement

To be appointed

> To be appointed: see s 135.

Appointment

> Appointment: 22 February 1999: see SI 1999/151, art 2.

100 Confidential journalistic material

(1) In section 97 "confidential journalistic material" means–

   (a)   material acquired or created for the purposes of journalism which–

      (i)   is in the possession of persons who acquired or created it for those purposes,

      (ii)   is held subject to an undertaking, restriction or obligation of the kind mentioned in section 99(3), and

      (iii)   has been continuously held (by one or more persons) subject to such an undertaking, restriction or obligation since it was first acquired or created for the purposes of journalism, and

   (b)   communications as a result of which information is acquired for the purposes of journalism and held as mentioned in paragraph (a)(ii).

(2) For the purposes of subsection (1), a person who receives material, or acquires information, from someone who intends that the recipient shall use it for the purposes of journalism is to be taken to have acquired it for those purposes.

Notes

Initial Commencement

To be appointed

> To be appointed: see s 135.

Appointment

> Appointment: 22 February 1999: see SI 1999/151, art 2.

...

Notes

Amendment

> Repealed by virtue of the Regulation of Investigatory Powers Act 2000, s 82(2), Sch 5.
> Date in force: 25 September 2000: see SI 2000/2543, art 2.

101 ...

...

Notes

Amendment

> Repealed by the Regulation of Investigatory Powers Act 2000, s 82(2), Sch 5.
> Date in force: 25 September 2000: see SI 2000/2543, art 2.

Complaints etc

102 ...

...

Notes

Amendment

Repealed by the Regulation of Investigatory Powers Act 2000, s 82(2), Sch 5.

Date in force: 2 October 2000 (except in relation to a complaint made to a Surveillance Commissioner before that date): see SI 2000/2543, art 6(1)(d), (5).

103 Quashing of authorisations etc

(1) Where, at any time, a Commissioner appointed under section 91(1)(b) is satisfied that, at the time an authorisation was given or renewed, there were no reasonable grounds for believing the matters specified in section 93(2), he may quash the authorisation or, as the case may be, renewal.

(2) Where, in the case of an authorisation or renewal to which section 97 does not apply, a Commissioner appointed under section 91(1)(b) is at any time satisfied that, at the time the authorisation was given or, as the case may be, renewed,–

(a) there were reasonable grounds for believing any of the matters specified in subsection (2) of section 97, and

(b) there were no reasonable grounds for believing the case to be one of urgency for the purposes of subsection (3) of that section,

he may quash the authorisation or, as the case may be, renewal.

(3) Where a Commissioner quashes an authorisation or renewal under subsection (1) or (2), he may order the destruction of any records relating to information obtained by virtue of the authorisation (or, in the case of a renewal, relating wholly or partly to information so obtained after the renewal) other than records required for pending criminal or civil proceedings.

(4) If a Commissioner appointed under section 91(1)(b) is satisfied that, at any time after an authorisation was given or, in the case of an authorisation renewed under section 95, after it was renewed, there were no reasonable grounds for believing the matters specified in section 93(2), he may cancel the authorisation.

(5) Where–

(a) an authorisation has ceased to have effect (otherwise than by virtue of subsection (1) or (2)), and

(b) a Commissioner appointed under section 91(1)(b) is satisfied that, at any time during the period of the authorisation, there were no reasonable grounds for believing the matters specified in section 93(2),

he may order the destruction of any records relating, wholly or partly, to information which was obtained by virtue of the authorisation after that time (other than records required for pending criminal or civil proceedings).

(6) Where a Commissioner exercises his powers under subsection (1), (2) or (4), he shall, if he is satisfied that there are reasonable grounds for doing so, order that the authorisation shall be effective, for such period as he shall specify, so far as it authorises the taking of action to retrieve anything left on property in accordance with the authorisation.

(7) Where a Commissioner exercises a power conferred by this section, he shall, as soon as is reasonably practicable, make a report of his findings–

    (a)   to the authorising officer who gave the authorisation or in whose absence it was given, and

    (b)   to the Chief Commissioner;

[and subsection (6A) of section 97 shall apply for the purposes of this subsection as it applies for the purposes of subsection (6) of that section].

(8) Where–

    (a)   a decision is made under subsection (1) or (2) and an order for the destruction of records is made under subsection (3), or

    (b)   a decision to order the destruction of records is made under subsection (5),

the order shall not become operative until the period for appealing against the decision has expired and, where an appeal is made, a decision dismissing it has been made by the Chief Commissioner.

(9) A Commissioner may exercise any of the powers conferred by this section notwithstanding any approval given under section 97.

Notes

Initial Commencement

To be appointed

    To be appointed: see s 135.

Appointment

    Appointment: 22 February 1999: see SI 1999/151, art 2.

Amendment

    Sub-s (7): words from "and subsection (6A)" to "of that section" in square brackets substituted by the Regulation of Investigatory Powers Act 2000, s 82(1), Sch 4, para 8(8).

    Date in force: 25 September 2000: see SI 2000/2543, art 2.

Appeals

104 Appeals by authorising officers

(1) An authorising officer who gives an authorisation, or in whose absence it is given, may, within the prescribed period, appeal to the Chief Commissioner against–

    (a)   any refusal to approve the authorisation or any renewal of it under section 97;

    (b)   any decision to quash the authorisation, or any renewal of it, under subsection (1) of section 103;

    (c)   any decision to quash the authorisation, or any renewal of it, under subsection (2) of that section;

    (d)   any decision to cancel the authorisation under subsection (4) of that section;

    (e)   any decision to order the destruction of records under subsection (5) of that section;

    (f)   any refusal to make an order under subsection (6) of that section;

(g)   ...

(2) In subsection (1), "the prescribed period" means the period of seven days beginning with the day on which the refusal, decision or, as the case may be, determination appealed against is reported to the authorising officer.

(3) In determining an appeal within subsection (1)(a), the Chief Commissioner shall, if he is satisfied that there are reasonable grounds for believing the matters specified in section 93(2), allow the appeal and direct the Commissioner to approve the authorisation or renewal under that section.

(4) In determining–

    (a)   an appeal within subsection (1)(b), ...

    (b)   ...

the Chief Commissioner shall allow the appeal unless he is satisfied that, at the time the authorisation was given or, as the case may be, renewed there were no reasonable grounds for believing the matters specified in section 93(2).

(5) In determining–

    (a)   an appeal within subsection (1)(c), ...

    (b)   ...

the Chief Commissioner shall allow the appeal unless he is satisfied as mentioned in section 103(2).

(6) In determining–

    (a)   an appeal within subsection (1)(d) or (e), ...

    (b)   ...

the Chief Commissioner shall allow the appeal unless he is satisfied that at the time to which the decision relates there were no reasonable grounds for believing the matters specified in section 93(2).

(7) In determining an appeal within subsection (1)(f), the Chief Commissioner shall allow the appeal and order that the authorisation shall be effective to the extent mentioned in section 103(6), for such period as he shall specify, if he is satisfied that there are reasonable grounds for making such an order.

(8) Where an appeal is allowed under this section, the Chief Commissioner shall–

    (a)   in the case of an appeal within subsection (1)(b) or (c), also quash any order made by the Commissioner to destroy records relating to information obtained by virtue of the authorisation concerned, ...

    (b)   ...

Notes

Initial Commencement

To be appointed
> To be appointed: see s 135.

Appointment
> Appointment: 22 February 1999: see SI 1999/151, art 2.

Amendment
> Sub-s (1): para (g) repealed by the Regulation of Investigatory Powers Act 2000, s 82(2), Sch 5.
> Date in force: 25 September 2000: see SI 2000/2543, art 2.

Sub-ss (4)–(6): para (b) and word omitted immediately preceding it repealed by the Regulation of Investigatory Powers Act 2000, s 82(2), Sch 5.

Date in force: 25 September 2000: see SI 2000/2543, art 2.

Sub-s (8): para (b) and word omitted immediately preceding it repealed by the Regulation of Investigatory Powers Act 2000, s 82(2), Sch 5.

Date in force: 25 September 2000: see SI 2000/2543, art 2.

105 Appeals by authorising officers: supplementary

(1) Where the Chief Commissioner determines an appeal under section 104–

    (a)   he shall give notice of his determination–

        (i)   to the authorising officer concerned, [and]

        (ii)   to the Commissioner against whose refusal, decision or determination the appeal was made, ...

        (iii)   ...

    (b)   if he dismisses the appeal, he shall make a report of his findings–

        (i)   to the authorising officer concerned,

        (ii)   to the Commissioner against whose refusal, decision or determination the appeal was made, and

        (iii)   under section 107(2), to the Prime Minister [and the Scottish Ministers].

(2) Subject to subsection (1)(b), the Chief Commissioner shall not give any reasons for a determination under section 104.

(3) Nothing in section 104 shall prevent a designated deputy from exercising the powers conferred by subsection (1) of that section on an authorising officer within paragraph (a), (c), (d), (f) or (g) of section 93(5).

Notes

Initial Commencement

To be appointed

To be appointed: see s 135.

Appointment

Appointment: 22 February 1999: see SI 1999/151, art 2.

Amendment

Sub-s (1): in para (a) word "and" in square brackets inserted by the Regulation of Investigatory Powers Act 2000, s 82(1), Sch 4, para 8(9).

Date in force: 25 September 2000: see SI 2000/2543, art 2.

Sub-s (1): sub-para (iii) and word omitted immediately preceding it repealed by the Regulation of Investigatory Powers Act 2000, s 82(1), (2), Sch 4, para 8(9), Sch 5.

Date in force: 25 September 2000: see SI 2000/2543, art 2.

Sub-s (1): in para (b)(iii) words "and the Scottish Ministers" in square brackets inserted by SI 1999/1747, art 3, Sch 6, Pt II, para 2(1), (3).

Date in force: 1 July 1999: see SI 1999/1747, art 1, and SI 1998/3178, art 3.

106 ...

...

Notes

Amendment

Repealed by the Regulation of Investigatory Powers Act 2000, s 82(2), Sch 5.
Date in force: 25 September 2000: see SI 2000/2543, art 2.

General

107 Supplementary provisions relating to Commissioners

(1) The Chief Commissioner shall keep under review the performance of functions under this Part.

(2) The Chief Commissioner shall make an annual report on [the matters with which he is concerned] to the Prime Minister [and to the Scottish Ministers] and may at any time report to him [or them (as the case may require)] on [anything relating to any of those matters].

(3) The Prime Minister shall lay before each House of Parliament a copy of each annual report made by the Chief Commissioner under subsection (2) together with a statement as to whether any matter has been excluded from that copy in pursuance of subsection (4) below.

[(3A) The Scottish Ministers shall lay before the Scottish Parliament a copy of each annual report made by the Chief Commissioner under subsection (2), together with a statement as to whether any matter has been excluded from that copy in pursuance of subsection (4) below.]

(4) The Prime Minister may exclude a matter from the copy of a report as laid before each House of Parliament, if it appears to him, after consultation with the Chief Commissioner [and the Scottish Ministers], that the publication of that matter in the report would be prejudicial to [any of the purposes for which authorisations may be given or granted under this Part of this Act or Part II of the Regulation of Investigatory Powers Act 2000 or under any enactment contained in or made under an Act of the Scottish Parliament which makes provision equivalent to that made by Part II of that Act of 2000 or] to the discharge of–

(a)   the functions of any police authority,

(b)   the functions of the Service Authority for the National Criminal Intelligence Service or the Service Authority for the National Crime Squad, or

(c)   the duties of the Commissioners of Customs and Excise.

(5) Any person having functions under this Part, and any person taking action in relation to which an authorisation was given, shall comply with any request of a Commissioner for documents or information required by him for the purpose of enabling him to discharge his functions.

[(5A) It shall be the duty of–

(a)   every person by whom, or on whose application, there has been given or granted any authorisation the function of giving or granting which is subject to review by the Chief Commissioner,

(b)   every person who has engaged in conduct with the authority of such an authorisation,

(c)   every person who holds or has held any office, rank or position with the same public authority as a person falling within paragraph (a),

(d)   every person who holds or has held any office, rank or position with any public authority for whose benefit (within the meaning of Part II of the Regulation of Investigatory Powers Act 2000) activities which are or may be subject to any such review have been or may be carried out, and

(e)   every person to whom a notice under section 49 of the Regulation of Investigatory Powers Act 2000 (notices imposing a disclosure requirement in respect of information protected by a key) has been given in relation to any information obtained by conduct to which such an authorisation relates,

to disclose or provide to the Chief Commissioner all such documents and information as he may require for the purpose of enabling him to carry out his functions.

(5B) It shall be the duty of every Commissioner to give the tribunal established under section 65 of the Regulation of Investigatory Powers Act 2000 all such assistance (including his opinion as to any issue falling to be determined by that tribunal) as that tribunal may require–

(a)   in connection with the investigation of any matter by that tribunal; or

(b)   otherwise for the purposes of that tribunal's consideration or determination of any matter.

(5C) In this section "public authority" means any public authority within the meaning of section 6 of the Human Rights Act 1998 (acts of public authorities) other than a court or tribunal.]

(6)   ...

Notes

Initial Commencement

To be appointed
To be appointed: see s 135.

Appointment
Appointment: 22 February 1999: see SI 1999/151, art 2.

Amendment
Sub-s (2): words "the matters with which he is concerned" in square brackets substituted by the Regulation of Investigatory Powers Act 2000, s 82(1), Sch 4, para 8(10)(a)(i).

Date in force: 25 September 2000: see SI 2000/2543, art 2.

Sub-s (2): words "and to the Scottish Ministers" in square brackets inserted by SI 1999/1747, art 3, Sch 6, Pt II, para 2(1), (5)(a)(i).

Date in force: 1 July 1999: see SI 1999/1747, art 1, and SI 1998/3178, art 3.

Sub-s (2): words "or them (as the case may require)" in square brackets inserted by SI 1999/1747, art 3, Sch 6, Pt II, para 2(1), (5)(a)(ii).

Date in force: 1 July 1999: see SI 1999/1747, art 1, and SI 1998/3178, art 3.

Sub-s (2): words "anything relating to any of those matters" in square brackets substituted by the Regulation of Investigatory Powers Act 2000, s 82(1), Sch 4, para 8(10)(a)(ii).

Date in force: 25 September 2000: see SI 2000/2543, art 2.

Sub-s (3A): inserted by SI 1999/1747, art 3, Sch 6, Pt II, para 2(1), (5)(b).

Date in force: 1 July 1999: see SI 1999/1747, art 1, and SI 1998/3178, art 3.

Sub-s (4): words "and the Scottish Ministers" in square brackets inserted by SI 1999/1747, art 3, Sch 6, Pt II, para 2(1), (5)(c).

Date in force: 1 July 1999: see SI 1999/1747, art 1, and SI 1998/3178, art 3.

Sub-s (4): words from "any of the purposes" to "Act of 2000 or" in square brackets substituted by the Regulation of Investigatory Powers Act 2000, s 82(1), Sch 4, para 8(10)(b).

Date in force: 25 September 2000: see SI 2000/2543, art 2.

Sub-ss (5A)–(5C): inserted by the Regulation of Investigatory Powers Act 2000, s 82(1), Sch 4, para 8(10)(c), (11).

Date in force: 25 September 2000: see SI 2000/2543, art 2.

Sub-s (6): repealed by the Regulation of Investigatory Powers Act 2000, s 82(2), Sch 5.

Date in force: 25 September 2000: see SI 2000/2543, art 2.

108 Interpretation of Part III

(1) In this Part–

["Assistant Commissioner of Police of the Metropolis" includes the Deputy Commissioner of Police of the Metropolis;]

"authorisation" means an authorisation under section 93;

"authorising officer" has the meaning given by section 93(5);

"criminal proceedings" includes–

(a) proceedings in the United Kingdom or elsewhere before a court-martial constituted under the Army Act 1955, the Air Force Act 1955 or the Naval Discipline Act 1957 ...,

(b) proceedings before the Courts-Martial Appeal Court, and

(c) proceedings before a Standing Civilian Court;

"customs officer" means an officer commissioned by the Commissioners of Customs and Excise under section 6(3) of the Customs and Excise Management Act 1979;

"designated deputy" has the meaning given in section 94(4);

"United Kingdom waters" has the meaning given in section 30(5) of the Police Act 1996; and

"wireless telegraphy" has the same meaning as in the Wireless Telegraphy Act 1949 and, in relation to wireless telegraphy, "interfere" has the same meaning as in that Act.

(2) Where, under this Part, notice of any matter is required to be given in writing, the notice may be transmitted by electronic means.

(3) For the purposes of this Part, an authorisation (or renewal) given–

(a) by the designated deputy of an authorising officer, or

(b) by a person on whom an authorising officer's powers are conferred by section 94,

shall be treated as an authorisation (or renewal) given in the absence of the authorising officer concerned; and references to the authorising officer in whose absence an authorisation (or renewal) was given shall be construed accordingly.

Notes

Initial Commencement

To be appointed

To be appointed: see s 135.

Appointment

Appointment: 22 February 1999: see SI 1999/151, art 2.

Amendment

Sub-s (1): definition "Assistant Commissioner of Police of the Metropolis" inserted by the Regulation of Investigatory Powers Act 2000, s 82(1), Sch 4, para 8(12).

Date in force: 25 September 2000: see SI 2000/2543, art 2.

Sub-s (1): in definition "criminal proceedings" in para (a) words omitted repealed by the Armed Forces Act 2001, s 38, Sch 7, Pt 1.

Date in force: 28 February 2002: see SI 2002/345, art 2.

INTELLIGENCE SERVICES ACT 1994

1994 CHAPTER 13

An Act to make provision about the Secret Intelligence Service and the Government Communications Headquarters, including provision for the issue of warrants and authorisations enabling certain actions to be taken and for the issue of such warrants and authorisations to be kept under review; to make further provision about warrants issued on applications by the Security Service; to establish a procedure for the investigation of complaints about the Secret Intelligence Service and the Government Communications Headquarters; to make provision for the establishment of an Intelligence and Security Committee to scrutinise all three of those bodies; and for connected purposes

[26th May 1994]

BE IT ENACTED by the Queen's most Excellent Majesty, by and with the advice and consent of the Lords Spiritual and Temporal, and Commons, in this present Parliament assembled, and by the authority of the same, as follows:–

The Secret Intelligence Service

1 The Secret Intelligence Service

(1) There shall continue to be a Secret Intelligence Service (in this Act referred to as "the Intelligence Service") under the authority of the Secretary of State; and, subject to subsection (2) below, its functions shall be–

    (a)   to obtain and provide information relating to the actions or intentions of persons outside the British Islands; and

    (b)   to perform other tasks relating to the actions or intentions of such persons.

(2) The functions of the Intelligence Service shall be exercisable only–

    (a)   in the interests of national security, with particular reference to the defence and foreign policies of Her Majesty's Government in the United Kingdom; or

    (b)   in the interests of the economic well-being of the United Kingdom; or

    (c)   in support of the prevention or detection of serious crime.

Notes

Initial Commencement

To be appointed
    To be appointed: see s 12(2).

Appointment
    Appointment (for the purposes of making any Orders in Council under s 12(4) hereof): 2 November 1994: see SI 1994/2734, art 2.
    Appointment (for remaining purposes): 15 December 1994: see SI 1994/2734, art 2.

---

2 The Chief of the Intelligence Service

(1) The operations of the Intelligence Service shall continue to be under the control of a Chief of that Service appointed by the Secretary of State.

(2) The Chief of the Intelligence Service shall be responsible for the efficiency of that Service and it shall be his duty to ensure–

(a)   that there are arrangements for securing that no information is obtained by the Intelligence Service except so far as necessary for the proper discharge of its functions and that no information is disclosed by it except so far as necessary–

   (i)   for that purpose;

   (ii)   in the interests of national security;

   (iii)   for the purpose of the prevention or detection of serious crime; or

   (iv)   for the purpose of any criminal proceedings; and

(b)   that the Intelligence Service does not take any action to further the interests of any United Kingdom political party.

(3)   Without prejudice to the generality of subsection (2)(a) above, the disclosure of information shall be regarded as necessary for the proper discharge of the functions of the Intelligence Service if it consists of–

(a)   the disclosure of records subject to and in accordance with the Public Records Act 1958; or

(b)   the disclosure, subject to and in accordance with arrangements approved by the Secretary of State, of information to the Comptroller and Auditor General for the purposes of his functions.

(4)   The Chief of the Intelligence Service shall make an annual report on the work of the Intelligence Service to the Prime Minister and the Secretary of State and may at any time report to either of them on any matter relating to its work.

Notes

Initial Commencement

To be appointed
   To be appointed: see s 12(2).

Appointment
   Appointment (for remaining purposes): 15 December 1994: see SI 1994/2734, art 2.
   Appointment (for the purposes of making any Orders in Council under s 12(4) hereof): 2 November 1994: see SI 1994/2734, art 2.

GCHQ

3   The Government Communications Headquarters

(1)   There shall continue to be a Government Communications Headquarters under the authority of the Secretary of State; and, subject to subsection (2) below, its functions shall be–

(a)   to monitor or interfere with electromagnetic, acoustic and other emissions and any equipment producing such emissions and to obtain and provide information derived from or related to such emissions or equipment and from encrypted material; and

(b)   to provide advice and assistance about–

   (i)   languages, including terminology used for technical matters, and

   (ii)   cryptography and other matters relating to the protection of information and other material, to the armed forces of the Crown, to Her Majesty's Government in the United Kingdom or to a Northern Ireland Department or to any other organisation which is determined for the purposes of this section in such manner as may be specified by the Prime Minister.

(2) The functions referred to in subsection (1)(a) above shall be exercisable only–

(a) in the interests of national security, with particular reference to the defence and foreign policies of Her Majesty's Government in the United Kingdom; or

(b) in the interests of the economic well-being of the United Kingdom in relation to the actions or intentions of persons outside the British Islands; or

(c) in support of the prevention or detection of serious crime.

(3) In this Act the expression "GCHQ" refers to the Government Communications Headquarters and to any unit or part of a unit of the armed forces of the Crown which is for the time being required by the Secretary of State to assist the Government Communications Headquarters in carrying out its functions.

Notes

Initial Commencement

To be appointed
To be appointed: see s 12(2).

Appointment
Appointment (for the purposes of making any Orders in Council under s 12(4) hereof): 2 November 1994: see SI 1994/2734, art 2.

Appointment (for remaining purposes): 15 December 1994: see SI 1994/2734, art 2.

---

4 The Director of GCHQ

(1) The operations of GCHQ shall continue to be under the control of a Director appointed by the Secretary of State.

(2) The Director shall be responsible for the efficiency of GCHQ and it shall be his duty to ensure–

(a) that there are arrangements for securing that no information is obtained by GCHQ except so far as necessary for the proper discharge of its functions and that no information is disclosed by it except so far as necessary for that purpose or for the purpose of any criminal proceedings; and

(b) that GCHQ does not take any action to further the interests of any United Kingdom political party.

(3) Without prejudice to the generality of subsection (2)(a) above, the disclosure of information shall be regarded as necessary for the proper discharge of the functions of GCHQ if it consists of–

(a) the disclosure of records subject to and in accordance with the Public Records Act 1958; or

(b) the disclosure, subject to and in accordance with arrangements approved by the Secretary of State, of information to the Comptroller and Auditor General for the purposes of his functions.

(4) The Director shall make an annual report on the work of GCHQ to the Prime Minister and the Secretary of State and may at any time report to either of them on any matter relating to its work.

Notes

Initial Commencement

To be appointed

> To be appointed: see s 12(2).

Appointment

> Appointment (for the purposes of making any Orders in Council under s 12(4) hereof): 2 November 1994: see SI 1994/2734, art 2.
>
> Appointment (for remaining purposes): 15 December 1994: see SI 1994/2734, art 2.

Authorisation of certain actions

5 Warrants: general

(1) No entry on or interference with property or with wireless telegraphy shall be unlawful if it is authorised by a warrant issued by the Secretary of State under this section.

(2) The Secretary of State may, on an application made by the Security Service, the Intelligence Service or GCHQ, issue a warrant under this section authorising the taking, subject to subsection (3) below, of such action as is specified in the warrant in respect of any property so specified or in respect of wireless telegraphy so specified if the Secretary of State–

    (a)   thinks it necessary for the action to be taken [for the purpose of] assisting, as the case may be,–

        (i)   the Security Service in carrying out any of its functions under the 1989 Act; or

        (ii)   the Intelligence Service in carrying out any of its functions under section 1 above; or

        (iii)   GCHQ in carrying out any function which falls within section 3(1)(a) above; and

    [(b)   is satisfied that the taking of the action is proportionate to what the action seeks to achieve;] and

    (c)   is satisfied that satisfactory arrangements are in force under section 2(2)(a) of the 1989 Act (duties of the Director-General of the Security Service), section 2(2)(a) above or section 4(2)(a) above with respect to the disclosure of information obtained by virtue of this section and that any information obtained under the warrant will be subject to those arrangements.

[(2A) The matters to be taken into account in considering whether the requirements of subsection (2)(a) and (b) are satisfied in the case of any warrant shall include whether what it is thought necessary to achieve by the conduct authorised by the warrant could reasonably be achieved by other means.]

[(3) A warrant issued on the application of the Intelligence Service or GCHQ for the purposes of the exercise of their functions by virtue of section 1(2)(c) or 3(2)(c) above may not relate to property in the British Islands.

(3A) A warrant issued on the application of the Security Service for the purposes of the exercise of their function under section 1(4) of the Security Service Act 1989 may not relate to property in the British Islands unless it authorises the taking of action in relation to conduct within subsection (3B) below.

(3B) Conduct is within this subsection if it constitutes (or, if it took place in the United Kingdom, would constitute) one or more offences, and either–

    (a)   it involves the use of violence, results in substantial financial gain or is conduct by a large number of persons in pursuit of a common purpose; or

    (b)   the offence or one of the offences is an offence for which a person who has attained the age of twenty-one [(eighteen in relation to England and Wales)] and has no previous convictions could reasonably be expected to be sentenced to imprisonment for a term of three years or more.]

(4) Subject to subsection (5) below, the Security Service may make an application under subsection (2) above for a warrant to be issued authorising that Service (or a person acting on its behalf) to take such action as is specified in the warrant on behalf of the Intelligence Service or GCHQ and, where such a warrant is issued, the functions of the Security Service shall include the carrying out of the action so specified, whether or not it would otherwise be within its functions.

(5) The Security Service may not make an application for a warrant by virtue of subsection (4) above except where the action proposed to be authorised by the warrant–

    (a)   is action in respect of which the Intelligence Service or, as the case may be, GCHQ could make such an application; and

    (b)   is to be taken otherwise than in support of the prevention or detection of serious crime.

Notes

Initial Commencement

To be appointed
    To be appointed: see s 12(2).

Appointment
    Appointment (for the purposes of making any Orders in Council under s 12(4) hereof): 2 November 1994: see SI 1994/2734, art 2.
    Appointment (for remaining purposes): 15 December 1994: see SI 1994/2734, art 2.

Amendment
    Sub-s (2): in para (a) words "for the purpose of" in square brackets substituted by the Regulation of Investigatory Powers Act 2000, s 74(1)(a).
    Date in force: 25 September 2000: see SI 2000/2543, art 2.
    Sub-s (2): para (b) substituted by the Regulation of Investigatory Powers Act 2000, s 74(1)(b).
    Date in force: 25 September 2000: see SI 2000/2543, art 2.
    Sub-s (2A): inserted by the Regulation of Investigatory Powers Act 2000, s 74(2).
    Date in force: 25 September 2000: see SI 2000/2543, art 2.
    Sub-ss (3)–(3B): substituted, for sub-s (3) as originally enacted, by the Security Service Act 1996 s 2.
    Sub-s (3B): in para (b) words "(eighteen in relation to England and Wales)" in square brackets inserted by the Criminal Justice and Court Services Act 2000, s 74, Sch 7, Pt II, para 119.
    Date in force: to be appointed: see the Criminal Justice and Court Services Act 2000, s 80(1).

Transfer of Functions
Functions under this section: certain functions under this section are transferred, in so far as they are exercisable in or as regards Scotland, to the Scottish Ministers, by the Scotland Act 1998 (Transfer of Functions to the Scottish Ministers etc) Order 1999, SI 1999/1750, art 2, Sch 1.

6 Warrants: procedure and duration, etc

(1) A warrant shall not be issued except–

    (a) under the hand of the Secretary of State [or, in the case of a warrant by the Scottish Ministers (by virtue of provision made under section 63 of the Scotland Act 1998), a member of the Scottish Executive]; or

    (b) in an urgent case where the Secretary of State has expressly authorised its issue and a statement of that fact is endorsed on it, under the hand of a senior official ... [; or

    (c) in an urgent case where, the Scottish Ministers have (by virtue of provision made under section 63 of the Scotland Act 1998) expressly authorised its issue and a statement of that fact is endorsed thereon, under the hand of a member of the staff of the Scottish Administration who is in the Senior Civil Service and is designated by the Scottish Ministers as a person under whose hand a warrant may be issued in such a case].

(2) A warrant shall, unless renewed under subsection (3) below, cease to have effect–

    (a) if the warrant was under the hand of the Secretary of State [or, in the case of a warrant issued by the Scottish Ministers (by virtue of provision made under section 63 of the Scotland Act 1998), a member of the Scottish Executive], at the end of the period of six months beginning with the day on which it was issued; and

    (b) in any other case, at the end of the period ending with the second working day following that day.

(3) If at any time before the day on which a warrant would cease to have effect the Secretary of State considers it necessary for the warrant to continue to have effect for the purpose for which it was issued, he may by an instrument under his hand renew it for a period of six months beginning with that day.

(4) The Secretary of State shall cancel a warrant if he is satisfied that the action authorised by it is no longer necessary.

(5) In the preceding provisions of this section "warrant" means a warrant under section 5 above.

(6) As regards the Security Service, this section and section 5 above have effect in place of section 3 (property warrants) of the 1989 Act, and accordingly–

    (a) a warrant issued under that section of the 1989 Act and current when this section and section 5 above come into force shall be treated as a warrant under section 5 above, but without any change in the date on which the warrant was in fact issued or last renewed; and

    (b) ... .

Notes

Initial Commencement

To be appointed
To be appointed: see s 12(2).

Appointment

Appointment (for the purposes of making any Orders in Council under s 12(4) hereof): 2 November 1994: see SI 1994/2734, art 2.

Appointment (for remaining purposes): 15 December 1994: see SI 1994/2734, art 2.

Amendment

Sub-s (1): in para (a) words "or, in the case of a warrant by the Scottish Ministers (by virtue of provision made under section 63 of the Scotland Act 1998), a member of the Scottish Executive" in square brackets inserted by SI 1999/1750, art 6(1), Sch 5, para 14(1), (2)(a)(i).

Date in force: 1 July 1999: see SI 1999/1750, art 1(1), and SI 1998/3178, art 3.

Sub-s (1): in para (b) words omitted repealed by the Regulation of Investigatory Powers Act 2000, ss 74(3), 82(2), Sch 5.

Date in force: 25 September 2000: see SI 2000/2543, art 2.

Sub-s (1): para (c) inserted by SI 1999/1750, art 6(1), Sch 5, para 14(1), (2)(a)(ii).

Date in force: 1 July 1999: see SI 1999/1750, art 1(1), and SI 1998/3178, art 3.

Sub-s (2): in para (a) words "or, in the case of a warrant issued by the Scottish Ministers (by virtue of provision made under section 63 of the Scotland Act 1998), a member of the Scottish Executive" in square brackets inserted by SI 1999/1750, art 6(1), Sch 5, para 14(1), (2)(b).

Date in force: 1 July 1999: see SI 1999/1750, art 1(1), and SI 1998/3178, art 3.

Sub-s (6): para (b) repeals the Security Service Act 1989, s 3.

Transfer of Functions

Functions under this section: certain functions under sub-ss (3) and (4) are transferred, in so far as they are exercisable in or as regards Scotland, to the Scottish Ministers, by the Scotland Act 1998 (Transfer of Functions to the Scottish Ministers etc) Order 1999, SI 1999/1750, art 2, Sch 1.

7 Authorisation of acts outside the British Islands

(1) If, apart from this section, a person would be liable in the United Kingdom for any act done outside the British Islands, he shall not be so liable if the act is one which is authorised to be done by virtue of an authorisation given by the Secretary of State under this section.

(2) In subsection (1) above "liable in the United Kingdom" means liable under the criminal or civil law of any part of the United Kingdom.

(3) The Secretary of State shall not give an authorisation under this section unless he is satisfied–

   (a)   that any acts which may be done in reliance on the authorisation or, as the case may be, the operation in the course of which the acts may be done will be necessary for the proper discharge of a function of the Intelligence Service [or GCHQ]; and

   (b)   that there are satisfactory arrangements in force to secure–

      (i)   that nothing will be done in reliance on the authorisation beyond what is necessary for the proper discharge of a function of the Intelligence Service [or GCHQ]; and

      (ii)   that, in so far as any acts may be done in reliance on the authorisation, their nature and likely consequences will be reasonable, having regard to the purposes for which they are carried out; and

   (c)   that there are satisfactory arrangements in force under section 2(2)(a) [or 4(2)(a)] above with respect to the disclosure of information obtained by virtue of this section and that any information obtained by virtue of anything done in reliance on the authorisation will be subject to those arrangements.

(4) Without prejudice to the generality of the power of the Secretary of State to give an authorisation under this section, such an authorisation–

(a) may relate to a particular act or acts, to acts of a description specified in the authorisation or to acts undertaken in the course of an operation so specified;

(b) may be limited to a particular person or persons of a description so specified; and

(c) may be subject to conditions so specified.

(5) An authorisation shall not be given under this section except–

(a) under the hand of the Secretary of State; or

(b) in an urgent case where the Secretary of State has expressly authorised it to be given and a statement of that fact is endorsed on it, under the hand of a senior official …

(6) An authorisation shall, unless renewed under subsection (7) below, cease to have effect–

(a) if the authorisation was given under the hand of the Secretary of State, at the end of the period of six months beginning with the day on which it was given;

(b) in any other case, at the end of the period ending with the second working day following the day on which it was given.

(7) If at any time before the day on which an authorisation would cease to have effect the Secretary of State considers it necessary for the authorisation to continue to have effect for the purpose for which it was given, he may by an instrument under his hand renew it for a period of six months beginning with that day.

(8) The Secretary of State shall cancel an authorisation if he is satisfied that any act authorised by it is no longer necessary.

[(9) For the purposes of this section the reference in subsection (1) to an act done outside the British Islands includes a reference to any act which–

(a) is done in the British Islands; but

(b) is or is intended to be done in relation to apparatus that is believed to be outside the British Islands, or in relation to anything appearing to originate from such apparatus;

and in this subsection "apparatus" has the same meaning as in the Regulation of Investigatory Powers Act 2000 (c 23).]

Notes

Initial Commencement

To be appointed
To be appointed: see s 12(2).

Appointment
Appointment (for the purposes of making any Orders in Council under s 12(4) hereof): 2 November 1994: see SI 1994/2734, art 2.
Appointment (for remaining purposes): 15 December 1994: see SI 1994/2734, art 2.

Amendment
Sub-s (3): in paras (a), (b)(i) words "or GCHQ" in square brackets inserted by the Anti-terrorism, Crime and Security Act 2001, s 116(1)(a).
Date in force: 14 December 2001: see the Anti-terrorism, Crime and Security Act 2001, s 127(2)(h).

Sub-s (3): in para (c) words "or 4(2)(a)" in square brackets inserted by the Anti-terrorism, Crime and Security Act 2001, s 116(1)(b).

Date in force: 14 December 2001: see the Anti-terrorism, Crime and Security Act 2001, s 127(2)(h).

Sub-s (5): in para (b) words omitted repealed by the Regulation of Investigatory Powers Act 2000, ss 74(3), 82(2), Sch 5.

Date in force: 25 September 2000: see SI 2000/2543, art 2.

Sub-s (9): inserted by the Anti-terrorism, Crime and Security Act 2001, s 116(2).

Date in force: 14 December 2001: see the Anti-terrorism, Crime and Security Act 2001, s 127(2)(h).

The Commissioner, the Tribunal and the investigation of complaints

---

Notes

Amendment

Repealed by virtue of the Regulation of Investigatory Powers Act 2000, s 82(2), Sch 5.

Date in force: to be appointed: see the Regulation of Investigatory Powers Act 2000, s 83(2).

---

8 ...

...

Notes

Amendment

Repealed by the Regulation of Investigatory Powers Act 2000, ss 59(8), 82(2), Sch 5.

Date in force: 2 October 2000: see SI 2000/2543, art 3.

---

9 ...

...

Notes

Amendment

Repealed by the Regulation of Investigatory Powers Act 2000, s 82(2), Sch 5.

Date in force: 2 October 2000 (except in relation to a complaint made to the tribunal before that date): see SI 2000/2543, arts 3, 6(1)(c), (4).

The Intelligence and Security Committee

10 The Intelligence and Security Committee

(1) There shall be a Committee, to be known as the Intelligence and Security Committee and in this section referred to as "the Committee", to examine the expenditure, administration and policy of–

  (a)   the Security Service;

  (b)   the Intelligence Service; and

  (c)   GCHQ.

(2) The Committee shall consist of nine members–

  (a)   who shall be drawn both from the members of the House of Commons and from the members of the House of Lords; and

(b)   none of whom shall be a Minister of the Crown.

(3) The members of the Committee shall be appointed by the Prime Minister after consultation with the Leader of the Opposition, within the meaning of the Ministerial and other Salaries Act 1975; and one of those members shall be so appointed as Chairman of the Committee.

(4) Schedule 3 to this Act shall have effect with respect to the tenure of office of members of, the procedure of and other matters relating to, the Committee; and in that Schedule "the Committee" has the same meaning as in this section.

(5) The Committee shall make an annual report on the discharge of their functions to the Prime Minister and may at any time report to him on any matter relating to the discharge of those functions.

(6) The Prime Minister shall lay before each House of Parliament a copy of each annual report made by the Committee under subsection (5) above together with a statement as to whether any matter has been excluded from that copy in pursuance of subsection (7) below.

(7) If it appears to the Prime Minister, after consultation with the Committee, that the publication of any matter in a report would be prejudicial to the continued discharge of the functions of either of the Services or, as the case may be, GCHQ, the Prime Minister may exclude that matter from the copy of the report as laid before each House of Parliament.

Notes

Initial Commencement

To be appointed

>   To be appointed: see s 12(2).

Appointment

>   Appointment (for the purposes of making any Orders in Council under s 12(4) hereof): 2 November 1994: see SI 1994/2734, art 2.
>   Appointment (for remaining purposes): 15 December 1994: see SI 1994/2734, art 2.

Supplementary

11 Interpretation and consequential amendments

(1) In this Act–

(a)   "the 1989 Act" means the Security Service Act 1989;

(b)   ...

(c)   "Minister of the Crown" has the same meaning as in the Ministers of the Crown Act 1975;

[(d)   "senior official" has the same meaning as in the Regulation of Investigatory Powers Act 2000;]

(e)   "wireless telegraphy" has the same meaning as in the Wireless Telegraphy Act 1949 and, in relation to wireless telegraphy, "interfere" has the same meaning as in that Act;

(f)   "working day" means any day other than a Saturday, a Sunday, Christmas Day, Good Friday or a day which is a bank holiday under the Banking and Financial Dealings Act 1971 in any part of the United Kingdom.

[(1A)   Section 81(5) of the Regulation of Investigatory Powers Act 2000 (meaning of "prevention" and "detection"), so far as it relates to serious crime, shall apply–

[(a)   for the purposes of section 3 above, as it applies for the purposes of Chapter 1 of Part 1 of that Act; and

(b)   for the other purposes of this Act, as it applies for the purposes of the provisions of that Act not contained in that Chapter].]

(2)   In consequence of the preceding provisions of this Act, the 1989 Act, the Official Secrets Act 1989 and the Official Secrets Act 1989 (Prescription) Order 1990 shall have effect subject to the amendments in Schedule 4 to this Act.

Notes

Initial Commencement

To be appointed
> To be appointed: see s 12(2).

Appointment
> Appointment (for the purposes of making any Orders in Council under s 12(4) hereof): 2 November 1994: see SI 1994/2734, art 2.
> Appointment (for remaining purposes): 15 December 1994: see SI 1994/2734, art 2.

Amendment
> Sub-s (1): para (b) repealed by the Regulation of Investigatory Powers Act 2000, s 82(2), Sch 5.
> Date in force: 2 October 2000: see SI 2000/2543, art 3.
> Sub-s (1): para (d) substituted by the Regulation of Investigatory Powers Act 2000, s 74(4).
> Date in force: 25 September 2000: see SI 2000/2543, art 2.
> Sub-s (1A): inserted by the Regulation of Investigatory Powers Act 2000, s 82(1), Sch 4, para 6.
> Date in force: 25 September 2000: see SI 2000/2543, art 2.
> Sub-s (1A): paras (a), (b) substituted by the Anti-terrorism, Crime and Security Act 2001, s 116(3).
> Date in force: 14 December 2001: see the Anti-terrorism, Crime and Security Act 2001, s 127(2)(h).

---

12   Short title, commencement and extent

(1)   This Act may be cited as the Intelligence Services Act 1994.

(2)   This Act shall come into force on such day as the Secretary of State may by an order made by statutory instrument appoint, and different days may be so appointed for different provisions or different purposes.

(3)   This Act extends to Northern Ireland.

(4)   Her Majesty may by Order in Council direct that any of the provisions of this Act specified in the Order shall extend, with such exceptions, adaptations and modifications as appear to Her to be necessary or expedient, to the Isle of Man, any of the Channel Islands or any colony.

Notes

Initial Commencement

To be appointed
> To be appointed: see sub-s (2) above.

Appointment

Appointment (for the purposes of making any Orders in Council under sub-s (4) above): 2 November 1994: see SI 1994/2734, art 2.

Appointment (for remaining purposes): 15 December 1994: see SI 1994/2734, art 2.

SCHEDULE 1

...

Notes

Amendment

Repealed by the Regulation of Investigatory Powers Act 2000, s 82(2), Sch 5.

Date in force: 2 October 2000 (except in relation to a complaint made to the tribunal before that date): see SI 2000/2543, arts 3, 6(1)(c), (4).

...

Notes

Amendment

Repealed by the Regulation of Investigatory Powers Act 2000, s 82(2), Sch 5.

Date in force: 2 October 2000 (except in relation to a complaint made to the tribunal before that date): see SI 2000/2543, arts 3, 6(1)(c), (4).

...

Notes

Amendment

Repealed by the Regulation of Investigatory Powers Act 2000, s 82(2), Sch 5.

Date in force: 2 October 2000 (except in relation to a complaint made to the tribunal before that date): see SI 2000/2543, arts 3, 6(1)(c), (4).

SCHEDULE 2

...

Notes

Amendment

Repealed by the Regulation of Investigatory Powers Act 2000, s 82(2), Sch 5.

Date in force: 2 October 2000 (except in relation to a complaint made to the tribunal before that date): see SI 2000/2543, arts 3, 6(1)(c), (4).

...

Notes

Amendment

Repealed by the Regulation of Investigatory Powers Act 2000, s 82(2), Sch 5.

Date in force: 2 October 2000 (except in relation to a complaint made to the tribunal before that date): see SI 2000/2543, arts 3, 6(1)(c), (4).

...

Notes

Amendment

Repealed by the Regulation of Investigatory Powers Act 2000, s 82(2), Sch 5.

Date in force: 2 October 2000 (except in relation to a complaint made to the tribunal before that date): see SI 2000/2543, arts 3, 6(1)(c), (4).

SCHEDULE 3
THE INTELLIGENCE AND SECURITY COMMITTEE

Section 10(4)

Tenure of office

1 (1) Subject to the provisions of this paragraph, a member of the Committee shall hold office for the duration of the Parliament in which he is appointed.

(2) A member of the Committee shall vacate office–

(a)   if he ceases to be a member of the House of Commons;

(b)   if he ceases to be a member of the House of Lords;

(c)   if he becomes a Minister of the Crown; or

(d)   if he is required to do so by the Prime Minister on the appointment, in accordance with section 10(3) of this Act, of another person as a member in his place.

(3) A member of the Committee may resign at any time by notice to the Prime Minister.

(4) Past service is no bar to appointment as a member of the Committee.

Procedure

2 (1) Subject to the following provisions of this Schedule, the Committee may determine their own procedure.

(2) If on any matter there is an equality of voting among the members of the Committee, the Chairman shall have a second or casting vote.

(3) The Chairman may appoint one of the members of the Committee to act, in his absence, as chairman at any meeting of the Committee, but sub-paragraph (2) above shall not apply to a chairman appointed under this sub-paragraph.

(4) The quorum of the Committee shall be three.

Access to information

3 (1) If the Director-General of the Security Service, the Chief of the Intelligence Service or the Director of GCHQ is asked by the Committee to disclose any information, then, as to the whole or any part of the information which is sought, he shall either–

(a)   arrange for it to be made available to the Committee subject to and in accordance with arrangements approved by the Secretary of State; or

(b)   inform the Committee that it cannot be disclosed either–

(i)   because it is sensitive information (as defined in paragraph 4 below) which, in his opinion, should not be made available under paragraph (a) above; or

(ii)   because the Secretary of State has determined that it should not be disclosed.

(2) The fact that any particular information is sensitive information shall not prevent its disclosure under sub-paragraph (1)(a) above if the Director-General, the Chief or the Director (as the case may require) considers it safe to disclose it.

(3) Information which has not been disclosed to the Committee on the ground specified in sub-paragraph (1)(b)(i) above shall be disclosed to them if the Secretary of State considers it desirable in the public interest.

(4) The Secretary of State shall not make a determination under sub-paragraph (1)(b)(ii) above with respect to any information on the grounds of national security alone and, subject to that, he shall not make such a determination unless the information appears to him to be of such a nature that, if he were requested to produce it before a Departmental Select Committee of the House of Commons, he would think it proper not to do so.

(5) The disclosure of information to the Committee in accordance with the preceding provisions of this paragraph shall be regarded for the purposes of the 1989 Act or, as the case may be, this Act as necessary for the proper discharge of the functions of the Security Service, the Intelligence Service or, as the case may require, GCHQ.

Sensitive information

4 The following information is sensitive information for the purposes of paragraph 3 above–

(a)   information which might lead to the identification of, or provide details of, sources of information, other assistance or operational methods available to the Security Service, the Intelligence Service or GCHQ;

(b)   information about particular operations which have been, are being or are proposed to be undertaken in pursuance of any of the functions of those bodies; and

(c)   information provided by, or by an agency of, the Government of a territory outside the United Kingdom where that Government does not consent to the disclosure of the information.

Notes

Initial Commencement

To be appointed

To be appointed: see s 12(2).

Appointment

Appointment (for the purposes of making any Orders in Council under s 12(4) hereof): 2 November 1994: see SI 1994/2734, art 2.

Appointment (for remaining purposes): 15 December 1994: see SI 1994/2734, art 2.

SCHEDULE 4
CONSEQUENTIAL AMENDMENTS

Section 11(2)

...

Notes

Initial Commencement

To be appointed

To be appointed: see s 12(2).

Appointment

Appointment (for the purposes of making any Orders in Council under s 12(4) hereof): 2 November 1994: see SI 1994/2734, art 2.

Appointment (for remaining purposes): 15 December 1994: see SI 1994/2734, art 2.

Amendment

This Schedule amends the Security Service Act 1989, ss 2, 4(3), Sch 1, para 4(1), the Official Secrets Act 1989, s 4(3)(b) and SI 1990/200, Sch 3.

Appendix 2

2003 No 3171

INVESTIGATORY POWERS

REGULATION OF INVESTIGATORY POWERS (DIRECTED SURVEILLANCE AND COVERT HUMAN INTELLIGENCE SOURCES) ORDER 2003

Made   5th December 2003
Coming into force   5th January 2004

Whereas a draft of this Order has been approved by a resolution of each House of Parliament;

Now, therefore, the Secretary of State, in exercise of the powers conferred on him by sections 30(1), (3), (5) and (6) and 78(5) of the Regulation of Investigatory Powers Act 2000, hereby makes the following Order:

Citation, commencement and interpretation

1 (1) This Order may be cited as the Regulation of Investigatory Powers (Directed Surveillance and Covert Human Intelligence Sources) Order 2003 and shall come into force one month after the day on which it is made.

(2) In this Order "the 2000 Act" means the Regulation of Investigatory Powers Act 2000.

Notes

Initial Commencement

Specified date

      Specified date: 5 January 2004: see para (1) above.

Amendments to Schedule 1 to the 2000 Act

2 (1) Part I of Schedule 1 to the 2000 Act shall be amended as follows.

(2) After paragraph 1 add the words–

    "**1A** The United Kingdom Atomic Energy Authority Constabulary.".

(3) After paragraph 13 add the words–

    "**13A** The Northern Ireland Office.".

(4) For paragraph 17 substitute–

    "**17** Any county council or district council in England, a London borough council, the Common Council of the City of London in its capacity as a local authority, the Council of the Isles of Scilly, and any county council or county borough council in Wales.".

(5) After paragraph 17 add the words–

"**17A** Any fire authority within the meaning of the Fire Services Act 1947 (read with paragraph 2 of Schedule 11 to the Local Government Act 1985).".

(6) After the heading "*Other bodies*" add the words–

"**17B** The Charity Commission.".

(7) After paragraph 20 add the words–

"**20A** The Gaming Board for Great Britain.

20B The Office of Fair Trading.

20C The Office of the Police Ombudsman for Northern Ireland.

20D The Postal Services Commission.".

Notes

Initial commencement

Specified date

Specified date: 5 January 2004: see art 1(1).

3 (1) Part II of Schedule 1 to the 2000 Act shall be amended as follows.

(2) After paragraph 27 add the words–

"**27A** Local Health Boards in Wales established under section 6 of the National Health Service Reform and Health Care Professions Act 2002.

Her Majesty's Chief Inspector of Schools in England

27B Her Majesty's Chief Inspector of Schools in England.

The Information Commissioner

27C The Information Commissioner.

The Royal Parks Constabulary

27D The Royal Parks Constabulary.".

Notes

Initial commencement

Specified date

Specified date: 5 January 2004: see art 1(1).

Prescribed offices, ranks and positions

4 (1) The offices, ranks and positions listed in column 2 of Part I of the Schedule to this Order (being offices, ranks or positions with the relevant public authorities listed in column 1 of Part I of that Schedule which are relevant public authorities for the purposes of sections 28 and 29 of the 2000 Act) are hereby prescribed for the purpose of section 30(1) of the 2000 Act, subject to the restrictions in articles 7, 8 and 9.

(2) The offices, ranks and positions listed in column 2 of Part II of the Schedule to this Order (being offices, ranks or positions with the relevant public authorities listed in column 1 of Part II of that Schedule which are relevant public authorities for the purposes only of section 28 of the 2000 Act) are hereby prescribed for the purpose of section 30(1) of the 2000 Act, subject to the restrictions in articles 7, 8 and 9.

Notes

Initial commencement

Specified date

   Specified date: 5 January 2004: see art 1(1).

More senior offices, ranks and positions

5 (1) Where an office, rank or position with a relevant public authority is prescribed by virtue of article 4, all more senior offices, ranks or positions with that authority are also prescribed for the purpose of section 30(1) of the 2000 Act, subject to article 10.

(2) Where an office, rank or position with a relevant public authority is described in column 2 of the Schedule to this Order by reference to an agency, unit, branch, division or other part of that authority, the reference in paragraph (1) to all more senior offices, ranks or positions with that authority is a reference to all more senior offices, ranks or positions with that agency, unit, branch, division or part.

Notes

Initial commencement

Specified date

   Specified date: 5 January 2004: see art 1(1).

Additional offices, ranks and positions prescribed for urgent cases

6 (1) The additional offices, ranks and positions listed in column 3 of the Schedule to this Order (being offices, ranks or positions with the relevant public authorities listed in column 1) are hereby prescribed for the purposes of section 30(1) of the 2000 Act, subject to the restrictions in articles 7, 8 and 9 in the circumstances described in paragraph (2).

(2) An individual holding an office, rank or position which is listed in column 3 of the Schedule to this Order may only grant an authorisation where it is not reasonably practicable, having regard to the urgency of the case, for the application to be considered by an individual with the same authority holding an office, rank or position listed in column 2 of the Schedule to this Order.

(3) Where an office, rank or position with a relevant public authority is described in column 3 of the Schedule to this Order by reference to an agency, unit, branch, division or other part of that authority, the reference in paragraph (2) to an individual with the same authority is a reference to an individual with that agency, unit, branch, division or part.

Notes

Initial commencement

Specified date

   Specified date: 5 January 2004: see art 1(1).

Restrictions on the granting of authorisations

7 The restriction in this article is that an individual holding an office, rank or position which is listed in column 2 or 3 of the Schedule to this Order may not grant an authorisation unless he believes it is necessary on the grounds set out in one or more of the paragraphs of sections 28(3) and 29(3) of the 2000 Act listed in the corresponding entry in column 4 of that Schedule.

Notes

Initial commencement

Specified date

   Specified date: 5 January 2004: see art 1(1).

8 The restriction in this article is that where any entry in column 2 or 3 of Part I of the Schedule to this Order is headed by a reference to an authorisation under section 28 or section 29 of the 2000 Act, an individual holding an office, rank or position which is listed in that entry may only grant an authorisation under the section of the 2000 Act with which that entry is headed.

Notes

Initial commencement

Specified date

   Specified date: 5 January 2004: see art 1(1).

9 The restriction in this article is that an individual holding an office, rank or position with the Food Standards Agency or the Rural Payments Agency may not grant an authorisation for conduct in Northern Ireland.

Notes

Initial commencement

Specified date

   Specified date: 5 January 2004: see art 1(1).

10 The restrictions on the granting of authorisations under section 28 and 29 of the 2000 Act that apply to an individual holding an office, rank or position with a relevant public authority listed in column 2 of the Schedule to this Order shall also apply to individuals holding all more senior offices, ranks or positions with that authority that are prescribed by article 5.

Notes

Initial commencement

Specified date

Specified date: 5 January 2004: see art 1(1).

Revocation

11 The Regulation of Investigatory Powers (Prescription of Offices, Ranks and Positions) Order 2000 is hereby revoked.

Notes

Initial commencement

Specified date

Specified date: 5 January 2004: see art 1(1).

Caroline Flint

Parliamentary Under-Secretary of State

Home Office

5th December 2003

SCHEDULE

Article 4

PART I
(PRESCRIPTIONS FOR PUBLIC AUTHORITIES IN PART I OF SCHEDULE 1 TO THE 2000 ACT THAT ARE RELEVANT PUBLIC AUTHORITIES FOR THE PURPOSES OF SECTIONS 28 AND 29 OF THE 2000 ACT)

(1) Relevant public authorities in Part I of Schedule 1 to the 2000 Act	(2) Prescribed offices etc	(3) Urgent cases	(4) Grounds set out in the paragraphs of sections 28(3) and 29(3) of the 2000 Act for which an authorisation can be given
A police force maintained under section 2 of the Police Act 1996 (police forces in England and Wales outside London)	Superintendent	Inspector	(a)(b)(c)(d)(e)
A police force maintained under or by virtue of section 1 of the Police (Scotland) Act 1967	Superintendent	Inspector	(a)(b)(c)(d)(e)
The metropolitan police force	Superintendent	Inspector	(a)(b)(c)(d)(e)
The City of London police force	Superintendent	Inspector	(a)(b)(c)(d)(e)
The Police Service of Northern Ireland	Superintendent	Inspector	(a)(b)(c)(d)(e)
The Ministry of Defence Police	Superintendent	Inspector	(a)(b)(c)
The Royal Navy Regulating Branch	Provost Marshal		(a)(b)(c)
The Royal Military Police	Lieutenant Colonel	Major	(a)(b)(c)
The Royal Air Force Police	Wing Commander	Squadron Leader	(a)(b)(c)
The British Transport Police	Superintendent	Inspector	(a)(b)(c)(d)(e)
The United Kingdom Atomic Energy Authority Constabulary	Superintendent	Inspector	(a)(b)

(1) Relevant public authorities in Part I of Schedule 1 to the 2000 Act	(2) Prescribed offices etc	(3) Urgent cases	(4) Grounds set out in the paragraphs of sections 28(3) and 29(3) of the 2000 Act for which an authorisation can be given
The National Criminal Intelligence Service	Superintendent, Level 2 or any individual on secondment to the National Criminal Intelligence Service who holds any office, rank or position in any other relevant public authority listed in column 2 of Part I of the Schedule to this Order	Inspector, Level 4 or any individual on secondment to the National Criminal Intelligence Service who holds any office, rank or position in any other relevant public authority listed in column 3 of Part I of the Schedule to this Order	(a)(b)(c)(d)(e)
The National Crime Squad	Superintendent	Inspector	(a)(b)(c)(d)(e)
The Serious Fraud Office	Assistant Director		(b)
Government Communications Headquarters	GC8		(a)(b)(c)
The Security Service	General Duties 3 or any other Officer at Level 3		(a)(b)(c)
The Secret Intelligence Service	Grade 6 or equivalent		(a)(b)(c)
The Royal Navy	Commander	Lieutenant Commander	(a)(b)(c)(d)(e)
The Army	Lieutenant Colonel	Major	(a)(b)(c)(d)(e)
The Royal Air Force	Wing Commander	Squadron Leader	(a)(b)(c)(d)(e)
The Commissioners of Customs and Excise	Band 9	Band 7 or 8	(a)(b)(c)(d)(e)(f)
The Commissioners of Inland Revenue	Band C1	Band C2	(b)(c)(f)
Ministry of Defence	Band C1	Band C2	(b)
Department for Environment, Food and Rural Affairs	Senior Investigation Officer in DEFRA Investigation Branch		(b)
	Senior Counter Fraud Officer in the Counter Fraud and Compliance Unit of the Rural Payments Agency		(b)
	Senior Investigation Officer in Centre for Environment, Fisheries and Aquaculture Science		(b)

(1) Relevant public authorities in Part I of Schedule 1 to the 2000 Act	(2) Prescribed offices etc	(3) Urgent cases	(4) Grounds set out in the paragraphs of sections 28(3) and 29(3) of the 2000 Act for which an authorisation can be given
	Section 28 authorisation Regional Horticultural Marketing Inspector in Horticultural Marketing Inspectorate		(b)
	Section 28 authorisation Senior Plant Health and Seed Inspector in Plant Health and Seed Inspectorate		(b)
	Section 28 authorisation Chief Egg Marketing Inspector in Egg Marketing Inspectorate		(b)
	Section 28 authorisation District Inspector in Sea Fisheries Inspectorate		(b)
The Department of Health	Integrated Payband 3 (Standard 2) in Medicines and Healthcare Products Regulatory Agency		(b)(d)(e)
The Home Office	**Section 28 authorisation** Area Manager in HM Prison Service		(a)(b)(d)
	Section 29 authorisation Prison Source System Manager in HM Prison Service	**Section 29 authorisation** A Governor, Duty Governor or Deputy Controller in HM Prison Service	(a)(b)(d)
	Immigration Inspector in the Immigration Service	Chief Immigration Officer in the Immigration Service	(b)(c)
	Section 28 authorisation The Head of the Unit responsible for Security and Anti Corruption within the Immigration and Nationality Directorate	**Section 28 authorisation** Senior Executive Officer within the Unit responsible for Security and Anti Corruption within the Immigration and Nationality Directorate	(b)

(1) Relevant public authorities in Part I of Schedule 1 to the 2000 Act	(2) Prescribed offices etc	(3) Urgent cases	(4) Grounds set out in the paragraphs of sections 28(3) and 29(3) of the 2000 Act for which an authorisation can be given
The Northern Ireland Office	Deputy Principal or Governor 3 in the Northern Ireland Prison Service	Staff Officer or Governor 4 in the Northern Ireland Prison Service	(b)(d)
The Department of Trade and Industry	Deputy Inspector of Companies in Companies Investigation Branch		(b)
	Chief Investigation Officer in the Investigation Officers Section of Legal Services Directorate D or a member of the Senior Civil Service in Legal Services Directorate D		(b)
	Section 28 authorisation Radio Specialist 5 or Range 9 Officer in Radiocommunications Agency	**Section 28 authorisation** Radio Specialist 4 or Range 8 Officer in Radiocommunications Agency	(b)
	Section 29 authorisation Member of Senior Civil Service in Radiocommunications Agency		(b)
	Section 28 authorisation Member of Senior Civil Service in British Trade International		(b)
	Section 28 authorisation Range 10 Officer in Coal Health Claims Unit	**Section 28 authorisation** Range 9 Officer in Coal Health Claims Unit	(b)
The Department for Transport	Head of Maritime Section		(b)(d)
	Assistant Director Transport Security		(b)(d)
	Head of Operational Support		(b)(d)
	Head of Land Transport Security		(b)(d)
	Head of Aviation Security Compliance		(b)(d)
	Head of Aviation Security Domestic Policy		(b)(d)

(1) Relevant public authorities in Part I of Schedule 1 to the 2000 Act	(2) Prescribed offices etc	(3) Urgent cases	(4) Grounds set out in the paragraphs of sections 28(3) and 29(3) of the 2000 Act for which an authorisation can be given
	Head of Aviation Security International Policy		(b)(d)
	Senior Transport Security Inspector		(b)(d)
	Section 28 authorisation Area Manager or National Intelligence Co-ordinator in the Vehicle and Operator Services Agency	**Section 28 authorisation** Senior Vehicle Examiner or Senior Traffic Examiner or Intelligence Officer in the Vehicle and Operator Services Agency	(b)(d)
	Section 29 authorisation Enforcement Manager in the Vehicle and Operator Services Agency	**Section 29 authorisation** Area Manager in the Vehicle and Operator Services Agency	(b)(d)(b)(d)
	Principal Enforcement Officer in the Maritime and Coastguard Agency	Enforcement Officer in the Maritime and Coastguard Agency	(b)(d)
The Department for Work and Pensions	Senior Executive Officer or equivalent grades in Jobcentre Plus	Higher Executive Officer or equivalent grades in Jobcentre Plus	(b)
	Senior Executive Officer or equivalent grades in DWP Internal Assurance Services		(b)
	Senior Executive Officer or equivalent grades in Child Support Agency	Higher Executive Officer or equivalent grades in Child Support Agency	(b)
National Assembly for Wales	Head of NHS Directorate	Member of NHS Directorate at a level equivalent to Grade 7	(b)(d)(e)
	Head of NHS Finance Division	Member of NHS Finance Division at a level equivalent to Grade 7	(b)(d)(e)
	Head of Common Agricultural Policy Management Division	Member of Common Agricultural Policy Management Division at a level equivalent to Grade 7	(b)(e)
	Regional Director in the Care Standards Inspectorate for Wales	Senior Inspector in the Care Standards Inspectorate for Wales	(b)(d)(e)

(1) Relevant public authorities in Part I of Schedule 1 to the 2000 Act	(2) Prescribed offices etc	(3) Urgent cases	(4) Grounds set out in the paragraphs of sections 28(3) and 29(3) of the 2000 Act for which an authorisation can be given
Any county council or district council in England, a London Borough Council, the Common Council of the City of London in its capacity as a local authority, the Council of the Isles of Scilly, and any county council or county borough council in Wales	Assistant Chief Officer, Assistant Head of Service, Service Manager or equivalent		(b)
Any fire authority within the meaning of the Fire Services Act 1947 (read with paragraph 2 of Schedule 11 to the Local Government Act 1985)	Divisional Officer 2	Divisional Officer 3	(b)(d)
The Charity Commission	Senior Investigations Manager	Investigations Manager	(b)
The Environment Agency	**Section 28 authorisation** Area Management Team Member	**Section 28 authorisation** Area Team Leader	(b)(d)(e)
	Section 29 authorisation Area Manager	**Section 29 authorisation** Area Management Team Member	(b)(d)(e)
The Financial Services Authority	Head of Department in Enforcement Division	Manager in Enforcement Division	(b)
The Food Standards Agency	**Section 28 authorisation** Head of Division or equivalent grade		(b)(d)(e)
	Section 29 authorisation Deputy Director of Legal Services or any Director		(b)(d)(e)
The Gaming Board for Great Britain	Chief Inspector	Deputy Chief Inspector	(b)
The Office of Fair Trading	Director of Cartel Investigations	Principal Investigation Officer in the Cartel Investigation Branch	(b)(c)
The Office of the Police Ombudsman for Northern Ireland	Senior Investigating Officer	Deputy Senior Investigating Officer	(b)

(1) Relevant public authorities in Part I of Schedule 1 to the 2000 Act	(2) Prescribed offices etc	(3) Urgent cases	(4) Grounds set out in the paragraphs of sections 28(3) and 29(3) of the 2000 Act for which an authorisation can be given
The Postal Services Commission	**Section 28 authorisation** Legal Adviser	**Section 28 authorisation** Deputy Director	(b)
	Section 29 authorisation Chief Legal Adviser		(b)
A Universal Service Provider within the meaning of the Postal Services Act 2000	Senior Investigation Manager in Royal Mail Group plc		(b)

Notes

Initial commencement

Specified date

Specified date: 5 January 2004: see art 1(1).

PART II
(PRESCRIPTIONS FOR PUBLIC AUTHORITIES IN PART II OF SCHEDULE 1 TO THE 2000 ACT THAT ARE RELEVANT PUBLIC AUTHORITIES FOR THE PURPOSES ONLY OF SECTION 28 OF THE 2000 ACT)

(1) Relevant public authorities in Part II of Schedule 1 to the 2000 Act	(2) Prescribed offices etc	(3) Urgent cases	(4) Grounds set out in the paragraphs of section 28(3) of the 2000 Act for which an authorisation can be given
The Health and Safety Executive	Band 2 Inspector		(b)(d)(e)
A Special Health Authority established under section 11 of the National Health Service Act 1977	Chief Executive		(b)(e)
	Senior Manager (Senior Manager Pay Range 14) in the Counter Fraud and Security Management Service		(b)

(1) Relevant public authorities in Part II of Schedule 1 to the 2000 Act	(2) Prescribed offices etc	(3) Urgent cases	(4) Grounds set out in the paragraphs of section 28(3) of the 2000 Act for which an authorisation can be given
A National Health Service trust established under section 5 of the National Health Service and Community Care Act 1990	Chief Executive		(b)(e)
Local Health Boards in Wales established under section 6 of the National Health Service Reform and Health Care Professions Act 2002	Chief Officer or Finance Officer		(b)(e)
Her Majesty's Chief Inspector of Schools in England	Band A in the Complaints, Investigation and Enforcement Team in the Office of Her Majesty's Chief Inspector of Schools in England (OFSTED)	Band B1 in the Complaints, Investigation and Enforcement Team in the Office of Her Majesty's Chief Inspector of Schools in England (OFSTED)	(b)
The Information Commissioner	Head of Investigations	Senior Investigating Officer	(b)
The Royal Parks Constabulary	Chief Officer	Inspector	(b)
The Royal Pharmaceutical Society of Great Britain	Director of Fitness to Practice and Legal Affairs or Director of Practice and Quality Improvement		(b)(d)(e)

Notes

Initial commencement

Specified date

Specified date: 5 January 2004: see art 1(1).

EXPLANATORY NOTE

(This note is not part of the Order)

Articles 2 and 3 of this Order amend Schedule 1 to the Regulation of Investigatory Powers Act 2000 ("the 2000 Act") by adding to it a number of new public authorities. Designated individuals in the public authorities listed in Part I of Schedule 1 are entitled to authorise directed surveillance and the use and conduct of covert human intelligence sources under sections 28 and 29 of the 2000 Act, respectively. Designated individuals in the public authorities listed in Part II of Schedule 1 are only entitled to authorise directed surveillance under section 28 of the 2000 Act. Article 4 of this Order prescribes offices, ranks and positions for the purposes of section 30(1) of the 2000 Act for both the public authorities already in Schedule 1 and those added to it by this Order. Individuals holding these prescribed offices, ranks or positions are designated under sections 28 and 29 of the 2000 Act as able to authorise directed surveillance and the use and conduct of covert human intelligence sources. An earlier Order that prescribed offices, ranks and positions in the public authorities that were in Schedule 1 when the 2000 Act was passed is revoked by article 10 of this Order.

Column 1 of the Schedule to this Order lists the public authorities. Column 2 specifies the individuals within each public authority that can authorise directed surveillance and the use and conduct of covert human intelligence sources. An individual holding an office, rank or position listed in column 2 of Part I of the Schedule may grant an authorisation under either section 28 or section 29 of the 2000 Act, other than where the Schedule indicates to the contrary. An individual holding an office, rank or position listed in column 2 of Part II of the Schedule may only grant an authorisation under section 28 of the 2000 Act. Individuals holding more senior offices, ranks or positions to those listed in column 2 may also authorise in the same circumstances as those to whom they are senior. Column 3 sets out certain less senior officials who can authorise in urgent cases. Column 4 sets out the grounds on which an authorisation can be given by reference to the grounds set out in the different paragraphs of sections 28(3) and 29(3) of the 2000 Act. For example, ground (b) is for the purpose of preventing or detecting crime or of preventing disorder.

2003 No 3172
INVESTIGATORY POWERS

REGULATION OF INVESTIGATORY POWERS (COMMUNICATIONS DATA) ORDER 2003

Made   5th December 2003
Coming into force   5th January 2004

Whereas a draft of this Order has been approved by resolution of each House of Parliament;

Now, therefore, the Secretary of State, in exercise of the powers conferred on him by paragraph (g) of the definition of "relevant public authority" in section 25(1) of the Regulation of Investigatory Powers Act 2000 and by sections 25(2) and (3) and 78(5) of that Act, hereby makes the following Order:

Citation, commencement and interpretation

1 (1) This Order may be cited as the Regulation of Investigatory Powers (Communications Data) Order 2003 and shall come into force one month after the day on which it is made.

(2) In this Order–

"the 2000 Act" means the Regulation of Investigatory Powers Act 2000;

"authorisation" means an authorisation under section 22(3) of the 2000 Act; and

"notice" means a notice under section 22(4) of the 2000 Act.

Notes

Initial commencement

Specified date
   Specified date: 5 January 2004: see para (1) above.

Prescribed offices, ranks and positions

2 The offices, ranks and positions listed in columns 2 and 3 of Schedule 1 (being offices, ranks and positions with the relevant public authorities in column 1 of that Schedule) are hereby prescribed for the purposes of section 25(2) of the 2000 Act, subject to the restrictions in articles 6, 7 and 10.

Notes

Initial commencement

Specified date
   Specified date: 5 January 2004: see art 1(1).

Additional public authorities

3 The public authorities set out in column 1 of Parts I, III and IV of Schedule 2 are hereby specified as relevant public authorities for the purposes of section 25(1) of the 2000 Act.

Notes

Initial commencement

Specified date
     Specified date: 5 January 2004: see art 1(1).

Prescribed offices, ranks and positions in the additional public authorities

4 The offices, ranks and positions listed in columns 2 and 3 of Parts I, II, III and IV of Schedule 2 (being offices, ranks and positions with the relevant public authorities in column 1 of that Schedule) are hereby prescribed for the purposes of section 25(2) of the 2000 Act, subject to the restrictions in articles 6, 7, 8 and 9.

Notes

Initial commencement

Specified date
     Specified date: 5 January 2004: see art 1(1).

More senior offices, ranks and positions

5 (1) Where an office, rank or position with a relevant public authority listed in column 2 of Schedule 1 or column 2 of Schedule 2 is prescribed by virtue of article 2 or 4, all more senior offices, ranks or positions with that authority are also prescribed for the purposes of section 25(2) of the 2000 Act, subject to article 11.

(2) Where an office, rank or position with a relevant public authority is described in column 2 of Schedule 1 or column 2 of Schedule 2 by reference to an agency, unit, branch, division or other part of that authority, the reference in paragraph (1) to all more senior offices, ranks or positions with that authority is a reference to all more senior offices, ranks or positions with that agency, unit, branch, division or part.

Notes

Initial commencement

Specified date
     Specified date: 5 January 2004: see art 1(1).

Restrictions on the granting of authorisations or the giving of notices

6 The restriction in this article is that an individual holding an office, rank or position which is listed in column 2 or 3 of Schedule 1 or column 2 or 3 of Schedule 2 may not grant an authorisation or give a notice unless he believes it is necessary on the grounds set out in one or more of the paragraphs of section 22(2) of the 2000 Act listed in the corresponding entry in column 4 of those Schedules.

Notes

Initial commencement

Specified date

Specified date: 5 January 2004: see art 1(1).

7 (1) The restriction in this paragraph is that an individual holding an office, rank or position which is listed in column 2 of Schedule 1 or column 2 of Schedule 2 may only grant an authorisation or give a notice that he believes is necessary on grounds other than those set out in paragraphs (a), (b), (c) and (g) of section 22(2) of the 2000 Act where that authorisation or notice satisfies the condition in paragraph (3).

(2) The restriction in this paragraph is that an individual holding an office, rank or position which is listed in column 3 of Schedule 1 or column 3 of Schedule 2 may only grant an authorisation or give a notice which satisfies the condition set out in paragraph (3).

(3) The condition referred to in paragraphs (1) and (2) is that the only communications data authorised to be obtained by the authorisation, or required to be obtained or disclosed by the notice, is communications data falling within section 21(4)(c) of the 2000 Act.

Notes

Initial commencement

Specified date

Specified date: 5 January 2004: see art 1(1).

8 (1) The restriction in this article is that an individual holding an office, rank or position which is listed in column 2 of Part II or Part III of Schedule 2 may only grant an authorisation or give a notice which satisfies the condition set out in paragraph (2).

(2) The condition referred to in paragraph (1) is that the only communications data authorised to be obtained by the authorisation, or required to be obtained or disclosed by the notice, is communications data falling within section 21(4)(b) or (c) of the 2000 Act.

Notes

Initial commencement

Specified date

Specified date: 5 January 2004: see art 1(1).

9 (1) The restriction in this article is that an individual holding an office, rank or position which is listed in column 2 of Part IV of Schedule 2 may only grant an authorisation or give a notice which satisfies the condition set out in paragraph (2).

(2) The condition referred to in paragraph (1) is that the only communications data authorised to be obtained by the authorisation, or required to be obtained or disclosed by the notice, is communications data relating to a postal service.

Notes

Initial commencement

Specified date

Specified date: 5 January 2004: see art 1(1).

10 (1)   The restriction in this article is that an individual holding an office, rank or position with the Commissioners of Inland Revenue (being a relevant public authority listed in Schedule 1) may only grant an authorisation or give a notice which satisfies the condition set out in paragraph (2).

(2) The condition referred to in paragraph (1) is that the only communications data falling with section 21(4)(a) of the 2000 Act authorised to be obtained by the authorisation, or required to be obtained or disclosed by the notice is communications data relating to a postal service.

Notes

Initial commencement

Specified date

Specified date: 5 January 2004: see art 1(1).

11 The restrictions on the granting of authorisations and the giving of notices that apply to an individual holding an office, rank or position with a relevant public authority listed in column 2 of Schedule 1 or column 2 of Schedule 2 shall also apply to all individuals holding all more senior offices, ranks or positions with that authority that are prescribed by article 5.

Notes

Initial commencement

Specified date

Specified date: 5 January 2004: see art 1(1).

Caroline Flint

Parliamentary Under-Secretary of State

Home Office

5th December 2003

SCHEDULE 1
INDIVIDUALS IN PUBLIC AUTHORITIES WITHIN SECTION 25(1) OF THE 2000 ACT

Article 2

(1) Relevant public authorities	(2) Prescribed offices etc (All authorisations/notices)	(3) Additional prescribed offices etc (Authorisations/notices relating solely to communications data falling within section 21(4)(c))	(4) Purposes within section 22(2) for which an authorisation may be granted or a notice given
Police Forces			
A police force maintained under section 2 of the Police Act 1996 (police forces in England and Wales outside London)	Superintendent	Inspector	(a)(b)(c)(d)(e)(g)
A police force maintained under or by virtue of section 1 of the Police (Scotland) Act 1967	Superintendent	Inspector	(a)(b)(c)(d)(e)(g)
The metropolitan police force	Superintendent	Inspector	(a)(b)(c)(d)(e)(g)
The City of London police force	Superintendent	Inspector	(a)(b)(c)(d)(e)(g)
The Police Service of Northern Ireland	Superintendent	Inspector	(a)(b)(c)(d)(e)(g)
The Ministry of Defence Police	Superintendent	Inspector	(a)(b)(c)(g)
The Royal Navy Regulating Branch	Provost Marshal	—	(a)(b)(c)(g)
The Royal Military Police	Lieutenant Colonel	Major	(a)(b)(c)(g)
The Royal Air Force Police	Wing Commander	Squadron Leader	(a)(b)(c)(g)
The British Transport Police	Superintendent	Inspector	(a)(b)(c)(d)(e)(g)
The National Criminal Intelligence Service	Superintendent, Level 2 or any individual on secondment to the National Criminal Intelligence Service who holds any other office, rank or position in any relevant public authority listed in column 2 of Schedule 1	Inspector, Level 4 or any individual on secondment to the National Criminal Intelligence Service who holds any other office, rank or position in any relevant public authority listed in column 3 of Schedule 1	(a)(b)(c)(d)(e)(g)

(1) Relevant public authorities	(2) Prescribed offices etc (All authorisations/notices)	(3) Additional prescribed offices etc (Authorisations/notices relating solely to communications data falling within section 21(4)(c))	(4) Purposes within section 22(2) for which an authorisation may be granted or a notice given
The National Crime Squad	Superintendent, Band I or any individual on secondment to the National Crime Squad who holds any other office, rank or position in any relevant public authority listed in column 2 of Schedule 1	Inspector, Band F or any individual on secondment to the National Crime Squad who holds any other office, rank or position in any relevant public authority listed in column 3 of Schedule 1	(a)(b)(c)(d)(e)(g)
The Commissioners of Customs and Excise	Band 9	Band 7 or 8	(b)(f)
The Commissioners of Inland Revenue	Band C1	Band C2	(b)(f)
The Intelligence Services			
Government Communications Headquarters	GC8	—	(a)(b)(c)
The Security Service	General Duties 3 or any other Officer at Level 3	General Duties 4	(a)(b)(c)
The Secret Intelligence Service	Grade 6 or equivalent	—	(a)(b)(c)

Notes

Initial commencement

Specified date

Specified date: 5 January 2004: see art 1(1).

SCHEDULE 2
INDIVIDUALS IN ADDITIONAL PUBLIC AUTHORITIES SPECIFIED BY THIS ORDER

Article 3

PART I
(INDIVIDUALS IN ADDITIONAL PUBLIC AUTHORITIES THAT MAY ACQUIRE ALL TYPES OF COMMUNICATIONS DATA WITHIN SECTION 21(4) OF THE 2000 ACT)

(1) Additional public authorities specified for the purposes of section 25(1) of the 2000 Act	(2) Prescribed offices etc (All authorisations/notices)	(3) Additional prescribed offices etc (Authorisations/notices relating solely to communications data falling within section 21(4)(c))	(4) Purposes within section 22(2) for which an authorisation may be granted or a notice given
The Financial Services Authority	Head of Department in Enforcement Division	—	(b)
The Scottish Crime Squad within the meaning of the Regulation of Investigatory Powers (Scotland) Act 2000	Superintendent	Inspector	(b)(d)(g)
The United Kingdom Atomic Energy Authority Constabulary	Superintendent	Inspector	(a)(b)
The Department of Trade and industry	Range 9 Officer in Radiocommunications Agency	—	(b)
The Office of the Police Ombudsman for Northern Ireland	Senior Investigating Officer	—	(b)
Emergency Services			
A National Health Service trust established under section 5 of the National Health Service and Community Care Act 1990 whose functions, as specified in its Establishment Order, include the provision of emergency ambulance services	Duty Officer responsible for the Control Function	—	(g)
The Welsh Ambulance Services NHS Trust	Regional Control Manager	—	(g)

(1) Additional public authorities specified for the purposes of section 25(1) of the 2000 Act	(2) Prescribed offices etc (All authorisations/notices)	(3) Additional prescribed offices etc (Authorisations/notices relating solely to communications data falling within section 21(4)(c))	(4) Purposes within section 22(2) for which an authorisation may be granted or a notice given
The Scottish Ambulance Service Board	Emergency Medical Dispatch Centre Officer in charge	—	(g)
The Northern Ireland Ambulance Service Health and Social Services Trust	Control Supervisor in Ambulance Control Room	—	(g)
The Department for Transport	Area Operations Manager in the Maritime and Coastguard Agency	—	(g)
Any fire authority within the meaning of the Fire Services Act 1947 (read with paragraph 2 of Schedule 11 to the Local Government Act 1985)	Fire Control Officer	—	(g)
A council constituted under section 2 of the Local Government etc (Scotland) Act 1994	Fire Control Officer	—	(g)
A joint Board constituted by an administration scheme under section 36 of the Fire Services Act 1947 or section 147 of the Local Government (Scotland) Act 1973	Fire Control Officer	—	(g)
The Fire Authority for Northern Ireland	Fire Control Officer	—	(g)

Notes

Initial commencement

Specified date

Specified date: 5 January 2004: see art 1(1).

PART II
(INDIVIDUALS IN THE PUBLIC AUTHORITIES SPECIFIED IN PART I THAT MAY ONLY ACQUIRE COMMUNICATIONS DATA FALLING WITHIN SECTIONS 21(4)(B) AND (C) OF THE 2000 ACT)

(1) Additional public authorities specified for the purposes of section 25(1) of the 2000 Act	(2) Prescribed offices etc (All authorisations/notices relating to communications data falling within sections 21(4)(b) and (c))	(3) Additional prescribed offices etc (Authorisations/notices relating solely to communications data falling within section 21(4)(c))	(4) Purposes within section 22(2) for which an authorisation may be granted or a notice given
The Department of Trade and Industry	Deputy Inspector of Companies in Companies Investigation Branch	—	(b)
	Deputy Chief Investigation Officer in the Investigation Officers Section of Legal Services Directorate D	—	(b)
Emergency Services			
A National Health Service Trust established under section 5 of the National Health Service and Community Care Act 1990 whose functions, as specified in its Establishment Order, include the provision of emergency ambulance services	Director of Operations or Director of Control and Communications	—	(b)
The Welsh Ambulance Services NHS Trust	Director of Operations	—	(b)
The Scottish Ambulance Service Board	Director of Operations	—	(b)
The Northern Ireland Ambulance Service Health and Social Services Trust	Director of Operations	—	(b)
The Department for Transport	Principal Enforcement Officer in the Maritime and Coastguard Agency	—	(b)(d)

(1) Additional public authorities specified for the purposes of section 25(1) of the 2000 Act	(2) Prescribed offices etc (All authorisations/notices relating to communications data falling within sections 21(4)(b) and (c))	(3) Additional prescribed offices etc (Authorisations/notices relating solely to communications data falling within section 21(4)(c))	(4) Purposes within section 22(2) for which an authorisation may be granted or a notice given
Any fire authority within the meaning of the Fire Services Act 1947 (read with paragraph 2 of Schedule 11 to the Local Government Act 1985)	Principal Fire Control Officer or Divisional Officer 2	—	(b)(d)
A council constituted under section 2 of the Local Government etc (Scotland) Act 1994	Assistant Chief Officer, Assistant Head of Service, Service Manager or equivalent	—	(b)
	Principal Fire Control Officer or Divisional Officer 2	—	(b)(d)
A joint Board constituted by an administration scheme under section 36 of the Fire Services Act 1947 or section 147 of the Local Government (Scotland) Act 1973	Principal Fire Control Officer or Divisional Officer 2	—	(b)(d)
The Fire Authority for Northern Ireland	Principal Fire Control Officer or Divisional Officer 2	—	(b)(d)

Notes

Initial commencement

Specified date

Specified date: 5 January 2004: see art 1(1).

PART III
(INDIVIDUALS IN FURTHER ADDITIONAL PUBLIC AUTHORITIES THAT MAY ONLY ACQUIRE COMMUNICATIONS DATA FALLING WITHIN SECTIONS 21(4)(B) AND (C) OF THE 2000 ACT)

(1) Additional public authorities specified for the purposes of section 25(1) of the 2000 Act	(2) Prescribed offices etc (All authorisations/notices relating to communications data falling within sections 21(4)(b) and (c))	(3) Additional prescribed offices etc (Authorisations/notices relating solely to communications data falling within section 21(4)(c))	(4) Purposes within section 22(2) for which an authorisation may be granted or a notice given
Government Departments			
The Department for Environment, Food and Rural Affairs	Senior Investigation Officer in DEFRA Investigation Branch	—	(b)
	Senior Investigation Officer in the Centre for Environment, Fisheries and Aquaculture Science	—	(b)
	Senior Counter Fraud Officer in the Counter Fraud and Compliance Unit of the Rural Payments Agency	—	(b)
The Food Standards Agency	Deputy Director of Legal Services or any Director	—	(b)(d)(e)
The Department of Health	Integrated Payband 3 (Standard 2) in the Medicines and Healthcare Products Regulatory Agency	—	(b)(d)(e)
The Home Office	Immigration Inspector in the Immigration Service	—	(b)
The Department of Enterprise, Trade and Investment for Northern Ireland	Deputy Chief Inspector in Trading Standards Service	—	(b)

(1) Additional public authorities specified for the purposes of section 25(1) of the 2000 Act	(2) Prescribed offices etc (All authorisations/notices relating to communications data falling within sections 21(4)(b) and (c))	(3) Additional prescribed offices etc (Authorisations/notices relating solely to communications data falling within section 21(4)(c))	(4) Purposes within section 22(2) for which an authorisation may be granted or a notice given
Local Authorities			
Any county council or district council in England, a London borough council, the Common Council of the City of London in its capacity as a local authority, the Council of the Isles of Scilly, and any county council or county borough council in Wales	Assistant Chief Officer, Assistant Head of Service, Service Manager or equivalent	—	(b)
A district council within the meaning of the Local Government Act (Northern Ireland) 1972	Assistant Chief Officer	—	(b)
NHS Bodies			
The Counter Fraud and Security Management Service	Senior Manager (Senior Manager Pay Range 14)	—	(b)
The Common Services Agency for the Scottish Health Service	Head of NHS Scotland Counter Fraud Services	—	(b)
The Northern Ireland Health and Social Services Central Services Agency	Head of the Counter Fraud Unit	—	(b)
Other Bodies			
The Charity Commission	Senior Investigations Manager	—	(b)
The Environment Agency	Area Management Team Member	—	(b)(d)(e)
The Gaming Board for Great Britain	Chief Inspector	—	(b)
The Health and Safety Executive	Band 2 Inspector	—	(b)(d)(e)(g)
The Information Commissioner	Head of Investigations	—	(b)

(1) Additional public authorities specified for the purposes of section 25(1) of the 2000 Act	(2) Prescribed offices etc (All authorisations/notices relating to communications data falling within sections 21(4)(b) and (c))	(3) Additional prescribed offices etc (Authorisations/notices relating solely to communications data falling within section 21(4)(c))	(4) Purposes within section 22(2) for which an authorisation may be granted or a notice given
The Office of Fair Trading	Director of Cartel Investigations	—	(b)
The Serious Fraud Office	Assistant Director	—	(b)
The Scottish Environment Protection Agency	Director of Operations, any other Director	—	(b)(d)(e)
A Universal Service Provider within the meaning of the Postal Services Act 2000	Senior Investigation Manager in Royal Mail Group plc	—	(b)

Notes

Initial commencement

Specified date

Specified date: 5 January 2004: see art 1(1).

PART IV
(INDIVIDUALS IN ADDITIONAL PUBLIC AUTHORITIES THAT MAY ONLY ACQUIRE COMMUNICATIONS DATA WITHIN SECTION 21(4) OF THE 2000 ACT RELATING TO A POSTAL SERVICE)

(1) Additional public authorities specified for the purposes of section 25(1) of the 2000 Act	(2) Prescribed offices etc (All authorisations/notices relating to communications data relating to postal services	(3) Additional prescribed offices etc (Authorisations/notices relating solely to communications data falling within section 21(4)(c))	(4) Purposes within section 22(2) for which an authorisation may be granted or a notice given
Postal Services Commission	Legal Adviser	—	(b)

Notes

Initial commencement

Specified date

Specified date: 5 January 2004: see art 1(1).

EXPLANATORY NOTE

(*This note is not part of the Order*)

This Order specifies additional public authorities for the purposes of section 25(1) of the Regulation of Investigatory Powers Act 2000 ("the 2000 Act"). Public authorities specified for the purposes of section 25 are entitled to acquire communications data under the provisions in Chapter II of Part I of the 2000 Act. The Order specifies which individuals within those public authorities, and the public authorities already listed in the 2000 Act, are entitled to acquire communications data. It also places restrictions on the grounds on which they may acquire communications data and the types of communications data they way acquire.

Column 1 of the two Schedules to the Order lists the public authorities. Column 1 of Schedule 1 contains the public authorities already listed within section 25(1) of the 2000 Act. The public authorities listed in Parts I, III and IV of column 1 of Schedule 2 are specified by article 3 as additional public authorities under the 2000 Act.

By virtue of articles 2 and 4 column 2 of the Schedules lists the individuals holding an office, rank or position within each public authority who may acquire communications data. Article 5 provides that more senior individuals with those public authorities may also acquire communications data in the same circumstances to those to whom they are senior. Certain less senior officials listed in column 3 of the Schedules can acquire communications date defined in section 21(4)(c) of the 2000 Act. This type of data is known as subscriber data.

An individual holding a particular office, rank or position can only acquire communications data on the particular grounds, set out in the different paragraphs of section 22(2) of the 2000 Act, found in the entry in column 4 of the Schedules corresponding to the entry for that individual in column 2 or 3. Where the grounds on which communications data is to be obtained is not national security, the prevention or detection of crime or the prevention of disorder, the economic well being of the UK, or in an emergency to prevent death or injury, then only subscriber data may be acquired.

Subject to these restrictions individuals holding offices, ranks or positions listed in Schedule 1 or Part I of Schedule 2 are entitled to acquire all types of communications data. Individuals holding offices, ranks or positions listed in Parts II and III of Schedule 2 are not entitled to acquire traffic data as defined in section 21(4)(a) (read with sections 21(6) and (7)) of the 2000 Act. Individuals within the Postal Services Commission can only acquire communications data about postal services. Individuals in the Inland Revenue can acquire all communications data other than traffic data that does not relate to a postal service.

2002 No 1931

INVESTIGATORY POWERS

REGULATION OF INVESTIGATORY POWERS (MAINTENANCE OF INTERCEPTION CAPABILITY) ORDER 2002

Made 22nd July 2002
Coming into force 1st August 2002

Whereas the Secretary of State has consulted the persons listed in section 12(9) and (11) of the Regulation of Investigatory Powers Act 2000 about this Order;

And whereas a draft of this Order has been laid before Parliament and approved by a resolution of each House;

Now, therefore, the Secretary of State, in exercise of the powers conferred on him by section 12(1), (2) and (5) and section 78(5) of that Act, hereby makes the following Order:

1 Citation, commencement and interpretation

(1) This Order may be cited as the Regulation of Investigatory Powers (Maintenance of Interception Capability) Order 2002 and shall come into force on 1st August 2002.

(2) In this Order "service provider" means a person providing a public postal service or a public telecommunications service, or proposing to do so.

Notes

Initial commencement

Specified date

> Specified date: 1 August 2002: see para (1) above.

---

2 Interception capability

(1) The Schedule to this Order sets out those obligations which appear to the Secretary of State reasonable to impose on service providers for the purpose of securing that it is and remains practicable for requirements to provide assistance in relation to interception warrants to be imposed and complied with.

(2) Subject to paragraph (3) the obligations in–

    (a) Part I of the Schedule only apply to service providers who provide, or propose to provide, a public postal service; and

    (b) Part II of the Schedule only apply to service providers who provide, or propose to provide, a public telecommunications service.

(3) The obligations in Part II of the Schedule shall not apply to service providers who–

    (a) do not intend to provide a public telecommunications service to more than 10,000 persons in any one or more parts of the United Kingdom and do not do so; or

    (b) only provide, or propose to provide, a public telecommunications service in relation to the provision of banking, insurance, investment or other financial services.

3 Interception capability notices

(1) The Secretary of State may give a service provider a notice requiring him to take all such steps falling within paragraph (2) as may be specified or described in the notice.

(2) Those steps are ones appearing to the Secretary of State to be necessary for securing that the service provider has the practical capability of meeting the obligations set out in the Schedule to this Order.

4 Referral of notices to the Technical Advisory Board

The period within which any person to whom a notice has been given under article 3 may refer the notice to the Technical Advisory Board is specified as being before the end of 28 days from the date of the notice.

Bob Ainsworth

Parliamentary Under-Secretary of State

Home Office

22nd July 2002

SCHEDULE

OBLIGATIONS ON SERVICE PROVIDERS

Article 2

PART I

INTERCEPTION CAPABILITY FOR PUBLIC POSTAL SERVICES

1 To ensure the interception and temporary retention of postal items destined for addresses in the United Kingdom for provision to the person on whose application the interception warrant was issued.

2 To provide for the interception and retention of postal items sent by identified persons where the carrier keeps records of who sent which item in the course of their normal business.

3 To maintain a system of opening, copying and resealing of any postal item carried for less than £1.

4 To comply with the obligations set out in paragraphs 1 to 3 above in such a manner that the chance of the interception subject or other unauthorised persons becoming aware of any interception is minimised.

Notes

Initial commencement

Specified date

   Specified date: 1 August 2002: see art 1(1).

PART II
INTERCEPTION CAPABILITY FOR PUBLIC TELECOMMUNICATION SERVICES

5 To provide a mechanism for implementing interceptions within one working day of the service provider being informed that the interception has been appropriately authorised.

6 To ensure the interception, in their entirety, of all communications and related communications data authorised by the interception warrant and to ensure their simultaneous (i.e. in near real time) transmission to a hand-over point within the service provider's network as agreed with the person on whose application the interception warrant was issued.

7 To ensure that the intercepted communication and the related communications data will be transmitted so that they can be unambiguously correlated.

8 To ensure that the hand-over interface complies with any requirements communicated by the Secretary of State to the service provider, which, where practicable and appropriate, will be in line with agreed industry standards (such as those of the European Telecommunications Standards Institute).

9 To ensure filtering to provide only the traffic data associated with the warranted telecommunications identifier, where reasonable.

10 To ensure that the person on whose application the interception warrant was issued is able to remove any electronic protection applied by the service provider to the intercepted communication and the related communications data.

11 To enable the simultaneous interception of the communications of up to 1 in 10,000 of the persons to whom the service provider provides the public telecommunications service, provided that those persons number more than 10,000.

12 To ensure that the reliability of the interception capability is at least equal to the reliability of the public telecommunications service carrying the communication which is being intercepted.

13 To ensure that the intercept capability may be audited so that it is possible to confirm that the intercepted communications and related communications data are from, or intended for the interception subject, or originate from or are intended for transmission to, the premises named in the interception warrant.

14 To comply with the obligations set out in paragraphs 5 to 13 above in such a manner that the chance of the interception subject or other unauthorised persons becoming aware of any interception is minimised.

Notes

Initial commencement

Specified date

Specified date: 1 August 2002: see art 1(1).

EXPLANATORY NOTE

(This note is not part of the Order)

Part I of the Regulation of Investigatory Powers Act 2000 ("the 2000 Act") contains provisions about the interception of communications transmitted by means of public postal service or a public telecommunications service. Interception is permitted under the 2000 Act by certain public authorities who obtain an interception warrant. This Order sets out the obligations which it appears to the Secretary of State reasonable to impose on the providers of public postal services or a public telecommunications services ("service providers") for the purpose of securing that it is and remains practicable for requirements to provide assistance in relation to interception warrants to be imposed and complied with.

These obligations are set out in the Schedule to the Order. The obligations in Part I of the Schedule relate only to persons who provide, or propose to provide, a public postal service. The obligations in Part II of the Schedule relate only to persons who offer, provide, or propose to provide a public telecommunications service to more than 10,000 persons in any one or more parts of the United Kingdom, other than service providers who only provide a public telecommunications service in relation to the provision of banking, insurance, investment or other financial services.

Article 3 enables the Secretary of State to ensure compliance with the obligations by providing that he may give a service provider a notice requiring it to take the steps described in the notice. The notice may only contain steps which appear to the Secretary of State necessary for securing that that service provider has the practical capability of meeting those obligations set out in the Schedule which apply to that service provider.

Article 4 specifies the period within which a person served with a notice may refer it to the Technical Advisory Board.

This Order was notified in draft to the European Commission in accordance with Directive 98/34/EC, as amended by Directive 98/48/EC.

2000 No 2418
INVESTIGATORY POWERS

REGULATION OF INVESTIGATORY POWERS (AUTHORISATIONS EXTENDING TO SCOTLAND) ORDER 2000

Made   7th September 2000
Laid before Parliament   8th September 2000
Coming into force   2nd October 2000

The Secretary of State, in exercise of the power conferred on him by section 46(4) of the Regulation of Investigatory Powers Act 2000, hereby makes the following Order:

Citation and commencement

1 This Order may be cited as the Regulation of Investigatory Powers (Authorisations Extending to Scotland) Order 2000 and shall come into force on 2nd October 2000.

Notes

Initial commencement

Specified date
> Specified date: 2 October 2000: see above.

Relevant public authorities for all parts of the United Kingdom

2 (1) Subject to paragraph (2), the public authorities listed in column 1 of the Schedule to this Order (being public authorities for the time being specified in Schedule 1 to the Regulation of Investigatory Powers Act 2000) are relevant public authorities for all parts of the United Kingdom.

(2) Where there is an entry in column 2 against a particular authority, that authority is a relevant public authority for all parts of the United Kingdom only to the extent specified in that column.

Notes

Initial commencement

Specified date
> Specified date: 2 October 2000: see art 1.

Charles Clarke

Minister of State

Home Office

7th September 2000

SCHEDULE

Article 2

(1)	(2)
The National Criminal Intelligence Service	
The Commissioners of Inland Revenue	
The Department of the Environment, Transport and the Regions	
The Department of Health	
The Home Office	The Immigration Service
The Department of Social Security	
The Department of Trade and Industry	
The Environment Agency	
The Financial Services Authority	
…	
[A universal service provider (within the meaning of the Postal Services Act 2000) acting in connection with the provision of a universal postal service (within the meaning of that Act)]	
The Health and Safety Executive	
The Royal Pharmaceutical Society of Great Britain	

Notes

Initial commencement

Specified date

Specified date: 2 October 2000: see art 1.

Amendment

Entry relating to "The Personal Investment Authority" (omitted) revoked by SI 2002/1555, art 42.

Date in force: 3 July 2002: see SI 2002/1555, art 1.

Entry relating to "A universal service provider" substituted by SI 2001/1149, art 3(1), Sch 1, para 144.

Date in force: 26 March 2001: see SI 2001/1149, art 1(2).

EXPLANATORY NOTE

(This note is not part of the Order)

This Order sets out the extent to which certain public authorities specified in Schedule 1 to the Regulation of Investigatory Powers Act 2000 ("the 2000 Act") are to be relevant public authorities "for all parts of the United Kingdom" and are to be treated as being included in the list of public authorities in section 46(3) of the 2000 Act.

The effect of a public authority specified in Schedule 1 to the 2000 Act, being included in the list of public authorities in section 46(3), is that authorisations may be granted or renewed under sections 28 and 29 of the 2000 Act, by or in relation to that authority, where all the conduct to be authorised is likely to take place in Scotland.

Such authorisations may be granted or renewed under sections 28 and 29 where the authority is specified in Part I of Schedule 1 to the Act and in relation to section 28 only where the authority is specified in Part II of Schedule 1 to the Act.

2000 No 2543 *(C 71)*

INVESTIGATORY POWERS

REGULATION OF INVESTIGATORY POWERS ACT 2000 (COMMENCEMENT NO 1 AND TRANSITIONAL PROVISIONS) ORDER 2000

Made   17th September 2000

In exercise of the powers conferred on him by sections 83(2) and 78(5) of the Regulation of Investigatory Powers Act 2000, the Secretary of State hereby makes the following Order:–

1 Citation

(1) This Order may be cited as the Regulation of Investigatory Powers Act 2000 (Commencement No 1 and Transitional Provisions) Order 2000.

(2) In this Order, "the Act" means the Regulation of Investigatory Powers Act 2000.

Notes

Initial commencement

Date Made

Date made: 17 September 2000: (no specific commencement provision).

---

2 Commencement on 25th September 2000

The following provisions of the Act shall come into force on 25th September 2000:

Part II (Surveillance and covert human intelligence sources)

the whole Part (sections 26 to 48).

Part IV (Scrutiny etc of investigatory powers and of the functions of the intelligence services)

section 61;

section 62, except subsection (1)(b) and (c);

sections 63 and 64;

sections 71 and 72, to the extent that they relate to Part II of the Act, section 5 of the Intelligence Services Act 1994 or Part III of the Police Act 1997.

Part V (Miscellaneous and supplemental)

sections 74 to 78;

sections 80 and 81;

in section 82, subsections (1) and (2) for the purpose of giving effect to those provisions in Schedules 4 and 5 that are brought into force by virtue of this article.

Schedules

Schedule 1;

in Schedule 4, paragraphs 4, 6 and 8;

in Schedule 5, the entries relating to sections 6 and 7 of the Intelligence Services Act 1994, the Police Act 1997 and the Crime and Disorder Act 1998.

Notes

Initial commencement

Date Made

Date made: 17 September 2000: (no specific commencement provision).

3 Commencement on 2nd October 2000

The following provisions of the Act shall come into force on 2nd October 2000:

Part I (*Communications*)

section 1, except for subsection (3);

sections 2 to 20;

section 21(4), for the purpose of giving effect to the definition of "related communications data" in section 20.

Part IV (*Scrutiny etc of investigatory powers and of the functions of the intelligence services*)

section 57 except subsection (2)(b), (c) and (d)(ii);

section 58 except the following paragraphs of subsection (1): (g), (h), (i) and, in respect of paragraphs (h) and (i), (j);

in section 59, subsections (1), (2)(a) and (3) to (10), and the rest of subsection (2) to the extent that it relates to Part II;

section 60;

in section 65, subsection (1), (2)(a) and (b) (subject to article 6), (3)(a), (b) and (d), (4), (5)(a), (b), (d) and (f), (6), (7), (8)(a), (c) and (f), (9) and (11);

in section 67, subsection (1) to the extent that it relates to section 65(2)(a) and (b), and the rest of the section except subsection (9);

section 68, except the following paragraphs of subsection (7): (g), (h), (m) and, in respect of paragraph (m), (n);

sections 69 and 70;

sections 71 and 72, to the extent that they relate to Chapter I of Part I of the Act.

Part V (*Miscellaneous and supplemental*)

section 73;

section 79;

section 82, to the extent that it is not in force by virtue of article 2, and subject to articles 5 and 6.

Schedules

Schedule 3;

Schedule 4, to the extent that it is not in force by virtue of article 2, and subject to article 5;

Schedule 5, to the extent that it is not in force by virtue of article 2, and subject to article 6.

Notes

Initial commencement

Date Made

Date made: 17 September 2000: (no specific commencement provision).

4 Commencement on 24th October 2000

Section 1(3) of the Act shall come into force on 24th October 2000.

Notes

Initial commencement

Date Made

Date made: 17 September 2000: (no specific commencement provision).

5 Transitional provision about the Telecommunications Act 1984

(1) The amendment made to section 45 of the Telecommunications Act 1984 by paragraph 3 of Schedule 4 to the Act shall come into force on 2nd October 2000 subject to the following provision.

(2) In respect of the disclosure, before the coming into force of sections 21 to 25 of the Act, of matter falling within paragraph (b) of section 45(1) of the Telecommunications Act 1984, the amendment shall not affect the continuing effect of paragraphs (a) and (c) of section 45(2), and of section 45(3).

Notes

Initial commencement

Date Made

Date made: 17 September 2000: (no specific commencement provision).

6 Transitional provisions about complaints

(1) Section 65(2)(b) of the Act, and the repeal by Schedule 5 of:

    (a)   section 7 of and Schedule 1 to the Interception of Communications Act 1985,

    (b)   section 5 of and Schedules 1 and 2 to the Security Service Act 1989,

    (c)   section 9 of and Schedules 1 and 2 to the Intelligence Services Act 1994, and

    (d)   section 102 of and Schedule 7 to the Police Act 1997,

shall come into force on 2nd October 2000 subject to the following provisions.

(2)   Any complaint made before 2nd October 2000 to the Tribunal established under section 7 of the Interception of Communications Act 1985 shall be dealt with by that Tribunal in accordance with that Act.

(3)   Any complaint made before 2nd October 2000 to the Tribunal established under section 5 of the Security Service Act 1989 shall be dealt with by that Tribunal in accordance with that Act, but the functions of the Commissioner in respect of those complaints shall be discharged by the Intelligence Services Commissioner.

(4)   Any complaint made before 2nd October 2000 to the Tribunal established under section 9 of the Intelligence Services Act 1994 shall be dealt with by that Tribunal in accordance with that Act, but the functions of the Commissioner in respect of those complaints shall be discharged by the Intelligence Services Commissioner.

(5)   Any complaint made before 2nd October 2000 to a Surveillance Commissioner by virtue of section 102 of the Police Act 1997 shall be dealt with by that Commissioner in accordance with that Act.

Notes

Initial commencement

Date Made

Date made: 17 September 2000: (no specific commencement provision).

Charles Clarke

Minister of State

Home Office

17th September 2000

EXPLANATORY NOTE

(*This note is not part of the Order*)

This Order brings into force much of the Regulation of Investigatory Powers Act 2000.

Part II, which regulates surveillance and the use of covert human intelligence sources, is brought into force on 25th September.

With the exception of subsection 1(3), Chapter I of Part I, which concerns the interception of communications and replaces the Interception of Communications Act 1985, is brought into force on 2nd October. This is also the commencement date for most of Part IV, which establishes judicial Commissioners to oversee the use of the powers conferred by the Act and a Tribunal to consider complaints and cases brought under section 7(1)(a) of the Human Rights Act 1988.

Section 1(3), which concerns interception by the controller of a private telecommunication system, is brought into force on 24th October. This is the date by which Article 5 of the Telecoms Data Protection Directive (97/66/EC) must be implemented.

2000 No 2665
INVESTIGATORY POWERS

INVESTIGATORY POWERS TRIBUNAL RULES 2000

Made   28th September 2000
Laid before Parliament   29th September 2000
Laid before the Scottish Parliament   29th September 2000
Coming into force   2nd October 2000

Whereas the Secretary of State may make Rules under section 69 of the Regulation of Investigatory Powers Act 2000;

And whereas subsections (9) and (10) of that section provide that the Rules made on the first occasion on which the power is exercised do not need to be approved by Parliament before being made, but must be approved after being made in accordance with subsection (10);

And whereas this is the first occasion on which the Secretary of State exercises the power;

Now, therefore, the Secretary of State, in exercise of the power conferred on him by section 69(1) of the Regulation of Investigatory Powers Act 2000 and after consultation with the Scottish Ministers as required by section 69(12) of that Act, hereby makes the following Rules:

PART I
GENERAL PROVISIONS

1 Citation and commencement

These Rules may be cited as the Investigatory Powers Tribunal Rules 2000, and shall come into force on 2nd October 2000.

Notes

Initial commencement

Specified date

Specified date: 2 October 2000: see above.

---

2 Interpretation

In these Rules:

"the Act" means the Regulation of Investigatory Powers Act 2000;

"Commissioner" means the Interception of Communications Commissioner, the Intelligence Services Commissioner, the Investigatory Powers Commissioner for Northern Ireland or any Surveillance Commissioner or Assistant Surveillance Commissioner;

"complainant" means a person who brings section 7 proceedings or, as the case may be, makes a complaint;

"complaint" means a complaint for which the Tribunal is the appropriate forum by virtue of section 65(2)(b) and section 65(4) of the Act;

"Convention right" has the same meaning as in the Human Rights Act 1998;

"section 7 proceedings" means proceedings under section 7(1)(a) of the Human Rights Act 1998 in relation to which the Tribunal is the only appropriate tribunal by virtue of section 65(2)(a) of the Act;

"the Tribunal" means the tribunal established under section 65(1) of the Act.

Notes

Initial commencement

Specified date

Specified date: 2 October 2000: see r 1.

3 Application of Rules

These Rules apply to section 7 proceedings, and to complaints.

Notes

Initial commencement

Specified date

Specified date: 2 October 2000: see r 1.

4 Exercise of Tribunal's jurisdiction

(1) The jurisdiction of the Tribunal may be exercised at any place in the United Kingdom, by any two or more members of the Tribunal designated for the purpose by the President; and different members of the Tribunal may carry out functions in relation to different complaints at the same time.

(2) This rule is subject to paragraph 3 of Schedule 3 to the Act (members of the Tribunal with special responsibilities).

Notes

Initial commencement

Specified date

Specified date: 2 October 2000: see r 1.

5 Functions exercisable by single member

(1) Subject to paragraph (2), the following powers and duties may be exercised or performed by a single member of the Tribunal:

(a)   the power under rule 7(4) or rule 8(4) to invite the complainant to supply information or make representations;

(b)   the power under section 68(2) of the Act to require a Commissioner to provide assistance;

(c)   the power under section 68(6) of the Act to require the disclosure or provision of documents or information;

(d)   the power under paragraph 5(2) of Schedule 3 to the Act to authorise an officer to obtain documents or information on the Tribunal's behalf;

    (e)   the power under section 7(5)(b) of the Human Rights Act 1998 to extend the time limit for section 7 proceedings;

    (f)   the power under section 67(5) of the Act to extend the time limit for complaints;

    (g)   the duty under rule 13 to notify the complainant of any of the determinations described in that rule;

    (h)   the duty, in considering a complaint, to investigate the matters described in paragraphs (a) and (b) of section 67(3) of the Act.

(2)   In relation to a case falling within paragraph 3(2) of Schedule 3 to the Act, a single member discharging any of these functions must be a member designated under paragraph 3(1) of that Schedule.

Notes

Initial commencement

Specified date
    Specified date: 2 October 2000: see r 1.

---

6 Disclosure of Information

(1) The Tribunal shall carry out their functions in such a way as to secure that information is not disclosed to an extent, or in a manner, that is contrary to the public interest or prejudicial to national security, the prevention or detection of serious crime, the economic well-being of the United Kingdom or the continued discharge of the functions of any of the intelligence services.

(2) Without prejudice to this general duty, but subject to paragraphs (3) and (4), the Tribunal may not disclose to the complainant or to any other person:

    (a)   the fact that the Tribunal have held, or propose to hold, an oral hearing under rule 9(4);

    (b)   any information or document disclosed or provided to the Tribunal in the course of that hearing, or the identity of any witness at that hearing;

    (c)   any information or document otherwise disclosed or provided to the Tribunal by any person pursuant to section 68(6) of the Act (or provided voluntarily by a person specified in section 68(7));

    (d)   any information or opinion provided to the Tribunal by a Commissioner pursuant to section 68(2) of the Act;

    (e)   the fact that any information, document, identity or opinion has been disclosed or provided in the circumstances mentioned in sub-paragraphs (b) to (d).

(3)   The Tribunal may disclose anything described in paragraph (2) with the consent of:

    (a)   in the case of sub-paragraph (a), the person required to attend the hearing;

    (b)   in the case of sub-paragraphs (b) and (c), the witness in question or the person who disclosed or provided the information or document;

    (c)   in the case of sub-paragraph (d), the Commissioner in question and, to the extent that the information or opinion includes information provided to the Commissioner by another person, that other person;

    (d)   in the case of sub-paragraph (e), the person whose consent is required under this rule for disclosure of the information, document or opinion in question.

(4)   The Tribunal may also disclose anything described in paragraph (2) as part of the information provided to the complainant under rule 13(2), subject to the restrictions contained in rule 13(4) and (5).

(5)   The Tribunal may not order any person to disclose any information or document which the Tribunal themselves would be prohibited from disclosing by virtue of this rule, had the information or document been disclosed or provided to them by that person.

(6)   The Tribunal may not, without the consent of the complainant, disclose to any person holding office under the Crown (except a Commissioner) or to any other person anything to which paragraph (7) applies.

(7)   This paragraph applies to any information or document disclosed or provided to the Tribunal by or on behalf of the complainant, except for the statements described in rule 7(2)(a) and (b) or, as the case may be, rule 8(2)(a) and (b).

Notes

Initial commencement

Specified date

    Specified date: 2 October 2000: see r 1.

PART II
PROCEEDINGS AND COMPLAINTS

7 Bringing section 7 proceedings

(1) Section 7 proceedings are brought by a complainant sending to the Tribunal a form and other information in accordance with this rule.

(2) The form must be signed by the complainant and must:

    (a)   state the name, address and date of birth of the complainant;

    (b)   state each public authority against which the proceedings are brought;

    (c)   describe the nature of the claim (including details of the Convention right which it is alleged has been infringed) and of the complainant's interest; and

    (d)   specify the remedy which the complainant seeks.

(3)   The complainant must also supply, either in or with the form, a summary of the information on which the claim is based.

(4)   At any time, the Tribunal may invite the complainant to supply further information or to make written representations on any matter.

Notes

Initial commencement

Specified date
      Specified date: 2 October 2000: see r 1.

8 Making a complaint

(1) A complaint is brought by a complainant sending to the Tribunal a form in accordance with this rule.

(2) The form must be signed by the complainant and must:

    (a)   state the name, address and date of birth of the complainant;

    (b)   state the person or authority whose conduct, to the best of the complainant's knowledge or belief, is the subject of the complaint; and

    (c)   describe, to the best of the complainant's knowledge or belief, that conduct.

(3)   The complainant must also supply, either in or with the form, a summary of the information on which the claim is based.

(4)   At any time, the Tribunal may invite the complainant to supply further information or to make written representations on any matter.

Notes

Initial commencement

Specified date
      Specified date: 2 October 2000: see r 1.

9 Forms of hearing and consideration

(1) The Tribunal's power to determine their own procedure in relation to section 7 proceedings and complaints shall be subject to this rule.

(2) The Tribunal shall be under no duty to hold oral hearings, but they may do so in accordance with this rule (and not otherwise).

(3) The Tribunal may hold, at any stage of their consideration, oral hearings at which the complainant may make representations, give evidence and call witnesses.

(4) The Tribunal may hold separate oral hearings which:

    (a)   the person whose conduct is the subject of the complaint,

    (b)   the public authority against which the section 7 proceedings are brought, or

    (c)   any other person specified in section 68(7) of the Act,

may be required to attend and at which that person or authority may make representations, give evidence and call witnesses.

(5)   Within a period notified by the Tribunal for the purpose of this rule, the complainant, person or authority in question must inform the Tribunal of any witnesses he or it intends to call; and no other witnesses may be called without the leave of the Tribunal.

(6)   The Tribunal's proceedings, including any oral hearings, shall be conducted in private.

Notes

Initial commencement

Specified date

Specified date: 2 October 2000: see r 1.

10 Representation

(1) A person entitled to make representations at an oral hearing may appear in person or may be represented by any person he may appoint for that purpose, subject to paragraph (2).

(2) The leave of the Tribunal is required except where the representative is:

  (a)   a member of the Bar of England and Wales or of Northern Ireland,

  (b)   a solicitor of the Supreme Court in England and Wales or in Northern Ireland,

  (c)   a member of the Faculty of Advocates, or

  (d)   a solicitor within the meaning of the Solicitors (Scotland) Act 1980.

Notes

Initial commencement

Specified date

Specified date: 2 October 2000: see r 1.

11 Evidence

(1) The Tribunal may receive evidence in any form, and may receive evidence that would not be admissible in a court of law.

(2) The Tribunal may require a witness to give evidence on oath.

(3) No person shall be compelled to give evidence at an oral hearing under rule 9(3).

Notes

Initial commencement

Specified date

Specified date: 2 October 2000: see r 1.

12 Remedies

(1) Before exercising their power under section 67(7) of the Act, the Tribunal shall invite representations in accordance with this rule.

(2) Where they propose to make an award of compensation, the Tribunal shall give the complainant and the person who would be required to pay the compensation an opportunity to make representations as to the amount of the award.

(3) Where they propose to make any other order (including an interim order) affecting the public authority against whom the section 7 proceedings are brought, or the person whose conduct is the subject of the complaint, the Tribunal shall give that authority or person an opportunity to make representations on the proposed order.

Notes

Initial commencement

Specified date
Specified date: 2 October 2000: see r 1.

13 Notification to the complainant

(1) In addition to any statement under section 68(4) of the Act, the Tribunal shall provide information to the complainant in accordance with this rule.

(2) Where they make a determination in favour of the complainant, the Tribunal shall provide him with a summary of that determination including any findings of fact.

(3) Where they make a determination:

    (a)   that the bringing of the section 7 proceedings or the making of the complaint is frivolous or vexatious;

    (b)   that the section 7 proceedings have been brought, or the complaint made, out of time and that the time limit should not be extended; or

    (c)   that the complainant does not have the right to bring the section 7 proceedings or make the complaint;

the Tribunal shall notify the complainant of that fact.

(4)   The duty to provide information under this rule is in all cases subject to the general duty imposed on the Tribunal by rule 6(1).

(5)   No information may be provided under this rule whose disclosure would be restricted under rule 6(2) unless the person whose consent would be needed for disclosure under that rule has been given the opportunity to make representations to the Tribunal.

Notes

Initial commencement

Specified date
Specified date: 2 October 2000: see r 1.

Charles Clarke

Minister of State

Home Office

28th September 2000

EXPLANATORY NOTE

(This note is not part of the Rules)

These Rules are for the Tribunal established under Part IV of the Regulation of Investigatory Powers Act 2000. The Tribunal has an extensive jurisdiction, set out in section 65(2) of the Act; these Rules only govern the jurisdiction described in paragraphs (a) and (b) of that subsection. The remainder of the subsection will be brought into force later, and there will be further rules for that purpose.

The Rules therefore cover:

(a)   cases brought under section 7(1)(a) of the Human Rights Act 1998 for which the Tribunal is the appropriate tribunal: this category of case is explained in subsections (3) and (5) to (8) of section 65 of the 2000 Act;

(b)   complaints for which the Tribunal is the appropriate forum: this function is explained in subsections (4), (5), (7) and (8) of section 65.

Section 68 of the 2000 Act provides that, subject to anything in these Rules, the Tribunal are entitled to determine their own procedure.

2000 No 2699

INVESTIGATORY POWERS

TELECOMMUNICATIONS (LAWFUL BUSINESS PRACTICE) (INTERCEPTION OF COMMUNICATIONS) REGULATIONS 2000

Made   2nd October 2000
Laid before Parliament   3rd October 2000
Coming into force   24th October 2000

The Secretary of State, in exercise of the powers conferred on him by sections 4(2) and 78(5) of the Regulation of Investigatory Powers Act 2000 ("the Act"), hereby makes the following Regulations:–

1   Citation and commencement

These Regulations may be cited as the Telecommunications (Lawful Business Practice) (Interception of Communications) Regulations 2000 and shall come into force on **24th October 2000**.

Notes

Initial commencement

Specified date

Specified date: 24 October 2000: see above.

---

2 Interpretation

In these Regulations–

- (a) references to a business include references to activities of a government department, of any public authority or of any person or office holder on whom functions are conferred by or under any enactment;

- (b) a reference to a communication as relevant to a business is a reference to–

  - (i) a communication–

    - (aa) by means of which a transaction is entered into in the course of that business, or

    - (bb) which otherwise relates to that business, or

  - (ii) a communication which otherwise takes place in the course of the carrying on of that business;

- (c) "regulatory or self-regulatory practices or procedures" means practices or procedures–

  - (i) compliance with which is required or recommended by, under or by virtue of–

    - (aa) any provision of the law of a member state or other state within the European Economic Area, or

    - (bb) any standard or code of practice published by or on behalf of a body established in a member state or other state within the

European Economic Area which includes amongst its objectives the publication of standards or codes of practice for the conduct of business, or

(ii) which are otherwise applied for the purpose of ensuring compliance with anything so required or recommended;

(d) "system controller" means, in relation to a particular telecommunication system, a person with a right to control its operation or use.

Notes

Initial commencement

Specified date

Specified date: 24 October 2000: see reg 1.

---

3 Lawful interception of a communication

(1) For the purpose of section 1(5)(a) of the Act, conduct is authorised, subject to paragraphs (2) and (3) below, if it consists of interception of a communication, in the course of its transmission by means of a telecommunication system, which is effected by or with the express or implied consent of the system controller for the purpose of–

(a) monitoring or keeping a record of communications–

(i) in order to–

(aa) establish the existence of facts, or

(bb) ascertain compliance with regulatory or self-regulatory practices or procedures which are–

applicable to the system controller in the carrying on of his business or

applicable to another person in the carrying on of his business where that person is supervised by the system controller in respect of those practices or procedures, or

(cc) ascertain or demonstrate the standards which are achieved or ought to be achieved by persons using the system in the course of their duties, or

(ii) in the interests of national security, or

(iii) for the purpose of preventing or detecting crime, or

(iv) for the purpose of investigating or detecting the unauthorised use of that or any other telecommunication system, or

(v) where that is undertaken–

(aa) in order to secure, or

(bb) as an inherent part of,

the effective operation of the system (including any monitoring or keeping of a record which would be authorised by section 3(3) of the Act if the conditions in paragraphs (a) and (b) thereof were satisfied); or

(b) monitoring communications for the purpose of determining whether they are communications relevant to the system controller's business which fall within regulation 2(b)(i) above; or

    (c)   monitoring communications made to a confidential voice-telephony counselling or support service which is free of charge (other than the cost, if any, of making a telephone call) and operated in such a way that users may remain anonymous if they so choose.

(2) Conduct is authorised by paragraph (1) of this regulation only if

    (a)   the interception in question is effected solely for the purpose of monitoring or (where appropriate) keeping a record of communications relevant to the system controller's business;

    (b)   the telecommunication system in question is provided for use wholly or partly in connection with that business;

    (c)   the system controller has made all reasonable efforts to inform every person who may use the telecommunication system in question that communications transmitted by means thereof may be intercepted; and

    (d)   in a case falling within–

        (i)   paragraph (1)(a)(ii) above, the person by or on whose behalf the interception is effected is a person specified in section 6(2)(a) to (i) of the Act;

        (ii)   paragraph (1)(b) above, the communication is one which is intended to be received (whether or not it has been actually received) by a person using the telecommunication system in question.

[(3) Conduct falling within paragraph (1)(a)(i) above is authorised only to the extent that Article 5 of Directive 2002/58/EC of the European Parliament and of the Council of 12 July 2002 concerning the processing of personal data and the protection of privacy in the electronic communications sector so permits.]

Notes

Initial commencement

Specified date
    Specified date: 24 October 2000: see reg 1.

Amendment
    Para (3): substituted by SI 2003/2426, reg 34.
    Date in force: 11 December 2003: see SI 2003/2426, reg 1.

Patricia Hewitt

Minister for Small Business and E-Commerce

Department of Trade and Industry

2nd October 2000

EXPLANATORY NOTE

(This note is not part of the Regulations)

These Regulations authorise certain interceptions of telecommunication communications which would otherwise be prohibited by section 1 of the Regulation of Investigatory Powers Act 2000. To the extent that the interceptions are also prohibited by Article 5.1 of Directive 97/66/EC, the authorisation does not exceed that permitted by Articles 5.2 and 14.1 of the Directive.

The interception has to be by or with the consent of a person carrying on a business (which includes the activities of government departments, public authorities and others exercising statutory functions) for purposes relevant to that person's business and using that business's own telecommunication system.

Interceptions are authorised for–

monitoring or recording communications–

to establish the existence of facts, to ascertain compliance with regulatory or self-regulatory practices or procedures or to ascertain or demonstrate standards which are or ought to be achieved (quality control and training),

in the interests of national security (in which case only certain specified public officials may make the interception),

to prevent or detect crime,

to investigate or detect unauthorised use of telecommunication systems or,

to secure, or as an inherent part of, effective system operation;

monitoring received communications to determine whether they are business or personal communications;

monitoring communications made to anonymous telephone helplines.

Interceptions are authorised only if the controller of the telecommunications system on which they are effected has made all reasonable efforts to inform potential users that interceptions may be made.

The Regulations do not authorise interceptions to which the persons making and receiving the communications have consented: they are not prohibited by the Act.

A regulatory impact assessment is available and can be obtained from Communications and Information Industries Directorate, Department of Trade and Industry, 151 Buckingham Palace Road, London SW1W 9SS. Copies have been placed in the libraries of both Houses of Parliament.

2000 No 2793
INVESTIGATORY POWERS

REGULATION OF INVESTIGATORY POWERS (JUVENILES) ORDER 2000

Made   10th October 2000
Laid before Parliament   16th October 2000
Coming into force   6th November 2000

The Secretary of State, in exercise of the powers conferred on him by sections 29(2)(c), 29(7)(a) and (b) and 43(8) of the Regulation of Investigatory Powers Act 2000, hereby makes the following Order:

1 Citation and commencement

This Order may be cited as the Regulation of Investigatory Powers (Juveniles) Order 2000 and shall come into force on 6th November 2000.

Notes

Initial commencement

Specified date
    Specified date: 6 November 2000: see above.

---

2 Interpretation

In this Order–

> "the 2000 Act" means the Regulation of Investigatory Powers Act 2000;

> "guardian", in relation to a source, has the same meaning as is given to "guardian of a child" by section 105 of the Children Act 1989;

> "relative" has the same meaning as it is given by section 105 of the Children Act 1989;

> "relevant investigating authority" has the meaning given by section 29(8) of the 2000 Act, and where the activities of a source are to be for the benefit of more than one public authority, each of these authorities is a relevant investigating authority;

> "source" means covert human intelligence source.

Notes

Initial commencement

Specified date
    Specified date: 6 November 2000: see art 1.

---

3 Sources under 16: prohibition

No authorisation may be granted for the conduct or use of a source if:

    (a)   the source is under the age of sixteen; and

(b)   the relationship to which the conduct or use would relate is between the source and his parent or any person who has parental responsibility for him.

Notes

Initial commencement

Specified date

Specified date: 6 November 2000: see art 1.

4 Sources under 16: arrangements for meetings

(1) Where a source is under the age of sixteen, the arrangements referred to in section 29(2)(c) of the 2000 Act must be such that there is at all times a person holding an office, rank or position with a relevant investigating authority who has responsibility for ensuring that an appropriate adult is present at meetings to which this article applies.

(2) This article applies to all meetings between the source and a person representing any relevant investigating authority that take place while the source remains under the age of sixteen.

(3) In paragraph (1), "appropriate adult" means:

(a)   the parent or guardian of the source;

(b)   any other person who has for the time being assumed responsibility for his welfare; or

(c)   where no person falling within paragraph (a) or (b) is available, any responsible person aged eighteen or over who is neither a member of nor employed by any relevant investigating authority.

Notes

Initial commencement

Specified date

Specified date: 6 November 2000: see art 1.

5 Sources under 18: risk assessments etc

An authorisation for the conduct or use of a source may not be granted or renewed in any case where the source is under the age of eighteen at the time of the grant or renewal, unless:

(a)   a person holding an office, rank or position with a relevant investigating authority has made and, in the case of a renewal, updated a risk assessment sufficient to demonstrate that:

  (i)   the nature and magnitude of any risk of physical injury to the source arising in the course of, or as a result of, carrying out the conduct described in the authorisation have been identified and evaluated; and

  (ii)   the nature and magnitude of any risk of psychological distress to the source arising in the course of, or as a result of, carrying out the conduct described in the authorisation have been identified and evaluated;

(b)   the person granting or renewing the authorisation has considered the risk assessment and has satisfied himself that any risks identified in it are justified and, if they are, that they have been properly explained to and understood by the source; and

(c)   the person granting or renewing the authorisation knows whether the relationship to which the conduct or use would relate is between the source and a relative, guardian or person who has for the time being assumed responsibility for the source's welfare, and, if it is, has given particular consideration to whether the authorisation is justified in the light of that fact.

Notes

Initial commencement

Specified date

Specified date: 6 November 2000: see art 1.

6 Sources under 18: duration of authorisations

In relation to an authorisation for the conduct or the use of a source who is under the age of eighteen at the time the authorisation is granted or renewed, section 43(3) of the 2000 Act shall have effect as if the period specified in paragraph (b) of that subsection were one month instead of twelve months.

Notes

Initial commencement

Specified date

Specified date: 6 November 2000: see art 1.

Charles Clarke

Minister of State

Home Office

10th October 2000

EXPLANATORY NOTE

(*This note is not part of the Order*)

Section 29 of the Regulation of Investigatory Powers Act 2000 allows authorisations to be granted for the use or conduct of covert human intelligence sources.

This Order contains special provisions for the cases of covert human intelligence sources who are under eighteen.

Appendix 3

Covert Human Intelligence Sources: Code of Practice

Pursuant to Section 71 of the Regulation of Investigatory Powers Act 2000

Commencement

This code applies to every authorisation of the use or conduct by public authorities of covert human intelligence sources carried out under Part II of the Regulation of Investigatory Powers Act 2000 which begins on or after the day on which this code comes into effect.

CONTENTS

1 Background

1.1 In this code the:

- "**1989 Act**" means the Security Service Act 1989;
- "**1994 Act**" means the Intelligence Services Act 1994;
- "**1997 Act**" means the Police Act 1997;
- "**2000 Act**" means the Regulation of Investigatory Powers Act 2000;
- "**RIP(S)A**" means the Regulation of Investigatory Powers (Scotland) Act 2000;

1.2 This code of practice provides guidance on the authorisation of the use or conduct of covert human intelligence sources ("a source") by public authorities under Part II of the 2000 Act.

1.3 The provisions of the 2000 Act are not intended to apply in circumstances where members of the public volunteer information to the police or other authorities, as part of their normal civic duties, or to contact numbers set up to receive information (such as Crimestoppers, Customs Confidential, the Anti Terrorist Hotline, or the Security Service Public Telephone Number). Members of the public acting in this way would not generally be regarded as sources.

1.4 Neither Part II of the 2000 Act or this code of practice is intended to affect the practices and procedures surrounding criminal participation of sources.

1.5 The 2000 Act provides that all codes of practice relating to the 2000 Act are admissible as evidence in criminal and civil proceedings. If any provision of the code appears relevant to any court or tribunal considering any such proceedings, or to the Investigatory Powers Tribunal established under the 2000 Act, or to one of the Commissioners responsible for overseeing the powers conferred by the 2000 Act, it must be taken into account.

General extent of powers

1.6 Authorisations can be given for the use or conduct of a source both inside and outside the United Kingdom. Authorisations for actions outside the United Kingdom can only validate them for the purposes of proceedings in the United Kingdom. An authorisation under Part II of the 2000 Act does not take into account the requirements of the country outside the United Kingdom in which the investigation or operation is taking place.

1.7 Members of foreign law enforcement or other agencies or sources of those agencies may be authorised under the 2000 Act in the UK in support of domestic and international investigations.

1.8 Where the conduct authorised is likely to take place in Scotland, authorisations should be granted under RIP(S)A, unless the authorisation is being obtained by those public authorities listed in section 46(3) of the 2000 Act and the Regulation of Investigatory Powers (Authorisations Extending to Scotland) Order 2000). Additionally, any authorisation granted or renewed for the purposes of national security or the economic well-being of the UK must be made under the 2000 Act. This code of practice is extended to Scotland in relation to authorisations made under Part II of the 2000 Act which apply to Scotland. A separate code of practice applies in relation to authorisations made under RIP(S)A.

Use of material in evidence

1.9 Material obtained from a source may be used as evidence in criminal proceedings. The proper authorisation of a source should ensure the suitability of such evidence under the common law, section 78 of the Police and Criminal Evidence Act 1984 and the Human Rights Act 1998. Furthermore, the product obtained by a source described in this code is subject to the ordinary rules for retention and disclosure of material under the Criminal Procedure and Investigations Act 1996, where those rules apply to the law enforcement body in question. There are also well-established legal procedures that will protect the identity of a source from disclosure in such circumstances.

2 General rules on authorisations

2.1 An authorisation under Part II of the 2000 Act will provide lawful authority for the use of a source. Responsibility for giving the authorisation will depend on which public authority is responsible for the source.

2.2 Part II of the 2000 Act does not impose a requirement on public authorities to seek or obtain an authorisation where, under the 2000 Act, one is available (see section 80 of the 2000 Act). Nevertheless, where there is an interference by a public authority with the right to respect for private and family life guaranteed under Article 8 of the European Convention on Human Rights, and where there is no other lawful authority, the consequences of not obtaining an authorisation under the 2000 Act may be that the action is unlawful by virtue of section 6 of the Human Rights Act 1998.

2.3 Public authorities are therefore strongly recommended to seek an authorisation where the use or conduct of a source is likely to interfere with a person's Article 8 rights to privacy by obtaining information from or about a person, whether or not that person is the subject of the investigation or operation. Obtaining an authorisation will ensure that the action is carried out in accordance with law and subject to stringent safeguards against abuse.

Necessity and proportionality

2.4 Obtaining an authorisation under the 2000 Act will only ensure that the authorised use or conduct of a source is a justifiable interference with an individual's Article 8 rights if it is necessary and proportionate for the source to be used. The 2000 Act first requires that the person granting an authorisation believe that the authorisation is necessary in the circumstances of the particular case for one or more of the statutory grounds in section 29(3) of the 2000 Act.

2.5 Then, if the use of the source is necessary, the person granting the authorisation must believe that the use of a source is proportionate to what is sought to be achieved by the conduct and use of that source. This involves balancing the intrusiveness of the use of the source on the target and others who might be affected by it against the need for the source to be used in operational terms. The use of a source will not be proportionate if it is excessive in the circumstances of the case or if the information which is sought could reasonably be obtained by other less intrusive means. The use of a source should be carefully managed to meet the objective in question and sources must not be used in an arbitrary or unfair way.

Collateral intrusion

2.6 Before authorising the use or conduct of a source, the authorising officer should also take into account the risk of intrusion into the privacy of persons other than those who are directly the subjects of the operation or investigation (collateral intrusion). Measures should be taken, wherever practicable, to avoid unnecessary intrusion into the lives of those not directly connected with the operation.

2.7 An application for an authorisation should include an assessment of the risk of any collateral intrusion. The authorising officer should take this into account, when considering the proportionality of the use and conduct of a source.

2.8 Those tasking a source should inform the authorising officer if the investigation or operation unexpectedly interferes with the privacy of individuals who are not covered by the authorisation. When the original authorisation may not be sufficient, consideration should be given to whether the authorisation needs to be amended and reauthorised or a new authorisation is required.

2.9 Any person granting or applying for an authorisation will also need to be aware of any particular sensitivities in the local community where the source is being used and of similar activities being undertaken by other public authorities which could impact on the deployment of the source. Consideration should also be given to any adverse impact on community confidence or safety that may result from the use or conduct of a source or of information obtained from that source. In this regard, it is recommended that where the authorising officers in the National Criminal Intelligence Service (NCIS), the National Crime Squad (NCS) and HM Customs and Excise (HMCE) consider that conflicts might arise they should consult a senior officer within the police force area in which the source is deployed. Additionally, the authorising officer should make an assessment of any risk to a source in carrying out the conduct in the proposed authorisation.

2.10 In a very limited range of circumstances an authorisation under Part II may, by virtue of sections 26(7) and 27 of the 2000 Act, render lawful conduct which would otherwise be criminal, if it is incidental to any conduct falling within section 26(8) of the 2000 Act which the source is authorised to undertake. This would depend on the circumstances of each individual case, and consideration should always be given to seeking advice from the legal adviser within the relevant public authority when such activity is contemplated. A source that acts beyond the limits recognised by the law will be at risk from prosecution. The need to protect the source cannot alter this principle.

Combined authorisations

2.11 A single authorisation may combine two or more different authorisations under Part II of the 2000 Act. For example, a single authorisation may combine authorisations for intrusive surveillance and the conduct of a source. In such cases the provisions applicable to each of the authorisations must be considered separately. Thus, a police superintendent can authorise the conduct of a source but an authorisation for intrusive surveillance by the police needs the separate authority of a chief constable, and in certain cases the approval of a Surveillance Commissioner will also be necessary. Where an authorisation for the use or conduct of a covert human intelligence source is combined with a Secretary of State authorisation for intrusive surveillance, the combined authorisation must be issued by the Secretary of State. However, this does not preclude public authorities from obtaining separate authorisations.

Directed surveillance against a potential source

2.12 It may be necessary to deploy directed surveillance against a potential source as part of the process of assessing their suitability for recruitment, or in planning how best to make the approach to them. An authorisation under this code authorising an officer to establish a covert relationship with a potential source could be combined with a directed surveillance authorisation so that both the officer and potential source could be followed. Directed surveillance is defined in section 26(2) of the 2000 Act. See the code of practice on Covert Surveillance.

Central record of all authorisations

2.13 A centrally retrievable record of all authorisations should be held by each public authority and regularly updated whenever an authorisation is granted, renewed or cancelled. The record should be made available to the relevant Commissioner or an Inspector from the Office of Surveillance Commissioners, upon request. These records should be retained for a period of at least three years from the ending of the authorisation.

2.14 Proper records must be kept of the authorisation and use of a source. Section 29(5) of the 2000 Act provides that an authorising officer must not grant an authorisation for the use or conduct of a source unless he believes that there are arrangements in place for ensuring that there is at all times a person with the responsibility for maintaining a record of the use made of the source. The Regulation of Investigatory Powers (Source Records) Regulations 2000; SI No: 2725 details the particulars that must be included in the records relating to each source.

2.15 In addition, records or copies of the following, as appropriate, should be kept by the relevant authority:

- a copy of the authorisation together with any supplementary documentation and notification of the approval given by the authorising officer;
- a copy of any renewal of an authorisation, together with the supporting documentation submitted when the renewal was requested;
- the reason why the person renewing an authorisation considered it necessary to do so;
- any authorisation which was granted or renewed orally (in an urgent case) and the reason why the case was considered urgent;
- any risk assessment made in relation to the source;
- the circumstances in which tasks were given to the source;
- the value of the source to the investigating authority;
- a record of the results of any reviews of the authorisation;
- the reasons, if any, for not renewing an authorisation;
- the reasons for cancelling an authorisation.
- the date and time when any instruction was given by the authorising officer to cease using a source.

2.16 The records kept by public authorities should be maintained in such a way as to preserve the confidentiality of the source and the information provided by that source. There should, at all times, be a designated person within the relevant public authority who will have responsibility for maintaining a record of the use made of the source.

Retention and destruction of the product

2.17 Where the product obtained from a source could be relevant to pending or future criminal or civil proceedings, it should be retained in accordance with established disclosure requirements for a suitable further period, commensurate to any subsequent review.

2.18 In the cases of the law enforcement agencies (not including the Royal Navy Regulating Branch, the Royal Military Police and the Royal Air Force Police), particular attention is drawn to the requirements of the code of practice issued under the Criminal Procedure and Investigations Act 1996. This requires that material which is obtained in the course of a criminal investigation and which may be relevant to the investigation must be recorded and retained.

2.19 There is nothing in the 2000 Act which prevents material obtained from properly authorised use of a source being used in other investigations. Each public authority must ensure that arrangements are in place for the handling, storage and destruction of material obtained through the use of a source. Authorising officers must ensure compliance with the appropriate data protection requirements and any relevant codes of practice produced by individual authorities in the handling and storage of material.

The Intelligence Services, MOD and HM Forces

2.20 The heads of these agencies are responsible for ensuring that arrangements exist to ensure that no information is stored by the authorities, except as necessary for the proper discharge of their functions. They are also responsible for arrangements to control onward disclosure. For the intelligence services, this is a statutory duty under the 1989 Act and the 1994 Act.

3 Special rules on authorisations

Confidential information

3.1 The 2000 Act does not provide any special protection for 'confidential information'. Nevertheless, particular care should be taken in cases where the subject of the investigation or operation might reasonably expect a high degree of privacy, or where confidential information is involved. Confidential information consists of matters subject to legal privilege, confidential personal information or confidential journalistic material.

3.2 In cases where through the use or conduct of a source it is likely that knowledge of confidential information will be acquired, the deployment of the source is subject to a higher level of authorisation. Annex A lists the authorising officer for each public authority permitted to authorise such use or conduct of a source.

Communications subject to legal privilege

3.3 Section 98 of the 1997 Act describes those matters that are subject to legal privilege in England and Wales. In Scotland, the relevant description is contained in section 33 of the Criminal Law (Consolidation) (Scotland) Act 1995. With regard to Northern Ireland, Article 12 of the Police and Criminal Evidence (Northern Ireland) Order 1989 should be referred to.

3.4 Legal privilege does not apply to communications made with the intention of furthering a criminal purpose (whether the lawyer is acting unwittingly or culpably). Legally privileged communications will lose their protection if there are grounds to believe, for example, that the professional legal adviser is intending to hold or use them for a criminal purpose. But privilege is not lost if a professional legal adviser is properly advising a person who is suspected of having committed a criminal offence. The concept of legal privilege applies to the provision of professional legal advice by any individual, agency or organisation qualified to do so.

3.5 The 2000 Act does not provide any special protection for legally privileged information. Nevertheless, such information is particularly sensitive and any source which acquires such material may engage Article 6 of the ECHR (right to a fair trial) as well as Article 8. Legally privileged information obtained by a source is extremely unlikely ever to be admissible as evidence in criminal proceedings. Moreover, the mere fact that use has been made of a source to obtain such information may lead to any related criminal proceedings being stayed as an abuse of process. Accordingly, action which may lead to such information being obtained is subject to additional safeguards under this code.

3.6 In general, an application for the use or conduct of a source which is likely to result in the acquisition of legally privileged information should only be made in exceptional and compelling circumstance. Full regard should be had to the particular proportionality issues such a use or conduct of a source raises. The application should include, in addition to the reasons why it is considered necessary for the use or conduct of a source to be used, an assessment of how likely it is that information subject to legal privilege will be acquired. The application should clearly state whether the purpose (or one of the purposes) of the use or conduct of the source is to obtain legally privileged information.

3.7 This assessment will be taken into account by the authorising officer in deciding whether the proposed use or conduct of a source is necessary and proportionate for a purpose under section 29 of the 2000 Act. The authorising officer may require regular reporting so as to be able to decide whether the authorisation should continue. In those cases where legally privileged information has been acquired and retained, the matter should be reported to the relevant Commissioner or Inspector during his next inspection and the material should be made available to him if requested.

3.8 A substantial proportion of the communications between a lawyer and his client(s) may be subject to legal privilege. Therefore, any case where a lawyer is the subject of an investigation or operation should be notified to the relevant Commissioner or Inspector during his next inspection and any material which has been retained should be made available to him if requested.

3.9 Where there is any doubt as to the handling and dissemination of information which may be subject to legal privilege, advice should be sought from a legal adviser within the relevant public authority before any further dissemination of the material takes place. Similar advice should also be sought where there is doubt over whether information is not subject to legal privilege due to the "in furtherance of a criminal purpose" exception. The retention of legally privileged information, or its dissemination to an outside body, should be accompanied by a clear warning that it is subject to legal privilege. It should be safeguarded by taking reasonable steps to ensure there is no possibility of it becoming available, or its contents becoming known to any person whose possession of it might prejudice any criminal or civil proceedings related to the information. Any dissemination of legally privileged material to an outside body should be notified to the relevant Commissioner or Inspector during his next inspection.

Communications involving confidential personal information and confidential journalistic material

3.10 Similar consideration must also be given to authorisations that involve confidential personal information and confidential journalistic material. In those cases where confidential personal information and confidential journalistic material has been acquired and retained, the matter should be reported to the relevant Commissioner or Inspector during his next inspection and the material be made available to him if requested. Confidential personal information is information held in confidence relating to the physical or mental health or spiritual counselling concerning an individual (whether living or dead) who can be identified from it. Such information, which can include both oral and written communications is held in confidence if it is held subject to an express or implied undertaking to hold it in confidence or it is subject to a restriction on disclosure or an obligation of confidentiality contained in existing legislation. Examples might include consultations between a health professional and a patient, or information from a patient's medical records.

3.11 Spiritual counselling means conversations between an individual and a Minister of Religion acting in his official capacity, where the individual being counselled is seeking or the Minister is imparting forgiveness, absolution or the resolution of conscience with the authority of the Divine Being(s) of their faith.

3.12 Confidential journalistic material includes material acquired or created for the purposes of journalism and held subject to an undertaking to hold it in confidence, as well as communications resulting in information being acquired for the purposes of journalism and held subject to such an undertaking.

Vulnerable individuals

3.13 A 'vulnerable individual' is a person who is or may be in need of community care services by reason of mental or other disability, age or illness and who is or may be unable to take care of himself, or unable to protect himself against significant harm or exploitation. Any individual of this description should only be authorised to act as a source in the most exceptional circumstances. In these cases, the attached table in Annex A lists the authorising officer for each public authority permitted to authorise the use of a vulnerable individual as a source.

Juvenile sources

3.14 Special safeguards also apply to the use or conduct of juvenile sources; that is sources under the age of 18 years. **On no occasion should the use or conduct of a source under 16 years of age be authorised to give information against his parents or any person who has parental responsibility for him**. In other cases, authorisations should not be granted unless the special provisions contained within The Regulation of Investigatory Powers (Juveniles) Order 2000; SI No. 2793 are satisfied. Authorisations for juvenile sources should be granted by those listed in the attached table at Annex A. The duration of such an authorisation is **one month** instead of twelve months.

4 Authorisation procedures for covert human intelligence sources

4.1 Under section 26(8) of the 2000 Act a person is a source if:

(a)   he establishes or maintains a personal or other relationship with a person for the covert purpose of facilitating the doing of anything falling within paragraph (b) or (c);

(b)   he covertly uses such a relationship to obtain information or to provide access to any information to another person; or

(c)   he covertly discloses information obtained by the use of such a relationship or as a consequence of the existence of such a relationship.

4.2 A source may include those referred to as agents, informants and officers working undercover.

4.3 By virtue of section 26(9)(b) of the 2000 Act a purpose is covert, in relation to the establishment or maintenance of a personal or other relationship, if and only if, the relationship is conducted in a manner that is calculated to ensure that one of the parties to the relationship is unaware of the purpose.

4.4 By virtue of section 26(9)(c) of the 2000 Act a relationship is used covertly, and information obtained as mentioned in paragraph 4.1(c) above is disclosed covertly, if and only if it is used or, as the case may be, disclosed in a manner that is calculated to ensure that one of the parties to the relationship is unaware of the use or disclosure in question.

4.5 The use of a source involves inducing, asking or assisting a person to engage in the conduct of a source or to obtain information by means of the conduct of such a source.

4.6 The conduct of a source is any conduct falling within section 29(4) of the 2000 Act, or which is incidental to anything falling within section 29(4) of the 2000 Act.

Authorisation procedures

4.7 Under section 29(3) of the 2000 Act an authorisation for the use or conduct of a source may be granted by the authorising officer where he believes that the authorisation is necessary:

- in the interests of national security[1], [2];
- for the purpose of preventing and detecting[3] crime or of preventing disorder;
- in the interests of the economic well-being of the UK;
- in the interests of public safety;
- for the purpose of protecting public health[4];
- for the purpose of assessing or collecting any tax, duty, levy or other imposition, contribution or charge payable to a government department; or
- for any other purpose prescribed in an order made by the Secretary of State[5].

4.8 The authorising officer must also believe that the authorised use or conduct of a source is proportionate to what is sought to be achieved by that use or conduct.

4.9 The public authorities entitled to authorise the use or conduct of a source are those listed in Schedule 1 to the 2000 Act. Responsibility for authorising the use or conduct of a source rests with the authorising officer and all authorisations require the personal authority of the authorising officer. An authorising officer is the person designated under section 29 of the 2000 Act to grant an authorisation for the use or conduct of a source. The Regulation of Investigatory Powers (Prescriptions of Offices, Ranks and Positions) Order 2000; SI No: 2417 designates the authorising officer for each different public authority and the officers entitled to act only in urgent cases. In certain circumstances the Secretary of State will be the authorising officer (see section 30(2) of the 2000 Act).

4.10 The authorising officer must give authorisations in writing, except that in urgent cases, they may be given orally by the authorising officer or the officer entitled to act in urgent cases. In such cases, a statement that the authorising officer has expressly authorised the action should be recorded in writing by the applicant as soon as is reasonably practicable.

4.11 A case is not normally to be regarded as urgent unless the time that would elapse before the authorising officer was available to grant the authorisation would, in the judgement of the person giving the authorisation, be likely to endanger life or jeopardise the operation or investigation for which the authorisation was being given. An authorisation is not to be regarded as urgent where the need for an authorisation has been neglected or the urgency is of the authorising officer's own making.

4.12 Authorising officers should not be responsible for authorising their own activities, e.g. those in which they, themselves, are to act as the source or in tasking the source. However, it is recognised that this is not always possible, especially in the cases of small organisations. Where an authorising officer authorises his own activity the authorisation record (see paragraphs 2.13 – 2.15) should highlight this and the attention of a Commissioner or Inspector should be invited to it during his next inspection.

4.13 The authorising officers within the police, NCIS and NCS may only grant authorisations on application by a member of their own force, Service or Squad. Authorising officers in HMCE may only grant authorisations on application by a customs officer[6].

Information to be provided in applications for authorisation

4.14 An application for authorisation for the use or conduct of a source should be in writing and record:

- the reasons why the authorisation is necessary in the particular case and on the grounds (e.g. for the purpose of preventing or detecting crime) listed in section 29(3) of the 2000 Act;
- the reasons why the authorisation is considered proportionate to what it seeks to achieve;
- the purpose for which the source will be tasked or deployed (e.g. In relation to an organised serious crime, espionage, a series of racially motivated crimes etc);
- where a specific investigation or operation is involved, nature of that investigation or operation;
- the nature of what the source will be tasked to do;
- the level of authority required (or recommended, where that is different).
- the details of any potential collateral intrusion and why the intrusion is justified;
- the details of any confidential information that is likely to be obtained as a consequence of the authorisation; and
- a subsequent record of whether authority was given or refused, by whom and the time and date.

4.15 Additionally, in urgent cases, the authorisation should record (as the case may be):

- the reasons why the authorising officer or the officer entitled to act in urgent cases considered the case so urgent that an oral instead of a written authorisation was given; and/or
- the reasons why it was not reasonably practicable for the application to be considered by the authorising officer.

4.16 Where the authorisation is oral, the detail referred to above should be recorded in writing by the applicant as soon as reasonably practicable.

Duration of authorisations

4.17 A written authorisation will, unless renewed, cease to have effect at the end of a period of **twelve months** beginning with the day on which it took effect.

4.18 Urgent oral authorisations or authorisations granted or renewed by a person who is entitled to act only in urgent cases will, unless renewed, cease to have effect after **seventy-two hours**, beginning with the time when the authorisation was granted or renewed.

Reviews

4.19 Regular reviews of authorisations should be undertaken to assess the need for the use of a source to continue. The review should include the use made of the source during the period authorised, the tasks given to the source and the information obtained from the source. The results of a review should be recorded on the authorisation record (see paragraphs 2.13 – 2.15). Particular attention is drawn to the need to review authorisations frequently where the use of a source provides access to confidential information or involves collateral intrusion.

4.20 In each case the authorising officer within each public authority should determine how often a review should take place. This should be as frequently as is considered necessary and practicable.

Renewals

4.21 Before an authorising officer renews an authorisation, he must be satisfied that a review has been carried out of the use of a source as outlined in paragraph 4.19.

4.22 If at any time before an authorisation would cease to have effect, the authorising officer considers it necessary for the authorisation to continue for the purpose for which it was given, he may renew it in writing for a further period of **twelve months**. Renewals may also be granted orally in urgent cases and last for a period of **seventy-two hours**.

4.23 A renewal takes effect at the time at which, or day on which the authorisation would have ceased to have effect but for the renewal. An application for renewal should not be made until shortly before the authorisation period is drawing to an end. Any person who would be entitled to grant a new authorisation can renew an authorisation. Authorisations may be renewed more than once, if necessary, provided they continue to meet the criteria for authorisation. The renewal should be kept/ recorded as part of the authorisation record (see paragraphs 2.13 – 2.15).

4.24 All applications for the renewal of an authorisation should record:

- whether this is the first renewal or every occasion on which the authorisation has been renewed previously;
- any significant changes to the information in paragraph 4.14;
- the reasons why it is necessary to continue to use the source;
- the use made of the source in the period since the grant or, as the case may be, latest renewal of the authorisation;
- the tasks given to the source during that period and the information obtained from the conduct or use of the source;
- the results of regular reviews of the use of the source;

Cancellations

4.25 The authorising officer who granted or renewed the authorisation must cancel it if he is satisfied that the use or conduct of the source no longer satisfies the criteria for authorisation or that satisfactory arrangements for the source's case no longer exist. Where the authorising officer is no longer available, this duty will fall on the person who has taken over the role of authorising officer or the person who is acting as authorising officer (see the Regulation of Investigatory Powers (Cancellation of Authorisations) Order 2000; SI No: 2794). Where necessary, the safety and welfare of the source should continue to be taken into account after the authorisation has been cancelled.

Management of sources

Tasking

4.26 Tasking is the assignment given to the source by the persons defined at sections 29(5)(a) and (b) of the 2000 Act, asking him to obtain information, to provide access to information or to otherwise act, incidentally, for the benefit of the relevant public authority. Authorisation for the use or conduct of a source is required prior to any tasking where such tasking requires the source to establish or maintain a personal or other relationship for a covert purpose.

4.27 The person referred to in section 29(5)(a) of the 2000 Act will have day to day responsibility for:

- dealing with the source on behalf of the authority concerned;
- directing the day to day activities of the source;
- recording the information supplied by the source; and
- monitoring the source's security and welfare;

4.28 The person referred to in section 29(5)(b) of the 2000 Act will be responsible for the general oversight of the use of the source.

4.29 In some instances, the tasking given to a person will not require the source to establish a personal or other relationship for a covert purpose. For example a source may be tasked with finding out purely factual information about the layout of commercial premises. Alternatively, a trading standards officer may be involved in the test purchase of items which have been labelled misleadingly or are unfit for consumption. In such cases, it is for the relevant public authority to determine where, and in what circumstances, such activity may require authorisation.

4.30 It is not the intention that authorisations be drawn so narrowly that a separate authorisation is required each time the source is tasked. Rather, an authorisation might cover, in broad terms, the nature of the source's task. If this changes, then a new authorisation may need to be sought.

4.31 It is difficult to predict exactly what might occur each time a meeting with a source takes place, or the source meets the subject of an investigation. There may be occasions when unforeseen action or undertakings occur. When this happens, the occurrence must be recorded as soon as practicable after the event and, if the existing authorisation is insufficient it should either be updated and reauthorised (for minor amendments only) or it should cancelled and a new authorisation should be obtained before any further such action is carried out.

4.32 Similarly where it is intended to task a source in a new way or significantly greater way than previously identified, the persons defined at section 29(5)(a) or (b) of the 2000 Act must refer the proposed tasking to the authorising officer, who should consider whether a separate authorisation is required. This should be done in advance of any tasking and the details of such referrals must be recorded.

Management responsibility

4.33 Public authorities should ensure that arrangements are in place for the proper oversight and management of sources, including appointing individual officers as defined in section 29(5)(a) and (b) of the 2000 Act for each source.

4.34 The person responsible for the day-to-day contact between the public authority and the source will usually be of a rank or position below that of the authorising officer.

4.35 In cases where the authorisation is for the use or conduct of a source whose activities benefit more than a single public authority, responsibilities for the management and oversight of that source may be taken up by one authority or can be split between the authorities.

Security and welfare

4.36 Any public authority deploying a source should take into account the safety and welfare of that source, when carrying out actions in relation to an authorisation or tasking, and to foreseeable consequences to others of that tasking. Before authorising the use or conduct of a source, the authorising officer should ensure that a risk assessment is carried out to determine the risk to the source of any tasking and the likely consequences should the role of the source become known. The ongoing security and welfare of the source, after the cancellation of the authorisation, should also be considered at the outset.

4.37 The person defined at section 29(5)(a) of the 2000 Act is responsible for bringing to the attention of the person defined at section 29(5)(b) of the 2000 Act any concerns about the personal circumstances of the source, insofar as they might affect:

- the validity of the risk assessment
- the conduct of the source, and
- the safety and welfare of the source.

4.38 Where deemed appropriate, concerns about such matters must be considered by the authorising officer, and a decision taken on whether or not to allow the authorisation to continue.

Additional rules

Recording of telephone conversations

4.39 Subject to paragraph 4.40 below, the interception of communications sent by post or by means of public telecommunications systems or private telecommunications systems attached to the public network may be authorised only by the Secretary of State, in accordance with the terms of Part I of the 2000 Act. Nothing in this code should be taken as granting dispensation from the requirements of that Part of the 2000 Act.

4.40 Part I of the 2000 Act provides certain exceptions to the rule that interception of telephone conversations must be warranted under that Part. This includes, where one party to the communication consents to the interception, it may be authorised in accordance with section 48(4) of the 2000 Act provided that there is no interception warrant authorising the interception. In such cases, the interception is treated as directed surveillance (see chapter 4 of the Covert Surveillance code of practice).

Use of covert human intelligence source with technical equipment

4.41 A source, whether or not wearing or carrying a surveillance device and invited into residential premises or a private vehicle, does not require additional authorisation to record any activity taking place inside those premises or vehicle which take place in his presence. This also applies to the recording of telephone conversations other than by interception which takes place in the source's presence. Authorisation for the use or conduct of that source may be obtained in the usual way.

4.42 However, if a surveillance device is to be used, other than in the presence of the source, an intrusive surveillance authorisation and if applicable an authorisation for interference with property should be obtained.

1   One of the functions of the Security Service is the protection of national security and in particular the protection against threats from terrorism. These functions extend throughout the United Kingdom, save that, in Northern Ireland, where the lead responsibility for investigating the threat from terrorism related to the affairs of Northern Ireland lies with the Police Service of Northern Ireland. An authorising officer in another public authority should not issue an authorisation under Part II of the 2000 Act where the operation or investigation falls within the responsibilities of the

Security Service, as set out above, except where it is to be carried out by a Special Branch or where the Security Service has agreed that another public authority can authorise the use or conduct of a source which would normally fall within the responsibilities of the Security Service.

2   HM Forces may also undertake operations in connection with a military threat to national security and other operations in connection with national security in support of the Security Service, the Police Service of Northern Ireland or other Civil Powers.

3   Detecting crime is defined in section 81(5) of the 2000 Act.

4   This could include investigations into infectious diseases, contaminated products or the illicit sale of pharmaceuticals.

5   This could only be for a purpose which satisfies the criteria set out in Article 8(2) of the ECHR.

6   As defined in section 81(1) of the 2000 Act.

5 Oversight by commissioners

5.1 The 2000 Act requires the Chief Surveillance Commissioner to keep under review (with the assistance of the Surveillance Commissioners and Assistant Surveillance Commissioners) the performance of functions under Part III of the 1997 Act and Part II of the 2000 Act by the police (including the Royal Navy Regulating Branch, the Royal Military Police and the Royal Air Force Police and the Ministry of Defence Police and the British Transport Police), NCIS, NCS, HMCE and of the 2000 Act the other public authorities listed in Schedule 1 and in Northern Ireland officials of the Ministry of Defence and HM Forces

5.2 The Intelligence Services Commissioner's remit is to provide independent oversight of the use of the powers contained within Part II of the 2000 Act by the Security Service, Secret Intelligence Service (SIS), the Governments Communication Headquarters (GCHQ) and the Ministry of Defence and HM Forces (excluding the Royal Navy Regulating Branch, the Royal Military Police and the Royal Air Force Police, and in Northern Ireland officials of the Ministry of Defence HM Forces).

5.3 This code does not cover the exercise of any of the Commissioners' functions. It is the duty of any person who uses these powers to comply with any request made by a Commissioner to disclose or provide any information he requires for the purpose of enabling him to carry out his functions.

5.4 References in this code to the performance of review functions by the Chief Surveillance Commissioner and other Commissioners apply also to Inspectors and other members of staff to whom such functions have been delegated.

6 Complaints

6.1 The 2000 Act establishes an independent Tribunal. This Tribunal will be made up of senior members of the judiciary and the legal profession and is independent of the Government. The Tribunal has full powers to investigate and decide any case within its jurisdiction.

6.2 This code does not cover the exercise of the Tribunal's functions. Details of the relevant complaints procedure can be obtained from the following address:

Investigatory Powers Tribunal

PO Box 33220

London

SW1H 9ZQ

Tel: 020 7273 4514

Annex A

Authorisation levels when knowledge of confidential information is likely to be acquired or when a vulnerable individual or juvenile is to be used as a source

Government Department/Public Authority	Authorisation level for when knowledge of Confidential Information is likely to be acquired	Authorisation level for when a vulnerable individual or a Juvenile is to be used as a source
Police Forces – Any police force maintained under section 2 of the Police Act 1996 (police forces in England and Wales outside London).	Chief Constable	Assistant Chief Constable
Police Forces – Any police force maintained under or by virtue of section 1 of the Police (Scotland) Act 1967.	Chief Constable	Assistant Chief Constable
The Metropolitan police force	Assistant Commissioner	Commander
The City of London police force	Commissioner	Commander
The Police Service of Northern Ireland	Deputy Chief Constable	Assistant Chief Constable
The Royal Navy Regulating Branch **Royal Military Police** **Royal Air Force Police**	Provost Marshal Provost Marshal Provost Marshal	Provost Marshal Provost Marshal Provost Marshal

Government Department/Public Authority	Authorisation level for when knowledge of Confidential Information is likely to be acquired	Authorisation level for when a vulnerable individual or a Juvenile is to be used as a source
National Criminal Intelligence Service (NCIS)	Director General	Assistant Chief Constable or Assistant Chief Investigation Officer
National Crime Squad (NCS)	Director General or Deputy Director General	Assistant Chief Constable
Serious Fraud Office	Director or Assistant Director	Director or Assistant Director
The Intelligence Services: Government Communications Headquarters Security Service Secret Intelligence Service	A Director of GCHQ Deputy Director General A Director of the Secret Intelligence Service	A Director of GCHQ Deputy Director General A member of the Secret Intelligence Service not below the equivalent rank to that of a Grade 5 in the Home Civil Service)
HM Forces: Royal Navy Army Royal Air Force	Rear Admiral Major General Air Vice-Marshal	Rear Admiral Major General Air Vice-Marshal
HM Customs and Excise	Director Investigation or Regional Heads of Investigation	Band 11 (Intelligence)
Inland Revenue	Deputy Chairman of Inland Revenue	Head of Special Compliance Office

Government Department/Public Authority	Authorisation level for when knowledge of Confidential Information is likely to be acquired	Authorisation level for when a vulnerable individual or a Juvenile is to be used as a source
Department for the Environment, Food and Rural Affairs: DEFRA Investigation Branch Horticultural Marketing Inspectorate Plant Health and Seed Inspectorate Egg Marketing Inspectorate Sea Fisheries Inspectorate (SFI) Centre for Environment, Fisheries & Aquaculture Science (CEFAS)	Immediate Senior Officer of Head of DEFRA Prosecution Division Immediate Senior Officer of Head of DEFRA Prosecution Division Immediate Senior Officer of Head of DEFRA Prosecution Division Immediate Senior Officer of Head of DEFRA Prosecution Division Immediate Senior Officer of Head of DEFRA Prosecution Division Immediate Senior Officer of Head of DEFRA Prosecution Division	Head of DEFRA Prosecution Division No No No No Head of DEFRA Prosecution Division
Ministry of Defence	Director General or equivalent	Director General or equivalent
Department for Transport, Local Government and the Regions: Vehicle Inspectorate Transport Security (Transec)	No Director of Transport Security	No Deputy Director of Transport Security

Government Department/Public Authority	Authorisation level for when knowledge of Confidential Information is likely to be acquired	Authorisation level for when a vulnerable individual or a Juvenile is to be used as a source
Department of Health: Medical Devices Agency Medicine Control Agency Welfare Foods Policy Unit Directorate of Counter Fraud Services (DFCS)	Chief Executive Chief Executive Deputy Chief Medical Officer Director of Counter Fraud Services	No Head of Division for Inspection and Enforcement No Director of Counter Fraud Services
Home Office: HM Prison Service Immigration Service	Deputy Director General Chief Inspector	Area Managers Director
Department of Work and Pensions: Benefits Agency	Chief Executive	Head of Fraud Investigation
Department of Trade and Industry: Radiocommunications Agency British Trade International Coal Health Claims Unit Companies Investigation Branch Legal Services Directorate D	No No Director of Coal Health Claims unit The Inspector of Companies The Director of Legal Service D	No No No The Inspector of Companies The Director of Legal Service D
National Assembly for Wales	Health – Director, NHS Wales Agriculture – Head, National Assembly for Wales Agriculture Department	Health – Director, NHS Wales Agriculture – Head, National Assembly for Wales Agriculture Department
Local Authorities	The Head of Paid Service or (in his absence) a Chief Officer	The Head of Paid Service or (in his absence) a Chief Officer
Environment Agency	Chief Executive	Executive Managers

Government Department/Public Authority	Authorisation level for when knowledge of Confidential Information is likely to be acquired	Authorisation level for when a vulnerable individual or a Juvenile is to be used as a source
Financial Services Authority	Chairman	Chairman
Food Standards Agency	Head of Group, Deputy Chief Executive and Chief Executive	Head of Group, Deputy Chief Executive and Chief Executive
The Intervention Board for Agricultural Produce	Chief Executive	Legal Director
Personal Investment Authority	Chairman	Chairman
Post Office	Director of Security	Head of Corporate Security/Head of Security for the Royal Mail/Head of Security for Counter Business

Interception of Communications: Code of Practice

Pursuant to Section 71 of the Regulation of Investigatory Powers Act 2000

CONTENTS

Section 8:   Oversight
Section 9:   Complaints
Section 10:   Interception without a warrant

1 General

1.1 This code of practice relates to the powers and duties conferred or imposed under Chapter I of Part I of the Regulation of Investigatory Powers Act 2000 ("the Act"). It provides guidance on the procedures that must be followed before interception of communications can take place under those provisions. It is primarily intended for use by those public authorities listed in section 6(2) of the Act. It will also prove useful to postal and telecommunication operators and other interested bodies to acquaint themselves with the procedures to be followed by those public authorities.

1.2 The Act provides that all codes of practice relating to the Act are admissible as evidence in criminal and civil proceedings. If any provision of this code appears relevant before any court or tribunal considering any such proceedings, or to the Tribunal established under the Act, or to one of the Commissioners responsible for overseeing the powers conferred by the Act, it must be taken into account.

2 General rules on interception with a warrant

2.1 There are a limited number of persons by whom, or on behalf of whom, applications for interception warrants may be made. These persons are:

- The Director-General of the Security Service.
- The Chief of the Secret Intelligence Service.
- The Director of GCHQ.
- The Director-General of the National Criminal Intelligence Service (NCIS handle interception on behalf of police forces in England and Wales).
- The Commissioner of the Police of the Metropolis (the Metropolitan Police Special Branch handle interception on behalf of Special Branches in England and Wales).
- The Chief Constable of the Police Service of Northern Ireland.
- The Chief Constable of any police force maintained under or by virtue of section 1 of the Police (Scotland) Act 1967.
- The Commissioners of Customs and Excise.
- The Chief of Defence Intelligence.
- A person who, for the purposes of any international mutual assistance agreement, is the competent authority of a country or territory outside the United Kingdom.

Any application made on behalf of one of the above must be made by a person holding office under the Crown.

2.2 All interception warrants are issued by the Secretary of State[1]. Even where the urgency procedure is followed, the Secretary of State personally authorises the warrant, although it is signed by a senior official.

2.3 Before issuing an interception warrant, the Secretary of State must believe that what the action seeks to achieve is necessary for one of the following section 5(3) purposes:

- in the interests of national security;
- for the purpose of preventing or detecting serious crime; or
- for the purpose of safeguarding the economic well-being of the UK

and that the conduct authorised by the warrant is proportionate to what is sought to be achieved by that conduct.

Necessity and proportionality

2.4 Obtaining a warrant under the Act will only ensure that the interception authorised is a justifiable interference with an individual's rights under Article 8 of the European Convention of Human Rights (the right to privacy) if it is necessary and proportionate for the interception to take place. The Act recognises this by first requiring that the Secretary of State believes that the authorisation is necessary on one or more of the statutory grounds set out in section 5(3) of the Act. This requires him to believe that it is necessary to undertake the interception which is to be authorised for a particular purpose falling within the relevant statutory ground.

2.5 Then, if the interception is necessary, the Secretary of State must also believe that it is proportionate to what is sought to be achieved by carrying it out. This involves balancing the intrusiveness of the interference, against the need for it in operational terms. Interception of communications will not be proportionate if it is excessive in the circumstances of the case or if the information which is sought could reasonably be obtained by other means. Further, all interception should be carefully managed to meet the objective in question and must not be arbitrary or unfair.

Implementation of warrants

2.6 After a warrant has been issued it will be forwarded to the person to whom it is addressed, in practice the intercepting agency which submitted the application. The Act (section 11) then permits the intercepting agency to carry out the interception, or to require the assistance of other persons in giving effect to the warrant. Warrants cannot be served on those outside the jurisdiction of the UK.

Provision of reasonable assistance

2.7 Any postal or telecommunications operator (referred to as communications service providers) in the United Kingdom may be required to provide assistance in giving effect to an interception. The Act places a requirement on postal and telecommunications operators to take all such steps for giving effect to the warrant as are notified to them (section 11(4) of the Act). But the steps which may be required are limited to those which it is reasonably practicable to take (section 11(5)). What is reasonably practicable should be agreed after consultation between the postal or telecommunications operator and the Government. If no agreement can be reached it will be for the Secretary of State to decide whether to press forward with civil proceedings. Criminal proceedings may also be instituted by or with the consent of the Director of Public Prosecutions.

2.8 Where the intercepting agency requires the assistance of a communications service provider in order to implement a warrant, they should provide the following to the communications service provider:

- A copy of the warrant instrument signed and dated by the Secretary of State (or in an urgent case, by a senior official);
- The relevant schedule for that service provider setting out the numbers, addresses or other factors identifying the communications to be intercepted;
- A covering document from the intercepting agency requiring the assistance of the communications service provider and specifying any other details regarding the means of interception and delivery as may be necessary. Contact details with respect to the intercepting agency will either be provided in this covering document or will be available in the handbook provided to all postal and telecommunications operators who maintain an intercept capability.

Provision of intercept capability

2.9 Whilst all persons who provide a postal or telecommunications service are obliged to provide assistance in giving effect to an interception, persons who provide a public postal or telecommunications service, or plan to do so, may also be required to provide a reasonable intercept capability. The obligations the Secretary of State considers reasonable to impose on such persons to ensure they have such a capability will be set out in an order made by the Secretary of State and approved by Parliament. The Secretary of State may then serve a notice upon a communications service provider setting out the steps they must take to ensure they can meet these obligations. A notice will not be served without consultation over the content of the notice between the Government and the service provider having previously taken place. When served with such a notice, a communications service provider, if he feels it unreasonable, will be able to refer that notice to the Technical Advisory Board (TAB) on the reasonableness of the technical requirements and capabilities that are being sought. Details of how to submit a notice to the TAB will be provided either before or at the time the notice is served.

2.10 Any communications service provider obliged to maintain a reasonable intercept capability will be provided with a handbook which will contain the basic information they require to respond to requests for reasonable assistance for the interception of communications.

Duration of interception warrants

2.11 All interception warrants are valid for an initial period of three months. Upon renewal, warrants issued on serious crime grounds are valid for a further period of three months. Warrants renewed on national security/ economic well-being grounds are valid for a further period of six months. Urgent authorisations are valid for five working days following the date of issue unless renewed by the Secretary of State.

2.12 Where modifications take place, the warrant expiry date remains unchanged. However, where the modification takes place under the urgency provisions, the modification instrument expires after five working days following the date of issue unless renewed following the routine procedure.

2.13 Where a change in circumstance prior to the set expiry date leads the intercepting agency to consider it no longer necessary or practicable for the warrant to be in force, it should be cancelled with immediate effect.

Stored communications

2.14 Section 2(7) of the Act defines a communication in the course of its transmission as also encompassing any time when the communication is being stored on the communication system in such a way as to enable the intended recipient to have access to it. This means that a warrant can be used to obtain both communications that are in the process of transmission and those that are being stored on the transmission system.

2.15 Stored communications may also be accessed by means other than a warrant. If a communication has been stored on a communication system it may be obtained with lawful authority by means of an existing statutory power such as a production order (under the Police and Criminal Evidence Act 1984) or a search warrant.

3 Special rules on interception with a warrant

Collateral intrusion

3.1 Consideration should be given to any infringement of the privacy of individuals who are not the subject of the intended interception, especially where communications relating to religious, medical, journalistic or legally privileged material may be involved. An application for an interception warrant should draw attention to any circumstances which give rise to an unusual degree of collateral infringement of privacy, and this will be taken into account by the Secretary of State when considering a warrant application. Should an interception operation

3.2 Particular consideration should also be given in cases where the subject of the interception might reasonably assume a high degree of privacy, or where confidential information is involved. Confidential information consists of matters subject to legal privilege, confidential personal information or confidential journalistic material (see paragraphs 3.9–3.11). For example, extra consideration should be given where interception might involve communications between a minister of religion and an individual relating to the latter's spiritual welfare, or where matters of medical or journalistic confidentiality or legal privilege may be involved.

Communications subject to legal privilege

3.3 Section 98 of the Police Act 1997 describes those matters that are subject to legal privilege in England and Wales. In relation to Scotland, those matters subject to legal privilege contained in section 33 of the Criminal Law (Consolidation) (Scotland) Act 1995 should be adopted. With regard to Northern Ireland, Article 12 of the Police and Criminal Evidence (Northern Ireland) Order 1989 should be referred to.

3.4 Legal privilege does not apply to communications made with the intention of furthering a criminal purpose (whether the lawyer is acting unwittingly or culpably). Legally privileged communications will lose their protection if there are grounds to believe, for example, that the professional legal advisor is intending to hold or use the information for a criminal purpose. But privilege is not lost if a professional legal advisor is properly advising a person who is suspected of having committed a criminal offence. The concept of legal privilege applies to the provision of professional legal advice by any individual, agency or organisation qualified to do so.

3.5 The Act does not provide any special protection for legally privileged communications. Nevertheless, intercepting such communications is particularly sensitive and is therefore subject to additional safeguards under this Code. The guidance set out below may in part depend on whether matters subject to legal privilege have been obtained intentionally or incidentally to some other material which has been sought.

3.6 In general, any application for a warrant which is likely to result in the interception of legally privileged communications should include, in addition to the reasons why it is considered necessary for the interception to take place, an assessment of how likely it is that communications which are subject to legal privilege will be intercepted. In addition, it should state whether the purpose (or one of the purposes) of the interception is to obtain privileged communications. This assessment will be taken into account by the Secretary of State in deciding whether an interception is necessary under section 5(3) of the Act and whether it is proportionate. In such circumstances, the Secretary of State will be able to impose additional conditions such as regular reporting arrangements so as to be able to exercise his discretion on whether a warrant should continue to be authorised. In those cases where communications which include legally privileged communications have been intercepted and retained, the matter should be reported to the Interception of Communications Commissioner during his inspections and the material be made available to him if requested.

3.7 Where a lawyer is the subject of an interception, it is possible that a substantial proportion of the communications which will be intercepted will be between the lawyer and his client(s) and will be subject to legal privilege. Any case where a lawyer is the subject of an investigation should be notified to the Interception of Communications Commissioner during his inspections and any material which has been retained should be made available to him if requested.

3.8 In addition to safeguards governing the handling and retention of intercept material as provided for in section 15 of the Act, caseworkers who examine intercepted communications should be alert to any intercept material which may be subject to legal privilege. Where there is doubt as to whether the communications are subject to legal privilege, advice should be sought from a legal adviser within the intercepting agency. Similar advice should also be sought where there is doubt over whether communications are not subject to legal privilege due to the "in furtherance of a criminal purpose" exception.

Communications involving confidential personal information and confidential journalistic material

3.9 Similar consideration to that given to legally privileged communications must also be given to the interception of communications that involve confidential personal information and confidential journalistic material. Confidential personal information is information held in confidence concerning an individual (whether living or dead) who can be identified from it, and the material in question relates to his physical or mental health or to spiritual counselling. Such information can include both oral and written communications. Such information as described above is held in confidence if it is held subject to an express or implied undertaking to hold it in confidence or it is subject to a restriction on disclosure or an obligation of confidentiality contained in existing legislation. For example, confidential personal information might include consultations between a health professional and a patient, or information from a patient's medical records.

3.10 Spiritual counselling is defined as conversations between an individual and a Minister of Religion acting in his official capacity, and where the individual being counselled is seeking or the Minister is imparting forgiveness, absolution or the resolution of conscience with the authority of the Divine Being(s) of their faith.

3.11 Confidential journalistic material includes material acquired or created for the purposes of journalism and held subject to an undertaking to hold it in confidence, as well as communications resulting in information being acquired for the purposes of journalism and held subject to such an undertaking.

4 Interception warrants (section 8(1))

4.1 This section applies to the interception of communications by means of a warrant complying with section 8(1) of the Act. This type of warrant may be issued in respect of the interception of communications carried on any postal service or telecommunications system as defined in section 2(1) of the Act (including a private telecommunications system). Responsibility for the issuing of interception warrants rests with the Secretary of State.

Application for a section 8(1) warrant

4.2 An application for a warrant is made to the Secretary of State. Interception warrants, when issued, are addressed to the person who submitted the application. This person may then serve a copy upon any person who may be able to provide assistance in giving effect to that warrant. Each application, a copy of which must be retained by the applicant, should contain the following information:

- Background to the operation in question.
- Person or premises to which the application relates (and how the person or premises feature in the operation).
- Description of the communications to be intercepted, details of the communications service provider(s) and an assessment of the feasibility of the interception operation where this is relevant[2].
- Description of the conduct to be authorised as considered necessary in order to carry out the interception[2a], where appropriate.
- An explanation of why the interception is considered to be necessary under the provisions of section 5(3).
- A consideration of why the conduct to be authorised by the warrant is proportionate to what is sought to be achieved by that conduct.
- A consideration of any unusual degree of collateral intrusion and why that intrusion is justified in the circumstances. In particular, where the communications in question might affect religious, medical or journalistic confidentiality or legal privilege, this must be specified in the application.
- Where an application is urgent, supporting justification should be provided.
- An assurance that all material intercepted will be handled in accordance with the safeguards required by section 15 of the Act.

Authorisation of a section 8(1) warrant

4.3 Before issuing a warrant under section 8(1), the Secretary of State must believe the warrant is necessary[3]

- in the interests of national security;
- for the purpose of preventing or detecting serious crime; or
- for the purpose of safeguarding the economic well-being of the United Kingdom.

4.4 In exercising his power to issue an interception warrant for the purpose of safeguarding the economic well-being of the United Kingdom (as provided for by section 5(3)(c) of the Act), the Secretary of State will consider whether the economic well-being of the United Kingdom which is to be safeguarded is, on the facts of each case, directly related to state security. The term "state security", which is used in Directive 97/66/EC (concerning the processing of personal data and the protection of privacy in the telecommunications sector), should be interpreted in the same way as the term "national security" which is used elsewhere in the Act and this Code. The Secretary of State will not issue a warrant on section 5(3)(c) grounds if this direct link between the economic well-being of the United Kingdom and state security is not established. Any application for a warrant on section 5(3)(c) grounds should therefore explain how, in the applicant's view, the economic well-being of the United Kingdom which is to be safeguarded is directly related to state security on the facts of the case.

4.5 The Secretary of State must also consider that the conduct authorised by the warrant is proportionate to what it seeks to achieve (section 5(2)(b)). In considering necessity and proportionality, the Secretary of State must take into account whether the information sought could reasonably be obtained by other means (section 5(4)).

Urgent authorisation of a section 8(1) warrant

4.6 The Act makes provision (section 7(1)(b)) for cases in which an interception warrant is required urgently, yet the Secretary of State is not available to sign the warrant. In these cases the Secretary of State will still personally authorise the interception but the warrant is signed by a senior official, following discussion of the case between officials and the Secretary of State. The Act restricts issue of warrants in this way to urgent cases where the Secretary of State has himself expressly authorised the issue of the warrant (section 7(2)(a)), and requires the warrant to contain a statement to that effect (section 7(4)(a)). A warrant issued under the urgency procedure lasts for five working days following the day of issue unless renewed by the Secretary of State, in which case it expires after 3 months in the case of serious crime or 6 months in the case of national security or economic well-being in the same way as other non-urgent section 8(1) warrants. An urgent case is one in which interception authorisation is required within a twenty four hour period.

Format of a section 8(1) warrant

4.7 Each warrant comprises two sections, a warrant instrument signed by the Secretary of State listing the subject of the interception or set of premises, a copy of which each communications service provider will receive, and a schedule or set of schedules listing the communications to be intercepted. Only the schedule relevant to the communications that can be intercepted by the specified communications service provider will be provided to that service provider.

4.8 The warrant instrument should include:

•   The name or description of the interception subject or of a set of premises in relation to which the interception is to take place
•   A warrant reference number
•   The persons who may subsequently modify the scheduled part of the warrant in an urgent case (if authorised in accordance with section 10(8) of the Act)

4.9 The scheduled part of the warrant will comprise one or more schedules. Each schedule should contain:

•   The name of the communication service provider, or the other person who is to take action
•   A warrant reference number
•   A means of identifying the communications to be intercepted[4]

Modification of Section 8(1) warrant

4.10 Interception warrants may be modified under the provisions of section 10 of the Act. The unscheduled part of a warrant may only be modified by the Secretary of State or, in an urgent case, by a senior official with the express authorisation of the Secretary of State. In these cases, a statement of that fact must be endorsed on the modifying instrument, and the modification ceases to have effect after five working days following the day of issue unless it is renewed by the Secretary of State. The modification will then expire upon the expiry date of the warrant.

4.11 Scheduled parts of a warrant may be modified by the Secretary of State, or by a senior official[5] acting upon his behalf. A modification to the scheduled part of the warrant may include the addition of a new schedule relating to a communication service provider on whom a copy of the warrant has not been previously served. Modifications made in this way expire at the same time as the warrant expires. There also exists a duty to modify a warrant by deleting a communication identifier if it is no longer relevant. When a modification is sought to delete a number or other communication identifier, the relevant communications service provider must be advised and interception suspended before the modification instrument is signed.

4.12 In an urgent case, and where the warrant specifically authorises it, scheduled parts of a warrant may be modified by the person to whom the warrant is addressed (the person who submitted the application) or a subordinate (where the subordinate is identified in the warrant). Modifications of this kind are valid for five working days following the day of issue unless the modification instrument is endorsed by a senior official acting on behalf of the Secretary of State. Where the modification is endorsed in this way, the modification expires upon the expiry date of the warrant.

Renewal of a section 8(1) warrant

4.13 The Secretary of State may renew a warrant at any point before its expiry date. Applications for renewals must be made to the Secretary of State and should contain an update of the matters outlined in paragraph 4.2 above. In particular, the applicant should give an assessment of the value of interception to the operation to date and explain why he considers that interception continues to be necessary for one or more of the purposes in section 5(3).

4.14 Where the Secretary of State is satisfied that the interception continues to meet the requirements of the Act he may renew the warrant. Where the warrant is issued on serious crime grounds, the renewed warrant is valid for a further three months. Where it is issued on national security/ economic well-being grounds, the renewed warrant is valid for six months. These dates run from the date of signature on the renewal instrument.

4.15 A copy of the warrant renewal instrument will be forwarded by the intercepting agency to all relevant communications service providers on whom a copy of the original warrant instrument and a schedule have been served, providing they are still actively assisting. A warrant renewal instrument will include the reference number of the warrant and description of the person or premises described in the warrant.

Warrant cancellation

4.16 The Secretary of State is under a duty to cancel an interception warrant if, at any time before its expiry date, he is satisfied that the warrant is no longer necessary on grounds falling within section 5(3) of the Act. Intercepting agencies will therefore need to keep their warrants under continuous review. In practice, cancellation instruments will be signed by a senior official on his behalf.

4.17 The cancellation instrument should be addressed to the person to whom the warrant was issued (the intercepting agency) and should include the reference number of the warrant and the description of the person or premises specified in the warrant. A copy of the cancellation instrument should be sent to those communications service providers who have held a copy of the warrant instrument and accompanying schedule during the preceding twelve months.

Records

4.18 The oversight regime allows the Interception of Communications Commissioner to inspect the warrant application upon which the Secretary of State based his decision, and the applicant may be required to justify the content. Each intercepting agency should keep the following to be made available for scrutiny by the Commissioner as he may require:

- all applications made for warrants complying with section 8(1) and applications made for the renewal of such warrants;
- all warrants, and renewals and copies of schedule modifications (if any);
- where any application is refused, the grounds for refusal as given by the Secretary of State;
- the dates on which interception is started and stopped.

4.19 Records shall also be kept of the arrangements by which the requirements of section 15(2) (minimisation of copying and destruction of intercepted material) and section 15(3) (destruction of intercepted material) are to be met. For further details see section on "Safeguards".

4.20 The term "intercepted material" is used throughout to embrace copies, extracts or summaries made from the intercepted material as well as the intercept material itself.

5 Interception warrants (section 8(4))

5.1 This section applies to the interception of external communications by means of a warrant complying with section 8(4) of the Act. External communications are defined by the Act to be those which are sent or received outside the British Islands. They include those which are both sent and received outside the British Islands, whether or not they pass through the British Islands in course of their transit. They do not include communications both sent and received in the British Islands, even if they pass outside the British Islands en route. Responsibility for the issuing of such interception warrants rests with the Secretary of State.

Application for a section 8(4) warrant

5.2 An application for a warrant is made to the Secretary of State. Interception warrants, when issued, are addressed to the person who submitted the application. This person may then serve a copy upon any person who may be able to provide assistance in giving effect to that warrant. Each application, a copy of which must be retained by the applicant, should contain the following information:

- Background to the operation in question.
- Description of the communications to be intercepted, details of the communications service provider(s) and an assessment of the feasibility of the operation where this is relevant[6].
- Description of the conduct to be authorised, which must be restricted to the interception of external communications, or to conduct necessary[7] in order to intercept those external communications, where appropriate.
- The certificate that will regulate examination of intercepted material.
- An explanation of why the interception is considered to be necessary for one or more of the section 5(3) purposes.
- A consideration of why the conduct to be authorised by the warrant is proportionate to what is sought to be achieved by that conduct.
- A consideration of any unusual degree of collateral intrusion, and why that intrusion is justified in the circumstances. In particular, where the communications in question might affect religious, medical or journalistic confidentiality or legal privilege, this must be specified in the application.
- Where an application is urgent, supporting justification should be provided.
- An assurance that intercepted material will be read, looked at or listened to only so far as it is certified, and it meets the conditions of sections 16(2)–16(6) of the Act.
- An assurance that all material intercepted will be handled in accordance with the safeguards required by sections 15 and 16 of the Act.

Authorisation of a section 8(4) warrant

5.3 Before issuing a warrant under section 8(4), the Secretary of State must believe that the warrant is necessary:[8]

- in the interests of national security;
- for the purpose of preventing or detecting serious crime; or
- for the purpose of safeguarding the economic well-being of the United Kingdom.

5.4 In exercising his power to issue an interception warrant for the purpose of safeguarding the economic well-being of the United Kingdom (as provided for by section 5(3)(c) of the Act), the Secretary of State will consider whether the economic well-being of the United Kingdom which is to be safeguarded is, on the facts of each case, directly related to state security. The term "state security", which is used in Directive 97/66/EC (concerning the processing of personal data and the protection of privacy in the telecommunications sector), should be interpreted in the same way as the term "national security" which is used elsewhere in the Act and this Code. The Secretary of State will not issue a warrant on section 5(3)(c) grounds if this direct link between the economic well-being of the United Kingdom and state security is not established. Any application for a warrant on section 5(3)(c) grounds should therefore explain how, in the applicant's view, the economic well-being of the United Kingdom which is to be safeguarded is directly related to state security on the facts of the case.

5.5 The Secretary of State must also consider that the conduct authorised by the warrant is proportionate to what it seeks to achieve (section 5(2)(b)). In considering necessity and proportionality, the Secretary of State must take into account whether the information sought could reasonably be obtained by other means (section 5(4)).

5.6 When the Secretary of State issues a warrant of this kind, it must be accompanied by a certificate in which the Secretary of State certifies that he considers examination of the intercepted material to be necessary for one or more of the section 5(3) purposes. The Secretary of State has a duty to ensure that arrangements are in force for securing that only that material which has been certified as necessary for examination for a section 5(3) purpose, and which meets the conditions set out in section 16(2) to section 16(6) is, in fact, read, looked at or listened to. The Interception of Communications Commissioner is under a duty to review the adequacy of those arrangements.

Urgent authorisation of a section 8(4) warrant

5.7 The Act makes provision (section 7(1)(b)) for cases in which an interception warrant is required urgently, yet the Secretary of State is not available to sign the warrant. In these cases the Secretary of State will still personally authorise the interception but the warrant is signed by a senior official, following discussion of the case between officials and the Secretary of State. The Act restricts issue of warrants in this way to urgent cases where the Secretary of State has himself expressly authorised the issue of the warrant (section 7(2)(a)), and requires the warrant to contain a statement to that effect (section 7(4)(a)).

5.8 A warrant issued under the urgency procedure lasts for five working days following the day of issue unless renewed by the Secretary of State, in which case it expires after 3 months in the case of serious crime or 6 months in the case of national security or economic well-being in the same way as other section 8(4) warrants.

Format of a section 8(4) warrant

5.9 Each warrant is addressed to the person who submitted the application. This person may then serve a copy upon such providers of communications services as he believes will be able to assist in implementing the interception. Communications service providers will not receive a copy of the certificate.

The warrant should include the following:

- A description of the communications to be intercepted
- The warrant reference number
- The persons who may subsequently modify the scheduled part of the warrant in an urgent case (if authorised in accordance with section 10(8) of the Act)

Modification of a section 8(4) warrant

5.10 Interception warrants may be modified under the provisions of section 10 of the Act. The warrant may only be modified by the Secretary of State or, in an urgent case, by a senior official with the express authorisation of the Secretary of State. In these cases a statement of that fact must be endorsed on the modifying instrument, and the modification ceases to have effect after five working days following the day of issue unless it is endorsed by the Secretary of State.

5.11 The certificate must be modified by the Secretary of State, save in an urgent case where a certificate may be modified under the hand of a senior official provided that the official holds a position in respect of which he is expressly authorised by provisions contained in the certificate to modify the certificate on the Secretary of State's behalf, or the Secretary of State has himself expressly authorised the modification and a statement of that fact is endorsed on the modifying instrument. Again the modification shall cease to have effect after five working days following the day of issue unless it is endorsed by the Secretary of State.

Renewal of a section 8(4) warrant

5.12 The Secretary of State may renew a warrant at any point before its expiry date. Applications for renewals are made to the Secretary of State and contain an update of the matters outlined in paragraph 5.2 above. In particular, the applicant must give an assessment of the value of interception to the operation to date and explain why he considers that interception continues to be necessary for one or more of purposes in section 5(3).

5.13 Where the Secretary of State is satisfied that the interception continues to meet the requirements of the Act he may renew the warrant. Where the warrant is issued on serious crime grounds, the renewed warrant is valid for a further three months. Where it is issued on national security/ economic well-being grounds the renewed warrant is valid for six months. These dates run from the date of signature on the renewal instrument.

5.14 In those circumstances where the assistance of communications service providers has been sought, a copy of the warrant renewal instrument will be forwarded by the intercepting agency to all those on whom a copy of the original warrant instrument has been served, providing they are still actively assisting. A warrant renewal instrument will include the reference number of the warrant and description of the communications to be intercepted.

Warrant cancellation

5.15 The Secretary of State shall cancel an interception warrant if, at any time before its expiry date, he is satisfied that the warrant is no longer necessary on grounds falling within Section 5(3) of the Act. In practice, cancellation instruments will be signed by a senior official on his behalf.

5.16 The cancellation instrument will be addressed to the person to whom the warrant was issued (the intercepting agency). A copy of the cancellation instrument should be sent to those communications service providers, if any, who have given effect to the warrant during the preceding twelve months.

Records

5.17 The oversight regime allows the Interception of Communications Commissioner to inspect the warrant application upon which the Secretary of State based his decision, and the applicant may be required to justify the content. Each intercepting agency should keep, so to be made available for scrutiny by the Interception of Communications Commissioner, the following:

- all applications made for warrants complying with section 8(4), and applications made for the renewal of such warrants;
- all warrants and certificates, and copies of renewal and modification instruments (if any);
- where any application is refused, the grounds for refusal as given by the Secretary of State;
- the dates on which interception is started and stopped.

Records shall also be kept of the arrangements in force for securing that only material which has been certified for examination for a purpose under section 5(3) and which meets the conditions set out in section 16(2) – 16(6) of the Act in accordance with section 15 of the Act. Records shall be kept of the arrangements by which the requirements of section 15(2) (minimisation of copying and distribution of intercepted material) and section 15(3) (destruction of intercepted material) are to be met. For further details see section on "Safeguards".

6 Safeguards

6.1 All material (including related communications data) intercepted under the authority of a warrant complying with section 8(1) or section 8(4) of the Act must be handled in accordance with safeguards which the Secretary of State has approved in conformity with the duty imposed upon him by the Act. These safeguards are made available to the Interception of Communications Commissioner, and they must meet the requirements of section 15 of the Act which are set out below. In addition, the safeguards in section 16 of the Act apply to warrants complying with section 8(4). Any breach of these safeguards must be reported to the Interception of Communications Commissioner.

6.2 Section 15 of the Act requires that disclosure, copying and retention of intercept material be limited to the minimum necessary for the authorised purposes. The authorised purposes defined in section 15(4) of the Act include:

- if the material continues to be, or is likely to become, necessary for any of the purposes set out in section 5(3) – namely, in the interests of national security, for the purpose of preventing or detecting serious crime, for the purpose of safeguarding the economic well-being of the United Kingdom;
- if the material is necessary for facilitating the carrying out of the functions of the Secretary of State under Chapter I of Part I of the Act;
- if the material is necessary for facilitating the carrying out of any functions of the Interception of Communications Commissioner or the Tribunal;
- if the material is necessary to ensure that a person conducting a criminal prosecution has the information he needs to determine what is required of him by his duty to secure the fairness of the prosecution;
- if the material is necessary for the performance of any duty imposed by the Public Record Acts.

6.3 Section 16 provides for additional safeguards in relation to material gathered under section 8(4) warrants, requiring that the safeguards:

- ensure that intercepted material is read, looked at or listened to by any person only to the extent that the material is certified;
- regulate the use of selection factors that refer to individuals known to be for the time being in the British Islands.

The Secretary of State must ensure that the safeguards are in force before any interception under warrants complying with section 8(4) can begin. The Interception of Communications Commissioner is under a duty to review the adequacy of the safeguards.

Dissemination of intercepted material

6.4 The number of persons to whom any of the material is disclosed, and the extent of disclosure, must be limited to the minimum that is necessary for the authorised purposes set out in section 15(4) of the Act. This obligation applies equally to disclosure to additional persons within an agency, and to disclosure outside the agency. It is enforced by prohibiting disclosure to persons who do not hold the required security clearance, and also by the need-to-know principle: intercepted material must not be disclosed to any person unless that person's duties, which must relate to one of the authorised purposes, are such that he needs to know about the material to carry out those duties. In the same way only so much of the material may be disclosed as the recipient needs; for example if a summary of the material will suffice, no more than that should be disclosed.

6.5 The obligations apply not just to the original interceptor, but also to anyone to whom the material is subsequently disclosed. In some cases this will be achieved by requiring the latter to obtain the originator's permission before disclosing the material further. In others, explicit safeguards are applied to secondary recipients.

Copying

6.6 Intercepted material may only be copied to the extent necessary for the authorised purposes set out in section 15(4) of the Act. Copies include not only direct copies of the whole of the material, but also extracts and summaries which identify themselves as the product of an interception, and any record referring to an interception which is a record of the identities of the persons to or by whom the intercepted material was sent. The restrictions are implemented by requiring special treatment of such copies, extracts and summaries that are made by recording their making, distribution and destruction.

Storage

6.7 Intercepted material, and all copies, extracts and summaries of it, must be handled and stored securely, so as to minimise the risk of loss or theft. It must be held so as to be inaccessible to persons without the required level of security clearance. This requirement to store intercept product securely applies to all those who are responsible for the handling of this material, including communications service providers. The details of what such a requirement will mean in practice for communications service providers will be set out in the discussions they will be having with the Government before a Section 12 Notice is served (see paragraph 2.9).

Destruction

6.8 Intercepted material, and all copies, extracts and summaries which can be identified as the product of an interception, must be securely destroyed as soon as it is no longer needed for any of the authorised purposes. If such material is retained, it should be reviewed at appropriate intervals to confirm that the justification for its retention is still valid under section 15(3) of the Act.

Personnel security

6.9 Each intercepting agency maintains a distribution list of persons who may have access to intercepted material or need to see any reporting in relation to it. All such persons must be appropriately vetted. Any person no longer needing access to perform his duties should be removed from any such list. Where it is necessary for an officer of one agency to disclose material to another, it is the former's responsibility to ensure that the recipient has the necessary clearance.

7 Disclosure to ensure fairness in criminal proceedings

7.1 Section 15(3) of the Act states the general rule that intercepted material must be destroyed as soon as its retention is no longer necessary for a purpose authorised under the Act. Section 15(4) specifies the authorised purposes for which retention is necessary.

7.2 This part of the Code applies to the handling of intercepted material in the context of criminal proceedings where the material has been retained for one of the purposes authorised in section 15(4) of the Act. For those who would ordinarily have had responsibility under the Criminal Procedure and Investigations Act 1996 to provide disclosure in criminal proceedings, this includes those rare situations where destruction of intercepted material has not taken place in accordance with section 15(3) and where that material is still in existence after the commencement of a criminal prosecution, retention having been considered necessary to ensure that a person conducting a criminal prosecution has the information he needs to discharge his duty of ensuring its fairness (section 15(4)(d)).

Exclusion of matters from legal proceedings

7.3 The general rule is that neither the possibility of interception nor intercepted material itself plays any part in legal proceedings. This rule is set out in section 17 of the Act, which excludes evidence, questioning, assertion or disclosure in legal proceedings likely to reveal the existence (or the absence) of a warrant issued under this Act (or the Interception of Communications Act 1985). This rule means that the intercepted material cannot be used either by the prosecution or the defence. This preserves "equality of arms" which is a requirement under Article 6 of the European Convention on Human Rights.

7.4 Section 18 contains a number of tightly-drawn exceptions to this rule. This part of the Code deals only with the exception in subsections (7) to (11).

Disclosure to a prosecutor

7.5 Section 18(7)(a) provides that intercepted material obtained by means of a warrant and which continues to be available, may, for a strictly limited purpose, be disclosed to a person conducting a criminal prosecution.

7.6 This may only be done for the purpose of enabling the prosecutor to determine what is required of him by his duty to secure the fairness of the prosecution. The prosecutor may not use intercepted material to which he is given access under section 18(7)(a) to mount a cross-examination, or to do anything other than ensure the fairness of the proceedings.

7.7 The exception does not mean that intercepted material should be retained against a remote possibility that it might be relevant to future proceedings. The normal expectation is, still, for the intercepted material to be destroyed in accordance with the general safeguards provided by section 15. The exceptions only come into play if such material has, in fact, been retained for an authorised purpose. Because the authorised purpose given in section 5(3)(b) ("*for the purpose of preventing or detecting serious crime*") does not extend to gathering evidence for the purpose of a prosecution, material intercepted for this purpose may not have survived to the prosecution stage, as it will have been destroyed in accordance with the section 15(3) safeguards. There is, in these circumstances, no need to consider disclosure to a prosecutor if, in fact, no intercepted material remains in existence.

7.8 Be that as it may, section 18(7)(a) recognises the duty on prosecutors, acknowledged by common law, to review all available material to make sure that the prosecution is not proceeding unfairly. 'Available material' will only ever include intercepted material at this stage if the conscious decision has been made to retain it for an authorised purpose.

7.9 If intercepted material does continue to be available at the prosecution stage, once this information has come to the attention of the holder of this material the prosecutor should be informed that a warrant has been issued under section 5 and that material of possible relevance to the case has been intercepted.

7.10 Having had access to the material, the prosecutor may conclude that the material affects the fairness of the proceedings. In these circumstances, he will decide how the prosecution, if it proceeds, should be presented.

Disclosure to a judge

7.11 Section 18(7)(b) recognises that there may be cases where the prosecutor, having seen intercepted material under subsection (7)(a), will need to consult the trial Judge. Accordingly, it provides for the Judge to be given access to intercepted material, where there are exceptional circumstances making that disclosure essential in the interests of justice.

7.12 This access will be achieved by the prosecutor inviting the judge to make an order for disclosure to him alone, under this subsection. This is an exceptional procedure; normally, the prosecutor's functions under subsection (7)(a) will not fall to be reviewed by the judge. To comply with section 17(1), any consideration given to, or exercise of, this power must be carried out without notice to the defence. The purpose of this power is to ensure that the trial is conducted fairly.

7.13 The judge may, having considered the intercepted material disclosed to him, direct the prosecution to make an admission of fact. The admission will be abstracted from the interception; but, in accordance with the requirements of section 17(1), it must not reveal the fact of interception. This is likely to be a very unusual step. The Act only allows it where the judge considers it essential in the interests of justice.

7.14 Nothing in these provisions allows intercepted material, or the fact of interception, to be disclosed to the defence.

8 Oversight

8.1 The Act provides for an Interception of Communications Commissioner whose remit is to provide independent oversight of the use of the powers contained within the warranted interception regime under Chapter I of Part I of the Act.

8.2 This Code does not cover the exercise of the Commissioner's functions. However, it will be the duty of any person who uses the above powers to comply with any request made by the Commissioner to provide any information as he requires for the purpose of enabling him to discharge his functions.

9 Complaints

9.1 The Act establishes an independent Tribunal. This Tribunal will be made up of senior members of the judiciary and the legal profession and is independent of the Government. The Tribunal has full powers to investigate and decide any case within its jurisdiction.

9.2 This code does not cover the exercise of the Tribunal's functions. Details of the relevant complaints procedure can be obtained from the following address:

The Investigatory Powers Tribunal

PO Box 33220

London

SW1H 9ZQ

Tel: 0207 273 4514

10 Interception without a warrant

10.1 Section 1(5) of the Act permits interception without a warrant in the following circumstances:

- where it is authorised by or under sections 3 or 4 of the Act (see below);
- where it is in exercise, in relation to any stored communication, of some other statutory power exercised for the purpose of obtaining information or of taking possession of any document or other property, for example, the obtaining of a production order under Schedule 1 to the Police and Criminal Evidence Act 1984 for stored data to be produced.

Interception in accordance with a warrant under section 5 of the Act is dealt with under parts 2, 3, 4 and 5 of this Code.

10.2 For lawful interception which takes place without a warrant, pursuant to sections 3 or 4 of the Act or pursuant to some other statutory power, there is no prohibition in the Act on the evidential use of any material that is obtained as a result. The matter may still, however, be regulated by the exclusionary rules of evidence to be found in the common law, section 78 of the Police and Criminal Evidence Act 1984, and/or pursuant to the Human Rights Act 1998.

Interception with the consent of both parties

10.3 Section 3(1) of the Act authorises the interception of a communication if both the person sending the communication and the intended recipient(s) have consented to its interception, or where the person conducting the interception has reasonable grounds for believing that all parties have consented to the interception.

Interception with the consent of one party

10.4 Section 3(2) of the Act authorises the interception of a communication if either the sender or intended recipient of the communication has consented to its interception, and directed surveillance by means of that interception has been authorised under Part II of the Act. Further details can be found in chapter 4 of the Covert Surveillance Code of Practice and in chapter 2 of the Covert Human Intelligence Sources Code of Practice.

Interception for the purposes of a communication service provider

10.5 Section 3(3) of the Act permits a communication service provider or a person acting upon their behalf to carry out interception for purposes connected with the operation of that service or for purposes connected with the enforcement of any enactment relating to the use of the communication service.

Lawful business practice

10.6 Section 4(2) of the Act enables the Secretary of State to make regulations setting out those circumstances where it is lawful to intercept communications for the purpose of carrying on a business. These regulations apply equally to public authorities.

These Lawful Business Practice Regulations can be found on the following Department of Trade and Industry website: www.dti.gov.uk/cii/regulation.html

1   Interception warrants may be issued on "serious crime" grounds by Scottish Ministers, by virtue of arrangements under the Scotland Act 1998. In this Code references to the "Secretary of State" should be read as including Scottish Ministers where appropriate. The functions of the Scottish Ministers also cover renewal and cancellation arrangements.
2   This assessment is normally based upon information provided by the relevant communication service provider.
2a This conduct may include the interception of other communications (section 5(6)(a)).
3   A single warrant can be justified on more than one of the grounds listed.
4   This may include addresses, numbers, apparatus or other factors, or combination of factors, that are to be used for identifying communications (section 8(2) of the Act).
5   Neither the senior official to whom the warrant is addressed, nor any of his subordinates may modify the scheduled parts of the warrant, except in an urgent case where the warrant contains an expressly authorised provision to this effect.
6   This assessment is normally based upon information provided by the relevant communications service provider.
7   This conduct may include the interception of other communications (section 5(6)(a)).
8   A single warrant can be justified on more than one of the grounds listed.

Covert Surveillance: Code of Practice

Pursuant to Section 71 of the Regulation of Investigatory Powers Act 2000

Commencement

This code applies to every authorisation of covert surveillance or of entry on or interference with property or with wireless telegraphy carried out under section 5 of the Intelligence Services Act 1994, Part III of the Police Act 1997 or Part II of the Regulation of Investigatory Powers Act 2000 by public authorities which begins on or after the day on which this code comes into effect.

CONTENTS

1 Background

1.1 In this code the:

- **"1989 Act"** means the Security Service Act 1989;
- **"1994 Act"** means the Intelligence Services Act 1994;
- **"1997 Act"** means the Police Act 1997;
- **"2000 Act"** means the Regulation of Investigatory Powers Act 2000;
- **"RIP(S)A"** means the Regulation of Investigatory Powers (Scotland) Act 2000.

1.2 This code of practice provides guidance on the use of covert surveillance by public authorities under Part II of the 2000 Act and on entry on, or interference with, property (or with wireless telegraphy) under section 5 of the 1994 Act or Part III of the 1997 Act. This code replaces the code of practice issued in 1999 pursuant to section 101(3) of the 1997 Act.

1.3 General observation forms part of the duties of many law enforcement officers and other public authorities and is not usually regulated by the 2000 Act. For example, police officers will be on patrol to prevent and detect crime, maintain public safety and prevent disorder or trading standards or HM Customs and Excise officers might covertly observe and then visit a shop as part of their enforcement function to verify the supply or level of supply of goods or services that may be liable to a restriction or tax. Such observation may involve the use of equipment to merely reinforce normal sensory perception, such as binoculars, or the use of cameras, where this does not involve systematic surveillance of an individual.

1.4 Although, the provisions of the 2000 Act or of this code of practice do not normally cover the use of overt CCTV surveillance systems, since members of the public are aware that such systems are in use, there may be occasions when public authorities use overt CCTV systems for the purposes of a specific investigation or operation. In such cases, authorisation for intrusive or directed surveillance may be necessary.

1.5 The 2000 Act provides that all codes of practice relating to the 2000 Act are admissible as evidence in criminal and civil proceedings. If any provision of the code appears relevant to any court or tribunal considering any such proceedings, or to the Investigatory Powers Tribunal established under the 2000 Act, or to one of the Commissioners responsible for overseeing the powers conferred by the 2000 Act, it must be taken into account.

General extent of powers

1.6 Authorisations under the 2000 Act can be given for surveillance both inside and outside the United Kingdom. Authorisations for actions outside the United Kingdom can only validate them for the purposes of proceedings in the United Kingdom. An authorisation under Part II of the 2000 Act does not take into account the requirements of the country outside the United Kingdom in which the investigation or operation is taking place.

1.7 Where the conduct authorised is likely to take place in Scotland, authorisations should be granted under RIP(S)A, unless the authorisation is being obtained by those public authorities listed in section 46(3) of the 2000 Act and the Regulation of Investigatory Powers (Authorisations Extending to Scotland) Order 2000; SI No. 2418). Additionally any authorisation granted or renewed for the purposes of national security or the economic well-being of the United Kingdom must be made under the 2000 Act. This code of practice is extended to Scotland in relation to authorisations made under Part II of the 2000 Act which apply to Scotland. A separate code of practice applies in relation to authorisations made under RIP(S)A.

Use of material in evidence

1.8 Material obtained through covert surveillance may be used as evidence in criminal proceedings. The proper authorisation of surveillance should ensure the admissibility of such evidence under the common law, section 78 of the Police and Criminal Evidence Act 1984 and the Human Rights Act 1998. Furthermore, the product of the surveillance described in this code is subject to the ordinary rules for retention and disclosure of material under the Criminal Procedure and Investigations Act 1996, where those rules apply to the law enforcement body in question.

Directed surveillance, intrusive surveillance and entry on or interference with property or with wireless telegraphy

1.9 Directed surveillance is defined in section 26(2) of the 2000 Act as surveillance which is covert, but not intrusive, and undertaken:

(a)   for the purposes of a specific investigation or specific operation;

(b)   in such a manner as is likely to result in the obtaining of private information about a person (whether or not one specifically identified for the purposes of the investigation or operation); and

(c)   otherwise than by way of an immediate response to events or circumstances the nature of which is such that it would not be reasonably practicable for an authorisation under Part II of the 2000 Act to be sought for the carrying out of the surveillance.

1.10 Directed surveillance investigations or operations can only be carried out by those public authorities who are listed in or added to Part I and Part II of schedule 1 of the 2000 Act.

1.11 Intrusive surveillance is defined in section 26(3) of the 2000 Act as covert surveillance that:

(a)   is carried out in relation to anything taking place on any residential premises or in any private vehicle; and

(b)   involves the presence of an individual on the premises or in the vehicle or is carried out by means of a surveillance device.

1.12 Applications to carry out intrusive surveillance can only be made by the senior authorising officer of those public authorities listed in or added to section 32(6) of the 2000 Act or by a member or official of those public authorities listed in or added to section 41(1).

1.13 Applications to enter on or interfere with property or with wireless telegraphy can only be made by the authorising officers of those public authorities listed in or added to section 93(5) of the 1997 Act. Under section 5 of the 1994 Act only members of the intelligence services are able to make applications to enter on or interfere with property or with wireless telegraphy.

2 General rules on authorisations

2.1 An authorisation under Part II of the 2000 Act will provide lawful authority for a public authority to carry out surveillance. Responsibility for authorising surveillance investigations or operations will vary, depending on whether the authorisation is for intrusive surveillance or directed surveillance, and which public authority is involved. For the purposes of Chapter 2 and 3 of this code the authorising officer, senior authorising officer or the person who makes an application to the Secretary of State will be referred to as an 'authorising officer'.

2.2 Part II of the 2000 Act does not impose a requirement on public authorities to seek or obtain an authorisation where, under the 2000 Act, one is available (see section 80 of the 2000 Act). Nevertheless, where there is an interference by a public authority with the right to respect for private and family life guaranteed under Article 8 of the European Convention on Human Rights, and where there is no other source of lawful authority, the consequence of not obtaining an authorisation under the 2000 Act may be that the action is unlawful by virtue of section 6 of the Human Rights Act 1998.

2.3 Public authorities are therefore strongly recommended to seek an authorisation where the surveillance is likely to interfere with a person's Article 8 rights to privacy by obtaining private information about that person, whether or not that person is the subject of the investigation or operation. Obtaining an authorisation will ensure that the action is carried out in accordance with law and subject to stringent safeguards against abuse.

Necessity and proportionality

2.4 Obtaining an authorisation under the 2000 Act, the 1997 Act and 1994 Act will only ensure that there is a justifiable interference with an individual's Article 8 rights if it is necessary and proportionate for these activities to take place. The 2000 Act first requires that the person granting an authorisation believe that the authorisation is necessary in the circumstances of the particular case for one or more of the statutory grounds in section 28(3) of the 2000 Act for directed surveillance and in section 32(3) of the 2000 Act for intrusive surveillance.

2.5 Then, if the activities are necessary, the person granting the authorisation must believe that they are proportionate to what is sought to be achieved by carrying them out. This involves balancing the intrusiveness of the activity on the target and others who might be affected by it against the need for the activity in operational terms. The activity will not be proportionate if it is excessive in the circumstances of the case or if the information which is sought could reasonably be obtained by other less intrusive means. All such activity should be carefully managed to meet the objective in question and must not be arbitrary or unfair.

Collateral intrusion

2.6 Before authorising surveillance the authorising officer should also take into account the risk of intrusion into the privacy of persons other than those who are directly the subjects of the investigation or operation (collateral intrusion). Measures should be taken, wherever practicable, to avoid or minimise unnecessary intrusion into the lives of those not directly connected with the investigation or operation.

2.7 An application for an authorisation should include an assessment of the risk of any collateral intrusion. The authorising officer should take this into account, when considering the proportionality of the surveillance.

2.8 Those carrying out the surveillance should inform the authorising officer if the investigation or operation unexpectedly interferes with the privacy of individuals who are not covered by the authorisation. When the original authorisation may not be sufficient, consideration should be given to whether the authorisation needs to be amended and reauthorised or a new authorisation is required.

2.9 Any person granting or applying for an authorisation or warrant will also need to be aware of particular sensitivities in the local community where the surveillance is taking place and of similar activities being undertaken by other public authorities which could impact on the deployment of surveillance. In this regard, it is recommended that where the authorising officers in the National Criminal Intelligence Service (NCIS), the National Crime Squad (NCS) and HM Customs and Excise (HMCE) consider that conflicts might arise they should consult a senior officer within the police force area in which the investigation or operation takes place.

2.10 The matters in paragraphs 2.1 – 2.9 above must also be taken into account when applying for authorisations or warrants for entry on or interference with property or with wireless telegraphy. In particular they must be necessary in the circumstances of the particular case for one of the statutory ground listed in section 93(2)(a) of the 1997 Act and section 5(2)(c) of the 1994 Act, proportionate and when exercised steps should be taken to minimise collateral intrusion.

Combined authorisations

2.11 A single authorisation may combine:

- two or more different authorisations under Part II of the 2000 Act;
- an authorisation under Part II of the 2000 Act and an authorisation under Part III of the 1997 Act;
- a warrant for intrusive surveillance under Part II of the 2000 Act and a warrant under section 5 of the 1994 Act.

2.12 For example, a single authorisation may combine authorisations for directed and intrusive surveillance. The provisions applicable in the case of each of the authorisations must be considered separately. Thus, a police superintendent can authorise the directed surveillance but the intrusive surveillance needs the separate authorisation of a chief constable, and in certain cases the approval of a Surveillance Commissioner will also be necessary. Where an authorisation for directed surveillance or the use or conduct of a covert human intelligence source is combined with a Secretary of State authorisation for intrusive surveillance, the combined authorisation must be issued by the Secretary of State. However, this does not preclude public authorities from obtaining separate authorisations.

2.13 In cases where one agency is acting on behalf of another, it is usually for the tasking agency to obtain or provide the authorisation. For example, where surveillance is carried out by the Armed Forces on behalf of the police, authorisations would be sought by the police and granted by the appropriate authorising officer. In cases where the Security Service is acting in support of the police or other law enforcement agencies in the field of serious crime, the Security Service would normally seek authorisations.

Central record of all authorisations

2.14 A centrally retrievable record of all authorisations should be held by each public authority and regularly updated whenever an authorisation is granted, renewed or cancelled. The record should be made available to the relevant Commissioner or an Inspector from the Office of Surveillance Commissioners, upon request. These records should be retained for a period of at least three years from the ending of the authorisation and should contain the following information:

- the type of authorisation;
- the date the authorisation was given;
- name and rank/grade of the authorising officer;
- the unique reference number (URN) of the investigation or operation;
- the title of the investigation or operation, including a brief description and names of subjects, if known;
- whether the urgency provisions were used, and if so why.
- if the authorisation is renewed, when it was renewed and who authorised the renewal, including the name and rank/grade of the authorising officer;
- whether the investigation or operation is likely to result in obtaining confidential information as defined in this code of practice;
- the date the authorisation was cancelled.

2.15 In all cases, the relevant authority should maintain the following documentation which need not form part of the centrally retrievable record:

- a copy of the application and a copy of the authorisation together with any supplementary documentation and notification of the approval given by the authorising officer;
- a record of the period over which the surveillance has taken place;
- the frequency of reviews prescribed by the authorising officer;
- a record of the result of each review of the authorisation;
- a copy of any renewal of an authorisation, together with the supporting documentation submitted when the renewal was requested;
- the date and time when any instruction was given by the authorising officer.

Retention and destruction of the product

2.16 Where the product of surveillance could be relevant to pending or future criminal or civil proceedings, it should be retained in accordance with established disclosure requirements for a suitable further period, commensurate to any subsequent review.

2.17 In the cases of the law enforcement agencies (not including the Royal Navy Regulating Branch, the Royal Military Police and the Royal Air Force Police), particular attention is drawn to the requirements of the code of practice issued under the Criminal Procedure and Investigations Act 1996. This requires that material which is obtained in the course of a criminal investigation and which may be relevant to the investigation must be recorded and retained.

2.18 There is nothing in the 2000 Act which prevents material obtained from properly authorised surveillance from being used in other investigations. Each public authority must ensure that arrangements are in place for the handling, storage and destruction of material obtained through the use of covert surveillance. Authorising officers must ensure compliance with the appropriate data protection requirements and any relevant codes of practice produced by individual authorities relating to the handling and storage of material.

The Intelligence Services, MOD and HM Forces

2.19 The heads of these agencies are responsible for ensuring that arrangements exist for securing that no information is stored by the authorities, except as necessary for the proper discharge of their functions. They are also responsible for arrangements to control onward disclosure. For the intelligence services, this is a statutory duty under the 1989 Act and the 1994 Act.

3 Special rules on authorisations

3.1 The 2000 Act does not provide any special protection for 'confidential information'. Nevertheless, particular care should be taken in cases where the subject of the investigation or operation might reasonably expect a high degree of privacy, or where confidential information is involved. Confidential information consists of matters subject to legal privilege, confidential personal information or confidential journalistic material. So, for example, extra care should be given where, through the use of surveillance, it would be possible to acquire knowledge of discussions between a minister of religion and an individual relating to the latter's spiritual welfare, or where matters of medical or journalistic confidentiality or legal privilege may be involved.

3.2 In cases where through the use of surveillance it is likely that knowledge of confidential information will be acquired, the use of surveillance is subject to a higher level of authorisation. Annex A lists the authorising officer for each public authority permitted to authorise such surveillance.

Communications subject to legal privilege

3.3 Section 98 of the 1997 Act describes those matters that are subject to legal privilege in England and Wales. In Scotland, the relevant description is contained in section 33 of the Criminal Law (Consolidation) (Scotland) Act 1995. With regard to Northern Ireland, Article 12 of the Police and Criminal Evidence (Northern Ireland) Order 1989 should be referred to.

3.4 Legal privilege does not apply to communications made with the intention of furthering a criminal purpose (whether the lawyer is acting unwittingly or culpably). Legally privileged communications will lose their protection if there are grounds to believe, for example, that the professional legal adviser is intending to hold or use them for a criminal purpose. But privilege is not lost if a professional legal adviser is properly advising a person who is suspected of having committed a criminal offence. The concept of legal privilege applies to the provision of professional legal advice by any individual, agency or organisation qualified to do so.

3.5 The 2000 Act does not provide any special protection for legally privileged information. Nevertheless, such information is particularly sensitive and surveillance which acquires such material may engage Article 6 of the ECHR (right to a fair trial) as well as Article 8. Legally privileged information obtained by surveillance is extremely unlikely ever to be admissible as evidence in criminal proceedings. Moreover, the mere fact that such surveillance has taken place may lead to any related criminal proceedings being stayed as an abuse of process. Accordingly, action which may lead to such information being acquired is subject to additional safeguards under this code.

3.6 In general, an application for surveillance which is likely to result in the acquisition of legally privileged information should only be made in exceptional and compelling circumstances. Full regard should be had to the particular proportionality issues such surveillance raises. The application should include, in addition to the reasons why it is considered necessary for the surveillance to take place, an assessment of how likely it is that information subject to legal privilege will be acquired. In addition, the application should clearly state whether the purpose (or one of the purposes) of the surveillance is to obtain legally privileged information.

3.7 This assessment will be taken into account by the authorising officer in deciding whether the proposed surveillance is necessary and proportionate under section 28 of the 2000 Act for directed surveillance and under section 32 for intrusive surveillance. The authorising officer may require regular reporting so as to be able to decide whether the authorisation should continue. In those cases where legally privileged information has been acquired and retained, the matter should be reported to the relevant Commissioner or Inspector during his next inspection and the material be made available to him if requested.

3.8 A substantial proportion of the communications between a lawyer and his client(s) may be subject to legal privilege. Therefore, any case where a lawyer is the subject of an investigation or operation should be notified to the relevant Commissioner during his next inspection and any material which has been retained should be made available to him if requested.

3.9 Where there is any doubt as to the handling and dissemination of information which may be subject to legal privilege, advice should be sought from a legal adviser within the relevant public authority before any further dissemination of the material takes place. Similar advice should also be sought where there is doubt over whether information is not subject to legal privilege due to the "in furtherance of a criminal purpose" exception. The retention of legally privileged information, or its dissemination to an outside body, should be accompanied by a clear warning that it is subject to legal privilege. It should be safeguarded by taking reasonable steps to ensure there is no possibility of it becoming available, or its contents becoming known, to any person whose possession of it might prejudice any criminal or civil proceedings related to the information. Any dissemination of legally privileged material to an outside body should be notified to the relevant Commissioner or Inspector during his next inspection.

Communications involving confidential personal information and confidential journalistic material

3.10 Similar consideration must also be given to authorisations that involve confidential personal information and confidential journalistic material. In those cases where confidential personal information and confidential journalistic material has been acquired and retained, the matter should be reported to the relevant Commissioner or Inspector during his next inspection and the material be made available to him if requested. Confidential personal information is information held in confidence relating to the physical or mental health or spiritual counselling concerning an individual (whether living or dead) who can be identified from it. Such information, which can include both oral and written communications, is held in confidence if it is held subject to an express or implied undertaking to hold it in confidence or it is subject to a restriction on disclosure or an obligation of confidentiality contained in existing legislation. Examples might include consultations between a health professional and a patient, or information from a patient's medical records.

3.11 Spiritual counselling means conversations between an individual and a Minister of Religion acting in his official capacity, where the individual being counselled is seeking or the Minister is imparting forgiveness, absolution or the resolution of conscience with the authority of the Divine Being(s) of their faith.

3.12 Confidential journalistic material includes material acquired or created for the purposes of journalism and held subject to an undertaking to hold it in confidence, as well as communications resulting in information being acquired for the purposes of journalism and held subject to such an undertaking.

4 Authorisation procedures for directed surveillance

4.1 Directed surveillance is defined in section 26(2) of the 2000 Act as surveillance which is covert, but not intrusive, and undertaken:

(a)   for the purposes of a specific investigation or specific operation;
(b)   in such a manner as is likely to result in the obtaining of private information about a person (whether or not one specifically identified for the purposes of the investigation or operation); and
(c)   otherwise than by way of an immediate response to events or circumstances the nature of which is such that it would not be reasonably practicable for an authorisation under Part II of the 2000 Act to be sought for the carrying out of the surveillance.

4.2 Covert surveillance is defined in section 26(9)(a) of the 2000 Act as any surveillance which is carried out in a manner calculated to ensure that the persons subject to the surveillance are unaware that it is or may be taking place.

4.3 Private information is defined in section 26(10) of the 2000 Act as including any information relating to a person's private or family life. The concept of private information should be broadly interpreted to include an individual's private or personal relationship with others. Family life should be treated as extending beyond the formal relationships created by marriage.

4.4 Directed surveillance does not include covert surveillance carried out by way of an immediate response to events or circumstances which, by their very nature, could not have been foreseen. For example, a police officer would not require an authorisation to conceal himself and observe a suspicious person that he came across in the course of a patrol.

4.5 By virtue of section 48(4) of the 2000 Act, surveillance includes the interception of postal and telephone communications where the sender or recipient consents to the reading of or listening to or recording of the communication (as the case may be). For further details see paragraphs 4.30 – 4.32 of this code.

4.6 Surveillance in residential premises or in private vehicles is defined as intrusive surveillance in section 26(3) of the 2000 Act and is dealt with in chapter 5 of this code. However, where surveillance is carried out by a device designed or adapted principally for the purpose of providing information about the location of a vehicle, the activity is directed surveillance and should be authorised accordingly.

4.7 Directed surveillance does not include entry on or interference with property or with wireless telegraphy. These activities are subject to a separate regime of authorisation or warrantry, as set out in chapter 6 of this code.

4.8 Directed surveillance includes covert surveillance within office premises (as defined in paragraph 6.31 of this code). Authorising officers are reminded that confidential information should be afforded an enhanced level of protection. Chapter 3 of this code provides that in cases where the likely consequence of surveillance is to acquire confidential information, the authorisation should be given at a higher level.

Authorisation procedures

4.9 Under section 28(3) of the 2000 Act an authorisation for directed surveillance may be granted by an authorising officer where he believes that the authorisation is necessary in the circumstances of the particular case:

- in the interests of national security[1], [2];
- for the purpose of preventing and detecting[3] crime or of preventing disorder;
- in the interests of the economic well-being of the UK;
- in the interests of public safety;
- for the purpose of protecting public health[4];
- for the purpose of assessing or collecting any tax, duty, levy or other imposition, contribution or charge payable to a government department; or
- for any other purpose prescribed by an order made by the Secretary of State[5].

4.10 The authorising officer must also believe that the surveillance is proportionate to what it seeks to achieve.

4.11 The public authorities entitled to authorise directed surveillance are listed in Schedule 1 to the 2000 Act. Responsibility for authorising the carrying out of directed surveillance rests with the authorising officer and requires the personal authority of the authorising officer. The Regulation of Investigatory Powers (Prescriptions of Offices, Ranks and Positions) Order 2000; SI No: 2417 designates the authorising officer for each different public authority and the officers entitled to act only in urgent cases. Where an authorisation for directed surveillance is combined with a Secretary of State authorisation for intrusive surveillance, the combined authorisation must be issued by the Secretary of State.

4.12 The authorising officer must give authorisations in writing, except that in urgent cases, they may be given orally by the authorising officer or the officer entitled to act in urgent cases. In such cases, a statement that the authorising officer has expressly authorised the action should be recorded in writing by the applicant as soon as is reasonably practicable.

4.13 A case is not normally to be regarded as urgent unless the time that would elapse before the authorising officer was available to grant the authorisation would, in the judgement of the person giving the authorisation, be likely to endanger life or jeopardise the investigation or operation for which the authorisation was being given. An authorisation is not to be regarded as urgent where the need for an authorisation has been neglected or the urgency is of the authorising officer's own making.

4.14 Authorising officers should not be responsible for authorising investigations or operations in which they are directly involved, although it is recognised that this may sometimes be unavoidable, especially in the case of small organisations, or where it is necessary to act urgently. Where an authorising officer authorises such an investigation or operation the central record of authorisations (see paragraphs 2.14 – 2.15) should highlight this and the attention of a Commissioner or Inspector should be invited to it during his next inspection.

4.15 Authorising officers within the Police, NCIS and NCS may only grant authorisations on application by a member of their own force, Service or Squad. Authorising officers in HMCE may only grant an authorisation on application by a customs officer[6].

Information to be provided in applications for authorisation

4.16 A written application for authorisation for directed surveillance should describe any conduct to be authorised and the purpose of the investigation or operation. The application should also include:

- the reasons why the authorisation is necessary in the particular case and on the grounds (e.g. for the purpose of preventing or detecting crime) listed in Section 28(3) of the 2000 Act;
- the reasons why the surveillance is considered proportionate to what it seeks to achieve;
- the nature of the surveillance;
- the identities, where known, of those to be the subject of the surveillance;
- an explanation of the information which it is desired to obtain as a result of the surveillance;

- the details of any potential collateral intrusion and why the intrusion is justified;
- the details of any confidential information that is likely to be obtained as a consequence of the surveillance.
- the level of authority required (or recommended where that is different) for the surveillance; and
- a subsequent record of whether authority was given or refused, by whom and the time and date.

4.17 Additionally, in urgent cases, the authorisation should record (as the case may be):

- the reasons why the authorising officer or the officer entitled to act in urgent cases considered the case so urgent that an oral instead of a written authorisation was given; and/or
- the reasons why it was not reasonably practicable for the application to be considered by the authorising officer.

4.18 Where the authorisation is oral, the detail referred to above should be recorded in writing by the applicant as soon as reasonably practicable.

Duration of authorisations

4.19 A written authorisation granted by an authorising officer will cease to have effect (unless renewed) at the end of a period of **three months** beginning with the day on which it took effect.

4.20 Urgent oral authorisations or written authorisations granted by a person who is entitled to act only in urgent cases will, unless renewed, cease to have effect after **seventy-two hours,** beginning with the time when the authorisation was granted or renewed.

Reviews

4.21 Regular reviews of authorisations should be undertaken to assess the need for the surveillance to continue. The results of a review should be recorded on the central record of authorisations (see paragraphs 2.14 – 2.15). Particular attention is drawn to the need to review authorisations frequently where the surveillance provides access to confidential information or involves collateral intrusion.

4.22 In each case the authorising officer within each public authority should determine how often a review should take place. This should be as frequently as is considered necessary and practicable.

Renewals

4.23 If at any time before an authorisation would cease to have effect, the authorising officer considers it necessary for the authorisation to continue for the purpose for which it was given, he may renew it in writing for a further period of **three months** unless it is a case to which paragraph 4.25 applies. Renewals may also be granted orally in urgent cases and last for a period of **seventy-two hours**.

4.24 A renewal takes effect at the time at which, or day on which the authorisation would have ceased to have effect but for the renewal. An application for renewal should not be made until shortly before the authorisation period is drawing to an end. Any person who would be entitled to grant a new authorisation can renew an authorisation. Authorisations may be renewed more than once, provided they continue to meet the criteria for authorisation.

4.25 If at any time before an authorisation for directed surveillance, granted on the grounds of it being in the interests of national security or in the interests of the economic well-being of the UK, would cease to have effect, an authorising officer who is a member of the intelligence services considers it necessary for it to continue, he may renew it for a further period of **six months**, beginning with the day on which it would have ceased to have effect but for the renewal.

4.26 All applications for the renewal of an authorisation for directed surveillance should record:

- whether this is the first renewal or every occasion on which the authorisation has been renewed previously;
- any significant changes to the information in paragraph 4.16;
- the reasons why it is necessary to continue with the directed surveillance;
- the content and value to the investigation or operation of the information so far obtained by the surveillance;
- the results of regular reviews of the investigation or operation.

4.27 Authorisations may be renewed more than once, if necessary, and the renewal should be kept/recorded as part of the central record of authorisations (see paragraphs 2.14 – 2.15).

Cancellations

4.28 The authorising officer who granted or last renewed the authorisation must cancel it if he is satisfied that the directed surveillance no longer meets the criteria upon which it was authorised. Where the authorising officer is no longer available, this duty will fall on the person who has taken over the role of authorising officer or the person who is acting as authorising officer (see the Regulation of Investigatory Powers (Cancellation of Authorisations) Order 2000; SI No: 2794).

Ceasing of surveillance activity

4.29 As soon as the decision is taken that directed surveillance should be discontinued, the instruction must be given to those involved to stop all surveillance of the subject(s). The date and time when such an instruction was given should be recorded in the central record of authorisations (see paragraphs 2.14 – 2.15) and the notification of cancellation where relevant.

ADDITIONAL RULES

Recording of telephone conversations

4.30 Subject to paragraph 4.31 below, the interception of communications sent by post or by means of public telecommunications systems or private telecommunications systems attached to the public network may be authorised only by the Secretary of State, in accordance with the terms of Part I of the 2000 Act. Nothing in this code should be taken as granting dispensation from the requirements of that Part of the 2000 Act.

4.31 Part I of the 2000 Act provides certain exceptions to the rule that interception of telephone conversations must be warranted under that Part. This includes, where one party to the communication consents to the interception, it may be authorised in accordance with section 48(4) of the 2000 Act provided that there is no interception warrant authorising the interception. In such cases, the interception is treated as directed surveillance.

4.32 The use of a surveillance device should not be ruled out simply because it may incidentally pick up one or both ends of a telephone conversation, and any such product can be treated as having been lawfully obtained. However, its use would not be appropriate where the sole purpose is to overhear speech which, at the time of monitoring, is being transmitted by a telecommunications system. In such cases an application should be made for an interception of communication warrant under section 5 of the 2000 Act.

5 Authorisation procedures for intrusive surveillance

5.1 Intrusive surveillance is defined in section 26(3) of the 2000 Act as covert surveillance that:

(a)   is carried out in relation to anything taking place on any residential premises or in any private vehicle; and

(b)   involves the presence of an individual on the premises or in the vehicle or is carried out by means of a surveillance device.

5.2 Covert surveillance is defined in section 26(9)(a) of the 2000 Act as any surveillance which is carried out in a manner calculated to ensure that the persons subject to the surveillance are unaware that it is or may be taking place.

5.3 Where surveillance is carried out in relation to anything taking place on any residential premises or in any private vehicle by means of a device, without that device being present on the premises, or in the vehicle, it is not intrusive unless the device consistently provides information of the same quality and detail as might be expected to be obtained from a device actually present on the premises or in the vehicle. Thus, an observation post outside premises, which provides a limited view and no sound of what is happening inside the premises would not be considered as intrusive surveillance.

5.4 Residential premises are defined in section 48(1) of the 2000 Act. The definition includes hotel rooms, bedrooms in barracks, and police and prison cells but not any common area to which a person is allowed access in connection with his occupation of such accommodation e.g. a hotel lounge.

5.5 A private vehicle is defined in section 48(1) of the 2000 Act as any vehicle which is used primarily for the private purposes of the person who owns it or of a person otherwise having the right to use it. A person does not have a right to use a motor vehicle if his right to use it derives only from his having paid, or undertaken to pay, for the use of the vehicle and its driver for a particular journey.

5.6 In many cases, a surveillance investigation or operation may involve both intrusive surveillance and entry on or interference with property or with wireless telegraphy. In such cases, both activities need authorisation. This can be done as a combined authorisation (see paragraph 2.11).

5.7 An authorisation for intrusive surveillance may be issued by the Secretary of State (for the intelligence services, the Ministry of Defence, HM Forces and any other public authority designated under section 41(1)) or by a senior authorising officer (for police, NCIS, NCS and HMCE).

5.8 All authorisations require the personal authority of the Secretary of State or the senior authorising officer. Any members or officials of the intelligence services, the Ministry of Defence and HM Forces can apply to the Secretary of State for an intrusive surveillance warrant. Under section 32(2) of the 2000 Act neither the Secretary of State or the senior authorising officer may authorise intrusive surveillance unless he believes–

(a) that the authorisation is necessary in the circumstances of the particular case on the grounds that it is:
  • in the interests of national security[7];
  • for the purpose of preventing or detecting serious crime; or
  • in the interests of the economic well-being of the UK;
  and
(b) the authorising officer must also believe that the surveillance is proportionate to what it seeks to achieve.

5.9 A factor which must be taken into account in deciding whether an authorisation is necessary and proportionate is whether the information which it is thought necessary to obtain by means of the intrusive surveillance could reasonably be obtained by other less intrusive means.

Authorisations procedures for Police, National Criminal Intelligence Service, the National Crime Squad and HM Customs and Excise

5.10 The senior authorising officer should generally give authorisations in writing. However, in urgent cases, they may be given orally. In an urgent oral case, a statement that the senior authorising officer has expressly authorised the conduct should be recorded in writing by the applicant as soon as is reasonably practicable.

5.11 If the senior authorising officer is absent then as provided for in section 12(4) of the Police Act 1996, section 5(4) of the Police (Scotland) Act 1967, section 25 of the City of London Police Act 1839, or sections 8 or 54 of the 1997 Act, an authorisation can be given in writing or, in urgent cases, orally by the designated deputy.

5.12 In an urgent case, where it is not reasonably practicable having regard to the urgency of the case for the designated deputy to consider the application, a written authorisation may be granted by a person entitled to act under section 34(4) of the 2000 Act.

5.13 A case is not normally to be regarded as urgent unless the time that would elapse before the authorising officer was available to grant the authorisation would, in the judgement of the person giving the authorisation, be likely to endanger life or jeopardise the investigation or operation for which the authorisation was being given. An authorisation is not to be regarded as urgent where the need for an authorisation has been neglected or the urgency is of the authorising officer's own making.

5.14 The consideration of an authorisation by the senior authorising officer is only to be regarded as not reasonably practicable (within the meaning of section 34(2) of the 2000 Act) if he is on annual leave, is absent from his office and his home, or is for some reason not able within a reasonable time to obtain access to a secure telephone or fax machine. Pressure of work is not normally to be regarded as rendering it impracticable for a senior authorising officer to consider an application. Where a designated deputy gives an authorisation this should be made clear and the reason for the absence of the senior authorising officer given.

5.15 A police, NCIS or NCS authorisation cannot be granted unless the application is made by a member of the same force, service or squad. For HMCE an authorisation cannot be granted unless the application is made by a customs officer. Where the surveillance is carried out in relation to any residential premises, the authorisation cannot be granted unless the residential premises are in the area of operation of the force, service, squad or organisation.

INFORMATION TO BE PROVIDED IN APPLICATIONS FOR AUTHORISATION

5.16 Applications should be in writing and describe the conduct to be authorised and the purpose of the investigation or operation. The application should specify:

- the reasons why the authorisation is necessary in the particular case and on the grounds (e.g. for the purpose of preventing or detecting serious crime) listed in section 32(3) of the 2000 Act;
- the reasons why the surveillance is considered proportionate to what it seeks to achieve;
- the nature of the surveillance;
- the residential premises or private vehicle in relation to which the surveillance will take place;
- the identities, where known, of those to be the subject of the surveillance;
- an explanation of the information which it is desired to obtain as a result of the surveillance;

- details of any potential collateral intrusion and why the intrusion is justified;
- details of any confidential information that is likely to be obtained as a consequence of the surveillance.
- A subsequent record should be made of whether authority was given or refused, by whom and the time and date.

5.17 Additionally, in urgent cases, the authorisation should record (as the case may be):

- the reasons why the authorising officer or designated deputy considered the case so urgent that an oral instead of a written authorisation was given; and/or
- the reasons why it was not reasonably practicable for the application to be considered by the senior authorising officer or the designated deputy.

5.18 Where the application is oral, the detail referred to above should be recorded in writing as soon as reasonably practicable.

APPROVAL OF SURVEILLANCE COMMISSIONERS

5.19 Except in urgent cases a police, NCIS, NCS or HMCE authorisation granted for intrusive surveillance will not take effect until it has been approved by a Surveillance Commissioner and written notice of the Commissioner's decision has been given to the person who granted the authorisation. This means that the approval will not take effect until the notice has been received in the office of the person who granted the authorisation within the relevant force, service, squad or HMCE.

5.20 When the authorisation is urgent it will take effect from the time it is granted provided notice is given to the Surveillance Commissioner in accordance with section 35(3)(b) (see section 36(3) of the 2000 Act).

5.21 There may be cases that become urgent after approval has been sought but before a response has been received from a Surveillance Commissioner. In such a case, the authorising officer should notify the Surveillance Commissioner that the case is now urgent (pointing out that it has become urgent since the notification). In these cases, the authorisation will take effect immediately.

NOTIFICATIONS TO SURVEILLANCE COMMISSIONERS

5.22 Where a person grants, renews or cancels an authorisation, he must, as soon as is reasonably practicable, give notice in writing to a Surveillance Commissioner, in accordance with whatever arrangements have been made by the Chief Surveillance Commissioner.

5.23 In urgent cases, the notification must specify the grounds on which the case is believed to be one of urgency. The urgency provisions should not be used routinely. If the Surveillance Commissioner is satisfied that there were no grounds for believing the case to be one of urgency, he has the power to quash the authorisation

5.24 The information to be included in the notification to the Surveillance Commissioner is set out in the Regulation of Investigatory Powers (Notification of Authorisations etc.) Order 2000; SI No: 2563.

Authorisation procedures for Secretary of State Authorisations

AUTHORISATIONS

5.25 An intrusive surveillance authorisation for any of the intelligence services, the Ministry of Defence, HM Forces or any other public authority designated for this purpose requires a Secretary of State authorisation/warrant, unless they are acting on behalf of another public authority that has obtained an authorisation. In this context, Secretary of State can mean any Secretary of State, although an authorisation or warrant should be obtained from the Secretary of State of the relevant department.

5.26 Intelligence services authorisations must be made by issue of a warrant. Such warrants will generally be given in writing by the Secretary of State. In urgent cases, a warrant may be signed (but not renewed) by a senior official, provided the Secretary of State has expressly authorised this.

5.27 Applications to the Secretary of State for authorisations should specify those matters listed in paragraph 5.16.

All intrusive surveillance authorisations

5.28 Paragraphs 5.29 to 5.42 deal with the duration, renewal and cancellation of authorisations. Unless otherwise specified the guidance below applies to all authorisations.

Duration of authorisations

ALL AUTHORISATIONS EXCEPT SECRETARY OF STATE INTELLIGENCE
SERVICES AUTHORISATIONS

5.29 A written authorisation granted by a Secretary of State, a senior authorising officer or a designated deputy will cease to have effect (unless renewed) at the end of a period of **three months**, beginning with the day on which it took effect.

5.30 Oral authorisations given in urgent cases by a Secretary of State, a senior authorising officers or their designated deputies, and written authorisations given by those only entitled to act in urgent cases (see paragraph 5.11), will cease to have effect (unless renewed) at the end of the period of **seventy-two hours** beginning with the time when they took effect.

SECRETARY OF STATE INTELLIGENCE SERVICES AUTHORISATIONS

5.31 A warrant issued by the Secretary of State will cease to have effect at the end of a period of **six months** beginning with the day on which it was issued.

5.32 Warrants expressly authorised by a Secretary of State, and signed on his behalf by a senior civil servant, will cease to have effect at the end of the **second working day** following the day of issue of the warrant unless renewed by the Secretary of State.

Renewals

ALL AUTHORISATIONS EXCEPT SECRETARY OF STATE INTELLIGENCE SERVICES AUTHORISATIONS

5.33 If at any time before an authorisation expires the senior authorising officer or, in his absence, the designated deputy considers the authorisation should continue to have effect for the purpose for which it was issued, he may renew it in writing for a further period of **three months**.

5.34 As with the initial authorisation, the senior authorising officer must (unless it is a case to which the urgency procedure applies) seek the approval of a Surveillance Commissioner. This means that the renewal will not take effect until the notice of it has been received in the office of the person who granted the authorisation within the relevant force, service, squad or HMCE (but not before the day on which the authorisation would have otherwise ceased to have effect). In urgent cases, a renewal can take effect immediately (provided this is not before the day on which the authorisation would have otherwise ceased to have effect). See section 35 and 36 of the 2000 Act and the Regulation of Investigatory Powers (Notification of Authorisations etc.) Order 2000; SI No: 2563.

5.35 Subject to paragraph 5.36, if at any time before the day on which a Secretary of State authorisation expires, the Secretary of State considers it necessary for the warrant to be renewed for the purpose for which it was issued, he may renew it in writing for a further period of **three months**, beginning with the day on which it would have ceased to have effect, but for the renewal.

SECRETARY OF STATE INTELLIGENCE SERVICES AUTHORISATIONS

5.36 If at any time before an intelligence service warrant expires, the Secretary of State considers it necessary for the warrant to be renewed for the purpose for which it was issued, he may renew it in writing for a further period of **six months**, beginning with the day on which it would have ceased to have effect, but for the renewal.

5.37 All applications for a renewal of an authorisation or warrant should record:

* whether this is the first renewal or every occasion on which the warrant/authorisation has been renewed previously;
* any significant changes to the information listed in paragraph 5.16;

- the reasons why it is necessary to continue with the intrusive surveillance;
- the content and value to the investigation or operation of the product so far obtained by the surveillance;
- the results of regular reviews of the investigation or operation.

5.38 Authorisations may be renewed more than once, if necessary, and the renewal should be kept/recorded as part of the central record of authorisations (see paragraphs 2.14 – 2.15).

Reviews

5.39 Regular reviews of authorisations should be undertaken to assess the need for the surveillance to continue. The results of a review should be recorded on the central record of authorisations (see paragraphs 2.14 – 2.15). Particular attention is drawn to the need to review authorisations frequently where the intrusive surveillance provides access to confidential information or involves collateral intrusion.

5.40 The senior authorising officer or, for those subject to Secretary of State authorisation, the member or official who made the application within each public authority should determine how often a review should take place. This should be as frequently as is considered necessary and practicable.

Cancellations

5.41 The senior authorising officer who granted or last renewed the authorisation must cancel it, or the person who made the application to the Secretary of State must apply for its cancellation, if he is satisfied that the surveillance no longer meets the criteria upon which it was authorised. Where the senior authorising officer or person who made the application to the Secretary of State is no longer available, this duty will fall on the person who has taken over the role of senior authorising officer or taken over from the person who made the application to the Secretary of State or the person who is acting as the senior authorising officer (see the Regulation of Investigatory Powers (Cancellation of Authorisations) Order 2000; SI No: 2794).

5.42 The Surveillance Commissioners must be notified where police, NCIS, NCS or HMCE authorisations are cancelled (see the Regulation of Investigatory Powers (Notification of Authorisations etc.) Order 2000; SI No: 2563).

Ceasing of surveillance activity

5.43 As soon as the decision is taken that the intrusive surveillance should be discontinued, instructions must be given to those involved to stop all surveillance of the subject(s). The date and time when such an instruction was given should be recorded in the central record of authorisations (see paragraphs 2.14 – 2.15) and the notification of cancellation where relevant.

POLICE, NATIONAL CRIMINAL INTELLIGENCE SERVICE, THE NATIONAL CRIME SQUAD AND HM CUSTOMS AND EXCISE AUTHORISATIONS

5.44 In cases where an authorisation is quashed or cancelled by a Surveillance Commissioner, the senior authorising officer must immediately instruct those carrying out the surveillance to stop monitoring, observing, listening or recording the activities of the subject of the authorisation. The date and time when such an instruction was given should be recorded on the central record of authorisations (see paragraphs 2.14 – 2.15).

6 Authorisation procedures for entry on or interference with property or with wireless telegraphy

6.1 The 1994 Act and 1997 Act provide lawful authority for entry on or interference with property or with wireless telegraphy by the intelligence services and the police, NCIS, NCS and HMCE.

6.2 In many cases a covert surveillance operation may involve both intrusive surveillance and entry on or interference with property or with wireless telegraphy. This can be done as a combined authorisation, although the criteria for authorisation of each activity must be considered separately (see paragraph 2.11).

Authorisations for entry on or interference with property or with wireless telegraphy by the police, National Criminal Intelligence Service, the National Crime Squad and HM Customs and Excise

6.3 Responsibility for such authorisations rests with the authorising officer as defined in section 93(5) of the 1997 Act, that is the chief constable or equivalent. Authorisations require the personal authority of the authorising officer (or his designated deputy) except in urgent situations, where it is not reasonably practicable for the application to be considered by such person. The person entitled to act in such cases is set out in section 94 of the 1997 Act.

6.4 Authorisations under the 1997 Act may not be necessary where the public authority is acting with the consent of a person able to give permission in respect of relevant property, although consideration should still be given to the need to obtain an authorisation under Part II of the 2000 Act.

6.5 Authorisations for the police, NCIS and NCS may only be given by an authorising officer on application by a member of his own force, Service or Squad for entry on or interference with property or with wireless telegraphy within the authorising officer's own area of operation. For HMCE an authorisation may only be given by an authorising officer on application by a customs officer. An authorising officer may authorise the taking of action outside the relevant area solely for the purpose of maintaining or retrieving any device, apparatus or equipment.

6.6 Any person giving an authorisation for entry on or interference with property or with wireless telegraphy under section 93(2) of the 1997 Act must believe that:

- it is necessary for the action specified to be taken for the purpose of preventing or detecting serious crime (or in the case of the Police Service of Northern Ireland, in the interests of national security)[8]; and
- that the taking of the action is proportionate to what the action seeks to achieve.

6.7 The authorising officer must take into account whether what it is thought necessary to achieve by the authorised conduct could reasonably be achieved by other means.

6.8 Any person granting or applying for an authorisation or warrant to enter on or interfere with property or with wireless telegraphy will also need to be aware of particular sensitivities in the local community where the entry or interference is taking place and of similar activities being undertaken by other public authorities which could impact on the deployment. In this regard, it is recommended that the authorising officers in NCIS, NCS and HMCE should consult a senior officer within the police force in which the investigation or operation takes place where the authorising officer considers that conflicts might arise. The Chief Constable of the Police Service of Northern Ireland should be informed of any surveillance operation undertaken by another law enforcement agency which involve its officers in maintaining or retrieving equipment in Northern Ireland.

Authorisation procedures for entry on or interference with property or with wireless telegraphy by the police, National Criminal Intelligence Service, the National Crime Squad and HM Customs and Excise

6.9 Authorisations will generally be given in writing by the authorising officer. However, in urgent cases, they may be given orally by the authorising officer. In such cases, a statement that the authorising officer has expressly authorised the action should be recorded in writing by the applicant as soon as is reasonably practicable. This should be done by the person with whom the authorising officer spoke.

6.10 If the authorising officer is absent then as provided for in section 12(4) of the Police Act 1996, section 5(4) of the Police (Scotland) Act 1967, section 25 of the City of London Police Act 1839, or sections 8 or 54 of the 1997 Act, an authorisation can be given in writing or, in urgent cases, orally by the designated deputy.

6.11 Where, however, in an urgent case, it is not reasonably practicable for the designated deputy to consider an application, then written authorisation may be given by the following:

- in the case of the police, by an assistant chief constable (other than a designated deputy);
- in the case of the Metropolitan Police and City of London Police, by a commander;
- in the case of NCIS and NCS, by a person designated by the relevant Director General[9];
- in the case of HMCE, by a person designated by the Commissioners of Customs and Excise[10].

6.12 Applications to the authorising officer for authorisation must be made in writing by a police or customs officer or a member of NCIS or NCS (within the terms of section 93(3) of the 1997 Act) and should specify:

- the identity or identities of those to be targeted (where known);
- the property which the entry or interference with will affect;
- the identity of individuals and/or categories of people, where known, who are likely to be affected by collateral intrusion;
- details of the offence planned or committed;
- details of the intrusive surveillance involved;
- how the authorisation criteria (as set out in paragraphs 6.6 and 6.7) have been met;
- any action which may be necessary to retrieve any equipment used in the surveillance;
- in case of a renewal, the results obtained so far, or a full explanation of the failure to obtain any results; and
- whether an authorisation was given or refused, by whom and the time and date.

6.13 Additionally, in urgent cases, the authorisation should record (as the case may be):

- the reasons why the authorising officer or designated deputy considered the case so urgent that an oral instead of a written authorisation was given; and
- the reasons why (if relevant) the person granting the authorisation did not consider it reasonably practicable for the application to be considered by the senior authorising officer or the designated deputy.

6.14 Where the application is oral, the information referred to above should be recorded in writing by the applicant as soon as reasonably practicable.

NOTIFICATIONS TO SURVEILLANCE COMMISSIONERS

6.15 Where a person gives, renews or cancels an authorisation, he must, as soon as is reasonably practicable, give notice of it in writing to a Surveillance Commissioner, in accordance with arrangements made by the Chief Surveillance Commissioner. In urgent cases which would otherwise have required the approval of a Surveillance Commissioner, the notification must specify the grounds on which the case is believed to be one of urgency.

6.16 There may be cases which become urgent after approval has been sought but before a response has been received from a Surveillance Commissioner. In such a case, the authorising officer should notify the Surveillance Commissioner that the case is urgent (pointing out that it has become urgent since the previous notification). In these cases, the authorisation will take effect immediately.

6.17 Notifications to Surveillance Commissioners in relation to the authorisation, renewal and cancellation of authorisations in respect of entry on or interference with property should be in accordance with the requirements of the Police Act 1997 (Notifications of Authorisations etc) Order 1998; SI No. 3241.

Duration of authorisations

6.18 Written authorisations given by authorising officers will cease to have effect at the end of a period of **three months** beginning with the day on which they took effect. In cases requiring prior approval by a Surveillance Commissioner this means from the time the Surveillance Commissioner has approved the authorisation and the person who gave the authorisation has been notified. This means that the approval will not take effect until the notice has been received in the office of the person who granted the authorisation within the relevant force, service, squad or HMCE. In cases not requiring prior approval, this means from the time the authorisation was given.

6.19 Oral authorisations given in urgent cases by:

- authorising officers;
- or designated deputies

and written authorisations given by:
- assistant chief constables (other than a designated deputy);
- commanders in the Metropolitan Police and City of London Police;
- the person designated to act by the Director General of NCIS or of NCS;
- the person designated for the purpose by the Commissioners of Customs and Excise;

will cease at the end of the period of **seventy-two** hours beginning with the time when they took effect.

Renewals

6.20 If at any time before the day on which an authorisation expires the authorising officer or, in his absence, the designated deputy considers the authorisation should continue to have effect for the purpose for which it was issued, he may renew it in writing for a period of **three months** beginning with the day on which the authorisation would otherwise have ceased to have effect. Authorisations may be renewed more than once, if necessary, and the renewal should be recorded on the authorisation record (see paragraph 6.27).

6.21 Commissioners must be notified of renewals of authorisations. The information to be included in the notification is set out in the Police Act 1997 (Notifications of Authorisations etc) Order 1998; SI No: 3241.

6.22 If, at the time of renewal, the criteria in paragraph 6.30 exist, then the approval of a Surveillance Commissioner must be sought before the renewal can take effect. The fact that the initial authorisation required the approval of a Commissioner before taking effect does not mean that its renewal will automatically require such approval. It will only do so if, at the time of the renewal, it falls into one of the categories requiring approval (and is not urgent).

Reviews

6.23 Authorising officers should regularly review authorisations to assess the need for the entry on or interference with property or with wireless telegraphy to continue. This should be recorded on the authorisation record (see paragraph 6.27). The authorising officer should determine how often a review should take place when giving an authorisation. This should be as frequently as is considered necessary and practicable and at no greater interval than one month. Particular attention is drawn to the need to review authorisations and renewals regularly and frequently where the entry on or interference with property or with wireless telegraphy provides access to confidential information or involves collateral intrusion.

Cancellations

6.24 The senior authorising officer who granted or last renewed the authorisation must cancel it, or the person who made the application to the Secretary of State must apply for its cancellation, if he is satisfied that the authorisation no longer meets the criteria upon which it was authorised. Where the senior authorising officer or person who made the application to the Secretary of State is no longer available, this duty will fall on the person who has taken over the role of senior authorising officer or taken over from the person who made the application to the Secretary of State or the person who is acting as the senior authorising officer (see the Regulation of Investigatory Powers (Cancellation of Authorisations) Order 2000; SI No: 2794).

6.25 The Surveillance Commissioners must be notified of cancellations of authorisations. The information to be included in the notification is set out in the Police Act 1997 (Notifications of Authorisations etc) Order 1998; SI No: 3421.

6.26 The Surveillance Commissioners have the power to cancel an authorisation if they are satisfied that, at any time after an authorisation was given or renewed, there were no reasonable grounds for believing the matters set out in paragraphs 6.6 and 6.7 above. In such circumstances, a Surveillance Commissioner may order the destruction of records, in whole or in part, other than any that are required for pending criminal or civil proceedings.

Authorisation record

6.27 An authorisation record should be created which records:

- the time and date when an authorisation is given;
- whether an authorisation is in written or oral form;
- the time and date when it was notified to a Surveillance Commissioner;
- and the time and date when the Surveillance Commissioner notified his approval (where appropriate).

The authorisation record should also record:
- every occasion when entry on or interference with property or with wireless telegraphy has occurred;
- the result of periodic reviews of the authorisation;

- the date of every renewal; and
- it should record the time and date when any instruction was given by the authorising officer to cease the interference with property or with wireless telegraphy.

Ceasing of entry on or interference with property or with wireless telegraphy

6.28 Once an authorisation or renewal expires or is cancelled or quashed, the authorising officer must immediately instruct those carrying out the surveillance to cease all the actions authorised for the entry on or interference with property or with wireless telegraphy. The time and date when such an instruction was given should be recorded on the authorisation record (see paragraph 6.27).

Retrieval of equipment

6.29 Where a Surveillance Commissioner quashes or cancels an authorisation or renewal, he will, if there are reasonable grounds for doing so, order that the authorisation remain effective for a specified period, to enable officers to retrieve anything left on the property by virtue of the authorisation. He can only do so if the authorisation or renewal makes provision for this. A decision by the Surveillance Commissioner not to give such an order can be the subject of an appeal to the Chief Surveillance Commissioner.

Special rules

CASES REQUIRING PRIOR APPROVAL OF A SURVEILLANCE COMMISSIONER

6.30 In certain cases, an authorisation for entry on or interference with property will not take effect until a Surveillance Commissioner has approved it and the notice has been received in the office of the person who granted the authorisation within the relevant force, service, squad or HMCE (unless the urgency procedures are used). These are cases where the person giving the authorisation believes that:

- any of the property specified in the authorisation:
  - is used wholly or mainly as a dwelling or as a bedroom in a hotel; or
  - constitutes office premises; or
- the action authorised is likely to result in any person acquiring knowledge of:
  - matters subject to legal privilege;
  - confidential personal information; or
  - confidential journalistic material.

6.31 Office premises are defined as any building or part of a building whose sole or principal use is as an office or for office purposes (which means purposes of administration, clerical work, handling money and telephone or telegraph operation).

Authorisations for entry on or interference with property or with wireless telegraphy by the intelligence services

6.32 Before granting a warrant, the Secretary of State must:

- think it necessary for the action to be taken for the purpose of assisting the relevant agency in carrying out its functions;
- be satisfied that the taking of the action is proportionate to what the action seeks to achieve;
- take into account in deciding whether an authorisation is necessary and proportionate is whether the information which it is thought necessary to obtain by the conduct authorised by the warrant could reasonably be obtained by other means; and
- be satisfied that there are satisfactory arrangements in force under the 1994 Act or the 1989 Act in respect of disclosure of any material obtained by means of the warrant, and that material obtained will be subject to those arrangements.

6.33 An application for a warrant must be made by a member of the intelligence services for the taking of action in relation to that agency. In addition, the Security Service may make an application for a warrant to act on behalf of the Secret Intelligence Service (SIS) and the Governments Communication Headquarters (GCHQ). SIS and GCHQ may not be granted a warrant for action in support of the prevention or detection of serious crime which relates to property in the British Islands.

6.34 A warrant shall, unless renewed, cease to have effect if the warrant was under the hand of the Secretary of State, at the end of the period of **six months** beginning with the day on which it was issued. In any other case, at the end of the period ending with the **second working day** following that day.

6.35 If at any time before the day on which a warrant would cease to have effect the Secretary of State considers it necessary for the warrant to continue to have effect for the purpose for which it was issued, he may by an instrument under his hand renew it for a period of **six months** beginning with that day. The Secretary of State shall cancel a warrant if he is satisfied that the action authorised by it is no longer necessary.

6.36 The intelligence services should provide the same information as the police, as and where appropriate, when making applications, requests for renewal and requests for cancellation of property warrants.

Retrieval of equipment

6.37 Because of the time it can take to remove equipment from a person's property it may also be necessary to renew a property warrant in order to complete the retrieval. Applications to the Secretary of State for renewal should state why it is being or has been closed down, why it has not been possible to remove the equipment and any timescales for removal, where known.

7 Oversight by commissioners

7.1 The 1997 and 2000 Acts require the Chief Surveillance Commissioner to keep under review (with the assistance of the Surveillance Commissioners and Assistant Surveillance Commissioners) the performance of functions under Part III of the 1997 Act and Part II of the 2000 Act by the police (including the Royal Navy Regulating Branch, the Royal Military Police and the Royal Air Force Police and the Ministry of Defence Police and the British Transport Police), NCIS, the NCS, HMCE and of the 2000 Act the other public authorities listed in Schedule 1 and in Northern Ireland officials of the Ministry of Defence and HM Forces.

7.2 The Intelligence Services Commissioner's remit is to provide independent oversight of the use of the powers contained within Part II of the 2000 Act and the 1994 Act by the Security Service, Secret Intelligence Service, GCHQ and the Ministry of Defence and HM Forces (excluding the Royal Navy Regulating Branch, the Royal Military Police and the Royal Air Force Police, and in Northern Ireland officials of the Ministry of Defence and HM Forces);

7.3 This code does not cover the exercise of any of the Commissioners' functions. It is the duty of any person who uses these powers to comply with any request made by a Commissioner to disclose or provide any information he requires for the purpose of enabling him to carry out his functions.

7.4 References in this code to the performance of review functions by the Chief Surveillance Commissioner and other Commissioners apply also to Inspectors and other members of staff to whom such functions have been delegated.

8 Complaints

8.1 The 2000 Act establishes an independent Tribunal. This Tribunal will be made up of senior members of the judiciary and the legal profession and is independent of the Government. The Tribunal has full powers to investigate and decide any case within its jurisdiction.

This code does not cover the exercise of the Tribunal's functions. Details of the relevant complaints procedure can be obtained from the following address:

Investigatory Powers Tribunal

PO Box 33220

London

SW1H 9ZQ

☎ 020 7273 4514

Annex A

Authorisation levels when knowledge of confidential information is likely to be acquired

Relevant Public Authorities	*Authorisation level*
Police Forces – Any police force maintained under section 2 of the Police Act 1996 (police forces in England and Wales outside London).	Chief Constable
Police Forces – Any police force maintained under or by virtue of section 1 of the Police (Scotland) Act 1967.	Chief Constable
The Metropolitan police force	Assistant Commissioner
The City of London police force	Commissioner
The Police Service of Northern Ireland	Deputy Chief Constable
The Royal Navy Regulating Branch	Provost Marshal
The Royal Military Police	Provost Marshal
The Royal Air Force Police	Provost Marshal
National Criminal Intelligence Service (NCIS)	Director General
National Crime Squad (NCS)	Director General or Deputy Director General
Serious Fraud Office	Director or Assistant Director
The Intelligence Services:	A Director of GCHQ
Government Communications Headquarters	Deputy Director General
Security Service	A Director of the Secret
Secret Intelligence Service	Intelligence Service
HM Forces:	Rear Admiral
Royal Navy	Major General
Army	Air Vice-Marshall
Royal Air Force	

Relevant Public Authorities	*Authorisation level*
HM Customs and Excise	Director Investigation or Regional Heads of Investigation
Inland Revenue	Deputy Chairman of Inland Revenue
Department for Environment, Food and Rural Affairs: DEFRA Investigation Branch Horticultural Marketing Inspectorate Plant Health and Seed Inspectorate Egg Marketing Inspectorate Sea Fisheries Inspectorate (SFI) Centre for Environment, Fisheries & Aquaculture Science (CEFAS)	Immediate Senior Officer of Head of DEFRA Prosecution Division Immediate Senior Officer of Head of DEFRA Prosecution Division Immediate Senior Officer of Head of DEFRA Prosecution Division Immediate Senior Officer of Head of DEFRA Prosecution Division Immediate Senior Officer of Head of DEFRA Prosecution Division Immediate Senior Officer of Head of DEFRA Prosecution Division Immediate Senior Officer of Head of DEFRA Prosecution Division
Ministry of Defence	Director General or equivalent
Department for Transport, Local Government and Regions: Vehicle Inspectorate Transport Security (Transec)	No Director of Transport Security
Department of Health: Medical Devices Agency Medicine Control Agency Welfare Foods Policy Unit Directorate of Counter Fraud Services (DFCS)	Chief Executive Chief Executive Deputy Chief Medical Officer Director of Counter Fraud Services
Home Office: HM Prison Service Immigration Service	Deputy Director General of the Prison Service Chief Inspector of the Immigration Service
Department of Work and Pensions: Benefits Agency	Chief Executive of the Benefits Agency

Relevant Public Authorities	*Authorisation level*
Department of Trade and Industry:	No
Radiocommunications Agency	No
British Trade International	Director of Coal Health Claims
Coal Health Claims Unit	unit
Companies Investigation Branch	The Inspector of Companies
Legal Services Directorate D	The Director of Legal Service D
National Assembly for Wales	Head of NHS Directorate in the National Assembly for Wales Head of NHS Finance Division in the National Assembly for Wales Head of Common Agricultural Policy Management Division in the National Assembly for Wales
Local Authorities	The Head of Paid Service or (in his absence) a Chief Officer
Environment Agency	Chief Executive of the Environment Agency
Financial Services Authority	Chairman of the Financial Services Authority
Food Standards Agency	Head of Group, Deputy Chief Executive and Chief Executive of the Foods Standards Agency
The Intervention Board for Agricultural Produce	Chief Executive of the Intervention Board for Agricultural Produce
Personal Investment Authority	Chairman of the Personal Investment Authority
Post Office	Director of Security

Relevant Public Authorities	*Authorisation level*
Health & Safety Executive	Director of Field Operations, Director of Hazardous Installations Directorate, Her Majesty's Chief Inspector of Nuclear Installations.
NHS bodies in England and Wales:	Chief Executive
A health authority established under section 8 of the National Health Service Act 1977	Chief Executive
A Special Health Authority established under section 11 of the National Health Service 1977	Chief Executive
A National Health Service Trust established under section 5 of the National Health Service and Community Care Act 1990	
Royal Pharmaceutical Society of Great Britain	Director of Professional Standards

1   One of the functions of the Security Service is the protection of national security and in particular the protection against threats from terrorism. These functions extend throughout the United Kingdom, save that, in Northern Ireland, where the lead responsibility for investigating the threat from terrorism related to the affairs of Northern Ireland lies with the Police Service of Northern Ireland. An authorising officer in another public authority should not issue an authorisation under Part II of the 2000 Act or under Part III of the 1997 Act where the operation or investigation falls within the responsibilities of the Security Service, as set out above, except where it is a directed surveillance investigation or operation that is to be carried out by a Special Branch or where the Security Service has agreed that another public authority can carry out a directed surveillance operation or investigation which would fall within the responsibilities of the Security Service.

2   HM Forces may also undertake operations in connection with a military threat to national security and other operations in connection with national security in support of the Security Service, the Police Service of Northern Ireland or other Civil Powers.

3   Detecting crime is defined in section 81(5) of the 2000 Act and is applied to the 1997 Act by section 134 of that Act (as amended).

4   This could include investigations into infectious diseases, contaminated products or the illicit sale of pharmaceuticals.

5   This could only be for a purpose which satisfies the criteria set out in Article 8(2) of the ECHR.

6   As defined in section 81(1) of the 2000 Act.

7   A senior authorising officer of a law enforcement agency should not issue an authorisation for intrusive surveillance or entry on or interference with property or with wireless telegraphy where the operation is within the responsibilities of one of the intelligence services and properly falls to be authorised by warrant issued by the Secretary of State under Part II of the 2000 Act or the 1994 Act. Also see footnotes 1 and 2.

8   See footnotes 1 and 2.

9   For police members of NCIS or NCS, this will be an officer who holds the rank of assistant chief constable in that Service or Squad. Additionally, in the case of NCIS, this may be an assistant chief investigation officer of HMCE.

10 This will be an officer of the rank of assistant chief investigation officer.

Accessing Communications Data: Draft Code of Practice

Pursuant to Section 71 of the Regulation of Investigatory Powers Act 2000

This is a draft code published under section 71(3)(a) of the Regulation of Investigatory Powers Act 2000 and laid before both Houses of Parliament.

CONTENTS

Introduction

1.1 This code of practice relates to the powers and duties conferred or imposed under Chapter II of Part I of the Regulation of Investigatory Powers Act 2000 ("the Act"). It provides guidance on the procedures that must be followed before access to communications data can take place under those provisions.

1.2 The code should be readily available to any members of a public authority who are involved in operations to access communications data.

1.3 The Act provides that the code is admissible in evidence in criminal and civil proceedings. If any provision of the code appears relevant to a question before any court or tribunal hearing any such proceedings, or to the Tribunal established under the Act, or to one of the Commissioners responsible for overseeing the powers conferred by the Act, it must be taken into account.

1.4 This code applies to relevant public authorities as described in Chapter II of Part I of the Act (see para 3.1 below).

1.5 This code **does not** cover conduct consisting in the interception of communications (contents of a communication).

1.6 This code extends to England, Wales, Scotland and Northern Ireland.

General

2.1 The code covers any conduct in relation to a postal service or telecommunication system for obtaining communications data and the disclosure to any person of such data. For these purposes, communications data includes information relating to the use of a postal service or telecommunication system but **does not include** the contents of the communication itself, contents of e-mails or interactions with websites. In this code "data", in relation to a postal item, means anything written on the outside of the item.

2.2 A person who engages in such conduct must be properly authorised and must act in accordance with that authority.

2.3 A test of *necessity* (see paras 4.1–4.3 below) must be met before any communications data is obtained. The assessment of necessity is one made by a designated person. (This is a person designated for the purposes of Chapter II of Part I of the Act (see para 3.2 below). A designated person has a number of obligations within the provisions of the Act which must be met before communications data is obtained. These are also laid out in this code). A designated person must not only consider it necessary to obtain the communications data but must also consider the conduct involved in obtaining the communications data to be *proportionate* (see para 4.4 below) to what it is sought to achieve.

Designated persons within relevant public authorities permitted to access communications data under the Act

3.1 Designated persons within the following *"relevant public authorities"*[1] are permitted under the Act to grant authorisations or serve notices[2], the two routes by which the Act allows communications data to be accessed (see further para 5.1 below):

- a police force (as defined in section 81(1) of the Act);
- the National Criminal Intelligence Service;
- the National Crime Squad;
- HM Customs and Excise;
- the Inland Revenue;
- the Security Service;

- the Secret Intelligence Service;
- the Government Communications Headquarters.

3.2 The appropriate level of official i.e. a designated person within each public authority for granting authorisations or giving notices will be as follows:

- to obtain any communications data defined by section 21(4) of the Act a minimum of Superintendent or equivalent;
- to obtain communications data defined by section 21(4)(c) only of the Act (such as account and subscriber information), a minimum of Inspector or equivalent.)

Purposes for which communications data may be sought

4.1 Under section 22(2) of the Act, communications data may be sought if a designated person believes it is necessary for one or more of the following purposes[3]:

- in the interests of national security;
- for the purpose of preventing or detecting crime or of preventing disorder;
- in the interests of the economic well-being of the United Kingdom (see para 4.2 below);
- in the interests of public safety;
- for the purpose of protecting public health;
- for the purpose of assessing or collecting any tax, duty, levy or other imposition, contribution or charge payable to a government department;
- for the purpose, in an emergency, of preventing death or injury or any damage to a person's physical or mental health, or of mitigating any injury or damage to a person's physical or mental health.

4.2 In exercising his power to grant an authorisation or give a notice in the interests of the economic well-being of the United Kingdom (as provided for by section 22(2)(c)) of the Act, a designated person will consider whether the economic well-being of the United Kingdom which it is in the interests of is, on the facts of each case, related to State security. The term "State security", which is used in Directive 97/66/EC (concerning the processing of personal data and the protection of privacy in the telecommunications sector), should be interpreted in the same way as the term "national security" which is used elsewhere in the Act and this code. A designated person will not grant an authorisation or give a notice on section 22(2)(c) grounds if this link is not established. Any application for an authorisation or a notice on section 22(2)(c) grounds should therefore explain how, in the applicant's view, the economic well-being of the United Kingdom which it is in the interests of is related to State security on the facts of the case.

4.3 For an action to be necessary in a democratic society the access to communications data must pursue a legitimate aim as listed in para 4.1; fulfil a pressing social need and be proportionate to that aim.

4.4 Under section 22(5) of the Act, a designated person must also consider the conduct involved in obtaining the communications data to be proportionate. Proportionality is a crucial concept. In both the Act and this code reference is made to the conduct being proportionate. This means that even if a particular case which interferes with a Convention right[4] is aimed at pursuing a legitimate aim (as listed in para 4.1 above) this will not justify the interference if the means used to achieve the aim are excessive in the circumstances. Any interference with a Convention right should be carefully designed to meet the objective in question and must not be arbitrary or unfair. Even taking all these considerations into account, in a particular case an interference may still not be justified because the impact on the individual or group is too severe.

Authorisations and notices

5.1 The Act provides two different ways of authorising access to communications data; through an authorisation under section 22(3) and by a notice under section 22(4). An authorisation would allow the relevant public authority to collect or retrieve the data itself. A notice is given to a postal or telecommunications operator and requires that operator to collect or retrieve the data and provide it to the public authority which served the notice. A designated person decides whether or not an authorisation should be granted or a notice given.

5.2 In order to illustrate, a section 22(3) authorisation may be appropriate where:

- the postal or telecommunications operator is not capable of collecting or retrieving the communications data[5];
- it is believed the investigation may be prejudiced if the postal or telecommunications operator is asked to collect the data itself;
- there is a prior agreement in place between the relevant public authority and the postal or telecommunications operator as to the appropriate mechanisms for the disclosure of communications data.

5.3 *Applications for communications data may only be made by persons in the same public authority as a designated person.*

(a) Single points of contact within relevant public authorities

5.4 Notices and where appropriate authorisations for communications data should be channelled through single points of contact within each public authority (unless the exemption in paras 5.13–5.14 applies). This will provide for an efficient regime, since the single points of contact will deal with the postal or telecommunications operator on a regular basis. It will also help the public authority to regulate itself. This will assist in reducing the burden on the postal or telecommunications operator by such requests. Single points of contact will be able to advise a designated person on whether an authorisation or a notice is appropriate.

5.5 Single points of contact should be in a position to:

- where appropriate, assess whether access to communications data is reasonably practical for the postal or telecommunications operator;
- advise applicants and designated persons on the practicalities of accessing different types of communications data from different postal or telecommunications operators;
- advise applicants and designated persons on whether communications data falls under section 21(4)(a), (b) or (c) of the Act;
- provide safeguards for authentication;
- assess any cost and resource implications to both the public authority and the postal or telecommunications operator.

(b) Applications to obtain communications data under the Act

5.6 The application form is subject to inspection by the Commissioner and both applicant and designated person may be required to justify their decisions. Applications to obtain communications data under the Act should be made on a standard form (paper or electronic) which must be retained by the public authority (see section 7 of this code) and which should contain the following minimum information:

- the name (or designation) of the officer requesting the communications data;
- the operation and person (if known) to which the requested data relates;
- a description, in as much detail as possible, of the communications data requested (there will also be a need to identify whether it is communications data under section 21(4)(a), (b) or (c) of the Act);
- the reason why obtaining the requested data is considered to be necessary for one or more of the purposes in paragraph 4.1 above (the relevant purpose also needs to be identified);
- an explanation of why obtaining the data constitutes conduct proportionate to what it seeks to achieve;
  - where appropriate, a consideration of collateral intrusion, the extent to which the privacy of others may be affected and why that intrusion is justified; and
- the timescale within which the communications data is required. Where the timescale within which the material is required is any greater than routine, the reasoning for this to be included.

5.7 The application form should subsequently record whether access to communications data was approved or denied, by whom and the date. Alternatively, the application form can be marked with a cross-reference to the relevant authorisation or notice.

(c) Considerations for designated person

5.8 A designated person must take account of the following points, so that he is in a position to justify decisions made:

- whether the case justifies the accessing of communications data for one or more of the purposes listed in paragraph 4.1 above, and why obtaining the data is *necessary* for that purpose;
- whether obtaining access to the data by the conduct authorised by the authorisation, or required of the postal or telecommunications operator in the case of a notice, is proportionate to what is sought to be achieved. (A designated person needs to have in mind the conduct which he is authorising or requiring in each case. In making a judgement as to proportionality, a designated person needs to have in mind whether he is granting an authorisation or issuing a notice, and also what the scope of the conduct is. For example, where the conduct covers the provision of ongoing communications data);
  - where appropriate, where accessing the communications data is likely to result in collateral intrusion, whether the circumstances of the case still justify that access; and
- whether any urgent timescale is justified.

(d) Content of an authorisation

5.9 An authorisation itself can only authorise conduct to which Chapter II of Part I of the Act applies. A designated person will make a decision whether to grant an authorisation based upon the application which is made. The application form and the authorisation itself is not served upon the holder of communications data. The authorisation should be in a standard format (written or electronic) which must be retained by the public authority (see section 7 of this code) and must contain the following information:

- a description of the conduct to which Chapter II of Part I of the Act applies that is authorised;
- a description of the required communications data;
- for which of the purposes in paragraph 4.1 above the data is required; and
- the name (or designation) and office, rank or position of the designated person.

5.10 The authorisation should also contain:

- a unique reference number.

(e) Content of a notice

5.11 A designated person will make a decision whether to issue a notice based upon the application which is made. The application form is not served upon the holder of communications data. The notice that they receive contains only enough information to allow them to fulfil their duties under the Act. The notice served upon the holder of the communications data should be in a standard format (written or electronic) which must be retained by the public authority (see section 7 of this code) and must contain the following information:

- a description of the required communications data;
- for which of the purposes in paragraph 4.1 above the data is required;

- the name (or designation) and office, rank or position of the designated person; and
- the manner in which the data should be disclosed.

5.12 The notice should also contain:

- a unique reference number;
- where appropriate, an indication of any urgency;
- a statement stating that data is sought under the provisions of Chapter II of Part I of the Act. i.e. an explanation that compliance with this notice is a legal requirement; and
- contact details so that the veracity of the notice may be checked.

[A specimen copy of a notice can be found at annex A to this code].

(f) Oral authority (urgent cases)

5.13 An application for communications data may only be made and approved orally, on an urgent basis, where it is necessary to obtain communications data for the purpose set out in section 22(2)(g) of the Act[6]:

> "for the purpose, in an emergency, of preventing death or injury or any damage to a person's physical or mental health, or of mitigating any injury or damage to a person's physical or mental health".

5.14 The fact of an oral application and approval must be recorded by the applicant and designated person at the time or as soon as possible. In this case, an authorisation under section 22(3) of the Act must be completed (in a written or electronic format) very shortly thereafter. In the case of a notice under section 22(4) of the Act, a designated person may make an oral request to a postal or telecommunications operator to disclose communications data which must be followed by a (written or electronic) notice to the postal or telecommunications operator very shortly thereafter. A section 22(4) notice may be issued directly to the postal or telecommunications operator, therefore relaxing the need to do so via a single point of contact.

(g) Disclosure of data

5.15 Notices under section 22(4) of the Act will only require the disclosure of data to:

- the person giving the notice i.e. the designated person; or
- to another specified person who must be from the same relevant public authority. In practice, this is likely to be the single points of contact.

Validity of authorisations and notices

(a) Duration

6.1 Authorisations and notices will only be valid for one month. This period will begin when the authorisation is granted or the notice given. A designated person should specify a shorter period if that is satisfied by the request, since this may go to the proportionality requirements. For 'future' communications data disclosure may only be required of data obtained by the postal or telecommunications operator **within** this period i.e. up to one month. For 'historical' communications data disclosure may only be required of data in the possession of the postal or telecommunications operator. A postal or telecommunications operator should comply with a section 22(4) notice as soon as is reasonably practicable. Furthermore, they will not be required to supply data unless it is reasonably practicable to do so.

(b) Renewal

6.2 An authorisation or notice may be renewed at any time during the month it is valid, by following the same procedure as in obtaining a fresh authorisation or notice.

6.3 A renewed authorisation or notice takes effect at the point at which the authorisation or notice it is renewing expires.

(c) Cancellation

6.4 A designated person shall cancel a notice given under section 22(4) of the Act as soon as it is no longer *necessary*, or the conduct is no longer *proportionate* to what is sought to be achieved. The duty to cancel a notice falls on the designated person who issued it.

6.5 The appropriate level of official within each public authority who may cancel a notice in the event of the designated person no longer being able to perform this duty is to be prescribed by Regulations made under section 23(9) of the Act.

6.6 As a matter of good practice, authorisations should also be cancelled in accordance with the procedure above.

6.7 In the case of a section 22(4) notice, the relevant postal or telecommunications operator will be informed of the cancellation.

Retention of records by public authorities

7.1 Applications, authorisations and notices for communications data must be retained by the relevant public authority until it has been audited by the Commissioner. The public authority should also keep a record of the dates on which the authorisation or notice is started and cancelled.

(a) Errors

7.2 Where any errors have occurred in the granting of authorisations or the giving of notices, a record should be kept, and a report and explanation sent to the Commissioner as soon as is practical.

7.3 Applications must also be retained to allow for the complaints Tribunal, under Part IV of the Act, to carry out its functions.

7.4 This code does not affect any other statutory obligations placed on public authorities to retain data under any other enactment. (Where applicable, in England and Wales, the relevant tests given in the Criminal Procedures and Investigations Act 1996[7], namely whether any material gathered might undermine the case for the prosecution against the accused, or might assist the defence, should be applied).

(b) Data protection safeguards

7.5 Communications data, and all copies, extracts and summaries of it, must be handled and stored securely. In addition, the requirements of the Data Protection Act 1998[8] and its data protection principles should be adhered to.

Oversight

8.1 The Act provides for an Interception of Communications Commissioner whose remit is to provide independent oversight of the use of the powers contained within Part I.

8.2 This code does not cover the exercise of the Commissioner's functions. However, it will be the duty of any person who uses the powers conferred by Chapter II of Part I to comply with any request made by the Commissioner to provide any information he requires for the purposes of enabling him to discharge his functions.

Complaints

9.1 The Act establishes an independent Tribunal, which is made up of senior members of the legal profession or judiciary and is independent of the Government. The Tribunal has full powers to investigate and decide any case within its jurisdiction.

9.2 This code does not cover the exercise of the Tribunal's functions. However, details of the relevant complaints procedure should be readily available, for reference purposes, at public offices of those public authorities permitted to access communications data under the provisions of Chapter II of Part I of the Act. Where this is not possible, copies should be made available by post or e-mail.

Annex A to draft code of practice

Unique reference number: [*to be completed by the public authority*]

[*an indication of any urgency*]

NOTICE UNDER SECTION 22(4) OF THE REGULATION OF INVESTIGATORY POWERS ACT 2000 REQUIRING COMMUNICATIONS DATA TO BE OBTAINED AND DISCLOSED

To: [NAME OF POSTAL OR TELECOMMUNICATIONS OPERATOR and address].

In accordance with section 22(4) of the Regulation of Investigatory Powers Act 2000, I hereby require you –

*(a)   if not already in possession of the data to which this notice relates, to obtain it; and *{for use in those cases where you are actually asking for data to be captured for the duration of the notice – this should be omitted where you are only requiring the disclosure of historical data}*.

(b)   to disclose all communications data to which this notice relates, whether in your possession or subsequently obtained by you.

Description of communications data to which this notice relates:

[enter details of the communications data required {distinguish here between data (a) to be obtained if not already in the possession of the operator (omitting if not relevant) and (b) to be disclosed – each should be described separately}].

*(a)   *[communications data to be obtained]*;
(b)   *[communications data to be disclosed]*.

This notice is valid from *[start date – issue date of this notice]* to *[end date]*. – This must be no more than one month from the date of this notice, or earlier if cancelled under section 23(8)). This notice may be renewed at any time before the end of the period of one month starting with *[issue date]* by the giving of a further notice.

I believe that it is necessary for this communications data to be obtained:

[List the purpose(s) that the communications data is required for (from Section 22(2)) – follow the statutory language exactly)].

In reaching this conclusion I have satisfied myself that obtaining this data by the conduct required by this notice is proportionate to what is sought to be achieved by so obtaining the data.

You are required to produce the said communications data to *[specify the person (a name or designation must be specified), office, rank or position to whom the data is to be disclosed]* of *[public authority]* for him to take away as specified below:

[*Specify the manner in which the data is to be disclosed*].

Date ....

Designated Person (a minimum of Superintendent or equivalent. For communications data falling under section 21(4)(c) of the Act, a minimum of Inspector or equivalent): [***Enter office, rank or position***] ....

This notice may be verified by contacting the following:

[*enter contact details i.e. of the Single Point of Contact*]

*Omit as appropriate

1   The Act permits the Secretary of State to add further public authorities to this list by means of an Order subject to the affirmative resolution procedure in Parliament.
2   The Secretary of State may by Order place restrictions on:
      ● the authorisations or notices that may be granted or given by designated persons; and
      ● the circumstances in which, or purposes for which, authorisations or notices may be granted or given.
      Relevant public authorities authorised to access communications data from the list in Chapter II of Part I of the Act may be removed, if deemed appropriate, by Order of the Secretary of State.
3   The Act permits the Secretary of State to add further purposes to this list by means of an Order subject to the affirmative resolution procedure in Parliament.
4   European Convention on Human Rights (ECHR).
5   Where possible, this assessment will be based upon information provided by the relevant postal or telecommunications operator.
6   To give effect to Article 2 (right to life) of the European Convention on Human Rights (ECHR).
7   Further guidance is available in the CPIA code of practice.
8   Further guidance is available from http://www.homeoffice.gov.uk/foi/datprot.html

Retention of Communications Data Under Part 11: Anti-Terrorism, Crime & Security Act 2001: Voluntary Code of Practice

Foreword

The Anti-Terrorism, Crime & Security Act was passed in December of 2001 (the Act). Part 11 of the Act aims to allow for the retention of communications data to ensure that the UK security, intelligence and law enforcement agencies have sufficient information available to them to assist them in protecting the UK's national security and to investigate terrorism.

Communications data are retained by the communications service providers to enable them to carry out their business effectively. Such information could be divided into three broad categories these being subscriber information (identifies user); traffic data (identifies whom was called etc); and use made of service (identifies what services are used). The Act recognises that communications data are an essential tool for the security, intelligence and law enforcement agencies in carrying out their work to safeguard United Kingdom national security. These agencies, which are authorised to acquire communications data under statutory provisions, would be greatly assisted if they could rely on the communications data being available when they required it.

Part 11 of the Act provides only for the retention of data that communication service providers already retain for business purposes. Its object is not to enlarge the fields of data which a communication service provider may (or must) retain, but to encourage communication service providers to retain that data for longer than they would otherwise need to do so for their own commercial purposes. The Act identifies that the purpose of the retention period is the safeguarding of national security or for the prevention or detection of crime or the prosecution of offences which relate directly or indirectly to national security.

This Code of Practice relates specifically to the need for communications service providers to retain data for extended periods of time in order to assist the security, intelligence and law enforcement agencies in carrying out their work of safeguarding national security or in the prevention or detection of crime or the prosecution of offences which relate directly or indirectly to national security.

This Code of Practice does not address issues relating to disclosure of data, it simply addresses the issues of what types of data can be retained and for how long it will be retained beyond a particular company's existing business practice. The Code explains why communications service providers have the ability to retain data beyond their normal business purposes for the reasons outlined in the Act.

Communications data may be obtained by security, intelligence and law enforcement agencies under the Regulation of Investigatory Powers Act 2000 and other statutory powers. This Code does not deal with these provisions.

The Data Protection Act 1998 requires that personal data are processed lawfully. In retaining communications data for longer than needed for their own business purposes and for the purposes identified in the Act communication service providers will process personal data. The Information Commissioner's Office (ICO) has accepted that such processing will not, on human rights grounds, contravene this requirement of the Act.

However, individual communication service providers must satisfy themselves that the processing is "necessary" for one of a range of functions. In doing so they are entitled to rely heavily on the Secretary of State's assurance that the retention of communications data for the periods as specified in this Code is necessary for the government's function of safeguarding national security, and on the fact that the Code has been approved by Parliament.

The ICO has though expressed concern about such retained data being acquired for purposes that do not relate to national security. Acquisition of communications data is not addressed in the Act and therefore is not within the proper ambit of this Code.

CONTENTS

Purpose of the Code
Human rights and data protection considerations
Jurisdiction and types of operators covered by the Code of Practice
Types of data and retention periods
Agreements
Costs arrangements
Acquisition of data retained under the terms of this Code of Practice
Oversight mechanism
Transitional arrangements
Criteria for assessing the effectiveness of the Code of Practice

Purpose of the Code

1.   In section 102 of the Act, Parliament has given the Secretary of State the power to issue a Code of Practice relating to the retention of communications data by communication service providers. This Code of Practice is intended to outline how communication service providers can assist in the fight against terrorism by meeting agreed time periods for retention of communications data that may be extended beyond those periods for which their individual company currently retains data for business purposes.

2.   After consultation with the security, intelligence and law enforcement agencies, the Secretary of State has determined that retention of communications data by communication service providers in line with the Appendix to this Code of Practice is necessary for the purposes set out in section 102(3) of the Act, namely;
      (a)   the purposes of safeguarding national security
      (b)   the purposes of prevention or detection of crime or the prosecution of offenders which may relate directly or indirectly to national security.

3.   The Code of Practice is intended to ensure that communication service providers may retain data for the two purposes identified at 2 a & b, after the need for retention for business purposes has elapsed and there is otherwise an obligation to erase or anonymise retained data. It does not provide guidance on the manner in which data retained for these purposes should be processed; nor does the Secretary of State consider it necessary to impose new standards on the conditions in which the data are stored, e.g. technical media, security, ease of access, indexing or other.

4.   The Code does not relate to the powers of public authorities to obtain communications data retained in accordance with the Appendix to the Code. Acquisition of communications data is provided for by Chapter II of Part I of the Regulation of Investigatory Powers Act 2000, as well as other relevant statutory powers. See paragraphs 25 to 28.

Human rights and data protection considerations

5.   This Code has been drawn up in accordance with existing legislation, including the Human Rights Act 1998, and the Data Protection Act 1998, and the Telecommunications (Data Protection and Privacy) Regulations 1999, together with their parent directives.

6.   Data retained under the Code are subject to the data protection principles found in the Data Protection Act 1998. Under the first data protection principle personal data may only be processed if at least one of the conditions in Schedule 2 to the 1998 Act is met. The processing of data retained under this Code falls within paragraph 5 of Schedule 2 of the Data Protection Act 1998 in that it is necessary for the communication service provider to retain data to enable the Secretary of State to fulfil his function for the protection of national security. Some communications data may in certain

circumstances constitute sensitive personal data. Processing of such data is permitted by virtue of Schedule 3, paragraph 7 of the 1998 Act.

7.   Data retained under the Code will, at least for a certain period, be data that are needed by the communication service provider for business purposes. Its processing will therefore initially be undertaken for a dual purpose: (a) business purposes, (b) national security purposes, where "national security purposes" includes both the purposes set out in section 102(3) of the Act. Since both purposes of retention will apply to all data simultaneously during the 'business purpose time period, there is no need for separate storage systems for "business data" and "national security data" under this dual-purpose scheme. However, once an individual company has exceeded the business purpose time period then data will be retained specifically for the purposes described in Section 102(3) of the Act. The system deployed by individual companies will need to identify that the data has exceeded the business purpose time period. Individual communication service providers will need to ensure that they do not access those data for their own purposes. At the end of the retention period necessary for 'business purposes' the only data that a communication service provider should retain are that data identified in the 'Technical Specification' attached as Appendix A to this Code.

8.   The fifth data protection principle provides that personal data processed for any purpose or purposes shall not be kept for any longer than is necessary for that purpose or those purposes. The periods for which it appears necessary to the Secretary of State for communication service providers to retain communications data for national security purposes are those set out in Appendix A. The periods for which it is necessary for communication service providers to retain communications data for business purposes is a matter for each communication service provider, and they might be longer or shorter than the retention periods the Secretary of State has set out are necessary for national security. Compliance with the fifth data protection principle under the dual-purpose scheme requires that after the expiry of the shorter of these two periods, communications data may only be retained further for the period required by the remaining purpose. When the retention periods for both purposes have expired, the data must be either anonymised or erased.

9.   As indicated the Secretary of State considers the retention of data in accordance with Appendix A to be necessary for the purpose of national security and accordingly retention for those periods should comply with the fifth data protection principle. However, because the purpose of retention is to safeguard national security were it to be suggested that retention in accordance with this Code did not comply with the fifth principle, the national security exemption in s 28 of the Data Protection Act 1998 could be relied on to exempt such data from the fifth principle so enabling it to be retained in accordance with the Code. If necessary the Secretary of State would issue a certificate under s 28.2 confirming the same.

10.   The data subject access provisions set out in the Data Protection Act 1998 continue to apply to communications data retained under this Code, that is to say that data subjects may request access to their personal data whether it is held for national security purposes or for the communication service provider's

business purposes. In addition, subscribers should be notified where their personal data will be retained for the purpose of the Act, as well as for the communication service providers business purposes, and that it may be disclosed to relevant public authorities, as set out in paragraph 27 of this Code. Every effort should be made to ensure that this is brought to the attention of the subscriber for example this could be added to billing information or sent by way of text message or e-mail.

NB. Communication service providers will need to ensure that their entry in the register of data controllers maintained by the Information Commissioner describes the processing of personal data involved in retention of communications data for the national security purposes. The Information Commissioner's advice is that they should notify that they are processing for the following purpose

"NATIONAL SECURITY: Retention of communications data for the purpose of safeguarding national security or for the purposes of prevention or detection of crime or the prosecution of offenders which may relate directly or indirectly to national security"

This is not one of the standard purpose descriptions that the Information Commissioner provides so communication service providers will need to complete it in full, together with details of the associated data subjects, classes and recipients, when they apply to add a new purpose to their existing notification.

11.   The retention specification set out in Appendix A to this Code has been drafted taking into account a number of factors, including the right to respect for private life under Article 8 of the European Convention of Human Rights. The Secretary of State considers the retention periods set out in Appendix A to be both necessary and proportionate in light of the individual's right to respect for private life and the national security purposes for which the retention of data is required.

Jurisdiction and types of operators covered by the Code of Practice

12.   The Code of Practice applies to all communication service providers who, provide a public telecommunications service in the United Kingdom as defined in section 2 of the Regulation of Investigatory Powers Act 2000, and who retain communications data in line with the provisions of the Act. The Secretary of State considers it necessary for the national security purposes outlined in the Act, for communications data held by communication service providers, which relates to subscribers resident in the UK or subscribing to or using a UK-based service, to be retained in accordance with the provisions of the Code, whether the data are generated or processed in the UK or abroad. However, if data relating to a service provided in the UK are stored in a foreign jurisdiction it may be subject to conflicting legal requirements prohibiting the retention of

data in accordance with this Code. In such cases, it is accepted that it may not be possible to adhere to the terms of this Code in respect of that communications data.

13.   The data categories and retention periods in the Appendix to this Code have been determined with regard to considerations of necessity and proportionality. The data categories and retention periods relate to communications data generated and retained by communication service providers who provide a service to the general public in the United Kingdom. This Code is not intended to apply to individuals or organisations who do not provide such a public service (e.g. private networks).

14.   In some cases, two or more legal entities may be involved in the provision of a public telecommunications service, e.g. backbone/virtual service provider model. In such cases, the provisions of this Code apply to data retained by each legal entity for their own business purposes.

Types of data and retention periods

15.   Communications data can be divided into three broad categories, corresponding to the definitions in section 21(4) of the Regulation of Investigatory Powers Act 2000, which can be summarised as follows:

(a)   **traffic data** – including telephone numbers called, email addresses, and location data etc.

(b)   **use made of service** – including services subscribed to, etc.

(c)   **other information relating to the subscriber** – including installation address, etc.

"communications data" as defined by RIPA means any of the following–

(i)   any traffic data comprised in or attached to a communication (whether by the sender or otherwise) for the purposes of any postal service or telecommunication system by means of which it is being or may be transmitted;

(ii)   any information which includes none of the contents of a communication [apart from any information falling within paragraph (i)] and is about the use made by any person–

(1)   of any telecommunications service; or

(2)   in connection with the provision to or use by any person of any telecommunications service, of any part of a telecommunication system;

(iii)   any information not falling within paragraph (i) or (ii) that is held or obtained, in relation to persons to whom he provides the service, by a person providing a telecommunications service.

"traffic data", as defined by the Regulation of Investigatory Powers Act 2000 in relation to any communication, means–

(i)   any data identifying, or purporting to identify, any person, apparatus or location to or from which the communication is or may be transmitted,

(ii)   any data identifying or selecting, or purporting to identify or select, apparatus through which, or by means of which, the communication is or may be transmitted,

(iii)   any data comprising signals for the actuation of apparatus used for the purposes of a telecommunication system for effecting (in whole or in part) the transmission of any communication, and

(iv)   any data identifying the data or other data as data comprised in or attached to a particular communication, but that expression includes data identifying a computer file or computer program access to which is obtained, or which is run, by means of the communication to the extent only that the file or program is identified by reference to the apparatus in which it is stored.

References, in relation to traffic data comprising signals for the actuation of apparatus, to a telecommunication system by means of which a communication is being or may be transmitted include references to any telecommunication system in which that apparatus is comprised; and references to traffic data being attached to a communication include references to the data and the communication being logically associated with each other.

16.   The maximum retention period for data held under the provisions of this Code is 12 months, without prejudice to any longer retention period which may be justified by the business practices of the communication service provider.

17.   For data categories 15(a) and 15 (b) above the period of retention begins at the point when the call ends, for subscriber-related data category 15 (c) the period of retention begins when the data are changed or subscriber leaves the service.

18.   The retention periods given in Appendix A recognise that types of communications data, as personal data, vary with respect both to their usefulness to the agencies, and to their sensitivity. It is recognised that the usefulness of different types of communications data for the purpose of safeguarding national security will vary and this is reflected in the different retention periods.

19.   The data categories listed in Appendix A will not all be relevant to every communication service provider. Whether or not a data type will be relevant to a communication service provider and therefore retained will depend on the services which it provides, for example, an internet service provider will not retain IMEI data. Communication service providers will not be expected to retain additional categories of data to those which they routinely retain for business purposes. In other words if a data type is not already captured for the business purposes of an individual company then there will be no expectation that this data type is retained for the purposes of the Act.

Agreements

20.   The Secretary of State may enter into agreements with individual communication service providers who receive requests for communications data stored under these provisions. The purpose of these agreements is to communicate the retention practices of those communication service provider to public authorities listed in Chapter II of Part I of the Regulation of Investigatory

Powers Act 2000. They will play the role of Service Level Agreements (SLAs) and will include any arrangements for payments to cover retention costs. These SLAs will be based on an open document outlining the agreement between the Secretary of State and the company concerned. Each of these will differ with respect to the appendices which will outline the services that a particular provider is able to deliver. Those parts of these agreements that do not contain commercially sensitive material will be publicly available. The appendices will remain commercially sensitive.

21.   The agreements will be drafted within the framework provided by this Code. An agreement may not set a retention period for any type of data which is greater than the period set out in Appendix A to this Code.

22.   Any agreement will be made between the Secretary of State and the communication service provider and must be entered into voluntarily by both sides. It may be terminated by either side subject to a period of notice set out in the agreement.

Costs arrangements

23.   Where the period of retention of data for national security purposes is not substantially larger than the period of retention for business purposes, the retention costs will continue to be borne by the communication service provider.

24.   Where data retention periods are significantly longer for national security purposes than for business purposes, the Secretary of State will contribute a reasonable proportion of the marginal cost as appropriate. Marginal costs may include, for example, the design and production of additional storage and searching facilities. This may be in the form of capital investment into retention and retrieval equipment or may include running costs.

Acquisition of data retained under the terms of this Code of Practice

25.   It is outside of the scope of this Code of Practice to address the issue of acquisition of data after it has been retained. It can only address the issue of retention of data for the purposes of the Act. The Act establishes the framework for communication service providers to retain data for the purposes of safeguarding national security and for the prevention or detection of crime and prosecution of offenders which may relate directly or indirectly to national security.

26.   The Code sets out a retention specification which is designed to meet the two aims set out above, both relating to national security. That is to say that any particular piece of data is retained because it belongs to a certain data type, and it is necessary to retain all data of that type for the purpose of safeguarding

national security or for the purpose of the prevention or detection of crime or the prosecution of offenders which may relate directly or indirectly to national security.

27.   The retention of such data is necessary so that it is available to be acquired by relevant public authorities under Chapter II of Part I of the Regulation of Investigatory Powers Act 2000, or otherwise, to assist them in safeguarding national security. However, whilst restrictions exist elsewhere, this Code cannot itself place restrictions on the ability of these bodies or other persons to acquire data retained under the Code for other purposes through the exercise of any statutory power. In particular, this Code cannot place any restrictions on the ability of the public authorities listed in Chapter II of Part I of the Regulation of Investigatory Powers Act 2000 to acquire data retained under this Code for any of the purposes set out in section 22 of that Act which do not relate to national security.

28.   In addition data access requests can also be received from data subjects under the Data Protection Act 1998 and from civil litigants.

Oversight mechanism

29.   The retention of communications data is a form of personal data processing. As such, it is subject to the Data Protection Act 1998. Oversight of the 1998 Act is by the Information Commissioner.

Transitional arrangements

30.   All data collected after the communication service provider adopts the Code should be processed in accordance with both the national security purposes and the business purposes from the point that it is generated. Data already held by the communication service providers at the time of adopting the Code will be processed only in accordance with the purpose for which it was originally collected.

31.   Subscribers should be notified of the new purpose for which data is being retained. This may be done by sending out a general notification to all customers. The national security purpose must be made clear to any new subscribers at the time they subscribe.

32.   During the period of time that a communications service provider is building the technical capacity to extend retention of specified data beyond their normal business time periods, the company's standard retention practice takes precedence. Once the individual communication service provider has the technical capacity to retain data for the extended time periods set out in this voluntary Code of Practice, then the communication service provider shall inform existing and new customers that the purpose for retention and the periods of retention have been varied to meet with the needs of the Act. Only after this information has been passed on to existing customers and new customers can the communication service provider then retain the data for the extended time

periods for the purposes of national security. There may be a period after the communication service provider has adopted the Code when he cannot retain data for the full period set out in Appendix A owing to the need to introduce technical adaptations. The agreement with the communication service provider will set out how long it will take to reach full compliance.

Criteria for assessing the effectiveness of the Code of Practice

33.   The Code will be reviewed three months from the date when it first receives parliamentary approval, in accordance with the following criteria:

(a)   Has it improved investigative work?

(b)   How many request for data have been made?

(c)   Is the voluntary system working?

(d)   What percentage of the market is covered by communication service providers who have adopted the Code of Practice?

(e)   Are sectors of the industry which have not adopted the Code enjoying an unfair commercial advantage?

The SLAs introduced under this Code will require communication service providers to keep records of all enquiries made for data retained under the Act from the date an individual service provider enters into a voluntary agreement with the Secretary of State, in order to enable a comprehensive survey to be undertaken.

Appendix A

Data retention: expansion of data categories

SUBSCRIBER INFORMATION   **12 months**

(From end of subscription/last change)

Subscriber details relating to the person

e.g. Name, date of birth, installation and billing address, payment methods, account/credit card details

Contact information (information held about the subscriber but not verified by the CSP)

e.g. Telephone number, email address

Identity of services subscribed to (information determined by the communication service provider)

e.g. Customer reference/account number, list of services subscribed to

Telephony:	telephone number(s), IMEI, IMSI(s)
Email:	email address(es), IP at registration
Instant messaging:	Internet Message Handle, IP at registration
ISP – dial-in:	Log-in, CLI at registration (if kept)
ISP – always-on:	Unique identifiers, MAC address (if kept), ADSL end points, IP tunnel address

TELEPHONY DATA   12 months

e.g. All numbers (or other identifiers e.g. name@bt) associated with call (e.g. physical/presentational/network assigned CLI, DNI, IMSI, IMEI, exchange/divert numbers)

Date and time of start of call

Duration of call/date and time of end of call

Type of call (if available)

Location data at start and/or end of call, in form of lat/long reference.

Cell site data from time cell ceases to be used.

IMSI/MSISDN/IMEI mappings.

For GPRS & 3G, date and time of connection, IMSI, IP address assigned.

Mobile data exchanged with foreign operators; IMSI & MSISDN, sets of GSM triples, sets of 3G quintuples, global titles of equipment communicating with or about the subscriber.

SMS, EMS and MMS DATA   6 months

e.g. Calling number, IMEI

Called number, IMEI

Date and time of sending

Delivery receipt – if available

Location data when messages sent and received, in form of lat/long reference.

EMAIL DATA   6 months

e.g. Log-on (authentication user name, date and time of log-in/log-off, IP address logged-in from)

Sent email (authentication user name, from/to/cc email addresses, date and time sent)

Received email (authentication user name, from/to email addresses, date and time received)

ISP DATA   6 months

e.g. Log-on (authentication user name, date and time of log-in/log-off, IP address assigned)

Dial-up:	CLI and number dialled
Always-on:	ADSL end point/MAC address (If available)

WEB ACTIVITY LOGS   4 days

e.g. Proxy server logs (date/time, IP address used, URL's visited, services)

The data types here will be restricted **solely to Communications Data and exclude content of communication**. This will mean that storage under this code can only take place to the level of www.homeoffice.gov.uk/......

OTHER SERVICES   Retention relative to service provided

e.g. Instant Message Type Services (log-on/off time) If available.

COLLATERAL DATA   Retention relative to data to which it is related

e.g. Data needed to interpret other communications data.for example – the mapping between cellmast identifiers and their location – translation of dialling (as supported by IN networks)

Notes:

All times should include an indication of which time zone is being used (Universal Co-ordinated Time is preferred).

An indication should also be given of the accuracy of the timing.

To assist in the interpretation of Internet terminology the Home Office have, with the permission of the Internet Crime Forum, reproduced at Appendix C the document written by the Data Retention Project Group of the Internet Crime Forum.

The Home Office recognises the effort that has gone into producing this document and would thank all those responsible for its production.

Appendix B

Agreements

To be written as single document outlining voluntary agreement and requirements of Appendix A. To include separate appendices relative to individual company's additional storage.

Appendix C

Principal Current Data Types

Howard Lamb

Chair

ICF Data Retention Project Group

1. Introduction

1.1 In December 2001, the Internet Crime Forum (ICF) established a project group the primary aim of which was to identify current data types in use by subscribers who have access to the Internet.

1.2 The group was not tasked with debating the legal issues in relation to the data types identified. There are many legal issues relating to data retention and these will undoubtedly be discussed in other documents.

1.3 The group was established with a view to producing a document that would provide a better understanding of the technology used and the information that law enforcement is seeking from its investigations. It is not intended to be a standard or a best practice document. The document is intended to be a reference to what data may be available and which of those data types are likely to be useful to law enforcement when conducting an investigation.

2. Group members

2.1 The group is restricted to technical and investigation experts, as explained in 1.2, this group does not hold a view on the value or legality of access to this data.

2.2 The ICF Data Retention Project Group called upon experts from the Internet industry who gave advice on the numerous data types that are created when a subscriber connects to and communicates via the Internet. This connection could be through an Internet Service Provider (ISP), a Virtual Internet Service Provider (VISP) or by other connection to the Internet.

2.3 The group also engaged the services of Computer Forensic experts whose work regularly involves liaising with various Law Enforcement Agencies and assisting with their investigation involving the Internet. Representatives of various Trade Associations were involved in the process together with several members of various Law Enforcement Agencies.

3. Acknowledgements

3.1 I would like to acknowledge the support given to this project by Chief Superintendent Len Hynds of the National High Tech Crime Unit, members of the Internet Crime Forum and to those experts from the Internet and Forensics Industry who have assisted in the process. All participants gave freely of their time as they agreed it was vital that this type of work be carried out.

4. Current data types

4.1 This document seeks to identify the principal known Data Types that a subscriber to an Internet Service may create whilst they are actively subscribing and utilising their Internet account.

4.2 It is accepted that this document could not be a definitive document of all data types due to the rapid development of technology.

5. Service providers

It must be appreciated by the reader of this document that not all Internet Service Providers retain the data types that are mentioned within this document.

Each service provider is aware of their current data retention practices and may be able to advise on the detail. Communication should in the first instance be routed through a Law Enforcement Single Point of Contact for Law Enforcement personnel. Requests for data retention policies made from outside the SPOC regime may be liable to conditions determined by individual ISPs.

There are service providers, known as Virtual Internet Service Providers (VISPs), who utilise most, if not all, the infrastructure of a large service provider. They may utilise various elements of a service, such as mail, sign up servers, radius servers, web cache and news and badge them as their own. In these cases the data that a subscriber generates may be spread across several companies.

Even amongst traditional ISPs some parts of their service may be provided by third parties. In this case as well, information may be held by many different companies and may or may not be accessible to the primary ISP.

Furthermore, some data types for example, web server log information, may be owned by and under the control of the customer rather than the ISP.

6. Glossary

There is a glossary attached to this document that informs the reader of what the various data types are and it is advisable that this is read in conjunction with the rest of the document.

7. Subscriber data types

7.1 This next section of the document identifies the principal data types that may be created when a subscriber accesses the Internet.

7.2 The data types have been broken down into two main areas. The first being the activity of the subscriber and the second the resources that a subscriber could utilise.

7.3   When matching events on the Internet with details recorded in ISP logs it is absolutely essential to ensure that time and date information is correctly recorded. It is Best Practice for ISPs to synchronize their systems with global time standards using protocols such as NTP, however consideration should always be given to this not being the case for particular logs. Equally it is essential that enquiries about logging information provide accurate timing information. A frequently encountered pitfall is incorrect handling of timezone offset information and careful attention should be paid to this.

8. Potential value

8.1   This section of the document identifies and details the potential value of the various data types to investigations. This is not a definitive list of data types and it must be appreciated that advances in technology may well mean that some of the data types that are currently of little value may at some stage in the future generate logs that could be useful for the purposes of investigations.

8.2   The table below identifies each of the data types and the data that could be generated by the subscriber.

8.3   Data can only be obtained in accordance with UK Law and international treaties. This document does not address this issue any further.

8.4   Internet Service Providers retain data for business purposes. The procedures surrounding this data retention may affect the way in which data could be used for evidential purposes.

Activity	Data Type	Comment
Content		
	URLs	A URL (Uniform/Unique Resource Locator) is the address of a file (resource) accessible on the Internet. The type of resource depends on the Internet application protocol. Using the World Wide Web's protocol, the Hypertext Transfer Protocol (**HTTP**), the resource can be an **HTML** page, an image file, a program such as a **common gateway interface** (CGI) application or Java **applet**, or any other file supported by HTTP. The URL contains the name of the protocol required to access the resource, a host name that identifies a specific computer on the Internet, and a hierarchical description of a file location on the computer. The host name can be used to determine the physical location of the computer and its logical ownership.

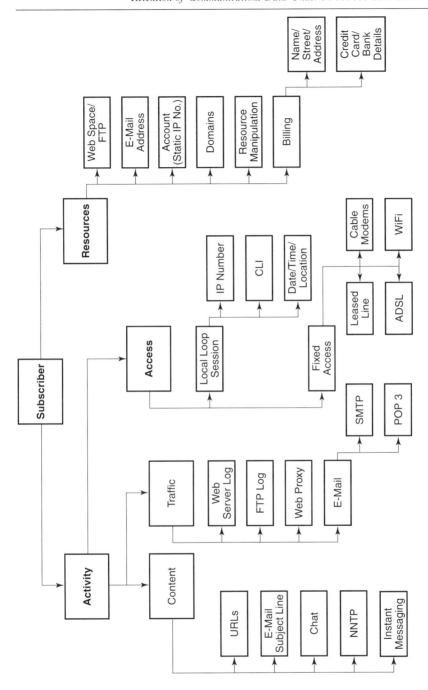

Activity	Data Type	Comment
	E-mail	ISPs may hold e-mail on behalf of subscribers. Much of the e-mail is content and a number of different legal regimes apply to the divulgence of this. Some of the header is communications data. In addition details of what e-mail has been sent and received may be recorded in logs. Some of the information in these logs may be content.
	Chat	Depending upon the technology the service provider will not normally retain the content of an individual Chat Room session but individual participants will be able to make their own record. It may be possible to trace and identify participants in a chat session providing the IP address or for some ISPs the screen name is obtained together with an accurate time stamp.
	NNTP/Usenet	In order to trace the author of a Usenet article, the article headers will need to be inspected. These will usually contain the posting IP address and time stamp. The system through which it was originally posted should then be able to identify the account responsible for creating the posting. Provision of Usenet services is increasingly performed by third parties so it may be necessary to make further enquiries with a connectivity ISP to determine where the account was used from. The content of an NNTP (Usenet) session will not be retained by a service provider. Therefore the readership of an article is unlikely to be available. Usenet postings are commonly exchanged between ISPs. This means that an article may well have been hosted on a different service provider from the one on which it is read.
	Instant Messaging	Instant messaging (sometimes called IM or Iming) is the ability to easily see whether a chosen friend or co-worker is connected to the Internet and, if they are, to exchange messages with them. Instant messaging differs from ordinary **e-mail** in the immediacy of the message exchange and also makes a continued exchange simpler than sending e-mail back and forth. Most exchanges are text-only. However, some services allow attachments.

Activity	Data Type	Comment
		In order for IMing to work, both users (who must subscribe to the service) must be online at the same time, and the intended recipient must be willing to accept instant messages. (It is possible to set your software to reject messages.) An attempt to send an IM to someone who is not online, or who is not willing to accept Ims, will result in notification that the transmission cannot be completed. The ISPs will not in general have any records of the messages which have been exchanged because they flow directly between the participants (Peer to Peer). If a 'rendez-vous' server is involved in the initial connection between the participants then some logging information about their identities may be retained. The rendez-vous server may be totally independent of any connectivity ISP.
Traffic		
	Web Server Logs	These typically contain the source IP address, requested content, submitted data e.g. username, password and previous site visited. Some of the data may be content rather than traffic data. Some of the data may be anonymised in near real time. Some of the IP addresses may be proxy caches rather than the actual requestor.
	FTP Logs	These contain source IP, account details and details of the file names uploaded into or downloaded from. Although most sites appear to have a username/password login, anonymous guest accounts are also common and although an e-mail address is traditionally provided as identification there is seldom any validation of this whatsoever. Some of the data may be content rather than traffic data. It is quite common for customers to upload the content of their web pages using FTP.

Activity	Data Type	Comment
	Web proxy	A proxy server is a **server** that acts as an intermediary between a user and the Internet. A proxy server receives a request for an Internet service (such as a Web page request) from a user. If it passes filtering requirements, the proxy server will access the remote site and pass the information to the user.
		A Web **cache** maintains a store of previously downloaded items from the Web such as an HTML page. If it is asked for a page that is already in its store, then it returns it to the user without needing to forward the request to the Internet, though it may need to check if its cached copy remains up-to-date. If the page is not in the cache then the cache server acting as a client, on behalf of the user, uses one of its own IP addresses to request the page from the server out on the Internet. When the page is returned, the proxy server relates it to the original request and forwards it on to the user.
		The user's general impression of using both proxy servers and caches will be of a direct connection to the remote site.
		In the ISP context it is usual to combine these two functions, and the result may be, rather confusingly, called a web cache, a web proxy or indeed a proxy-cache.
		Some ISPs use a "transparent" scheme that intercepts, for example, all HTTP (port 80) traffic and sends it via a proxy-cache. In other cases the use of a proxy-cache is entirely under the users' control, though the ISP may encourage usage by means of the default configurations shipped to its customers.
		These servers can produce logs of the data handled, giving the local customer IP address, details of the requested content and details of any connections made to remote sites. Complete logging may only be enabled for troubleshooting, but even incomplete logging can create very substantial volumes of data and these logs are not kept for long periods of time.

Activity	Data Type	Comment
		The presence of a proxy may mean that the user never accesses the target web site. The access that is made will show the IP address of the server. The server may be configured to pass information to the target web site giving some details of the user, but some servers are configured specifically to obscure the true identity of the user. Some web pages are designed so that they cannot be cached and so this traffic will flow directly and hence proxy-cache logs will be incomplete. Similar effects will be caused by the use of protocols such as HTTPS which often avoid the use of a proxy-caches altogether.
E-mail		SMTP (Simple Mail Transfer Protocol) is a **TCP protocol** used in sending and receiving e-mail between permanently connected machines. However, because mail is "pushed" rather than "pulled" it works very poorly with intermittently connected machines. Therefore is usual to provide mail delivery to dialup customers via **POP3 or IMAP**. These provide a store and forward system, so that users can periodically "pull" any new e-mail.
		SMTP is the standard method for ISP customers to send their e-mail. Although delivery can be made directly to remote systems it is common to relay e-mail traffic via an SMTP server at the ISP called a "smart host". Some ISPs will intercept outgoing SMTP (port 25) traffic and force it to use the smart host. POP3 is a relatively simple protocol for e-mail reception. It is usual to configure clients to delete the e-mail once it has been fetched. If it is not deleted then the ISP will delete it after a preset period. Long term storage is done on the client machine. IMAP is somewhat more complex and provides a client/server implementation of a fully featured e-mail interface – with all the e-mail held on the server machine, possibly for very long periods. IMAP clients will hold very little state from one session to another.

Activity	Data Type	Comment
	SMTP	Mail will be held on the server until it can be passed to a destination but most service providers do not routinely keep content thereafter. A service provider may retain summary logging details of e-mail that has been received from or sent to their customers. This would include a unique message identifier, who the mail was alleged to be from, who the mail was addressed to, the IP address of the immediately previous hop and the time and date the mail was sent. Further information such as size and content such as the subject line may sometimes be recorded. When the intended destination of e-mail is unavailable it may be routed via intermediate machines (using lower priority MX records). This will reduce the usefulness of IP address logging details. It is also essential to view the "from" details with caution since they are trivial to forge. Finally, many ISPs have outsourced virus scanning and "spam" deletion services. Initial delivery is made to a third party who will only forward genuine e-mail to the ISP's systems. In all cases, the e-mail itself should contain full details of all the machines it has passed through, but these machines will almost invariably only record one part of its journey.
	IMAP & POP3	IMAP & POP3 logs typically contain just brief summary details of connections. These may extend as far as recording the connecting IP address and how many e-mails were read or deleted. It would be very unusual indeed to record anything which references the content, sender or path associated with transmission of the e-mail. IMAP & POP3 servers can usually be accessed from anywhere on the Internet so any IP address recorded may well require further tracing to be useful.

Activity	Data Type	Comment
	Webmail	Acesss to e-mail via a web interface ("webmail") may be provided as a front end to POP3 services or as a service in its own right. Logging will typically record the IP address that accesses the mail box and may record which items of mail were looked at. Webmail services are almost invariably designed to be used from any Internet address.
Access		
Circuit Switched		
	IP Address	An IP address can either be static (allocated on permanent basis) or dynamic (a different IP address allocated each time authentication is made). When mapping a dynamic address to an account it is therefore essential to provide accurate timing information (date, time and timezone).
	Account Usage	Logging of account usage will record the date and time that the connection was established, and the date and time that it. Further details such as the number of packets transferred may also be available from some ISPs. Account authorisation if often done using a system called RADIUS so these logs are often referred to as RADIUS logs. Further logs, holding much the same information, from the Network Access Servers (NASs) may also be available at some ISPs. A number of different versions of RADIUS are in use, so that the actual format of the logs (and indeed the format of the time and date information) may vary from ISP to ISP.
	CLI	If CLI is captured by the service provider it is most likely to be recorded within the RADIUS logs. Not all types of accounts will require CLI to be presented to the ISP. Some types of account will require access only from authorised CLI. At present, ISP equipment will not usually record the CLI if it is marked to be withheld.

Activity	Data Type	Comment
Fixed access		Unlike circuit switched (dial-up) services which may be provided "free", fixed access systems are invariably charged for. This means that a valid billing address will be present in the ISP's accounting systems. In addition an installation address will be recorded, though in some cases the service may be moved to another address without the ISP becoming aware of it or bothering to record the change.
	Leased Line	A leased line is a link via the local exchange that has been provided for private use. In some contexts, it's called a *dedicated* line. A leased line is usually contrasted with a *switched line* or *dial-up line*.
	Cable Modem	The connection may be a dedicated modem or integrated into a television set top box.
	ADSL	A method of providing broadband access over a standard local loop. Within the UK this is mainly provided by British Telecom who route the traffic over an ATM cloud and provide an IP data connection to the ISP.
	Satellite	A system designed for rural areas to provide high bandwidth Internet access. The return path from the user to the ISP may be direct or via the satellite.
	WiFi	A fixed base station is connected by one of the previously described methods to the Internet. Clients may access by wireless within a limited distance. Currently these systems are insecure even where encryption has been used to protect the connection. Logs may only show that someone (necessarily physically close to the base station) has been using the system but local logging may provide further traceability. Some WiFi installations are deliberately made open for public access and some commercial operations provide access for payment, which may be made in cash.

Activity	Data Type	Comment
Resources		
	Shell Sessions	Details pertaining to telnet and other 'shell' login sessions may be held in several files (telnet connections are typically logged in 'last' and 'messages' files on UNIX based systems). Shell sessions may log a variety of data including start/stop and source IP.
	Web/FTP Space	Web and FTP Space may be provided separately or as part of a service package. All of the remarks relating to billing (to identify the owner) to server logs (to identify readers) and to FTP Logs (to identify up loaders) apply to this section.
	E-mail Addresses	There is a mapping between the e-mail address and the account. This may vary between ISPs. An account may have one or more e-mail addresses associated with it. Users may have the ability to change e-mail addresses at will. Some ISPs may not hold data on previous e-mail addresses.
	Domains	ISPs provide Domain Name Service (DNS) to allow mapping between domain names and IP addresses as well as information such as where to deliver e-mail. Details of who actually owns the domain name will be held by the appropriate registrar. The ISP will have some records as to which of their customers is controlling it. There may be limited records of historical settings.
	Resource manipulation	Many services provided by ISPs and particularly those provided by third parties can be configured by the user for example e-mail may be redirected to another account, web space requests may be directed to another server or DNS settings may be rearranged. The system that is used for this configuration may keep logs that allow historic configurations to be reconstructed.

Activity	Data Type	Comment
Billing		Many forms of access are paid for. Billing data may relate to an individual or could also be that of an organization. Some systems may be sub-let and billing records will relate to the 'letting company'. Many services are re-sold. Some systems may be insecure and used without permission.
	Name, Street, Address	A service provider does not necessarily verify a subscriber's name and address details. This is dependant upon the service a subscriber utilises whilst on the Internet. In many instances the subscriber will provide CLI (Caller Line Identifier) as a part of the authentication process prior to their use of that service. This CLI can often be mapped to a geographical location by the appropriate telco.
	Credit Card/Bank Details	For accounts where payments are made, credit card, debit card, direct debit, cheques or standing order will provide traceability through the banking system. Where postal orders or cash payments are made or accepted, these will not always be verified. It should be noted that billing information may not be retained by the backbone ISP but by the Virtual ISP who has ownership of the customer.

Glossary of terms used within this document

Access	Data access is being able to get to (usually having permission to use) particular data on a computer.
ADSL	Asymmetric Digital Subscriber Line is a technology for transmitting **digital** information at a high **bandwidth** on existing phone lines.
ATM	Asynchronous Transfer Mode. A switching technology for transferring packets of data. ATM was originally developed for voice application, but is now used for Internet transports and underpins current broadband technologies.
Cable Modem	A cable modem is a device that enables you to hook up your PC to a local **cable** TV connection in order to send and receive data packets.
CGI	Common Gateway Interface. A method of providing dynamic content within "web pages".
Chat	Facility to talk with others whilst on line.

Access	Data access is being able to get to (usually having permission to use) particular data on a computer.
CLI	Calling Line Identifier is the telephone number that a person has used to access their required service.
DNS	Domain Name System. Protocol for providing mappings from domain names to resource identifiers such as IP addresses.
Domain name	A domain name is a user-friendly method of identifying the location of resources on the Internet.
E-mail	E-mail is the exchange of text-based electronic messages by telecommunication.
E-mail Subject Line	A conventional e-mail header that is intended to provide a brief description of the contents of an email.
FTP	File Transfer Protocol. A standard TCP protocol for transferring files between machines. FTP is often used to upload the content of web sites onto servers.
HTML	Hypertext Markup Language. This is the language which is used for "web pages" to indicate the structure of documents so that browsers can display them in a standardised manner.
HTTP	Hypertext Transport Protocol. A standard TCP protocol for transferring "web pages" from one machine to another.
HTTPS	Secure HTTP. Transfer of "web pages" over an encrypted transport protocol.
ICF	Internet Crime Forum. A body formed "To promote, maintain and enhance an effective working relationship between industry and law enforcement to tackle crime and foster business and public confidence in the use of the Internet in ways that respect human rights and are sympathetic to the needs of industry."
Instant Messaging	A quick and easy way of exchanging messages with others who are also online.
IM	Instant Messaging
IMAP	Internet Message Access Protocol. A standard TCP protocol for accessing e-mail that is received, organised and stored on a remote server.
MX record	DNS record entry that indicates where e-mail for a domain is to be delivered.
IP	Internet Protocol. The basic protocol used for communication between computers on the Internet.
IP address	Internet Protocol Address. A numeric value that serves to uniquely identify an interface that is connected to the Internet.
ISP	Internet Service Provider. An organisation that makes Internet services to its customers. ISPs usually provide connectivity, often many other services as well.
Java applet	A way of providing "mobile code" on web pages so as to enable extra functionality on web pages.
Leased Line	A method of providing a fixed connection to the Internet.

Access	Data access is being able to get to (usually having permission to use) particular data on a computer.
Local Loop	In telephony, a local loop is the wired connection from a telephone company's **central office** in a locality to its customers' telephones at homes and businesses.
NNTP	Network News Transfer Protocol. A standard TCP protocol for transferring Usenet articles over the Internet.
POP3	Post Office Protocol 3. A standard TCP protocol for collecting e-mail from a server.
RADIUS	Remote Authentication Dial-in User Service. A standard TCP protocol for communicating authentication information and establishing parameters for dial-up connections to the Internet.
SMTP	Simple Mail Transfer Protocol. A standard **protocol** used for the transport of e-mail over the Internet.
SPOC	Single Point of Contact. A scheme whereby requests from law enforcement organisations are funnelled through a single part of that organisation and passed to a single contact point within ISPs.
TCP	Transport Control Protocol. A protocol layered over IP that provides a reliable delivery service for data.
URL	Unique/Uniform Resource Locator. A stylised naming system for web resources.
VISP	Virtual ISP. An ISP whose infrastructure is completely provided by third parties.
Web Cache	A cache is a server that retains copies of web content so as to provide timely local delivery for repeat requests.
Web Proxy	A proxy is a **server** that acts as an intermediary between a workstation user and the Internet.
WiFi	Wireless systems (such as 802.11) that provide Internet connectivity.

CCTV: Code of Practice

Foreword

Closed circuit television (CCTV) surveillance is an increasing feature of our daily lives. There is an ongoing debate over how effective CCTV is in reducing and preventing crime, but one thing is certain, its deployment is commonplace in a variety of areas to which members of the public have free access. We might be caught on camera while walking down the high street, visiting a shop or bank or travelling through a railway station or airport. The House of Lords Select Committee on Science and Technology expressed their view that if public confidence in CCTV systems was to be maintained there needed to be some tighter control over their deployment and use (5th Report – Digital Images as Evidence).

There was no statutory basis for systematic legal control of CCTV surveillance over public areas until 1 March 2000 when the Data Protection Act came into force. The definitions in this new Act are broader than those of the Data Protection Act 1984 and so more readily cover the processing of images of individuals caught by CCTV cameras than did the previous data protection legislation. The same legally enforceable information handling standards as have previously applied to those processing personal data on computer now cover CCTV. An important new feature of the recent legislation is a power for me to issue a Commissioner's Code of Practice (section 51(3)(b) DPA '98) setting out guidance for the following of good practice. In my 14th Annual Report to Parliament I signalled my intention to use this power to provide guidance on the operation of CCTV as soon as those new powers became available to me. This Code of Practice is the first Commissioner's Code to be issued under the Data Protection Act 1998.

This code deals with surveillance in areas to which the public have largely free and unrestricted access because, as the House of Lords Committee highlighted, there is particular concern about a lack of regulation and central guidance in this area. Although the Data Protection Act 1998 covers other uses of CCTV this Code addresses the area of widest concern. Many of its provisions will be relevant to other uses of CCTV and will be referred to as appropriate when we develop other guidance. There are some existing standards that have been developed by representatives of CCTV system operators and, more particularly, the British Standards Institute. While such standards are helpful, they are not legally enforceable. The changes in data protection legislation mean that for the first time legally enforceable standards will apply to the collection and processing of images relating to individuals.

This Code of Practice has the dual purpose of assisting operators of CCTV systems to understand their legal obligations while also reassuring the public about the safeguards that should be in place. It sets out the measures which must be adopted to comply with the Data Protection Act 1998, and goes on to set out guidance for the following of good data protection practice. The Code makes clear the standards which must be followed to ensure compliance with the Data Protection Act 1998 and then indicates those which are not a strict legal requirement but do represent the following of good practice.

Before issuing this Code I consulted representatives of relevant data controllers and data subjects, and published a draft copy of the Code on my website. I am grateful to all those consultees who responded and have taken account of their comments in producing this version.

Our experience of the Codes of Practice which were put forward under the 1984 Act was that they needed to remain relevant to the day to day activities of data controllers. They need to be 'living' documents, which are updated as practices, and understanding of the law develops.

This code will therefore be kept under review to ensure that it remains relevant in the context of changing technology, use and jurisprudence. In this context it is likely that the Human Rights Act 1998, which comes into force on 2 October 2000, and provides important legal safeguards for individuals, will lead to developments in legal interpretation which will require review of the Code.

It is my intention that this Code of Practice should help those operating CCTV schemes monitoring members of the public to do so in full compliance of the Data Protection Act 1998 and in adherence to high standards of good practice. There does seem to be public support for the widespread deployment of this surveillance technology, but public confidence has to be earned and maintained. Compliance with this Code will not only help CCTV scheme operators' process personal data in compliance with the law but also help to maintain that public confidence without which they cannot operate.

Elizabeth France

Data Protection Commissioner

July 2000

Introduction

This is a code of practice issued by the Data Protection Commissioner in accordance with her powers under Section 51 (3)(b) of the Data Protection Act 1998 (the "1998 Act"). It is intended to provide guidance as to good practice for users of CCTV (closed circuit television) and similar surveillance equipment.

It is not intended that the contents of this Code should apply to:–

- Targeted and intrusive surveillance activities, which are covered by the provisions of the forthcoming Regulation of Investigatory Powers Act.
- Use of surveillance techniques by employers to monitor their employees' compliance with their contracts of employment[1].
- Security equipment (including cameras) installed in homes by individuals for home security purposes[2].
- Use of cameras and similar equipment by the broadcast media for the purposes of journalism, or for artistic or literary purposes.

This Code of Practice is drafted in two parts:

Part I

This sets out:

- the standards which must be met if the requirements of the 1998 Act are to be complied with. These are based on the Data Protection Principles which say that data must be
    - fairly and lawfully processed;
        - processed for limited purposes and not in any manner incompatible with those purposes;
    - adequate, relevant and not excessive;
    - accurate;
    - not kept for longer than is necessary
    - processed in accordance with individuals' rights;

- secure;
    - not transferred to countries without adequate protection.
- guidance on good practice,
    - examples of how to implement the standards and good practice.

The Data Protection Commissioner has the power to issue Enforcement Notices where she considers that there has been a breach of one or more of the Data Protection Principles. An Enforcement Notice[3] would set out the remedial action that the Commissioner requires to ensure future compliance with the requirements of the Act. The Data Protection Commissioner will take into account the extent to which users of CCTV and similar surveillance equipment have complied with this Code of Practice when determining whether they have met their legal obligations when exercising her powers of enforcement.

Part II – Glossary

This sets out the interpretation of the 1998 Act on which Part I is based. Part I is cross-referenced to Part II to try to clarify the reasoning behind the standard or guidance.

It is intended that this Code of Practice will be revised on a regular basis in order to take account of developments in the interpretation of the provisions of the data protection legislation, developments in the technology involved in the recording of images, and developments in the use of such technologies, the use of sound recording, facial recognition techniques and the increased use of digital technology.

Please Note

Italicised text indicates good practice.

Initial assessment procedures

Before installing and using CCTV and similar surveillance equipment, users will need to establish the purpose or purposes for which they intend to use the equipment.[4] This equipment may be used for a number of different purposes – for example, prevention, investigation and detection of crime, apprehension and prosecution of offenders (including use of images as evidence in criminal proceedings), public and employee safety, monitoring security of premises etc.

Standards

1. establish who is the person(s) or organisation(s) legally responsible for the proposed scheme.[5]

2.   assess the appropriateness of, and reasons for, using CCTV or similar surveillance equipment (First Data Protection Principle).

3.   *document this assessment process and the reasons for the installation of the scheme.*

4.   establish the purpose of the Scheme (First and Second Data Protection Principle).[6]

5   *document the purpose of the scheme.*

6.   ensure that the notification lodged with the Office of the Data Protection Commissioner covers the purposes for which this equipment is used[7]

7.   *establish and document the person(s) or organisation(s) who are responsible for ensuring the day-to-day compliance with the requirements of this Code of Practice (if different from above)*

8.   *establish and document security and disclosure policies.*

Siting the cameras

It is essential that the location of the equipment is carefully considered, because the way in which images are captured will need to comply with the First Data Protection Principle. Detailed guidance on the interpretation of the First Data Protection Principle is provided in Part II, but the standards to be met under this Code of Practice are set out below.

Standards

1.   The equipment should be sited in such a way that it only monitors those spaces which are intended to be covered by the equipment (First and Third Data Protection Principles).

2.   If domestic areas such as gardens or areas not intended to be covered by the scheme border those spaces which are intended to be covered by the equipment, then the user should consult with the owners of such spaces if images from those spaces might be recorded. In the case of back gardens, this would be the resident of the property overlooked (First and Third Data Protection Principles).

3.   Operators must be aware of the purpose(s) for which the scheme has been established (Second and Seventh Data Protection Principles).

4.   Operators must be aware that they are only able to use the equipment in order to achieve the purpose(s) for which it has been installed (First and Second Data Protection Principles).

5.   If cameras are adjustable by the operators, this should be restricted so that operators cannot adjust or manipulate them to overlook spaces which are not intended to be covered by the scheme (First and Third Data Protection Principles).

6.   If it is not possible physically to restrict the equipment to avoid recording images from those spaces not intended to be covered by the scheme, then operators should be trained in recognising the privacy implications of such spaces being covered (First and Third Data Protection Principles).

For example – individuals sunbathing in their back gardens may have a greater expectation of privacy than individuals mowing the lawn of their front garden.

For example – it may be appropriate for the equipment to be used to protect the safety of individuals when using ATMs, but images of PIN numbers, balance enquiries etc should not be captured.

7. Signs should be placed so that the public are aware that they are entering a zone which is covered by surveillance equipment (First Data Protection Principle).

8. The signs should be clearly visible and legible to members of the public (First Data Protection Principle)

9. The size of signs will vary according to circumstances:

    For example – a sign on the entrance door to a building society office may only need to be A4 size because it is at eye level of those entering the premises.

    For example – signs at the entrances of car parks alerting drivers to the fact that the car park is covered by such equipment will usually need to be large, for example, probably A3 size as they are likely to be viewed from further away, for example by a driver sitting in a car.

10. The signs should contain the following information:
    a) Identity of the person or organisation responsible for the scheme.
    b) The purposes of the scheme.
    c) Details of whom to contact regarding the scheme.

(First Data Protection Principle)

    For example – Where an image of a camera is not used on a sign – the following wording is recommended:

    "Images are being monitored for the purposes of crime prevention and public safety. This scheme is controlled by the Greentown Safety Partnership. For further information contact 01234–567-890"

    For example – Where an image of a camera is used on a sign – the following wording is recommended:

    "This scheme is controlled by the Greentown Safety Partnership. For further information contact 01234–567-890"

11. In exceptional and limited cases, if it is assessed that the use of signs would not be appropriate, the user of the scheme must ensure that they have:
    a) Identified specific criminal activity.
    b) Identified the need to use surveillance to obtain evidence of that criminal activity.
    c) Assessed whether the use of signs would prejudice success in obtaining such evidence.
    d) Assessed how long the covert monitoring should take place to ensure that it is not carried out for longer than is necessary.
    e) *Documented (a) to (d) above.*[8]

12. Information so obtained must only be obtained for prevention or detection of criminal activity, or the apprehension and prosecution of offenders[9]. It should not be retained and used for any other purpose. If the equipment used has a sound recording facility, this should not be used to record conversations between members of the public (First and Third Data Protection Principles).

Quality of the images

It is important that the images produced by the equipment are as clear as possible in order that they are effective for the purpose(s) for which they are intended. This is why it is essential that the purpose of the scheme is clearly identified. For example if a system has been installed to prevent and detect crime, then it is essential that the images are adequate for that purpose. The Third, Fourth and Fifth Data Protection Principles are concerned with the quality of personal data, and they are outlined in more detail in Part II. The standards to be met under this Code of Practice are set out below.

Standards

1.   Upon installation an initial check should be undertaken to ensure that the equipment performs properly.
2.   If tapes are used, it should be ensured that they are good quality tapes (Third and Fourth Data Protection Principles).
3.   The medium on which the images are captured should be cleaned so that images are not recorded on top of images recorded previously (Third and Fourth Data Protection Principles).
4.   The medium on which the images have been recorded should not be used when it has become apparent that the quality of images has deteriorated. (Third Data Protection Principle).
5.   If the system records features such as the location of the camera and/or date and time reference, these should be accurate (Third and Fourth Data Protection Principles).
6.   *If their system includes such features, users should ensure that they have a documented procedure for ensuring their accuracy.*
7.   Cameras should be situated so that they will capture images relevant to the purpose for which the scheme has been established (Third Data Protection Principle)

      For example, if the purpose of the scheme is the prevention and detection of crime and/or apprehension and prosecution of offenders, the cameras should be sited so that images enabling identification of perpetrators are captured.

      For example, if the scheme has been established with a view to monitoring traffic flow, the cameras should be situated so that they do not capture the details of the vehicles or drivers.
8.   If an automatic facial recognition system is used to match images captured against a database of images, then both sets of images should be clear enough to ensure an accurate match (Third and Fourth Data Protection Principles).
9.   If an automatic facial recognition system is used, procedures should be set up to ensure that the match is also verified by a human operator, who will assess the match and determine what action, if any, should be taken (First and Seventh Data Protection Principles).[10]
10.   *The result of the assessment by the human operator should be recorded whether or not they determine there is a match.*

11.   When installing cameras, consideration must be given to the physical conditions in which the cameras are located (Third and Fourth Data Protection Principles).

      For example – infrared equipment may need to be installed in poorly lit areas.

12.   Users should assess whether it is necessary to carry out constant real time recording, or whether the activity or activities about which they are concerned occur at specific times (First and Third Data Protection Principles)

      For example – it may be that criminal activity only occurs at night, in which case constant recording of images might only be carried out for a limited period e.g. 10.00 pm to 7.00 am

13.   Cameras should be properly maintained and serviced to ensure that clear images are recorded (Third and Fourth Data Protection Principles)

14.   Cameras should be protected from vandalism in order to ensure that they remain in working order (Seventh Data Protection Principle)

15.   *A maintenance log should be kept.*

16.   If a camera is damaged, there should be clear procedures for:

      a)   *Defining the person responsible for making arrangements for ensuring that the camera is fixed.*

      b)   Ensuring that the camera is fixed within a specific time period (Third and Fourth Data Protection Principle).

      c)   *Monitoring the quality of the maintenance work.*

Processing the images

Images, which are not required for the purpose(s) for which the equipment is being used, should not be retained for longer than is necessary. While images are retained, it is essential that their integrity be maintained, whether it is to ensure their evidential value or to protect the rights of people whose images may have been recorded. It is therefore important that access to and security of the images is controlled in accordance with the requirements of the 1998 Act. The Seventh Data Protection Principle sets out the security requirements of the 1998 Data Protection Act. This is discussed in more depth at Part II. However, the standards required by this Code of Practice are set out below.

Standards

1.   Images should not be retained for longer than is necessary (Fifth Data Protection Principle)

     For example – publicans may need to keep recorded images for no longer than seven days because they will soon be aware of any incident such as a fight occurring on their premises.

     For example – images recorded by equipment covering town centres and streets may not need to be retained for longer than 31 days unless they are required for evidential purposes in legal proceedings.

For example – images recorded from equipment protecting individuals' safety at ATMs might need to be retained for a period of three months in order to resolve customer disputes about cash withdrawals. The retention period of three months is based on the interval at which individuals receive their account statements.

2.   Once the retention period has expired, the images should be removed or erased (Fifth Data Protection Principle).

3.   If the images are retained for evidential purposes, they should be retained in a secure place to which access is controlled (Fifth and Seventh Data Protection Principles).

4.   On removing the medium on which the images have been recorded for the use in legal proceedings, the operator should ensure that they have documented:

    a)   The date on which the images were removed from the general system for use in legal proceedings.

    b)   The reason why they were removed from the system.

    c)   Any crime incident number to which the images may be relevant.

    d)   The location of the images.

For example – if the images were handed to a police officer for retention, the name and station of that police officer.

    e)   The signature of the collecting police officer, where appropriate (see below) (Third and Seventh Data Protection Principles).

5.   Monitors displaying images from areas in which individuals would have an expectation of privacy should not be viewed by anyone other than authorised employees of the user of the equipment (Seventh Data Protection Principle).

6.   Access to the recorded images should be restricted to a manager or designated member of staff who will decide whether to allow requests for access by third parties in accordance with the user's documented disclosure policies (Seventh Data Protection Principle).[11]

7.   Viewing of the recorded images should take place in a restricted area, for example, in a manager's or designated member of staff's office. Other employees should not be allowed to have access to that area when a viewing is taking place (Seventh Data Protection Principle).

8.   *Removal of the medium on which images are recorded, for viewing purposes, should be documented as follows:*

    a)   The date and time of removal

    b)   The name of the person removing the images

    c)   The name(s) of the person(s) viewing the images. If this should include third parties, this include the organisation of that third party

    d)   The reason for the viewing

    e)   The outcome, if any, of the viewing

    f)   The date and time the images were returned to the system or secure place, if they have been retained for evidential purposes

9.   All operators and employees with access to images should be aware of the procedure which need to be followed when accessing the recorded images (Seventh Data Protection Principle).

10.   All operators should be trained in their responsibilities under this Code of Practice i.e. they should be aware of:

a)   The user's security policy e.g. procedures to have access to recorded images.
b)   The user's disclosure policy.[12]
c)   Rights of individuals in relation to their recorded images.[13]

(Seventh Data Protection Principle)

Access to and disclosure of images to third parties

It is important that access to, and disclosure of, the images recorded by CCTV and similar surveillance equipment is restricted and carefully controlled, not only to ensure that the rights of individuals are preserved, but also to ensure that the chain of evidence remains intact should the images be required for evidential purposes. Users of CCTV will also need to ensure that the reason(s) for which they may disclose copies of the images are compatible with the reason(s) or purpose(s) for which they originally obtained those images. These aspects of this Code are to be found in the Second and Seventh Data Protection Principles, which are discussed in more depth at Part II. However, the standards required by this Code are set out below.

Standards

All employees should be aware of the restrictions set out in this code of practice in relation to access to, and disclosure of, recorded images.

1.   Access to recorded images should be restricted to those staff who need to have access in order to achieve the purpose(s) of using the equipment (Seventh Data Protection Principle).[14]

2.   All access to the medium on which the images are recorded should be documented (Seventh Data Protection Principle).[15]

3.   Disclosure of the recorded images to third parties should only made in limited and prescribed circumstances (Second and Seventh Data Protection Principles).

   For example – if the purpose of the system is the prevention and detection of crime, then disclosure to third parties should be limited to the following:

   - Law enforcement agencies where the images recorded would assist in a specific criminal enquiry
   - Prosecution agencies
   - Relevant legal representatives
   - The media, where it is decided that the public's assistance is needed in order to assist in the identification of victim, witness or perpetrator in relation to a criminal incident. As part of that decision, the wishes of the victim of an incident should be taken into account
   - People whose images have been recorded and retained (unless disclosure to the individual would prejudice criminal enquiries or criminal proceedings)

4. All requests for access or for disclosure should be recorded. If access or disclosure is denied, the reason should be documented (Seventh Data Protection Principle)
5. *If access to or disclosure of the images is allowed, then the following should be documented:*
    a) *The date and time at which access was allowed or the date on which disclosure was made*
    b) *The identification of any third party who was allowed access or to whom disclosure was made*
    c) *The reason for allowing access or disclosure*
    d) *The extent of the information to which access was allowed or which was disclosed[16]*
6. Recorded images should not be made more widely available – for example they should not be routinely made available to the media or placed on the Internet (Second, Seventh and Eighth Data Protection Principles).
7. If it is intended that images will be made more widely available, that decision should be made by the manager or designated member of staff. The reason for that decision should be documented (Seventh Data Protection Principle).
8. If it is decided that images will be disclosed to the media (other than in the circumstances outlined above), the images of individuals will need to be disguised or blurred so that they are not readily identifiable (First, Second and Seventh Data Protection Principles).
9. *If the system does not have the facilities to carry out that type of editing, an editing company may need to be hired to carry it out.*
10. If an editing company is hired, then the manager or designated member of staff needs to ensure that:
    a) There is a contractual relationship between the data controller and the editing company.
    b) That the editing company has given appropriate guarantees regarding the security measures they take in relation to the images.
    c) The manager has checked to ensure that those guarantees are met
    d) The written contract makes it explicit that the editing company can only use the images in accordance with the instructions of the manager or designated member of staff.
    e) The written contract makes the security guarantees provided by the editing company explicit.
    (Seventh Data Protection Principle)
11. If the media organisation receiving the images undertakes to carry out the editing, then (a) to (e) will still apply (Seventh Data Protection Principle).

Access by data subjects

This is a right, which is provided by section 7 of the 1998 Act. A detailed explanation of the interpretation of this right is given in Part II. The standards of this Code of Practice are set out below.

Standards

1.   All staff involved in operating the equipment must be able to recognise a request for access to recorded images by data subjects (Sixth and Seventh Data Protection Principles).

2.   *Data subjects should be provided with a standard subject access request form which:*
     a)   Indicates the information required in order to locate the images requested.
     ***For example** – an individual may have to provide dates and times of when they visited the premises of the user of the equipment.*
     b)   Indicates the information required in order to identify the person making the request.
     ***For example** – if the individual making the request is unknown to the user of the equipment, a photograph of the individual may be requested in order to locate the correct image.*
     c)   Indicates the fee that will be charged for carrying out the search for the images requested. A maximum of £10.00 may be charged for the search.
     d)   Asks whether the individual would be satisfied with merely viewing the images recorded.
     e)   Indicates that the response will be provided promptly and in any event within 40 days of receiving the required fee and information.
     f)   Explains the rights provided by the 1998 Act.

3.   Individuals should also be provided with a leaflet which describes the types images which are recorded and retained, the purposes for which those images are recorded and retained, and information about the disclosure policy in relation to those images (Sixth Data Protection Principle).[17]

4.   This should be provided at the time that the standard subject access request form is provided to an individual (Sixth Data Protection Principle).[18]

5.   *All subject access requests should be dealt with by a manager or designated member of staff.*

6.   *The manager or designated member of staff should locate the images requested*

7.   The manager or designated member of staff should determine whether disclosure to the individual would entail disclosing images of third parties (Sixth Data Protection Principle).[19]

8.   The manager or designated member of staff will need to determine whether the images of third parties are held under a duty of confidence (First and Sixth Data Protection Principle).[20]
     For example – it may be that members of the public whose images have been recorded when they were in town centres or streets have less expectation that their images are held under a duty of confidence than individuals whose images have been recorded in more private space such as the waiting room of a doctor's surgery.

9.   If third party images are not to be disclosed, the manager or designated member of staff shall arrange for the third party images to be disguised or blurred (Sixth Data Protection Principle).[21]

10. *If the system does not have the facilities to carry out that type of editing, a third party or company may be hired to carry it out*

11. If a third party or company is hired, then the manager or designated member of staff needs to ensure that:

a)　There is a contractual relationship between the data controller and the third party or company.

b)　That the third party or company has given appropriate guarantees regarding the security measures they take in relation to the images.

c)　The manager has checked to ensure that those guarantees are met.

d)　The written contract makes it explicit that the third party or company can only use the images in accordance with the instructions of the manager or designated member of staff.

e)　The written contract makes the security guarantees provided by the third party or company explicit

(Seventh Data Protection Principle)

12.　*If the manager or designated member of staff decides that a subject access request from an individual is not to be complied with, the following should be documented:*

a)　The identity of the individual making the request

b)　The date of the request

c)　The reason for refusing to supply the images requested

d)　The name and signature of the manager or designated member of staff making the decision.[22]

13.　All staff should be aware of individuals' rights under this section of the Code of Practice (Seventh Data Protection Principle)

Other rights

A detailed explanation of the other rights under Sections 10, 12 and 13 of the Act are provided in Part II of this Code. The standards of this Code are set out below.

Standards

1.　All staff involved in operating the equipment must be able to recognise a request from an individual to:

a)　Prevent processing likely to cause substantial and unwarranted damage to that individual.[23]

b)　Prevent automated decision taking in relation to that individual.[24]

2.　*All staff must be aware of the manager or designated member of staff who is responsible for responding to such requests.*

3.　In relation to a request to prevent processing likely to cause substantial and unwarranted damage, the manager or designated officer's response should indicate whether he or she will comply with the request or not.[25]

4.　The manager or designated member of staff must provide a written response to the individual within 21 days of receiving the request setting out their decision on the request.[26]

5.　If the manager or designated member of staff decide that the request will not be complied with, they must set out their reasons in the response to the individual.[27]

6.　*A copy of the request and response should be retained.*

7. If an automated decision is made about an individual, the manager or designated member of staff must notify the individual of that decision.[28]

8. If, within 21 days of that notification, the individual requires, in writing, the decision to be reconsidered, the manager or designated staff member shall reconsider the automated decision.[29]

9. On receipt of a request to reconsider the automated decision, the manager or designated member of staff shall respond within 21 days setting out the steps that they intend to take to comply with the individual's request.[30]

10. *The manager or designated member of staff shall document:*
    a) *The original decision.*
    b) *The request from the individual.*
    c) *Their response to the request from the individual.*

Monitoring compliance with this code of practice

Standards

1. The contact point indicated on the sign should be available to members of the public during office hours. Employees staffing that contact point should be aware of the policies and procedures governing the use of this equipment.

2. *Enquiries should be provided on request with one or more of the following:*
   a) *The leaflet which individuals receive when they make a subject access request as general information*
   b) *A copy of this code of practice*
   c) *A subject access request form if required or requested*
   d) *The complaints procedure to be followed if they have concerns about the use of the system*
   e) *The complaints procedure to be followed if they have concerns about non-compliance with the provisions of this Code of Practice*

3. *A complaints procedure should be clearly documented.*

4. *A record of the number and nature of complaints or enquiries received should be maintained together with an outline of the action taken.*

5. *A report on those numbers should be collected by the manager or designated member of staff in order to assess public reaction to and opinion of the use of the system.*

6. A manager or designated member of staff should undertake regular reviews of the documented procedures to ensure that the provisions of this Code are being complied with (Seventh Data Protection Principle).

7. *A report on those reviews should be provided to the data controller(s) in order that compliance with legal obligations and provisions with this Code of Practice can be monitored.*

8. *An internal annual assessment should be undertaken which evaluates the effectiveness of the system.*

9. *The results of the report should be assessed against the stated purpose of the scheme. If the scheme is not achieving its purpose, it should be discontinued or modified.*

10. *The result of those reports should be made publicly available.*

PART II – Glossary

The Data Protection Act 1998

1. Definitions

There are several definitions in Sections 1 and 2 of the 1998 Act which users of CCTV systems or similar surveillance equipment must consider in order to determine whether they need to comply with the requirements of the 1998 Act, and if so, to what extent the 1998 Act applies to them:

a)   **Data Controller**

"A person who (either alone or jointly or in common with other persons) determines the purposes for which and the manner in which any personal data are, or are to be, processed".

For example: if a police force and local authority enter into a partnership to install CCTV in a town centre with a view to:–

- Preventing and detecting crime.
- Apprehending and prosecuting offenders.
- Protecting public safety.

They will both be data controllers for the purpose of the scheme.

For example – if a police force, local authority and local retailers decide to install a CCTV scheme in a town centre or shopping centre, for the purposes of:

- Prevention or detection crime.
- Apprehending or prosecuting offenders.
- Protecting public safety.

All will be data controllers for the purposes of the scheme. It is the data controllers who should set out the purposes of the scheme (as outlined above) and who should set out the policies on the use of the images (as outlined in the Standards section of this Code of Practice).

The data controller(s) may devolve day-to-day running of the scheme to a manager, but that manager is not the data controller – he or she can only manage the scheme according to the instructions of the data controller(s), and according to the policies set out by the data controller(s).

If the manager of the scheme is an employee of one or more of the data controllers, then the manager will not have any personal data protection responsibilities as a data controller. However, the manager should be aware that if he or she acts outside the instructions of the data controller(s) in relation to obtaining or disclosing the images, they may commit a criminal offence contrary to Section 55 of the 1998 Act, as well as breach their contract of employment.

If the manager is a third party such as a security company employed by the data controller to run the scheme, then the manager may be deemed a data processor. This is "any person (other than an employee of the data controller) who processes the personal data on behalf of the data controller. If the data controller(s) are considering using a data processor, they will need to consider their compliance with the Seventh Data Protection Principle in terms of this relationship.

b)   **Personal Data**
"Data which relate to a living individual who can be identified:
a)   from those data, or
b)   from those data and other information which is in the possession of, or is likely to come into the possession of, the data controller".
The provisions of the 1998 Act are based on the requirements of a European Directive[31], which at, Article 2, defines, personal data as follows:
"Personal data" shall mean any information relating to an identified or identifiable natural person; an identifiable person is one who can be identified, directly or indirectly, in particular by reference to an identification number or to one or more factors specific to his physical, physiological, mental, economic, cultural or social identity.
The definition of personal data is not therefore limited to circumstances where a data controller can attribute a name to a particular image. If images of distinguishable individuals' features are processed and an individual can be identified from these images, they will amount to personal data.

c)   **Sensitive Personal Data**
Section 2 of the 1998 Act separates out distinct categories of personal data, which are deemed sensitive. The most significant of these categories for the purposes of this code of practice are information about:[32]
●   the commission or alleged commission of any offences
●   any proceedings for any offence committed, or alleged to have been committed, the disposal of such proceedings or the sentence of any court in such proceedings.
This latter bullet point will be particularly significant for those CCTV schemes which are established by retailers in conjunction with the local police force, which use other information to identify known and convicted shoplifters from images, with a view to reducing the amount of organised shoplifting in a retail centre.
It is essential that data controllers determine whether they are processing sensitive personal data because it has particular implications for their compliance with the First Data Protection Principle.

d)   **Processing**
Section 1 of the 1998 Act sets out the type of operations that can constitute processing:
"In relation to information or data, means obtaining, processing, recording or holding the information or data or carrying out any operation or set of operations on the information or data, including:
a)   organisation, adaptation or alteration of the information or data,

b)   retrieval, consultation or use of the information or data,

c)   disclosure of the information or data by transmission, dissemination or otherwise making available, or

d)   alignment, combination, blocking, erasure or destruction of the information or data."

The definition is wide enough to cover the simple recording and holding of images for a limited period of time, even if no further reference is made to those images. It is also wide enough to cover real-time transmission of the images. Thus if the images of individuals passing in front of a camera are shown in real time on a monitor, this constitutes "transmission, dissemination or otherwise making available". Thus even the least sophisticated capturing and use of images falls within the definition of processing in the 1998 Act.

2. Purposes for which personal data/images are processed

Before considering compliance with the Data Protection Principles, a user of CCTV or similar surveillance equipment, will need to determine two issues:

- What type of personal data are being processed i.e. are there any personal data which fall within the definition of sensitive personal data as defined by Section 2 of the 1998 Act.

- For what purpose(s) are both personal data and sensitive personal data being processed?

Users of surveillance equipment should be clear about the purposes for which they intend to use the information/images captured by their equipment. The equipment may be used for a number of purposes:

- Prevention, investigation and/or detection of crime.

- Apprehension and/or prosecution of offenders (including images being entered as evidence in criminal proceedings).

- Public and employee safety.

- Staff discipline.

- Traffic flow monitoring.

Using information captured by a surveillance system will not always require the processing of personal data or the processing of sensitive personal data. For example, use of the system to monitor traffic flow in order to provide the public with up to date information about traffic jams, will not necessarily require the processing of personal data.

3. Data protection principles

The first data protection principle

This requires that

"Personal data shall be processed fairly and lawfully, and, in particular, shall not be processed unless:

a)   at least one of the conditions in Schedule 2 is met, and
b)   in the case of sensitive personal data, at least one of the conditions in Schedule 3 is also met".

To assess compliance with this Principle, it is recommended that the data controller address the following questions:

a)   **Are personal data and/or sensitive personal data processed?**
The definition of sensitive personal data[33] has been discussed above and it is essential that the data controller has determined whether they are processing information/images, which fall into that category in order to assess which criteria to consider when deciding whether there is a legitimate basis for the processing of that information/images.

b)   **Has a condition for processing been met?**
The First Data Protection Principle requires that the *data controller* have a legitimate basis for processing. It is for the data controller to be clear about which grounds to rely on in this respect. These are set out in Schedules 2 and 3 to the Act.
Users of schemes which monitor spaces to which the public have access, such as town centres, may be able to rely on Paragraph 5 (d) of Schedule 2 because the processing is for the exercise of any other function of a public nature exercised in the public interest by any person. This could include purposes such as prevention and detection of crime, apprehension and prosecution of offenders or public/employee safety.
Users of schemes which monitor spaces in shops or retail centres to which the public have access may be able to rely on Paragraph 6(1) of Schedule 2 because the processing is necessary for the purposes of legitimate interests pursued by the data controller or the third party or third parties to whom the data are disclosed, except where the processing is unwarranted in any particular case by reason of prejudice to the rights and freedoms or legitimate interests of the data subject.
It should be noted that while this criterion may provide a general ground for processing, in an individual case, the interests of the data controller i.e. the user of the surveillance equipment might not outweigh the rights of an individual.
If the data controller has determined that he or she is processing sensitive personal data, then the data controller will also need to determine whether he

or she has a legitimate basis for doing so under Schedule 3. It should be noted that Schedule 3 does not contain the grounds cited above in relation to Schedule 2.

Users of surveillance equipment in town centres, particularly where the local authority or police force (or a partnership of the two) are the data controllers may be able to rely on Paragraph 7(1)(b) of Schedule 3 because the processing is necessary for the exercise of any functions conferred on any person by or under an enactment. It may be that the use of such information/images by a public authority in order to meet the objectives of the Crime and Disorder Act 1998 would satisfy this criterion.

Users of information/images recorded in a shop or retail centre may be able to rely on one of the grounds contained in the Order made under Schedule 3(10) of the 1998 Act.[34]

For example –
> "(1)   The processing:
> a)   is in the substantial public interest;
> b)   is necessary for the purposes of the prevention and detection of any unlawful act; and
> c)   must necessarily be carried out without the explicit consent of the data subject so as not to prejudice those purposes"

It is for the data controller to be sure that he or she has legitimate grounds for their processing and therefore it is essential that the data controller has identified:
- what categories of data are processed, and
- why?

c)   **Are the information/images processed lawfully?**

The fact that the data controller has a legitimate basis for processing does not mean that this element of the First Data Protection Principle is automatically satisfied. The data controller will also need to consider whether the information/images processed are subject to any other legal duties or responsibilities such as the common law duty of confidentiality. Public sector bodies will need to consider their legal powers under administrative law in order to determine whether there are restrictions or prohibitions on their ability to process such data. They will also need to consider the implications of the Human Rights Act 1998.

d)   **Are the information/images processed fairly?**

The fact that a data controller has a legitimate basis for processing the information/images will not automatically mean that this element of the First Data Protection Principle is satisfied.

The interpretative provisions[35] of the Act set out what is required in order to process fairly. In order to process fairly, the following information, at least, must be provided to the individuals at the point of obtaining their images:
- the identity of the data controller
- the identity of a representative the data controller has nominated for the purposes of the Act

- the purpose or purposes for which the data are intended to be processed, and
- any information which is necessary, having regard to the specific circumstances in which the data are or are to be processed, to enable processing in respect of the individual to be fair.

e)   **Circumstances in which the requirement for signs may be set aside**

The Act does not make specific reference to the use of covert processing of (sensitive) personal data but it does provide a limited exemption from the requirement of fair processing. Because fair processing (as indicated above) requires that individuals are made aware that they are entering an area where their images may be captured, by the use of signs, it follows that the use of covert processing i.e. removal or failure to provide signs, is prima facie a breach of the fairness requirement of the First Data Protection Principle. However, a breach of this requirement will not arise if an exemption can be relied on. Such an exemption may be found at Section 29(1) of the Act, which states that:

"Personal data processed for any of the following purposes:

a)   prevention or detection of crime

b)   apprehension or prosecution of offenders

are exempt from the first data protection principle (except to the extent to which it requires compliance with the conditions in Schedules 2 and 3) ... in any case to the extent to which the application of those provisions to the data would be likely to prejudice any of the matters mentioned ..."

This means that if the data controller processes images for either or both of the purposes listed in the exemption, he or she may be able to obtain and process images without signs without breaching the fairness requirements of the First Data Protection Principle.

The second data protection principle

This requires that

"Personal data shall be obtained only for one or more specified and lawful purposes, and shall not be further processed in any manner incompatible with that purpose or those purposes".

In order to ascertain whether the data controller can comply with this Data Protection Principle, it is essential that he or she is clear about the purpose(s) for which the images are processed.

Specified purposes may be those, which have been notified to the Commissioner or to the individuals.

There are a number of issues to be considered when determining lawfulness:

- Whether the data controller has a legitimate basis (see First Data Protection Principle) for the processing.

- Whether the images are processed in accordance with any other legal duties to which the data controller may be subject e.g. the common law duty of confidence, administrative law in relation to public sector powers etc.

It is quite clear from the interpretative provisions to the Principle that the requirement of compatibility is particularly significant when considering making a disclosure to a third party or developing a policy on disclosures to third parties. If the data controller intends to make a disclosure to a third party, regard must be had to the purpose(s) for which the third party may process the data.

This means, for example, that if the purpose(s) for which images are processed is:

- Prevention or detection of crime
- Apprehension or prosecution of offenders

The data controller may only disclose to third parties who intend processing the data for compatible purposes. Thus, for example, where there is an investigation into criminal activity, disclosure of footage relating to that criminal activity to the media in order to seek assistance from the public in identifying either the perpetrator, the victim or witnesses, may be appropriate. However, it would be an incompatible use if images from equipment installed to prevent or detect crime were disclosed to the media merely for entertainment purposes. For example, it might be appropriate to disclose to the media images of drunken individuals stumbling around a town centre on a Saturday night to show proper use of policing resources to combat anti-social behaviour. However, it would not be appropriate for the same images to be provided to a media company merely for inclusion in a "humorous" video.

If it is determined that a particular disclosure is compatible with the purposes for which the data controller processes images, then the extent of disclosure will need to be considered. If the footage, which is to be disclosed contains images of unrelated third parties, the data controller will need to ensure that those images are disguised in such a way that they cannot be identified.

If the data controller does not have the facilities to carry out such editing, he or she may agree with the media organisation that it will ensure that those images are disguised. This will mean that the media organisation is carrying out processing, albeit of a limited nature on behalf of the data controller which is likely to render it a data processor. In which case the data controller will need to ensure that the relationship with the media organisation complies with the Seventh Data Protection Principle.

The third data protection principle

This requires that

> "Personal data shall be adequate, relevant and not excessive in relation to the purpose or purposes for which they are processed".

This means that consideration must be given to the situation of the cameras so that they do not record more information than is necessary for the purpose for which they were installed. For example cameras installed for the purpose of recording acts of vandalism in a car park should not overlook private residences. Furthermore, if the recorded images on the tapes are blurred or indistinct, it may well be that this will constitute inadequate data. For example, if the purpose of the system is to collect evidence of criminal activity, blurred or indistinct images from degraded tapes or poorly maintained equipment will not provide legally sound evidence, and may therefore be inadequate for its purpose.

The fourth data protection principle

This requires that

"Personal data shall be accurate and, where necessary, kept up to date".

This principle requires that the personal information that is recorded and stored must be accurate. This is particularly important if the personal information taken from the system is to be used as evidence in cases of criminal conduct or in disciplinary disputes with employees. The Commissioner recommends that efforts are made to ensure the clarity of the images, such as using only good quality tapes in recording the information, cleaning the tapes prior to re-use and not simply recording over existing images, and replacing tapes on a regular basis to avoid degradation from over-use.

If the data controller's system uses features such as time references and even location references, then these should be accurate. This means having a documented procedure to ensure the accuracy of such features are checked and if necessary, amended or altered.

Care should be exercised when using digital-enhancement and compression technologies to produce stills for evidence from tapes because these technologies often contain pre-programmed presumptions as to the likely nature of sections of the image. Thus the user cannot be certain that the images taken from the tape are an accurate representation of the actual scene. This may create evidential difficulties if they are to be relied on either in court or an internal employee disciplinary hearing.

The fifth data protection principle

This requires that

"Personal data processed for any purpose or purposes shall not be kept for longer than is necessary for that purpose or those purposes".

This principle requires that the information shall not be held for longer than is necessary for the purpose for which it is to be used. The tapes that have recorded the relevant activities should be retained until such time as the proceedings are completed and the possibility of any appeal has been exhausted. After that time, the tapes should be erased. Apart from those circumstances, stored or recorded images should not be kept for any undue length of time. A policy on periods for retention of the images should be developed which takes into account the nature of the information and the purpose for which it is being collected. For example where images are being recorded for the purposes of crime prevention in a shopping area, it may be that the only images that need to be retained are those relating to specific incidents of criminal activity; the rest could be erased after a very short period. The Commissioner understands that generally town centre schemes do not retain recorded images for more than 28 days unless the images are required for evidential purposes.

The sixth data protection principle

This requires that

"Personal data shall be processed in accordance with the rights of data subjects under this Act".

The Act provides individuals with a number of rights in relation to the processing of their personal data. Contravening the following rights will amount to a contravention of the Sixth Data Protection Principle:

- The right to be provided, in appropriate cases, with a copy of the information constituting the personal data held about them – Section 7.[36]
- The right to prevent processing which is likely to cause damage or distress – Section 10.[37]
- Rights in relation to automated decision-taking – Section 12[38]

The seventh data protection principle[39]

This requires that

"Appropriate technical and organisational measures shall be taken against unauthorised or unlawful processing of personal data and against accidental loss or destruction of, or damage to, personal data".

In order to assess the level of security the data controller needs to take to ensure compliance with this Principle, he or she needs to assess–

- the harm that might result from unauthorised or unlawful processing or accidental loss, destruction or damage of the personal data[40]. While it is clear that breach of this Principle may have a detrimental effect on the purpose(s) of the scheme e.g. the evidence or images might not stand up in court, or the public may lose confidence in your use of surveillance equipment due to inappropriate disclosure, the harm test required by the Act also requires primarily the effect on the people recorded to be taken into account;
- the nature of the data to be protected must be considered. Sensitive personal data was defined at the beginning of this part of the Code, but there may be other aspects, which need to be considered. For example, a town centre scheme may coincidentally record the image of a couple kissing in a parked car, or a retailer's scheme may record images of people in changing rooms (in order to prevent items of clothing being stolen). Whilst these images may not fall within the sensitive categories as set in Section 2 (described above), it is clear that the

people whose images have been captured will consider that information or personal data should be processed with greater care.

The eighth data protection principle

This requires that

"Personal data shall not be transferred to a country or territory outside the European Economic Area unless that country or territory ensures an adequate level of protection for the rights and freedoms of data subjects in relation to the processing of personal data".

This Principle places limitations on the ability to transfer personal data to countries and territories outside of the EEA.[41] It is unlikely that the data controller would want, in general, to make such transfers of personal data overseas, but the data controller should refrain from putting the images on the Internet or on their website. In order to ensure that this Principle is not breached, the data controller should consider the provisions of Schedule 4 of the 1998 Act.

4. Right of subject access

Upon making a request in writing (which includes transmission by electronic means) and upon paying the fee to the data controller an individual is entitled:

- To be told by the data controller whether they or someone else on their behalf is processing that individual's personal data.
- If so, to be given a description of:
  a) the personal data,
  b) the purposes for which they are being processed, and
  c) those to whom they are or may be disclosed.
- To be told, in an intelligible manner, of:
  a) all the information, which forms any such personal data. This information must be supplied in permanent form by way of a copy, except where the supply of such a copy is not possible or would involve disproportionate effort or the individual agrees otherwise. If any of the information in the copy is not intelligible without explanation, the individual should be given an explanation of that information, e.g. where the data controller holds the information in coded form which cannot be understood without the key to the code, and
  b) any information as to the source of those data. However, in some instances the data controller is not obliged to disclose such information where the source of the data is, or can be identified as, an individual.

A data controller may charge a fee (subject to a maximum) for dealing with subject access. A data controller must comply with a subject access request promptly, and in any event within forty days of receipt of the request or, if later, within forty days of receipt of:

- the information required (i.e. to satisfy himself as to the identity of the person making the request and to locate the information which that person seeks); and
- the fee.

However, unless the data controller has received a request in writing, the prescribed fee and, if necessary, the said information the data controller need not comply with the request. If the data controller receives a request without the required fee and/or information, they should request whichever is outstanding as soon as possible in order that they can comply with the request promptly and in any event within 40 days. A data controller does not need to comply with a request where they have already complied with an identical or similar request by the same individual unless a reasonable interval has elapsed between compliance with the previous request and the making of the current request. In deciding what amounts to a reasonable interval, the following factors should be considered: the nature of the data, the purpose for which the data are processed and the frequency with which the data are altered.

The information given in response to a subject access request should be all that which is contained in the personal data at the time the request was received. However, routine amendments and deletions of the data may continue between the date of the request and the date of the reply. To this extent, the information revealed to the individual may differ from the personal data which were held at the time the request was received, even to the extent that data are no longer held. But, having received a request, the data controller must not make any special amendment or deletion which would not otherwise have been made. The information must not be tampered with in order to make it acceptable to the individual.

A particular problem arises for data controllers who may find that in complying with a subject access request they will disclose information relating to an individual other than the individual who has made the request, who can be identified from that information, including the situation where the information enables that other individual to be identified as the source of the information. The Act recognises this problem and sets out only two circumstances in which the data controller is obliged to comply with the subject access request in such circumstances, namely:

- where the other individual has consented to the disclosure of the information, or
- where it is reasonable in all the circumstances to comply with the request without the consent of the other individual.

The Act assists in interpreting whether it is reasonable in all the circumstances to comply with the request without the consent of the other individual concerned. In deciding this question regard shall be had, in particular, to:

- any duty of confidentiality owed to the other individual,
- any steps taken by the data controller with a view to seeking the consent of the other individual,
- whether the other individual is capable of giving consent, and
- any express refusal of consent by the other individual.

If a data controller is satisfied that the individual will not be able to identify the other individual from the information, taking into account any other information which, in the reasonable belief of the data controller, is likely to be in (or to come into) the possession of the individual, then the data controller must provide the information.

If an individual believes that a data controller has failed to comply with a subject access request in contravention of the Act they may apply to Court for an order that the data controller complies with the request. An order may be made if the Court is satisfied that the data controller has failed to comply with the request in contravention of the Act.

5. Exemptions to subject access rights

There are a limited number of exemptions to an individuals right of access. One of potential relevance to CCTV images is found at Section 29 of the Act. This provides an exemption from the subject access rights, which is similar to that discussed in relation to the exemption to the fairness requirements of the First Data Protection Principle. This means that where personal data are held for the purposes of:–

- prevention or detection of crime,
- apprehension or prosecution of offenders,

the data controller will be entitled to withhold personal data from an individual making a subject access request, where it has been adjudged that to disclose the personal data would be likely to prejudice one or both of the above purposes. Like the exemption to the fairness requirements of the First Data Protection Principle, this judgement must be made on a case-by-case basis, and in relation to each element of the personal data held about the individual. It is likely that this exemption may only be appropriately relied upon where the data controller has recorded personal data about an individual in accordance with guidance set out in relation to the fairness requirements of the First Data Protection Principle.[42]

6. Other rights

Right to prevent processing likely to cause damage or distress

Under Section 10 of the Act, an individual is entitled to serve a notice on a data controller requiring the data controller not to begin, or to cease, processing personal data relating to that individual. Such a notice could only be served on the grounds that the processing in question is likely to cause substantial, unwarranted damage or distress to that individual or another person. There are certain limited situations where this right to serve a notice does not apply. These are where the individual has consented; the processing is in connection with performance of a contract with the data subject, or in compliance with a legal obligation on the data controller, or in order to protect the vital interests of the individual. If a data controller receives such a notice they must respond within 21 days indicating either compliance with the notice or why the notice is not justified.

Rights in relation to automated decision-taking

Under section 12 of the Act individuals also have certain rights to prevent automated decision taking where a decision, which significantly affects them is based solely on automated processing. The Act draws particular attention to decisions taken aimed at evaluating matters such as the individual's performance at work and their reliability or conduct. The Act does provide exemption for certain decisions reached by automated means and these cover decisions which have been taken in the course of contractual arrangements with the individual, where a decision is authorised or required by statute, where the decision is to grant a request of the individual or where steps have been taken to safeguard the legitimate interests of individuals. This latter point may include matters such as allowing them to make representations about a decision before it is implemented.

Where no notice has been served by an individual and a decision which significantly affects the individual based solely on automated processing will be made, then there is still an obligation on the data controller to notify the individual that the decision was taken on the basis of automated processing as soon as reasonably practicable. The individual may, within 21 days of receiving such a notification, request the data controller to reconsider the decision or take another decision on a new basis. Having received such a notice the data controller has 21 days in which to respond, specifying the steps that they intend to take to comply with the notice.

In the context of CCTV surveillance it may be the case that certain automated decision-making techniques are deployed, such as with automatic facial recognition. It is important therefore that any system takes account of an individual's rights in relation to automated decision taking. It should be noted that these rights are founded on decisions, which are taken solely on the basis of automated processing. If a decision whether to take particular action in relation to a particular identified individual is taken further to human intervention, then such a decision would not be based solely on automated processing.

The individual's rights to prevent processing in certain circumstances and in connection with automated decision taking are underpinned by an individual's right to seek a Court Order should any notice served by the individual not be complied with.

Compensation for failure to comply with certain requirements

Under Section 13 of the Act, individuals who suffer unwarranted damage or damage and distress as a result of any contravention of the requirements of the Act are entitled to go to court to seek compensation in certain circumstances. This right to claim compensation for a breach of the Act is in addition to an individual's right to request the Data Protection Commissioner to make an assessment as to whether processing is likely or unlikely to comply with the Act.

1   It is intended that employers' use of personal data to monitor employee compliance with contracts of employment will be covered by the Data Protection Commissioner's forthcoming code of practice on use of employee personal data.

2   It is likely that the use of cameras by individuals to protect their own property is excluded from the provisions of the Act under the exemption at Section 36 of the Act.

3   The Commissioner's powers to issue an Enforcement Notice may be found in section 40 of the Act.

4   The First Data Protection Principle requires data controllers to have a legitimate basis for processing personal data, in this case images of individuals. The Act sets out criteria for processing, one of which must be met in order to demonstrate that there is a legitimate basis for processing the images.

5   Section 4(4) of the Act places all data controllers under a duty to comply with the data protection principles in relation to all personal data with respect to which he is the data controller as defined by section 1(1) of the Act. See the section on definitions.

6   See the First Data Protection Principle requires data controllers to have a legitimate basis for processing, one of which must be met in order to demonstrate that there is a legitimate basis for processing the images.

7   Section 17 of the Act prohibits the processing of personal data unless the data controller has notified the Data Protection Commissioner. The notification scheme requires that the purpose(s) of the processing be identified.

8   Section 29 of the Act sets out the circumstances in which the fair processing requirements of the First Data Protection Principle are set aside.

9   It may be that the particular problem identified is theft from cars in a car park. Following the appropriate assessment, surveillance equipment is installed but signs are not. If the equipment co-incidentally records images relating to other criminality for example a sexual assault, it will not be inappropriate for those images to be used in the detection of that crime or in order to apprehend and prosecute the offender. However, it might be inappropriate for images so obtained to be used in civil proceedings or disciplinary proceedings e g the car park attendant is recorded committing a minor disciplinary misdemeanour.

10 Users of such systems should be aware of the affect of Section 12 of the 1998 Act regarding individuals' rights in relation to automated decision taking.

11 See the section on access to and disclosure of images to third parties.

12 See the section on access to and disclosure of images to third parties.

13 See the section on individual's rights.

14 See the section on the seventh data protection principle.

15 See the section on access to and disclosure of images to third parties.

16 See the section on access to and disclosure of images to third parties.

17 See the section on the right of subject access.

18 See the section on the right of subject access.

19 See the section on the right of subject access.

20 See the section on the right of subject access.

21 See the section on the right of subject access.

22 See the section on the right of subject access.

23 Section 10 of the Act provides individuals with the right to prevent processing likely to cause damage or distress. See the section on other rights.

24 Users of such a system should be aware of the effects of section 12 of the Act regarding individuals' rights in relation to automated decision taking.

25 Section 10 of the Act provides individuals with the right to prevent processing likely to cause substantial damage or distress. See the section on other rights.

26 Section 10 of the Act provides individuals with the right to prevent processing likely to cause substantial damage or distress. See the section on other rights.

27 Section 10 of the Act provides individuals with the right to prevent processing likely to cause substantial damage or distress. See the section on other rights.

28 Users of such systems should be aware of the effect of section 12 of the 1998 Act regarding individuals' rights in relation to automated decision taking.

29 Users of such systems should be aware of the effect of section 12 of the 1998 Act regarding individuals' rights in relation to automated decision taking.

30 Users of such systems should be aware of the effect of section 12 of the 1998 Act regarding individuals' rights in relation to automated decision taking.

31 European Directive 95/46/EC on the protection of individuals with regard to the processing of personal data and on the free movement of such data.

32   Section 2 of Act sets out the full list of categories of sensitive personal data. This part of the Code only refers to some of the categories, which may have particular relevance for users of CCTV. For a full list, please see the relevant section of the Act.

33   Section 2 of Act sets out the full list of categories of sensitive personal data. This part of the Code only refers to some of the categories, which may have particular relevance for users of CCTV. For a full list, please see the relevant section of the Act.

34   The Data Protection (Processing of Sensitive Personal Data) Order 2000 (S.I No 417).

35   Schedule 1 Part II Sections 1 – 4 of the Act.

36   See the section on the right of subject access.

37   Section 2 of the Act sets out the full list of categories of sensitive personal data. This part of the Code only refers to some of the categories, which may have particular relevance for users of CCTV. For a full list, please see the relevant section of the Act.

38   Users of such systems should be aware of the effect of section 12 of the 1998 Act regarding individuals' rights in relation to automated decision taking.

39   British Standard Institute – BS 7958:1991 "Closed Circuit Television (CCTV) – Management and Operation Code of Practice" provides guidance on issues of security, tape management etc.

40   Schedule 1, Part II, Paragraph 9 of the Act.

41   Schedule 1, Part II, Paragraphs 13 – 15 of the Act.

42   See the subsection on circumstances in which the requirements for signs may be set aside.

The Employment Practices Data Protection Code

Part 3: Monitoring at work

CONTENTS

Section 1:   About the Code
Section 2:   Monitoring workers
Section 3:   Good practice recommendations

Section 1: About the Code

Our aim:

This Code is intended to help employers comply with the Data Protection Act and to encourage them to adopt good practice. The Code aims to strike a balance between the legitimate expectations of workers that personal information about them will be handled properly and the legitimate interests of employers in deciding how best, within the law, to run their own businesses. It does not impose new legal obligations.

Who is the Code for?

The Employment Practices Data Protection Code deals with the impact of data protection laws on the employment relationship. It covers such issues as the obtaining of information about workers, the retention of records, access to records and disclosure of them. Not every aspect of the Code will be relevant to every organisation – this will vary according to size and the nature of its business. Some of the issues addressed may arise only rarely – particularly for small businesses. Here the Code is intended to serve as a reference document to be called on when necessary.

This part of the Code recommends how your organisation can meet the requirements of the Data Protection Act through the adoption of good practice where you wish to monitor the activities of your workers.

The benefits of the code:

The Data Protection Act 1998 places responsibilities on any organisation to process personal information that it holds in a fair and proper way. Failure to do so can ultimately lead to a criminal offence being committed.

The effect of the Act on how an organisation processes information on its workers is generally straightforward. But in some areas it can be complex and difficult to understand, especially if your organisation has only limited experience of dealing with data protection issues. The Code therefore covers the points you need to check, and what action, if any, you may need to take. Following the Code should produce other benefits in terms of relationships with your workers, compliance with other legislation and efficiencies in storing and managing information.

Benefits of the Employment Practices Code:

Following the Code will:

- increase trust in the workplace – there will be transparency about information held on individuals, thus helping to create an open atmosphere where workers have trust and confidence in employment practices.
- encourage good housekeeping – following the Code encourages organisations to dispose of out-of-date information, freeing up both physical and computer-ised filing systems and making valuable information easier to find.
- protect organisations from legal action – adhering to the Code will help employers to protect themselves from challenges against their data protection practices.
- encourage workers to treat customers' personal data with respect – following the Code will create a general level of awareness of personal data issues, helping to ensure that information about customers is treated properly.
- help organisations to meet other legal requirements – the Code is intended to be consistent with other legislation such as the Human Rights Act 1998 and the Regulation of Investigatory Powers Act 2000 (RIPA).
- assist global businesses to adopt policies and practices which are consistent with similar legislation in other countries – the Code is produced in the light of EC Directive 95/46/EC and ought to be in line with data protection law in other European Union member states.

- help to prevent the illicit use of information by workers – informing them of the principles of data protection, and the consequences of not complying with the Act, should discourage them from misusing information held by the organisation.

What is the legal status of the Code?

The Code has been issued by the Information Commissioner under section 51 of the Data Protection Act. This requires him to promote the following of good practice, including compliance with the Act's requirements, by data controllers and empowers him, after consultation, to prepare Codes of Practice giving guidance on good practice.

The basic legal requirement on each employer is to comply with the Act itself. The Code is designed to help. It sets out the Information Commissioner's recommendations as to how the legal requirements of the Act can be met. Employers may have alternative ways of meeting these requirements but if they do nothing they risk breaking the law.

Any enforcement action would be based on a failure to meet the requirements of the Act itself. However, relevant parts of the Code are likely to be cited by the Commissioner in connection with any enforcement action that arises in relation to the processing of personal information in the employment context.

Who does data protection cover in the workplace?

The Code is concerned with information that employers might collect and keep on any individual who might wish to work, work, or have worked for them. In the Code the term 'worker' includes:

- applicants (successful and unsuccessful)
- former applicants (successful and unsuccessful)
- employees (current and former)
- agency staff (current and former)
- casual staff (current and former)
- contract staff (current and former)

Some of this Code will also apply to others in the workplace, such as volunteers and those on work experience placements.

What information is covered by the Code?

It is likely that most information about individuals that is processed by an organisation in the employment context will fall within the scope of the Data Protection Act and therefore within the scope of this Code.

Personal information

The Code is concerned with 'personal information'. That is, information which:

relates to a living person, and
identifies an individual, whether by itself, or together with other information in the
organisation's possession or that is likely to come into its possession.

All automated and computerised personal information is covered by the Act. It also
covers personal information put on paper or microfiche and held in any 'relevant
filing system'. In addition, information recorded with the intention that it will be put
in a relevant filing system or held on computer is covered. A relevant filing system
essentially means any set of information about workers in which it is easy to find a
piece of information about a particular individual.

[Note: At the date of publication the case of *Durrant v the Financial Services
Authority* is still before the courts. The explanation of 'relevant filing system' is based
on the Information Commissioner's previously published advice. This may need to
be amended as the case law develops.]

Processing

The Act applies to personal information that is subject to 'processing'. For the
purposes of the Act, the term 'processing' applies to a comprehensive range of
activities. It includes the initial obtaining of personal information, the retention and
use of it, access and disclosure and final disposal.

Examples of personal information likely to be covered by the Act include:

- details of a worker's salary and bank account held on an organisation's
  computer system or in a manual filing system
- an e-mail about an incident involving a named worker
- a supervisor's notebook containing sections on several named workers
- a supervisor's notebook containing information on only one individual but
  where there is an intention to put that information in that person's file
- a set of completed application forms

Examples of information unlikely to be covered by the Act include:
- information on the entire workforce's salary structure, given by grade, where
  individuals are not named and are not identifiable
- a report on the comparative success of different recruitment campaigns where
  no details regarding individuals are held
- a report on the results of "exit interviews" where all responses are anonymised
  and where the results are impossible to trace back to individuals
- manual files that contain some information about workers but are not stored in
  an organised way, such as a pile of papers left in a basement

In practice, therefore, nearly all employment-related useable information held about
individuals will be covered by the Code.

Sensitive personal information:

What are sensitive data?

Sensitive data are information concerning an individual's;

- racial or ethnic origin
- political opinions
- religious beliefs or other beliefs of a similar nature
- trade union membership (within the meaning of the Trade Union and Labour Relations (Consolidation) Act 1992)
- physical or mental health or condition
- sexual life
- commission or alleged commission of any offence, or
- proceedings for any offence committed or alleged to have been committed, the disposal of such proceedings or the sentence of any court in such proceedings

Sensitive data found in a worker's record might typically be about their;

- physical or mental health – as a part of sickness records
- disabilities – to facilitate adaptations in the workplace
- racial origin – to ensure equality of opportunity
- trade union membership – to enable deduction of subscriptions from payroll

In the context of monitoring, typical circumstances in which sensitive personal information might be held include;

- health information in e-mails sent by a worker to his or her manager, a personnel department or an occupational health advisor
- trade union membership revealed by internet access logs which show that a worker routinely accesses a particular trade union website
- information about a worker's political opinions or religious beliefs obtained by intercepting and recording a private conversation.

The Act sets out a series of conditions, at least one of which has to apply before an employer can collect, store, use, disclose or otherwise process sensitive data.

See Supporting Guidance page 23 which explains more about the conditions for processing sensitive data

What responsibilities do workers have under the Act?

Workers – as well as employers – have responsibilities for data protection under the Act. Line managers have responsibility for the type of personal information they collect and how they use it. No-one at any level should disclose personal information outside the organisation's procedures, or use personal information held on others for their own purposes. Anyone disclosing personal information without the authority of the organisation may commit a criminal offence, unless there is some other legal justification, for example under 'whistle-blowing' legislation.

Of course, applicants for jobs ought to provide accurate information and may breach other laws if they do not. However, the Act does not create any new legal obligation for them to do so.

Managing Data Protection Page 21 explains more about allocating responsibility.

Other Parts of the Code:

The Employment Practices Data Protection Code has three additional parts,

- **recruitment and selection** – is about job applications and preemployment vetting.
- **employment records** – is about collecting, storing, disclosing and deleting records
- **medical information** – is about occupational health, medical testing, drug and genetic screening

Each part of the Code has been designed to stand alone. Which parts of the Code you choose to use will depend on the relevance to your organisation of each area covered.

Ask the Information Commissioner for copies of any parts you require or for any further information.

See Supporting Guide, page 39, for contact details or view our website: www.informationcommissioner.gov.uk

Section 2: Monitoring workers

Data protection and monitoring at work

A number of the requirements of the Data Protection Act will come into play whenever an employer wishes to monitor workers. The Act does not prevent an employer from monitoring workers, but such monitoring must be done in a way which is consistent with the Act. Employers – especially in the public sector – must also bear in mind Article 8 of the European Convention on Human Rights which creates a right to respect for private and family life and for correspondence.

How does the Data Protection Act regulate monitoring?

Monitoring is a recognised component of the employment relationship. Most employers will make some checks on the quantity and quality of work produced by their workers. Workers will generally expect this. Many employers carry out monitoring to safeguard workers, as well as to protect their own interests or those of their customers. For example, monitoring may take place to ensure that those in hazardous environments are not being put at risk through the adoption of unsafe working practices. Monitoring arrangements may equally be part of the security mechanisms used to protect personal information. In other cases, for example in the context of financial services, the employer may be under legal or regulatory obligations which it can only realistically fulfil if it undertakes monitoring. However where monitoring goes beyond one individual simply watching another and involves the manual recording or any automated processing of personal information, it must be done in a way that is both lawful and fair to workers.

Monitoring may, to varying degrees, have an adverse impact on workers. It may intrude into their private lives, undermine respect for their correspondence or interfere with the relationship of mutual trust and confidence that should exist between them and their employer. The extent to which it does this may not always be immediately obvious. It is not always easy to draw a distinction between work-place and private information. For example monitoring e-mail messages from a worker to an occupational health advisor, or messages between workers and their trade union representatives, can give rise to concern.

In broad terms, what the Act requires is that any adverse impact on workers is justified by the benefits to the employer and others. This Code is designed to help employers determine when this might be the case.

What does this part of the Code cover?

This part of the Code applies where activities that are commonly referred to as "monitoring" are taking place or are planned. This means activities that set out to collect information about workers by keeping them under some form of observation, normally with a view to checking their performance or conduct. This could be done either directly, indirectly, perhaps by examining their work output, or by electronic means.

This part of Code is primarily directed at employers – especially larger organisations – using or planning some form of **systematic monitoring**. This is where the employer monitors all workers or particular groups of workers as a matter of routine, perhaps by using an electronic system to scan all e-mail messages or by installing monitoring devices in all company vehicles.

The Act still applies to **occasional monitoring**. This is where the employer introduces monitoring as a short term measure in response to a particular problem or need, for example by keeping a watch on the e-mails sent by a worker suspected of racial harassment or by installing a hidden camera when workers are suspected of drug dealing on the employer's premises.

This part of the Code deals with both types of monitoring, but it is likely to be of most relevance to employers involved in systematic monitoring, which will generally be larger organisations.

Examples of monitoring

There is no hard-and-fast definition of 'Monitoring' to which this part of the Code applies. Examples of activities addressed in this part of the Code include:

- gathering information through point of sale terminals, to check the efficiency of individual supermarket check-out operators
- recording the activities of workers by means of CCTV cameras, either sothat the recordings can be viewed routinely to ensure that health and safety rules are being complied with, or so that they are available to check on workers in the event of a health and safety breach coming to light
- randomly opening up individual workers' e-mails or listening to their voice-mails to look for evidence of malpractice
- using automated checking software to collect information about workers, for example to find out whether particular workers are sending or receiving inappropriate e-mails
- examining logs of websites visited to check that individual workers are not downloading pornography
- keeping recordings of telephone calls made to or from a call centre, either to listen to as part of workers training, or to simply to have a record to refer to in the event of a customer complaint about a worker
- systematically checking logs of telephone numbers called to detect use of premium-rate lines
- videoing workers outside the workplace, to collect evidence that they are not in fact sick
- obtaining information through credit reference agencies to check that workers are not in financial difficulties

Outside the Code

There are other activities that this part of the Code does not specifically address. Most employers will keep some business records that contain information about workers but are not collected primarily to keep a watch on their performance or conduct. An example could be records of customer transactions – including paper records, computer records or recordings of telephone calls. This part of the Code is **not** concerned with occasional access to records of this type in the course of an investigation into a specific problem, such as a complaint from a customer.

See Part 2: Employment Records, Page 47, for guidance relating to grievance and disciplinary investigations.

Examples of activities **not** directly addressed in this part of the Code include;

- looking back through customer records in the event of a complaint, to check that the customer was given the correct advice
- checking a collection of e-mails sent by a particular worker which is stored as a record of transactions, in order to ensure the security of the system or to investigate an allegation of malpractice
- looking back through a log of telephone calls made that is kept for billing purposes, to establish whether a worker suspected of disclosing trade secrets has been contacting a competitor

The Data Protection Act does not prevent monitoring. Indeed in some cases monitoring might be necessary to satisfy its requirements. However, any adverse impact of monitoring on individuals must be justified by the benefits to the employer and others. We use the term "impact assessment" to describe the process of deciding whether this is the case.

In all but the most straightforward cases, employers are likely to find it helpful to carry out a formal or informal 'impact assessment' to decide if and how to carry out monitoring. This is the means by which employers can judge whether a monitoring arrangement is a proportionate response to the problem it seeks to address. This Code does not prejudge the outcome of the impact assessment. Each will necessarily depend on the particular circumstances of the employer. Nor does the Code attempt to set out for employers the benefits they might gain from monitoring. What it does do is assist employers in identifying and giving appropriate weight to the other factors they should take into account.

Impact assessments

An impact assessment involves;

- identifying clearly the **purpose(s)** behind the monitoring arrangement and the benefits it is likely to deliver
- identifying any likely **adverse impact** of the monitoring arrangement
- considering **alternatives** to monitoring or different ways in which it might be carried out
- taking into account the **obligations** that arise from monitoring
- judging whether monitoring is **justified**.

Adverse impact

Identifying any likely adverse impact means taking into account the consequences of monitoring, not only for workers, but also for others who might be affected by it, such as customers. Consider:

- what intrusion, if any, will there be into the private lives of workers and others, or interference with their private e-mails, telephone calls or other correspondence? Bear in mind that the private lives of workers can, and usually will, extend into the workplace.
- to what extent will workers and others know when either they, or information about them, are being monitored and then be in a position to act to limit any intrusion or other adverse impact on themselves?
- whether information that is confidential, private or otherwise sensitive will be seen by those who do not have a business need to know, e.g. IT workers involved in monitoring e-mail content
- what impact, if any, will there be on the relationship of mutual trust and confidence that should exist between workers and their employer?
- what impact, if any, will there be on other legitimate relationships, e.g. between trades union members and their representatives?
- what impact, if any, will there be on individuals with professional obligations of confidentiality or secrecy, e.g. solicitors or doctors?
- whether the monitoring will be oppressive or demeaning?

Alternatives

Considering alternatives, or different methods of monitoring, means asking questions such as:

*   can established or new methods of supervision, effective training and/or clear communication from managers, rather than electronic or other systemic monitoring, deliver acceptable results?
*   can the investigation of specific incidents or problems be relied on, for example accessing stored e-mails to follow up an allegation of malpractice, rather than undertaking continuous monitoring?
*   can monitoring be limited to workers about whom complaints have been received, or about whom there are other grounds to suspect of wrongdoing?
*   can monitoring be targeted at areas of highest risk, e.g. can it be directed at a few individuals whose jobs mean they pose a particular risk to the business rather than at everyone?
*   can monitoring be automated? If so, will it be less intrusive, e.g. does it mean that private information will be 'seen' only by a machine rather than by other workers?
*   can spot-checks or audit be undertaken instead of using continuous monitoring? Remember though that continuous automated monitoring could be less intrusive than spot-check or audit that involves human intervention.

Obligations

Taking into account the obligations that arise from monitoring means considering such matters as:

*   whether and how workers will be notified about the monitoring arrangements
*   how information about workers collected through monitoring will be kept securely and handled in accordance with the Act.

See Part 2 – Employment Records, Page 19 for more information on security requirements.

*   the implications of the rights that individuals have to obtain a copy of information about them that has been collected through monitoring.

See Part 2 – Employment Records, Page 32 which explains more about rights to access.

Justified?

Making a conscious decision as to whether the current or proposed method of monitoring is justified involves;

*   establishing the benefits of the method of monitoring
*   considering any alternative method of monitoring
*   weighing these benefits against any adverse impact
*   placing particular emphasis on the need to be fair to individual workers

- ensuring, particularly where monitoring electronic communications is involved, that any intrusion is no more than absolutely necessary
- bearing in mind that significant intrusion into the private lives of individuals will not normally be justified unless the employer's business is at real risk of serious damage
- taking into account the results of consultation with trade unions or other representatives, if any, or with workers themselves

See Supporting Guidance Page 27 for a chart to help assess the degree of intrusiveness involved in monitoring the content of various types of communication

Making an impact assessment need not be a complicated or onerous process. It will often be enough for an employer to make a simple mental evaluation of the risks faced by his or her business and to assess whether the carrying out of monitoring would reduce or eradicate those risks. In other cases the impact assessment will be more complicated, for example where an employer faces a number of different risks of varying degrees of seriousness. In such cases appropriate documentation would be advisable.

Is a worker's consent needed?

There are limitations as to how far consent can be relied on in the employment context to justify the processing of personal data. To be valid, for the purposes of the Data Protection Act, consent must be "freely given", which may not be the case in the employment environment. Once given, consent can be withdrawn. In any case, employers who can justify monitoring on the basis of an impact assessment will not generally need the consent of individual workers.

Are there special rules for electronic communications?

Electronic communications are broadly telephone calls, fax messages, emails and internet access. Monitoring can involve the 'interception' of such communications. The Regulation of Investigatory Powers Act, and the Lawful Business Practice Regulations made under it, set out when interception can take place despite the general rule that interception without consent is against the law. It should be remembered that – whilst the Regulations deal only with interception – the Data Protection Act is concerned more generally with the processing of personal information. Therefore when monitoring involves an interception which results in the recording of personal information an employer will need to satisfy both the Regulations and the requirements of the Data Protection Act.

See Supporting Guidance page 28, for more details on The Lawful Business Practice Regulations.

Section 3: Good practice recommendations

There are seven sub-sections in this section of the Code:

1. **Managing data protection**
2. **The general approach to monitoring**
3. **Monitoring electronic communications**
4. **Video and audio monitoring**
5. **Covert monitoring**
6. **In-vehicle monitoring**
7. **Monitoring through information from third parties**

The good practice recommendations may be relevant to either large or small employers, but they primarily address activities that are likely to be undertaken by those involved with systematic monitoring. As such they are most likely to be relevant to larger organisations. However, how far they are applicable and what is needed to achieve them will, of course, depend very much on the nature and size of each organisation.

Supporting guidance, aimed mainly at those in larger organisations who are responsible for ensuring that employment policies and practices comply with data protection law, includes more detailed notes and examples. These notes and examples, do not form part of this Code.

For Supporting Guidance go to: www.informationcommissioner.gov.uk

3.1 Managing data protection

Data protection compliance should be seen as an integral part of employment practice. It is important to develop a culture in which respect for private life, data protection, security and confidentiality of personal information is seen as the norm.

3.1.1 Identify the person within the organisation responsible for ensuring that employment policies and procedures comply with the Act and for ensuring that they continue to do so. Put in place a mechanism for checking that procedures are followed in practice
Key points and possible actions
- The nature and size of the organisation will influence where responsibility should rest.
- Ensure the person responsible reads all relevant parts of the Code.
- Check employment policies and procedures, including unwritten practices, against the relevant parts of the Code.
- Eliminate areas of non-compliance.
- Inform those who need to know why certain procedures have changed.
- Introduce a mechanism for checking that procedures are followed in practice, for example, occasional audits and spot checks and/or a requirement for managers to sign a compliance statement.

3.1.2 Ensure that business areas and individual line managers who process information about workers understand their own responsibility for data protection compliance and if necessary amend their working practices in the light of this.
Key points and possible actions
- Prepare a briefing to departmental heads and line managers about their responsibilities.

3.1.3 Assess what personal information about workers is in existence and who is responsible for it.
Key points and possible actions
- Use the various parts of this Code as the framework to assess what personal information your organisation keeps and where responsibility for it lies.
- Remember that personal information may be held in different departments as well as within the personnel/human resource function.

3.1.4 Eliminate the collection of personal information that is irrelevant or excessive to the employment relationship. If sensitive data are collected ensure that a sensitive data condition is satisfied.
Key points and possible actions
- Consider each type of personal information that is held and decide whether any information could be deleted or not collected in the first place.
- Check that the collection and use of any sensitive personal data satisfies at least one of the sensitive data conditions.

See Supporting Guidance Page 23 which explains more about the conditions for processing sensitive data.

3.1.5 Ensure that all workers are aware how they can be criminally liable if they knowingly or recklessly disclose personal information outside their employer's policies and procedures. Make serious breaches of data protection rules a disciplinary matter.
Key points and possible actions
- Prepare a guide explaining to workers the consequences of their actions in this area.
- Make sure that the serious infringement of data protection rules is clearly indicated as a disciplinary matter.
- Ensure that the guide is brought to the attention of new workers.
- Ensure that workers can ask questions about the guide.

3.1.6 Ensure that your organisation has a valid notification in the register of data controllers that relates to the processing of personal information about workers, unless it is exempt from notification.
Key points and possible actions
- Consult the Data Protection Register website – www.dpr.gov.uk – to check the notification status of your organisation.
- Check whether your organisation is exempt from notification using the website.
- Check whether all your processing of information about workers is correctly described there – unless your organisation is exempt.

- Allocate responsibility for checking and updating this information on a regular basis, for example every 6 months.

3.1.7 Consult workers, and/or trade unions or other representatives, about the development and implementation of employment practices and procedures that involve the processing of personal information about workers.

Key points and possible actions

- Consultation is not currently mandatory under employment law, but should help to ensure that processing of personal information is fair.
- When formulating new employment practices and procedures, assess the impact on collection and use of personal data.

3.2 The general approach to monitoring

CORE PRINCIPLES
- **It will usually be intrusive to monitor your workers.**
- **Workers have legitimate expectations that they can keep their personal lives private and that they are also entitled to a degree of privacy in the work environment.**
- **If employers wish to monitor their workers, they should be clear about the purpose and satisfied that the particular monitoring arrangement is justified by real benefits that will be delivered.**
- **Workers should be aware of the nature, extent and reasons for any monitoring, unless (exceptionally) covert monitoring is justified.**
- **In any event, workers' awareness will influence their expectations.**

3.2.1 Identify who within the organisation can authorise the monitoring of workers and ensure they are aware of the employer's responsibilities under the Act.

Key points and possible actions

- There are non-compliance risks if line mangers introduce monitoringar-rangements without due authority.
- Those who monitor workers, or who can authorise such monitoring, should be briefed on the Act and this Code.

3.2.2 Before monitoring, identify clearly the purpose(s) behind the monitoring and the specific benefits it is likely to bring. Determine – preferably using an impact assessment – whether the likely benefits justify any adverse impact.

Key points and possible actions

- Identify the monitoring that currently takes place in your organisation.
- Identify any monitoring that you plan to implement.
- Consider conducting an impact assessment on either current or planned monitoring based on the guidance on page 15.

3.2.3 If monitoring is to be used to enforce the organisation's rules and standards make sure that the rules and standards are clearly set out in a policy which also refers to the nature and extent of any associated monitoring. Ensure workers are aware of the policy.

Key points and possible actions

- Identify which of your organisation's rules and standards are enforced partly or wholly through the use of monitoring.

- Ensure that these rules and standards are set out in policies that are clearly communicated to workers.

3.2.4 Tell workers what monitoring is taking place and why, and keep them aware of this, unless covert monitoring is justified.

Key points and possible actions

- Ensure that workers are aware of the nature and extent of any monitoring.
- Set up a system (for example by using the workers handbook or via an intranet) to ensure workers remain aware that monitoring is being conducted.
- Tell workers when significant changes are introduced.

3.2.5 If sensitive data are collected in the course of monitoring, ensure that a sensitive data condition is satisfied.

Key points and possible actions

- If monitoring workers' performance or conduct results in the collection of information on such matters as health, racial origin, trade union activities or sex life, check that at least one of the sensitive data conditions is met.

See Supporting Guidance Page 23 which explains more about the conditions for processing sensitive data.

3.2.6 Keep to a minimum those who have access to personal information obtained through monitoring. Subject them to confidentiality and security requirements and ensure that they are properly trained where the nature of the information requires this.

Key points and possible actions

- Assess whether the organisation could reduce the number of staff involved in monitoring workers.
- Consider whether monitoring is more appropriately carried out by security or personnel functions rather than by line managers.
- Ensure that the training for workers who may come across personal information whilst monitoring makes them aware of data protection obligations

3.2.7 Do not use personal information collected through monitoring for purposes other than those for which the monitoring was introduced unless:

(a) it is clearly in the individual's interest to do so; or

(b) it reveals activity that no employer could reasonably be expected to ignore.

Key points and possible actions

- Ensure that only senior management can authorise the use of personal information obtained through monitoring for new or different purposes.
- Ensure that they are familiar with the Act and the relevant parts of this Code.

3.2.8 If information gathered from monitoring might have an adverse impact on workers, present them with the information and allow them to make representations before taking action.

Key points and possible actions

- Equipment or systems malfunction can cause information collected through monitoring to be misleading or inaccurate. Information can also be misinterpreted or even deliberately falsified.
- Ensure that, within or alongside disciplinary or grievance procedures, workers can see, and if necessary explain or challenge, the results of any monitoring.

3.2.9 Ensure that the right of access of workers to information about them which is kept for, or obtained through, monitoring is not compromised. Monitoring systems must be capable of meeting this and other data protection requirements.

Key points and possible actions

- Assess whether monitoring systems collect information in a way that enables you to respond readily to access requests.
- If they do not, ensure that a mechanism that will allow you to do so is built into the system.
- Check that any electronic monitoring system, bought 'off-the-shelf', has the capability to enable you to meet access requests.

3.2.10 Do not monitor workers just because a customer for your products or services imposes a condition requiring you to do so, unless you can satisfy yourself that the condition is justified.

Key points and possible actions

- Monitoring is not justified simply because it is a condition of business. Such a condition cannot over-ride the employer's obligations to comply with the Act.
- Consider carrying out an impact assessment to assess whether meeting any external stipulation means that your organisation is in breach of the Act. If so, cease monitoring on this basis

3.3 Monitoring electronic communications

This sub-section deals with the monitoring of telephone, fax, e-mail, voicemail, internet access and other forms of electronic communication.

3.3.1 If you wish to monitor electronic communications, establish a policy on their use and communicate it to workers – see 'Policy for the use of electronic communications' below.

Key points and possible actions

- If your organisation does not have a policy on the use of electronic communications, decide whether you should establish one.
- Review any existing policy to ensure that it reflects data protection principles
- Review any existing policies and actual practices to ensure that they are not out of line, e.g. whether private calls are banned in the policy but generally accepted in practice.
- Check that workers are aware of the policy and if not bring it to their attention.

Policy for the use of electronic communications

Employers should consider integrating the following data protection features into a policy for the use of electronic communications:–

- Set out clearly to workers the circumstances in which they may or may not use the employer's telephone systems (including mobile phones), the email system and internet access for private communications.

- Make clear the extent and type of private use that is allowed, for example restrictions on overseas phone calls or limits on the size and/or type of email attachments that they can send or receive.

- In the case of internet access, specify clearly any restrictions on material that can be viewed or copied. A simple ban on 'offensive material' is unlikely to be sufficiently clear for people to know what is and is not allowed. Employers may wish to consider giving examples of the sort of material that is considered offensive, for example material containing racist terminology or nudity.

- Advise workers about the general need to exercise care, about any relevant rules, and about what personal information they are allowed to include in particular types of communication.

- Make clear what alternatives can be used, e.g. the confidentiality of communications with the company doctor can only be ensured if they are sent by internal post, rather than by e-mail, and are suitably marked.

- Lay down clear rules for private use of the employer's communication equipment when used from home or away from the workplace, e.g. the use of facilities that enable external dialling into company networks

- Explain the purposes for which any monitoring is conducted, the extent of the monitoring and the means used.

- Outline how the policy is enforced and penalties which exist for a breach of policy.

There may, of course, be other matters that an employer also wants to address in its policy.

3.3.2 Ensure that where monitoring involves the interception of a communication it is not outlawed by the Regulation of Investigatory Powers Act 2000.

Key points and possible actions

- Interception occurs when, in the course of its transmission, the contents of a communication are made available to someone other than the sender or intended recipient. It does not include access to stored e-mails that have been opened.

- The intended recipient may be the business, but it could be a specified individual.

- Check whether any interception is allowed under the Lawful Business Practice Regulations.

- Take any necessary action to bring such monitoring in line with RIPA and these Regulations.

See Supporting Guidance Page 28 for more information about the Lawful Business Practice Regulations.

3.3.3 Consider – preferably using an impact assessment – whether any monitoring of electronic communications can be limited to that necessary to ensure the security of the system and whether it can be automated.

Key points and possible actions

- Automated systems can be used to provide protection from intrusion, malicious code such as viruses and Trojans, and to prevent password misuse. Such systems may be less intrusive than monitoring of communications to or from workers.

3.3.4 If telephone calls or voice-mails are, or are likely to be, monitored, consider – preferably using an impact assessment – whether the benefits justify the adverse impact. If so, inform workers about the nature and extent of such monitoring.

Key points and possible actions

- If telephone calls or voice-mails are monitored, or will be monitored in the future, consider carrying out an impact assessment.
- If voice-mails need to be checked for business calls when workers are away, make sure they know this may happen and that it may be unavoidable that some personal messages are heard.
- In other cases, assess whether it is essential to monitor the content of calls and consider the use of itemised call records instead.
- Ensure that workers are aware of the nature and extent of telephone monitoring.

3.3.5 Ensure that those making calls to, or receiving calls from, workers are aware of any monitoring and the purpose behind it, unless this is obvious.

Key points and possible actions

- Consider the use of recorded messages, informing external callers that calls may be monitored.
- If this is not feasible, encourage workers to tell callers that their conversations may be monitored.

3.3.6 Ensure that workers are aware of the extent to which you receive information about the use of telephone lines in their homes, or mobile phones provided for their personal use, for which your business pays partly or fully. Do not make use of information about private calls for monitoring, unless they reveal activity that no employer could reasonably be expected to ignore.

Key points and possible actions

- Remember that expectations of privacy are likely to be significantly greater at home than in the workplace.
- If any workers using mobiles or home telephone lines, for which you pay, are currently subjected to monitoring ensure that they are aware of the nature and the reasons for monitoring.

3.3.7 If e-mails and / or internet access are, or are likely to be, monitored, consider, preferably using an impact assessment, whether the benefits justify the adverse impact. If so, inform workers about the nature and extent of all e-mail and internet access monitoring.

Key points and possible actions

- If e-mails and/or internet access are presently monitored, or will be monitored in the future, consider carrying out an impact assessment.

- Check that workers are aware of the nature and extent of e-mail and internet access monitoring

3.3.8 Wherever possible avoid opening e-mails, especially ones that clearly show they are private or personal.

Key points and possible actions

- Ensure that e-mail monitoring is confined to address / heading unless it is essential for a valid and defined reason to examine content.
- Encourage workers to mark any personal e-mails as such and encourage them to tell those who write to them to do the same.
- If workers are allowed to access personal e-mail accounts from the workplace, such e-mails should only be monitored in exceptional circumstances.

3.3.9 Where practicable, and unless this is obvious, ensure that those sending emails to workers, as well as workers themselves, are aware of any monitoring and the purpose behind it.

Key points and possible actions

- It may be practicable – for example when soliciting e-mail job applications – to provide information about the nature and extent of monitoring.
- In some cases, those sending e-mails to a work-place address will be aware that monitoring takes place without the need for specific information.

3.3.10 If it is necessary to check the e-mail accounts of workers in their absence, make sure that they are aware that this will happen.

Key points and possible actions

- If e-mail accounts need to be checked in the absence of workers, make sure they know this will happen.
- Encourage the use of a marking system to help protect private or personal communications.
- Avoid, where possible, opening e-mails that clearly show they are private or personal communications.

3.3.11 Inform workers of the extent to which information about their internet access and e-mails is retained in the system and for how long.

Key points and possible actions

- Check whether workers are currently aware of the retention period of e-mail and internet usage.
- If it is not already in place, set up a system (e.g. displaying information online or in a communication pack) that informs workers of retention periods.

3.4. Video and audio monitoring

Some – though not all – of the data protection issues that arise when carrying out video monitoring in public places will arise in the workplace. Employers carrying out video monitoring of workers will therefore find the guidance in the Information Commissioner's CCTV Code useful. Audio monitoring means the recording of face-to-face conversations, not recording telephone calls.

See www.informationcommissioner.gov.uk and search for the CCTV Code of Practice

3.4.1 If video or audio monitoring is (or is likely) to be used, consider – preferably using an impact assessment – whether the benefits justify the adverse impact.
Key points and possible actions
- Where possible, any video or audio monitoring should be targeted at areas of particular risk and confined to areas where expectations of privacy are low.
- Continuous video or audio monitoring of particular individuals is only likely to be justified in rare circumstances

3.4.2 Give workers a clear notification that video or audio monitoring is being carried out and where and why it is being carried out.
Key points and possible actions
- Unless covert monitoring is justified, ensure that workers are informed of the extent and nature of any monitoring that is taking place and the reasons for it.

3.4.3 Ensure that people other than workers, such as visitors or customers, who may inadvertently be caught by monitoring, are made aware of its operation and why it is being carried out.
Key points and possible actions
- Ensure that there are adequate notices, or other means, to inform such people about the monitoring and its purpose(s).

3.5. Covert monitoring.

Covert monitoring means monitoring carried out in a manner calculated to ensure those subject to it are unaware that it is taking place. This sub-section is largely directed at covert video or audio monitoring, but will also be relevant where electronic communications are monitored when workers would not expect it.

3.5.1 Senior management should normally authorise any covert monitoring. They should satisfy themselves that there are grounds for suspecting criminal activity or equivalent malpractice and that notifying individuals about the monitoring would prejudice its prevention or detection.
Key points and possible actions
- Covert monitoring should not normally be considered. It will be rare for covert monitoring of workers to be justified. It should therefore only be used in exceptional circumstances.

3.5.2 Ensure that any covert monitoring is strictly targeted at obtaining evidence within a set timeframe and that the covert monitoring does not continue after the investigation is complete
Key points and possible actions
- Deploy covert monitoring only as part of a specific investigation and cease once the investigation has been completed

3.5.3 Do not use covert audio or video monitoring in areas which workers would genuinely and reasonably expect to be private.

Key points and possible actions

- If embarking on covert monitoring with audio or video equipment, ensure that this is not used in places such as toilets or private offices.
- There may be exceptions to this in cases of suspicion of serious crime but there should be an intention to involve the police.

3.5.4 If a private investigator is employed to collect information on workers covertly make sure there is a contract in place that requires the private investigator to only collect information in a way that satisfies the employer's obligations under the Act.

Key points and possible actions

- Check any arrangements for employing private investigators to ensure your contracts with them impose requirements on the investigator to only collect and use information on workers in accordance with your instructions and to keep the information secure.

3.5.5 Ensure that information obtained through covert monitoring is used only for the prevention or detection of criminal activity or equivalent malpractice. Disregard and, where feasible, delete other information collected in the course of monitoring unless it reveals information that no employer could reasonably be expected to ignore.

Key points and possible actions

- In a covert monitoring exercise, limit the number of people involved in the investigation.
- Prior to the investigation, set up clear rules limiting the disclosure and access to information obtained.
- If information is revealed in the course of covert monitoring that is tangential to the original investigation, delete it from the records unless it concerns other criminal activity or equivalent malpractice.

3.6. In-vehicle monitoring

Devices can record or transmit information such as the location of a vehicle, the distance it has covered and information about the user's driving habits. Monitoring of vehicle movements, where the vehicle is allocated to a specific driver, and information about the performance of the vehicle can therefore be linked to a specific individual, will fall within the scope of the Data Protection Act.

3.6.1 If in-vehicle monitoring is or will be used, consider – preferably using an impact assessment – whether the benefits justify the adverse impact.

Key points and possible actions

- Where private use of a vehicle is allowed, monitoring its movements when used privately, without the freely given consent of the user, will rarely be justified.
- If the vehicle is for both private and business use, it ought to be possible to provide a 'privacy button' or similar arrangement to enable the monitoring to be disabled.
- Where an employer is under a legal obligation to monitor the use of

vehicles, even if used privately, for example by fitting a tacograph to a lorry, then the legal obligation will take precedence

3.6.2 Set out a policy that states what private use can be made of vehicles provided by, or on behalf of, the employer, and any conditions attached to use.

Key points and possible actions

- Make sure, either in the policy or separately, that details of the nature and extent of monitoring are set out.
- Check that workers using vehicles are aware of the policy.

3.7 Monitoring through information from third parties

Employers need to take special care when wishing to make use of information held by third parties, such as credit reference or electoral roll information.

This section also applies to information held by employers in a nonemployment capacity, such as when a bank monitors its workers' bank accounts. Where an employer wishes to obtain information about a worker's criminal convictions, a disclosure must be obtained via the Criminal Records Bureau.

See Part 1 – Recruitment and Selection, Page 34, for more information about the Criminal Records Bureau.

3.7.1 Before undertaking any monitoring which uses information from third parties, ensure – preferably using an impact assessment – that the benefits justify the adverse impact.

Key points and possible actions

- A worker's financial circumstances should not be monitored unless there are firm grounds to conclude that financial difficulties would pose a significant risk to the employer.

3.7.2 Tell workers what information sources are to be used to carry out checks on them and why the checks are to be carried out.

Key points and possible actions

- Set up a system to tell workers the nature and extent of any monitoring which uses information from third parties. (This could be via a workers handbook, notice board or on-line.)
- Where a specific check is to be carried out, the workers should be directly informed, unless to do so would be likely to prejudice the prevention or detection of crime.

3.7.3 Ensure that, if workers are monitored through the use of information held by a credit reference agency, the agency is aware of the use to which the information is put. Do not use a facility provided to conduct credit checks on customers to monitor or vet workers.

Key points and possible actions

- If your organisation uses a credit reference agency to check customers, make sure this facility is not being used to monitor or vet workers. If such practices are in place, stop them immediately.

3.7.4 Take particular care with information about workers which you have as a result of a non-employment relationship with them.

Key points and possible actions
- Check whether your organisation routinely uses information about workers that has been obtained from them because they are also (or have been) your customers, clients or suppliers. If such practices are in place, stop them unless they are justified by a risk you face.

3.7.5 Ensure that workers carrying out monitoring which involves information from third parties are properly trained. Put in place rules preventing the disclosure or inappropriate use of information obtained through such monitoring.

Key points and possible actions
- Identify who may carry out monitoring using information from third parties.
- Assess whether the organisation could reduce the number of workers involved in this activity without compromising necessary monitoring.
- Set up instructions or training for workers involved in this monitoring, making them aware of the data protection principles involved.
- Consider placing confidentiality clauses in the contracts of relevant staff.

3.7.6 Do not retain all the information obtained through such monitoring. Simply record that a check has taken place and the result of this.

Key points and possible actions
- Review procedures on retaining information. Unless there is a legal or regulatory obligation, check that information is not normally retained for more than 6 months.

If you wish to contact us:

Information Commissioner,

Wycliffe House, Water Lane,

Cheshire, SK9 5AF

Telephone: 01625 545700

Fax: 01625 524510

E-mail@ico.gsi.gov.uk

Website: www.informationcommissioner.gov.uk

Index